Principles of
Business, Marketing, and Finance

Robert L. Dansby, PhD

Chairperson of the Division of Business and Social Sciences
Instructor of Business
Chattahoochee Valley Community College
Phenix City, Alabama

Chris Gassen, MBA, CFA

Faircourt Valuation Investments
Grosse Point Woods, Michigan

Brenda Clark, EdD

Professional Development Manager
MBA Research and Curriculum Center
Columbus, Ohio

Publisher
The Goodheart-Willcox Company, Inc.
Tinley Park, Illinois
www.g-w.com

Introduction

What career goals have you set for your future? You may have been talking all of your life about what you want to be when you grow up. Now, the time is here and you are making career plans. No matter what your career aspirations may be, your life will be touched by business. Business is all around you and affects everything you do.

As a student, studying *Principles of Business, Marketing, and Finance* can help you in many ways. Learning basic principles and concepts about commerce can help you become a more valuable employee. Becoming knowledgeable about how business operates and contributes to our society can assist you in becoming a better citizen. Understanding how the economy operates can make you a better consumer. Studying various career options in this text can influence the career you choose.

Principles of Business, Marketing, and Finance provides an opportunity for you to maximize and refine your knowledge. As you explore and discover business, marketing, and finance in this text, you will learn life-long skills that will follow you wherever your interests may lead.

About the Authors

Robert (Bob) Dansby is an instructor of accounting, business, and personal finance at Chattahoochee Valley Community College in Alabama, where he also serves as Chairperson of the Division of Business and Social Science. In addition, Bob is a small business, tax, and personal finance consultant. He is the author of numerous textbooks and workbooks in the areas of accounting, cost accounting, managerial accounting, business math, and personal finance. He has also written several articles for professional journals, served a five-year term as editor of the Georgia Business Education Association Journal, and has given more than 30 presentations at national and regional business education and accounting conferences. Bob holds a PhD in business education from Southern Illinois University at Carbondale.

Chris M. Gassen is the principal of an investment firm and was formerly an equity mutual fund manager, financial analyst, accountant, and college instructor. Chris writes educational materials and business valuations. He holds a master of business administration degree with a concentration in finance from Indiana University and a bachelor of science degree in management from Oakland University. He is a Chartered Financial Analyst (CFA) and served as a grader for the national CFA exam.

Brenda Clark is a retired CTE director, marketing instructor, SBE advisor, and DECA advisor for Jenison, Michigan Public Schools. She was named Marketing Teacher of the Year at state and national levels. She currently serves as the Professional Development Manager for MBA Research and Curriculum Center and is the coauthor of *Marketing Dynamics* and *Entrepreneurship*. Brenda's marketing program was named Business of the Year by the Jenison Chamber of Commerce. Two of her marketing department's school-based enterprises have earned numerous Gold Certifications. She earned a bachelor degree in marketing education, a master degree in educational leadership, and an EdD in educational leadership with a concentration in career and technical education from Western Michigan University.

Reviewers

Goodheart-Willcox Publisher would like to thank the following instructors and professionals who reviewed selected manuscript chapters and provided input for the development of *Principles of Business, Marketing, and Finance.*

Jason Barth
Executive Vice President, Human Resources
Town and Country Financial Corporation
Springfield, Illinois

Jeffery Biersach
Chair, Department of Economics and Financial
   Literacy
Durham Academy
Durham, North Carolina

Jennifer Culpepper
Marketing Teacher
Crisp County High School
Cordele, Georgia

Dawn Eisenhardt
Business, Marketing, and Cooperative Education
   Teacher
School Store Manager
Cherokee High School
Marlton, New Jersey

Deborah Gonzalez
CTE Coordinator
Plano Independent School District
Plano, Texas

Angela Hartman
Business Instructor
Underwood High School
Underwood, Minnesota

Nicholas Haug
Business and Marketing Education Teacher
St. Croix Central High School
Hammond, Wisconsin

Leesa Holloway
CTE Business Department Chair
Spruce Creek High School
Port Orange, Florida

Julie Hutto
CTAE Business and Marketing Teacher
Bleckley County High School
Cochran, Georgia

Dena Irwin
Business Teacher
Shakamak Jr./Sr. High School
Jacksonville, Indiana

Nicole Mallory
Business and Computer Science Instructor
Monroe High School
Albany, Georgia

Lena Marietti
CTE Department Chair, Accounting Teacher
Sunset High School
Dallas, Texas

Donna W. Martin
Director, Academy of Entrepreneurship
Buchholz High School
Gainesville, Florida

Darren McCauley
Marketing Education, CTE Dept. Chairman
Fluvanna County High School
Palmyra, Virginia

Timothy O'Dell, AAMS®
Junior Planner
Delco Financial Group
Shorewood, Illinois

Karen S. Phipps
CTE Lead Instructor
Ansonia High School
Ansonia, Connecticut

Marie Polzer
CTE Business Teacher
Vines High School
Plano, Texas

Tony Saccone, LUTCF
Licensed Insurance Agent
State Farm Insurance
Steger, Illinois

Karissa Samuel
CTE Instructor for Business and Media
Horn High School
Mesquite, Texas

George A. Smith, EA
Enrolled to Practice before the IRS
George A. Smith EA, INC
Highland, Indiana

Belinda Speer
CTE Teacher
Ennis High School
Ennis, Texas

Anjanette Stewart
High School Business Teacher
Sol C. Johnson High School
Savannah, Georgia

Michael Vialpando
CTE Business/Marketing Education
La Joya Community High School
Avondale, Arizona

Cathy Wojcik
Business Teacher
Victor J. Andrew High School
Tinley Park, Illinois

Precision Exams Certification

Goodheart-Willcox is pleased to partner with Precision Exams by correlating *Principles of Business, Marketing, and Finance* to the Standards, Objectives, and Indicators for Precision Exams Business Management Exam. Precision Exams were created in concert with industry and subject matter experts to match real-world job skills and marketplace demands. Students who pass the exam and performance portion of the exam can earn a Career Skills Certification™. To see how *Principles of Business, Marketing, and Finance* correlates to the Precision Exam Standards, please visit www.g-w.com/principles-business-marketing-finance-2017 and click on the Correlations tab. For more information on Precision Exams, please visit www.precisionexams.com.

I earned a CAREER SKILLS™ Certificate in BUSINESS MANAGEMENT. You can earn one too!

Ask your instructor how you can earn a CAREER SKILLS™ Certificate for your resume.

800.470.1215   PRECISION EXAMS   precisionexams.com

Contents in Brief

Expanded Table of Contents

Features

—Exploring Careers —

Ethics

You Do the Math

Green

Prepare for Your Future

As you prepare for college and career, your life will be touched by business. Business is all around you and affects everything you do. By studying *Principles of Business, Marketing, and Finance*, you can become more knowledgeable about business and how it will influence your future.

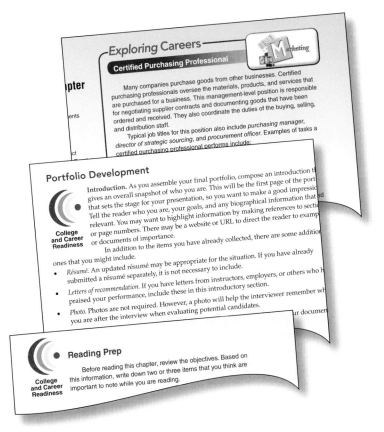

It is all about getting ready for college and career. College and career readiness activities address literacy skills to help prepare you for the real world.

- English/Language Arts standards for reading, writing, speaking, and listening are incorporated in **Reading Prep** activities, as well as in end-of-chapter applications.

- **Exploring Careers** features present information about potential career opportunities in the Business, Management, & Administration career cluster. By studying these, you can investigate career possibilities for your future.

- **Portfolio Development** activities provide guidance to create a personal portfolio for use when exploring volunteer, education and training, and career opportunities.

Practical information helps prepare for your future. Special features add realism and interest to enhance learning.

- **Ethics** offers insight into ethical issues with which you will be confronted in the workplace.

- **Green Business** illustrates the importance of respecting the environment in the workplace.

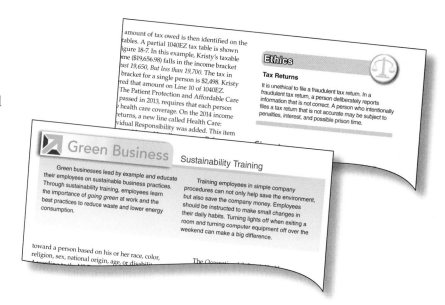

Amplify Your Learning

Content is presented in an easy-to-comprehend and relevant format. Practical activities provide everyday learning opportunities which enable you to experience real-life situations and challenges.

- Each chapter opens with a **pretest** and concludes with a **posttest**. The pretest will help you evaluate your prior knowledge of the chapter content. The posttest will help you evaluate what you have learned after studying the chapter.

- The **Essential Question** at the beginning of each section will engage you as you uncover the important points presented in the content.

- A **You Do the Math** activity in each chapter focuses on skills that are important to your understanding of math for business. You are given an opportunity to apply math concepts in that context of business applications.

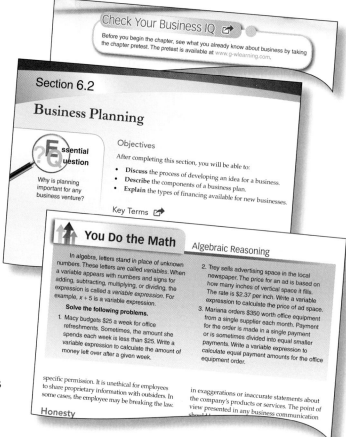

- Research skills are critical for college and career. **Internet Research** activities at the end of each chapter provide opportunities to put them to work.

- **Event Prep** presents information to use when preparing for competitive activities in career and technical student organization (CTSO) competitions.

- A **Math Skills Handbook** provides you with a quick reference for basic math functions. This helpful information will help clarify business math that is presented in the chapters.

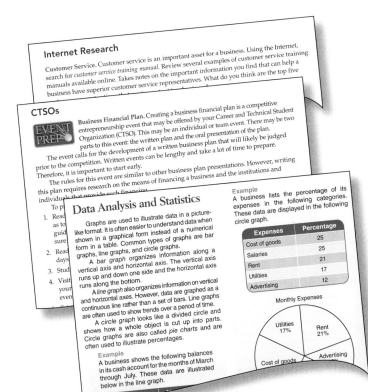

Assess Your Progress

It is important to assess what you learn as you progress through the textbook. Multiple opportunities are provided to confirm learning as you explore the content. *Formative assessment* includes the following:

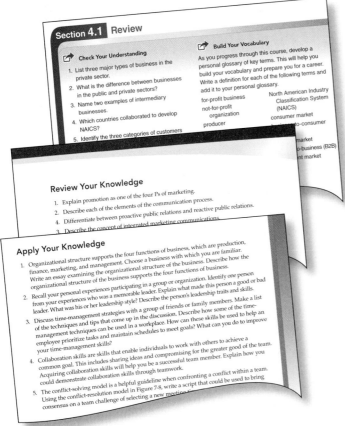

- **Check Your Understanding** questions at the end of each chapter section provide an opportunity to review what you have learned before moving on to additional content.

- **Build Your Vocabulary** activities review the key terms presented in each section. By completing these activities, you will be able to demonstrate your understanding of communication terms.

- **Review Your Knowledge** activities cover the basic concepts presented in the chapter so you can evaluate your understanding of the material.

- **Apply Your Knowledge** activities challenge you to relate what you learned in the chapter with your own ideas, experiences, and goals.

- **Communication Skills** activities provide ways for you to demonstrate the literacy and career readiness skills you have mastered.

- **Teamwork** activities encourage a collaborative experience to help you learn how to interact with other students in a productive manner.

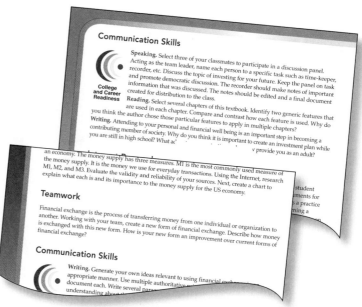

Maximize the Impact

G-W Learning Companion Website

Technology is an important part of your world. So, it should be part of your everyday learning experiences. G-W Learning for *Principles of Business, Marketing, and Finance* is a study reference that contains activity files, vocabulary exercises, interactive quizzes, and more.

Visit www.g-wlearning.com/business/

G-W Learning provides you with opportunities for hands-on interactivity so you can study on the go. Look for the activity icon in the text next to the following activities:

- Chapter **pretests** allow you to assess what you know before you begin the chapter.

- Chapter **posttests** allow you to assess what you have learned at the completion of your study.

- **E-flash cards** and **matching activities** for every key term in each chapter will reinforce the vocabulary learned and enable you to study on the go.

G-W Integrated Learning Solution

The G-W Integrated Learning Solution offers easy-to-use resources for both students and instructors. Digital and blended learning content can be accessed through any Internet-enabled device, such as a computer, smartphone, or tablet. Students spend more time learning, and instructors spend less time administering.

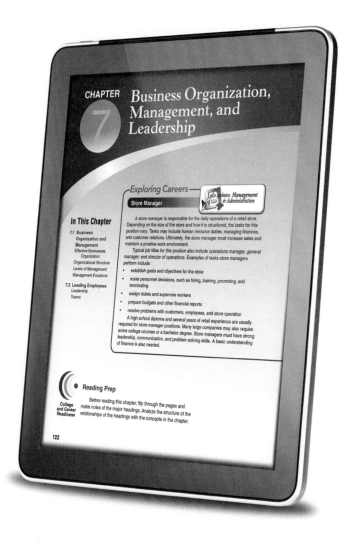

G-W Learning Companion Website/ Student Textbook

The G-W Learning companion website is a study reference that contains e-flash cards, vocabulary exercises, interactive quizzes, and more! Accessible from any digital device, the G-W Learning companion website complements the textbook and is available to the student at no charge.
Visit www.g-wlearning.com.

Online Learning Suite

Available as a classroom subscription, the Online Learning Suite provides the foundation of instruction and learning for digital and blended classrooms. An easy-to-manage, shared classroom subscription makes it a hassle-free solution for both students and instructors. An online student text and workbook, along with rich supplemental content, bring digital learning to the classroom. All instructional materials are found on a convenient online bookshelf and are accessible at home, at school, or on the go.

Online Learning Suite/Student Textbook Bundle

Looking for a blended solution? Goodheart-Willcox offers the Online Learning Suite bundled with the printed text in one easy-to-access package. Students have the flexibility to use the print version, the Online Learning Suite, or a combination of both components to meet their individual learning style. The convenient packaging makes managing and accessing content easy and efficient.

Online Instructor Resources

Online Instructor Resources provide all the support needed to make preparation and classroom instruction easier than ever. Available in one accessible location, support materials include Answer Keys, Lesson Plans, Instructor Presentations for PowerPoint®, ExamView® Assessment Suite, and more! Online Instructor Resources are available as a subscription and can be accessed at school or at home.

G-W Integrated Learning Solution

For the Student:

Student Textbook (print)

Student Workbook (print)

G-W Learning Companion Website (free)

Online Learning Suite (subscription)

Online Learning Suite/Student Textbook Bundle

For the Instructor:

Instructor's Presentations for PowerPoint® (CD)

ExamView® Assessment Suite (CD)

Instructor Resources (CD)

Online Instructor Resources (subscription)

Business Environment

Focus on Business

Business is the term for all activities involved in developing and exchanging products. *Economics* is a science that examines how goods and services are produced, sold, and used. Economics plays a vital role in today's business activities. The economic decisions of individuals, businesses, and governments have a direct impact on the activity and health of the economy. There are many signs that indicate the health of an economy. The US government monitors economic activity and takes action to maintain economic stability.

The government also establishes and enforces laws that apply to business operations and activities. Understanding and respecting the laws is necessary to operate in our society. Demonstrating ethical conduct and social responsibility is also expected behavior of businesses.

In our free enterprise system, businesses may organize for profit or not for profit. They may be producers, intermediaries, or service providers that meet the needs and wants of different types of customers. The number of owners and size of a business are major considerations when choosing to structure the business as a proprietorship, partnership, corporation, or an alternative form of ownership.

Business is global. Trade barriers are disappearing and communication is constantly improving. Modern communication technology allows businesses to participate in the economies of countries around the world. These business opportunities open new markets, create jobs, and develop political relationships.

Social Media for Business

Social media refers to the websites and apps that allow individual users to network online by creating and sharing content with one another. For many individuals, social media is an important part of everyday life. People use it to build their personal brand, to develop a community, and to communicate with others. Unlike other forms of media, such as television, radio, and newspapers, social media allows for interaction between people.

Businesses and governments also have learned the many advantages that social media can provide. Platforms such as Facebook, Twitter, and LinkedIn are no longer just for personal use. Social media is a tool that can complement a company's business strategy when used wisely. For example, by communicating regular updates on products, events, or customer feedback, a company can help keep its brand in front of customers. This awareness brings the need for writers who are capable of presenting information in an appropriate format for the medium.

While studying, look for the activity icon ⬆️ for:

- Pretests and posttests
- Vocabulary terms with e-flash cards and matching activities
- Self-assessment

G-WLEARNING.com

3

Introduction to Business and Economics

In This Chapter

1.1 Introduction to Business
Impact of Business
Functions of Business

1.2 Introduction to Economics
Economics
Economic Systems
Market Forces

Exploring Careers

Economist

Business Management & Administration

Economic activity is essential for businesses to succeed, but it can be difficult to predict. Economists study, analyze, and interpret economic issues. They observe financial markets, employment rates, and government economic policies. Economists typically work with statistics, charts, and surveys to organize economic data. Based on their studies, they make recommendations to a business or government.

Typical job titles for this position also include *economic consultant*, *project economist*, and *research analyst*. Examples of tasks that economists perform include:

- predict market trends by using sampling to collect data

- compare current and historic economic conditions

- advise businesses on economic trends and problems

Economists are required to have a bachelor degree. Coursework in economics, calculus, and statistics is required for entry-level jobs. A master degree or doctorate degree in economics is needed for higher-level positions. Economists should have advanced computer and math skills.

Reading Prep

As you read this chapter, determine the point of view or purpose of the author. What aspects of the text help to establish this purpose or point of view?

College and Career Readiness

Check Your Business IQ

Before you begin the chapter, see what you already know about business by taking the chapter pretest. The pretest is available at www.g-wlearning.com.

Introduction to Business

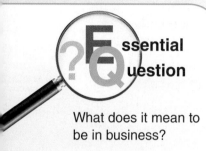

Objectives

After completing this section, you will be able to:

- **Define** business and its benefits.
- **Describe** the four functions of business.

Key Terms

business	consumer	profit
product	need	wages
good	want	standard of living
service	utility	
customer	market	

Impact of Business

What career goals have you set for your future? No matter what your passions or career aspirations, your life will be touched by business. Business is all around you and affects everything you do.

As a student, studying business can help you in many ways. Learning the basic principles of business will help you become a more valuable employee by understanding how the economy operates. Employers seek workers who are knowledgeable about how business operates and contributes to our society.

Not everyone wants to work for an employer. Maybe owning your own business is in your career plans. Think about the businesses in your community. How many are independently owned and operated? Understanding business concepts will help you learn the processes necessary to create a business and become your own boss.

Learning about business can also help you be a more informed citizen. Having business knowledge can help you be a better consumer and investor in your personal life. You can gain personal satisfaction by understanding the business world. The possibilities are endless.

What is business? A *business* is a specific organization, such as Ford Motor Company or a local pet walking service. However, **business** is the term for all the activities involved in developing and exchanging products. A **product** is anything that can be bought or sold. Products are commonly known as goods and services. A **good** is a physical item that can be touched. A **service** is an action or task that is performed, usually for a fee. Products may be bought or sold to individuals, businesses, and governments.

To be successful, a business must be organized and focused on the customer. A **customer** is an individual or group who buys products. The customer of a service business is often called a *client*. A customer can be an individual, a business, a nonprofit organization, or a governmental agency. Customers who purchase goods and services for their own use are **consumers**. The *consumer market* is comprised of customers who buy products for their own use. The *business market* consists of customers who buy products for use in a business.

Ethics

Business Ethics

Ethics is a set of rules that define what is wrong and right. Ethics helps people make good decisions in both their personal and professional lives. *Business ethics* is a set of rules that help define appropriate behavior in a business setting.

In general, the benefits created by business include:

- providing products
- creating markets
- generating economic benefits

Business Provides Products

Some of the products you use every day meet a need, and others satisfy wants. A **need** is something a person must have in order to survive, such as food, clothing, and shelter. A **want** is something that a person desires but can survive without. Needs and wants are unlimited. Businesses focus on satisfying customer needs and wants. A business could not continue without satisfied customers.

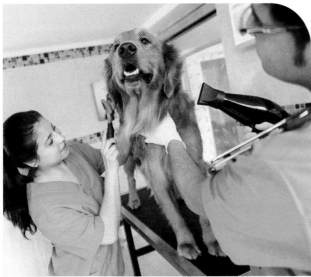

Andresr/Shutterstock.com

A product is anything that can be bought or sold, which includes both goods and services.

A major task of business is to provide utility. In business, **utility** describes the characteristics of a product that satisfy wants and needs. Utility means usefulness. There are five types of utility, as shown in Figure 1-1.

- *Form utility* is added when a business changes the form of a good or service to make it more useful.
- *Place utility* is added when products are available at convenient places.
- *Time utility* is added when products are made available at the times that customers need and want them.
- *Information utility* is added when facts and details about a product are made available to a customer.
- *Possession utility* is added when it becomes easier for customers to acquire a product.

Business sometimes refers to the process of adding utility as adding value. *Adding value* means enhancing a feature or service to motivate customers to make a purchase.

Examples of Utility	
Form	Smartphones are designed to be ergonomic, compatible with popular apps, and have high enough capacity to be useful.
Place	Shopping malls make a wide variety of stores available in one convenient location.
Time	Banks offer early morning teller services to meet the needs of businesses that are open in the morning, as well.
Information	Many electronics manufacturers have digital versions of installation and troubleshooting guides that are accessible anytime on their websites.
Possession	Convenience stores and drive-thru pharmacies offer quick product access.

Goodheart-Willcox Publisher

Figure 1-1 One of the major tasks of business is to provide utility in order to satisfy the wants and needs of customers.

Business Creates Markets

Think about a typical day, and consider all of the individual goods and services you use. Getting each of those products to you involved business activities that take place in a market. A market, or *marketplace*, does not have to be a physical place, like a shopping mall or a grocery store. Instead, a **market** is anywhere buyers and sellers meet to buy and sell goods and services.

When buying back-to-school supplies at an office supply store or other retail store, you are shopping in a physical market. Downloading apps for your smartphone is an example of shopping in an online market. A community rummage sale can even be a marketplace. Anywhere a business exchange takes place is a market.

Business Generates Economic Benefits

Economic benefits are gains that are measured in terms of money. The main reason businesses operate is to earn a profit. **Profit** is the difference between the income earned and expenses incurred by a business during a specific period of time. It is income generated from sales after the costs of producing and selling products are subtracted. By earning a profit, a business can continue to operate. It can also contribute to the economy by employing workers and paying taxes that help fund the economy.

One of the economic benefits businesses provide is employment. People are employed by a business in exchange for wages. **Wages** are money earned in exchange for work. People use their wages to buy goods and services, such as groceries, car repairs, and clothing. Local businesses that hire people within the community benefit because the people who earn money, in turn, buy more goods and services from local businesses.

Consumers also enjoy the economic benefits of business. Businesses create products that allow consumers to determine their standard of living. **Standard of living** is a level of material comfort measured by the goods, services, and luxuries available. Businesses provide goods and services that give customers choices.

Another economic benefit of business is taxes. The profits of a business are taxed by local, state, and federal governments. The taxes help pay for services that benefit the community. Businesses must also pay real estate taxes if they own their business location. Employees of the business pay payroll taxes, which also fund government activities.

Functions of Business

In the process of satisfying customers and making a profit, businesses perform many activities, or functions. *Function* is a general

cdrin/Shutterstock.com

A market is anywhere buyers and sellers come together to participate in business transactions.

word for a category of activities. The functions of business are production, finance, marketing, and management, as shown in Figure 1-2.

- *Production* is any activity related to making a product. There are many activities included in the production function, such as farming, mining, construction, and manufacturing.

- *Finance* includes all business activities that involve money. These activities include receiving money from customers, paying money to suppliers, and paying wages to employees.

- *Marketing* consists of all activities that identify, anticipate, and satisfy customer demand while making a profit. Marketing activities focus on customers.

- *Management* is the process of controlling and making decisions about a business. It includes all of the activities required to plan, coordinate, and monitor a business, as well as hiring and training employees.

In order for a business to be successful, all the functions must work together.

Goodheart-Willcox Publisher

Figure 1-2 Each of the four functions of business work together to create customer satisfaction and business success.

Section 1.1   Review

 Check Your Understanding

1. What is the difference between the consumer market and the business market?
2. List the five types of utility provided by business.
3. What is the main reason a business operates?
4. What are three economic benefits generated by businesses in an economy?
5. List the four functions of business.

 Build Your Vocabulary

As you progress through this course, develop a personal glossary of key terms. This will help you build your vocabulary and prepare you for a career. Write a definition for each of the following terms and add it to your personal glossary.

business	want
product	utility
good	market
service	profit
customer	wages
consumer	standard of living
need	

Introduction to Economics

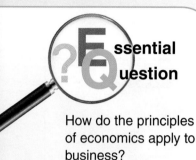

Objectives

After completing this section, you will be able to:

- **Explain** the importance of economics.
- **Describe** the four economic systems.
- **Discuss** the impact of market forces on businesses.

Key Terms

economics	scarcity	command economy
factors of production	trade-off	market economy
labor	opportunity cost	capitalism
capital	systematic	mixed economy
capital goods	decision-making	law of supply and
entrepreneurship	economic system	demand
entrepreneur	traditional economy	competition

Economics

Economics is a science that examines how goods and services are produced, sold, and used. It involves how people, governments, and businesses make choices about using limited resources to satisfy unlimited wants. Understanding the role of economics in the buying decisions of consumers helps businesses make better plans and decisions.

Economic Resources

All economic resources are limited. Individuals, businesses, and governments must decide how to use resources in order to meet their needs. Unlimited needs and wants cannot be met with limited resources. Decisions must be made about which goods or services will be created.

Factors of production are the economic resources a nation uses to make goods and supply services for its population. The factors of production are land, labor, capital, and entrepreneurship, as shown in Figure 1-3.

Land includes all of a nation's natural resources. *Natural resources* are raw materials found in nature. These can include soil, water, minerals, plants, and animals. Every good produced uses some form of natural resources. Many natural resources are scarce and take a very long time to replenish. Even developed nations, like the United States, have limited natural resources.

Labor is the work performed by people in organizations. It is also called *human resources*. This includes workers producing goods, accountants managing company finances, human resources staff interviewing and hiring

Factors of Production

Land	Labor	Capital	Entrepreneurship
• Soil • Water • Minerals • Plants • Animals • Climate	• Agricultural workers • Construction workers • Factory workers • Miners • Professionals • Service workers	• Tools • Equipment • Machinery • Buildings • Vehicles • Transportation systems • Utilities	• Business owners

Goodheart-Willcox Publisher

Figure 1-3 The factors of production include the economic resources of land, labor, capital, and entrepreneurship.

employees, sales people selling products in retail stores, and all other business activity performed by people.

As a factor of production, **capital** is all the tools, equipment, and machinery used to produce goods or provide services. **Capital goods** are the products businesses use to produce other goods. Capital goods are used to make final products, which are then sold to consumers.

The final factor of production is entrepreneurship. **Entrepreneurship** is the willingness and ability to start a new business. **Entrepreneurs** are people who start a new business or purchase an existing business. They organize the other three factors of production to produce a good or service and earn a profit.

Economic Problem

Individuals, businesses, and governments must constantly make choices about using limited resources to satisfy unlimited wants. This is known as the basic *economic problem*. **Scarcity** develops when demand is higher than the available resources, as illustrated in Figure 1-4.

Every economic decision has a cost. Scarcity forces choices to be made. Choosing one option means giving up other options that may have been available. A **trade-off** is when something is given up in order to gain something else. When a trade-off occurs, an opportunity cost is created. **Opportunity cost** is the value of the next best option that was not selected. *Value* is the relative worth of something.

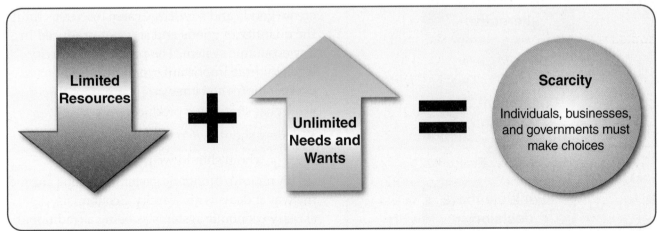

Goodheart-Willcox Publisher

Figure 1-4 Scarcity is the result of an imbalance of limited resources and unlimited wants.

Individuals make economic decisions based on what is most valuable to them. Nations also have many economic needs and wants, but most resources are scarce. As a result, nations have to make economic choices with bigger opportunity costs.

When making economic decisions, a systematic decision-making process can help identify the best option. **Systematic decision-making** is a process of choosing an option after evaluating the available information and weighing the costs and benefits of the alternatives. A systematic decision-making process can be used by both businesses and individuals. The process involves five steps, as shown in Figure 1-5.

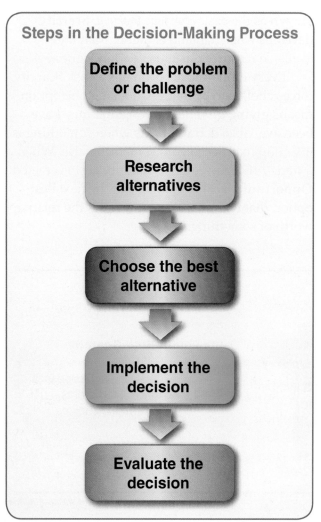

Steps in the Decision-Making Process

Define the problem or challenge

↓

Research alternatives

↓

Choose the best alternative

↓

Implement the decision

↓

Evaluate the decision

Goodheart-Willcox Publisher

Figure 1-5 A systematic decision-making process can be a helpful tool when making economic decisions.

1. *Define the decision to be made.* Have a clear understanding of the end goal. For a business, it may be to offer a new product line or change the image of the business. For an individual, it may be a purchasing decision or where to cut expenses.

2. *Explore all alternatives.* Analyze all the options available. What is the benefit of each option? What is the disadvantage of each? What is the financial cost of each option?

3. *Choose the best alternative.* After considering all alternatives, decide which option is better. The decision may be a single option or a combination of several options.

4. *Act on the decision.* Carry out the plan.

5. *Evaluate the solution or decision.* Evaluation is an ongoing process. Evaluate how effective the choice is in reaching the end goal. Did the plan work? How can it be improved? The evaluation process can help an individual or business stay on track and make better decisions in the future.

Economic Systems

A *system* is a way to manage, control, or organize something that follows a set of rules. An **economic system** is an organized way in which a nation chooses to use its resources to create goods and services. Scarce resources limit the quantity of goods and services produced in any economic system. The problem of scarcity leads to three important economic questions every nation must answer.

• What should we produce?

• How should we produce it?

• For whom should we produce it?

A nation's economic system develops around the way it deals with scarcity. Economists classify economic systems as being a traditional, command, or market economy. However, many economies today are mixed. Mixed economies have elements of both command and market economies.

Taina Sohlman/Shutterstock.com; Goodluz/Shutterstock.com; rodho/Shutterstock.com; wavebreakmedia/Shutterstock.com

Nations must choose how to use their scarce resources of land, labor, capital, and entrepreneurship to create goods and services.

Traditional Economy

Tradition is a way of thinking, behaving, or acting that has been used by a group of people for a long period of time. A **traditional economy** is one in which economic decisions are based on a society's values, culture, and customs. Traditional economies existed early in human history and are still found today in underdeveloped nations.

Countries with traditional economies typically have large rural populations that rely on farming and hunting activities to meet basic needs. Most citizens in a traditional economy have just enough to survive. There is usually little to no manufacturing in this type of economy. So, most people trade or barter for goods and services they cannot produce on their own. To *barter* is to exchange one good or service for another good or service.

Command Economy

In a **command economy**, the government makes all the economic decisions for its citizens. The government decides how to answer the three economic questions. A command economy is also called a *centrally-planned economy* because a central government makes all decisions.

Command economies are found in communist and socialist societies. In this type of economy, the government owns and controls all the factors of production, decides how much will be produced, and sets the prices of goods and services. Ideally, the government makes sure that all citizens get an equal share of the limited resources available. It ensures that jobs are available to everyone and provides education, medical care, and housing. However, citizens give up much individual freedom in a command economy. The nations of North Korea and Cuba are current examples of command economies.

Market Economy

A **market economy** is one in which individuals are free to make their own economic decisions. It is also known as *free enterprise* or *private enterprise*. The characteristics of a free enterprise system are shown in Figure 1-6 and include the following:

- *Private property*. Individuals have the right to own property.

- *Profit*. Individuals and businesses have the right to make a profit.

- *Economic freedom*. Individuals are free to make their own economic decisions. They can decide what to buy, when to buy, and how to use what they have bought.

- *Voluntary exchange*. Individuals have the right to buy and sell in a marketplace where prices are freely set by the forces of supply and demand.

- *Competition*. Businesses can compete to sell goods and services and decide what to produce, how to produce, and for whom to produce.

People and businesses decide what and how much to produce. They also choose what to buy based on how much money they have. The government does not set prices. Instead, consumers in the marketplace determine prices by how much they are willing to pay for items. A market economy is also called a *consumer economy*.

The United States has maintained the largest market economy of the 20th and 21st centuries. Capitalism is another name for the US economic system. **Capitalism** is an economic system where the economic resources are privately owned by individuals rather than the government.

Mixed Economy

In a **mixed economy**, both the government and individuals make decisions about economic resources. Many economies are mixed, having elements of both command and market economies. In most countries, for example, public roads are built and maintained by departments of the government. The government also handles law enforcement and national defense. However, private businesses operate with little government

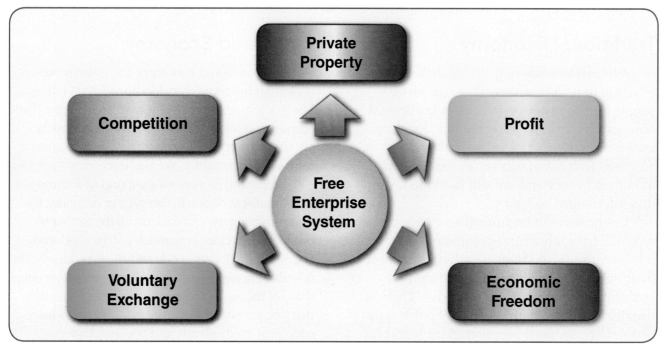

Figure 1-6 The characteristics of a free enterprise system enable consumers in the marketplace to make decisions.

Green Business — Environmental Protection Agency

The United States Environmental Protection Agency (EPA) is a government organization with a mission to protect human health and the environment. The EPA is a rich resource of information on environmental issues, such as pollution, climate change, protecting wildlife, and hazardous waste disposal.

The EPA publishes information on environmental regulations by business sector. It is important for businesses to do their part to protect the environment. Every type of business must follow laws enforced by the EPA. Visit www.epa.gov to learn more about what individuals and businesses can do to preserve the Earth.

Additionally, businesses can go above and beyond what is legally required. Green businesses lead by example and educate their employees on sustainable business practices. Through sustainability training, employees learn the importance of *going green* at work and the best practices to reduce waste and lower energy consumption.

involvement and citizens are free to make their own economic decisions. The amount of government involvement in mixed economies can vary from one economy to another.

Market Forces

Market forces are economic factors that affect the price, demand, and availability of a good or service. In a free enterprise system, the decisions related to market forces result in the production of the best goods and services at the most attractive prices. Market forces include supply and demand, the profit motive, and competition.

Supply and Demand

The principle of supply and demand is critical to business because it determines the price of goods and services. *Supply* is the quantity of goods available for purchase. *Demand* is the quantity of goods that consumers want to purchase. The **law of supply and demand** says that the price of a product is determined by the relationship of the supply of a product and the demand for the product.

Generally, higher demand results in higher prices, and lower demand results in lower prices. An increase in the supply of a product often lowers prices. When the supply of a product decreases, the price usually increases. The *price* is the amount charged for a product.

The *market price* is determined at the point where supply equals demand for a product. This point is called *equilibrium*.

The law of supply and demand can be illustrated with a supply and demand curve, as shown in Figure 1-7. The *supply curve* shows that producers are willing to supply a greater quantity of goods at higher prices.

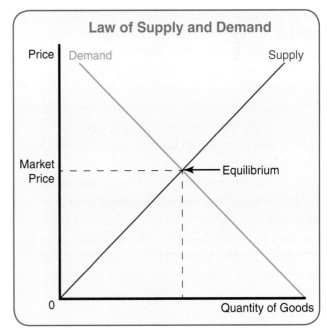

Goodheart-Willcox Publisher

Figure 1-7 A supply and demand curve shows the relationship between the quantity of goods producers are willing to supply and the quantity consumers are willing to buy.

You Do the Math   Numeric Reasoning

Real numbers are all whole and fractional or decimal numbers on a continuous number line that are not imaginary. *Whole numbers* are numbers with no fractional or decimal portion. *Decimals* are numbers with digits to the right of the decimal point. An *imaginary number* is any number that results in a negative number when squared. An imaginary number always includes the notation *i*, such as 2*i*.

To add a positive number, move to the right on the number line. To subtract a positive number, move to the left on the number line.

Find the solution to these equations.

1. $5.87 + 4.956 + 2.011 + 4 =$
2. $34 + 9 - 127 + 783 =$
3. $73 + 8 - 12 =$

The *demand curve* shows that consumers are willing to buy fewer goods at higher prices. The market price of a product is the point at which the supply and demand are equal. The equilibrium is where the supply curve and demand curve intersect.

The law of supply and demand applies to a constant environment. A *constant environment* means that other factors do not change, which is rarely the case. For example, the demand for goods and services can quickly change in reaction to fluctuations in the economy. When the economy is strong, many consumers have more money to spend. They demand more products to satisfy their wants. If the demand for a product becomes greater than the available supply, a *shortage* develops. In this case, consumers compete to buy the available supply, which forces the price up.

When the economy weakens, consumers typically have less money to spend and they demand fewer products. If the demand for a product becomes less than the available supply, a *surplus* develops. In this case, sellers compete to sell the available supply, which forces the price down.

Demand can also be influenced by changes in society. For example, many people today are more concerned about living healthier lifestyles

wavebreakmedia/Shutterstock.com

Demand for goods and services can be affected by changes in society.

than people were several decades ago. The result is a greater and growing demand for products like fitness equipment and foods with high nutritional value.

Profit Motive

Profit is a powerful market force. Profit is the difference between the income earned and expenses incurred by a business. The *profit motive* is one reason people choose to start and expand businesses. Even though many businesses are created because the owners are looking for

personal satisfaction, independence, and other advantages, profit is the driving force.

Competition

Competition among businesses is an important factor in a free enterprise system. **Competition** is the action taken by two or more businesses attempting to attract the same customers. Because consumers have the freedom to choose the goods and services they buy, businesses must work to win each consumer's business.

Section 1.2   Review

 Check Your Understanding

1. What is the basic economic problem?
2. List the four factors of production a nation uses to make goods and supply services for its population.
3. What are the four economic systems?
4. What are market forces?
5. Identify three market forces that impact business.

 Build Your Vocabulary

As you progress through this course, develop a personal glossary of key terms. This will help you build your vocabulary and prepare you for a career. Write a definition for each of the following terms and add it to your personal glossary.

economics
factors of production
labor
capital
capital goods
entrepreneurship
entrepreneur
scarcity
trade-off
opportunity cost

systematic
   decision-making
economic system
traditional economy
command economy
market economy
capitalism
mixed economy
law of supply and demand
competition

Review and Assessment

Chapter Summary

Section 1.1 Introduction to Business

- Business is all the activities involved in developing and exchanging products. Products are goods and services that can be bought or sold to meet needs or satisfy wants. Business provides economic benefits such as providing products, creating markets, and generating economic benefits.

- The functions of business are production, finance, marketing, and management. In order for business to be successful, all the functions must work together.

Section 1.2 Introduction to Economics

- Economics is a science that examines how goods and services are produced, sold, and used. It involves how individuals, governments, and businesses make choices about using limited economic resources to satisfy unlimited wants. Factors of production are the economic resources a nation uses to make goods and to supply services for its population.

- An economic system is an organized way in which a state or nation chooses to use its resources to create goods and services. Economic systems are classified as being traditional, command, market, or mixed economies.

- Market forces are economic factors that affect the price, demand, and availability of a good or service. Market forces include supply and demand, the profit motive, and competition.

Online Activities

Complete the following activities to help you learn, practice, and expand your knowledge and skills.

 Posttest. Now that you have finished the chapter, see what you learned by taking the chapter posttest.

 Vocabulary. Practice vocabulary for this chapter using the e-flash cards, matching activity, and vocabulary game until you are able to recognize their meanings.

Review Your Knowledge

1. Differentiate between goods and services.
2. What are the benefits created by business?
3. Explain the five types of utility provided by business.
4. How does business create economic benefits?
5. Describe the four functions of business.
6. Explain how economic resources determine what goods and services will be produced.

7. Describe the factors of production.

8. Summarize the characteristics of the private enterprise system.

9. How does the law of supply and demand affect the market price of a product?

10. Explain *profit motive* as a market force.

Apply Your Knowledge

1. A major task of business is to provide utility. Explain how the five types of utility can be added to a common product, such as milk or gasoline. List each form of utility and write your explanation next to each.

2. Create a flow chart of the decision-making process to use as a reference as you study this text. For each step, write a brief explanation of what is included. Write any additional notes in the chart that will provide clarification for your future use.

3. Compare and contrast the types of economic systems: traditional, command, market economy, and mixed economy. How are these systems the same? How are they different? Summarize your findings. Create a Venn diagram or other graphic organizer to visually display the information.

4. A private enterprise system has specific characteristics. List each of these characteristics and summarize what each characteristic means to the American public.

5. Explain the basic principles of supply and demand. What effect do you think this principle has on human behavior? Give an example in which the principles of supply and demand result in positive behavior. Give an example in which behavior becomes negative.

Communication Skills

College and Career Readiness

Reading. Skimming means to quickly glance through an entire document. Skimming will give you a preview of the material to help comprehension when you read the chapter. You should notice headings, key words, phrases, and visual elements. The goal is to identify the main idea of the content. Skim this chapter. Provide an overview of what you read.

Writing. Generate ideas for writing a paper that describes the concept of business as you interpret it. Gather information to support your thoughts and ideas. Keep careful and accurate records of any sources that you use as references. Create the notes that you could use to write a paper to distribute for discussion with your classmates.

Speaking. Career ready individuals understand that demonstrating leadership qualities is a way to make a positive contribution to the team. Identify leadership characteristics that you believe all team members should possess. Use a graphic organizer to record your ideas. Share with the class.

Internet Research

Economic systems. Countries throughout the world have their own economic system. Select a country that you would be interested in learning more about. Research the economic system of that country. Using the Internet, visit the Central Intelligence Agency of the United States government at www.cia.gov and select the library tab. The World Factbook on the page provides information on countries of the world. Summarize the information that you find about the country you select. How does the country you selected compare with the United States?

Teamwork

Working as a team, select a product that uses multiple economic resources in its production. Describe how each factor of production was used to create the end product.

Portfolio Development

College and Career Readiness

Portfolio Overview. When you apply for a job, community service, or college, you will need to tell others why you are qualified for the position. To support your qualifications, you will need to create a portfolio. A *portfolio* is a selection of related materials that you collect and organize to show your qualifications, skills, and talents to support a career or personal goal. For example, a certificate that shows you have completed lifeguard and first-aid training could help you get a job at a local pool as a lifeguard. An essay you wrote about protecting native plants could show that you are serious about eco-friendly efforts and help you get a volunteer position at a park. A transcript of your school grades could help show that you are qualified for college. A portfolio is a *living document*, which means it should be reviewed and updated on a regular basis.

Artists and other communication professionals have historically presented portfolios of their creative work when seeking jobs or admission to educational institutions. However, portfolios are now used in many professions.

Two types of portfolios commonly used are print portfolios and digital portfolios. A digital portfolio may also be called an *e-portfolio*.

1. Use the Internet to search for *print portfolio* and *digital portfolio*. Read articles about each type.

2. In your own words, compare and contrast a print portfolio with a digital one.

CTSOs

Student Organizations. Career and technical student organizations (CTSOs) are a valuable asset to any educational program. These organizations support student learning and the application of skills learned in real-world situations. Competitive events may be written, oral, or a combination of both. There is a variety of organizations from which to select, depending on the goals of your educational program.

To prepare for any competitive event, complete the following activities.

1. Go to the website of your organization to find specific information for the events. Visit the site often as information changes quickly. If the organization has an app, download it to your digital device.

2. Read all the organization's guidelines closely. These rules and regulations must be strictly followed, or disqualification can occur.

3. Communication plays a role in all the competitive events, so read which communication skills are covered in the event you select. Research and preparation are important keys to a successful competition.

4. Select one or two events that are of interest to you. Print the information for the events and discuss your interest with your instructor.

Economic Activity

In This Chapter

Exploring Careers

Environmental Economist

Business Management & Administration

Every action taken by a business impacts the well-being of the company. However, these actions also have an impact on the environment. Environmental economists conduct economic analyses related to the environment. Their research focuses on the protection of water, air, and land. They also analyze the use of renewable energy sources. An important aspect of this job is to evaluate and quantify benefits, costs, and options by applying economic principles.

Typical job titles for this position also include *natural resource economist* and *principal research economist*. Examples of tasks that environmental economists perform include:

- assess the costs and benefits of activities, policies, and regulations that affect the environment

- conduct research on economic and environmental topics

- write documents to communicate results or economic forecasts

Most environmental economist positions require a master or doctorate degree. Having integrity, innovation, initiative, and persistence are also necessary. Environmental economists have analytical-thinking skills and great attention to detail.

Reading Prep

Before you begin reading this chapter, consider how the author developed and presented information. How does the information in this chapter provide a foundation for the next chapter?

College and Career Readiness

Check Your Business IQ

Before you begin the chapter, see what you already know about business by taking the chapter pretest. The pretest is available at www.g-wlearning.com.

Measuring Economic Activity

How does the health of an economy affect businesses?

Objective

After completing this section, you will be able to:

- **Describe** common indicators used to measure the strength of an economy.
- **Explain** the four stages of a business cycle.

Key Terms

gross domestic product (GDP)	interest	bond
inflation	interest rate	business cycle
inflation rate	labor force	expansion
consumer price index (CPI)	unemployment rate	peak
deflation	productivity	recession
	specialization	depression
	stock market	trough

Economic Measurement

The market forces of supply and demand, the profit motive, and competition influence the economic decisions of individuals, businesses, and governments. The economic decisions made have a direct impact on the activity and health of the economy.

The strength of an economy can be measured using certain economic indicators. An *indicator* is a sign that shows the condition or existence of something. Some of the most widely followed indicators of the economy are gross domestic product (GDP), inflation, interest rates, unemployment rate, and the stock and bond markets.

Gross Domestic Product (GDP)

Gross domestic product (GDP) is the market value of all final products produced in a country during a specific time period. It is also known as *economic output*. GDP is measured in dollars and is one of the most closely followed economic indicators. GDP is used by the president and congress to prepare the budget for the federal government. It is used by companies when preparing business plans and sales forecasts. Financial institutions also use GDP as an indicator of economic activity, which can affect interest rates.

Per capita GDP is the GDP of a nation divided by its population. It shows the amount of economic output for each person in the country. When per capita GDP is high, there is more economic output per person. When per capita GDP is low, it may indicate that the economy is suffering. Per capita GDP is one way to measure a country's standard of living. One of the goals of a government is to increase the standard of living for its citizens. Measuring the standard of living with per capita GDP has some drawbacks. Per capita GDP does not consider quality-of-life factors. These factors are important, but are difficult to measure, such as health, safety, environmental concerns, and political freedom.

Measuring GDP

One way to measure GDP is to add the total amount of money spent in the economy to buy goods and services. The four components of GDP are consumer spending, business investment, government spending, and net exports, as shown in Figure 2-1.

Consumer spending includes everything people buy for personal use, such as food, clothing, cars, medical care, and recreation. When consumer spending is high, economic growth is often strong. If consumer spending is low, the economy tends to be weak.

Business spending includes all purchases made for capital goods and construction. These may include factories, machines, and warehouses. Business spending is also called *investment spending.*

Government spending includes spending by national, state, and local governments. The government spends on projects and services, such as national defense, police and fire protection, roads, and many social programs.

Net exports are a country's exports minus imports. If a country imports more goods and services than it exports, it is spending more on trade than it is earning.

Growth Rate of GDP

GDP changes over time as referenced in Figure 2-2. The *economic growth rate* shows the amount and direction of the change in GDP for a specific time period, such as a quarter or year. When GDP is rising, the economy is growing. When GDP growth is above average, it indicates a strong economy. When the rate of GDP growth is below average, it is a sign that the economy is weakening. Sometimes economic growth turns negative and GDP falls, which can indicate a recession.

In the United States, long-term economic growth has averaged between 6 and 7 percent, including inflation. This is the range of growth for many industrialized countries. Many fast-growing countries have growth rates that are higher.

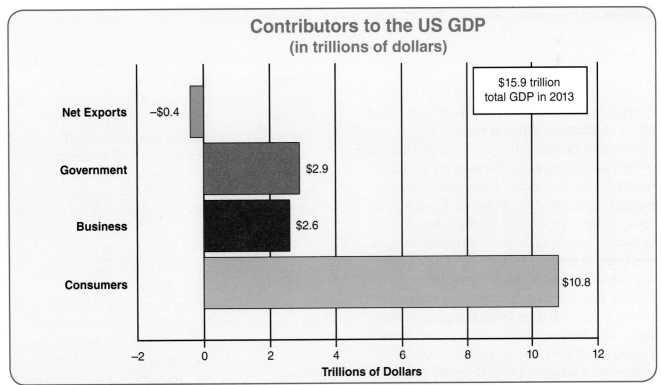

Source: US Bureau of Economic Analysis; Goodheart-Willcox Publisher

Figure 2-1 The GDP includes consumer, business, and government spending, as well as net exports.

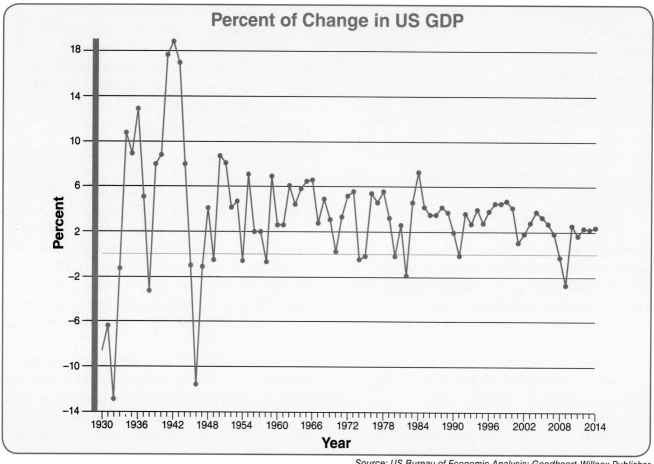

Figure 2-2 The GDP changes from year to year. It can rise, fall, or be negative, depending on consumer, business, and government spending for that year.

Inflation

Inflation is the general rise in prices throughout an economy. The most significant effect of inflation is that it reduces the purchasing power of money. The **inflation rate** is the rate of change in prices calculated on a monthly or yearly basis. It is expressed as a percent. Low inflation, between 1 and 4 percent, usually does not cause a problem for an economy. However, higher rates of inflation can create some economic challenges. For example, high inflation hurts people who live on a fixed income because they have less purchasing power. High inflation leads to higher interest rates, which makes borrowing money more expensive. It also disrupts the financial planning of workers because prices rise faster than wages. In general, high inflation adds uncertainty to an economy.

Inflation tends to increase during periods of economic expansion. This happens because increased consumer demand forces prices to rise. Increased employee hiring during an expansion also leads to an increase in wages overall. However, the inflation rate tends to decline during a recession. Falling consumer demand forces many businesses to lower prices. In addition, the growth of wages falls as businesses cut back on hiring.

There are several indicators of inflation, but the consumer price index is the most widely used. The **consumer price index (CPI)** is a measure of the average change in the prices paid by consumers for typical consumer goods and services over time. The CPI is compiled by the US Bureau of Labor Statistics.

Inflation can be divided into four levels: low, moderate, severe, and hyperinflation. Each level is based on the inflation rate, as shown in Figure 2-3.

Levels of Inflation		
Inflation Level	**Inflation Rate**	**Effect on Economy**
Low	1% to 4%	Economy remains stable
Medium	5% to 9%	Prices start rising faster than wages
Severe	10% or higher	Purchasing power falls more quickly
Hyperinflation	Over 1,000%	Value of money and the economy is destroyed

Goodheart-Willcox Publisher

Figure 2-3 The terms for inflation levels are usually applied to changes that occur on a month-to-month or year-to-year basis.

Severe inflation is also called *double-digit inflation*. Inflation in the United States has averaged around 3 percent annually over the past 100 years. *Hyperinflation* is an extremely rapid, out-of-control rise in inflation. A country's currency is severely devalued by hyperinflation. The United States has never experienced hyperinflation.

Deflation is a general decline in prices throughout an economy. It is the opposite of inflation. This situation usually occurs when the economy is very weak. The last time there was significant deflation in the United States was during the Great Depression in the 1930s.

Interest Rates

Interest is the amount a borrower pays to a lender for a loan. An **interest rate** represents the cost of a loan and is expressed as a percent of the amount borrowed. Many different interest

rates can be found in an economy, because there are many different borrowers, lenders, and types of loans.

Borrowers may be consumers, businesses, and government agencies. Lenders include banks, finance companies, and investors. Loans are made in the form of home mortgages, auto loans, student loans, business loans, and for other purposes.

The interest rate on a loan is determined by the forces of supply and demand. An increase in demand to borrow money tends to increase interest rates. Interest rates usually decrease when the demand for loans falls. As a result, interest rates typically rise when the economy is strong and there is more demand to borrow money to buy various goods and services. Interest rates often decline when the economy is weak and there is less demand to borrow money.

 You Do the Math   Algebraic Reasoning

The order of operations is a set of rules stating which operations in an equation are performed first. The order of operations is often stated using the acronym *PEMDAS*. PEMDAS stands for parentheses, exponents, multiplication and division, and addition and subtraction. Anything inside parentheses is computed first. Exponents are computed next. Then, any multiplication and division operations are computed. Finally, any addition and subtraction

operations are computed to find the answer to the problem. Equations are solved from left to right when applying PEMDAS.

Find the solution to these equations.

1. $8 - (4 \times 3) + 2^3 \div 2 =$
2. $3 + 4.5 - 27 \div 9 =$
3. $11^2 + (45 \times 2) =$

An increase in the supply of money available for lending may also lower interest rates. The supply is influenced by the amount of money that is saved in an economy and made available for loans. The government can change the supply of money to influence interest rates.

Labor

All of the people in a nation who are capable of working and want to work are called the **labor force**. It does not include children, individuals who are retired, or people who choose not to work. The total labor force includes civilian workers, as well as those in the military.

Labor is important in an economy. Without labor, goods and services would not be available. Those who provide labor receive wages. Workers spend their wages on goods and services, which supports business and economic activity.

Unemployment Rate

The civilian labor force is divided into two categories: employed and unemployed. *Employed* includes everyone who is working. *Unemployed* includes those who do not have a job but are actively looking for one. The **unemployment rate** is the percentage of the civilian labor force that is unemployed.

If every person who is willing and able to work has a job, the economy would be at *full employment*. Interestingly, even when the economy is considered to be at full employment, the unemployment rate is still about 4 percent. This is because there are always people who are not working for many different reasons. They may be entering or

kurhan/Shutterstock.com

The labor force includes all civilian workers in an economy.

reentering the workforce or may be between jobs. As a result, an unemployment rate between 4 and 5 percent indicates a healthy economy. A rising unemployment rate indicates a weakening economy because it means businesses are not hiring or are eliminating part of their labor force.

The unemployment rate does not immediately rise or fall with changes in the economy. Rising consumer demand for goods and services causes the economy to strengthen. Businesses react by increasing production and eventually hire more workers. This is when the unemployment rate declines. However, the unemployment rate typically does not change until after economic expansion has been underway for six to nine months. When the economy falls into a recession, businesses react by decreasing production and eventually cutting their workforce. This causes the unemployment rate to rise. The unemployment rate does rise until after the economic contraction has been underway for a while.

Productivity

Productivity is a measure of a worker's production in a specific amount of time, such as an hour, a day, or a week. The more products a worker produces in the amount of time specified, the higher his or her productivity. Higher productivity means more products can be produced at the same cost, often in a shorter amount of time. It also means fewer workers are needed, so employers have lower costs. This, in turn, generally results in more profits. More profit enables companies to reinvest more money in their businesses.

Productivity can also lead to a higher standard of living for consumers. *Standard of living* refers to the financial well-being of the average person in a country. When the selection of products is greater, individuals have more choices when making purchase decisions.

Businesses are always looking for ways to increase productivity that will also increase profitability. One way to increase productivity is to increase efficiency through specialization. **Specialization** is focusing on the production

of specific goods so that more products can be produced with the same amount of labor. Specialization is often centered on the factors of production. Nations often specialize in products for which they have the resources and talent to produce. Trying to produce all the products to meet all the needs of every consumer is not always efficient or profitable.

Specialization can also apply to labor. Henry Ford was one of the first to apply specialization in his company by using the assembly line. Before the assembly line, ten Ford workers produced ten cars in a day. With an assembly line, each worker specialized in one-tenth of the car's assembly. Work was much more efficient and the same ten workers produced thirty cars in a day.

Air Images/Shutterstock.com

Specializing in one part of a larger process increases worker productivity.

Stock and Bond Markets

The **stock market** is a system and marketplace for buying and selling stocks. A *stock* represents the right of ownership in a corporation. Ownership of a corporation is divided into *shares*. Each share represents a partial ownership. Buying partial ownership in a corporation is a form of investment. People who buy shares of stock in a company are called *stockholders*.

When the value of the stock market increases, it indicates that the value of businesses is rising. Investors make decisions based on their expectations of economic growth and profits for a corporation. As a result, they often buy stocks when they think the economy will get stronger. This sends the value of the stock market higher. A falling stock market means the market value of businesses is falling. Investors tend to sell stocks when they think the economy will get weaker. This sends the value of the stock market lower.

The values in stock markets continually go up and down and do not always reflect the actual state of an economy. History has shown that stock markets tend to peak right before a downturn in the economy. However, nobody really knows when a market has reached its peak. As a result, many investors are surprised when stock markets fall.

A **bond** is a certificate of debt issued by an organization or government. Corporations and governments issue bonds to borrow large amounts of money. The bonds are sold to investors, who are essentially the lenders to corporations and governments. Bondholders are paid interest for the use of their money.

After bonds are issued, they can be traded among investors in a bond market. *Trading* means to buy or sell. There are markets for various corporate and government bonds. The largest market is for bonds issued by the US government. The interest rates in the bond markets can change every day. Rising rates tend to reflect a stronger economy. Lower rates tend to reflect a weaker economy.

Lisa S./Shutterstock.com

The New York Stock Exchange (NYSE) provides a marketplace for buyers and sellers to trade stocks and bonds.

Business Cycle

The economy of the United States has been very successful and has experienced growth over many years. However, the economy does not grow at the same rate each year. In some years, the economy and gross domestic product (GDP) grow by more than the average amount. At other times, it grows less than the average amount or may even decline. These alternating periods of expansion and contraction in the economy are called the **business cycle**.

There are four stages of the business cycle: expansion, peak, recession, and trough. Each stage can vary in length. The graph in Figure 2-4 illustrates the cyclical movement in our economy. Understanding these stages helps businesses make better decisions.

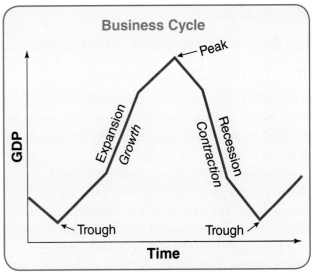

Goodheart-Willcox Publisher

Figure 2-4 A single business cycle includes all the economic activity from the beginning of one trough to the beginning of the next.

Expansion

Economic **expansion** is a period when the economy is growing and the GDP is rising. It usually begins with an increase in consumer demand for goods and services. Businesses react to expansion by increasing production and hiring more workers. During an expansion, wages also begin to increase. More workers and higher wages produce an even greater demand for goods and services. This fuels more growth and continued expansion.

Peak

The **peak** marks the end of expansion and is the highest point in the business cycle. At this point, consumer demand for goods and services starts to slow. Businesses react by reducing production and cutting workers. Wages also grow more slowly, if at all. Overall economic growth slows. Economic expansion may end for a reason that is obvious, such as the great recession of 2008 that started with a financial crisis and housing market collapse. Other times, the reason is not clear.

 Green Business   Environmentally Friendly Electronics

A variety of electronic equipment, such as computers and cell phones, are necessary to communicate efficiently. It is important to purchase environmentally friendly devices as older equipment is replaced. Lead-free and mercury-free computers that are built using reduced amounts of chemicals are available. Many manufacturers phased out the use of arsenic in the production of glass display screens. Some manufacturers use recycled materials in the construction of their products. Additionally, many electronics retailers offer electronics recycling services.

These retailers often partner with responsible recyclers who use the best practices available to repair, repurpose, or recycle the equipment.

Many businesses focus on purchasing equipment that respects the environment. Various organizations, such as *Green Seal*, use rigid criteria to evaluate products for sustainability. If a product meets all of the requirements, it earns an official green seal of approval. A product with a seal of approval sends the message that your company values preserving the environment.

Recession

Recession follows a peak in the business cycle. **Recession** is a period of significant decline in the total output, income, employment, and trade in an economy. It usually lasts from twelve to eighteen months, but may be less. Recession is marked by widespread contraction, or decline, in many parts of the economy.

A period of economic contraction that is severe and lasts a long time is called a **depression**. The last period of depression in the United States was from 1929 to 1940. During this time, many banks failed, unemployment reached over 20 percent, and many people lost their homes. There was widespread poverty. The causes of the Great Depression are still debated by economists. However, some reasons include the crash of stock prices, a decline in business spending, and a reduction in the money supply.

Trough

A **trough** is the lowest stage of a business cycle and marks the end of a recession. The period of

Dragon Images/Shutterstock.com

A severe drop in stock prices may contribute to an economic recession or period of depression.

expansion that follows a trough is called *economic recovery*. The reasons a recession comes to an end are not always clear. However, the economy begins to grow again and is fueled by increased consumer demand for goods and services. The business cycle continues again into another period of expansion.

Section 2.1 Review

 Check Your Understanding

1. List five of the most widely followed indicators of the economy.
2. Identify four components that are used to measure the GDP.
3. What are the four levels of inflation?
4. Name the four stages of the business cycle.
5. What is the effect of economic expansion on employment and wages?

 Build Your Vocabulary

As you progress through this course, develop a personal glossary of key terms. This will help you build your vocabulary and prepare you for a career. Write a definition for each of the following terms and add it to your personal glossary.

gross domestic product (GDP)

inflation

inflation rate

consumer price index (CPI)

deflation

interest

interest rate

labor force

unemployment rate

productivity

specialization

stock market

bond

business cycle

expansion

peak

recession

depression

trough

Government and the Economy

Objective

After completing this section, you will be able to:

- **Describe** the four basic market structures in a free enterprise system.
- **Explain** the government's role in the economy.

Key Terms 📇

market structure	price competition	Federal Reserve
monopoly	nonprice	System
oligopoly	competition	money supply
monopolistic	commerce	antitrust laws
competition	fiscal policy	price fixing
perfect competition	monetary policy	collusion

Market Structure

Market structure is how a market is organized based on the number of businesses competing for sales in an industry. In our free enterprise system, competition is the backbone of our economy. As shown in Figure 2-5, there are four basic market structures that represent varying degrees of competition.

- **Monopoly.** A monopoly is a market structure with one business that has complete control of a market's entire supply of goods or services.

- **Oligopoly.** An oligopoly is a market structure with a small number of businesses selling the same or similar products.

- **Monopolistic competition.** Monopolistic competition is a large number of businesses selling similar, but not the same, products and at different prices. This is also known as *imperfect competition*.

- **Perfect competition.** Perfect competition is characterized by a large number of businesses selling the same product at the same prices.

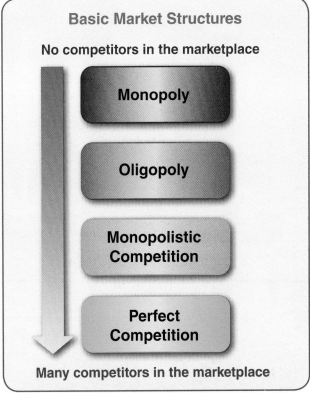

Goodheart-Willcox Publisher

Figure 2-5 Four basic market structures represent various levels of competition in an economy.

Most businesses operate in a market structure of monopolistic competition. Each business competes for customers using price or nonprice competition. **Price competition** is when a lower price is the main reason for customers to buy from one business over another. Although lowering prices may attract more customers, it may have a negative effect on overall business profits. **Nonprice competition** is a competitive advantage based on factors other than price. Better service or more convenient store hours are ways businesses compete and potentially increase sales.

Role of Government in the Economy

Government plays an important role in a nation's economy. Compared with many other nations, the US government plays a small role in the economy. The US economy has been more successful and has created more wealth than any other economic system. Like other market economies, the foundation of our free enterprise system is freedom of choice by individuals. This implies that the government should not interfere with market forces at work. *Laissez-faire* describes an economic policy that allows businesses to operate with very little interference from the government. It is a French term that means "let them do as they please."

However, even a free enterprise system needs some government involvement. The question is, how much? Some want the government to address many problems that a market economy creates or cannot fix. Others think the role of government should be very limited.

The Constitution of the United States gives Congress the power to regulate commerce and become involved in business and labor matters. **Commerce** is the activities involved in buying and selling goods on a large scale, such as state-wide or nation-wide commerce.

Orhan Cam/Shutterstock.com

The US Congress has the power to regulate commerce and become involved in business and labor matters.

The government protects individual liberties and private property rights and enforces contractual agreements. It provides political stability and laws necessary for economic interaction. These government roles enable individuals and businesses to carry out productive economic activities.

As a *regulator*, the government enacts and enforces laws and regulations to control individual and business activities. As a *provider*, it makes available goods and services for the public benefit in various areas, such as safety, education, and various welfare programs. Examples of specific roles the government plays in the operation of our economy include the following:

- manages the economy
- provides public goods and services
- provides a legal framework
- promotes competition
- corrects for externalities

The economy is incredibly complex and difficult to predict. Government policies can help a free enterprise system operate in an efficient manner.

Manage the Economy

The government takes a role to manage the economy. This is done through fiscal and monetary policies.

Fiscal Policy

Fiscal policy is the tax and spending decisions made by the president and Congress. The government often uses fiscal policies to boost the economy when it is weak. Fiscal policy may also be used to reduce the extreme highs and lows of the business cycle. For example, the government may choose to lower taxes during an economic contraction. This would give people more money to spend and may reduce the impact of a sharp fall in the economy. However, consumers and businesses may choose to save the money from lower taxes instead of spending it. Fiscal policy is the decision made by government, but the action taken by the people can be unpredictable.

Ethics

Collusion

It is unethical for a business to participate in acts of collusion. *Collusion* occurs when competing businesses work together to eliminate competition by misleading customers, fixing prices, or other fraudulent practices. Unethical businesses sometimes collude with others so they can dominate the marketplace. Collusion is not only unethical—it is illegal.

Monetary Policy

Monetary policy is policy that regulates the supply of money and interest rates by a central bank in an economy. The **Federal Reserve System** is the central bank of the United States, created by Congress in 1913. It carries out the nation's monetary policy "to promote effectively the goals of maximum employment, stable prices, and moderate long-term interest rates."

The Federal Reserve, also called the *Fed*, looks at many economic indicators to evaluate the condition of the economy. When the economy is slow or weak, it may take action to increase the money supply and lower interest rates. **Money supply** is the total money circulating at any one time in a country. It includes both cash and money in the bank.

When interest rates are lowered, it makes borrowing money easier, which may encourage consumers and business to spend more. When more money is spent, the economy grows faster.

If the economy is growing too fast, the Federal Reserve can raise interest rates to slow the economy and avoid inflation. When the demand for goods and services grows faster than the supply, inflation can increase. Higher interest rates make borrowing money more expensive. As a result, individuals and businesses become more cautious about spending and demand is reduced.

Harry Hu/Shutterstock.com

Police services and protection are an example of a public service provided by the government.

Provide Public Goods and Services

The government provides certain public goods and services that are available to everyone in the economy. Government agencies collect taxes to pay for these goods and services. Public education is an example of a public service provided by the government. A nation benefits when its population is well educated. This can result in a society that is generally more productive and stable. However, education is expensive. If private schools were the only options, few people could afford the cost of education. Other public services include construction and maintenance of roads, police and fire protection, postal services, and public parks.

The main motives in a market economy are money and profit. People who have money can get what they need and want. However, people with little money may struggle to meet basic needs. These people often include retirees, disabled citizens, veterans, disaster victims, and unemployed workers. The government has developed social programs to offer goods and services to citizens in need. Medicare and Social Security are among the largest social programs that benefit retirees and the disabled. Unemployment compensation provides some money to workers who have lost their jobs. The Federal Emergency Management Agency (FEMA) provides relief to victims of disasters, such as hurricanes and earthquakes. There are many other programs at the federal, state, and local levels.

Provide a Legal Framework

A legal framework is necessary for a market economy to function. Laws are needed to define and enforce property rights and provide for public safety. They establish boundaries and define acceptable behavior. They help protect individuals and businesses from dishonest business practices. Laws are made and enforced at all levels of government. Criminal laws define conduct that threatens public safety and outlines punishment for such acts. Civil laws define conduct between individuals in situations such as contracts and property.

Federal Antitrust Laws	
Sherman Antitrust Act (1890)	This act supports fair commerce and trade by making the formation of monopolies and agreements to practice price fixing illegal. Violations of this act are punishable as criminal felonies.
Clayton Antitrust Act (1914)	This act helps prevent the formation of monopolies that will reduce competition. Businesses planning a merger or acquisition must notify the Department of Justice Antitrust Division and the Federal Trade Commission.
Federal Trade Commission Act (1914)	This act prohibits unfair competition in interstate commerce. It also created the Federal Trade Commission to oversee related business activity.

Source: US Department of Justice; Goodheart-Willcox Publisher

Figure 2-6 The federal antitrust laws are enforced by departments of the federal government. Individual states also enforce their own antitrust laws.

Promote Competition

The government creates laws to control unfair business practices. **Antitrust laws** promote fair trade and competition among businesses. As shown in Figure 2-6, there are three major federal antitrust laws: Sherman Antitrust Act, Clayton Antitrust Act, and Federal Trade Commission Act. The US Department of Justice and the Federal Trade Commission enforce antitrust laws in the US economy.

Antitrust laws attempt to ensure that markets are open and fair. These laws have been established to prevent monopolies and price fixing. **Price fixing** occurs when two or more businesses in an industry agree to sell the same good or service at a set price. This practice eliminates price competition. When two or more businesses work together to remove their competition, set prices, and control distribution, it is called **collusion**.

The *Sherman Antitrust Act* in 1890 was the first antitrust law in the United States. It removed limits on competitive trade and kept companies from monopolizing markets.

In 1914, the *Clayton Antitrust Act* gave the federal government more power to detect companies in the early stages of creating monopolies and to prevent them. Some public utility companies, such as electric, natural gas, and water suppliers, have been allowed to remain monopolies. However, the rates they charge are regulated by the government to protect consumers.

The *Federal Trade Commission Act* was also signed into law in 1914. It created the US Federal Trade Commission (FTC), whose mission is to protect consumers and promote fair competition in the marketplace. Over the years the role of the FTC has expanded and evolved with changes in the economy and society. It is now involved in monitoring telemarketing activity and violations, deceptive advertising, and breaches in data security.

Correct for Externalities

An *externality* is something that is not directly connected to an economic activity, but that affects people. For example, emissions from a factory can be harmful to those living close to the business. It can cause problems for those who inhale the fumes. Controlling emissions is not an economic activity. However, the government can impose fines and taxes on industries to reduce this type of externality.

Section 2.2   Review

Check Your Understanding

1. What are the four basic market structures?
2. How do businesses compete for customers?
3. List examples of specific roles that the US government plays in the operation of the economy.
4. How can the government use fiscal policies to manage the economy?
5. Why is a legal framework needed for a market economy to function?

Build Your Vocabulary

As you progress through this course, develop a personal glossary of key terms. This will help you build your vocabulary and prepare you for a career. Write a definition for each of the following terms and add it to your personal glossary.

market structure	fiscal policy
monopoly	monetary policy
oligopoly	Federal Reserve System
monopolistic competition	money supply
perfect competition	antitrust laws
price competition	price fixing
nonprice competition	collusion
commerce	

Review and Assessment

Chapter Summary

Section 2.1 Measuring Economic Activity

- The strength of an economy can be measured using certain economic indicators. Some of the most widely followed indicators of the economy are gross domestic product (GDP), inflation, interest rates, unemployment rate, and the stock and bond markets.

- The economy moves through alternating periods of expansion and contraction called the business cycle. The four stages of the business cycle include expansion, peak, recession, and trough. Expansion is a period of when the economy is growing and the GDP is rising. The peak is the highest point in the business cycle. Recession is a period of significant economic decline. Trough is the lowest stage of the business cycle.

Section 2.2 Government and the Economy

- Market structure is how a market is organized based on the number of businesses competing for sales in an industry. There are four basic market structures: monopoly, oligopoly, perfect competition, and monopolistic competition. Businesses compete for customers using price or nonprice competition.

- The government plays specific roles in the operation of the US economy. It manages the economy, provides public goods and services, establishes a legal framework, promotes competition, and corrects for externalities.

Online Activities

Complete the following activities to help you learn, practice, and expand your knowledge and skills.

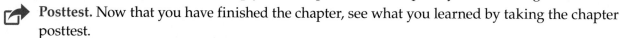 **Posttest.** Now that you have finished the chapter, see what you learned by taking the chapter posttest.

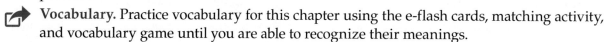 **Vocabulary.** Practice vocabulary for this chapter using the e-flash cards, matching activity, and vocabulary game until you are able to recognize their meanings.

Review Your Knowledge

1. Explain how the GDP can be used to measure the strength of the economy.
2. Summarize the difference between inflation and interest rates.
3. How is the unemployment rate used to measure the strength of an economy?
4. Explain how the stock and bond markets reflect economic strength.
5. Describe each of the four stages of the business cycle.
6. Describe each of the four basic market structures.

7. Explain how the government functions as both a regulator and a provider in the free enterprise economy.

8. How does the Federal Reserve regulate monetary policy?

9. Describe the government's role in providing public safety and well-being.

10. Explain the three major federal antitrust laws.

Apply Your Knowledge

1. An interest rate represents the cost of a loan and is expressed as a percent of the amount borrowed. How do interest rates affect the average consumer? Describe how interest rates have affected your personal financial activities.

2. Explain the concept of productivity. Choose a type of business and create a chart to illustrate areas of specialization and division of labor within the business operations. Analyze the impact of specialization and division of labor on the overall productivity of the business type you chose.

3. Businesses compete for customers using both price and nonprice competition. What are some examples of nonprice factors you have experienced as a consumer? Have nonprice factors ever influenced your buying decisions? Explain your answer.

4. The government plays specific roles in our economy to aid business operations. Create a chart that lists each role that government plays in our economy. Next to each role, indicate if the government serves as a regulator or provider.

5. Make a list of ten activities that your local government performs in the community. Do any of these overlap with state or federal government activities?

Communication Skills

College and Career Readiness

Speaking. All careers require that individuals be able to participate and contribute to one-on-one discussions. Developing intrapersonal communication skills is one way to achieve career opportunities. As your instructor lectures on this chapter, contribute thoughtful comments when participation is invited.

Listening. Hearing is a physical process. Listening combines hearing with evaluation. Listen to your instructor as a lesson is presented. Analyze the effectiveness of the presentation. Listen carefully and take notes about the main points. Then organize the key information that you heard.

Writing. Contributing citizens pay their fair share of taxes to support the government. Select two tax laws that generate funds for government services and analyze how they work. Write several paragraphs to describe how the revenue generated from these taxes helps contribute to the betterment of the community.

Internet Research

Business Cycles. In what stage of the business cycle do you think our economy is in today? Research the current state of our economy using various Internet resources including data on the gross domestic product (GDP) from the Bureau of Economic Analysis website. Information on the unemployment rate, interest rate, and the stock market can also be helpful as you make your determination. Synthesize and organize the information so that you may present it to your class.

Teamwork

Working with your team, make a list of three businesses you would expect to do well in the expansion stage of the business cycle. Next, make a list of three businesses you would expect to do well in the recession stage of the business cycle. Why do these businesses perform differently in the business cycle?

Portfolio Development

College and Career Readiness

Objective. Before you begin collecting information for your portfolio, write an objective for the finished product. An *objective* is a complete sentence or two that states what you want to accomplish.

The language in your objective should be clear and specific. Include enough details so you can easily judge when you have accomplished it. Consider this objective: "I will try to get into college." Such an objective is too general. A better, more detailed objective might read: "I will get accepted into the communications program at one of my top three colleges of choice." Creating a clear objective is a good starting point for beginning to work on your portfolio.

1. Decide the purpose of the portfolio you are creating, such as short-term employment, career, community service, or college application.

2. Set a time line to finish the final product.

3. Write an objective for your portfolio.

CTSOs

 **Performance.** Some competitive events for CTSOs have a performance component. The activity could potentially be a decision-making scenario for which your team will provide a solution and present to the judges.

To prepare for the performance component of a presentation, complete the following activities.

1. On your CTSO's website, locate a rubric or scoring sheet for the event.

2. Confirm whether visual aids may be used in the presentation and the amount of setup time permitted.

3. Review the rules to confirm whether questions will be asked or if the team will need to defend a case or situation.

4. Make notes on index cards about important points to remember. Use these notes to study. You may also be able to use these notes during the event.

5. Practice the performance. You should introduce yourself, review the topic that is being presented, defend the topic being presented, and conclude with a summary.

6. After the practice performance is complete, ask for feedback from your instructor. You may also consider having a student audience listen and give feedback.

CHAPTER 3

Business Law and Ethics

Exploring Careers

Business Ethics Consultant

Business Management & Administration

Business ethics is a set of rules that helps define appropriate behavior in a business setting. A business ethics consultant evaluates the culture and value system of a company. That information is used to decide whether the company's practices are ethical. If not, the business ethics consultant assists the business in developing an ethical culture.

Typical job titles for this position also include *ethics and compliance officer* and *ethics officer*. Examples of tasks that business ethics consultants perform include:

- ensure practices and policies of an organization conform to laws and regulations
- help solve problems that occur within an organization
- advise on crisis control when problems occur with customers and governmental agencies
- educate employees in the legal, ethical, and reputation interests of the organization

Most business ethics consultant jobs require a bachelor or master degree in business administration. A business ethics consultant should have an understanding of regulations and compliance procedures for the field in which they work. Strong oral and written communication skills are important. Related job experience is also helpful.

Reading Prep

As you read the chapter, record any questions that come to mind. Indicate where the answer to each question can be found: within the text, by asking your teacher, in another book, on the Internet, or by reflecting on your own knowledge and experiences. Pursue the answers to your questions.

**College
and Career
Readiness**

Check Your Business IQ

Before you begin the chapter, see what you already know about business by taking the chapter pretest. The pretest is available at www.g-wlearning.com.

Legal Environment

?**E**ssential **Q**uestion

How is the US government involved in business activities?

Objectives

After completing this section, you will be able to:

- **Describe** the purpose of contracts.
- **Discuss** the role of the legal system in business.
- **Explain** workplace laws and regulations.
- **Identify** laws and regulations that protect consumers.

Key Terms 🗘

contract
offer
acceptance
consideration
capacity
contract law

breach of contract
sales and service contract
lease
employment contract

employer identification number (EIN)
Consumer Bill of Rights
recall

Contracts

A **contract** is a legally binding agreement between two or more people or businesses. Each person who participates in a contract agreement is called a *party*. The purpose of a contract is to formalize an agreement between the parties involved. Business contracts protect the interests of the business and help to ensure all parties perform as expected. Contracts ensure that:

- customers understand their role and rights in a sales transaction
- businesses have the materials and resources needed to operate
- all parties understand the terms of the agreement and consequences for not performing

A contract may be a written document or a verbal agreement. Whether written or verbal, all the parties involved in a contract are expected to perform according to the contract agreement.

Legal experts recommend that all contracts be in writing. Written contracts are easier to enforce and can avoid misinterpretations. Written contracts include electronic contracts that parties sign using electronic signatures. Electronic contracts are as legal and enforceable as contracts printed on paper.

Elements of a Contract

Certain elements must be included in a contract to be enforceable. The following are some of the required elements of a legal contract.

- *Offer.* An **offer** is a proposal to provide a good or service.
- *Acceptance.* **Acceptance** means that all parties involved must agree to the terms of the contract.
- *Consideration.* **Consideration** means that something of value must be promised in return.

Ethics

Ethical Messages

Sometimes it is necessary to write a sales message or other type of document for your organization. Embellishing a message about a product or intentionally misrepresenting a product is unethical and may be illegal. There are truth-in-advertising laws that must be followed. Focus on the truths of the message and use your communication skills in a positive manner to create interest or demand for the good or service.

- *Intention of legal consequences.* The parties entering into the contract must understand that it can be enforced by law.

Additionally, the goods, services, and actions involved in a contract must be legal.

In order for a contract to be legally binding, all parties involved must enter the contract voluntarily and be competent. They must be of legal age and be of sound mind to understand their actions. **Capacity** means that a person is legally able to enter into a binding agreement.

The US legal system provides a framework for creating and enforcing legal contracts. **Contract law** regulates how contracts are written, executed, and enforced. A **breach of contract** is when one or more parties do not follow the agreed terms of a contract without having a legitimate reason. It is basically a broken promise. A breach of contract lawsuit is a civil action and damages are usually settled in the form of money.

Business Contracts

Contracts are used in many areas of business and professional activities, such as with product vendors, business partners, property leasing companies, and landscape contractors. Some contracts commonly used by businesses include:

- sales and service contracts
- property or equipment leases
- partnership agreements
- employment contracts

Sales and service contracts list the goods or services provided by a business and the price the customer pays in exchange. This type of contract may simply be a receipt that is printed after a retail purchase. Other types may include more details, such as a list of all materials and labor provided. They may also include a time frame for delivery, payments terms, and a product guarantee.

A **lease** is a contract to rent something. This type of contract typically applies to real estate and vehicles used by a business. For example, if a business needs to rent office space, a property lease is issued. A property lease includes the type of activities that will take place in the space. It also includes the length of time use of the space will be provided and how much will be paid in rent to use the space.

Goodluz/Shutterstock.com

It is important to carefully read and understand all legal documents before signing.

A vehicle lease is a type of business sales and service contract.

A *software license* may be considered a type of lease because the software publisher keeps ownership of the software. The software can only be used in the ways described in the software license. The user agrees to this contract when the software is installed.

A *partnership agreement* is a contract used when two or more individuals create a business. The agreement usually states how much each partner will invest in the business, each partner's responsibilities, and how profits and losses are distributed.

An **employment contract** describes the terms of employment between a business and an employee. The contract describes how long employment will last, how much the employee will be paid, and the benefits provided by the business. An employment contract can also include information about trade secrets and termination of employment.

Areas of Business Regulation	
Administrative Law	Laws that regulate the activities and procedures of governmental agencies
Antitrust Law	Laws that support fair business practices in a free market economy
Common Law	Laws and authority based on previous court rulings and judicial decisions
Intellectual Property Law	Regulations on establishing and enforcing ownership rights for inventions, artistic creations, ideas, and many other types of original work
Maritime Law	Laws that apply to interstate and international commerce activity on bodies of water
Uniform Commercial Code	Laws established to make commercial transactions, such as sales, contracts, and loans, more consistent in all fifty states

Goodheart-Willcox Publisher

Figure 3-1 Business-related laws and regulations provide a framework for legal business activity in the United States.

Role of the Legal System

In addition to enforcing legal contracts, an important activity performed by government is regulating certain business activities. Some areas of business-related regulation are described in Figure 3-1. Many federal and state laws reinforce honest business practices and financial responsibility. The US legal system may become involved in enforcing business laws and deciding the action that should be taken. Local, state, and federal governmental agencies and departments all play a role in enforcing business operation regulations.

Businesses, regardless of type or size, are subject to various laws and regulations. These include fair competition, e-commerce, business finances, and environmental protection.

Fair Competition

Laws regulating the day-to-day activities and practices of businesses help ensure fair competition in the marketplace. The Federal Trade Commission Act of 1914 created the Federal Trade Commission (FTC) to enforce US antitrust laws. Antitrust laws, such as the Sherman Act and Clayton Act, regulate against unfair business practices that prevent competition in the marketplace. Unfair business practices include forming monopolies and exclusive distribution agreements. By enforcing antitrust laws, consumers are free to choose goods and services that range in quality and price in an open and fair marketplace.

Fair pricing plays a role in fair competition. Many factors affect the price a business charges for goods and services. However, intentionally pricing products to mislead customers or to put a competitor out of business is illegal. Regulations on price fixing and predatory pricing were put in place by the Sherman Act. The Robinson-Patman Act brings additional fair pricing regulations to business activities. These regulations prevent price discrimination among distributors and sellers. This means that businesses are expected to sell their products at the same price to all buyers, regardless of who the buyers are or the quantity they purchase.

E-Commerce

Businesses that operate online have additional e-commerce guidelines and laws that they must follow. Some examples are described in Figure 3-2. Typically, these laws regulate how online business is conducted, the use of customer information, data security, and online advertising. The FTC has information and many resources for businesses on e-commerce regulations available through the agency's website.

E-Commerce Laws	
Electronic Fund Transfer Act (1978)	Protects consumers who use electronic fund transfer (EFT) services, including ATMs, point-of-sale terminals, automated bill-payment arrangements, and remote banking programs
Children's Online Privacy Protection Act—COPPA (1998)	Protects the personal information of children under 13 years of age who are using online services or websites
Electronic Signatures in Global and National Commerce Act—ESIGN (2000)	Allows electronic signatures to be used for interstate and international commerce transactions that require written signatures
CAN-SPAM Act (2003)	Sets rules for commercial e-mail messages and gives recipients the right to stop receiving unwanted e-mails
US Safe Web Act (2006)	Increases the scope of cooperation to enforce regulations related to spam, spyware, false advertising, breaches in security, and consumer privacy

Goodheart-Willcox Publisher

Figure 3-2 Businesses that participate in e-commerce activities must follow e-commerce laws in addition to US business regulations.

Business Finances

There are many US laws that regulate the financial activities of businesses. These laws are meant to promote competition and protect businesses and financial investors.

- *Antitrust laws.* The financial regulations of antitrust laws relate to businesses buying or investing in other businesses. These regulations promote fair competition and discourage monopolies.

- *Bankruptcy laws.* Bankruptcy laws apply to the handling of business debts when a business is no longer profitable.

- *Securities laws.* Securities include stocks and other financial investments. Securities laws regulate businesses that have publicly traded stocks and bonds. These regulations are enforced by the US Securities and Exchange Commission (SEC) and cover areas like financial reporting, issuance of securities, and use of information by company insiders.

The Internal Revenue Service (IRS) is a bureau of the US Department of Treasury. It is responsible for enforcing US tax laws. Businesses are required to pay taxes on their profits and to file federal and state tax documents on a regular basis. In addition, businesses are responsible for collecting employment taxes from employee paychecks and sales taxes from customers. The type of taxes paid and forms required depend on the business type.

For tax purposes, most businesses are required to have an **employer identification number (EIN)**. This number is assigned by the IRS for businesses to use when preparing federal tax returns and forms. Partnerships and corporations must have an EIN. Sole proprietorships with at least one employee must also have an EIN. Sole proprietorships without employees can obtain an EIN, but are usually not required to have one. Instead, the business owner can use his or her personal Social Security Number for business tax purposes. State governments also require business owners to have a state tax identification number. The Internal Revenue Service and the Department of Revenue in each state provide information and resources to help businesses understand their legal tax obligations.

Environmental Protection

Environmental laws and regulations apply to every type of business in every industry. Among many others, the United States has laws regulating:

- toxic chemicals released by industrial businesses

- importing and exporting materials that pose a risk to the environment

- handling and removal of asbestos

- vehicle emissions

- use of pesticides

- quality of drinking water

US businesses must make responsible decisions about their actions that relate to the environment. Examples of environmental laws are shown in Figure 3-3.

Environmental Protection Laws	
Clean Air Act (1970)	Establishes the allowable air pollutant levels emitted by US businesses
Clean Water Act (1972)	Establishes the allowable water pollutant levels emitted by US businesses
Noise Control Act (1972)	Protects the public from excessive noise created by business operations
Energy Policy Act (2005)	Provides tax incentives for companies that use energy-efficient methods in the operation of their business
Energy Independence and Security Act (2007)	Requires companies to increase the energy efficiency of the products they create, as well as the buildings used for operations

Goodheart-Willcox Publisher

Figure 3-3 Environmental laws and regulations apply differently to businesses within different industries.

The *Environmental Protection Agency (EPA)* is a governmental agency that enforces federal laws regarding human health and the environment. The EPA offers information and resources for individuals, businesses, and communities about environmental protection. Organizations looking for sustainable business practices can contact the EPA for guidance.

Workplace Laws

All businesses in the United States are required to protect employees and treat them fairly. The *US Department of Labor (DOL)* enforces workplace laws and regulations. The DOL works with many other governmental agencies to protect employees. Some of the laws that protect employees:

- enforce fair-wage laws and work-hours laws
- prevent discrimination and harassment in the workplace
- ensure employee safety

Some of the laws that protect employees in the United States are presented in Figure 3-4.

Labor Relations and Compensation

Labor relations laws regulate the relationships between employees and their employers. Labor laws cover a wide variety of employment issues. These include work hours and overtime pay. They also cover employee retirement income, medical leave, workplace safety, child labor, and many others.

In many industries, workers are part of a union that negotiates the terms of employment with employers. This negotiation is called *collective bargaining*. Representatives meet with an employer to discuss wages, hours of work, and other business practices that affect a group of workers. Even businesses that do not employ union workers must follow state and federal fair compensation laws for their employees. These laws address minimum wage, overtime pay, and equal pay. They also include how and when employees are paid and benefits employers may be required to offer.

Equal Employment Opportunity

Businesses are required to give all workers equal employment and advancement opportunities. State and federal laws on equal employment address employee hiring, training, promotion, termination, harassment, wages, and benefits. The *US Equal Employment Opportunity Commission (EEOC)* enforces federal laws that regulate unfair employment practices. It is illegal to discriminate against a job applicant or employee because of the person's race, ethnicity, religion, gender, national origin, age, disability, or genetic information.

Employee Protection Laws	
Fair Labor Standards Act (1938)	Establishes the minimum wage, overtime pay, recordkeeping, and youth employment standards
Comprehensive Omnibus Budget Reconciliation Act (1985)	Gives workers who lose their health benefits the option to continue the group health benefits provided by their group health plan
Worker Adjustment and Retraining Notification Act–WARN (1988)	Protects workers and communities by requiring employers to provide notice 60 days in advance of plant closings and mass layoffs
Family and Medical Leave Act (1993)	Requires that eligible employees be allowed to take unpaid, job-protected leave for specified family and medical reasons

Goodheart-Willcox Publisher

Figure 3-4 The US Department of Labor enforces workplace laws and regulations that protect employees in several ways.

Employers cannot deny someone a job or a promotion based on any of these characteristics alone. Some Equal Employment Opportunity (EEO) laws are described in Figure 3-5.

In addition to employment practices, EEOC regulations require businesses to keep certain records. These records include those on personnel, payroll, and employee evaluation. Employers are also required to educate employees about workplace discrimination. Businesses must be knowledgeable about Equal Employment Opportunity laws, how the laws apply to different businesses, and the legal responsibilities of employers. The EEOC provides education and guidance for employers and employees on equal employment opportunity laws and regulations.

Employee Health and Safety

Businesses must protect the health and safety of employees while in the workplace.

Employers are expected to make sure working conditions are safe for employees. The workplace should be secure so that accidents are less likely to occur. The *Occupational Safety and Health Association (OSHA)* was established by the US Department of Labor in 1970. The goal of the agency is to assure safe and healthful working conditions for employees. OSHA sets and enforces safety standards. It also provides training, outreach, education, and assistance to businesses.

Consumer Protection Laws

The government also protects consumers from unfair and unsafe business practices and products. Consumer protection laws aim to protect consumers from false advertising, harmful goods and services, and many other consumer issues. Some of the laws protecting consumers are shown in Figure 3-6.

Equal Employment Opportunity Laws	
Title VII of the Civil Rights Act–Title 7 (1964)	Employers cannot discriminate based on the race, color, religion, national origin, or gender of an individual.
Pregnancy Discrimination Act (1978)	An addition to Title VII that makes it illegal to discriminate against a woman because of pregnancy, childbirth, or a medical condition related to pregnancy or childbirth.
Equal Pay Act (1963)	Employers cannot pay different wages to men and women if they perform equal work in the same workplace.
Age Discrimination in Employment Act–ADEA (1967)	It is illegal for employers to discriminate against people who are age 40 and older based on age.
Title I of the Americans with Disabilities Act–ADA (1990)	It is illegal for employers to discriminate against a qualified person with a disability in both the private sector and in government departments. Employers must make reasonable accommodations for known physical or mental limitations of an otherwise qualified individual.
Section 501 of the Rehabilitation Act (1973)	The federal government cannot discriminate against a qualified employment candidate with a disability.
The Genetic Information Nondiscrimination Act of 2008 (GINA)	Employers cannot discriminate against employees or applicants because of genetic information, such as information about any disease, disorder, or condition of an individual's family members.

Goodheart-Willcox Publisher

Figure 3-5 The US Equal Employment Opportunity Commission enforces federal laws that regulate unfair employment practices.

Consumer Protection Laws	
Federal Food, Drug, and Cosmetic Act (1938)	Gives the US Food and Drug Administration the power to oversee the safety of all food, drugs, and cosmetics
Fair Packaging and Labeling Act (1966)	Requires that product labels identify the product and list the manufacturer's name and location and net amount of contents
Truth-in-Lending Act (1968)	Requires the disclosure of all finance charges on consumer credit agreements and in the advertising for credit plans
Child Protection and Toy Safety Act (1969)	Protects children from toys and other products that contain thermal, electrical, or mechanical hazards
Fair Credit Reporting Act (1970)	Gives individuals the right to examine and correct their own credit history records
Consumer Product Safety Act (1972)	Gives the Consumer Product Safety Commission the power to protect the public against risks of injury or death from unsafe products
Nutrition Labeling and Education Act (1990)	Requires food labels to list the amount of calories, fat, cholesterol, sodium, and fiber per serving
Country of Origin Labeling Law (2009)	Requires that product labels list a product's country of origin

Goodheart-Willcox Publisher

Figure 3-6 Consumer protection laws protect consumers from unfair and unsafe business practices and products.

President John F. Kennedy presented four basic consumer rights in a speech to Congress in 1962. These became the **Consumer Bill of Rights**, which are basic expectations of fair treatment of consumers. The Consumer Bill of Rights has expanded over time from four to a set of eight basic consumer rights.

- The right to safety.
- The right to be informed.
- The right to choose freely.
- The right to be heard.
- The right to satisfy basic needs.
- The right to redress.
- The right to consumer education.
- The right to a healthy environment.

The *US Consumer Product Safety Commission (CPSC)* is a governmental agency in charge of protecting consumers from products that pose unreasonable risks of injury or death.

Ditty_about_summer/Shutterstock.com

Labeling laws support the right of consumers to know the ingredients and nutritional facts about food products.

If the CPSC determines that a product is unsafe for consumers, the agency orders a recall. A **recall** is an order to remove or repair unsafe products in the market. In some cases, products are taken off store shelves and consumers are asked to return an unsafe product for a full refund. Recalls on larger and more complex products, like vehicles and some electronics, usually require repairs to be made. The manufacturer must fix the unsafe component of the product free of charge for the consumers affected.

The Federal Trade Commission (FTC) works to prevent unfair competition and deceptive acts or practices in business. The FTC enforces truth-in-advertising laws, such as the false advertising regulations in the Lanham Act of 1946. The FTC offers helpful guides and resources for both businesses and consumers. Truthful advertising helps consumers make knowledgeable purchasing decisions. It also encourages fair competition in the marketplace.

Section 3.1   Review

 Check Your Understanding

1. List the required elements of a legal contract.
2. Identify the types of laws and regulations that apply to every business, regardless of type or size.
3. Which governmental agency enforces federal laws regarding human health and the environment?
4. What personal characteristics does the EEOC use to define discrimination against a job applicant or employee?
5. List the eight basic consumer rights that are stated in the Consumer Bill of Rights.

 Build Your Vocabulary

As you progress through this course, develop a personal glossary of key terms. This will help you build your vocabulary and prepare you for a career. Write a definition for each of the following terms and add it to your personal glossary.

contract
offer
acceptance
consideration
capacity
contract law
breach of contract
sales and service contract

lease
employment contract
employer identification number (EIN)
Consumer Bill of Rights
recall

Ethics and Social Responsibility

?EQ **Essential Question**

In what ways do businesses demonstrate ethics and social responsibility?

Objectives

After completing this section, you will be able to:

- **Explain** how businesses encourage ethical behavior.
- **Discuss** the actions businesses take to promote social good.

Key Terms

ethics	confidentiality	social responsibility
integrity	proprietary	corporate social
morals	information	responsibility
code of ethics	trade secret	corporate culture
code of conduct	false advertising	philanthropy

Business Ethics

Ethics are rules of behavior based on a group's ideas about what is right and wrong. Groups that define ethics may be social groups, organizations, or society. *Business ethics* are principles that help define appropriate behavior in a business setting. These principles help businesses, governments, and employees make decisions. Many governmental agencies enforce business laws to support private enterprise, encourage fair competition, and protect consumers. However, businesses are expected to demonstrate ethical behavior and practices even when governmental regulations do not apply. Unethical actions that involve crime or theft can be punishable by law.

Integrity is the honesty of a person's actions. Those actions may be motivated by ethical, moral, or legal decisions. **Morals** are an individual's ideas of what is right and wrong. A person's morals guide his or her overall behavior and actions. However, an individual's morals may conflict with the ethics of a business or with legal definitions of right and wrong.

Ethical actions result when a person, business, or organization applies ethics and moral behavior. Many businesses encourage ethical behavior by creating a code of ethics and a code of conduct. They also establish confidentiality and communication guidelines for employees to follow.

Code of Ethics

Within a business or organization, a **code of ethics** is a document that dictates how business should be conducted. This document provides an outline of the appropriate channels of communication for the company. It also describes how business or official activities should take place.

Companies may define specific issues as inappropriate, as well as unethical or illegal. When making decisions that represent an organization, the following questions can be used to analyze if the action is ethical.

- Is the action legal?
- Will the privacy and confidentiality of the company be protected?

Unethical actions may also be illegal.

- Who is affected by these actions?
- Is the information presented factual and honest?

Code of Conduct

Businesses typically have a **code of conduct** handbook that outlines expectations of employee behavior. This applies to employees at work and when representing the company outside the workplace. The following examples may be part of a code of conduct to discourage unethical behavior in the workplace.

- Office equipment should not be used for personal business. This includes using the photocopier and office telephone.
- To avoid the appearance of conflicting interests, employees are not allowed to accept gifts from vendors.
- Internet access provided by the company should be used for business purposes only. Checking personal e-mail and shopping online by employees is not acceptable.

Confidentiality

In business, **confidentiality** means that specific information about a company or its employees is never shared, except with those who have clearance to receive it. Before hiring an employee, a company may require the person sign a confidentiality agreement. A *confidentiality agreement* typically states that the employee will not share any company information with those outside the company. Confidentiality agreements can also prevent former employees from working for a competitor for a specified length of time.

Proprietary information is any work created by company employees on the job that is owned by that company. Proprietary information may be called a **trade secret** because it is confidential information a company needs to keep private and protect from theft. Proprietary information can include many things, such as product formulas, customer lists, manufacturing processes, or sales strategies. The code of conduct should explain that company information may only be shared with

You Do the Math Algebraic Reasoning

In algebra, letters stand in place of unknown numbers. These letters are called *variables*. When a variable appears with numbers and signs for adding, subtracting, multiplying, or dividing, the expression is called a *variable expression*. For example, *x* + 5 is a variable expression.

Solve the following problems.

1. Macy budgets $25 a week for office refreshments. Sometimes, the amount she spends each week is less than $25. Write a variable expression to calculate the amount of money left over after a given week.

2. Trey sells advertising space in the local newspaper. The price for an ad is based on how many inches of vertical space it fills. The rate is $2.37 per inch. Write a variable expression to calculate the price of ad space.

3. Mariana orders $350 worth of office equipment from a single supplier each month. Payment for the order is made in a single payment or is sometimes divided into equal smaller payments. Write a variable expression to calculate equal payment amounts for the office equipment order.

specific permission. It is unethical for employees to share proprietary information with outsiders. In some cases, the employee may be breaking the law.

Honesty

Those who create communication documents for an organization must carefully consider the impact that communication has on the public. It may be tempting to get caught up in

YanLev/Shutterstock.com

The formula for a product may be the secret to a company's success in the marketplace.

exaggerations or inaccurate statements about the company's goods or services. The point of view presented in any business communication should be unbiased and honest.

Marketing messages that persuade the reader to buy something or respond in some way must be written according to the law. **False advertising** is overstating the features and benefits of products or making false claims about them. The *Federal Trade Commission (FTC)* enforces laws that uphold truth in advertising. Misrepresenting information, whether intentionally or unintentionally, can result in lawsuits, lost customers, or employees being dismissed.

Social Responsibility

Social responsibility is behaving with sensitivity to social, environmental, and economic issues. **Corporate social responsibility** includes all the actions taken by a business to promote social good. These actions go beyond the profit interests and legal requirements of a business. The term **corporate culture** describes how the owners and employees of a company think, feel, and act as a business. The level of social responsibility is part of corporate culture.

Organizations must be sensitive to the world around them. Negative communication about society or the environment reflects negatively on the company. Business communications should be analyzed to make certain they are not offensive. To measure whether an action is socially responsible, certain questions may be asked to analyze the action.

- Is the information presented factual and unbiased?

- Are any negative comments stated or implied about social issues?

- Does the message include any personal opinions about social responsibility?

Socially responsible businesses are civic-minded and work with the community in multiple ways. Societal issues, economic issues, and the environment are some areas that businesses may address.

Philanthropy is promoting the welfare of others. Protecting natural resources or donating money or products are examples of ways businesses give back to society. Many organizations encourage employees to volunteer their time for charitable organizations. Giving back to the community creates goodwill for a business.

Businesses that support the local economy also support themselves. Hiring employees from the community or using local vendors are both good business practices. Providing jobs for local people helps keep the community employment rate stable and strengthens the local economy. Hiring local vendors also contributes to the employment of a community. Both also generate taxes that go back to the local economy.

Social responsibility includes concern for the environment. Air, water, noise, and land pollution are examples of concerns to businesses that are socially responsible.

wavebreakmedia/Shutterstock.com

Corporate culture may encourage employees to participate in activities that promote social good.

Green Business Electronic Waste

Recycling is important so that landfills do not become overloaded. Paper and cans are often recycled, but electronics should also be recycled. Digital devices, such as cell phones and computers, are considered electronic waste. All electronic waste should be properly disposed of and should not be placed in the trash. Batteries are also considered electronic waste. The batteries in digital devices are hazardous and will harm the environment if discarded in a landfill.

Old electronic equipment can be donated to charities or community organizations to be refurbished and used to support their activities. However, if the equipment is beyond repair, locate a reputable electronic manufacturer, reseller, or community service center that will make sure the equipment is properly recycled.

Governments and businesses spend billions of dollars every year to try to reduce harmful pollution.

The normal operations of any type of business can be harmful to the environment. For example, the disposal of waste materials and use of chemicals may be harmful if handled improperly. There are many ways for socially responsible businesses to protect the environment. Using environmentally friendly, or *green*, products in business operations and for product packaging is a responsible choice. Also, recycling as many materials as possible, such as paper, printer cartridges, and glass bottles, is an environmentally responsible business behavior.

Section 3.2 Review

 ### Check Your Understanding

1. What are *business ethics*?
2. List the questions that can be used to analyze if an action is ethical.
3. What is the purpose of a confidentiality agreement?
4. Which governmental agency enforces laws that uphold truth in advertising?
5. Explain how businesses benefit from giving back to the community.

 ### Build Your Vocabulary

As you progress through this course, develop a personal glossary of key terms. This will help you build your vocabulary and prepare you for a career. Write a definition for each of the following terms and add it to your personal glossary.

ethics
integrity
morals
code of ethics
code of conduct
confidentiality
proprietary information

trade secret
false advertising
social responsibility
corporate social responsibility
corporate culture
philanthropy

Review and Assessment

Chapter Summary

Section 3.1 Legal Environment

- A contract is a legally binding agreement between two or more people or businesses. Business contracts protect the interests of the business and help to ensure all parties perform as expected.

- An important function of government is regulating certain business activities. Many federal and state laws reinforce honest business practices and financial responsibility. Local, state, and federal governmental agencies and departments all play a role in enforcing business operation regulations.

- All businesses in the United States are required to protect employees and treat them fairly. The US Department of Labor (DOL) works with many other governmental agencies to enforce workplace laws and regulations and protect employees.

- The government protects consumers from unfair and unsafe business practices and products. The Consumer Bill of Rights describes basic expectations of fair treatment of consumers.

Section 3.2 Ethics and Social Responsibility

- Ethics are rules of behavior based on ideas about what is right and wrong. *Business ethics* are principles that help define appropriate behavior in a business setting. Businesses are expected to demonstrate ethical behavior and practices even when governmental regulations do not apply. Businesses encourage ethical behavior by creating a code of ethics and a code of conduct.

- Social responsibility is behaving with sensitivity to social, environmental, and economic issues. Corporate social responsibility includes all the actions taken by a business to promote social good. Businesses have a responsibility to support their communities and to have a positive impact on society.

Online Activities

Complete the following activities to help you learn, practice, and expand your knowledge and skills.

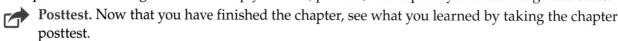 **Posttest.** Now that you have finished the chapter, see what you learned by taking the chapter posttest.

Vocabulary. Practice vocabulary for this chapter using the e-flash cards, matching activity, and vocabulary game until you are able to recognize their meanings.

Review Your Knowledge

1. Describe the purpose of contracts.
2. Explain the role of the legal system in business.
3. List four areas of business that are regulated by environmental protection laws.
4. List three ways that workplace laws protect employees.
5. Identify two governmental agencies that work to protect consumers.
6. What are some ways in which businesses encourage ethical behavior from employees?
7. List several examples of behavior that may be found in a code of conduct.
8. What is the difference between the focus of a code of ethics and the focus of a code of conduct?
9. What questions can be asked to measure whether an action is socially responsible?
10. What actions can businesses take to promote social good?

Apply Your Knowledge

1. Review the eight items listed in the Consumer Bill of Rights. Describe how businesses support these rights for their customers.
2. The EPA enforces laws that regulate air and water pollutants emitted by businesses. Which businesses in your community need to be mindful of these particular laws? Explain the goods or services the businesses provide. How are the pollutants created?
3. Write an essay contrasting ethical, moral, and legal choices that relate to the decision-making process in business situations. Provide examples that distinguish between ethical and unethical business practices.
4. Socially responsible businesses are civic-minded and work with the community in many different ways. Identify a business in your area that actively supports the local community. Explain how the business demonstrates this type of social responsibility.
5. Like the code of conduct handbook in a workplace, schools have a code of conduct that applies to students. This may include an honor code, behavior policy, and other policies that apply to conduct and ethical behavior. Identify and describe three policies at your school that apply to student conduct. How do students benefit from following the policies you identified? How does the school community benefit from the policies?

Communication Skills

College and Career Readiness

Writing. There will be many instances when you will be required to persuade the listener. When you persuade, you convince a person to take a proposed course of action. Prepare for a conversation with a person in the community about who should be responsible for paying for a clean environment. Ask for assistance to help you plan a focused presentation that argues your case and shows solid reasoning that will influence the listener's understanding of the topic.

Reading. Imagery is descriptive language that indicates how something looks, feels, smells, sounds, or tastes. After you have read this chapter, find an example of how the author used imagery to appeal to the five senses. Analyze the presentation of the material. Why did you think this appealed to the senses? How did this explanation create imagery? Describe how it influenced your mood.

Speaking. Most people in the United States act as responsible and contributing citizens. How can a person demonstrate social and ethical responsibility in times when disaster relief is needed in the community? Participate in a group discussion about how citizens can go beyond the minimum expectations of helping others in the community.

Internet Research

Role of law in business. Primary research is conducted by gathering information. Using the Internet, research the role of law in business. How does the legal system and laws help businesses understand their roles in commerce? Gather appropriate relevant sources and cite each. Summarize your findings.

Teamwork

Ethics are discussed in this chapter. Working with your team, make a list of five current ethical issues that have been in the news. Indicate if the ethics issues involve the owner, employees, or other specific individuals. Your team should give suggestions on how to remedy each ethics violation. Discuss your opinions with your class. What did you learn from this exercise?

Portfolio Development

College and Career Readiness

Digital Presentation Options. Before you begin collecting items for a digital portfolio, you will need to decide how you are going to present the final product. For example, you could create an electronic presentation with slides for each section. The slides could have links to documents, videos, graphics, or sound files. This will dictate file naming conventions and file structure.

Websites are another option for presenting a digital portfolio. You could create a personal website to host the files and have a main page with links to various sections. Each section page could have links to pages containing your documents, videos, graphics, or sound files. (Be sure you read and understand the user agreement for any site on which you place your materials.)

Another option is to place the files on a CD or flash drive. The method you choose should allow the viewer to easily navigate and find items. There are many creative ways to present a digital portfolio.

1. Establish the types of technology that are available for you to create a digital portfolio. Will you have access to cameras or studios? Do you have the level of skill needed to create videos?

2. Decide the type of presentation you will use. Research what will be needed to create the final portfolio product.

CTSOs

Ethics. Many competitive CTSO events include an ethics component that covers multiple topics. The ethics component of an event may be part of an objective test. However, ethics may also be a part of the competition in which teams participate to defend a given position on an ethical dilemma or topic.

To prepare for an ethics event, complete the following activities.

1. Read the guidelines provided by your organization.

2. Make notes on index cards about important points to remember. Use these notes to study.

3. To get an overview of various ethical situations that individuals encounter, read each of the Ethics features that appear throughout this text.

4. Ask someone to practice role-playing with you by asking questions or taking the other side of an argument.

5. Use the Internet to find more information about ethical issues. Find and review ethics cases that involve business situations.

CHAPTER 4

Business in the Free Enterprise

In This Chapter

4.1 Business in the Private Sector

Types of Businesses

North American Industry Classification System

Types of Customers

4.2 Business Organization

Forms of Business Ownership

Alternative Forms of Ownership

Exploring Careers

Product Manager

Retail stores offer a wide variety of products that includes several different brands. Who decides which products a store will carry? A product manager investigates new products, analyzes buying trends, and reviews sales records of current products to determine how profitable each is likely to be. Based on this information, the product manager buys products for resale to the store's customers.

Typical job titles for a product manager include *buyer*, *merchandiser*, *purchasing manager*, and *procurement specialist*. Examples of tasks that product managers perform include:

- use spreadsheet software to organize and analyze sales figures

- meet with sales personnel to get customer information

- analyze sales records and trends

- negotiate prices and discounts with vendors

- determine markups and selling prices

Product managers must be able to analyze product performance based on financial figures. They also need good negotiation skills in order to get the best prices and terms for purchases. Most jobs in this field require an associate degree or equivalent training in a vocational school, but on-the-job training may be substituted.

College and Career Readiness

Reading Prep

Read the chapter title and tell a classmate what you have experienced or already know about the topic. Write a paragraph describing what you would like to learn about the topic. After reading the chapter, share two things you have learned with the classmate.

Check Your Business IQ

Before you begin the chapter, see what you already know about business by taking the chapter pretest. The pretest is available at www.g-wlearning.com.

Business in the Private Sector

Objectives

After completing this section, you will be able to:

- **Describe** three general types of business in the private sector.
- **Define** the North American Industry Classification System (NAICS).
- **Identify** three types of customers businesses serve.

Key Terms

for-profit business
not-for-profit
   organization
producer
extractor
manufacturer
intermediary
wholesaler

retailer
service business
North American
   Industry
   Classification
   System (NAICS)
consumer market

business-to-consumer
   (B2C)
business market
business-to-business
   (B2B)
government market
institution

Types of Businesses

In the United States, there are many different types of businesses that provide goods and services to customers. A **for-profit business** is an organization that generates revenue. One of its sole purposes is to be productive and generate money for its owners. A **not-for-profit organization** is an organization that exists to serve some public purpose. The money it raises is used to support a cause rather than make money for its owners.

Organizations are either part of the public sector or private sector. Governmental organizations are part of the *public sector*. Schools, the military, and the Internal Revenue Service are part of the public sector. Their purpose is to serve the public.

The *private sector* consists of all other organizations that provide goods and services.

Ethics

Integrity

Integrity is defined as the honesty of a person's actions. Integrity and ethics go hand-in-hand in both personal and professional lives. Employees and employers help establish the reputation of a business in the community. Company employees who display integrity help create a positive culture for the business, customers, and the community.

In general, businesses in the private sector can be divided into three categories, as shown in Figure 4-1.

- Producers
- Intermediaries
- Service businesses

Businesses in the Private Sector		
Producers	**Intermediaries**	**Service Business**
• Organic farmer • Logging contractor • Automobile manufacturer	• New car dealership • Floral supply wholesaler • Grocery store	• Tax accounting firm • Beauty salon • Currency exchange

Goodheart-Willcox Publisher

Figure 4-1 Many different businesses fall into each of the categories of private sector businesses.

Producers

Producers are businesses that create goods and services. Producers are important in the economy because they create products that can be used by individuals, businesses, and government.

Extractors are an example of producers. **Extractors** are businesses or people that take natural resources from the land. Natural resources are also called *raw materials*. Extractors sell natural resources to manufacturers.

Manufacturers are businesses that use supplies from other producers to make products. Some manufacturers use raw materials purchased from extractors. These businesses are called *raw-materials manufacturers*. They are also known as *raw-materials producers*. Manufacturers generally use assembly lines to mass produce identical products. They create an end product that is sold for use by individuals, businesses, or governmental agencies.

Goodluz/Shutterstock.com

Farmers function as producers in the private sector.

Farmers are another type of producer. They raise crops and livestock that are sold to either end users or other producers.

Intermediaries

People and businesses that sell the goods and services from producers to customers are called **intermediaries**. Intermediaries make sure goods and services are in the right place at the right time to meet consumer needs and wants. Wholesalers and retailers are the most common intermediary businesses.

Wholesalers

A **wholesaler** is a business that purchases large quantities of products directly from producers and sells the products in smaller quantities to retailers. An example of a wholesaler is a business that purchases truckloads of lumber from a producer. The wholesaler divides the lumber into smaller quantities. These smaller quantities are sold to retailers like Lowe's or Home Depot.

Wholesalers are often called *distributors*. In addition to providing retailers with the products to sell to customers, wholesalers may offer product storage and transportation services. These services may be used by both producers and retailers.

Retailers

Retailers are businesses that buy products from wholesalers or directly from producers, and sell them to consumers to make a profit. Consumers are also called *end users*. In the private enterprise system, retailers directly provide consumers with the products that meet their needs and wants. Food, clothing, and electronics are some of the products provided by retailers.

Solis Images/Shutterstock.com

The skills of an architect are provided through service businesses.

Service Businesses

A **service business** earns profits by providing consumers with services that meet their needs and wants. Service businesses do not sell products. These businesses perform activities and provide expertise for their customers. Examples of service businesses include moving companies, law firms, and interior design firms.

In 2015, the Bureau of Labor Statistics (BLS) of the US Department of Labor reported that 70 percent of all nonfarm jobs in the country are in service industries. Additionally, the BLS estimates that most of the 15 million new jobs created in the next ten years will be in service industries. In the United States, the number of service businesses is growing faster than any other type of business.

North American Industry Classification System

Businesses are classified by industry. An *industry* is a group of businesses that produce the same type of goods or services. One way to distinguish businesses is to use NAICS codes. The **North American Industry**

Classification System (NAICS) (pronounced nākes) is a numeric system used to classify businesses and collect economic statistics. This system was developed by the United States, Canadian, and Mexican governments for trade purposes.

Standard categories of businesses were developed to define the business types and to gather and track trade data. The codes are used to classify businesses based on the activity that takes place within each business. Each category may have subcategories to further compare and analyze the business type.

Figure 4-2 lists the major industrial categories of NAICS. More information on NAICS is available through the US Census Bureau.

NAICS Business Classifications	
11	Agriculture, Forestry, Fishing and Hunting
21	Mining, Quarrying, and Oil and Gas Extraction
22	Utilities
23	Construction
31-33	Manufacturing
42	Wholesale Trade
44-45	Retail Trade
48-49	Transportation and Warehousing
51	Information
52	Finance and Insurance
53	Real Estate Rental and Leasing
54	Professional, Scientific, and Technical Services
55	Management of Companies and Enterprises
56	Administrative and Support and Waste Management and Remediation Services
61	Educational Services
62	Health Care and Social Assistance
71	Arts, Entertainment, and Recreation
72	Accommodation and Food Services
81	Other Services (except Public Administration)
92	Public Administration

Source: US Census Bureau; Goodheart-Willcox Publisher

Figure 4-2 Each major NAICS category is subdivided into smaller, more specific categories.

Types of Customers

Each type of business works to meet the needs of its customers. A customer is an individual or group who buys products. The customer of a service business is often called a *client*. The types of customers businesses serve can be separated into three categories, as shown in Figure 4-3.

- Consumer market
- Business market
- Government and institutions

Consumer Market

The **consumer market** consists of customers who buy products for their own use. Consumers are actually the end users of the products. Businesses that sell primarily to individual consumers are in the **business-to-consumer (B2C)** market. Businesses in the consumer market are some of the most familiar and well-known businesses. Customers in the consumer market buy clothes, cars, gifts, and many other goods and services. Most of the commercials on television are aimed at the consumer market.

Business Market

The **business market** consists of customers who buy products for use in a business. A customer in the business market is a *business* that buys products from another *business*. Businesses that sell primarily to other businesses are in the **business-to-business (B2B)** market. For example, a computer sales business sells computer systems to a law firm. The employees of the law firm will use the computers for various business activities. This is a B2B sale.

Government and Institutions

The **government market** includes national, state, and local governmental offices and agencies. Government customers buy a wide variety of products. These products range from airplanes and ground vehicles to office supplies

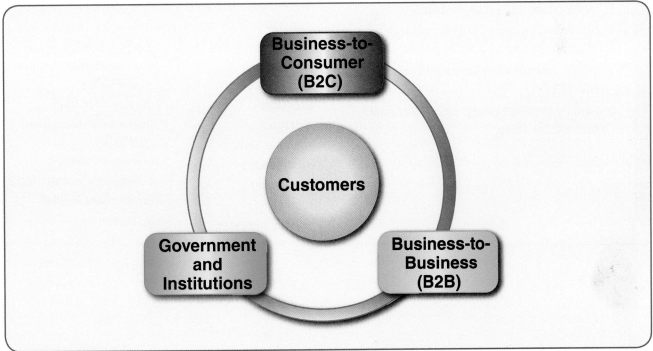

Goodheart-Willcox Publisher

Figure 4-3 Businesses can serve any of the three types of customers or multiple types of customers.

and electronics. Governments also buy services, such as food preparation, education, security, and medical care.

Institutions are nonprofit organizations that may be either public or private. A nonprofit organization is an entity that exists to serve a public purpose. These include schools, hospitals, museums, and organizations, such as United Way and the American Cancer Society. Like government customers, institutions also buy a wide variety of goods and services to support their activities.

littleny/Shutterstock.com

The American Red Cross is an example of a nonprofit organization that buys a variety of goods and services in order to operate.

Section 4.1 Review

 Check Your Understanding

1. List three categories of business in the private sector.
2. What is the difference between businesses in the public and private sectors?
3. Name two examples of intermediary businesses.
4. Which countries collaborated to develop NAICS?
5. Identify the three categories of customers businesses serve.

 Build Your Vocabulary

As you progress through this course, develop a personal glossary of key terms. This will help you build your vocabulary and prepare you for a career. Write a definition for each of the following terms and add it to your personal glossary.

for-profit business
not-for-profit
    organization
producer
extractor
manufacturer
intermediary
wholesaler
retailer
service business

North American Industry
    Classification System
    (NAICS)
consumer market
business-to-consumer
    (B2C)
business market
business-to-business (B2B)
government market
institution

Business Organization

?ⁱ**E**ssential
Question

How do business
owners choose a form
of ownership?

Objectives

After completing this section, you will be able to:

- **Describe** the three basic forms of business ownership.
- **Explain** alternative ways a business can be organized.

Key Terms 📤

proprietorship
liability
partnership
partnership agreement

corporation
stock
dividend
board of directors

limited liability
    company (LLC)
cooperative

Forms of Business Ownership

Private businesses can be structured, or owned, in different ways. The number of owners and size of the business are important factors when choosing the best form of ownership. There are three basic forms of business ownership:

- proprietorship
- partnership
- corporation

Each form of business ownership has unique characteristics, as shown in Figure 4-4.

Proprietorships

A **proprietorship** is a business that is owned and often operated by a single individual. This individual is called the *sole proprietor*. A proprietorship is the simplest and most common form of business ownership. It is also the easiest to establish because no formal action is necessary. In most cases, the owner simply decides he or she is going to start a business. As long as there is only one owner, the status of "proprietorship" automatically comes from business activities.

Common Forms of Business Ownership			
	Proprietorships	**Partnerships**	**Corporations**
Limited liability	No	No	Yes
Number of owners restricted	Yes	No	No
Limited life	Yes	Yes	No
Easy to transfer ownership	No	No	Yes
Double taxation	No	No	Yes
Formation costs	None	Low	High

Goodheart-Willcox Publisher

Figure 4-4 When choosing a form of ownership, the number of owners and size of the business should be considered.

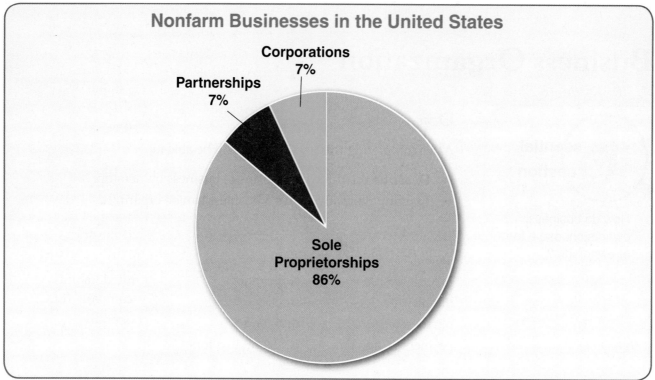

Source: US Small Business Administration; Goodheart-Willcox Publisher

Figure 4-5 There are more proprietorships in the United States than any other type of business.

A proprietorship can operate under the name of its owner or under a business name. However, a proprietorship cannot be named in a way that implies more than one owner or another ownership structure. For example, names such as Gordy and Associates or Gordy Corp. cannot be used. Also, a sole proprietor cannot choose a business name that is already in use.

Licenses or permits may be required in the locality where the business operates. A *doing business as (DBA)* license may be required if using a business name other than the owner's name. The DBA license, also known as *fictitious name registration*, allows the owner to officially register the business. Some types of business activities may require certain licenses or permits from the local or state government. For example, hair stylists are typically required to have a state-issued cosmetology license to provide their services to customers.

Proprietorships comprise a large percentage of the nonfarm businesses operating in the United States. Figure 4-5 shows the percentages of partnerships, corporations, and sole proprietorships included in a report by the Small Business Administration in 2014.

Most proprietorships are small businesses, but they do not always remain small operations. Many American success stories begin with good ideas and entrepreneurs who start as sole proprietors and grew their businesses into huge corporations.

Advantages of Proprietorships

There are several advantages of the proprietorship form of business ownership:

- *Easy to start.* Once the owner opens the business, a proprietorship is formed.

- *Easy to close.* The business can be closed simply by making the decision to do so. There is no formal or legal process to close operations.

- *Retain all profits.* Since a proprietorship has only one owner, all the profits from the business belong to the owner. Profits do not have to be shared with anyone else.

- *Complete control of operations.* The owner has complete control over all business decisions. A sole proprietor is not required to consult with anyone else when making decisions about the business.

- *Simple tax structure.* A proprietorship is not taxed separately from the business owner. The profit of the business is added to the personal tax return of the business owner. This makes tax preparation simple.

Disadvantages of Proprietorships

Many of the advantages of a proprietorship involve the fact that there is only one owner. However, being the sole owner of a business also has disadvantages:

- *Unlimited liability.* **Liability** means legal responsibility. *Unlimited liability* means the business owner is held personally responsible for all debts and losses of the business. If a business fails, a sole proprietor could lose personal property, savings, investments, and other personal items of value.

- *Limited expertise.* A sole proprietor is in charge of every aspect of operating a business. While the sole proprietor may be extremely good at a trade, he or she may not have enough business skills and experience to run a successful business alone.

- *Limited life of business.* A *limited life* means a proprietorship business exists only as long as the owner wants or is able to run the business. A change in ownership automatically dissolves a proprietorship. For the business to continue, the new owner must form a new proprietorship.

Partnerships

A **partnership** is an association of two or more persons who co-own a business with the objective of earning a profit. If the objective of an organization is something different, such as a charity or a religious activity, the partnership form of business ownership cannot be used. There must be at least two parties involved to form a partnership. However, there is no limit to the maximum number of partners involved in a business.

There are two common types of partnerships: general partnerships and limited partnerships. A *general partnership* is a business that is co-owned by two or more general partners who are responsible for business operations.

 You Do the Math Problem Solving and Reasoning

Word problems are exercises in which the problem is set up in text, rather than as a mathematical notation. Many word problems tell a story. You must identify the elements of the math problem and solve it. There are several strategies for solving word problems. Some of the common strategies include making a list or table, working backward, making a guess and then checking and revising, and substituting simpler numbers to solve the problem.

Solve the following problems.

1. An online bookseller must earn a profit of 27 percent on each book it sells. The bookseller's cost for each book is $5.58. How much must the bookseller charge to make the required profit?

2. A delivery service charges a fuel surcharge whenever the price of gasoline exceeds $4.00 per gallon. The surcharge is 45 percent of the amount over $4.00 for each gallon of gasoline used. The current price of gasoline is $4.32 per gallon. If the price of the delivery service is $6.95 and the driver uses 5.25 gallons of gasoline for the delivery, what is the total charged for the delivery?

3. Avery Johnson owns a graphic design firm. He must price a job for a client. The labor cost is $4,053 and the material cost is $605. A 15 percent markup is added to the costs. Sales tax of 6.25 percent must be added to the materials cost. What is the total price Avery must quote to the customer?

The general partners and the partnership are considered to be one and the same. Typical responsibilities of a *general partner,* or *managing partner,* include:

- authority to make decisions
- active in the day-to-day business operations
- unlimited liability for all partnership debts

A *limited partnership* is a business co-owned by at least one general partner and one or more limited partners. A *limited partner* is a business partner who does not participate in managing the business. The liability of general partners is limited to the amount of investment they have made in the business. Limited partners invest money in the business, but have no authority to make decisions.

Partnership Agreement

A partnership is formed when two or more persons voluntarily enter into an agreement or a legally-binding contract. The **partnership agreement**, also called the *articles of partnership,* is a written contract that establishes a partnership. There is not a standard format for the articles of partnership, but it should contain the following common details:

- date of the agreement
- names of the partners
- name and location of the business
- nature of the business activity
- duties of each partner
- investment of each partner
- division of profit and losses
- plan for dissolving the partnership
- signatures of the partners

Partnership agreements can be prepared by the business partners or by an attorney. Most experts recommend the services of an attorney.

Advantages of Partnerships

Many of the advantages of a partnership are similar to those of a sole proprietorship:

- *Easy to start.* A partnership is easy to establish. The partnership agreement is created by the partners to define the important terms of the partnership.

Dean Drobot/Shutterstock.com

A partnership agreement is a legally-binding contract.

 Green Business   Power Strips

Power strips allow many devices to be powered through a single electrical outlet. Computer workstations should be set up so all of the computer equipment is plugged into a power strip. Doing this allows the employee to have control of the power to an entire workstation.

New "smart" power strips make it easy and convenient to save power each day. A power strip with a timer feature can be set to automatically turn the power strip off at a designated time. Occupancy power strips have a motion detector that senses when a person has been away from the workstation for a specified period of time. Once time elapses, the power strip turns off. Because electronic devices to draw power even in sleep mode, a power-sensing strip can turn off the power supply when sleep mode is detected.

- *Combined financial resources.* Several partners can usually contribute more money overall to a business than a single owner can alone.

- *Skills and resources.* Each partner brings his or her skills and experience into the business. Business decisions are based on the combined knowledge, special skills, and experience of all the partners.

- *Simple tax structure.* A partnership is not taxed separately from the partners. Each partner pays income taxes based on his or her share of the business profit.

Disadvantages of Partnerships

The partnership business structure also has some disadvantages:

- *Unlimited liability.* General partners are personally liable for all debts of the partnership, including debts created by other partners.

- *Limited life.* A partnership is dissolved when a partner leaves the business, no matter the reason. A new partnership agreement is needed when a new partner enters the business.

- *Potential disagreements.* All of the partners will not always agree when making important business decisions. This can lead to disagreements, which could weaken the partnership.

Corporations

A **corporation** is defined by the US Supreme Court as "an artificial being, invisible, intangible, and existing only in contemplation of the law." It is a business that is legally separate from its owners. A corporation has been described an "artificial person" because it has most of the legal rights of an actual person. A corporation can:

- buy and sell property;

- hire and fire employees;

- borrow money;

- enter into binding contracts;

- sue or be sued; and

- make gifts to charitable causes.

A corporation exists only on paper. However, the law recognizes a corporation as a separate legal entity that can act on its own behalf.

Establishing a Corporation

Forming a corporation is more complex than starting a proprietorship or partnership. To form a corporation, articles of incorporation must be filed with the Secretary of State's office in the state of operation. The *articles of incorporation* are a document that includes the names of the corporation's founders, name of the corporation, and type of business that will be conducted.

In the United States, a business does not have to incorporate in the same state where the company headquarters are located. The choice is usually based on two factors:

- the cost of incorporating in a particular state compared to other states

- how favorable a state's incorporation laws and taxes are compared to other states

The corporation's founders create *corporate bylaws* that explain the practices and procedures to be followed in conducting business. The bylaws typically include the name and address of the business, the type of stock that will be issued, the number of shares of stock that will be issued, and procedures for stockholder meetings. **Stock** is a share of ownership in a corporation. Those who own stock are stockholders, or shareholders, of the corporation. Shareholders are paid dividends on their stock. A **dividend** is a portion of the corporation's earnings distributed to stockholders.

The stock of public corporations is listed on an organized stock exchange. A *stock exchange* is where securities are bought and sold through stockbrokers. The New York Stock Exchange (NYSE) is a well known example. Anyone who wishes can buy stock of a public corporation. All financial information of public corporations must be made public. Private corporations do not sell company stock on stock exchanges. All the stock is privately owned and sales or profit information does not have to be released to the public.

Stockholders are the owners of the corporation. They participate in managing the business by electing a board of directors. The **board of directors** is a group of individuals who make high-level management decisions for the business and establish company policies. The board also selects a chief executive officer (CEO) and other corporate officers to run the day-to-day operations of the company. Figure 4-6 shows the typical organizational structure of a corporation.

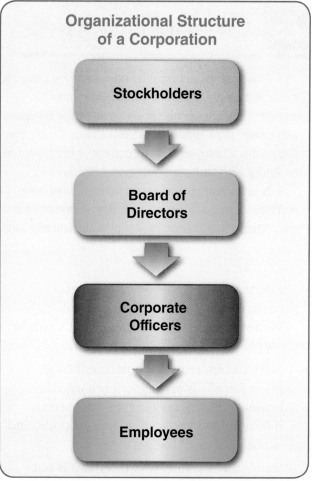

Goodheart-Willcox Publisher

Figure 4-6 The organizational structure of a corporation is more complex than most other business types.

Advantages of Corporations

The corporation form of businesses offers a number of advantages that are not available to proprietorships or partnerships. Many businesses choose to incorporate once the business is large enough to justify the costs of forming a corporation. The advantages of forming a corporation include:

- *Limited liability. Limited liability* means stockholders are not personally responsible for the debts and obligations of the business. The corporation is responsible for business debts and obligations.

- *Ability to raise capital.* A corporation can raise large sums of capital by selling stock. The ability to raise money helps corporations grow and become more profitable.

- *Continued life.* Corporations continue to operate as long as the business is profitable and the majority of the stockholders want the corporation to continue.

- *Transferring ownership.* The stock of a corporation can be transferred to another investor without affecting the operations of the business.

- *Professional management.* Stockholders elect a board of directors to govern the corporation. The board appoints knowledgeable corporate officers to run the daily business activities.

Disadvantages of Corporations

With all its advantages, the corporation form of business ownership also has a number of disadvantages:

- *Expensive to form.* Forming a corporation requires a great deal of paperwork. In addition to attorney fees, there are application fees, registration fees to sell stock, publication fees, and many others. The fees involved usually total several thousands of dollars.

- *Many governmental regulations.* There are many standards and regulations a corporation must follow to sell stock, which require annual financial reports to be filed with the federal and state governments.

- *Double taxation.* Since a corporation is a separate legal entity, it must pay state and federal income taxes on its profit.

Stockholders must add stock dividends to their personal income tax returns. Because of this, the profit of a corporation is taxed twice.

Alternative Forms of Ownership

There are certain business ownership structures that combine elements of proprietorships, partnership, and corporations. Depending on the goals of the business and the individuals involved, an alternative ownership structure may be beneficial. As with other forms of ownership, tax and legal requirements must be considered when considering an alternative business ownership structure.

Three examples of alternative business ownership structures are S corporations, limited liability companies, and cooperatives. The characteristics of these alternative forms of ownership are compared in Figure 4-7.

S Corporations

An S corporation is a form of business ownership that provides limited liability to its owners, but is taxed as a partnership. S corporations are restricted to no more than 100 shareholders. All shareholders must be US citizens or residents.

The S corporation is taxed as a partnership because the business does not pay corporate income tax on profits. Instead, individual owners report

Alternative Business Ownership Structures			
	S Corporations	**Limited Liability Companies**	**Cooperatives**
Limited liability	Yes	Yes	Yes
Double taxation	No	No	No
Board of Directors	Yes	No	Yes
Number of owners restricted	Yes	No	No
Limited life	No	Yes	No
Formation cost	High	Low	Low

Goodheart-Willcox Publisher

Figure 4-7 Limited liability companies and cooperatives combine many of the characteristics of proprietorships, partnership, and corporations.

their share of business profits on their personal income tax returns. This provides small business owners with the protection of limited liability without the double taxation of a corporation.

However, being classified as a type of corporation requires that governmental regulations and standard practices be followed. For example, S corporations must schedule regular board of directors and shareholder meetings, file annual financial reports, and follow regulations for selling stock. Complying with some of the regulations and standard practices may be costly for a small business.

Limited Liability Companies

A **limited liability company (LLC)** is a form of business ownership that combines the benefits of a corporation with those of proprietorships and partnerships. Like stockholders of a corporation, owners of an LLC have limited liability. Also, there is no limit to the number of business owners. Other features of an LLC are more like those of a partnership or a proprietorship.

These advantages make the LLC form of business ownership popular with owners of new businesses.

- The profit of an LLC is taxed to the owners, not the business.
- LLCs are not subject to the heavy governmental regulations that apply to corporations.
- The cost of forming an LLC is low.

Each state has its own regulations for starting an LLC. The following are some of the common guidelines that apply to naming an LLC business.

- The name cannot be the same as an LLC that already exists in the state.
- The name must include LLC as part of its name.
- The name cannot include words prohibited by the state in which it is created.

Cooperatives

A **cooperative**, or *co-op*, is a business that is owned and operated by those using its services. The members of a co-op pool their resources and work together to produce quality goods and services.

Michaelpuche/Shutterstock.com

The success of a cooperative business depends on the full participation of members.

For example, several supermarkets may join together to pool their resources and operate as a wholesaler. When purchasing in larger quantities, they may be able to get better prices on the goods their businesses need to operate.

Co-ops are run democratically and usually have an elected board of directors. All members of a co-op have voting rights when deciding the actions of the organization. This democratic form of operation ensures that the needs of all members are met.

A cooperative offers important benefits to its members. In addition to strength in numbers, the members of a cooperative are taxed only once on income from the cooperative. This is similar to the taxation of a proprietorship and

an LLC. The cooperative is not recognized as a separate business entity. The cooperative form of ownership also offers continued life. Members can join and leave the co-op without affecting the ownership status. In addition, formation costs are low.

There are some disadvantages to the co-op form of business ownership. The participation of members in the activities of a co-op may depend on how much they use or benefit from the cooperative. The business cannot operate effectively if all members do not fully participate. If the co-op does not operate effectively and produce benefits for its members, it could lose members, which reduces the pool of resources available.

Section 4.2 Review

 Check Your Understanding

1. Identify the three basic forms of business ownership.
2. What is unlimited liability?
3. List five details commonly found on a partnership agreement.
4. What are some disadvantages of the corporation form of business ownership?
5. List three alternative forms of business ownership.

 Build Your Vocabulary

As you progress through this course, develop a personal glossary of key terms. This will help you build your vocabulary and prepare you for a career. Write a definition for each of the following terms and add it to your personal glossary.

proprietorship	dividend
liability	board of directors
partnership	limited liability company
partnership agreement	(LLC)
corporation	cooperative
stock	

Review and Assessment

Chapter Summary

Section 4.1 Business in the Private Sector

- Three general types of businesses in the private sector are producers, intermediaries, and service businesses. Producers are businesses that create goods and services. Businesses that sell the goods and services directly to customers are called intermediaries. A service business provides consumers with services that meet their needs and wants.

- The North American Industry Classification System (NAICS) was developed to define the types of businesses and to gather and track trade data. NAICS was developed by the US, Canadian, and Mexican governments for trade purposes. NAICS codes are used to classify businesses based on their activities.

- A customer is an individual or group who buys products. Customers can be classified as consumers, businesses, and government and institutions. Businesses that sell primarily to individual consumers are in the business-to-consumer (B2C) market. Businesses that sell primarily to other businesses are in the business-to-business (B2B) market.

Section 4.2 Business Organization

- Businesses can be structured in different ways. The number of owners and size of the business are important factors in determining the best form of ownership. There are three basic forms of business ownership: proprietorship, partnership, and corporation. Each form has unique advantages and disadvantages.

- Alternative forms of business ownership combine elements of proprietorships, partnerships, and corporations. These alternative forms include S corporations, limited liability companies, and cooperatives. Like other forms of ownership, each of these has advantages and disadvantages.

Online Activities

Complete the following activities to help you learn, practice, and expand your knowledge and skills.

Posttest. Now that you have finished the chapter, see what you learned by taking the chapter posttest.

Vocabulary. Practice vocabulary for this chapter using the e-flash cards, matching activity, and vocabulary game until you are able to recognize their meanings.

Review Your Knowledge

1. Describe three general types of business in the private sector.
2. Describe the role of service businesses. Give an example of a service business.
3. What is the purpose of the North American Industry Classification System?
4. Explain the difference between the consumer market and the business market.
5. Describe the three basic forms of business ownership.
6. What are some advantages and disadvantages of a proprietorship?
7. Explain the difference between a general partnership and a limited partnership.
8. Describe how corporations are established.
9. What are common guidelines that apply to naming an LLC business?
10. Explain how the participation of members impacts the effectiveness of a co-op.

Apply Your Knowledge

1. Make a list of four natural resources. Give examples of products that are created from each resource. What role do producers, intermediaries, and service businesses play in creating the products you listed?
2. Create a chart listing ten businesses in your community. Identify which businesses are for-profit and which are not-for-profit. For each business, indicate if it is part of the public sector or the private section.
3. Identify an example of a non-profit organization with which you are familiar. What services does this organization provide? How does this organization raise funds?
4. Compare the forms of business ownership discussed in this chapter. What characteristics do they have in common? How are the ownership structures different? Create a chart that compares the features of the forms of business ownership.
5. A group of students plans to start a delivery service. Which business ownership structure should they choose? Consider the size of the business, the type of business activities performed, and the number of owners. Write a paper explaining your answer.

Communication Skills

College and Career Readiness

Speaking. A presentation is usually a speech given to a group of people. This chapter discussed different ways to start a business. Plan and deliver a speech to a group of business people about an idea you have to start a business. Be clear in your perspective for the idea and demonstrate solid reasoning.

Listening. Passive listening is casually listening to someone speak. Passive listening is appropriate when you do not have to interact with the speaker. Listen to a classmate as he or she is having a conversation with you. Focus attention on the message. Ask for clarification for anything that you do not understand. Provide verbal and nonverbal feedback while the person is talking.

Writing. Becoming a business owner in your community would require that you model integrity, ethical leadership, and effective management. Make a list of actions that you could take to meet these requirements.

Internet Research

Business ownership. Primary research is conducted by the writer in preparation for writing a report. The most common types of primary research are interviews, surveys, and experiments. Before research begins, questions should be formulated. Using the Internet as a resource, formulate research questions that should be answered when investigating types of business ownership. Next, decide how you would approach getting answers to these questions. Would it be interviews, surveys, or experiments? Explain your reasoning.

Teamwork

Working with your team, discuss the three major types of business in the private sector. Which type of business does your team think is most important to the economy? Make a list of reasons why the team thinks their choice is most important to the economy. Did everyone agree?

Portfolio Development

College and Career Readiness

Hard Copy Organization. As you collect material for your portfolio, you will need an effective strategy to keep the items clean, safe, and organized for assembly at the appropriate time. Structure and organization are important when working on an on-going project that includes multiple pieces. A large manila envelope works well to keep hard copies of documents, photos, awards, and other items. A three-ring binder with sleeves is another good way to store your materials.

Plan to keep similar items together and label the categories. For example, store sample documents that illustrate your writing or technology skills together. Use notes clipped to the documents to identify each item and state why it is included in the portfolio. For example, a note might say, "Newsletter that illustrates desktop publishing skills."

1. Select a method for storing hard copy items you will be collecting.

2. Create a master spreadsheet to use as a tracking tool for the components of your portfolio. You may list each document alphabetically, by category, date, or other convention that helps you keep track of each document that you are including.

3. Record the name of each item and the date that you stored it.

CTSOs

Teamwork. Some competitive events for CTSOs have a teamwork component. If it is a team event, it is important that the competing team prepare to operate as a cohesive unit.

To prepare for teamwork activities, complete the following activities.

1. Review the rules to confirm whether questions will be asked or if the team will need to defend a case or situation.

2. Practice performing as a team by completing the team activities at the end of each chapter in this text. This will help members learn how to interact with each other and participate effectively.

3. Locate a rubric or scoring sheet for the event on your organization's website to see how the team will be judged.

4. Confirm whether visual aids may be used in the presentation and the amount of setup time permitted.

5. Make notes on index cards about important points to remember. Team members should exchange note cards so that each evaluates the other person's notes. Use these notes to study. You may also be able to use these notes during the event.

6. Assign each team member a role for the presentation. Practice performing as a team. Each team member should introduce him- or herself, review the case, make suggestions for the case, and conclude with a summary.

7. Ask your instructor to play the role of competition judge as your team reviews the case. After the presentation is complete, ask for feedback from your instructor. You may also consider having a student audience to listen and give feedback.

CHAPTER 5

Business in a Global Economy

In This Chapter

Exploring Careers

Freight Forwarder

Business Management & Administration

Producers of goods ship their items to businesses that, in turn, sell those goods to end users. On each end of these transactions is a freight forwarder. Freight forwarders advise clients on transportation and payment methods for shipping merchandise, both domestically and internationally. They research and estimate shipping rates, arrange delivery of shipments, and track shipments. In addition, they prepare bills, invoices, and other shipping documents.

Typical job titles for this position also include *export agent*, *export coordinator*, and *route specialist*. The following are examples of tasks that freight forwarders perform:

- record shipment costs and weights

- keep records of all goods shipped, received, and stored

- check import or export documentation

- estimate shipping costs

- arrange transport of goods with shipping companies

Freight forwarders are required to have a high school diploma, though a college degree is preferred. Excellent organization skills, good attention to detail, and the ability to work cooperatively with diverse groups are necessary. Good technology and math skills are also required.

Reading Prep

College and Career Readiness

Arrange a study session to read the chapter aloud with a classmate. Take turns reading each section. Stop at the end of each section to identify and discuss its main points. Take notes during your study session to prepare for class discussions and quizzes.

Check Your Business IQ

Before you begin the chapter, see what you already know about business by taking the chapter pretest. The pretest is available at www.g-wlearning.com.

Exploring Global Business

How is the government involved in the trade activities of businesses?

Objectives

After completing this section, you will be able to:

- **Describe** the impact of globalization on business.
- **Explain** the role of currency in foreign trade.
- **Discuss** trade policy.

Key Terms

globalization	comparative advantage	embargo
culture	balance of trade	trade sanctions
international trade	balance of payments	tariff
domestic business	foreign exchange rate	quota
exports	floating currency	trade agreement
imports	trade policy	trading bloc
absolute advantage	trade barrier	

Globalization

Globalization is the connection made among nations when economies freely move goods, labor, and money across borders. Modern technology allows communication to flow easily around the world. It has created opportunities for nations to connect by opening new markets, creating jobs, and developing political relationships. Workers travel around the world, bringing their culture and diversity to businesses. **Culture** is the shared beliefs, customs, practices, and social behavior of a particular group or nation. It affects how people think, work, interact, and communicate with others.

Nations and businesses can sell goods to countries across their borders or across oceans. **International trade** is the buying and selling of goods and services across national borders. It involves people, businesses, and governments of different nations. International trade is also known as *international business* or *world trade*.

Companies that conduct business among many different nations must respect cultures, laws, and other rules and regulations of doing business internationally.

Exports and Imports

Much of a nation's business activities take place within its home country. **Domestic business** is all the business activity involved in making, buying, and selling product within a nation's borders. *Product* includes both goods and services. Companies looking to expand a domestic business have the potential to export and sell product globally. **Exports** are goods and services that are produced within a country's borders and sold in another country. Figure 5-1 shows US exports in 2014. By exporting product, several benefits are created. Companies can realize potential new markets and increase their profits. Creating products for export also generates jobs. These jobs mean employment for the citizens of the origin country, as well as new

US Export Totals for 2014		
Country/Region	**Export Dollar Amount**	**Percent of Total US International Exports**
Canada	$287,818,800,000	19.3%
Mexico	221,437,000,000	14.8%
China	111,792,500,000	7.5%
Japan	61,185,700,000	4.1%
United Kingdom	49,031,300,000	3.3%
Germany	45,668,000,000	3.0%
South Korea	40,720,800,000	2.7%
Netherlands	40,031,300,000	2.6%
Brazil	39,280,900,000	2.6%
Hong Kong	37,578,800,000	2.5%

Source: US Dept. of Commerce: International Trade Administration; Goodheart-Willcox Publisher

Figure 5-1 This list reflects the top ten 2014 US exports.

tax dollars for that country. The positive ripple effect is felt throughout that country's economy.

Exporting is one way a business can generate additional profits. Importing is another way a domestic company can increase sales potential. **Imports** are goods, services, and capital that are brought into a country from outside its borders. Businesses can import new or different products that the domestic company or country does not produce. For example, the United States does not grow bananas. By importing bananas, new sales are generated for the importing company. Just as when exporting, new sales put money into the local economy.

Absolute and Comparative Advantage

Nations trade with each other because most countries do not have the factors of production needed to produce all the goods and services needed by their population. The available land, labor, capital, and entrepreneurship vary by country. Trading the goods and services produced by each country's businesses allows more of the needs and wants of consumers to be met. This has created a *global dependency* in which countries depend on each other for products.

Absolute advantage exists when a country can produce goods more efficiently and at a lower cost than another country. The United States has an absolute advantage over Costa Rica in producing wheat. Costa Rica has an absolute advantage over the United States in producing bananas. The United States can benefit from trading wheat for bananas.

anekoho/Shutterstock.com

Goods are sent all around the world to fuel the global market.

A **comparative advantage** exists when a country specializes in producing a product at which it is relatively more efficient. For example, the United States might be very efficient at producing both aircraft and certain items of clothing. However, producing aircraft might be much more profitable. As a result, the United States can benefit by specializing in aircraft production and importing clothing from another country.

Measures of Trade

All countries measure and record the economic exchanges that take place with all other trading countries. The **balance of trade** is the difference between a nation's exports and its imports. A nation that has more exports than imports has a positive balance of trade, or a *trade surplus*. When a nation imports more products than it exports, the result is a negative balance of trade, or a *trade deficit*.

The **balance of payments** is the total amount of money that comes into a country, minus the total amount of money that goes out for a specific period of time. This includes all the goods and services a country imports and exports, as well as all the country's international financial transactions. Financial transactions include investments in stocks, real estate, and international companies. It also includes tourism.

A country has a *positive* balance of payments when more money comes into the country than leaves it. If more money leaves a country than comes into it, a *negative* balance of payments is created.

Currency

When businesses, individuals, or governments in the same country buy and sell goods to one another, they use the same currency. *Currency* is money. Most countries have their own currencies and typically only accept their own currency for business exchanges. For example, a US business that buys from Europe needs to exchange dollars for euros to complete the financial transaction. This can become complicated because the value of each country's currency is different when compared to other currencies.

Foreign Exchange Rate

The **foreign exchange rate** is the cost to convert one currency into another. Exchange rates are needed because currencies have different values. For example, the value of one US dollar (USD) is not equal to one British pound (GBP). The exchange rate helps determine how much in British pounds is needed to equal one US dollar. Figure 5-2 shows a sample of five foreign currency exchange rates at the end of years 2013 and 2014.

Today, most currencies are floating. A **floating currency** means that its exchange rate is set by the market forces of the supply and demand in the foreign exchange market.

Currency Exchange Rates (value per USD)		
Currency	December 31, 2013	December 31, 2014
British Pound	£0.60 GBP	£0.64 GBP
Canadian Dollar	$1.06 CAD	$1.16 CAD
European Union Euro	€0.72 EUR	€0.82 EUR
Japanese Yen	¥119.76 JPY	¥119.76 JPY
Mexican Peso	$13.10 MXN	$14.74 MXN

Source: Board of Governors of the Federal Reserve System; Goodheart-Willcox Publisher

Figure 5-2 The value of foreign currencies tends to fluctuate over time.

Green Business   Paperless Society

Even though much written communication today is in the form of e-mail, paper helps people communicate. At school and in the office, paper is used to take notes, write reports, and for countless other tasks. Take measures to reduce the consumption of paper. By sending an e-mail to communicate with a coworker or friend, the message is still communicated, but paper, ink, and other costs associated with mailing a physical letter are saved.

Our "paperless society" still creates many reasons to print rather than to save our information digitally. According to the EPA, the average office worker in the United States will use approximately 10,000 sheets of paper in a year. Considering how much paper, ink, toner, and electricity is needed to print those pages, we can conserve resources by planning our printing needs.

Exchange rates can vary from day to day and even hour to hour. This fluctuation in exchange rates can make financial exchanges complicated.

Businesses, governments, and individuals need assistance when buying or selling with other countries. When buying and selling products in countries that use different currencies, it is important to understand the value of the foreign currencies. The *foreign exchange market (FOREX)* is a financial marketplace for buying and selling the currencies of different countries. It works like a stock market for foreign currencies.

Currency Value

The exchange rate of currency is often considered to be an indicator of the economy's health. The rates can be influenced by many factors:

- political stability or instability in the world

- nations changing their laws

- nations in dispute with other nations

- economic conditions, such as interest rates

The US dollar is a floating currency. It can strengthen or weaken against other currencies. Sometimes, the value of a foreign currency declines in US dollars. When this happens, it means the value of the US dollar has strengthened. A stronger dollar can buy more imports. However, exports then become more expensive to foreign buyers. When the price of foreign currency increases in US dollars, it

means the value of the US dollar has weakened. A weaker dollar can buy fewer foreign products. US exports are less expensive to foreign buyers, which makes them more attractive. But, imports become more expensive for US consumers.

Trade Policy

Trade policy is the body of laws related to the exchange of goods and services for international trade. Most governments believe that fair and open trade among nations benefits everyone. Governments are constantly negotiating trade terms with one another. Disagreements among governments are often related to access to markets.

vinnstock/Shutterstock.com

The value of foreign currencies fluctuates and may or may not benefit US-based businesses.

You Do the Math

Measurement Reasoning

Different systems of measurement are used throughout the world. The United States uses a system called the US Customary System that consists of feet, pounds, and degrees Fahrenheit. However, most of the world uses a variation of the metric system called the *Système International d'Unités* (SI), or International System of Units. The SI system consists of meters, grams, and degrees Celsius. The following are some common conversions:

- To convert degrees Fahrenheit to degrees Celsius, subtract 32, multiply by 5, and divide by 9.
- One inch is equal to 25.4 millimeters.
- One pound is equal to 0.45 kilogram.

Solve the following problems.

1. If a carton ready for shipping weighs 18.7 kilograms, how many pounds does it weigh?

2. Marion must ship a temperature-sensitive good to a country that uses the metric system. The product cannot be exposed to temperatures below 0 degrees Fahrenheit. She must place a label on the package indicating this temperature in Celsius. What temperature must she write on the label?

3. Luis must order a length of specialized steel rod from a company in Germany. He needs 0.3 feet of the rod. However, the rod must be ordered in increments of 10 millimeters. What length of rod must be ordered?

Trade disputes may arise over certain policies and practices. This can create an unfair advantage or disadvantage for at least one of the trading partners.

Trade Restrictions

Trade restrictions may be used to prevent hazardous goods from entering the country. They are also used to put pressure on foreign governments for political reasons. Most governments try to protect domestic businesses from foreign competitors. Governmental policies can restrict or discourage import activity through trade barriers. A **trade barrier** is any government action taken to control or limit the amount of imports. There are several types of trade barriers, including embargos, tariffs, and quotas.

An **embargo** is a government order that prohibits trade with a foreign country. A *total embargo* is the most severe trade restriction. **Trade sanctions** are embargoes that affect only certain goods. For example, trade sanctions can prohibit the import of a specific product for public health reasons.

A **tariff** is a governmental tax on imported goods. A tariff may also be called a *duty, customs duty,* or *import duty.* There are two reasons governments impose tariffs: revenue and protection. Tariffs generate revenue for the government

Martina I. Meyer/Shutterstock.com

Fruits and vegetables are not permitted to be brought into some countries due to potential diseases they may carry.

because the tax is paid on each related product. Imposing tariffs also protects domestic businesses. The additional tax makes imported products more expensive for consumers than competing products available from domestic businesses.

A **quota** is a limit on the amount of a product imported into a country during a specific period of time. For example, the United States has quotas on sugar, some textiles, tuna, dried milk, and peanuts. Import quotas are meant to protect domestic producers by limiting foreign competition.

Governments use import restrictions to protect the health and safety of citizens from dangerous imported goods. The United States has laws controlling hazardous materials, firearms, and drugs coming into the country. There are also laws restricting plants, animals, and food that may bring pests or diseases into the country. Endangered plant and animal species, and goods made from them, are banned under the US Endangered Species Act.

Trade Agreements

The United States has trade agreements and partnerships with many individual nations and regions around the world. A **trade agreement** is a document listing the conditions and terms for importing and exporting products between countries. The goal of trade agreements is to create economic benefits and opportunities for all participating nations by allowing free trade and investing across their borders.

A **trading bloc** is a group of countries that has joined together to trade as if they were a single country. A trading bloc is usually a free-trade zone, as well. A *free-trade zone* is a group of countries that have reduced or eliminated trade barriers among themselves.

The *European Union (EU)* is a major trading bloc and free-trade zone in the modern global economy. It consists of 28 countries in Europe and is the largest trade sector in the world, as shown in Figure 5-3.

Figure 5-3 The countries of the European Union compose the largest trade sector in the world.

The EU has one of the largest GDPs and is the largest importer and exporter of goods and services. Eighteen of the EU countries share a common currency called the *euro*. The main trading partners of the EU include the United States, China, Switzerland, and Russia.

The *North American Free Trade Agreement (NAFTA)* is a trade agreement between the United States, Canada, and Mexico that was established in 1994. The agreement lowered trade barriers and opened markets among the three countries. Canada and Mexico are top trading partners of the United States. Trade has increased dramatically among the three nations since NAFTA went into effect.

Section 5.1 Review

 Check Your Understanding

1. What benefits are created when a business exports and sells product globally?
2. Name the condition created when a nation has more exports than imports.
3. What are some factors that can influence the exchange rate of currency?
4. Identify three types of trade barriers used by governments.
5. What is NAFTA?

 Build Your Vocabulary

As you progress through this course, develop a personal glossary of key terms. This will help you build your vocabulary and prepare you for a career. Write a definition for each of the following terms and add it to your personal glossary.

globalization	foreign exchange rate
culture	floating currency
international trade	trade policy
domestic business	trade barrier
exports	embargo
imports	trade sanction
absolute advantage	tariff
comparative advantage	quota
balance of trade	trade agreement
balance of payments	trading bloc

Entering Global Business

?E ssential Q uestion

How do culture and established laws affect the operations of a multinational corporation?

Objectives

After completing this section, you will be able to:

- **Identify** considerations that must be taken when doing business off shore.
- **Discuss** ways to enter global markets.

Key Terms

logistics
diversity
intercultural communication

English as a second language (ESL)
multinational corporation
licensing

franchise
franchisor
franchisee
joint venture

Offshore Business

Many businesses looking for growth opportunities consider going off shore. Technology has changed the way we communicate, making it somewhat easier to enter global markets than it was decades ago. However, there are considerations that should be addressed before taking business into another country. Common considerations involved in taking business to another country include labor laws in force, legal documents required, logistics of offshore business operations, incorporating a diverse workforce, and effective intercultural communications. Every detail of going global must be planned, organized, and well executed for the best chance of success.

Labor Laws

Labor laws must be considered when doing business offshore. US businesses with overseas operations must be sure to abide by US labor laws. They must also make sure the labor laws of the offshore country are followed.

The United States has labor laws that apply to doing business in foreign countries. For example, US laws on child labor do not allow children under the age of 14 to work. The typical 8-hour workday common in the United States should also be honored. The US Bureau of International Labor Affairs (ILAB) and the Office of International Relations (OIR) offer businesses assistance with both cultural differences and labor laws in other countries.

Legal Documents

Engaging in international business requires specific legal documentation. Many government and private establishments, such as foreign customs offices, security, and overseas harbors and airports, may require documents. Some of the documents required may include air waybills, certificates of origin, dock receipts, ocean bills of lading, and special packing lists.

Logistics

Logistics is planning and managing the flow of goods, services, and people to a destination.

leungchopan/Shutterstock.com

The labor and business laws in a foreign territory, such as Hong Kong, must be researched and considered when doing business offshore.

When a business expands off shore, goods must be moved over at least one country's border by air, rail, or trucking transportation. Moving goods internationally is much more complex than domestic transport. When distances increase, it is more likely that many different forms of transportation will be needed. For example, moving goods and supplies overseas often requires air or ocean freight. It might also require rail or trucking to reach the final destination. Using several forms of transportation usually results in longer shipping times and greater expense.

Diverse Workforce

Businesses that operate globally must consider their human resources. Hiring people from other countries or operating in another country brings diversity to the workplace. **Diversity** is having people from different backgrounds, cultures, or demographics coming together in a group. Characteristics of diversity include age, race, nationality, and gender. It also includes mental ability, physical ability, and other qualities that make an individual unique.

A diverse workforce can help an organization be more creative. It can guide a business to be more receptive to customer needs. It can also

©iStock.com/Rawpixel Ltd

A diverse workforce can help increase creativity and expand the markets of a business, but it may also present challenges in communication.

help a company find new ways of thinking and looking at business. Diverse employees can help a company create goods and services that may be new and unique in the marketplace. Diversity also increases the pool of potential qualified and talented candidates, which may result in a more effective workforce.

Diversity, however, does not come without some challenges. Special training may be required for employees to learn how to effectively communicate in a diverse workplace. Employees may need to adjust their ways of thinking and day-to-day habits in order to work with a diverse population. Potential employees in the native country of a business may even lose job opportunities to diverse candidates.

Intercultural Communication

Intercultural communication is the process of sending and receiving messages between people of various cultures. To communicate successfully, businesses must understand the culture of their employees. Not understanding another person's culture may result in misinterpreting verbal and nonverbal communication. For example, during a business meeting in the United States, when a topic is "tabled," it is put off to be addressed at another time. However, the same phrase in Great Britain means to "bring it to the table" for discussion.

Listening is one of the most important skills a person in business can develop. Extra attention should be given when listening to individuals from diverse backgrounds. English may not be their first language. **English as a second language (ESL)** is the use of English by people with a different native language. Imagine yourself in another country trying to speak a foreign language. It could be frustrating trying to express a thought or idea if you are not fluent in the language. Be patient and attentive when communicating with those who are not fluent in English.

Business communication requires that individuals speak clearly. Using simple language and short sentences can help avoid misunderstandings when communicating with a diverse group. Speaking loudly will not necessarily help another person understand

what you are saying. Humor should be avoided, as well as topics that are not appropriate in the other person's culture. Business communication should not include slang words, jargon, or expressions that someone from another country would not understand.

When doing business globally, some businesses use an interpreter. An *interpreter* translates a conversation between individuals who do not speak the same language. Many companies that do business internationally employ an interpreter.

Body language is an important form of nonverbal communication. People from different countries and cultures interpret specific meanings from nonverbal behavior, which may not always be the same meanings intended. For example, direct eye contact is not acceptable in some cultures, while it is favored in others. Many cultures have different standards of how much personal space is acceptable. Shaking hands may be inappropriate when meeting someone from a certain culture, while it is a common greeting in others.

koh sze kiat/Shutterstock.com

When communicating with a diverse population, whether in person, by phone, or in e-mail, speak clearly and use simple language.

Ethics

Sourcing

Ethical businesses purchase raw materials or goods from reputable suppliers where products are created in safe conditions. Factories in which products are created should be clean and safe for workers. Manufacturers in other countries may have different work safety standards than the United States. Purchasing products at the expense of others to save money is unethical.

Ways to Enter the Global Market

There are various ways that a domestic business can enter a global market. Importing and exporting are obvious ways of conducting international business. Some businesses take it a step further. They produce and sell goods both domestically and in another country. A **multinational corporation** is a business that operates in more than one country. Multinational corporations often have their corporate headquarters in one country and divisions of the business in another country, or located offshore. General Motors and Johnson & Johnson are examples of multinational companies.

For companies that want to establish a business in another country, there are some options. Some of the ways to start a business in a foreign country include licensing, franchising, and joint ventures, as shown in Figure 5-4.

Licensing

Licensing is when a business sells the right to manufacture its products or use its trademark. Licensing involves selling the rights in exchange for a fee, also known as a *royalty*. The company that sells the license is the *licensor*. The buyer of the license is the *licensee*.

Licensing can benefit both parties. The licensor earns revenue, often for little or no extra work. The licensee gets product into the market quickly. A familiar example of a licensing agreement is the Walt Disney Company. Disney entered a foreign market in Japan through a long-term licensing agreement with Oriental Land Company. Tokyo Disneyland and Tokyo DisneySea are operated by Oriental Land Company.

However, there are potential problems that arise when licensing. Examples are improper use of the trademark or product and failure to deliver the material or property to the licensee.

Franchising

A **franchise** is the right to sell a company's goods or services in a specific area. A **franchisor** is the parent company that owns the chain and the brand. The **franchisee** is the person or company that buys the rights to use the brand. The franchisee pays a fee to the franchisor in addition to royalties on every dollar the business earns.

Global Business Options		
Type	**Pro**	**Con**
Licensing	• Licensor earns revenue for little or no extra work • Licensee gets product into the market quickly	• Potential for conflict between licensor and licensee
Franchise	• Product is already known in the market • Effective standards and procedures are provided	• Can be expensive to buy • May be difficult to maintain proper standards
Joint Venture	• Each company is independent • Profits and losses are shared • Effective way to start a business off shore	• May not be allowed in all foreign countries

Goodheart-Willcox Publisher

Figure 5-4 Global business ownership options include licensing, franchise business, and joint venture.

Franchising enables the franchisee to enter a market where the good or service is already known. The franchisor provides standards and procedures to get the company organized and in operation.

However, buying a franchise can be expensive and maintaining established franchise standards can be challenging. Examples of popular international franchise businesses include Chem-Dry Carpet Cleaning, Ziebart, Anytime Fitness, and Minuteman Press. Each franchise is independently owned and operated.

Joint Venture

A **joint venture** is a partnership of two or more companies that work together for a specific business purpose. Each company remains independent. They work together for a specific purpose and share the profits or losses. Joint ventures may be formed among domestic businesses, as well as internationally.

An international joint venture allows a company in one country to enter a foreign market without assuming all the risk. Also, some countries do not allow foreign companies to enter and establish a business. However, a company may be allowed to participate in a joint venture with a foreign company. In some cases, an international joint venture may be the only way to start a business off shore.

For example, the Campbell Soup Company entered into joint ventures with Japanese and Malaysian companies to compete for a greater portion of the soup market in Japan and Malaysia.

JStone/Shutterstock.com

Entering the global market through a franchise business is beneficial because the product is known and established within the market.

Section 5.2 Review

 Check Your Understanding

1. Identify five common considerations involved in taking business to another country.
2. Why is moving products internationally much more complex than domestic transport?
3. List some of the benefits that a diverse workforce can provide to a business.
4. List three ways a business can enter a global market.
5. How does licensing benefit both the licensor and licensee?

 Build Your Vocabulary

As you progress through this course, develop a personal glossary of key terms. This will help you build your vocabulary and prepare you for a career. Write a definition for each of the following terms and add it to your personal glossary.

logistics
diversity
intercultural communication
English as a second
　language (ESL)
multinational corporation

licensing
franchise
franchisor
franchisee
joint venture

Review and Assessment

Chapter Summary

Section 5.1 Exploring Global Business

- Globalization is the connection made among nations when economies freely move goods, labor, and money across borders. International trade is the buying and selling of goods and services across national borders. Nations trade with each other because most countries do not have the factors of production needed to produce all the goods and services needed by their population. By trading with other countries, the needs and wants of consumers are more likely to be met.

- Most countries have their own currencies and typically only accept their own currency for business exchanges. The foreign exchange rate is the cost to convert one currency into another. When buying and selling products in countries that use different currencies, it is important to understand the value of the foreign currencies.

- Trade policy is the body of laws related to the exchange of goods and services for international trade. It includes trade restrictions and trade agreements. Many forms of trade restrictions are used to prevent or limit the amount of certain products from entering the country. The goal of trade agreements is to create economic benefits and opportunities for all participating nations.

Section 5.2 Entering Global Business

- Many businesses looking for growth opportunities consider going off shore. However, there are considerations that should be addressed before taking business into another country. Common considerations involved in taking business to another country include labor laws in force, legal documents required, logistics of offshore business operations, incorporating a diverse workforce, and effective intercultural communications.

- A business can enter the global market in various ways. They can import and export goods and services internationally. Businesses can also expand into a foreign country to produce and sell goods. Some ways to start a business in a foreign country include licensing, franchising, and joint ventures.

Online Activities

Complete the following activities to help you learn, practice, and expand your knowledge and skills.

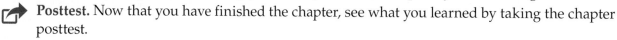 **Posttest.** Now that you have finished the chapter, see what you learned by taking the chapter posttest.

Vocabulary. Practice vocabulary for this chapter using the e-flash cards, matching activity, and vocabulary game until you are able to recognize their meanings.

Review Your Knowledge

1. Explain the role of business in a global society.
2. Compare the activities involved in world trade with the activities involved in domestic business.
3. Explain why currency makes global trade complex.
4. Describe three types of trade barriers.
5. What is the purpose and goal of a trade agreement?
6. What is a free-trade zone?
7. How do US labor laws affect business conducted in another country?
8. Explain why logistics is a consideration when taking business to another country.
9. Explain the importance of effective intercultural communication for business.
10. Discuss three ways to enter global markets.

Apply Your Knowledge

1. Explain the impact of imports and exports on the United States economy. How does the population benefit? Are there negative aspects to participating in import and export activities? Write several paragraphs to support your opinion.
2. How does the foreign exchange rate affect the buying power of the US dollar?
3. Consider the logistics of moving product to be sold overseas. Create an illustration that depicts the movement of goods produced in Cincinnati, Ohio, to a distributor in London, England. How many different forms of transportation are involved? Who is responsible for the product in each step of the transport? Write a brief summary of the process to accompany your illustration.
4. Communication includes verbal, nonverbal, and written forms of expression. Describe the communication barriers that can be involved in carrying out international business. What forms of communication are commonly used for business? How can a business prepare itself for intercultural communication?
5. Describe the benefits and importance of international business for workers, consumers, and citizens.

Communication Skills

College and Career Readiness

Reading. After you have read this chapter, identify the explicit details, as well as the author's main idea for the chapter. Apply appropriate reading techniques to identify the main ideas and purpose of the information that is presented. Draw conclusions about the author's purpose. Share your findings with the class.

Writing. Standard English means that word choice, sentence structure, paragraphs, and the format of communication follow standard conventions used by those who speak English. Research the topic of ways to take a business global. Write an informative report, consisting of several paragraphs to describe your findings. Edit the writing for proper syntax, tense, and voice.

Speaking. The workplace requires that employees adapt to diversity of the many individuals with whom they will come in contact. The interaction can be in formal or informal situations. Make a list of potential barriers that can evolve and solutions to eliminate those barriers. Did you uncover any that were not presented in this chapter? Share your list with the class.

Internet Research

Exporting Opportunities. Primary research is conducted by gathering information. Conduct research on the topic of international business and how US companies can get help from the government to learn how to export product. The governmental website www.export.gov provides helpful assistance about exporting. Write several paragraphs explaining opportunities available to businesses.

Teamwork

Working with your team, discuss the topic of international business and its impact on consumers, business, and government. Discuss why your team thinks that exporting is good for the United States. Make a list of pros and cons to present to the class.

Portfolio Development

College and Career Readiness

Checklist. Once you have written your portfolio objective, consider how you will achieve it. It is helpful to have a checklist of components that will be included in your portfolio. The checklist will be used to record ideas for documents and other items that you might include. Starting with a checklist will help you brainstorm ideas that you want to pursue.

The elements that you select to include in your portfolio will reflect your portfolio's purpose. For example, if you are seeking acceptance into art school, create a portfolio that includes your best artwork.

1. Ask your instructor for a checklist. If one is not provided, use the Internet and research Student Portfolio checklists. Find an example that works for your purpose.

2. Create a checklist. This will be your road map for your portfolio.

CTSOs

Objective Test. Some competitive events for CTSOs require that entrants complete an objective component of the event. This event will typically be an objective test that includes terminology and concepts related to a selected subject area. Participants are usually allowed one hour to complete the objective test component of the event. The Global Business event may also include a team activity, case, or role play.

To prepare for an objective test, complete the following activities.

1. Read the guidelines provided by your organization.

2. Visit the organization's website and look for objective tests that were used in previous years. Many organizations post these tests for students to use as practice for future competitions.

3. Look for the evaluation criteria or rubric for the event. This will help you determine what the judge will be looking for in your presentation.

4. Create flash cards for each vocabulary term with its definition on the other side. Ask a friend to use these cards to review with you.

5. Ask your instructor to give you practice tests for this chapter of the text that would prepare you for the subject area of the event. It is important that you are familiar with answering multiple choice and true/false questions. Have someone time you as you take a practice test.

Business Management

Focus on Management

Management is the process of controlling and making decisions about a business. Strong management skills are needed in order to be an effective business person and entrepreneur.

Anyone has the opportunity to be an entrepreneur in the US free enterprise system. Entrepreneurs are only limited by their drive, creativity, desire, and available resources.

Most successful entrepreneurs start with a great idea that has the potential to meet the needs or wants of a large number of people. Entrepreneurs may choose to start a new business, purchase an existing business, or buy a franchise. No matter how the new business is started, a detailed business plan provides a road map to help establish and grow the business.

Once a new business is operating, an important factor for success is strong management. Performing the management functions of planning, organizing, staffing, leading and controlling helps managers reach their goals and the goals of the company. One of the many important responsibilities of management is to oversee the production of goods. This requires planning products and resources, purchasing materials and equipment, scheduling resources, inventory control, and quality control.

Human resource management is another crucial focus of management. The human resource department provides guidance for the people who provide labor for a business. Businesses would not exist without their human resources. Human resource management responsibilities include hiring and supporting capable employees, as well as fostering the corporate culture.

Social Media for Business

LinkedIn® is a social media website for professional networking. A business can create a LinkedIn profile at no charge and then invite others to join its network. For a fee, businesses can post open jobs on the site. These postings are available for any LinkedIn member to view and submit an application. Creating a professional network provides businesses the opportunity to recruit candidates, as well as obtain referrals for job applicants. By using keywords to target skill sets or other criteria, the profiles of qualified candidates can be reviewed. The candidates may be contacted directly or through people who know them.

LinkedIn also offers professional groups that include people who represent different companies. These groups allow companies to network with others within their industry. LinkedIn offers solutions and tips to help employers make the most of the social media site, as well as enhanced features to engage followers and track data about profile activity.

While studying, look for the activity icon ↱ for:

- Pretests and posttests
- Vocabulary terms with e-flash cards and matching activities
- Self-assessment

G-WLEARNING.com

Entrepreneurship

In This Chapter

Exploring Careers

Chief Executive

Business Management & Administration

Businesses are run by people in a variety of management levels. In many businesses, the chief executive is the person in charge. Chief executives are responsible for creating policies for a business. They hold the highest position within the company and often have the most authority. Their responsibilities include overseeing the overall direction of their company established by a company's board of directors.

Typical job titles for this position also include *chief executive officer (CEO)*, *chief financial officer (CFO)*, and *president*. Examples of tasks that chief executives perform include:

- direct financial activities

- appoint department heads and managers

- analyze operations

- determine areas of cost reduction, program improvement, and policy change

Chief executive positions require a bachelor degree, but a postgraduate degree may be preferred. Chief executives must also have effective leadership and communication skills, as well as strong analytical and problem-solving abilities.

Reading Prep

College and Career Readiness

Before reading the chapter, skim the photos and their captions. As you read, determine how these concepts contribute to the ideas presented in the text.

Check Your Business IQ

Before you begin the chapter, see what you already know about business by taking the chapter pretest. The pretest is available at www.g-wlearning.com.

Entrepreneurs in a Free Enterprise System

?**E**ssential **Q**uestion

What are common elements of success in new businesses?

Objectives

After completing this section, you will be able to:

- **Describe** common skills and traits of successful entrepreneurs.
- **Explain** the criteria to qualify as a small business.
- **Identify** sources of professional advice for entrepreneurs.
- **List** common reasons that new businesses fail.

Key Terms

trait	job-specific skills	planning
leadership	transferable skills	mentor

Entrepreneurs

An *entrepreneur* is a person who starts a new business or purchases an existing business. According to the US Small Business Administration (SBA), an entrepreneur is "a person who organizes and manages a business undertaking, assuming the risk for the sake of profit." *Entrepreneurship* is willingly risking resources to start and run a business in pursuit of profit.

Anyone has the opportunity to be an entrepreneur in the US free enterprise system. A college degree, prior business experience, one million dollars, or permission from anyone are not needed. As shown in Figure 6-1, there are no boundaries in becoming an entrepreneur. As long as the activity is legal, a person is free to pursue it. Individuals of all personality types can be entrepreneurs. Some entrepreneurs are extroverts, and some are introverts. Some prefer working with the public, while others prefer working quietly behind the scenes. Entrepreneurs are only limited by their drive, creativity, desire, and available resources.

Five Ps of Entrepreneurship

A common model of successful entrepreneurial ventures addresses five qualities, as shown in Figure 6-2. These are known as the *five Ps of entrepreneurship*:

- **Purpose.** Entrepreneurs have a *purpose*. They are driven to be independent and successful. They set goals and work hard to achieve them.

- **Passion.** Entrepreneurs follow their *passion*, which is something they believe in or that they are enthusiastic about. Most successful entrepreneurs combine what they are good at with what they enjoy.

- **Persistence.** Entrepreneurs are *persistent* in achieving success. Determination to work through obstacles is key in becoming a successful entrepreneur.

- **People.** Entrepreneurs need a support system of *people*. Professional connections and business associations can offer helpful resources and shared experiences.

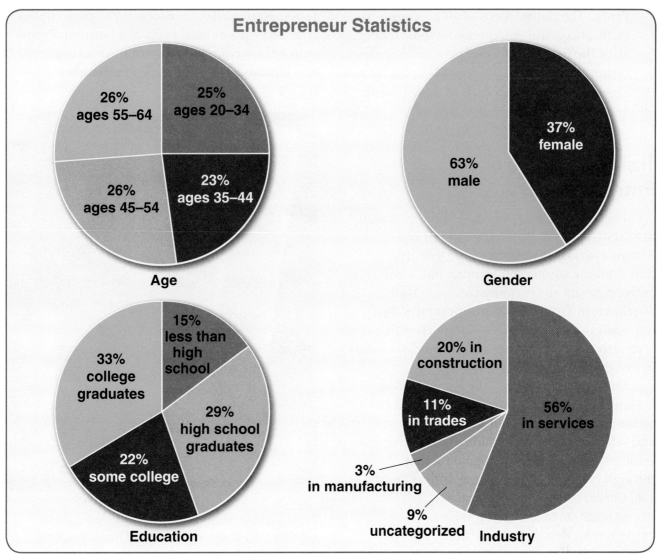

Source: Kauffman Foundation; Goodheart-Willcox Publisher

Figure 6-1 The statistics about entrepreneurs in the US prove that anyone can become an entrepreneur.

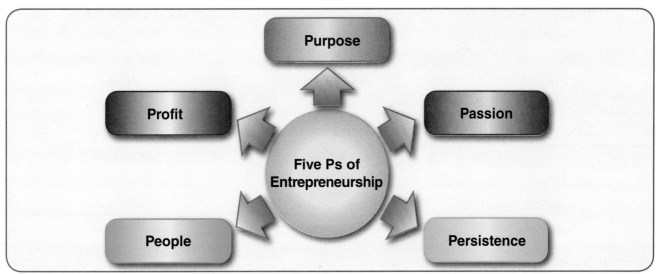

Goodheart-Willcox Publisher

Figure 6-2 The five Ps are common qualities of successful entrepreneurial businesses.

- **Profit.** The central focus of all businesses is *profit*. Successful entrepreneurs must manage all of the finances of a business and keep the business profitable.

Defining and planning for each of these contributes to the chances of business success.

Traits and Skills of Entrepreneurs

There are many traits and skills common to successful entrepreneurs. A **trait** is a distinguishing characteristic or quality that makes each person unique. Successful entrepreneurs share many common traits, as shown in Figure 6-3. Entrepreneurs do not need to be accomplished in each trait. Strength in one area can overcome a weakness in another.

Entrepreneurs are usually recognized as leaders. **Leadership** is the ability to influence others to reach a goal. Honesty, competence, and self-confidence are qualities of effective leadership. Being able to set goals, follow through on tasks, and be forward-thinking are also important leadership abilities.

In addition to leadership skills, an entrepreneur needs job-specific skills.

Job-specific skills are necessary to perform the required work-related tasks of a position. People gain job-specific skills through work experience and education or training. These are also

Monkey Business Images/Shutterstock.com

Entrepreneurs willingly take the risks involved in starting a business in the hope of making a profit.

Common Traits of Successful Entrepreneurs

Achievement-oriented	Enthusiastic	Passionate
Adaptable	Fast learner	Persistence
Competitive	Goal-oriented	Perseverance
Confident	Good with money	Planner
Creative	Honest	Positive attitude
Customer focused	Independent	Receptive
Disciplined	Intuitive	Resourceful
Driven	Motivated	Risk-tolerant
Dynamic	Nonjudgmental	Self-starter
Empathetic	Optimistic	Versatile
Energetic	Organized	Visionary

Goodheart-Willcox Publisher

Figure 6-3 Most successful entrepreneurs have these traits in common.

You Do the Math   Geometric Reasoning

The area of a two-dimensional shape considers measurements of its perimeter. The area of a rectangle, for example, is calculated by multiplying the length of two sides that meet at a right angle. The area of a circle is calculated by multiplying the constant pi (3.14) by the radius of the circle squared. To calculate the volume of a cylinder, multiply its height by the area of its base.

Solve the following problems.

1. Catalina must calculate the area of a parking lot in order to estimate the cost of repaving it. The parking lot measures 75 feet by 125 feet. What is the area of the parking lot?

2. Tim must order cleaning fluid for his cleaning service. The cleaning fluid comes in buckets that are 12 inches in diameter and 2 feet in height. What is the volume of cleaning fluid in each bucket?

3. Geoff must buy enough plywood to cover the floor in a room that is 12 feet by 25 feet. One sheet of plywood is 4 feet by 8 feet. How many sheets of plywood must be purchased?

known as *skills of the trade*. This means that entrepreneurs must have basic expertise in the type of business they want to run. For example, to open an income tax preparation business, a person must understand tax laws and regulations.

Transferrable skills are also necessary to become an effective entrepreneur. **Transferable skills**, also known as *foundation skills*, help an individual perform in the workplace or gain success in a career. Examples of transferable skills include effective communication, presentation, and time management skills. Most of these skills are gained through life experience or while working on a job.

Basic Skills

Certain basic skills are necessary to operate a successful business. These skills are not specific to any one career, but they are valuable in any professional position. Some of the basic skills every entrepreneur should master include:

- basic math functions
- reading and writing
- effective speaking and listening
- knowledge of current technology

The better an entrepreneur's basic skills, the greater his or her chances of success. These basic skills will help the business owner:

- keep accurate financial records
- understand and meet legal business requirements
- deal with customers and suppliers effectively
- manage general business operations

Problem-Solving and Decision-Making Skills

Entrepreneurs can count on the fact that problems will always arise. To keep a business running smoothly, they must be able to take charge of situations and quickly make decisions. Many people put off making decisions because they are afraid of doing the wrong thing. However, postponing a decision often makes a situation worse. Effective decisions are made after weighing all options and choosing the best solution or action.

Planning Skills

Planning is the process of setting goals and deciding how to accomplish them. Planning is important in any type of business. The ability to organize and manage resources is necessary in order to make a profit. Lack of effective planning is a common reason that businesses fail.

Small Businesses

According to the Small Business Administration (SBA), "To be a small business, you must adhere to industry size standards established by the US Small Business Administration." The business size standards are based on industry groups, as illustrated in Figure 6-4. These standards help to identify and categorize small businesses. For most industries, a small business is defined either in terms of the *average number of employees* over the past 12 months or *average annual receipts* over the past three years.

In addition, the SBA requires that a small business:

- is organized for profit
- has a place of business in the United States
- operates primarily within the United States or makes a significant contribution to the US economy through payment of taxes or use of American products, materials, or labor
- is independently owned and operated
- is not dominant in its field on a national scale

The small business may be a sole proprietorship, partnership, corporation, or any other legal form. The operation of small businesses makes large contributions to the US economy, as shown in Figure 6-5.

Professional Advice

Most new entrepreneurs are not experienced in all aspects of operating a business. Seeking advice from experienced professionals can help entrepreneurs become more knowledgeable about the process and have confidence about starting a new business.

Small Business Size Standards	
Industry Group	**Size Standard**
Wholesale trade	100 employees
Manufacturing	500 employees
Publishing industries	500 employees
Mining	500 employees
Agriculture	$750,000
Ground passenger transportation	$15 million
Specialty trade contractors	$15 million
Travel agencies	$20.5 million
General and heavy construction	$36.5 million
Professional and personal services:	
Dry cleaning and laundry services	$5.5 million
Beauty salons and barbershops	$7.5 million
Architectural, drafting, interior design, and graphic design services	$7.5 million
Engineering, surveying, and mapping services	$15 million

Source: The US Small Business Administration; Goodheart-Willcox Publisher

Figure 6-4 The SBA small business size standards help categorize small businesses and identify assistance that may be available.

Economic Contribution of Small Businesses
• Represent 99.7 percent of all employer firms
• Employ about 50 percent of all private sector employees
• Create more than 50 percent of the nonfarm, private GDP
• Pay 43 percent of total US private payroll
• Hire 43 percent of high-tech workers
• Produce 16.5 times more patents per employee than large patenting firms

Source: The US Small Business Administration; Goodheart-Willcox Publisher

Figure 6-5 Small businesses in the United States have made significant contributions to the economy.

Mentors

Finding a business mentor can lend helpful advice and direction. A **mentor** is someone with experience who can provide advice, suggestions, and ideas. The person must have knowledge and experience and be willing to devote the time necessary to help an entrepreneur. The experience and knowledge of an enthusiastic mentor can help take a business to the next level of success.

Small Business Administration

The US Small Business Administration (SBA) is an independent agency of the federal government dedicated to helping entrepreneurs start, build, and grow their business. The SBA provides information on starting a small business and expanding an existing business. Every year, thousands of small business owners take advantage of the assistance provided by the SBA.

baranq/Shutterstock.com

Mentors and other business professionals can offer their experience and connections to new entrepreneurs.

Managing inventory can help a new business succeed.

The agency's website provides a variety of online education and resources.

Service Corps of Retired Executives

The *Service Corps of Retired Executives (SCORE)* is a nonprofit association of more than 13,000 retired and active businesspeople. These professionals volunteer their services to help small businesses succeed. Created in 1964, SCORE has 348 local chapters and provides advice on over 500 skills. Small business entrepreneurs can visit the SCORE website to request a meeting with a local mentor, find free local and online workshops, and access free business templates and tools.

Why Businesses Fail

Unfortunately, many new businesses fail. The reasons are personal to the entrepreneur and they are varied. Some common reasons for failure include:

- *Lack of money.* New business owners must have enough funds available to support business operations before the business generates enough profit to pay for itself.

- *Lack of business experience.* Many business owners are skilled at their trade or profession but lack experience in operating a business.

- *Poor management skills.* Managing a business involves people skills, organizational skills, patience, and willingness to adapt and accept change.

- *Inefficient inventory control.* Too much inventory on hand means money is tied up that could be used for other vital activities. Too little inventory results in lost sales and frustrated customers. Inventory should be ordered in the proper amounts at the best prices available.

- *Poor credit management.* Using credit responsibly is important to the financial success of a business. Credit should only be used when absolutely necessary.

- *Poor location.* The least expensive business location is not always the best location.

The main consideration should be customer convenience. Customers must be able to find and want to come into the business.

- *Improper budgeting.* There are many expenses associated with running a business. Expenses can get out of control if business owners do not properly budget.

- *Lack of advertising.* Getting the word out about a new business is critical. Many new businesses cannot afford to adequately advertise.

Potential business owners who plan and seek advice are more likely to avoid failure. However, there is no strategy that guarantees the success of any business.

Section 6.1 Review

 Check Your Understanding

1. How does the US Small Business Administration define *entrepreneur*?

2. What are the five Ps of entrepreneurship?

3. How does the US Small Business Administration define small business in most industries?

4. Identify three resources an entrepreneur can use for business advice.

5. List some reasons that many new businesses fail.

 Build Your Vocabulary

As you progress through this course, develop a personal glossary of key terms. This will help you build your vocabulary and prepare you for a career. Write a definition for each of the following terms and add it to your personal glossary.

trait
leadership
job-specific skills

transferable skills
planning
mentor

Business Planning

Objectives

After completing this section, you will be able to:

- **Discuss** the process of developing an idea for a business.
- **Describe** the components of a business plan.
- **Explain** the types of financing available for new businesses.

Key Terms

market research
market
cash flow
business plan
mission
  statement
start-up capital

pro forma financial
  statements
pro forma balance
  sheet
pro forma income
  statement
pro forma cash flow
  statement

capital structure
debt financing
collateral
assets
equity financing
venture capital
angel investors

Developing a Business Idea

Most successful entrepreneurs start with a great idea, or a *vision*. Whether the idea is for a new good or service, or an improvement on an existing good or service, it must be something that appeals to a large number of people. The opportunity to meet a customer want or need must be established. In order to do this, extensive market research must be conducted to test the idea. **Market research** is the gathering and analyzing of information about a business. Market research helps analyze if the idea is feasible. Feasible means that something can be done successfully. If the idea is not a good one, the business will not succeed.

To appeal to the greatest number of consumers, entrepreneurs must know their market. A **market** is all the people and organizations that might purchase a product.

Knowing the market allows an entrepreneur to focus on the most effective way to develop, advertise, and deliver a product.

The next step is to consider start-up strategies. Will the business be a service business, retail business, or manufacturing business? The entrepreneur can choose to:

- start a new business
- purchase an existing business
- buy a franchise

Each option offers unique advantages, as well as disadvantages.

Start a New Business

To start a business from scratch, entrepreneurs need a new product or operating strategy that sets the business apart from the competition. Additionally, a new business must have a detailed plan to attract customers.

Konstantin Chagin/Shutterstock.com

Brainstorming is one way of generating new business ideas.

Entrepreneurs who start new businesses have the unique opportunity to build a reputation and establish a customer base on their own terms.

Purchase an Existing Business

Buying an established business removes some of the risks typically involved in opening a new business. An existing business has an established location and customer base, as well as relationships with suppliers. An important advantage is that the entrepreneur will probably have cash flow from the business starting on day one of ownership. **Cash flow** is the movement of money into and out of a business. Other potential advantages of purchasing an existing business include:

- history of profitable operations
- proven products and sales strategies
- experienced employees and operating procedures are in place
- easier to secure financing for an established business
- guidance and advice from the previous owner

Buying an existing business can also have disadvantages. The purchase price of an established business may be more expensive than starting a business from scratch. The current owners may place a high value on the business they are trying to sell. There is also a risk that the inventory or equipment being sold with the business is old or out of date. In addition, a buyer may need to agree to keep current employees on the payroll, which could be an advantage or disadvantage.

Buying an existing business requires careful research and consideration. It is suggested that an attorney or other professional assist in the purchase decision.

Buy a Franchise

A *franchise* is a license to sell a company's goods or services within a certain territory or location. Buying a franchise gives a person the right to sell an established product. A *franchisee* is a person or company that buys a franchise. A *franchisor* is the person or company that grants a franchise.

TK Kurikawa/Shutterstock.com

A franchise provides the benefit of a business name that is already known in the market.

The franchisee pays a franchise fee to the franchisor and is usually responsible for the startup costs of the business. The franchisee gets a proven business system and a business name that is already known in the market. In return, the franchisor receives a portion of the earnings of the business.

There are many different types of franchise businesses, including automotive sales and repair, health and fitness clubs, pet care, lawn maintenance, and many others. A popular franchise in a good location improves the chances of business success.

Business Plan

Once the business idea is established and the startup strategy is underway, a business plan should be written. A **business plan** is a written statement of goals and objectives for a business with a strategy to achieve them. It is a road map to help an entrepreneur establish and grow a business. A complete business plan is also needed to apply for financing through banks and other financial institutions.

In general, a business plan includes the following sections:

- executive summary
- company description
- market analysis
- organization and management
- service or line of goods
- marketing and sales
- funding request (if applicable)
- financial projections
- appendix

Executive Summary

The executive summary is a description of the business and why it will be successful. It should include a **mission statement**, which is a sentence describing the purpose of the business. The founders of the business and their roles should also be explained in this part of the business plan. The executive summary should be one to two pages that grab the attention of readers and makes them want to learn more about the business and its plans.

vgstudio/Shutterstock.com

A business plan provides a road map when creating a new business.

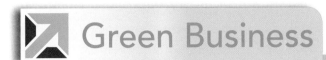

Green Business

Green Team

There are many ways to go green in the workplace. Assembling an employee green team is a good place to start. Most green teams start out by addressing employee habits in the workplace, such as implementing a recycling program and eliminating the use of plastic water bottles. Some green teams evolve their mission to help employees make environmentally friendly decisions in their personal lives as well. A green team can prepare a presentation about hybrid vehicles or about the importance of eating locally grown produce.

Green teams may also look for ways to make the operations of the business more environmentally friendly. Companies can improve shipping routes to consume less fuel, implement online systems that replace paperwork, and keep electronic records. Another way for a green team to expand its mission is to involve consumers and customers. Businesses that work toward sustainability are socially responsible and create goodwill.

Company Description

The company description gives details about the business activities, describes the market it serves, and explains why the business will be successful.

- Describe the business activity. Is the business a provider of goods or services? Will there be a physical location, online store, or both?

- Identify the market need. How do the goods or services meet a need in the market? Who is the customer?

- Explain competitive advantages. Why will this business succeed? What advantages does this business have over its competitors?

Market Analysis

The market analysis provides an overview of the industry and market that the business will serve. It presents the current and projected size of the entire market and identifies competitors. The plan should also estimate how much of the market the entrepreneur hopes to capture. This section describes characteristics of the target market and customer needs the business will satisfy.

Organization and Management

The organization and management section details how the company is organized and run.

This includes the business structure, such as proprietorship, partnership, corporation, or LLC. It may include an organizational chart showing the chain of command within the business. Biographies of company leaders are presented, along with their ownership in the business and how much they will be involved in the business. Any special licenses and permits held by the business are also listed.

Products

The products section details what the business will sell, as well as the product's life cycle and a plan for pricing. The issue of *competitiveness* should be discussed. This includes why the goods or services will be successful despite competition from other companies.

Marketing and Sales Strategy

The marketing and sales strategy section describes how the business will reach its market. The information in this section should include:

- strategy for building and growing the business

- plan for reaching customers, such as promotions, advertising, and public relations

- system for selling the product, such as retail location with sales associates, direct sales representatives, or online store

- average sale amount per customer to make a profit

Financial Plans

Financial plans are necessary to convince investors to participate in a new business. A new business usually needs **start-up capital** which is the money necessary to start and open a business. It is also known as *seed capital*. To investors and lenders, the financial plans section is an important part of the business plan and helps them decide if they should invest.

The financial plans section of the business plan contains pro forma financial statements. **Pro forma financial statements** are financial statements based on estimates of future business performance, sales, and expenses. Three financial statements should be included:

- A **pro forma balance sheet** reports the assets, liabilities, and net worth of the business.

- A **pro forma income statement** projects revenues and expenses to show whether or not a business is profitable.

- A **pro forma cash flow statement** reports anticipated sources and uses of cash from operations, investing, and financing activities.

Pro forma financial statements for a proposed business should contain cost estimates for a one year period of time, as well as a summary of start-up costs.

Goodluz/Shutterstock.com

An entrepreneur may need to obtain capital through financing when starting a new business.

Appendix

The appendix may include company brochures, copies of published articles about the business, and photographs of products. It may include résumés of those in leadership roles as well as permits and contracts. The material contained in the appendix may not be relevant to all readers and can be referenced as needed.

Business Financing

Capital structure refers to the way a business is financed. Capital structure determines who has control of the business and decision-making power. If the capital structure consists primarily of loans, the owner retains more control and usually has more decision-making authority. If the capital structure includes money from investors, the business is owned by investors who each have a vote in the management of the company.

The ability to secure funding is an important factor in the success of any business venture. Businesses in different stages of development have specific financial requirements. Most businesses get needed capital through financing at some point. Financing may be necessary when a business is formed. The business may also need financing when capital is needed to take advantage of opportunities for growth. Two common sources of financing are debt financing and equity financing.

Debt Financing

Debt financing is borrowing money that must be repaid for use in the business. Loans typically come from family, friends, or financial institutions. Banks and other financial institutions require entrepreneurs to have enough collateral to back up the loan. **Collateral** is an asset pledged that will be claimed by the lender if the loan is not repaid. **Assets** are the property or items of value a business owns. The entrepreneur must have property that is worth as much as the amount loaned. Property may include real estate, vehicles, investment accounts, and other items of value.

If a business does not qualify for a traditional loan, banks and other lending institutions offer a number of small business loan programs guaranteed by the US Small Business Administration. The SBA itself does not make loans, but it does guarantee loans made to small businesses by private banks and other financial institutions.

Equity Financing

Equity financing is capital brought into the business in exchange for a percent of ownership in the business. When equity financing is used, the investors gain a percentage of ownership in the business. Two sources of equity financing are venture capitalists and angel investors.

Venture capital is money invested in a business by investors who form partnerships or groups to pool investments. In return for their investment, venture capitalists receive a portion of the business equity. They typically provide a significant portion of financing for a business and usually get a voice in major company decisions.

Angel investors are private investors who fund start-up businesses. The investors expect returns on their investments. However, they generally do not participate in the management of the businesses.

Section 6.2 Review

 Check Your Understanding

1. Why is it important for entrepreneurs to know their market?
2. What is an advantage of buying a franchise?
3. Identify the sections of a business plan.
4. List the three financial statements that should be included in the financial plans section of a business plan.
5. Name two sources of equity financing.

 Build Your Vocabulary

As you progress through this course, develop a personal glossary of key terms. This will help you build your vocabulary and prepare you for a career. Write a definition for each of the following terms and add it to your personal glossary.

market research
market
cash flow
business plan
mission statement
start-up capital
pro forma financial statements
pro forma balance sheet
pro forma income statement
pro forma cash flow statement
capital structure
debt financing
collateral
assets
equity financing
venture capital
angel investors

Review and Assessment

Chapter Summary

Section 6.1 Entrepreneurs in a Free Enterprise System

- Entrepreneurship is willingly risking resources to start and run a business in pursuit of profit. Successful entrepreneurs share many common skills and traits such as basic skills, problem-solving skills, decision-making skills, and planning skills.

- The US Small Business Administration sets business size standards based on industry groups. These standards help to identify and categorize small businesses.

- Most new entrepreneurs are not experienced in all aspects of running a business. There are many sources of assistance available to entrepreneurs, including mentors, the US Small Business Administration, and the Service Corps of Retired Executives.

- Many new businesses fail. The reasons can range from poor management skills to a bad business location.

Section 6.2 Business Planning

- Most successful entrepreneurs start with a great idea. Then, they do extensive research to test the idea and get to know their market before starting a business. An entrepreneur may choose to start a new business, purchase an existing business, or buy a franchise business.

- A business plan is a written statement of goals and objectives for a business with a strategy to achieve them. The business plan includes several sections, including summaries of the company, its organization and management structures, product lines, marketing and sales plan, and financial projections.

- Most businesses get needed capital through financing at some point. The ability to secure funding is an important factor in the success of any business venture. Two common sources of financing are debt financing and equity financing.

Online Activities

Complete the following activities to help you learn, practice, and expand your knowledge and skills.

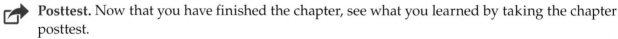

Posttest. Now that you have finished the chapter, see what you learned by taking the chapter posttest.

Vocabulary. Practice vocabulary for this chapter using the e-flash cards, matching activity, and vocabulary game until you are able to recognize their meanings.

Review Your Knowledge

1. Describe common skills and traits of successful entrepreneurs.
2. List five SBA requirements of a small business not related to business size.
3. Explain how the Service Corps of Retired Executives can be a resource in operating a small business.
4. How can inefficient inventory control contribute to the failure of a business?
5. Discuss the process of developing an idea for a business.
6. Identify the start-up strategies discussed and explain the benefits of each.
7. Describe the components of a business plan.
8. What kind of information do pro forma financial statements provide?
9. How does capital structure affect a business?
10. What are two common sources of financing for businesses?

Apply Your Knowledge

1. Could you be an entrepreneur? Why do you think that starting your own business would be a good venture for you? Incorporate the five Ps of entrepreneurship in your explanation.
2. Make a list of all of the skills you think you would need as an entrepreneur. For each skill, rate yourself on a scale of one to five, with five being very skilled. For each skill that you rate at less than three, brainstorm ideas of how you can improve through training or by partnering with someone else.
3. Write several paragraphs about a business idea you would consider developing. What is the best way to start your business—start a new business, purchase an existing business, or buy a franchise? Explain your choice.
4. Franchises are a popular way for entrepreneurs to start a business. Make a list of some of the popular franchises that are in your neighborhood. Would any of these businesses be of interest to you? Why or why not?
5. If you decided to start a business, which forms of financing would you prefer to use? Explain why. List the pros and cons of each form of financing, as they apply to your business.

Communication Skills

College and Career Readiness

Reading. Read a magazine, newspaper, or online article about business. Analyze the article and distinguish the facts from the author's point of view on the subject. Write a report in which you draw conclusions about the importance of business. Use visual support, such as graphs, to share specific evidence from the article with your class to support your understanding of the topic.

Speaking. Select three of your classmates to participate in a cooperative learning situation such as a discussion panel. Acting as the team leader, name each person to a specific task such as timekeeper, recorder, etc. Discuss the topic of buying a franchise or a business that is available for sale. What are the advantages and disadvantages of not starting a business from scratch? Keep the panel on task and promote democratic discussion.

Writing. Making small improvements in the way things are done can bring about great benefits. Choose three entrepreneurs and explain how they used innovation to start a new business or improve an existing product.

Internet Research

Locating Information. Using a web browser, navigate to the website for the Service Corps of Retired Executives (www.score.org). There are many topics that are covered on this site pertaining to business. Make a list of five topics that are of interest to you. Read one article that is most intriguing. Synthesize the information and write several paragraphs to summarize your thoughts. Create a visual, such as a graphic organizer, to accompany your written summary.

Teamwork

Working with a teammate, make a list of personality traits that you have observed in a famous entrepreneur such as Mark Zuckerberg or Bill Gates. Then, have your teammate make a list of your personality traits. Discuss your opinions with each other. Do you think either of you would make good entrepreneurs? Why or why not?

Portfolio Development

College and Career Readiness

Digital File Formats. A portfolio will contain documents you created electronically as well as documents that you have in hard copy format that will be scanned. It will be necessary to decide file formats to use for both types of documents. Before you begin, consider the technology that you might use for creating and scanning documents. You will need access to desktop publishing software, scanners, cameras, and other digital equipment or software.

For documents that you create, consider using the default format to save the files. For example, you could save letters and essays created in Microsoft Word in DOCX format. You could save worksheets created in Microsoft Excel in XLSX format. If your presentation will include graphics or video, confirm the file formats that are necessary for each item. Use the appropriate formats as you create the documents.

Hard copy items will need to be converted to digital format. Portable document format, or PDF, is a good choice for scanned items, such as awards and certificates.

Another option is to save all documents as PDF files. Keep in mind that the person reviewing your digital portfolio will need programs that open these formats to view your files. Having all of the files in the same format can make viewing them easier for others who need to review your portfolio.

1. Establish the types of technology that are available for you to create a digital portfolio. Will you have access to cameras or studios? Do you have the level of skill needed to create videos?

2. Decide the type of presentation you will use. Research what will be needed to create the final portfolio product.

CTSOs

Promoting the Benefits of Entrepreneurship. Some Career and Technical Student Organizations (CTSOs) have competitive events where the chapter spends the school year developing and carrying out a marketing campaign that promotes entrepreneurship. This event provides chapters with the opportunity to demonstrate knowledge of entrepreneurial concepts while making presentations to audiences in their community. For the competition, the chapter is required to prepare a report detailing a marketing campaign and present the report to a panel of judges. To prepare for an entrepreneurship marketing campaign chapter project, complete the following activities.

1. Read the guidelines provided by your organization. Make certain that you ask any questions about points you do not understand. It is important to follow each specific item that is outlined in the competition rules.

2. Contact the association immediately at the end of the state conference to prepare for next year's event.

3. As a team, select a theme for the marketing campaign to promote entrepreneurship.

4. Decide which roles are needed for the team. There may be one person who is the captain, one person who is the secretary, and any other roles that will be necessary to create the plan. Ask your instructor for guidance in assigning roles to team members.

5. Identify your target audience, which may include business, school, and community groups.

6. Brainstorm with members of your chapter. Make a list of the benefits and opportunities available through entrepreneurship that can be communicated beyond your chapter membership.

7. This project will probably span the school year. During regular chapter meetings, create a draft of the report based on direction from the CTSO. Write and refine drafts until the final report is finished.

Business Organization, Management, and Leadership

Exploring Careers

Store Manager

A store manager is responsible for the daily operations of a retail store. Depending on the size of the store and how it is structured, the tasks for this position vary. Tasks may include human resource duties, managing finances, and customer relations. Ultimately, the store manager must increase sales and maintain a positive work environment.

Typical job titles for this position also include *operations manager*, *general manager*, and *director of operations*. Examples of tasks store managers perform include:

- establish goals and objectives for the store

- make personnel decisions, such as hiring, training, promoting, and terminating

- assign duties and supervise workers

- prepare budgets and other financial reports

- resolve problems with customers, employees, and store operation

A high school diploma and several years of retail experience are usually required for store manager positions. Many large companies may also require some college courses or a bachelor degree. Store managers must have strong leadership, communication, and problem-solving skills. A basic understanding of finance is also needed.

In This Chapter

Reading Prep

College and Career Readiness

Before reading this chapter, flip through the pages and make notes of the major headings. Analyze the structure of the relationships of the headings with the concepts in the chapter.

Check Your Business IQ

Before you begin the chapter, see what you already know about business by taking the chapter pretest. The pretest is available at www.g-wlearning.com.

Business Organization and Management

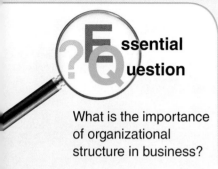

Objectives

After completing this section, you will be able to:

- **Explain** effective business organization.
- **Describe** the purpose of organizational structure.
- **Discuss** the roles of different levels of management.
- **Identify** the five functions of management.

Key Terms

goal
policy
procedure
chain of command
organization chart
organizational chart
management

top management
middle management
first-line management
plan
strategic plans
tactical plans

operational plans
contingency plans
organizing
staffing
leading
controlling

Effective Business Organization

Effective businesses establish guidelines for their organization. These guidelines are sometimes called *principles*. In general, these principles include vision, structure of the business, chain of command, roles of employees, and accountability, as shown in Figure 7-1. Many of these principles are determined in the business plan when an organization begins. However, business principles are evolving guidelines that develop and expand as a business matures.

A business that has an effective organization has a clear picture of its direction. This begins with writing a mission statement as part of the business plan when the company is formed. A *mission statement* is a sentence describing the purpose of the company and why it exists.

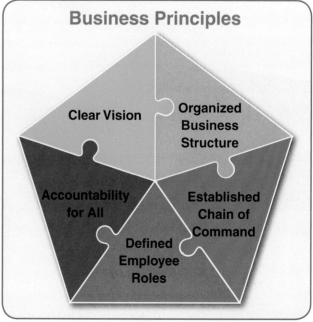

Goodheart-Willcox Publisher

Figure 7-1 The principles of an organization are determined in the business plan and expand as the business matures.

Establishing goals helps a business define success.

It should remind employees and customers what the company aims to accomplish. A mission statement defines what a company does, how it is done, and for whom it is done. It should be considered for all decisions and actions of the business and should not be forgotten.

A company's mission statement may be very simple or be descriptive. For example, the mission statement of Nike, Inc. is very brief, while The Walt Disney Company's is more detailed.

- Nike, Inc.: "To bring inspiration and innovation to every athlete in the world."

- The Walt Disney Company: "The mission of The Walt Disney Company is to be one of the world's leading producers and providers of entertainment and information, using its portfolio of brands to differentiate its content, services, and consumer products. The company's primary financial goals are to maximize earnings and cash flow, and to allocate capital toward growth initiatives that will drive long-term shareholder value."

No matter the length, the mission statement creates the foundation for everything that the company strives to accomplish.

Once the mission is established, the company can create goals. A **goal** is something to be achieved in a specified period of time. A *short-term goal* is one that is accomplished in a short period of time, generally less than a year. A *long-term goal* is one that takes more than a year to reach.

A company may create goals that relate to many different areas of the business, including finances, sales, production volume, staffing, and service efficiency. Goals help define what the company must do to be successful. Meeting goals allows businesses to continue operating and to grow.

Establishing policies and procedures is necessary for any organization. A **policy** outlines how company decisions are made. Company policies may include hiring practices, schedule of management meetings, and employee code of conduct. A **procedure** describes how tasks should be completed. Some common business procedures include operation guides for using equipment, workflow charts, and employee training manuals. Policies and procedures help create consistency in business operations.

Ethics

Bribes

A *bribe* is an exchange of something of value for special consideration when doing business. Bribes are unethical, as well as illegal in the United States. In some foreign countries, however, bribes are considered legal. Regardless of where a company is located, US companies should not accept a bribe from an individual, government, or business entity.

Organizational Structure

The *organizational structure* of a business identifies the hierarchy of the employees within the business. The structure determines employee roles, authority, and how communication flows within an organization. Structure helps identify responsibility and determine who should carry out a job. It also defines who has the authority to make decisions and how jobs should be completed.

©iStock.com/GlobalStock

Every company has an established chain of command.

Organizational structure supports the four functions of business, which are production, finance, marketing, and management. It helps the efficiency of the flow of communication between the functions. Structure also helps a business create customer satisfaction and business success.

Career paths for employees can be a positive benefit of organizational structure. Employees may aspire to move to higher levels of authority through work experience and education. This creates a corporate culture that encourages success and promotion within a business.

Organizations decide the most appropriate structure for their business based on the type of business and its mission. Two common organizational structures are *functional* and *matrix*.

- *Functional organizational structure.* Workers that share the same skill set and expertise are brought together for a specific function. The group has specific goals and responsibilities it must meet. This structure is common in organizations that have marketing, sales, and production teams.

- *Matrix organizational structure.* Workers with various skills and experience are brought together to solve a specific problem or task. This type of group includes many different perspectives and may be called a *task force* or *cross-functional team*. Task forces are effective for solving issues that affect an entire organization.

Within the organizational structure, there must be clear understanding of who is leading the team, roles of team members, and how decisions are made. The **chain of command** is the authority structure in a company from the highest to the lowest levels. It is also called the *line of authority*. Chain of command helps define decision-making responsibilities for team members.

Most companies create an organizational chart so that employees understand the lines of authority. An **organization chart** is a diagram that shows the structure of an organization. This chart identifies departments, shows how business operations tasks are divided, and indicates levels of authority, as shown in Figure 7-2.

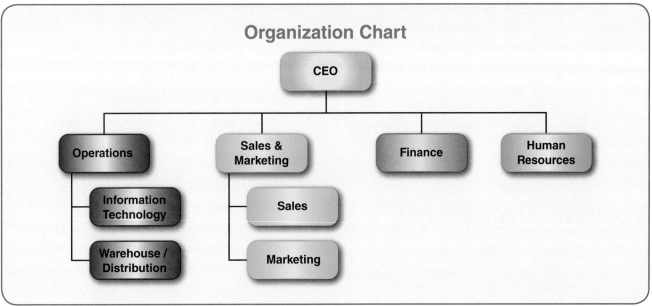

Figure 7-2 An *organization chart* illustrates the structure of an organization.

An **organizational chart** is a diagram showing how each employee position within the company interacts with others in the chain of command. As shown in Figure 7-3, an organizational chart identifies who answers to whom.

The division of authority within a company may also vary depending on the type of business, size of the company, or the wishes of owners or top management. The authority within a business may be organized in different ways:

- *Centralized organization.* All of the authority within a business rests with top management.

- *Decentralized organization.* Authority within a business is given to various managers that run their own departments.

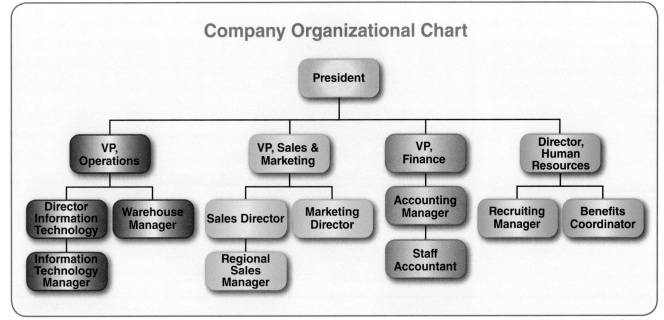

Figure 7-3 An *organizational chart* identifies each employee position and shows the channels of authority.

- *Departmentalization.* Responsibilities and authority are divided among certain areas or departments within the business.

There is no right or wrong way to distribute power within an organization. The structure depends on various factors within the business, such as experience of the employees, size of the company, or location of the management team.

Levels of Management

Management is the process of controlling and making decisions about a business. Most organizations have levels of management. The number of management levels often depends on the size of the company. As shown in Figure 7-4, there are three general levels of management: top management, middle management, and first-line management.

Top management consists of a company's board of directors, president, and other high-ranking managers. Typical duties of managers at this level include:

- develop major goals and broad policies
- prepare strategic plans
- appoint lower-level managers
- control and coordinate the activities of all departments and divisions
- provide guidance, motivation, and direction
- take responsibility for the performance of the business

Middle management consists of a company's division managers and department heads. Typical duties of middle management include:

- carry out plans developed by top management
- manage activities of assigned divisions or departments
- participate in hiring and training of lower management
- explain policies of top management to lower management

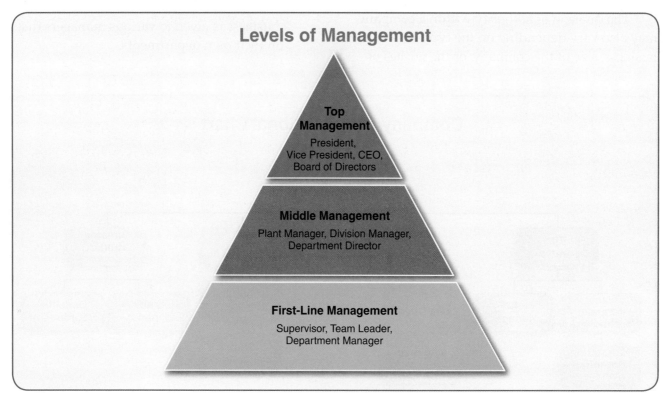

Goodheart-Willcox Publisher

Figure 7-4 Although the number of management levels may vary from company to company, there are three general levels of management.

- evaluate the performance of lower managers
- inspire and lead first-line managers

First-line management coordinates and supervises the activities and duties of employees. This level of management includes supervisors, foreman, and shift managers. Typical duties of managers at this level include:

- assign jobs and tasks to employees
- supervise and guide daily activities and duties of employees
- maintain the quality of work
- communicate employee problems, suggestions, and recommendations to higher management
- help solve employee grievances
- train employees
- motivate employees

Management Functions

Business management includes all the activities necessary to operate a business. Successful businesses typically have good managers who diligently perform their duties. They also carefully consider the potential results of their decisions. As shown in Figure 7-5, the *five functions of management* are planning, organizing, staffing, leading, and controlling.

Planning

Planning is the process of setting goals and deciding how to accomplish them. Management is responsible for the success of an organization. Planning is important to the success of any type of organization. Managers set goals and then develop strategies to achieve them. The steps involved in reaching goals are then developed into a *plan*. A **plan** is an outline of the actions needed to accomplish a goal. There are four basic types of management plans: strategic, tactical, operational, and contingency.

- **Strategic plans** are created for the long-term goals of an organization. They involve major goals of an organization or business.
- **Tactical plans** are developed for the short-term goals of a company.

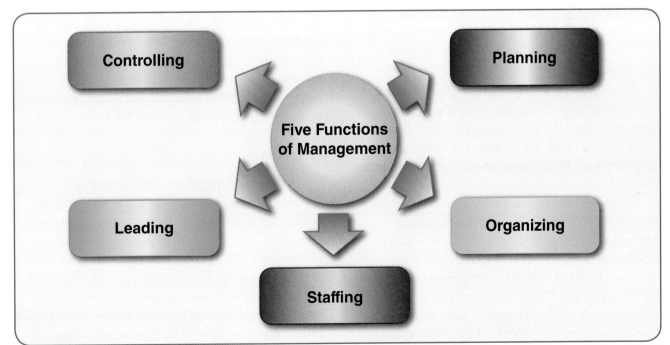

Goodheart-Willcox Publisher

Figure 7-5 Business management activities address the five functions of management.

Monkey Business Images/Shutterstock.com

First-line managers supervise the employees of a business.

- **Operational plans** are designed to reach the day-to-day goals of a business. They give precise details on how to accomplish specific goals.

- **Contingency plans** are backup plans. They outline alternative actions that can be taken if the organization's other plans are unsuccessful.

A well-written management plan is detailed. Goals, strategies for meeting those goals, and dates by which the goals must be met should all be stated. Roles are assigned to individual employees and their tasks identified to help meet the goals.

Management plans are written by various managers within an organization. In many organizations, management plans are written by each department or team. They are then combined into an overall management plan for the company. There may be short-term management plans that span a year. Long-term management plans may also be written that span multiple years.

Organizing

When goals are set and planning is complete, managers can begin the task of organizing. **Organizing** is the coordination of activities and resources needed to reach its goals. Managers perform the organizing function by making schedules, assigning tasks, and coordinating efforts among different departments. A clear organization chart is important so that everyone understands his or her role in the business.

Staffing

Staffing is the process of recruiting, hiring, training, evaluating, and compensating employees. Effective staffing is essential to the success of a business. Most people believe that a business is only as good as the people who run it. *Human resources* are the employees who work for a company. The *human resource (HR) department* helps an organization hire employees and handles other employee-related functions, including compensation, benefit programs, code of conduct, and following employment regulations.

Monkey Business Images/Shutterstock.com

Planning is one of the five functions of management.

Leading

To accomplish goals, managers need to lead their staff members. **Leading** is the process of influencing others to work toward common goals. Managers motivate employees and should lead by example.

Controlling

Controlling is a continuous process of evaluating the progress in reaching goals and making corrections to plans, when necessary. Part of this process is comparing expected outcomes to actual outcomes. Managers must also evaluate the goals that have not been met and create a plan to achieve them.

Section 7.1   Review

 Check Your Understanding

1. Identify the general principles that should be determined for an organization.
2. What is organizational structure?
3. List three ways in which authority within a business may be organized.
4. What are the typical duties of first-line managers?
5. What are the five functions of management?

 Build Your Vocabulary

As you progress through this course, develop a personal glossary of key terms. This will help you build your vocabulary and prepare you for a career. Write a definition for each of the following terms and add it to your personal glossary.

goal	plan
policy	strategic plans
procedure	tactical plans
chain of command	operational plans
organization chart	contingency plans
organizational chart	organizing
management	staffing
top management	leading
middle management	controlling
first-line management	

Leading Employees

How do effective leaders benefit a business?

Objectives

After completing this section, you will be able to:

- **Identify** the qualities and skills of effective leadership.
- **Explain** the importance of teams in business.

Key Terms

SMART goal
time management
personal information
   management (PIM)
interpersonal skills
critical-thinking skills

verbal skills
nonverbal skills
listening skills
collaboration skills
compromise
team

teamwork
conflict management
conflict-resolution
   skills
negotiation
mediation

Leadership

Leadership is the ability to influence others to reach a goal. Organizations count on their managers to show leadership qualities. Certain traits such as honesty, competence, self-confidence, communication skills, problem-solving skills, and dependability, are examples of leadership characteristics. The ability to set goals, follow through on tasks, and be forward-thinking are also important leadership abilities.

Management Theory

Every manager is different in his or her approach and style of leadership. To identify how managers view employees, American social psychologist Douglas McGregor developed two theories: Theory X and Theory Y. *Theory X* managers believe that employees dislike work and need close supervision in order to get their work done. As a result, Theory X managers maintain total control over the duties of employees. *Theory Y* managers believe that

employees like to work and do not need close supervision to get their work done. According to this theory, workers have potential and are capable of self-direction.

The research of William Ouchi added another component to the Theory Y approach. In the 1980s, the productivity rate in the United States was much lower than that of Japan. Ouchi compared the Japanese management style, which leans towards Theory Y, with the American management style. He developed *Theory Z*, which is a middle-ground approach that includes characteristics of both the Japanese and American styles of management. According to Ouchi, Theory Z managers believe that workers are motivated to work and can make sound decisions. This type of manager is more likely to act as coach, and let workers make most of the decisions. A summary of Theories X, Y, and Z is shown in Figure 7-6.

Leadership Styles

Being in a leadership position is not always an easy job. Some team members can be easy to work

Green Business — Carbon Footprints

A *carbon footprint* is a measurement of how much the everyday behaviors of an individual, company, or community impact the environment. This includes the amount of carbon dioxide put into the air from the consumption of energy and fuel used in homes, for travel, and business operations.

Online carbon footprint calculators can be used to determine areas and practices that need to change. Companies can reduce their carbon footprints by recycling, reducing waste, and using responsible energy options. For example, video communication can be used to hold business meetings across the country. This reduces the fossil fuel emissions for travel by automobile, train, or airplane.

Management Theories

Type	Characteristics
Theory X	• Leadership is autocratic • Close supervision needed at all times • Workers dislike work • Workers prefer direction and seek security
Theory Y	• Leadership is democratic • Leader maintains control, but seeks input from workers • Workers like work and are innately motivated
Theory Z	• Leadership is laissez-faire • Leader is trusting of workers to make sound decisions • Leader provides direction, but allows workers to make decisions • Workers are naturally self-motivated

Goodheart-Willcox Publisher

Figure 7-6 The approach managers take with their employees can typically be categorized as Theory X, Theory Y, or Theory Z.

with, but others can be difficult. Leaders have to be able to work with different personalities and motivate the group to accomplish its goals. Each leader has his or her style or may develop a style based on the personalities of the team.

Three common leadership styles are autocratic, democratic, and laissez-faire, as seen in Figure 7-7. The *autocratic* leadership style describes a leader who maintains all of the power within a team. Autocratic managers tend to have Theory X attitudes. Other leaders use the democratic style. *Democratic* leadership style is one in which the leader shares decision-making with the group. Democratic leaders encourage other team members to participate in the leadership process. These managers tend to have Theory Y attitudes. The last common type of leadership is laissez-faire.

Common Leadership Styles

Leadership Style	Characteristics of Leader
Autocratic	• Maintains power within the group • Keeps close control over members of the team • Makes all decisions for the group
Democratic	• Open and collegial • Invites participation from team • Shares decision-making with team members
Laissez-faire	• Hands-off approach • Provides little or no direction • Makes decisions only if requested by the team

Goodheart-Willcox Publisher

Figure 7-7 Every leader has an individual style for managing his or her team.

Laissez-faire leadership style is a hands-off approach to leadership. This style leaves the decision-making to the group to decide and manage. Laissez-faire managers tend to have Theory Z attitudes.

Individuals in leadership positions need to possess certain skills. A *skill* is something a person does well. There are many skills that effective leaders possess. Examples of needed skills are goal setting, time management, and interpersonal skills.

Goal Setting Skills

Successful leaders set clear goals. Goals focus on an end-result, not the ways to get to the result. For goals to be as effective as possible, they should be written as SMART goals. A **SMART goal** is one that is specific, measurable, attainable, realistic, and timely as shown in Figure 7-8.

- *Specific.* A goal should be specific and straightforward.

- *Measurable.* Progress toward a goal should be measurable.

- *Attainable.* A goal needs to be attainable.

- *Realistic.* A goal must be realistic.

- *Timely.* A goal should have a starting point and an ending point.

By setting SMART goals, managers can organize the activities of their team to accomplish the plans for the business. It also helps them manage their own activities.

Goodheart-Willcox Publisher

Figure 7-8 Setting SMART goals helps leaders clearly communicate objectives and plans.

Time Management Skills

Time management is the practice of organizing time and work tasks to increase personal efficiency. Goals are created to help optimize results. Goals are then broken down into manageable tasks. To manage several tasks at the same time, the tasks must be prioritized to determine which should be completed before others. Schedules must be followed and time must be used wisely.

Personal information management (PIM) is a system used to acquire, organize, maintain, retrieve, and use information. An example of a PIM system is Microsoft Outlook. This PIM allows users to keep schedules, record contact information, and complete other activities that help organize personal information. A schedule should identify all required tasks for completing a project or meeting goals.

Interpersonal Skills

Interpersonal skills are skills that help people communicate and work well with each other. There are many interpersonal skills that can help a leader be effective. The following are some examples of important interpersonal skills:

- **Critical-thinking skills** are the ability to analyze a situation, interpret information, and make reasonable decisions. Applying critical-thinking skills as a leader can help the team problem-solve in a more efficient manner.

- **Verbal skills** are the ability to communicate effectively using spoken or written words. Good verbal skills help leaders describe plans and procedures when writing or speaking to a team member.

- **Nonverbal skills** are the ability to communicate effectively using body language, eye contact, personal space, behavior, and attitude.

- **Listening skills** are the ability to hear what a person says and understand what is being said. Listening is required for all team members.

- **Collaboration skills** are skills that enable individuals to work with others to achieve a common goal. This includes sharing ideas and compromising for the greater good of the team. To **compromise** is to give up an individual idea, or part of an idea, so that the group can come to a solution.

You Do the Math   Measurement Reasoning

Three-dimensional figures have length, width, and height. In other words, they have volume. Volume is an important measurement for shipping boxes, bottles, containers, and many other items. The area of a rectangular figure is calculated by multiplying its length, height, and width. The volume of a cylinder is calculated by multiplying the area of its base by its height.

Solve the following problems.

1. The inside of a shipping container is 6 feet by 18 feet by 8 feet. If a single box is 1 foot by 2 feet by 6 inches, how many boxes can fit inside the shipping container?

2. If a rectangular box has a volume of 161.28 cubic inches and its base measures 3.5 inches by 7.2 inches, what is the height of the box?

3. If a cylindrical fuel tank is 4.25 feet tall and holds 122.6 cubic feet of fuel, what is the area of the base of the cylinder?

Teams

Many businesses develop and organize teams within the company. A **team** is a group of two or more people working together to achieve a common goal. The terms *team* and *group* are used interchangeably. Small businesses may only have one or two teams. Larger organizations may have multiple teams. Teams can be physically located under one roof or they may have members located around the country or around the world. By creating teams, individual roles in the organization can become better defined.

Effective teams accomplish the defined goals. This happens only when the members are cooperative and focus on their assigned tasks. Effective team members contribute ideas and personal effort. **Teamwork** is the cooperative efforts by individual team members to achieve a goal. Team members are expected to be cooperative and work well with others. This includes individuals on their team and outside of the team. Successful team members are productive and work to achieve team goals. Individuals who contribute in a positive way demonstrate leadership qualities, even if they are not in a leadership role.

Team Meetings

The primary way teams come together is through meetings. Meetings are an organized format for the discussion of topics and issues. Informal meetings allow members to come together for a short period of time and casually discuss a topic. However, formal meetings should be run in a more structured and organized manner. Formal meetings usually require an agenda and someone to lead the meeting. *Parliamentary procedure* is a process for holding meetings so that they are orderly and democratic.

John Kropewnicki/Shutterstock.com

Successful teams work together to achieve goals, both in business and personal life.

Team meetings may include a virtual component for members not at the same location. For example, a real-time video conferencing tool, such as Skype, may be used to include off-site team members. To use this type of virtual connection, a dependable Internet connection is necessary. Specific software may also be required and should be installed before the meeting begins. A high-quality microphone is required so that conversations are clear. It is also important to position the camera so the people who are speaking can be clearly seen.

If a meeting is conducted using a web seminar website, such as GoTo Meeting, guidelines similar to video conferencing apply. There is no camera, but an Internet connection and quality microphone are important. The software required should be downloaded before the conference begins.

Team Conflict

Group dynamics are the interacting forces within a group. The forces include attitudes, behaviors, and personalities of all team members. The dynamics of a team are made up of the attitudes of the members and how they interact with each other. Group dynamics can positively or negatively influence how a team reaches its goals. It can also influence a company's profitability.

Every group faces conflict at some point when working as a team. However, conflict is not always negative. Creative solutions can result when team members disagree on a subject. Conflict is negative when it becomes destructive and stops the team from reaching its goals.

When conflict arises, some team members show passive behavior. *Passive behavior* is accepting the things that happen without trying to change them. Other members show aggressive behavior. *Aggressive behavior* is expressing individual needs with little interest in or respect to the needs of others. Still other team members are assertive. *Assertive behavior* is expressing personal opinions while showing respect for others.

The team leader and members are responsible for being proactive and monitoring conflicts that can potentially hold back the success of the team. **Conflict management** is the process of

recognizing and resolving team disputes in a balanced and effective way. Negative conflicts can throw a group off course. When it is clear that a dispute is escalating, members should actively work to resolve the negative conflict.

Conflict-resolution skills are the skills required to resolve a situation that could lead to hostile behavior, such as shouting or fighting. A model for solving conflict can help a team develop conflict-resolution skills. See Figure 7-9 for an example of a conflict-resolution model.

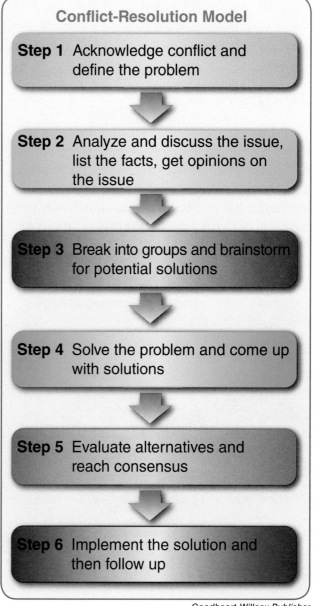

Conflict-Resolution Model

Step 1 Acknowledge conflict and define the problem

Step 2 Analyze and discuss the issue, list the facts, get opinions on the issue

Step 3 Break into groups and brainstorm for potential solutions

Step 4 Solve the problem and come up with solutions

Step 5 Evaluate alternatives and reach consensus

Step 6 Implement the solution and then follow up

Goodheart-Willcox Publisher

Figure 7-9 Establishing a conflict-resolution model can help a team resolve issues more efficiently.

1. Acknowledge the conflict and define the problem. Team members should apply positive verbal and nonverbal skills during this stage.

2. Analyze and discuss the issue. List the facts and get opinions on the issue. Analyze all the information related to the issue.

3. Break into small groups or brainstorm as a large group for potential solutions. *Brainstorming* is discussion within a group where individuals generate as many ideas as possible within a set amount of time. There are no bad ideas when brainstorming and all are listed for consideration. Critical-thinking skills are required.

4. Solve the problem and come up with a solution. After all alternatives have been discussed, the team should be able to recommend one or more solutions. Collaboration is needed from individual team members.

5. Evaluate recommended solutions and reach consensus. Individual team members agree on the decision that the team makes.

6. Implement the solution and follow up. Apply the solution or process and review the outcome.

Formal methods, such as negotiation or mediation, may be required to settle some group conflicts. **Negotiation** is when individuals involved in a conflict come together to discuss a compromise. With negotiation, both parties enter the process willing to give up something in order to solve the conflict. For extreme conflicts, mediation may be needed. **Mediation** is a process in which a neutral person meets with each side of a negotiation in an attempt to find a solution that both sides will accept. A *mediator* is a neutral person who helps the parties involved in the conflict to resolve their dispute and reach an agreement.

If handled well, conflicts can strengthen the bonds between group members. Learning from disputes can help the group avoid them as they move forward toward their goals. However, if a conflict is not caught early enough or is not fully resolved, it can result in a reoccurring problem within the group.

Section 7.2 Review

 Check Your Understanding

1. List three common leadership styles.
2. Explain how an effective goal should be written.
3. What is *parliamentary procedure*?
4. List three behaviors that can arise from team conflict.
5. What is *brainstorming*?

 Build Your Vocabulary

As you progress through this course, develop a personal glossary of key terms. This will help you build your vocabulary and prepare you for a career. Write a definition for each of the following terms and add it to your personal glossary.

SMART goal	collaboration skills
time management	compromise
personal information management (PIM)	team
	teamwork
interpersonal skills	conflict management
critical-thinking skills	conflict-resolution skills
verbal skills	negotiation
nonverbal skills	mediation
listening skills	

Review and Assessment

Chapter Summary

Section 7.1 Business Organization and Management

- Successful businesses establish principles, or guidelines, including vision, structure of the business, chain of command, roles of employees, and accountability. A business that has an effective organization has a clear picture of its direction.

- The organizational structure of a business identifies the hierarchy of the employees within the business. The structure determines employee roles, authority, and how communication flows within an organization.

- Most organizations have levels of management. There are three general levels of management: top management, middle management, and first-line management.

- Business management includes all the activities necessary to operate a business. Good business managers master the *five functions of management*: planning, organizing, staffing, leading, and controlling.

Section 7.2 Leading Employees

- Leadership is the process of influencing others or making things better. Certain traits such as honesty, competence, self-confidence, communication skills, problem-solving skills, and dependability, are examples of leadership characteristics. The ability to set goals, follow through on tasks, and be forward-thinking are also important leadership abilities.

- Effective teams accomplish the defined goals. Team members are expected to be cooperative and work well with others. Successful team members are productive and work to achieve team goals.

Online Activities

Complete the following activities to help you learn, practice, and expand your knowledge and skills.

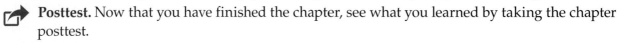

- **Posttest.** Now that you have finished the chapter, see what you learned by taking the chapter posttest.

- **Vocabulary.** Practice vocabulary for this chapter using the e-flash cards, matching activity, and vocabulary game until you are able to recognize their meanings.

Review Your Knowledge

1. Explain effective business organization.
2. Describe the purpose of organizational structure.
3. What is the difference between a functional organizational structure and a matrix organizational structure?
4. Explain the role of each level of management.
5. Explain each of the five functions of management.
6. Describe each of the three common leadership styles.
7. Give an example of a personal information management (PIM) system and describe how it aids in time management.
8. Identify important interpersonal skills that can help a leader be effective.
9. Explain the importance of teams in a business.
10. Define the role of a mediator.

Apply Your Knowledge

1. Organizational structure supports the four functions of business, which are production, finance, marketing, and management. Choose a business with which you are familiar. Write an essay examining the organizational structure of the business. Describe how the organizational structure of the business supports the four functions of business.
2. Recall your personal experiences participating in a group or organization. Identify one person from your experiences who was a memorable leader. Explain what made this person a good or bad leader. What was his or her leadership style? Describe the person's leadership traits and skills.
3. Discuss time-management strategies with a group of friends or family members. Make a list of the techniques and tips that come up in the discussion. Describe how some of the time-management techniques can be used in a workplace. How can these skills be used to help an employee prioritize tasks and maintain schedules to meet goals? What can you do to improve your time-management skills?
4. Collaboration skills are skills that enable individuals to work with others to achieve a common goal. This includes sharing ideas and compromising for the greater good of the team. Acquiring collaboration skills will help you be a successful team member. Explain how you could demonstrate collaboration skills through teamwork.
5. The conflict-solving model is a helpful guideline when confronting a conflict within a team. Using the conflict-resolution model in Figure 7-9, write a script that could be used to bring consensus on a team challenge of selecting a new meeting time.

Communication Skills

College and Career Readiness

Writing. Writing style is the way in which a writer uses language to convey an idea. Select a page or pages of notes you have taken during a class. Evaluate your writing style and the relevance, quality, and depth of the information. Once you have done so, write a one-page paper that synthesizes your notes into complete sentences and thoughts. Organize your material so that it is logical to the reader. Describe what you have learned to the class.

Reading. After you have read this chapter, determine the central ideas and review the conclusions made by the author. Take notes to identify the chapter's purpose and intended audience. Demonstrate your understanding of the information by retelling or summarizing what you read.

Speaking. To become career ready, it is necessary to utilize critical-thinking skills in order to solve problems. Give an example of a problem that you needed to solve that was important to your success at work or school. How did you apply critical-thinking skills to arrive at a solution? Explain your solution to the class.

Internet Research

Personal Information Management (PIM). Using the Internet, research personal information management (PIM) systems. Identify a system that would work for you. Make a list of the ways that a PIM system can help you prioritize tasks and follow schedules. In addition, write a paragraph that describes how it could help you create and tend to goal-relevant activities and use your time wisely to maximize efficiency and results. When you finish with your evaluation, reflect on how you can apply a PIM system to your daily schedule to help you complete projects and other tasks.

Management Theories. Use the Internet to research Theories X, Y, and Z. Compare and contrast the details of each management theory. Which management style do you prefer? Explain your preference.

Teamwork

Working with your team, create a one-page handout that describes each management style. Under each style, make a list of bullets that describe the characteristics of that type of manager. Photocopy enough of these handouts to distribute to your classmates. Ask if they will participate in an anonymous survey and select the characteristics that apply to him or her. Tally the responses. Which type of manager style was most dominant in your class?

Portfolio Development

College and Career Readiness

File Structure. After you have chosen a file format for your documents, determine a strategy for storing and organizing the materials. The file structure for storing digital documents is similar to storing hard copy documents.

First, you need a place to store each item. Ask your instructor where to save your documents. This could be on the school's network or a flash drive of your own. Next, decide how to organize related files into categories. For example, certificates might be the name of a folder with a subfolder Community Service Certificates and a subfolder that says School Certificates. Appropriate certificates would be saved in each subfolder. The names for folders and files should be descriptive but not too long.

1. Decide on the file structure for your documents.

2. Create folders and subfolders on the school's network drive or flash drive on which you will save your files.

CTSOs

Parliamentary Procedures. The *Parliamentary Procedure* competitive event is an event in which the participants must demonstrate understanding of parliamentary procedures such as *Roberts Rules of Order*. This is a team event in which the group will demonstrate how to conduct an effective meeting. An objective test may be administered to each person on the team that will be evaluated and included in the overall team score.

To prepare for the parliamentary procedure, complete the following activities.

1. Read the guidelines provided by your organization.

2. Study parliamentary procedure principles by reviewing *Roberts Rules of Order*.

3. Practice proper procedures for conducting a meeting. Assign each team member a role for the presentation.

4. Visit the organization's website and look for the evaluation criteria or rubric for the event. This will help you determine what the judges will be looking for in your presentation.

Production of Goods

Exploring Careers

Forecasting Manager

Business Management & Administration

One of the many tasks that contributes to a company's success is managing product flow. Forecasting managers are responsible for managing the flow of products through a company. They coordinate the activities of the production, purchasing, warehousing, and distribution departments to ensure that products flow smoothly and efficiently from production or purchase through final sales and distribution.

Typical job titles for this position also include *supply chain manager*, *supply chain director*, and *supply chain coordinator*. Examples of tasks forecasting managers perform include:

- analyze inventories to determine how quickly products are turned over

- create demand and supply plans to ensure the timely availability of materials or products

- monitor industry forecasts to identify trends that may affect the supply chain

- coordinate purchasing, manufacturing, sales, marketing, warehousing, and distribution of products

Most forecasting manager jobs require a bachelor or master degree in accounting or a related field, as well as several years of experience. Forecasting managers need to have knowledge of production processes and should understand transportation and distribution. In addition, they must have excellent math skills and an ability to analyze data.

Reading Prep

As you read this chapter, take time to answer the Section Review questions. Were you able to answer the questions without referring to the chapter content?

College and Career Readiness

Check Your Business IQ

Before you begin the chapter, see what you already know about business by taking the chapter pretest. The pretest is available at www.g-wlearning.com.

Producing Product

How does managing the production process impact business operations?

Objectives

After completing this section, you will be able to:

- **Explain** production as a function of business.
- **Identify** the steps in the production process.
- **Discuss** ways a business can improve productivity.

Key Terms

operations management
conversion
materials processing
division of labor
mass production
custom manufacturing
production process
sourcing
supplier

inventory
inventory management
direct materials inventory
work in process inventory
finished goods inventory
perpetual inventory-control system

electronic data interchange (EDI)
periodic inventory-control system
inventory shrinkage
just-in-time (JIT) inventory-control system
quality control

Producing Goods

Businesses generate revenue by creating and selling products that meet the needs and wants of customers. In order for a business to stay in operation, quality goods and services must be produced. **Operations management** is the area of management responsible for the activities necessary to produce goods and services.

Production is one of the four functions of business, as shown in Figure 8-1. It includes any activity related to making a product. *Producers* are businesses that create goods and services. *Manufacturers* are a type of producer that uses raw materials from other producers and converts them into finished goods. **Conversion** is the process of changing and improving resources to create goods or services.

Goodheart-Willcox Publisher

Figure 8-1 Production is one of the four functions of business.

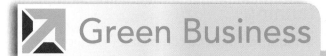

Green Business · Lighting

Every building must be well-lit in order for employees and customers to work and visit safely. Simple behavioral changes can make an impact in the cost of lighting. Businesses should take advantage of the natural daylight that comes in through windows and skylights. Employees should be reminded to turn off lights when not in use, such as when leaving a room. Lights can be dimmed when strong lighting is not needed, such as around computer monitors.

Lighting can also be modified to be more environmentally friendly. Removing or disconnecting unnecessary light fixtures saves energy because the fixtures draw power whether they are on or off. Replacing or retrofitting light fixtures that are not energy efficient also helps the environment. Installing automatic sensors to turn lights on and off when people enter and exit rooms saves energy. Outdoor lighting can be fitted with timers or photocells to turn on only when it gets dark outside.

One of the purposes of manufacturing is to create form utility. *Utility* describes the characteristics of a product that satisfy wants and needs. It also means usefulness. There are five types of utility as shown in Figure 8-2. Form utility is important in production because it includes the conversion of raw materials into finished product.

To create form utility, multiple manufacturing processes are used. Raw materials must be processed so they can be used to create product. Natural resources, such as timber, water, and minerals, are raw materials that can be processed to be used in a product. **Materials processing** is changing the form of raw materials for another use.

Productivity is a measure of a worker's production in a specific amount of time, such as an hour. The more products a worker produces each hour, the higher his or her productivity. Manufacturing is organized by processes, which are further broken into smaller tasks. Employees are assigned specific tasks to complete on a repetitive basis. **Division of labor** is the specialization of individuals who perform specific tasks. Workers who perform repetitive tasks generally become fast and accurate because of the repetition. Mastering the smaller tasks in a process, also called *specialization*, enables workers to become efficient at specific roles. This, in turn, leads to increased productivity and profits for a company.

Mass production is one method of manufacturing. **Mass production** is the manufacturing of goods in large quantities using standard techniques. In this type of manufacturing, workers repeat the same task using the same techniques. Factory automation is typically introduced with mass production.

Examples of Utility	
Form	Smartphones are designed to be ergonomic, compatible with popular apps, and have high enough capacity to be useful.
Place	Shopping malls make a wide variety of stores available in one convenient location.
Time	Banks offer early morning teller services to meet the needs of businesses that are open in the morning, as well.
Information	Many electronics manufacturers have digital versions of installation and troubleshooting guides that are accessible any time on their websites.
Possession	Convenience stores and drive-thru pharmacies offer quick product access.

Goodheart-Willcox Publisher

Figure 8-2 A major task of business is to provide utility.

When automation is introduced, productivity of employees tends to increase.

Custom manufacturing is converting resources to a product that fits the specifications of a particular customer. The manufacturer creates a product to fit the requirements of the buyer. For example, a home builder can be considered a custom manufacturer because raw materials are converted to create a building that fits a customer's unique needs or requirements.

Production Process

The **production process** is all the activities required to create a product. Production is focused on converting raw materials and labor into goods and services in an efficient manner. Typical activities in an effective production process include:

- planning
- purchasing
- scheduling
- inventory control
- quality control

©iStock.com/microolga

Automation is common in mass production operations, such as vehicle manufacturing.

Planning

Planning must be completed to determine resources needed for production. It requires executing the short-term and long-term goals stated in the business plan. In some situations, building a new facility may be necessary. Other situations may require the purchase of specialized equipment. Hiring new employees with specific skill sets or retraining current employees may also be required.

Part of the planning process includes finding the raw materials to create the product. This is known as sourcing. **Sourcing** is finding suppliers of materials needed for the production of a product. A **supplier**, or *vendor*, is a business that sells materials, supplies, or services to an organization that creates product.

Purchasing

After the needed materials, equipment, and supplies have been identified for production, the items must be purchased. Business *purchasing* is the activity of acquiring materials, supplies, or services necessary to create a product.

Purchasing agents are the individuals responsible for sourcing and buying the materials needed for producing goods and services. Their goal is to purchase materials and supplies that meet the company's specification for quality and timely delivery at the best possible price.

Scheduling

Scheduling personnel, material deliveries, shipments, and many other items are crucial to business operation. For example, manufacturing businesses must have enough raw materials and labor on hand to meet the product demand of customers. This requires scheduling deliveries of material from vendors to make products. Employees must also be scheduled to produce the amount of work required. Careful scheduling is necessary for a business to operate efficiently and prevent material shortages or production problems. Purchasing too much material or scheduling too many labor hours can cause unnecessary cost increases.

Inventory Control

Inventory is the assortment or selection of items that a business has on hand at a particular point in time. **Inventory management** is the area of management involved in ordering goods, receiving them into stock on arrival, and paying vendors. It also includes managing the costs of shipping, storage, and other activities to keep inventory-related costs low. Carrying too much inventory can reduce the profitability of a company. Carrying too little inventory can result in lost sales. As shown in Figure 8-3, manufacturers usually have three types of inventory: direct materials, work in process, and finished goods inventory.

Direct materials inventory is the raw materials needed to produce a finished product. The purchasing agent must plan to have enough materials for production to operate efficiently. These materials must be stored, which takes up valuable space. Also, materials cost money. Businesses do not want cash to be tied up in materials that will not be used in a reasonable amount of time. However, it is also important not to underestimate the materials needed.

Work in process inventory consists of products that are partially completed. This type of inventory is also referred to as *unfinished product*. This type of inventory consists of products going through the production process. Once these items are finished, they become part of the finished goods inventory.

Finished goods inventory is the assortment or selection of finished items for sale that a business has in stock. As with materials, it is important to have the appropriate amount of products that will sell in a projected amount of time. Too much inventory costs space and ties up money that can be used elsewhere in the business. Inventory can also become obsolete. Too little inventory could result in lost sales.

Baloncici/Shutterstock.com

Materials and equipment must be purchased and ready for production.

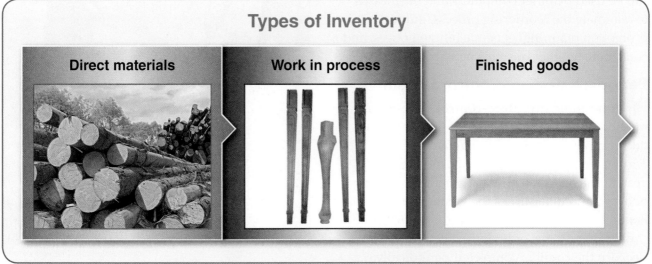

smereka/Shutterstock.com; Margrit Hirsch/Shutterstock.com; Horiyan/Shutterstock.com; Goodheart-Willcox Publisher

Figure 8-3 Manufacturers typically have three types of inventory for material and product.

Businesses need to have enough on hand to meet customer demand and not lose sales.

In order to track inventory, a system of inventory control must be used. There are three primary types of inventory-control systems: perpetual, periodic, and just-in-time.

Perpetual Inventory-Control System

A **perpetual inventory-control system** is a method of counting inventory that shows the quantity on hand at all times. The system tracks each good as it is received, placed in stock, and then sold. There are two types of perpetual inventory systems: manual and computerized.

In a *manual perpetual inventory-control system*, the inventory is calculated by physically counting and recording individual items. A person records each item that comes into inventory and each item that leaves inventory as a sale or vendor return. This information is recorded on a spreadsheet or entered into a software program. The important part to note is that the inventory is recorded manually, *not* electronically.

Most businesses use a *computerized inventory-control system* for more precise control and information access. Inventory software programs track incoming inventory and outgoing product. Computerized inventory-control systems are an important part of electronic data interchange. **Electronic data interchange (EDI)** is the standard transfer of electronic data for business transactions between organizations. It can be used by other computers and businesses to automate the reordering process, guide promotion planning, generate billing notices, and contribute to other business activities.

Periodic Inventory-Control System

A **periodic inventory-control system** is a method of measuring inventory that involves taking a physical count of merchandise at regular periods, such as weekly, monthly, or yearly. The business physically counts all items on hand and determines the value of those items. Taking a physical inventory is often time consuming, so it is only done at certain intervals. Because the count is completed periodically, the actual inventory data is not accurate on a day-to-day basis.

No matter the inventory system used, businesses should complete a physical inventory annually. The results are compared to the perpetual inventory records. The two inventories are rarely exactly the same. **Inventory shrinkage** is the difference between the perpetual inventory and the physical inventory. There are three main causes for inventory shrinkage.

- Data input errors can occur during receiving, stocking, or selling.
- Product damage or breakage may occur when products are moved from the receiving dock to storage to store shelves.
- Theft can occur by employees or outsiders, such as customers or burglars. Theft is the largest cause of inventory shrinkage.

The physical inventory usually shows fewer items in stock than the perpetual inventory indicates.

bikeriderlondon/Shutterstock.com

It is important to take a physical count of inventory at regular intervals.

You Do the Math   Connections

Mathematics is an educational discipline that is extensively used in many other educational disciplines. Science, business, economics, accounting, engineering, and many other areas feature mathematics as an integral part of the discipline. For example, accountants must use math to calculate balance sheets, engineers must use math to calculate loads, and economists must use math to calculate the gross domestic product.

Solve the following problems.

1. An accountant must calculate the final account balance from a starting balance of $1,593.86 after these transactions:
   - Income: $28.65, $18.04, $21.73, and $67.81
   - Expenses: $45.39, $106.45, $289.63, and $547.20.

What is the final account balance?

2. A scientist must convert the volume of liquid in a flask from cubic centimeters to cubic inches. One cubic centimeter is equal to 0.06 cubic inches. The flask contains 28.6 cubic centimeters of liquid. How many cubic inches of liquid are in the flask?

3. A restaurateur must calculate how much flour to order for the week. Each day the restaurant sells 356 biscuits and 48 loaves of bread. One biscuit requires 0.045 pounds of flour and each loaf of bread requires 0.62 pounds of flour. How many pounds of flour must be ordered for the week (seven days)?

Just-in-Time (JIT) Inventory-Control System

The **just-in-time (JIT) inventory-control system** is a method of managing inventory that keeps a minimal amount of raw materials on hand to meet production needs. In a JIT system, raw materials are received *just in time* for the production needs of the day. Manufacturing companies that use JIT systems aim to operate with a minimum of raw materials in storage. They make sure raw materials are delivered right before they are needed in the assembly process.

Advantages of JIT include increased efficiency, reduced waste, reduced storage space, and cash available for other purposes. A disadvantage of JIT occurs when production or delivery is not timed correctly. If raw materials are late in arriving, a manufacturing production line may be forced to shut down until materials arrive. JIT systems are difficult to completely implement because many suppliers cannot meet demands for frequent deliveries.

Quality Control

Checking products in inventory for damages, shortages, and overages is considered quality control. **Quality control** is the activity of checking products as they are produced or received to ensure the quality meets expectations. Quality control may involve visual inspection or physical testing.

Manufacturers have quality control procedures established to ensure the quality of the raw materials they use, as well as the products they produce. Quality control takes place throughout the production process—from the time raw materials are received to when the finished goods are completed.

Improving Productivity

Most successful businesses study their processes on a regular basis with the goal of becoming more efficient. *Continuous process improvement (CPI)* is an ongoing effort to improve production processes to meet goals and increase profit.

Technology continues to evolve in ways that make manufacturing more efficient. Industry-specific engineering processes enable businesses to focus on their continuous process improvement strategies. Robotics, computer-aided design software, and many other technologies improve productivity.

There are formal programs that offer training to improve processes in a business. Individuals can enroll in courses at an educational institution to learn how to become more efficient in manufacturing processes. Six Sigma® is an example of formal education in the area of process improvement. Individuals who successfully complete the courses are awarded Six Sigma certification.

RGtimeline/Shutterstock.com

Quality control takes place throughout the production process and includes both testing and inspection.

Section 8.1 Review

 Check Your Understanding

1. What is the difference between producers and manufacturers?
2. Explain the meaning of scheduling in the production process.
3. List three types of inventory usually used by manufacturers.
4. List three primary types of inventory-control systems.
5. Explain *continuous process improvement (CPI)*.

 Build Your Vocabulary

As you progress through this course, develop a personal glossary of key terms. This will help you build your vocabulary and prepare you for a career. Write a definition for each of the following terms and add it to your personal glossary.

operations management
conversion
materials processing
division of labor
mass production
custom manufacturing
production process
sourcing
supplier
inventory
inventory management
direct materials inventory

work in process inventory
finished goods inventory
perpetual inventory-
    control system
electronic data
    interchange (EDI)
periodic inventory-control
    system
inventory shrinkage
just-in-time (JIT)
    inventory-control system
quality control

Product Development

Objectives

After studying this section, you will be able to:

- **Explain** the product planning process.
- **Identify** the steps in new product development.

Key Terms

product planning
new product
product life cycle
repositioning

repackaging
image
brand
prototype

trial run
test marketing
commercialization
trade show

Product Planning

Before production begins for a product, planning must take place. **Product planning** is the process of deciding which products will be most strategic for the organization to produce. These decisions are made based on market research and development, as well as past company experience. Most companies cannot continue to be profitable by producing the same product year after year. Consumers may stop buying products because they have lost their appeal, become dated, are no longer useful, or a multitude of other reasons. In order to stay competitive, companies must have a strategy to keep their offerings current and appealing to the consumer. As part of product planning strategy, a business can create new product, reposition current product, or repackage current product to appeal to consumers.

A **new product** is a product that is different in some way from existing products. The **product life cycle** is the series of stages a product goes through from its beginning to the end. When a product comes to the end of its life cycle, a new product usually replaces it. A new invention can generate an idea for a complementary product. A product may also be changed or adapted to suit new customer needs. A small change made to an existing product is often considered to be a new product. Many new products are simple variations of existing products. Other products are developed to meet a specific need.

Repositioning is marketing an existing product in a new way to create a new opinion or view of the product in the minds of customers to increase sales. Many existing products can be valuable for uses other than the original purpose. For example, baking soda is a common product that was originally intended as an ingredient for baking. However, it has been proven to serve other purposes, such as a cleaning agent or antacid.

Repackaging is using new packaging for an existing product. The product stays the same, but the packaging is different. Repackaging may make the product more efficient or attractive to the consumer. For example, Materne North America began packaging applesauce in plastic pouches, rather than in cups. The Go Go squeeZ

A company makes product planning decisions based on market research and development, as well as previous business experience.

product does not require a spoon to eat, which provides convenience and efficiency to Materne's customers.

Developing New Product

A great deal of thought and planning goes into identifying the best products to meet the needs of customers in a target market. A new product must meet customer needs and wants, as well as fulfill company profit goals. Marketing research is necessary to make sure a new product is the best business decision. The development process for a new product generally follows seven steps, as shown in Figure 8-4.

Idea Generation

New product ideas may be prompted by alterations to an existing product, new technology, a design that meets a new need, or many other factors. Product ideas are usually the result of trend research, observation, customer feedback, and brainstorming.

Ethics

Code of Ethics

Most companies establish a set of ethics that employees must follow. The code of ethics outlines acceptable behavior when interacting with coworkers, suppliers, and customers. Some businesses even post their code of ethics on their websites. As an employee, it is important to know the code of ethics so you can make correct decisions on behalf of the company.

Tracking trends in consumer and market activity can lead to product ideas. Many large companies hire marketing research firms that specialize in trend research and new product ideas. An organization may choose to conduct its own research to identify the latest trends within an industry.

Observation is a common source of product ideas. Observing people and activities within the environment may reveal unfilled customer needs.

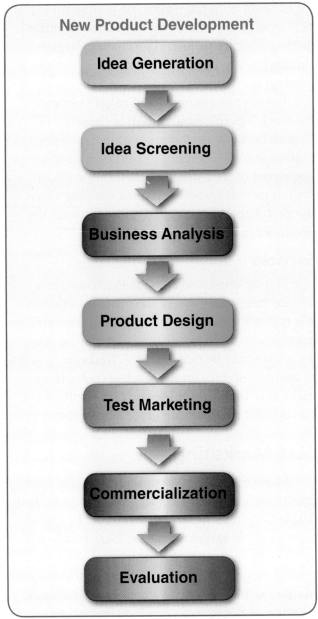

New Product Development

Idea Generation

⬇

Idea Screening

⬇

Business Analysis

⬇

Product Design

⬇

Test Marketing

⬇

Commercialization

⬇

Evaluation

Goodheart-Willcox Publisher

Figure 8-4 There are seven common steps in the process of developing a new product.

Finding a way to fulfill a need often leads to a new product idea.

Customer feedback is critical for companies that follow the marketing concept. Customer ideas, unmet needs, complaints, and suggestions for product improvement provide important information for product development. Apple Inc. is an example of a company that produces innovative products by listening to customers and keeping up with trends in technology.

Brainstorming is a creative process that focuses on new product ideas. Bringing people together with different experiences, skills, and backgrounds can generate ideas and new ways of looking at a product.

Idea Screening

Once a list of new product ideas is generated, it must be reviewed. The goal of idea screening is to choose the best and, hopefully, most profitable ideas. During idea screening, new product ideas are evaluated from the customer viewpoint. This is the time to conduct research to learn if the new product will meet customer needs and wants. Idea screening needs to take place before the company makes a large investment to develop and produce a new product.

Business Analysis

Developing a new product can be expensive. A company must determine if it has the necessary people, expertise, equipment, and money to develop and promote the new product. Performing a business analysis for a new product idea involves researching the projected costs and forecasting product sales.

Analysis includes calculating the cost of modifying a current product or bringing a new product to market. Market research should help determine if the product can generate enough sales to cover costs and make the desired profit.

Canadapanda/Shutterstock.com

The Apple Watch was introduced in 2015 in response to trends in the personal use of technology in the market.

A detailed financial analysis of a new product plan is a necessary step.

Any new product must be consistent with the company image, mission, and goals. An **image** is the idea that people have about someone or something. Many companies choose to develop a specific image through their brand. A **brand** is a name, term, or design that sets a product or business apart from its competition. For example, Hallmark is a brand of greeting cards and other stationery items. The products the company offers under the Hallmark brand are known to be different from competitor products.

Product Design

After proving the new product meets a need in the market and can meet company profit goals, the next step is product design. This is the stage where the product idea becomes a reality. During the design phase, the details of producing the product are planned. Determining the product brand is also part of the design phase. The name, image, logo, slogan, and packaging of the good or service are usually created at this stage.

Goods

A **prototype** is a working model of a new product for testing purposes. Product designers

Monkey Business Images/Shutterstock.com
Product designers plan the details of a product.

experiment with the prototype to determine if it performs as expected. Any problems identified are fixed before full-scale production begins. Prototypes are particularly important for any product with moving parts.

Prototypes are also used to get customer feedback before a final design is chosen. Researchers ask customers within the target market to test different prototypes. The responses from testers help determine which prototype and features will sell the best. Once the prototype is researched and approved, the product can go into full production.

Services

Testing must also be done to make sure a service meets the goals of the business. However, it is typically not possible to create a prototype for a service. To test new services that may be offered, a trial run may be performed. A **trial run** consists of testing a service on a few select customers to make sure that everything runs smoothly. A trial run is like a dress rehearsal for a business.

Test Marketing

Many companies do not immediately start producing a new product in large numbers. **Test marketing** introduces a new product to a small portion of the target market to learn how it will sell. Customer feedback within the test market helps a business solve unexpected problems. Test marketing may also help a company determine whether or not to mass produce the product.

Commercialization

Commercialization is the introduction stage of a new product. Businesses select a release date to make the new product available for sale. Activities to promote the new product are critical at this point and often start before the product is even released. The production and shipping functions must have the product ready for shipment to be available to customers by the release date.

New products are often introduced at industry trade shows to monitor customer response. A **trade show** is a large gathering of businesses for the purpose of displaying goods and services for sale.

Companies often introduce new products at industry trade shows.

There are trade shows for every industry and type of B2C product, as well as many B2B products.

Evaluation

All businesses need to know if their products are successful. The success of any product is evaluated on an ongoing basis. It is important to frequently evaluate both new and existing products. The success of a product is based on how well it meets the sales and other goals set for the product during the business analysis. The evaluation process typically involves reviewing financial records and marketing data.

Section 8.2 Review

Check Your Understanding

1. What three options does a business have when choosing a product planning strategy?
2. When developing new products, what four activities usually result in product ideas?
3. What activities are part of the product design process?
4. How does a company use feedback from test marketing?
5. How is the success of a product evaluated?

Build Your Vocabulary

As you progress through this course, develop a personal glossary of key terms. This will help you build your vocabulary and prepare you for a career. Write a definition for each of the following terms and add it to your personal glossary.

product planning	brand
new product	prototype
product life cycle	trial run
repositioning	test marketing
repackaging	commercialization
image	trade show

Chapter Summary

Section 8.1 Producing Product

- Businesses create product to meet the needs and wants of customers while generating revenue. *Production* is one of the four functions of business and includes any activity related to making a product. *Producers* are businesses that create goods and services. *Manufacturers* are a type of producer that use raw materials from other producers and convert them into finished goods.

- The production process is all the activities required to create a product. Typical activities in an effective production process include planning, purchasing, scheduling, inventory control, and quality control.

Section 8.2 Product Development

- Before production begins on a product, planning must take place. Product planning is the process of deciding which products will be produced. Businesses use market research and past experience to help make these decisions. They can create new product, reposition current product, or repackage current product.

- A new product must meet customer needs and wants, as well as fulfill company profit goals. The development process for a new product generally follows seven steps: idea generation, idea screening, business analysis, product design, test marketing, commercialization, and evaluation.

Online Activities

Complete the following activities to help you learn, practice, and expand your knowledge and skills.

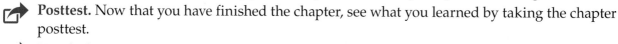

Posttest. Now that you have finished the chapter, see what you learned by taking the chapter posttest.

Vocabulary. Practice vocabulary for this chapter using the e-flash cards, matching activity, and vocabulary game until you are able to recognize their meanings.

Review Your Knowledge

1. Explain the concept of productivity.
2. Identify the typical activities in the production process.
3. List and describe three primary types of inventory-control systems.

4. What are some advantages of just-in-time inventory-control?

5. Explain the importance of quality control.

6. Explain the product planning process.

7. Identify the steps in new product development.

8. How can observation lead to a new product idea?

9. Explain the business analysis step of the new product development process.

10. How is product testing performed for services?

Apply Your Knowledge

1. Manufacturers choose locations for their operations based on their business strategy. Some prefer to be located close to the raw materials that they use to create product. Others prefer to be located close to the customers who will buy the product. Create a table with two columns. In the first column, enter a heading for *Close to raw materials*. In the second column, enter a heading that says *Close to customers*. In each column, list reasons that support the column heading. In your opinion, which strategy is better?

2. When individuals become specialists in their work, efficiency increases. Select a manufacturer with which you are familiar, such as one that produces clothing or automobiles. How do you think specialization impacts the profitability of that company? Discuss the impact of specialization on productivity for that business.

3. Division of labor can have a positive effect on productivity in business and personal situations. You can apply division of labor to daily tasks to accomplish both small and large jobs. Assume you are hired to cut grass for three neighbors and must complete all the yards in one afternoon. This job includes cutting the grass, trimming, and raking. How could you employ friends and use division of labor to tackle the job?

4. New product ideas can come from simple strategies, such as repackaging a current product to make it more appealing to the customer or easier to use. Sometimes repackaging can make a product more affordable to purchase. Select a product that you currently purchase. Identify ways this product could be repackaged to become more appealing to the consumer.

5. Many products are created with a specific purpose in mind, but other uses develop. This chapter offered baking soda as an example of a product with creative uses in addition to baking. Is there a product you use regularly that has more uses than the manufacturer specified? Name a product and describe its alternative uses.

Communication Skills

College and Career Readiness

Speaking. The way you communicate with others will have a significant impact on the success of the relationships you build with them. Create a speech that explains the production process for producing goods. Deliver the speech to your class. How did the style, words, phrases, and tone you used influence the way the audience responded to the speech?

Reading. As you read this chapter, you learned that materials are processed to create finished goods. Choose an everyday object and make a list of the steps that are necessary to manufacture the finished product.

Listening. Engage in a conversation with someone you have not spoken with before. Ask the person his or her definition of a *quality product*. Actively listen to what that person shares. Build on his or her ideas by sharing your own. Try this again with other people you have not spoken to before. How clearly were the different people able to articulate themselves? How is having a conversation with someone you do not normally speak with different from a conversation with a familiar friend or family member?

Internet Research

Manufacturing Time Line. Manufacturing in the United States has a long history. Using the Internet, research manufacturing in the United States from 1900 to the present day. Create a poster that shows a time line of important people, events, and processes in the history and development of manufacturing. Use photos or other visuals to highlight important data.

Teamwork

Developing a new product can be a fun and exciting activity. Working with your team, think of products that are missing from today's market. Using the Idea Generation step of the new product development process, create a list of five products that you think consumers would be eager to purchase. Next to each new product, write a short description of the product and how it meets customer needs or wants. Share your ideas with your class.

Portfolio Development

College and Career Readiness

Diversity Skills. As part of an interview with an organization, you may be asked about your travels or experiences with people from other cultures. Many different organizations serve people from a variety of geographic locations and cultures. Some have offices or other types of facilities in more than one region or country. You may need to interact with people from diverse cultures or travel to facilities in different countries. Speaking more than one language and having traveled, studied, or worked in other countries can be valuable assets. You may be able to help an organization understand the needs and wants of diverse people. You may also be better able to communicate and get along with others.

1. Identify travel and other educational experiences that helped you learn about another culture, such as foreign languages studied or trips taken.

2. Create a Microsoft Word document that describes the experience. Use the heading "Diversity Experience" and your name. Explain how the information you learned might help you better understand classmates, customers, or coworkers from this culture. Save the document in an appropriate folder.

3. Place a printed copy in the container for future reference.

4. Update your checklist to reflect the file format and location of the document.

CTSOs

Financial Math. Financial math is a competitive event you might enter with your career and technical student organization (CTSO). The financial math event may include an objective test that includes financial literacy topics. If you decide to participate in this event, review basic banking and business finance concepts to prepare for the test.

To prepare for a financial math event, complete the following activities.

1. Read the guidelines provided by your organization. Make certain that you ask any questions about items you do not understand. It is important you follow each specific item that is outlined in the competition rules.

2. Download any posted practice tests.

3. Time yourself taking the tests with the aid of a non-graphing calculator. Check the answers and correct any mistakes you may have made.

4. Review the You Do the Math features in this text for additional practice.

5. Visit the organization's website often to make sure information regarding the event has not changed.

Human Resources Management

In This Chapter

Exploring Careers

Compensation and Benefits Specialist

Full-time employees typically receive a salary and benefits in return for their work. A compensation and benefits specialist designs benefits plans for businesses. These benefits can include employer-paid health and life insurance, a retirement plan, and additional bonuses. These specialists also ensure the company's compensation and benefits plans fit within federal regulations.

Typical job titles for this position also include *compensation analyst*, *benefits analyst*, and *benefits administrator*. Examples of tasks that a compensation and benefits specialist performs include:

• determine standard salary and benefits for positions

• maintain current knowledge of federal and state laws

• analyze and negotiate the details of complex benefits plans

• develop methods for compensating and evaluating employees

• explain benefits plans and answer related questions

A bachelor degree in human resources or a related field is required. Many positions also require a master degree and professional certification. Decision-making, speaking, listening, and interpersonal skills are essential for this position.

College and Career Readiness

Reading Prep

Before reading this chapter, review the objectives. Based on this information, write down two or three items that you think are important to note while you are reading.

Check Your Business IQ

Before you begin the chapter, see what you already know about business by taking
the chapter pretest. The pretest is available at www.g-wlearning.com.

Human Resources

Why is human resource management important in any type of business?

Objectives

After completing this section, you will be able to:

- **Describe** the role of human resources within an organization.
- **Explain** the role of organized labor in society.

Key Terms

human resources

human resources
  management (HRM)

job analysis

job description

compensation

professional
  development

salary

incentive

bonus

commission

piecework

benefit

labor union

white-collar worker

blue-collar worker

collective
  bargaining

arbitration

strike

Role of Human Resources

No matter the type of work performed, businesses cannot exist without their human resources. **Human resources** are the employees who work for a business. The *human resources (HR) department* is the division that oversees the human resources within an organization. HR is responsible for hiring and supporting capable employees.

Human resources planning is the process of creating a strategy to meet the employment needs of a company. This starts with recruiting talent from the labor force. The labor force consists of all individuals age 16 or over who are working or actively looking for work. The US labor force has experienced significant changes in the last 100 years. Advances in technology have changed the qualities that many businesses look for in employment candidates. Additionally, the labor force has become more diverse as technology provides global access for businesses.

Human resources management (HRM) is the process of hiring, training, and developing employees. As shown in Figure 9-1, HRM consists of five basic functions:

- recruiting and hiring
- training and development
- compensation
- performance evaluation
- legal compliance

Recruiting and Hiring

Recruiting and hiring is one of the most basic HRM functions. Businesses spend a great deal of time, resources, and money in hiring employees. This function involves:

- developing job descriptions
- advertising available jobs
- screening applicants

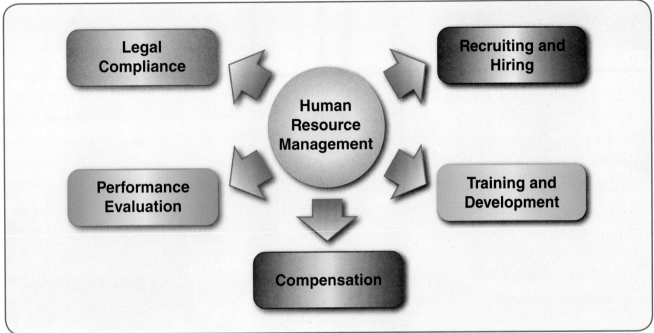

Goodheart-Willcox Publisher

Figure 9-1 The five basic functions of human resources management.

- conducting interviews
- drafting job offers
- negotiating salary and benefits

Before the recruiting process begins, the job that needs to be filled must be identified. Then, the qualities and skills needed for the position are identified. It is HR's responsibility to perform a job analysis. A **job analysis** is a process that identifies the job requirements for a position, employee qualifications, and how success will be evaluated. With this information, HR can develop a job description. A **job description** defines the position and expectations of the job.

Recruiting

Recruiting is the next step in finding potential employees. *Recruiting* is the strategy used to find people who are qualified for the position. Once the job description is developed, a job posting can be written and recruiting can begin. Job postings may be advertised on employment websites, job boards, and social media.

Candidates who respond to job postings are typically asked to complete a job application form. The application asks for information about the applicant and his or her work experience and skills. Personal information on an application includes applicant's name, address, phone number, and social security number. Work-related information includes dates of employment at previous businesses, positions held, degrees earned, and reason for leaving previous jobs. A résumé and other information may also be required.

Ethics

Bias-Free Language

As you go to work or school each day, you may encounter others who categorize people using biased words and comments. Using age, gender, race, disability, or ethnicity as a way to describe others is unethical and sometimes illegal. Use bias-free language in all of your communication, whether verbal or printed, to show respect for those with whom you come in contact.

HR reviews applications received for a position and invites qualified applicants to interview.

Screening Candidates

As the company begins to receive applications for a position, HR begins the screening process. HR reviews applications and selects applicants who appear to have the qualifications needed for the position.

After applications are screened, the top applicants are invited to an interview. The hiring process often involves several interviews. The first interview is called the *screening interview*. This is usually an interview conducted by HR to confirm the candidate's qualifications for the job. If the applicant meets the expectations for the position, he or she will likely be contacted for a second interview.

The second interview is typically conducted by the hiring manager. This interview is a more in-depth examination of the candidate's qualifications and how well he or she fits the position. Other managers, staff, or team members may participate in this interview, as well. In general, the interviewing process can be lengthy and involves interviews with multiple candidates.

Hiring

After the top applicants have been interviewed and their references have been checked, the company makes its hiring decision. HR may make the job offer to the selected applicant by phone, letter, or in person.

An important part of the job offer is the compensation package. **Compensation** is payment to an employee for work performed including wages or salaries, incentives, and benefits. The job offer also involves working through the terms of the offer, such as work location, start date, and job expectations.

Training

After an employee is hired, training must be provided to prepare the new employee for the job. HR is responsible for employee training and development. Training is specific and job-related. It starts with new employee orientation and becomes ongoing.

Orientation

New employees must be trained how to satisfactorily perform their duties. New employee training is often divided into two phases:

- orientation
- job-specific training

The orientation phase is an overview of the company and its operations. New employees learn about the company's philosophy, mission statement, policies, and goals. They are also given information about employee benefits, such as health insurance, retirement plan, vacation time, and other benefits.

Job-specific training usually combines group learning in a classroom setting and hands-on training. Hands-on training often includes job shadowing. The new employee works side-by-side with an experienced employee to learn the specific tasks of the job.

Ongoing Training

Existing employees often need training, as well. This training may involve:

- learning how to use new computer hardware and software
- learning new or updated operating procedures
- sharing some of the best practices within the industry

Professional development is an important part of the training services provided by HR. **Professional development** is education for people who have already completed their formal schooling and training. It gives employees the skills and knowledge needed for personal growth and career development. Some examples of professional development opportunities include:

- seminars on public speaking
- conferences about new industry practices
- presentations on sexual harassment in the workplace

Compensation

Compensation is wages or salaries, incentives, and benefits paid to employees. HR is responsible for making sure the compensation offered by a business is in line with its competition and industry standards. The compensation offered by a company should align with the goals of the business, as well.

Wages or Salaries

A *wage* is payment for work and is usually calculated on an hourly, daily, or weekly basis. Wages are paid on a schedule—often every week or every two weeks. For example, an hourly wage is a fixed amount paid for each hour worked. An employee who is paid $12 an hour and works 40 hours during a week will earn $480 (40 hours × $12) before taxes. *Competitive wages* are wages that are at least equal to those paid by similar businesses in an area. For example, if most department stores in an area pay associates $10 per hour, a retail business needs to pay close to that amount to attract and keep employees.

auremar/Shutterstock.com

New employees may work side-by-side with experienced employees to learn job tasks and procedures.

You Do the Math   Probabilistic Reasoning

The fundamental counting principle is a way to calculate the sample space for multiple independent events. The sample space is the set of all possible outcomes when determining probability. To use the fundamental counting principle, simply multiply the total possible outcomes of all events to find the sample space. For example, if a restaurant offers five entrées with one of seven side dishes and four beverage choices: $5 \times 7 \times 4 = 140$ possible combinations.

Solve the following problems.

1. Chad must price the printing of his business's annual report. The printer he has selected offers four choices of page size, three choices for binding, and nine choices for paper. How many total combinations are possible?

2. Rita must purchase a new work truck for her construction company. The dealership offers three choices for engine size, 14 choices for paint color, two choices for drive train, five choices for wheels and tires, and three choices for seat configuration. How many total combinations are possible for the work truck?

3. A marketing company specializes in promotional items. It offers a package in which a company's logo is printed as stickers in one of three sizes, magnets in one of five shapes, key chains in two styles, and water bottles in one of four styles. How many different packages are available?

A **salary** is fixed payment for work and is expressed as an annual figure. It is paid in periodic equal payments. The payment period is usually weekly, biweekly (every other week), semimonthly (twice a month), or monthly.

The annual salary amount is divided by the number of pay periods in the year. For example, a high school teacher earns $45,000 a year and is paid once per month. The teacher's monthly salary, before taxes, is $3,750 ($45,000 ÷ 12).

Incentives

Incentives are a type of compensation based on performance. It is also known as *pay for performance*. It can be based on the company performance or the company and employee performance. A bonus is an example of an incentive. A **bonus** is money added to an employee's base pay. It is usually a reward for performance or a share of business profits. Bonuses are incentives to encourage workers to perform better. Bonus income is usually based on worker performance, length of time with the company, or company performance.

A **commission** is income paid as a percentage of sales made by a salesperson. This is another example of pay for performance. Some employees may work on a commission-only basis. Others may receive a combination of base pay plus commission. Many people in sales positions are paid a commission. The amount of commission paid is a percentage of the dollar amount in sales the salesperson generated during a specific period.

Sean Locke Photography/Shutterstock.com

Compensation for real estate agents includes commission earned from the properties they sell.

Another form of incentive pay is the piecework system. **Piecework** is a wage based on a rate per unit of work completed. An employee receives a specific dollar amount for each unit of work completed. For example, garment workers may be paid by the number of garments completed. Piecework systems are common in the manufacturing and agriculture industries.

Benefits

A **benefit** is a form of noncash compensation received in addition to a wage or salary. Many employees view benefits to be as important as actual pay. Benefits provided by employers may include:

- medical and dental insurance
- retirement plan
- sick leave
- vacation time
- flexible work schedule
- childcare
- profit-sharing program
- opportunities for continuing education and professional development

By offering competitive benefits, a business can attract qualified candidates and increase employee job satisfaction.

Performance Evaluation

Performance evaluations, or appraisals, are used to assess how well employees are performing their jobs. A *performance appraisal* is an assessment of an employee's job performance and the progress made toward achieving set goals. Most organizations conduct performance evaluations for employees on an annual basis. Pay raises, bonuses, and promotions are often based on performance evaluations. HR is responsible for developing an evaluation system that is reliable and fair.

The performance evaluation is usually conducted by the employee's supervisor. The supervisor discusses the results of the evaluation with the employee. A copy of the evaluation is sent to HR and becomes part of the employee's permanent personnel file.

Andresr/Shutterstock.com

By offering vacation time as a benefit, employees can take paid time off work.

Promoting Employees

Employees who perform their jobs well, are reliable, and are loyal to a company may be promoted. A job *promotion* is the advancement of an employee within a company to a position of greater responsibility. A promotion also typically leads to increased pay and a higher status within the company.

The possibility of a promotion helps motivate employees to do their best work. Promotions also allow employees to apply their skills and talent and take ownership in the business.

Reducing the Labor Force

If an employee's performance does not meet expectations or the employee has violated company policy, it may be necessary to terminate the employee. *Termination* is the process of ending the relationship between an employer and an employee. The employee is relieved of all company-related duties. Terminations should be made carefully and be within the law.

Downsizing is a general reduction in the number of employees within a company. This typically occurs due to a change in economic conditions. An employer reduces its payroll by eliminating employee positions, which also eliminates employees from the business operations. Reducing the size of the workforce reduces employee-related business expenses. However, fewer employees may also reduce the amount of work produced. Companies carefully evaluate the effects of downsizing on operations and production, as well as business finances.

Legal Compliance

An important function of HRM is staying up-to-date with changes in labor laws and regulations. The most common laws affecting HR involve fair and equal treatment and working conditions. Some of these laws are described in Figure 9-2.

Laws Affecting Human Resource Management		
Law	**Year**	**Description**
Fair Labor Standards Act	1938	Supports workers rights by establishing the federal minimum wage, 40-hour workweek, requirements for overtime pay, and restrictions on child labor
Equal Pay Act	1963	Requires that women and men receive equal pay for equal work
Civil Rights Act	1964	Outlaws discrimination and segregation based on race, color, religion, sex, or national origin
Age Discrimination in Employment Act	1967	Protects employees age 40 and older from discrimination on the basis of age in hiring, promotion, discharge, and compensation
Occupational Safety and Health Act	1970	Requires employers to provide a workplace free of hazards that could affect the health and safety of workers
Americans with Disabilities Act	1990	Prohibits discrimination against people with disabilities in employment, transportation, public accommodation, communications, and governmental activities
Family and Medical Leave Act	1993	Requires certain employees be granted temporary, job-protected leave based on qualifying events

Goodheart-Willcox Publisher

Figure 9-2 It is essential for HR to stay up-to-date as labor laws and regulations are updated and new laws are enacted.

Employment laws change often and may be different from state to state. HR is often responsible for training managers to ensure they understand and follow the various laws. HR must stay up-to-date on laws and policies regarding:

- working conditions and hours
- tax allowances
- minimum wage and overtime
- discrimination policies
- family and medical leave

Complying with employment laws is vital. Fines and penalties can be imposed on a business for noncompliance. In extreme cases of noncompliance, employees may file lawsuits or the government may shut down a business.

Organized Labor

In the late nineteenth century and early twentieth century, American business was expanding rapidly. However, many employers of the time did not treat employees well. Low wages, long hours, and poor working conditions were standard. As a result, workers started to band together and form labor unions. A **labor union**, also called *organized labor*, is a group of workers united as a single body to protect and advance the rights and interests of its members.

Business relies on labor for business activities and, ultimately, profit and success. Jobs within businesses are commonly classified as white-collar and blue-collar. A **white-collar worker** is one who primarily uses mental abilities and knowledge acquired in higher education. Most white-collar jobs require a college degree. A **blue-collar worker** is one whose job involves physical labor. Blue-collar workers are typically employed in factories, warehouses, on farms, and on construction sites. Some examples of blue-collar jobs include electricians, welders, building maintenance personnel, and assembly line workers.

The role of organized labor in society impacts both the labor force and business. As early as the 1900s, organized labor brought many changes to the American labor force. These changes included fair wages, standardized hours of work, and a safer working environment. Many labor management laws protect the rights of workers and unions, as shown in Figure 9-3.

Labor Management Legislation		
Law	**Year**	**Description**
Norris-LaGuardia Act	1932	Supported organized labor and the formation of unions
National Labor Relations Act (Wagner Act)	1935	Established protection for the right of workers to organize and bargain collectively with their employers
Fair Labor Standards Act	1938	Established standards for minimum wage, overtime pay, child labor, and recordkeeping
Labor Management Relations Act (Taft-Hartley Act)	1947	Established rules of fair conduct that apply equally to unions and businesses
Labor Management Reporting and Disclosure Act (Landrum-Griffen Act)	1959	Protected union membership rights of workers from unfair practices by unions

Goodheart-Willcox Publisher

Figure 9-3 US labor management laws protect both union and worker rights.

A union helps its members when issues arise between management and employees. **Collective bargaining** is the formal negotiation process between management and unions to resolve issues. If the negotiation process does not solve the issues, they may try mediation. *Mediation* is a process in which a neutral person meets with each side in an attempt to find a solution that both sides will accept. If mediation is unsuccessful, the last resort is arbitration. In **arbitration**, a third party reviews the case made by both sides of a negotiation. The arbitrator makes a decision that is legally binding for both sides.

When union members are unhappy with the bargaining process, they may choose to strike. A **strike** is when union workers temporarily refuse to work. Workers may strike when bargaining reaches a *impasse*, or neither side is willing to continue negotiating. Unions may also use a strike to emphasize the importance of certain bargaining issues, such as wages, job security, or work hours. Workers who participate in a union-approved strike have some protection against being fired.

When an agreement is reached or imposed by an arbitrator, both the union members and the business sign a *labor contract*. This contract describes the details of the agreement. The entire bargaining process is called *labor relations*. HR must understand the labor relations process and comply with union rules and contracts for organized laborers.

In the United States, any group of non-management employees has the right to unionize. The US National Labor Relations Board helps workers organize and works to prevent unfair labor practices. Labor unions are typically specific to particular types of labor. Some examples of labor unions include:

- steel workers union
- auto workers union
- aviation workers union
- teachers union
- truck drivers union
- heavy equipment operators union
- nurses union

Teachers are an example of a group of employees that is unionized.

In the last 30 years, union membership in the United States has steadily declined. According to the US Department of Labor's Bureau of Labor Statistics, the percentage of union wage and salary workers declined from 20.1 percent in 1983 to 11.1 percent in 2014. Unions formed largely in reaction to working conditions in the manufacturing industry. Over time, the nature of work in the United States has changed a great deal. In addition, there are now many laws regulating the fair treatment and safety of workers. The evolution of the labor force and the US economy has made the role of unions less necessary for many workers.

Section 9.1   Review

 Check Your Understanding

1. List the five basic functions of human resources management.

2. What are the two phases of new employee training?

3. What is the purpose of a performance appraisal?

4. Why did labor unions begin to appear in the late nineteenth and early twentieth century?

5. Why do unions and union workers choose to strike?

 Build Your Vocabulary

As you progress through this course, develop a personal glossary of key terms. This will help you build your vocabulary and prepare you for a career. Write a definition for each of the following terms and add it to your personal glossary.

human resources

human resources management (HRM)

job analysis

job description

compensation

professional development

salary

incentive

bonus

commission

piecework

benefit

labor union

white-collar worker

blue-collar worker

collective bargaining

arbitration

strike

Workplace Environment

How do companies develop their corporate culture?

Objectives

After completing this section, you will be able to:

- **Explain** corporate culture in the workplace.
- **Describe** components of an effective workplace environment.

Key Terms

personal leave
family leave
flextime

job sharing
telecommuting
work environment

discrimination
harassment
ergonomics

Corporate Culture

The term *corporate culture* describes how the owners and employees of a company think, feel, and act as a business. It is also known as *organizational culture*. It is a set of shared values and practices held by the members of an organization. Culture is reflected in how an organization operates and how it accomplishes its objectives. Some common ways that the culture of an organization is noticeable include:

- how an organization conducts business
- treatment of employees and customers
- extent of employee freedom in decision making and personal expression
- commitment of employees to the organization

Corporate culture also includes social responsibility. As you recall, *social responsibility* is behaving with sensitivity to social, environmental, and economic issues. Corporate social responsibility includes all the actions taken by a business to promote social good.

Work-Life Balance

Less than a hundred years ago, most workers were expected to work six to seven days a week from sunrise to sunset. This left little time for life outside of work. Working that many hours was harmful to employee health and decreased job productivity.

Many organizations recognize that employees have responsibilities and obligations outside of work. To create a positive organizational culture, employees may be offered various ways to balance job responsibilities with family and life responsibilities. Some of the ways an organization may offer balance include personal leave, family leave, flextime, job sharing, and telecommuting.

Personal leave is a few days each year employees can use for personal reasons. In most organizations, personal time can be taken an hour at a time or days at a time.

Family leave is time off work for certain life events. These may include the birth or adoption of a child, caring for a sick family member, and other family-related emergencies.

Flextime is a policy allowing employees to adjust work schedules to better match personal schedules. For example, it is more practical for some employees to begin work early in the morning and leave early in the afternoon.

Monkey Business Images/Shutterstock.com

Many companies offer employees options to help balance their work and life responsibilities.

Job sharing is an arrangement where two part-time employees handle the responsibilities of a single full-time position. Together, their hours and duties are equal to one full-time employee.

Telecommuting is an arrangement where employees work away from the business site. Most telecommuters work from home and use the Internet, fax, and telephone to communicate with managers, co-workers, and customers.

Employee Motivation

Personal motivation plays a major part in the productivity of employees. In the 1950s, psychologist Abraham Maslow developed *Maslow's Hierarchy of Needs*. According to this theory, needs motivate people to act. However, some needs must be satisfied before others for survival. This means there is a hierarchy, or order of importance, of needs. The *Hierarchy of Needs* relates to general factors of motivation. In the workplace, employees must meet basic needs in order to be motivated in their jobs.

Psychologist Frederick Herzberg developed a list of factors related to workplace motivation. According to Herzberg, factors that motivate employees and lead to job satisfaction are different from those that cause employee dissatisfaction. To explain the difference, he developed the *motivation/hygiene theory*, or the *two-factor theory*.

Motivation factors are factors that lead to employee satisfaction. They are therefore called *satisfiers*. Motivation factors include recognition of work well done, achievement, opportunity for growth and advancement, responsibility, and meaningful and interesting work.

Hygiene factors are factors that, when adequate, do not lead to increased employee satisfaction. As a result, hygiene factors are called *dissatisfiers*. The lack of hygiene factors, however, also leads to employee dissatisfaction. Hygiene factors include physical working conditions, company policies, job benefits, job security, status, and interpersonal relations.

Employers who focus on motivating employees can improve the quality of work produced. Motivated employees generally work harder and are better performers.

Employer/Employee Relationships

An effective relationship between employer and employees is important to the success of any organization. Both the employer and the employees must want to create a profitable business. From the moment a new employee is hired, a relationship is created. The most common characteristics of effective employer/employee relationships are mutual respect, mutual reliance, openness, and gratitude.

- *Mutual respect.* Any relationship is more effective when all parties respect one another. Employers who respect employees consider what is best for both employees and the business. An employee who respects the employer is loyal and works toward the company's objectives.

Pressmaster/Shutterstock.com

Positive relationships among employers and employees contribute to business success.

- *Mutual reliance.* Employers and employees should recognize that they need one another. This understanding creates a more harmonious work environment. Managers who involve employees in planning and decision-making end up with better plans and decisions. Also, employees are more likely to work hard to accomplish those plans and objectives.

- *Openness.* Open lines of communication between the employer and employees promote effective relationships. Employees want clear, concise, and honest feedback. They want to know that their voices will be heard.

- *Gratitude.* A more effective relationship is created when both employers and employees appreciate each other's efforts. Numerous studies have shown that employees value the gratitude shown by their employer.

The type of relationship between employer and employees varies from organization to organization.

Workplace Diversity

Every year thousands of immigrants come to the United States in search of a better life. They come from different countries, have different physical features, speak different languages, and have different religious beliefs. A diverse population means a diverse workplace. *Diversity* is having people from different backgrounds, cultures, or demographics coming together in a group. Workplace diversity is achieved by employing people without regard to gender, age, ethnicity, or racial background. However, diversity for diversity's sake can hurt a business. All employees should be the ones best suited for the job.

Work Environment

How an organization operates is reflected in the work environment. The **work environment** is the location, physical conditions, and emotional atmosphere in which

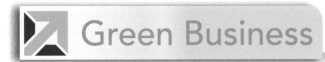

Green Business — Sustainability Training

Green businesses lead by example and educate their employees on sustainable business practices. Through sustainability training, employees learn the importance of *going green* at work and the best practices to reduce waste and lower energy consumption.

Training employees in simple company procedures cannot only help save the environment, but also save the company money. Employees should be instructed to make small changes in their daily habits. Turning lights off when exiting a room and turning computer equipment off over the weekend can make a big difference.

employees work. The conditions of a workplace are affected by the environment created by conduct and company policies, as well as the physical surroundings.

Workplace Conduct

Many US laws describe the proper treatment expected for employees in the workplace. Workplace **discrimination** occurs when an individual is treated unfairly because of his or her race, gender, religion, national origin, disability, or age. It is illegal for an employer to discriminate during any part of the employment process. Examples of discrimination include:

- excluding certain groups of people from employment
- asking a woman during a job interview if she plans to have children
- paying different wages to equally-qualified employees in the same position
- denying the use of company facilities to certain employees
- unfairly evaluating certain employees for promotions

Harassment can create an unhealthy work environment. **Harassment** is uninvited conduct toward a person based on his or her race, color, religion, sex, national origin, age, or disability. According to the US Equal Employment Opportunity Commission (EEOC), harassment becomes unlawful when:

- enduring offensive conduct becomes a condition of employment, *or*
- conduct creates a work environment that a reasonable person would consider intimidating, hostile, or abusive

Examples of offensive conduct include inappropriate jokes, name calling, physical assaults, threats, intimidation, and insults. Offensive conduct also includes displaying offensive pictures or objects. The victim does not have to be the target of the harassing behavior. Anyone affected by offensive conduct is considered a victim. For example, suppose a person at work overhears an offensive joke. Even though the joke was told to someone else, the person overhearing it can be considered a victim. Harassment increases employee turnover, lowers morale, and hurts employee productivity.

Workplace Safety

The work environment must be safe and promote employee health and well-being. A positive and safe work environment is good for the mental and physical health of employees. Also, employee productivity and efficiency increase in a positive work environment.

The *Occupational Safety & Health Administration (OSHA)* was established by the US Department of Labor in 1970. Its mission is to assure safe and healthful working conditions for employees by setting and enforcing safety standards. OSHA also provides safety training, outreach, education, and assistance.

Maintaining a safe workplace is the responsibility of both employers and employees. Employees are expected to use common sense and care while working, and follow safety instructions and procedures provided by the business.

Falls are the most common workplace accident in an office setting. Preventing workplace falls is relatively simple:

- close drawers completely
- do not stand on a chair or box to reach
- secure cords, rugs, and mats
- obey safety signs

Lifting hazards are sources of potential injury from improperly lifting or carrying items. Most back injuries are caused by improper lifting. To avoid injuries from lifting, employees should be instructed to:

- make several small trips with items rather than one trip with a heavy load
- use dollies or handcarts whenever possible
- lift with the legs, not with the back
- never carry an item that blocks vision
- obey safety signs

Material-storage hazards are sources of potential injury that come from the improper storage of files, books, office equipment, or other items. A cluttered workplace is an unsafe workplace. Material stacked too high can fall on employees. Paper and files that are stored on the floor or in a hallway are a fire risk. Both employers and employees can prevent material-storage injuries.

- Do not stack boxes or papers on top of tall cabinets.
- Store heavier objects on lower shelves.
- Keep aisles and hallways clear.
- Obey safety signs.

Emergency Procedures

Emergency procedures are a series of actions taken to minimize risks during an emergency. There are many types of emergencies that can happen in any type of workplace. Employees must be trained on how to react and the appropriate actions to take in a workplace emergency.

The first line of defense in all emergencies is to stay calm and follow the emergency procedures. Evaluate the seriousness of the emergency to determine the type of help required. Everyone in the workplace should be aware of exits and how to evacuate the premises, if necessary. If there is a medical emergency, employees should understand the procedures for giving assistance and calling for help. Employees should be trained and prepared for common emergency situations, including:

- fires
- natural disasters, such as a tornado, earthquake, or hurricane
- medical emergencies, such as heart attack, stroke, fainting, burns, and cuts
- bomb threats

Ergonomics

Ergonomics is a science concerned with designing and arranging things people use so that they can interact efficiently and safely.

©iStock.com/bunsview

It is important to know workplace safety protocol and emergency procedures.

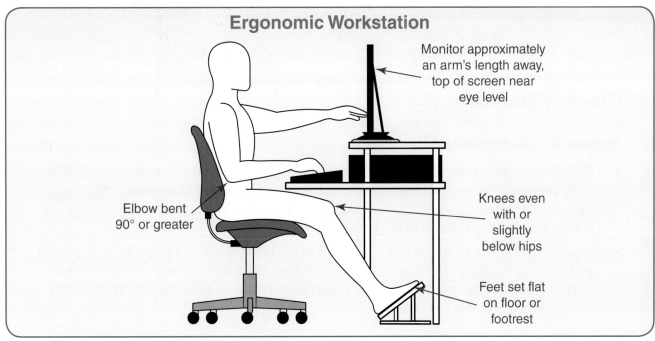

Ergonomic Workstation

Monitor approximately an arm's length away, top of screen near eye level

Elbow bent 90° or greater

Knees even with or slightly below hips

Feet set flat on floor or footrest

Goodheart-Willcox Publisher

Figure 9-4 An ergonomic workstation helps prevent back and neck pain, eyestrain, and headaches.

In the workplace, this can include designing workstations to fit the unique needs of workers and the equipment they use. Applying ergonomic principles results in a comfortable, efficient, and safe working environment.

Ergonomics can improve the workspace of employees who spend long periods of time working at computer stations. There are many types of ergonomic accessories that may improve the comfort of reading on a screen, including wrist rests, specially designed chairs, and back supports. In addition, Figure 9-4 identifies actions that can be taken for comfort while working at computer stations and to help prevent injury or strain to the worker's body.

Section 9.2 Review

 Check Your Understanding

1. List five examples of methods businesses can use to promote a healthy work-life balance.
2. What are common characteristics of an effective employer/employee relationship?
3. How is workplace diversity achieved?
4. According to the EEOC, when does harassment become unlawful?
5. What are some ergonomic accessories that may improve the comfort of reading on a computer screen?

 Build Your Vocabulary

As you progress through this course, develop a personal glossary of key terms. This will help you build your vocabulary and prepare you for a career. Write a definition for each of the following terms and add it to your personal glossary.

personal leave   work environment

family leave   discrimination

flextime   harassment

job sharing   ergonomics

telecommuting

Review and Assessment

Chapter Summary

Section 9.1 Human Resources

- Businesses cannot exist without human resources. Human resources management (HRM) is the process of hiring, training, and developing employees. HRM consists of five basic functions: recruiting and hiring, training and development, compensation, performance evaluation, and legal compliance.

- Organized labor, or Labor unions, is a group of workers united as a single body to protect and advance the rights and interests of its members. Unions help resolve issues between management and its members through collective bargaining. Labor unions are typically specific to particular types of labor.

Section 9.2 Workplace Environment

- Corporate culture is a set of shared values and practices held by the members of an organization. Social responsibility, work-life balance, employer/employee relationships, and workplace diversity contribute to organizational culture.

- The conditions of a workplace are affected by the environment created by conduct and company policies, as well as the physical surroundings. This includes considerate treatment of employees in the workplace and a commitment to employee safety and well-being.

Online Activities

Complete the following activities to help you learn, practice, and expand your knowledge and skills.

 Posttest. Now that you have finished the chapter, see what you learned by taking the chapter posttest.

 Vocabulary. Practice vocabulary for this chapter using the e-flash cards, matching activity, and vocabulary game until you are able to recognize their meanings.

Review Your Knowledge

1. Describe the role of human resources within an organization.
2. Describe the five basic functions of human resources management.
3. Explain the role of organized labor in society.
4. Who has the right to unionize in the United States?
5. Differentiate between a white-collar worker and a blue-collar worker.
6. Explain corporate culture in the workplace.

7. Explain mutual reliance as part of employer/employee relationships.

8. Give three examples of discrimination in the workplace.

9. What is the purpose of OSHA?

10. What is the first line of defense in all workplace emergencies?

Apply Your Knowledge

1. Recruiting and hiring is a major focus of most human resource departments. Review the functions of HRM shown in Figure 9-1. Which of the functions do you consider most important? Write several paragraphs to defend your choice.

2. What do you think *social responsibility* means for a business? Give examples of ways businesses can demonstrate their corporate culture through social responsibility.

3. There are times when employees need to be terminated for performance or behavioral issues. Create a list of inappropriate work habits that you think could lead to termination. Explain actions an employee could take to correct the inappropriate work habits.

4. Even though union membership in the United States has steadily declined, union activity is still commonly seen in many communities. Describe a union-related activity or advertisement you have recently seen. What was the purpose of the activity or advertisement?

5. Select a business in your community with which you are familiar. What positions do you think exist within the business in order for it to operate? Make a list of the positions for the business you chose and classify them as white collar or blue collar. Which type of position is dominant? Why do you think that type of position is important to the company?

Communication Skills

College and Career Readiness

Reading. Carefully consider the use of the term *human resources* in the chapter. What connotation does this word have? How does using the term human resources today compare with the word *personnel* that was common in the last century? Do you think the term readily conveys its meaning to the reader? Why or why not?

Listening. Practice active-listening skills while listening to your teacher present this chapter. Focus on the message and monitor it for understanding. Were there any barriers to effective listening? How did you use prior knowledge to help you understand what was being said? Share your ideas in the group discussion.

Speaking. Successful employees model integrity. What role do you think ethics and integrity have in decision-making? Think of a time when your ideals and principles helped you make a decision. What process did you use to make the decision? In retrospect, do you think you made the correct decision? Make an informal presentation to your class to share your thoughts.

Internet Research

History of Organized Labor. Organized labor plays an important role in society. Using the Internet, research the history of organized labor. Make notes as you perform the research. Next, synthesize the information that you have gathered. Write several paragraphs on what you think organized labor has contributed to society.

Motivation. Employees who are motivated are more productive. Using the Internet, research Maslow's Hierarchy of Needs and Herzberg's two-factor theory. Create a table that lists the characteristics of each theory. How do the theories compare?

Teamwork

Working as a team, write a job description for an administrative assistant for the human resources team. Start by listing the tasks that will be performed in this position. Define the personal qualifications the candidates must have to be considered for an interview. After the information is gathered, write a job description.

Portfolio Development

College and Career Readiness

Certificates. Exhibiting certificates you have received in your portfolio reflects your accomplishments. For example, a certificate might show that you have completed a training class. Another one might show that you can key at a certain speed.

Include any certificates that show tasks completed or that exhibit your skills and talents. Remember that this is an ongoing project. Plan to update when you have new certificates to add.

1. Scan the certificates that will be in your portfolio.

2. Give each document an appropriate name and save in a folder or subfolder.

3. Place the hard copy certificates in a container for future reference.

4. Record these documents on your master spreadsheet that you started earlier to record hardcopy items. You may list each document alphabetically, by category, date, or other convention that helps you keep track of each document that you are including.

CTSOs

Extemporaneous speaking. Extemporaneous speaking is a competitive event you might enter with your CTSO. This event allows you to display your communication skills, specifically your ability to organize and deliver an oral presentation. At the competition, you will be given several topics from which to choose. You will also be given a time limit to create and deliver the speech. You will be evaluated on your verbal and nonverbal skills as well as the tone and projection of your voice.

To prepare for an extemporaneous speaking event, complete the following activities.

1. Ask your instructor for several practice topics so you can practice making impromptu speeches.

2. Once you have a practice topic, jot down the ideas and points to cover. An important part of making this type of presentation is that you will have only a few minutes to prepare. Being able to write down your main ideas quickly will enable you to focus on what you will actually say in the presentation.

3. Practice the presentation. You should introduce yourself, review the topic that is being presented, defend the topic, and conclude with a summary.

4. Ask your instructor to play the role of competition judge as you give the presentation. Afterward, ask for feedback from your instructor. You may also consider having a student audience listen and give feedback.

5. For the event, bring paper and pencils to record notes. Supplies may or may not be provided.

Marketing

Focus on Marketing

Marketing is a term that has been around for centuries. The word *market* is derived from the Latin word *mercaris*, which means *to trade*. Sometime in twelfth century Europe, market came to mean the meeting of buyers and sellers of livestock or other goods. Today, a market is anywhere a buyer and seller come together.

Marketing means different things to different people. Some people think of advertising when they hear the term *marketing*. Others think it means to talk to customers and see what they need from a business. Ultimately, marketing activities identify and satisfy customer needs and wants.

Product, price, place, and promotion are the four Ps of marketing. They lay the groundwork and tell the story of marketing. *Product* includes both goods and services. Without product, marketing would not be necessary. The *price* of products must be an amount customers are willing to pay but also that generates profit. *Place* refers to the activities involved in getting goods or services to the end user. This includes producers, wholesalers, retailers, and others in the supply chain.

Businesses communicate with potential customers in an effort to influence their buying behavior. This is the process of *promotion*. The promotional mix can include advertising, sales promotion, public relations, and personal selling. Without promotion, customers would not have information about a company or product. Businesses communicate with customers both during and after a sale. Good customer service should be provided by all employees in a company as a part of the marketing concept.

TRACKING
RETINA PATH

Social Media for Business

Companies are using social media more and more to reach their customers. Social media is considered a free way to engage with both current and potential customers. Technically, social media does cost companies money. It is free to create a Facebook page, Twitter account, and Pinterest account. However, companies must still bring customers to those pages. To do that, they must invest employee time, possibly pay for social endorsements, or even pay for display ads on the social media sites. Paying for display ads is a popular way to communicate. They are easy to start and reach most target customers.

Metrics are ways to measure the effectiveness of marketing activities. *Social-media analytics* is the gathering of information from social media activities. It is important for a business to measure the returns of using social media as a tool. There are many programs available that measure how many responses are received from an activity, how many dollars have been generated, and other important data. This information helps determine if the investment of time and money has been productive. Marketing plans should include an approach for analyzing the effectiveness of the social media marketing used for the business.

While studying, look for the activity icon ⬀ for:

- Pretests and posttests
- Vocabulary terms with e-flash cards and matching activities
- Self-assessment

G-WLEARNING.com

CHAPTER 10

Marketing

Exploring Careers

Marketing Professional

A company's marketing activities play a large role in the success of the goods or services it offers. Marketing professionals identify potential customers and develop strategies to market products to these customers. They also help keep the company on track by monitoring customer wants and needs and suggesting new ways to satisfy those needs.

Typical job titles for this position also include *marketing manager*, *marketing coordinator*, and *brand manager*. Examples of tasks marketing professionals perform include:

- coordinate marketing activities and policies to promote the company's goods or services;

- develop marketing and pricing strategies;

- perform market research and analysis; and

- coordinate or participate in promotional activities and trade shows to showcase the company's products.

Marketing professional positions require a bachelor degree in marketing, advertising, communications, or a related field. They need a strong background in sales and marketing strategy. Experience in customer service and employee management is preferred. Solid knowledge of the English language, business and management principles, media production, and communication are also needed. Marketing professionals must also be able to think creatively and use critical-thinking skills to solve problems.

In This Chapter

Reading Prep

College and Career Readiness

Examine the visuals in the chapter before you read it. Write down questions you have about them. Try and answer the questions as you read.

Check Your Business IQ

Before you begin the chapter, see what you already know about business by taking the chapter pretest. The pretest is available at www.g-wlearning.com.

Introduction to Marketing

Objectives

After completing this section, you will be able to:

- **Describe** marketing and its focus on the customer.
- **Explain** marketing strategies.

Key Terms

marketing

marketing concept

four Ps of marketing

product

price

place

promotion

target market

marketing strategy

marketing plan

market segmentation

geographic segmentation

demographic segmentation

psychographic segmentation

behavioral segmentation

customer profile

mass marketing

marketing mix

Importance of Marketing

The American Marketing Association defines *marketing* as "the activity, set of institutions, and processes for creating, communicating, delivering, and exchanging offerings that have value for customers, clients, partners, and society at large." Without marketing efforts, it would be a challenge for businesses to reach customers and meet their needs and wants.

Marketing consists of dynamic activities that identify, anticipate, and satisfy customer demand while making a profit. It is one of the four functions of business, as shown in Figure 10-1. In order for a business to be successful, all the functions must work together. Marketing efforts can identify the best potential customers, research how to improve a product, and find new ways to sell it.

Functions of Business	
Production	Any activity related to making a product
Finance	All business activities that involve money
Management	Process of controlling and making decisions about a business
Marketing	Activities that identify, anticipate, and satisfy customer demand while making a profit

Goodheart-Willcox Publisher

Figure 10-1 Each of the four functions of business work together to create customer satisfaction and business success.

Marketing Concept

Marketing activities are aimed at the customer. The **marketing concept** is an approach to business that focuses on satisfying customers

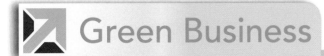

Green Business | Green Presentations

Many companies find that being good stewards of the environment can help increase sales and profits. This is because consumers often hold companies in higher regard when they act responsibly and have environmentally friendly policies.

When making presentations to customers and other audiences, many companies request that presenters make green presentations. Green presentations avoid waste of paper, supplies, and energy.

Presentations typically consist of slideshows, website demonstrations, and handouts of important points for the audience. Green presenters take advantage of technology to post presentations on YouTube, Facebook, or company websites. Interested audience members can visit the sites to review presentation information, download or view the presentation itself, and download electronic handouts. This practice saves resources, such as paper for handouts and energy to run the presentation with lights and audio equipment.

as the means of achieving profit goals. The three elements of the marketing concept are customer satisfaction, total company approach, and profit, as shown in Figure 10-2.

- *Customer satisfaction* is the degree to which customers are pleased with a company's goods or services.

- *Total company approach* is all functions of a company working together to achieve goals.

- *Profit* is the difference between the income earned and expenses incurred by a business during a specific period of time.

Successful businesses focus on the customers and listen to their needs and wants. In turn, customer satisfaction can be achieved and repeated business can be earned.

Four Ps of Marketing

Many people think of advertising when they hear the term *marketing*. However, marketing is much more than just advertising. It includes the **four Ps of marketing**, which are product, price, place, and promotion.

- **Product** is anything that can be bought or sold.

- **Price** is an amount of money requested or exchanged for a product.

- **Place** includes the activities involved in getting goods and services to customers.

- **Promotion** is the process of communicating with potential customers in an effort to influence their buying behavior.

Successful businesses consider each of the four Ps to provide customer satisfaction.

Goodheart-Willcox Publisher

Figure 10-2 The marketing concept focuses on every aspect of the business to keep the customer satisfied, because that is the key to long-term profit.

Functions of Marketing

Marketing consists of hundreds of activities. These marketing activities can be organized by the seven functions of marketing, as shown in Figure 10-3. The seven functions of marketing are channel management, marketing-information management (MIM), market planning, pricing, product/service management, promotion, and selling.

- *Channel management* handles activities involved in getting products through the different routes from the producers to the customers. These routes are called *channels*.

- *Marketing-information management (MIM)* involves gathering and analyzing information about markets, customers, industry trends, new technology, and competing businesses. MIM is also called *marketing research*.

- The *market planning* function is creating an actionable marketing plan designed to achieve business goals. Activities in market planning include identifying the target market. A **target market** is the specific group of customers whose needs a company will focus on satisfying.

- *Pricing* directly affects the profit of a business. The pricing function handles all activities involved in setting acceptable prices for products. Financial information is used to set prices that cover costs and include a reasonable profit, as well as to adjust prices when conditions change.

- The *product/service management* function determines which products a business should offer to meet customer needs. Activities can include developing new goods or services or improving a current one.

- *Promotion* refers to the nonpersonal communication with customers that influences purchasing. It includes decisions about advertising, such as the type of ads to use and where to place them. It also includes decisions about personal selling, customer service, publicity, promotional events, and store design and layout.

Goodheart-Willcox Publisher

Figure 10-3 The seven functions of marketing incorporate hundreds of activities.

- *Selling* is all personal communications with customers. Selling activities include helping customers in a store, making sales presentations or product demonstrations, and providing customer service.

Marketing Strategies

Marketing strategy is the plan that helps a business meet its overall goals and objectives. A well-designed strategy first addresses the target market. It then addresses the four Ps of marketing. Marketing strategies provide the groundwork for writing the marketing plan. The **marketing plan** is a document describing business and marketing objectives and the strategies and tactics to achieve them. Marketing plans are generally written each year and updated throughout the year, as needed.

Target the Market

The first step in developing a marketing strategy is to identify the target market. This is

Teens are the target market for many companies that produce school supplies, such as backpacks.

also known as *market identification*. A market is the group of people who might buy a product. A target market is the specific group of people at which a company aims to promote its goods and services. These are the individuals whose wants and needs are fulfilled by the products offered by a business. They are also the people most likely to buy the goods or services. Correctly choosing the best target market is one of the most important decisions a marketer makes. Selecting the wrong target market can mean the business loses an opportunity for success in a different target market.

After the target market is selected, the market is segmented. **Market segmentation** is the process of dividing the market into smaller groups. The segments are determined by different variables. The variables used for market segmentation are geographic, demographic, psychographic, and behavioral, as shown in Figure 10-4. Within those groups, customer types can be refined even further by using additional variables.

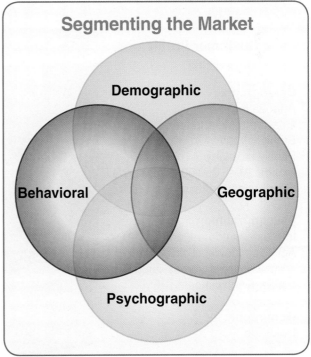

Figure 10-4 Market segmentation divides the market into smaller groups based on certain variables.

Research has found that customers in the same market segments have similar buying patterns and behaviors.

- **Geographic segmentation** is segmenting a market based on where customers live. Customers can be segmented by region, climate, or population density.

- **Demographic segmentation** is dividing the market of potential customers by their personal statistics. This information can be found in census data. A *census* is a count of the people in a country made by the government on a regular basis. Some of the census data collected includes age, gender, income, ethnicity, education level, occupation, marital status, and family size.

- **Psychographic segmentation** is dividing the market by certain preferences or lifestyle choices. *Psychographics* are data about the preferences or choices of a group of people. This includes information about individual values, attitudes, activities, and interests that affect purchasing decisions.

- **Behavioral segmentation** divides a market by the relationships between customers and the good or service. Behavioral variables include benefits sought, usage rate, buying status, brand loyalty, and special occasions.

Once marketers have divided a market into segments, they choose which segments to target for marketing purposes. When the market segments are chosen, a customer profile is created for each segment. A **customer profile** is a detailed description of the typical consumer in a market segment. The profile includes geographic, demographic, psychographic, and behavioral characteristics about this typical customer. A sample customer profile is shown in figure 10-5.

Accurate customer profiles help determine the best promotional strategies. By knowing who is most interested in the company's products, promotional dollars can be used wisely.

Segmenting the market is an efficient use of time and money. However, some marketing plans include mass marketing. **Mass marketing** is marketing to a larger group of people who might buy a product. An example of using mass marketing is a product advertisement shown on TV.

Customer Profile
Skier

Demographic
Age: 25 to 40
Gender: male and female
Ethnicity: any
Family size: any
Income level: $50,000 and above
Occupation: professional

Psychographic
Interests: outdoors, adventure
Activities: downhill skiing, snowboarding, cross-country skiing, snowshoeing

Geographic
Colorado

Ipatov/Shutterstock.com; Goodheart-Willcox Publisher

Figure 10-5 A customer profile for a ski shop in Colorado lists demographic, psychographic, and geographic characteristics about consumers in the market segment.

Andresr/Shutterstock.com

An example of mass marketing is when a bank sends a direct mailing about banking services to all high school graduates in the hopes that some will open an account.

The audience is everyone watching rather than a chosen segmented market. The larger group will likely include people who are not interested in the product. Media advertising, in some situations, can be a good use of marketing dollars.

Identify the Marketing Mix

The next step in developing a strategy is to identify the marketing mix. The **marketing mix** is the strategy for using the elements of product, price, place, and promotion. It consists of the decisions made about each of the four Ps for that product, shown in Figure 10-6. A marketing mix can also be developed for a group of products or an entire business.

The marketing mix strategy adapts when needed for marketing a good versus a service. Goods are tangible and can be touched, whereas services are intangible and cannot be touched. A good can be photographed for an advertisement, but a service may not lend itself to a picture. A good can often be sampled, but a service cannot always be experienced

before purchasing. A dissatisfied customer can return a good, but cannot return a service with which he or she is unhappy. Because of

Goodheart-Willcox Publisher

Figure 10-6 The marketing mix for a product must be carefully identified in order for a business to achieve success.

these differences, the four Ps must recognize if the product is a good or service and adapt appropriately.

- *Product* can be changed by adding new features. Product includes goods and services. Product strategies include decisions about quality, quantity, size, color, features, technical support, packaging, warranties, brand name, and image.

- *Price* can be changed to match new features. Price strategies include decisions about the desired profit, discounts, and selling prices. Pricing can also have an impact on the image of a product.

- *Place* can be changed based on where a product is offered. Place strategies include all of the decisions made about where the product will be sold. It includes decisions about transporting, warehousing, inventory controlling, and order processing for the product.

- *Promotion* can be changed to appeal more to the target market. Promotion strategies include all of the decisions made about how to promote the product. It includes decisions about advertising, personal selling, customer service, publicity, promotional events, and store design and layout.

One marketing mix usually does not meet the needs of all customers. The key to finding a successful mix is to:

- choose the right product

- sell it at the right price

- make it available at the right place

- promote it in a way that will reach the target audience

An effective marketing mix is a balance of each of the four Ps. Not all of the elements must be used at one time. Each marketing mix should be unique to the product for a given target market.

Section 10.1 Review

 Check Your Understanding

1. How is marketing related to the other functions of business?
2. What are the three elements of the marketing concept?
3. What are the seven functions of marketing?
4. Explain the concept of market identification.
5. List the four variables used to identify market segments.

 Build Your Vocabulary

As you progress through this course, develop a personal glossary of key terms. This will help you build your vocabulary and prepare you for a career. Write a definition for each of the following terms and add it to your personal glossary.

marketing

marketing concept

four Ps of marketing

product

price

place

promotion

target market

marketing strategy

marketing plan

market segmentation

geographic segmentation

demographic segmentation

psychographic segmentation

behavioral segmentation

customer profile

mass marketing

marketing mix

Customers

Objectives

After completing this section, you will be able to:

- **Describe** the types of customers that a business serves.
- **Differentiate** between consumer and business buying decisions.

Key Terms

relationship selling
database marketing
customer relationship
  management
  (CRM) system
social influence
psychological
  influence

situational influence
personal influence
impulse buying
  decision
routine buying
  decision
limited buying
  decision

extensive buying
  decision
internal influence
external influence
situational influence

Customer Types

Some businesses only sell to one type of customer. Other businesses sell to multiple types of customers. There are three basic types of customers:

- consumers, also known as the *business-to-consumer (B2C) market*
- businesses, also known as the *business-to-business (B2B) market*
- government and institutions

Relationship marketing is important for all types of customers. Personal selling and other marketing activities help customers learn to trust and depend on certain businesses to meet their needs. Customers are more likely to buy from companies they know and trust.

For consumers, some businesses reward customers for their continued business through loyalty programs. The most popular ones involve giving customers free goods or services after a certain number of purchases has been made.

Many purchases made by business, government, and industry customers are based on relationship selling. **Relationship selling** focuses on building long-term relationships with customers. Because business sales are usually large, the sales process is lengthy and the customers may need follow-up service. These customers value personal contact with sales people with whom they trust.

To help manage customer relationships, many businesses use database marketing. **Database marketing** is a system of gathering, storing, and using customer data for marketing directly to customers based on their histories. An example of a marketing database is a customer relationship management (CRM) system. A **customer relationship management (CRM) system** is a system to track contact and other information for current and potential customers.

Adam Gregor/Shutterstock.com

Relationship selling is common in the B2B market. Many deals are finalized with a handshake which signifies trust.

Using such a system helps marketers efficiently identify customers, their buying habits, and other important information to help a business be profitable.

Customer Buying Decisions

Customer buying behavior is, in part, based on influences. An *influence* is the power to sway or produce an effect. Each type of customer has very different ways of making buying decisions.

Business-to-Consumer

A consumer buys products for personal use. Businesses that sell primarily to individual consumers are in the *business-to-consumer (B2C) market*. Consumer buying behavior is typically based on social, psychological, situational, and personal influences.

- **Social influences** are the influences that come from the society in which a person lives. There are many sources of social influence, including family, peers, culture, and media.

- **Psychological influences** are the influences that come from within a person or why a person has specific needs and wants. In the 1950s, psychologist Abraham Maslow developed *Maslow's Hierarchy of Needs*, as shown in Figure 10-7. According to this theory, needs motivate people to act. However, some needs must be satisfied before others. This means there is a hierarchy, or order of importance, of needs. Maslow noticed that people fulfill physical needs before other needs that are not as important to survival.

- **Situational influences** for B2C are the influences that come from the environment. The weather, store location, time of day, and current sales promotions affect buying choices. Mood, physical health, and how much money is in the consumer's pocket are also situational influences that impact buying habits.

- **Personal influences** are the influences that make each individual unique. These include demographics, such as gender, age, and race, as well as individual personality, lifestyle, and finances.

Figure 10-7 Abraham Maslow believed physical needs must be met before all other needs and wants.

The decision-making process used by individual consumers is similar to the process used by business and government consumers. The decision-making process helps consumers make the decision to purchase or not to purchase. The stages in the decision-making process are shown in Figure 10-8.

- *Define the problem or need.* Consumers become aware of a problem when they have a need or want to be satisfied. Defining the need or want is the first step in the decision-making process.

- *Research.* The next step is to search for information on how to fulfill the need or want. Consumers may recall past experiences or ask family and friends for recommendations. Many consumers research product features and reviews on websites.

- *Choose the best option.* When research is complete, all of the available options are reviewed. Consumers evaluate and compare many factors for each option, including price, brand, features, and convenience.

Figure 10-8 Consumers use some or all of the steps in the decision-making process to make buying decisions.

- *Implement the decision.* When an option is selected, consumers choose where and when to make their purchase. They may decide to delay the purchase for various reasons, such as to save up money or wait for a newer model of the product to be available.

- *Evaluate the purchase.* After a purchase, consumers evaluate their purchasing experience. This includes their expectations of the goods, store, and service they received.

Consumers do not always use all the steps in the decision-making process to make buying decisions. Some purchases may require a great deal of research and evaluation, and others may need little or none.

There are different levels of decision making for consumers when making decisions about a purchase, as shown in Figure 10-9. There are four levels of buying decisions: impulse, routine, limited, and extensive.

- An **impulse buying decision** is a purchase made with no planning or research. This type of purchase typically does not involve any steps in the decision-making process.

- A **routine buying decision** is a purchase made quickly and with little thought. These purchases are made when a consumer has experience with a product or prefers a certain brand.

- A **limited buying decision** is one that requires some amount of research and planning. This process is used when buying unfamiliar products or those that are purchased only occasionally.

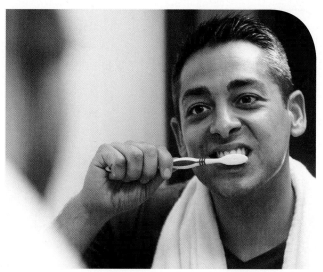

Dragon Images/Shutterstock.com

An example of a routine buying decision for a B2C sale is toothpaste. Little thought is given to purchasing a familiar product.

- An **extensive buying decision** involves a great deal of research and planning. It is usually used when buying higher-priced items, such as cars and real estate. These purchases typically have a major impact on an individual's daily life, safety, and finances.

Business-to-Business

The business market consists of customers who buy products for use in a business. A customer in the business market is a business that buys products from another business. Businesses that sell primarily to other businesses are in the *business-to-business (B2B) market.*

Levels of Consumer Buying Decisions	
Impulse Purchase	No prior planning; spur-of-the-moment purchase
Routine Purchase	Little thought or planning; familiar products purchased often
Limited Buying Decision	Some research and planning; new purchase
Extensive Buying Decision	A great deal of research, time, and planning; usually an expensive good or service

Goodheart-Willcox Publisher

Figure 10-9 Some consumer buying decisions involve little planning and no research, while others may involve a great deal of thought and research.

You Do the Math   Statistical Reasoning

There are three measures of the center of a data set. The mode is the value that occurs most frequently in the data set. The median is the middle number in a data set. To find the median, the numbers must be listed in numerical order. The mean is the average of all values in the data set. Mean is calculated by adding all values and dividing that sum by the total number of values.

Solve the following problems.

1. A recent survey of gasoline prices for a region reported these prices per gallon: $3.49, $3.67, $3.52, $3.58, and $3.56. What is the mean price per gallon?

2. A business ships telephone headsets all across the country. The various shipping costs it charged last week are: $0.99, $1.05, $0.75, $1.07, $0.99, $1.05, and $1.05. What is the mode shipping charge?

3. For the data in question #2, what is the median shipping charge?

The B2B market is very different than the B2C market. Business customers have different needs and motives than consumers. Businesses buy product to manufacture new product, resell, or use for their operations. B2B sales usually take a long time and may be based on relationship selling. These purchases typically have to go through an approval process. In a B2C purchase, the consumer is the final decision maker and may make on-the-spot buying decisions. Another important distinction is that a consumer buys products to use personally.

The needs of an organization are the primary motivating force of B2B buying decisions. However, other influences affect final purchase decisions. These influences fall into three categories:

- **Internal influences** are motivators or change factors that come from within the business itself. These include the structure, goals, and management team of a company.

- **External influences** are motivators or change factors from outside the business. These include competitors, new technology, and product trends.

- **Situational influences** for B2B are those from the environment in which the business exists. These include the economy, political environment, and regulations or laws.

Even though the quantity and motivation for purchasing is different for businesses, purchasing decisions must still be made. As shown in Figure 10-10, there are three levels

Levels of Business Buying Decisions	
New Purchase	Great deal of research and planning, including product specifications and expectations
Repeat Purchase	Little research and thought; typical for items purchased on a regular basis
Modified Purchase	Some planning and research; used when purchasing a familiar product with certain changes or modifications

Goodheart-Willcox Publisher

Figure 10-10 Like consumer buying decisions, the levels of buying decisions for businesses range in amount of planning and research.

of buying decisions for business purchases: new purchase, repeat purchase, and modified purchase.

- A *new purchase* is a decision to buy a new product, which requires a great deal of research and thought. A business will likely outline product specifications and expectations for the new product. The new-purchase level of business-buying decisions is similar to the extensive decision-making process for consumers.

- A *repeat purchase* is a buying decision that requires little research and thought. Many businesses purchase the same items on a regular basis. Repeat purchase decisions occur when the buyer is satisfied with the product, vendor, and terms of sale. This is similar to the routine buying decisions of consumers.

- A *modified purchase* is a decision to buy a familiar product but with some changes

or modifications. The buyer may ask for bids for the modified product. This gives the current vendor and new vendors the opportunity to meet the needs of the business. This is similar to the limited decision-making process of consumers.

The amount of research and planning varies among the levels of buying decisions for business purchases. A business must consider the needs of both the business and customers when making buying decisions.

Government and Institutions

The government market includes national, state, and local government offices and agencies. Government customers buy a wide variety of products. These products range from airplanes and ground vehicles to office supplies and electronics. Governments also buy services, such as food preparation, education, security, and medical care.

Ken Wolter/Shutterstock.com

Universities are an example of nonprofit institutions to which B2B sales are made.

Ethics

Using Social Networking Media

Social networking media is commonly used by organizations to reach customers and find new ones. Because it is readily available and easy to use, those who are writing communication for the organization must be ethical when using websites, such as Facebook or Twitter, for business purposes. Use good judgment and represent the organization in a professional manner.

Institutions are nonprofit organizations that may be either public or private. A nonprofit organization is an entity that exists to serve a public purpose. These include schools, hospitals, and museums. It also includes organizations, such as United Way and the American Cancer Society. Like government customers, institutions also buy a wide variety of goods and services to support their activities.

Section 10.2 Review

 Check Your Understanding

1. Identify three types of customers that a business serves.
2. What are four influences that typically affect consumer buying behavior?
3. What are the stages of the decision-making process?
4. List the three influences that affect the buying decisions of organizations.
5. What are the levels of buying decisions for business purchases?

 Build Your Vocabulary

As you progress through this course, develop a personal glossary of key terms. This will help you build your vocabulary and prepare you for a career. Write a definition for each of the following terms and add it to your personal glossary.

relationship selling
database marketing
customer relationship
    management (CRM)
    system
social influence
psychological influence
situational influence

personal influence
impulse buying decision
routine buying decision
limited buying decision
extensive buying decision
internal influence
external influence
situational influence

Review and Assessment

Chapter Summary

Section 10.1 Introduction to Marketing

- Marketing consists of dynamic activities that identify, anticipate, and satisfy customer demand while making a profit. The marketing concept is an approach to business that focuses on satisfying customers as the means of achieving profit goal. To help accomplish the marketing concept, the four Ps of marketing address product, price, place, and promotion. Applying the seven functions of marketing help a business organize its marketing activities.

- Marketing strategy is the plan that helps a business meet its overall goals and objectives. Strategies provide the groundwork for creating the marketing plan that describes marketing objectives and tactics to meet them. The first step in developing a marketing strategy is to identify the target market. The next step in developing a strategy is to identify the marketing mix.

Section 10.2 Customers

- Customer relationships are essential to business. Three basic types of customers are B2C, B2B, and government/institutions. To help manage customer relationships, many businesses use databases to gather, store, and use customer data for marketing directly to their customers. A customer service relationship management (CRM) is used to accomplish those tasks. It identifies customers, their buying habits, and other important information to help the business.

- The buying decisions made by customers of all types are affected by various influences. Consumer buying behavior is typically based on social, psychological, situation, and personal influences. The purchases made by a consumer are based on impulsive, routine, limited, or extensive buying decisions. In contrast, business purchases are influenced by internal factors, external factors, and situational factors. Purchases by a business are new, repeat, or modified.

Online Activities

Complete the following activities to help you learn, practice, and expand your knowledge and skills.

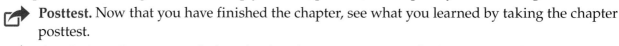

Posttest. Now that you have finished the chapter, see what you learned by taking the chapter posttest.

Vocabulary. Practice vocabulary for this chapter using the e-flash cards, matching activity, and vocabulary game until you are able to recognize their meanings.

Review Your Knowledge

1. What is the American Marketing Association definition of marketing?
2. Explain the marketing concept.
3. List the seven functions of marketing and describe their related activities.
4. Explain the concept of marketing strategies.
5. Define and explain the importance of a target market.
6. Explain the difference between market segmentation and mass marketing.
7. What is Maslow's Hierarchy of Needs?
8. Define each component of the marketing mix.
9. What are the four levels of consumer buying decisions?
10. Explain the three levels of business buying decisions.

Apply Your Knowledge

1. Select a student organization in your school of which you are a member or would consider becoming a member. For this organization to recruit members, it must first identify the target market. How would you identify a target market for a student organization? Explain how the concepts of marketing and market identification apply. How would you use market segmentation to identify the group that would be most likely to join when recruiting for the organization?

2. Select a product that appeals to people in your age group, such as an electronics item or automobile. Imagine that you are creating a marketing strategy for that product. Identify examples of an effective marketing mix that would have the most influence on the target market. Which of the four Ps would you use? Explain your reasoning.

3. In the last question, you identified examples of an effective marketing mix for a product. Create examples for each of the elements to market your chosen product. Identify each element and how you would use it in a marketing strategy. Explain why different marketing strategies are used for services versus goods. How would your marketing strategy change if your product was a service?

4. Describe a memorable commercial or print advertisement you have seen recently. What was the product being promoted? What do you think the target market was for that particular advertisement? Explain your answer.

5. There are four levels of consumer buying decisions: impulse, routine, limited, and extensive. Give examples of purchases you have recently made that fit into each level. Did you make good purchasing decisions? Explain your answer.

Communication Skills

College and Career Readiness

Reading. This chapter is about the importance of marketing to the success of business. After you read the chapter, identify and analyze the audience, purpose, and message of the author's writing.

Writing. Generate ideas for writing a paper that describes the concept of marketing as you interpret it. Gather information to support your thoughts and ideas. Keep careful and accurate records of any sources that you use as references. Create the notes that you could use to write a paper to distribute for discussion with your classmates.

Speaking. To become career ready, it will be important to learn how to communicate clearly and effectively by using reason. Create an outline that includes information about the importance of loyalty programs for businesses. Consider your audience as you prepare the information. Using the outline, make a presentation to your class.

Internet Research

Customer Relationships. Explore the topic of the importance of customer relationships for a business. Use multiple sources for your research. Take notes on key ways a business can build relationships with its target market and why this activity is important. Write your findings in several paragraphs. Cite any sources that you used.

Teamwork

Working with a partner, identify advertisements in a newspaper or magazine that you agree are appealing to the reader. Select several examples and create a poster. Sort the advertisements by target market. What did you learn from this experience? Share your project with the class.

Portfolio Development

College and Career Readiness

Community Service. Community service is an important quality to show in a portfolio. Serving the community shows that a candidate is well rounded and socially aware. In this activity, you will create a list of your contributions to nonprofit organizations. Many opportunities are available for young people to serve the community. You might volunteer for a park clean-up project. Perhaps you might enjoy reading to residents in a senior-living facility. Maybe raising money for a pet shelter appeals to you. Whatever your interests, there is sure to be a related service project.

1. Create a Microsoft® Word document that lists service projects or volunteer activities in which you have taken part. Use the heading "Community Service" on the document along with your name. List the name of the organization or person you helped, the date(s) of service, and the activities that you performed. If you received an award related to this service, mention it here.

2. Save the document in an appropriate folder.

3. Update your spreadsheet to reflect the inclusion of this Community Service document.

CTSOs

 **Written Events.** Many competitive events for career and technical student organizations (CTSOs) require students to write a paper and submit it either before the competition or when the student arrives at the event. Written events can be lengthy and take a lot of time to prepare, so it is important to start early. To prepare for a written event, complete the following activities.

1. Read the guidelines provided by the organization. The topic to be researched will be specified in detail. Also, all final format guidelines will be given, including how to organize and submit the paper. Make certain you ask questions about any points you do not understand.

2. Do your research early. Research may take days or weeks, and you do not want to rush the process.

3. Set a deadline for yourself so that you write at a comfortable pace.

4. After you write the first draft, ask an instructor to review it for you and give feedback.

5. Once you have the final version, go through the checklist for the event to make sure you have covered all of the details. Your score will be penalized if you do not follow instructions.

6. To practice, visit your organization's website and select a written event in which you might be interested. Research the topic and then complete an outline. Create a checklist of guidelines that you must follow for this event. After you have completed these steps, decide if this is the event or topic that interests you. If you are still interested, move forward and start the writing process.

CHAPTER
11

Product, Price, and Place

Exploring Careers

Certified Purchasing Professional

Many companies purchase goods from other businesses. Certified purchasing professionals oversee the materials, goods, and services that are purchased for a business. This management-level position is responsible for negotiating supplier contracts and documenting goods that have been ordered and received. They also coordinate the duties of the buying, selling, and distribution staff.

Typical job titles for this position also include *purchasing manager*, *director of strategic sourcing*, and *procurement officer*. Examples of tasks a certified purchasing professional performs include:

- direct and coordinate the work of purchasing department employees

- identify and interview suppliers of needed goods

- develop detailed needs for goods or services to be purchased

- facilitate payment to suppliers for products received

Most certified purchasing professional positions require a bachelor degree, as well as Certified Purchasing Professional certification or Certified Purchasing Manager certification. Because this is a manager-level position, experience as a buyer, product manager, or purchasing agent is needed.

Reading Prep

Skim the chapter by reading the first sentence of each paragraph. Use this information to create an outline for the chapter before you read it.

College and Career Readiness

Check Your Business IQ ↪

Before you begin the chapter, see what you already know about business by taking the chapter pretest. The pretest is available at www.g-wlearning.com.

Section 11.1

Product

What is a product?

Objectives

After studying this section, you will be able to:

- **Explain** product as one of the four Ps of marketing.
- **Describe** common elements of product.
- **Define** product mix.

Key Terms

intangible	quality	product line
inseparable	packaging	product width
variable	warranty	product item
perishable	guarantee	product depth
feature	product mix	product planning

Product

A product is what a business sells to satisfy customer needs. It is one of the four Ps of marketing, which are product, place, price, and promotion. Product is an important part of the marketing mix. Without product, marketing would not be necessary.

Collectively, goods and services are called *products*. Goods are physical items, and services are activities performed by others. Services are considered products, but they are different from goods in four important ways. Services are intangible, inseparable, variable, and perishable.

- **Intangible** means something that cannot be touched. Services cannot be tried out before purchased or be returned.

- **Inseparable** means a service cannot be separated from the person who performs it. For example, a computer repair does not exist until the technician performs the service on the equipment. Because services are inseparable from the provider, customers often think of the service and the service provider as one and the same.

Odua Images/Shutterstock.com

An example of a service is an outpatient center that provides x-ray tests for patients.

- **Variable** means each service is almost always unique. A service only exists once and is rarely repeated in exactly the same way.

- **Perishable** means that services cannot be stored for later use.

Because the service is the product, service businesses must pay close attention to how services are provided and to the unique needs of each customer. Customers remember how well a service was performed and how well the service met their individual needs.

Product Elements

All products have certain elements that may be changed to meet customer needs. These elements can be organized into three categories:

- features
- usage
- protection

Understanding these elements can enable a business to more effectively fulfill the marketing concept of attaining customer satisfaction.

Features

Features are facts about a good or service. For example, a feature of a tablet computer as a *good* is the size of its display screen. A *service* feature for the tablet can be technical support or data services.

An *option* is a feature that can be added to a product by customer request. Sometimes, options are called *optional features*. Many products have a basic design and customers can choose features to add. For example, options on an automobile might include a sunroof and leather seats. Options allow consumers to customize products to their specific needs and wants.

Quality is an indicator of a product's excellence. Price and quality are often directly related. There are three general quality levels:

- *Premium quality* is the highest level of quality available in products. Premium-quality products usually have the highest prices.

- *Moderate quality* is the middle range of product quality. These products usually combine good-quality materials with moderate prices.

- *Value quality* is an adequate level of product quality. Value-quality products are typically functional, but are not made to last a long time.

Kmannn/Shutterstock.com

Digital products come with many features, including service plans and limited warranties to protect them.

wavebreakmedia/Shutterstock.com

Technical support is available when usage problems arise with a product.

Usage

Usage means the way something is used. Product usage includes the available instructions, installation, and technical support.

- *Instructions* are steps that must be carried out in a specific order to successfully complete a task.

- *Installation* is the act or process of putting a good in a certain place and getting it ready for use. Installation is a service offered with many large or complex products.

- *Technical support* includes the people and resources available to help customers with any usage problems.

Protection

Protection is a broad category that includes safety inspections, packaging, warranties, and maintenance and repair services. The various forms of protection may be intended to protect the product, the user, or both.

Safety Inspections

Most manufacturers work diligently to verify product safety through quality control checks during the manufacturing process. In addition, certain laws establish safety standards for some products. Special governmental agencies may be involved in setting and enforcing safety standards for some products. For example, the National Highway Traffic Safety Administration (NHTSA) regulates safety standards for automobiles. Automobile manufacturers must meet minimum safety standards before their products are sold. The safety features of products may influence consumer buying decisions.

Packaging

Packaging protects products until customers are ready to use them. Some items, such as fresh food products, require special packaging to keep them fresh and healthful. Packaging also contains information about the product, such as contents, nutritional information, and weight.

Niloo/Shutterstock.com

Packaging is particularly important for items that can spoil.

Some packaging contains safety precautions and directions to prevent injury to the user. Special governmental agencies may be involved in packaging standards for some products.

Warranties and Guarantees

A **warranty** is a written document that states the quality of a product with a promise to correct certain problems that might occur. The warranty promises that the manufacturer will replace or repair faulty items. A **guarantee** is a promise that a product has a certain quality or will perform in a specific way. A guarantee is similar to a warranty, but is not a written document. The term *guarantee* is usually used in promotions, such as "Satisfaction guaranteed or your money back."

Maintenance and Repair Services

Complex machinery, vehicles, and other equipment often require regular maintenance to remain in safe, working order. The availability and cost of maintenance and repair services can affect consumer buying decisions.

Consumers in the B2B and B2C markets may make purchases based on services available from the vendor.

Product Mix

A **product mix** is all the goods and services that a business sells. Some businesses sell only a few products, while others may offer thousands of different products. Usually, the product mix consists of goods and services that relate to each other in some way. For example, the product mix for a bicycle store may include bicycle equipment and clothing, in addition to bicycles.

Retail businesses generally organize products into product lines. A **product line** is a group of closely related products within the product mix. For example, a sporting goods store may sell several different lines of tennis racquets, such as children and adult sizes. The **product width** is the number of product lines a company offers.

pio3/Shutterstock.com

Athletic shoes are a product line within the product mix at sporting goods stores.

You Do the Math   Functions

A function involves relating an input to an output. Each value in a discrete function is one of a specified set. For example, the number of children in a family must be a whole number, so the function for how many children are in a family is a discrete function. The values in a continuous function do not have to be one of a specific set. For example, the average age of students in a class does not need to be a whole number, so the function for average age is a continuous function.

Solve the following problems.

1. The sales tax in a particular town. Is this a discrete or continuous function?
2. The average age of a business's training staff. Is this a discrete or continuous function?
3. The speed at which a delivery truck travels. Is this a discrete or continuous function?

A **product item** is the specific model, color, or size of products in a line. For example, the product items in a sporting goods store include the different styles, colors, and sizes of athletic shoes. Perhaps the store has five identical, size-ten running shoes. They are not considered different items, but the quantity (five) of one item (size-ten running shoes). **Product depth** is the number of product items within a product line.

Product planning is the process of deciding which products will appeal to the target market. These decisions are made with the target customer profile in mind. Product planning helps marketers make decisions on how to distinguish their products from others.

Consumer Products

In the B2C market, *consumer products* are those sold to consumers for their personal use. The three basic categories of consumer products are convenience goods, shopping goods, and specialty goods, as shown in Figure 11-1.

- *Convenience goods* are goods that are bought often and with little effort. These goods are typically for immediate use. Convenience goods include most grocery items and gasoline.

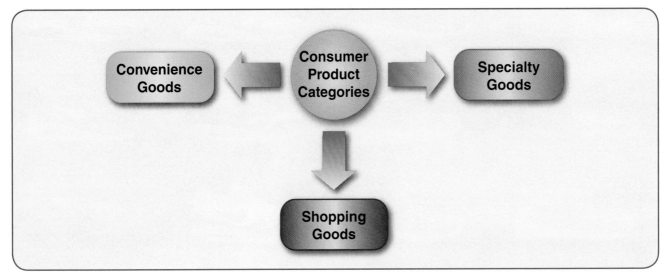

Goodheart-Willcox Publisher

Figure 11-1 The categories of consumer products are marketed specifically to consumers for their personal use.

Dmitry Kalinovsky/Shutterstock.com

Consumers usually research features and compare prices before purchasing shopping goods, such as home appliances.

- *Shopping goods* are goods usually purchased after making the effort to compare price, quality, and style in more than one store. Shopping goods are purchased less often than convenience goods. They include more expensive, durable items, such as appliances and furniture.

- *Specialty goods* are unique items that consumers are willing to spend considerable time, effort, and money to buy. Examples of specialty products include unique sports cars and rare antiques.

The product mix for consumers has to be broad enough to meet their needs and wants. Otherwise, customers will go elsewhere to shop.

Business Products

In the B2B market, *business products* are items sold to businesses for use in their operations. The target markets for business products are based primarily on the business type and how the products are used. Business products tend to fall into one of six categories: raw materials, process materials, component parts, major equipment, office equipment and supplies, and business services.

- *Raw materials* are natural or man-made materials that become part of a manufactured product. Raw materials include wood, plastic pellets, metal, and other substances. They are sold to various manufacturers for different uses.

- *Process materials* are used in product manufacturing, but are not identifiable. Examples of process materials include food preservatives and industrial glue. These are sold to different product manufacturers.

- *Component parts* become a part of a finished product, but are already assembled. Component parts are items like computer chips, tires, and switches. They are sold to companies that produce final products, such as car and computer manufacturers.

- *Major equipment* is large machines and other equipment used for production purposes, such as furnaces, cranes, and conveyors.

Serg64/Shutterstock.com

Office supplies are an example of products sold by a business to other businesses for use in their daily operations.

Every size and type of manufacturing company needs different equipment.

- *Office equipment and supplies* are products for basic office needs. These products may include computers, calculators, paper, pens, and other office items. Every type of business needs these products.

- *Business services* are the tasks necessary to keep a business running. Examples of business services include building maintenance, equipment repair, and accounting.

The needs of an organization are the primary motivating force of B2B buying decisions. If the product mix is not adequate, the business will be taken to a competitor.

Section 11.1 Review

 Check Your Understanding

1. In what four ways are services different from goods?
2. List the three categories of product elements.
3. Explain the three general quality levels of products.
4. List the three basic categories of consumer products.
5. What are the six categories of business products?

 Build Your Vocabulary

As you progress through this course, develop a personal glossary of key terms. This will help you build your vocabulary and prepare you for a career. Write a definition for each of the following terms and add it to your personal glossary.

intangible	guarantee
inseparable	product mix
variable	product line
perishable	product width
feature	product item
quality	product depth
packaging	product planning
warranty	

Price

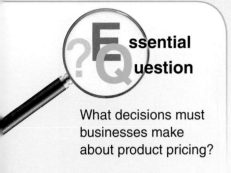

Objectives

After completing this section, you will be able to:

- **Explain** price as one of the four Ps of marketing.
- **Describe** pricing strategies.
- **Identify** unfair pricing practices.
- **Discuss** governmental price controls.

Key Terms

price
value proposition
list price
selling price
manufacturer's suggested retail price (MSRP)

pricing objective
break-even point
markup
base price
psychological pricing
bait and switch
price discrimination

deceptive pricing
predatory pricing
loss leader
price gouging
price ceiling
price floor

Price

Price is the amount of money requested or exchanged for a product. Price is an important element of the marketing mix. Every business faces the challenge of correctly pricing goods and services. The price of a good and service must:

- cover the costs of producing and selling the product
- generate the desired level of profit for the business
- be what customers are willing to pay for the product

As a function of marketing, businesses use price to establish and communicate the value of products. *Value* is the relative worth of something to a person. Some businesses use price to influence customer perception.

The **value proposition** is an explanation of the value of a certain product over others that are similar. Customers may be willing to pay more if they believe in the value of the goods or service. Individual customers often place different values on the same product.

Most businesses have several tiers, or levels, of pricing. The **list price** of a product is the established price printed in a catalog, on a price tag, or on a price list. The list price does not include any discounts. The **selling price** is the actual price a customer pays for a product after any discounts or coupons are deducted.

Another type of price is the MSRP, which is often associated with car buying. The **manufacturer's suggested retail price (MSRP)** is the price recommended by the manufacturer. Some retailers use the MSRP as the list price. However, retailers do not have to sell items at the MSRP.

Tupungato/Shutterstock.com

Pricing can convey value in the minds of consumer. This is especially true for luxury items.

Pricing Objectives

The price of a product plays a major role in determining whether the product and the company are successful. For that reason, it is important that companies set pricing objectives. **Pricing objectives** are goals defined in the business and marketing plans for the overall pricing policies of the company. Pricing objectives may be based on both the short- and long-term goals of a company. The price must be at a level that encourages customers to purchase the product, but also generates profits for the business.

Typical pricing objectives are to maximize sales or maximize profit. *Maximizing sales* is a pricing objective based on offering the lowest price possible to get the largest number of customers to buy the product. *Maximizing profit* is a pricing objective that aims to generate as much revenue as possible in relation to total cost. A marketer charges the highest price a customer will pay before deciding that the price exceeds the value for customers.

Price Factors

Many factors influence the price of a product. Factors include company goals, expenses, customer perception, competition, supply and demand, economic conditions, and product life cycle.

bikeriderlondon/Shutterstock.com

To maximize profit, marketers charge the highest price customers will pay.

Ethics

Going out of Business Sale

A going out of business sale must be actual sales because the business is closing. It is unethical for a retailer to advertise a going out of business sale as an advertising scheme to lure customers into the business.

Company Goals

Prices must be consistent with the overall company goals. The image a company projects is, in part, determined by the prices it charges. High prices tend to create an image of high-end products. Low prices often create an image of discount products.

Expenses

All products have expenses related to their creation and distribution. These costs influence the price of the product. The price must consider the cost to make the product, as well as the profit to be gained.

Customer Perception

Customers often perceive price as an indicator of the value or quality of a product. Sometimes, customers believe that a high price means a better-quality product. However, if the price of a product is too high, customers may not buy it. Their perception of the product is that it is not worth the money.

Competition

If a business suddenly lowers its prices, that could mean trouble for the competition. *Price competition* is competing on the basis of price alone. *Nonprice competition* is having a competitive advantage based on factors other than price. Nonprice competition is often used to build brand loyalty. If customers prefer a brand, they are not easily influenced to buy another brand because of a lower price.

Supply and Demand

The law of supply and demand is tied directly to price. When demand is high and the supply is low, businesses usually raise prices. Customers are willing to pay higher prices for products they really want. When demand is low and supply is high, businesses usually cut prices to increase sales. Customers are often willing to buy more of a product when the price is low. However, for some products, demand is not affected by price.

Economic Conditions

Economic conditions change. One day the economy seems stable. The next day the stock market may fall and the economy takes a turn for the worse. Business cycles affect the prices of many products. Prices tend to rise during good economic times, or expansion. Prices tend to fall during bad economic times, or recession. When demand falls, prices also typically fall.

Product Life Cycle

Product life cycle is the stages a product goes through from its beginning to end.

Ariwasabi/Shutterstock.com

If a product is priced too high, customers may choose not to make a purchase.

The product lifecycle is shown in Figure 11-2. The stage of a product within the product life cycle affects pricing strategies.

- In the *introduction stage*, the price of a brand new product is often high. The business aims to recover some of the new product development costs. The company may be the only one making the new product, so the supply is low and demand may be high.

Other times, new products are introduced at low prices to encourage customers to make a purchase and generate demand.

- During the *growth stage*, more competitors enter the market and the price of high-priced new products usually falls. This is particularly true for technology products.
- During the *maturity stage*, the sales and price of products are stable.
- During the *decline stage*, some products are eliminated. The price is often significantly reduced to quickly sell the remaining products in inventory.

The product life cycle does not have a specific time frame. Some products are short-lived but others, like Levi's® jeans, are sold for many years.

Pricing Product

The *selling price* is the amount a customer pays for an item. In order to set a selling price that generates profits, the costs of creating the product have to be considered. All products have

studiog/Shutterstock.com

Typewriters are an example of a product that was eliminated at the end of its life cycle to make way for new technology.

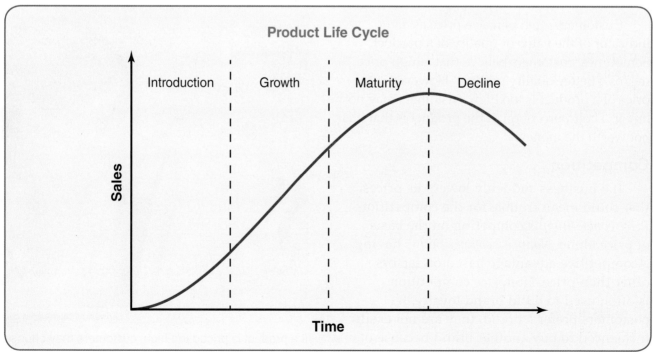

Goodheart-Willcox Publisher

Figure 11-2 The product life cycle is based on the overall industry sales of a product over time.

costs related to creating and delivering them to the end user. For manufacturers, the selling price must cover the cost of making the goods and marketing them to customers. For retailers, the price must cover the cost of buying the goods and reselling them to consumers. Operating expenses, which include wages and utilities, are included in the cost of the product.

A product starts making profit after reaching the **break-even point**, or the point at which revenue from sales equals the costs. The break-even point is often explained as cost of the items that is necessary to recover the money spent to create or buy them. At this point, the company is not losing or making money, it is breaking even. Any revenue made from sales after the break-even point is profit.

To arrive at a selling price, a business starts with a break-even price for an item. Then, the markup is added. **Markup** is the amount added to the cost to determine the selling price. Using a *percentage markup* is the most common way to determine a markup. Management decides the percent of profit necessary for each item. The percentage markup for each product is turned into a dollar figure and added to the cost.

$$\text{cost} \times \text{markup \%} = \text{markup \$}$$
$$\text{cost} + \text{markup \$} = \text{price}$$

The selling price is sometimes known as the base price. The **base price** of a product is the general price at which the company expects to sell the product. This is the price that is typically used before any discounts are given to the customer. In order to be competitive, businesses may adjust this base price to sell to consumers.

The last step in pricing products is to select the pricing tactic that will work best for the product. Businesses typically use one or more of the psychological- or discount-pricing tactics, depending on the situation or product type.

Psychological Pricing

Psychological pricing strategies are pricing techniques that create an image of a product and entice customers to buy. The following are some common B2C psychological pricing techniques.

- *Odd pricing* sets the prices to end in an odd number, such as 5 or 9. Prices such as $9.99 or $99.95 convey the perception of a bargain. Discount-store prices and sale items usually end in odd numbers.

- *Even pricing* sets the prices to end in an even number, most often 0. Prices might be set at $40, $100, or $14,000. Even pricing conveys quality.

- *Prestige pricing* sets prices high to convey quality and status. Customers see a higher price and think the product is better than lower-priced competing products.

- *Price lining* sets various prices for the same type of product to indicate different levels of quality.

- *Buy one, get one (BOGO) pricing* gives customers a free or reduced-price item when another is purchased at full price. The BOGO technique conveys savings and value.

- *Bundling* combines two or more services or products for one price. Bundling can reduce the overall price when compared to buying the items separately.

Tupungato/Shutterstock.com

Some stores use BOGO pricing to attract customers to make purchases.

Goodheart-Willcox Publisher

Figure 11-3 These discount pricing strategies are popular in the B2B market.

Discount Pricing

In retail businesses, when items are discounted from the list price, they are *on sale*. Marketers for companies that sell to other businesses (B2B) use different discount pricing strategies as pricing techniques. As shown in Figure 11-3, the most popular B2B discount pricing strategies marketers use are cash discounts, promotional discounts, quantity discounts, seasonal discounts, and trade discounts.

Cash Discount

A *cash discount* is usually a percentage deducted from the total invoice amount. It is offered to encourage a customer to pay a bill early. A cash discount often shows up in a format similar to *2/10, net 30*. The *2* reflects the percentage off the invoice total. The *10* indicates the number of days the customer has to pay the bill in order to receive the discount. The *30* stands for the number of days the customer has to pay the bill without receiving a penalty. This discount would be read, "2 percent off if paid within 10 days, otherwise the entire bill is due in 30 days." Cash discounts encourage customers to pay bills early, which also helps the cash flow of the business.

Promotional Discount

A *promotional discount* is given to businesses that agree to advertise or promote a manufacturer's product. The discount may be a dollar amount or a percentage of the product order. When you see a product advertised in an ad sponsored by

a manufacturer, the retail store probably got a promotional discount on that product.

Quantity Discount

A *quantity discount* offers a reduced per-item price for larger numbers of an item purchased. Many companies offer a quantity discount as an incentive for buying more products. The more a customer buys, the more money is saved on each item.

Seasonal Discount

If retailers buy goods well in advance of the season, they are often given a *seasonal discount*. Seasonal discounts help manufacturers plan production and reduce inventories.

wavebreakmedia/Shutterstock.com

Manufacturers and other companies that sell to businesses use various B2B discount pricing strategies.

Trade Discount

A *trade discount* is not really a discount. It is actually the way that manufacturers quote prices to wholesalers and retailers. Some manufacturers suggest retail prices for their products (MSRP). The MSRP is often used as a list price. The manufacturer then offers the wholesaler or retailer a percentage off the list price. A trade discount may be 20 percent or more off the list price.

Unfair Pricing Practices

Both businesses and consumers are affected by unfair and unethical pricing practices. Businesses that use unfair pricing practices are breaking laws in addition to being unethical. The following pricing practices are both harmful to consumers and illegal.

- **Bait and switch** is the practice of advertising one product with the intent of persuading customers to buy a more expensive item when they arrive in the store.

- *Price fixing* is when a group of competitors get together and set the price for a specific product, which is usually high.

- **Price discrimination** occurs when a company sells the same product to different customers at different prices based on personal characteristics of the customers.

- **Deceptive pricing** is the illegal pricing of products in a way that intentionally misleads customers.

- **Predatory pricing** is the practice of setting very low prices to remove competition. Some foreign companies price their products below the same domestic products to drive the domestic companies out of business.

Some US states have laws against several additional pricing practices. However, there are no federal laws banning these practices, so they are enforced on the state level. Businesses must be aware of the pricing laws in the state in which they operate.

Twenty-two US states have *sales-below-cost (SBC) laws* that ban loss-leader pricing. A **loss leader** is pricing an item much lower than the current market price or the cost of acquiring the product. The purpose of loss leaders is to draw customers into a business by advertising a product for a very low price. The business hopes that once in the store, consumers will buy enough other products to make up for the lost profit. Some state laws consider loss-leader pricing to be a predatory and misleading pricing practice.

Thirty-four US states have laws that protect consumers from price gouging practices. **Price gouging** is the raising of prices on certain kinds of goods to an excessively high level during an emergency. The state laws consider price gouging a form of price fixing.

There are state and federal laws that regulate pricing to prevent unfair pricing policies and practices used by some businesses. The government also prevents the formation of monopolies, which interfere with the workings of a market economy. Recall that a monopoly

Valkar/Shutterstock.com

Businesses must be aware of the wording in their advertisements to avoid intentionally misleading customers.

controls the market for a single product and can set whatever price it wants. As a result, a monopoly usually sets unfair high prices that hurt consumers. Specific laws that regulate or affect pricing are shown in Figure 11-4.

Governmental Price Controls

The government may intervene in the pricing of some products to control the economy or help consumers. Price controls are often set when the public becomes alarmed about a fast-growing rate of inflation. Most economists believe price controls can help suppliers and/or consumers in certain circumstances.

However, there are times when price controls can actually lead to the problems the government is trying to solve.

The government may set maximum prices called **price ceilings** for certain goods and services that it thinks are being priced too high. The government may believe that consumers need some help to purchase the products. Price ceilings on some products may be set during war times when shortages can drive prices unreasonably high. However, price ceilings can also cause the very shortages the government is trying to prevent. Existing businesses or producers must accept the lower price set by the government for their goods or services, which may cause many to leave the business.

Laws That Regulate Pricing	
Law	**What it Regulates**
Sherman Antitrust Act (1890)	This law regulates price-fixing.
Clayton Antitrust Act (1914)	Passed in 1914, this law makes price discrimination illegal.
Robinson-Patman Act (1936)	This law strengthened the Clayton Act by specifically prohibiting a seller from charging different prices to different customers for the same product and the same quantity.
Wheeler Lea Act (1938)	This law prohibits deceptive advertising of prices. Companies cannot advertise that their prices are lower unless they can prove it. They cannot advertise lowered prices unless the original price was higher. Also, list prices cannot be used in reference to a sale price unless the product was actually sold at the list price.
Unit-Pricing Laws	These laws vary from state to state. Retailers must display pricing that shows the price of an item per unit. Most packaged items are priced per package, which makes it hard to compare the prices of certain items.
Minimum Price Laws or Sales-Below-Cost Laws	These laws vary from state to state. Retailers cannot sell a product for less than its cost.
Federal Trade Commission Price Advertising Guidelines	These FTC guidelines prohibit any deceptive or bait-and-switch advertising.

Goodheart-Willcox Publisher

Figure 11-4 The federal government passed a number of laws to prevent monopolies and promote fair price competition.

Price floors are minimum prices set by the government for certain goods and services that it thinks are being priced too low. Price floors are set to help the producers. However, if the price floor is set higher than the market price, a surplus will develop. A surplus happens because consumers will not buy the higher-priced products. In many cases, a surplus situation also forces the government to buy the excess inventory to prevent rampant waste.

Section 11.2 Review

 Check Your Understanding

1. Identify seven factors that influence the price of a product.
2. What is the formula for calculating a percentage markup?
3. Give examples of pricing strategies used for the B2B market.
4. What is the purpose of loss-leader pricing?
5. How can a price floor cause a surplus?

 Build Your Vocabulary

As you progress through this course, develop a personal glossary of key terms. This will help you build your vocabulary and prepare you for a career. Write a definition for each of the following terms and add it to your personal glossary.

price
value proposition
list price
selling price
manufacturer's suggested
    retail price (MSRP)
pricing objectives
break-even point
markup
base price

psychological pricing
bait and switch
price discrimination
deceptive pricing
predatory pricing
loss leader
price gouging
price ceiling
price floor

Distribution

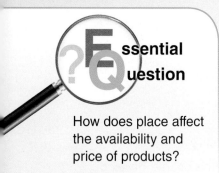

Essential Question

How does place affect the availability and price of products?

Objectives

After completing this section, you will be able to:

- **Define** place as one of the four Ps of marketing.
- **Explain** distribution as an important element of place.

Key Terms

supply chain
channel of
  distribution
direct channel
indirect channel

nonstore retailer
e-tailer
multi-channel
  retailer
trade industry

bulk-breaking
freight forwarder
transportation
pipeline

Place

Place is one of the four Ps of marketing. *Place* refers to the activities involved in getting a product to the end user. It involves determining when, where, and how products get to customers. Place is also known as *distribution*.

A **supply chain** is the businesses, people, and activities involved in turning raw materials into products and delivering them to end users. The supply chain includes producers, intermediaries, and service businesses.

A major part in the decision of place is selecting the channel of distribution. A **channel of distribution** is the *path* that goods take through the supply chain. A **direct channel** is the path of selling goods or services directly from a manufacturer to end users without using intermediaries. An **indirect channel** uses intermediaries to get the product from the manufacturer to the end users. Examples of direct and indirect channels of distribution are illustrated in Figure 11-5.

Producers

Producers are businesses that create goods and services. Producers provide a specific role in the economy. In order for business to meet consumer needs and wants, producers are needed to create the end product. This industry produces three basic types of product: natural resources, agricultural products, and finished goods.

Natural Resources

Natural resources, such as timber, water, or minerals, are one type of product produced by the industry. Natural resources are also called *raw materials*. *Extractors* are businesses or people that take natural resources from the land.

Agricultural Products

Farmers raise crops and livestock that are sold to end users, such as consumers. These products may also be used by manufacturers to create other products.

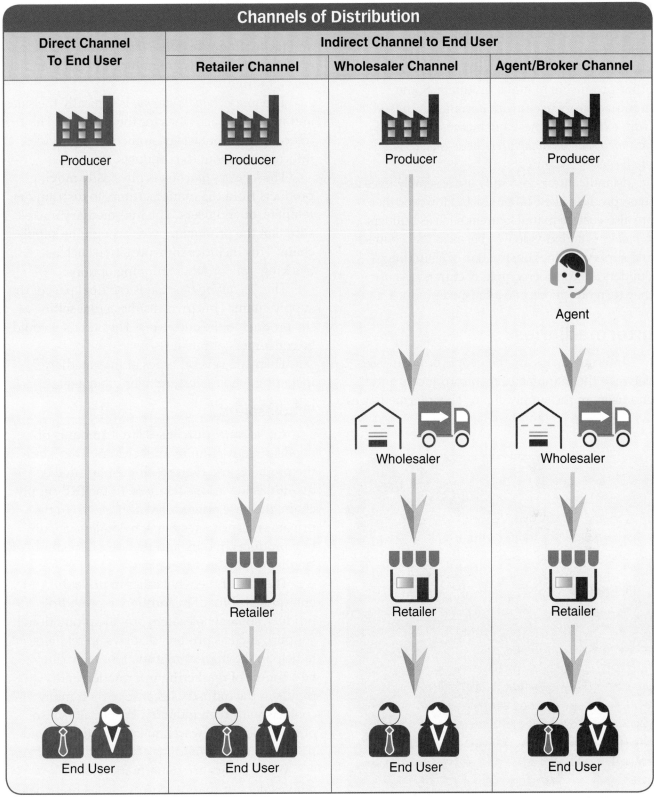

Figure 11-5 Depending on the number of intermediaries used, the channel of distribution may be very short (direct) or long (indirect).

Finished Goods

Finished goods are another type of product created by producers. *Manufacturers* are businesses that use supplies from other producers to make products. Some manufacturers use raw materials purchased from extractors. These businesses are called *raw-materials manufacturers* or *raw-materials producers*.

Manufacturers generally use assembly lines to mass produce identical products. However, there are also custom manufacturers, such as builders. A *builder* is an individual or business that contracts and supervises the construction of a building. Builders are considered manufacturers because they turn raw goods into a finished product.

Intermediaries

Intermediaries are the people or businesses between the manufacturers or producers and the end users in the supply chain. The intermediaries are also called *channel members*. Intermediaries serve three functions: transactional, logistical, and facilitating functions. These functions help make sure the goods are in the right place and at the right time.

The *transactional function* is typically the sales and marketing activities for the business. The intermediary contacts customers and provides information about the products.

The *logistics function* is physically moving products from the manufacturers to distributors, retailers, or end users. The intermediary makes sure that the product moves through the supply chain. This includes transportation such as trucking, rail, or other shipping options.

The *facilitating function* is the final part of the supply chain. This involves the actual selling of the product to the end users. The end user could be consumers or businesses.

There are several types of intermediaries, including wholesalers, retailers, and agents.

Wholesalers

A *wholesaler* purchases large amounts of goods directly from manufacturers. They store the products and then resell them in smaller quantities to various retailers. In the B2B supply chain, they are often called *distributors*. In the private enterprise system, wholesalers usually buy products in bulk and then resell them in smaller quantities to retailers.

The role of the wholesaler in private enterprise is broad. In addition to providing product, some wholesalers provide promotional support, such as product displays, to retailers to help in the marketing function. They can be a source of marketing information and trends in the industry because of their many contacts within an industry. Wholesalers also offer services like warehousing, or storage, and transportation of goods.

Wholesalers are usually merchant wholesalers or manufacturer's sales branches. Merchant wholesalers own the merchandise that they sell. They are sometimes called *drop shippers* because they ship the merchandise directly to the retailer to sell to customers. *Rack jobbers* provide full service to the retailer

Alexander Raths/Shutterstock.com

Agricultural products may be used by manufacturers to create other products.

Intermediaries provide the logistics function of moving products from the producer to the distributors.

and set up racks, maintain stock, and other activities. They bill the retailer only for the items that are sold.

Manufacturer's sales branches are similar to factory outlets. The manufacturer sells the merchandise directly to the customers.

Retailers

A *retailer* is a business that buys products from wholesalers or directly from producers, and sells them to consumers to make a profit. Retailers play multiple roles in the private enterprise system. Primarily, retailers directly provide consumers with the products that meet their needs and wants. Other functions they perform include promotion, offering credit, and handling returns. On a larger scale, retailers provide employment in communities and contribute to local economies.

Many retailers have physical brick-and-mortar stores, but some do not. A **nonstore retailer** is a business that sells directly to consumers in ways that do not involve a physical store location. Nonstore retail businesses include catalog sales, direct sales, and e-tailers.

Catalog sales generally use direct mailings. Retail businesses mail product catalogs to customers, who can then shop from the comfort of their home or office. *Direct sales retailers* have sales representatives who approach customers outside of a fixed location. The sales representatives sell products to customers either in their homes or by telephone. For many years, businesses like Avon and Tupperware have sold products in this manner. Direct sales companies also sell products through their websites.

Retailers are also considered intermediaries in the supply chain. They typically buy products from wholesalers then sell to consumers.

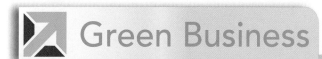

Green Business   Lightbulbs

Switching from traditional 60-watt incandescent lightbulbs to new energy-efficient lightbulbs can save a business a lot of money. Two lightbulbs commonly used in place of the traditional incandescent lightbulb are the 15-watt compact fluorescent lamp (CFL) and the 12-watt light emitting diode (LED).

CFLs can save up to 75 percent of the energy used by an incandescent lightbulb. Regular lightbulbs last around 1,000 hours, while CFLs can last up to 10,000 hours—ten times longer. LEDs can save up to 80 percent of the energy used by a regular lightbulb, and last up to 25,000 hours. Using one of these alternative lightbulbs can save a lot of money over time. Not only will there be money saved on energy costs, but because they last longer, they do not need to be replaced as often. However, CFLs can contain mercury, so they must be recycled properly.

E-tailers are retailers that sell products through websites. **Multi-channel retailers** are those that sell products through both brick-and-mortar stores and online sites.

Agents

Agents bring buyers and sellers together. They buy and sell goods for a commission and never take direct ownership of the products. An agent is someone working on the behalf of another party. Agents are also known as *brokers*. An agent may be hired by either the buyer or the seller. The goal of this intermediary is to create a favorable exchange for both buyer and seller.

Twin Design/Shutterstock.com

Amazon is an example of a retailer that sells through its website.

Agents can be used anywhere in the supply-chain process. They are especially useful in facilitating international trade.

Service Businesses

A *service business* earns profits by providing consumers with services that meet their needs and wants. Service businesses do not sell goods. These businesses perform activities and provide expertise for their customers. Examples of service businesses include travel agencies, law firms, and interior design firms.

Trade industries are another example of a service business. The **trade industry** provides labor based on specialized knowledge and skills. Trade laborers provide services in many different business activities and include electricians, plumbers, carpenters, welders, mechanics, and many others.

Functions of Distribution

Physical distribution is one of the most important parts of place. The selling function helps to transfer ownership to the end user. However, the physical distribution actually gives the end user possession of the goods. Physical distribution also plays a competitive role in product promotion. It makes products available where needed, correctly fills orders, and provides on-time delivery.

Patryk Kosmider/Shutterstock.com

Bulk breaking is a service provided by intermediaries. They buy goods in bulk and break them into smaller quantities to sell to distributors.

Distribution influences the final price of a product and affects company profitability. Distribution strategies include decisions about transportation, storage, and utility costs. The goal is to provide the best distribution services for the lowest cost. Efficient distribution services help to keep the customer prices lower. Examples of distribution services are bulk breaking, freight forwarding, and transportation.

Bulk-Breaking

Breaking bulk is one service that intermediaries can provide. **Bulk-breaking** is the process of separating a large quantity of goods into smaller quantities for resale. An intermediary buys goods in bulk and then breaks the bulk into smaller quantities of goods. For example, it is easier and cheaper to ship a bushel of apples rather than 100 separate apples. The grocery store buys apples by the bushel and then sells them to customers a few at a time.

Freight Forwarder

Intermediaries may also provide the services of freight forwarders. A **freight forwarder** is a company that organizes shipments. It is not a shipper or carrier; it functions as an agent. Freight forwarders generally combine shipments from various companies. They combine the shipments and hire a transportation company to move them as one large shipment. By putting these smaller shipments together, money is saved for the companies shipping the goods.

gpointstudio/Shutterstock.com

The trade industry provides many valuable services needed by consumers.

Transportation

Transportation is the physical movement of products through the channel of distribution. Transportation decisions impact the price of a product and the length of time it takes to reach the end user. The cost of transportation can add up to 10 percent to the price of a product.

Each type of transportation has different costs, efficiencies, and time constraints. For example, a less expensive and slower mode of transportation may be fine to ship large quantities of durable products. However, when shipping perishable goods, a more expensive, faster mode of transportation may be necessary.

There are six main methods of transportation as shown in Figure 11-6. These transportation methods are road, rail, air, water, pipeline, and digital.

- *Road transportation* includes any motor vehicle that moves products on highways and roads. Vehicles used are trucks, buses, vans, and automobiles. According to the US Department of Transportation, trucking is the most common method of distribution in the United States.

Transportation Modes for Distribution		
Transportation Mode	**Advantages**	**Disadvantages**
Road	• Can deliver door to door • Flexible schedules • Can be modified for specific cargo (i.e., refrigerator trucks)	• Weather delays • Traffic delays • Maintenance problems
Rail	• Send large quantities over long distances • Inexpensive • Can carry trucks closer to the destination • Can be modified for cargo (flatbed railcars for intermodal containers)	• Slower method of transportation • Minimal destination flexibility • Needs a second mode of transportation to get to final destination
Air	• Fastest mode of transportation • Less chance of damage to items • Can save on warehousing as products arrive as needed	• Most expensive • Weather delays • Maintenance problems • Needs a second mode of transportation to get to final destination
Water	• Send large quantities over long distances • Can be modified for cargo (i.e., tankers for oil) • Inexpensive	• Slowest method • No destination flexibility • Needs a second mode of transportation to get to final destination
Pipeline	• Not subject to weather delays • Fewer maintenance issues • Low operating costs	• Can only carry products that flow (i.e., gasoline) • Expensive to build • Leaks linked to environmental damage • Needs a second mode of transportation to get to final destination
Digital	• Low to no operating cost • Easy access • Very fast delivery	• Only for electronic goods or services

Goodheart-Willcox Publisher; Source: US Census Statistical Abstract

Figure 11-6 There are pros and cons for each method of transportation.

- *Rail transportation* is the second most often used mode of transportation in the United States, based on findings from the US Department of Transportation. Rail transportation is one of the least expensive modes of transportation and is good for long-distance shipping of large, bulky items.

- *Air transportation* is the most expensive method of transporting products. High-value, low-weight items are often shipped by air.

- *Water transportation* includes ocean-going ships, inland ships, and coastal ships. *Ocean-going ships* transport products across the ocean, normally between countries. *Inland ships* use rivers and lakes to transport products. *Coastal ships* move products up and down the coastline of a country.

- A **pipeline** is a line of connected pipes that are used for carrying liquids and gases over a long distance. Products carried through pipelines move slowly, but continuously.

- *Digital transportation* is used to download books and music onto digital devices. Products can be shipped instantly after an order is placed.

Physical distribution involves responsibilities associated with the transfer of ownership of products from the producer to the end user. The original owner is at the beginning of the distribution channel. The final owner is the end user at the end of the distribution channel.

When ownership is transferred to intermediaries in the distribution channel, each one assumes the risk and responsibility for the product. The new owner is the one who will suffer any loss if the product is damaged or lost. For that reason, producers must use caution when hiring intermediaries to transport their products to the end user.

Vytautas Kielaitis/Shutterstock.com

DHL is a worldwide provider of transportation for both land and air.

Section 11.3 Review

 ### Check Your Understanding

1. List three basic types of product that come from producers.
2. Describe the three functions of intermediaries.
3. Identify examples of wholesalers.
4. What is the goal of distribution?
5. What are the six main methods for the transportation of goods?

 ### Build Your Vocabulary

As you progress through this course, develop a personal glossary of key terms. This will help you build your vocabulary and prepare you for a career. Write a definition for each of the following terms and add it to your personal glossary.

supply chain	multi-channel retailer
channel of distribution	trade industry
direct channel	bulk-breaking
indirect channel	freight forwarder
nonstore retailer	transportation
e-tailer	pipeline

Review and Assessment

Chapter Summary

Section 11.1 Product

- A product is what a business sells to satisfy customer needs and is one of the four Ps. Products can be goods or services. Goods are physical items that can be touched. Services are intangible, inseparable, variable, and perishable.

- All products have certain elements that can be changed to meet customer needs: features, usage, and protection. Understanding these elements can enable a business to more effectively fulfill the marketing concept of attaining customer satisfaction.

- A product mix is all the goods and services that a business sells. Products are organized into product lines and further organized by product item, width, and depth. The products offered vary depending on whether the target market is consumers or businesses.

Section 11.2 Price

- Price is one of the four Ps of marketing. It is the amount of money requested or exchanged for a product. As a function of marketing, businesses use price to establish and communicate the value of products. In addition, the price must be at a level that encourages customers to purchase the product, but also generates profits for the business.

- All products have costs related to creating and delivering them to the end user. Businesses calculate their break-even price for a product and then apply a markup to determine the selling price.

- Both businesses and consumers are affected by unfair and unethical pricing practices. Common unfair pricing practices include bait and switch, price fixing, price discrimination, deceptive pricing, and predatory pricing. There are state and federal laws that regulate pricing to prevent unfair pricing policies and practices used by some businesses.

- The government may intervene in the pricing of some products to control the economy or help consumers. Price controls are often set when the public becomes alarmed about a fast-growing rate of inflation. Price controls may be a price ceiling, which sets the maximum price of a product, or a price floor, which sets the minimum price of a product.

Section 11.3 Distribution

- *Place*, also known as *distribution*, refers to the activities involved in getting goods or services to the end user. Place is one of the four Ps of marketing and involves determining when, where, and how products get to customers. The path that products take to customers is known as the channel of distribution.

- Physical distribution is one of the most important parts of place. Distribution influences the final price of the product and company profitability. Distribution strategies include decisions about transportation, storage, and utility costs. The goal is to provide the best distribution services for the lowest cost.

Online Activities

Complete the following activities to help you learn, practice, and expand your knowledge and skills.

 Posttest. Now that you have finished the chapter, see what you learned by taking the chapter posttest.

 Vocabulary. Practice vocabulary for this chapter using the e-flash cards, matching activity, and vocabulary game until you are able to recognize their meanings.

Review Your Knowledge

1. Explain product as one of the four Ps of marketing.
2. Describe the product mix for consumer products and for business products.
3. Explain price as one of the four Ps of marketing.
4. Describe popular B2B discount pricing strategies.
5. Identify five unfair pricing practices.
6. How can price ceilings and price floors create negative outcomes?
7. Explain *place* as one of the four Ps of marketing.
8. What is the role of wholesalers in a private enterprise system?
9. Explain the role of retailers in a private enterprise system.
10. Explain the activities and decisions involved in distribution.

Apply Your Knowledge

1. In the private enterprise system, retailers directly provide consumers with the products that meet their needs and wants. List four types of retailers and an example of each. Describe the consumer needs and wants met by each of the retailers identified.
2. Customers often perceive price as an indicator of the value or quality of a product. Make a list of five products for which price affects your perception of value. Give your opinion of each product compared to competing products. Explain how price is a factor in your perception of each product.
3. Describe examples of psychological pricing strategies you have seen in the B2C market. Do you think these strategies are effective? Which do you think is most effective in your market? Explain your answers.

4. The supply chain includes producers, intermediaries, and service businesses. A channel of distribution is the path that goods take through the supply chain. Choose a product that you purchase regularly. Create a flowchart that identifies each business, person, and activity involved in the process of making the product and getting it to you.

5. What are trade industries? Give examples of businesses in the trade industry. How do trade industries participate in providing place?

Communication Skills

College and Career Readiness

Speaking. Participate actively and effectively in a one-on-one oral communication with a classmate about the importance of the product mix for a business. Prepare for the conversation by creating notes that outline your opinions.

Writing. Create a Venn diagram to show the relationships between pricing factors and pricing objectives. Where do the circles overlap? What do you think this overlap signifies?

Reading. There are many new vocabulary terms in this chapter that relate to marketing. Make a list of the terms and the words that are italicized. Use reference guides to confirm the meanings of new words or concepts.

Internet Research

Product Life Cycle. Fashion, entertainment, and electronics trends change regularly. Businesses watch these trends in an effort to determine the demand of products. Choose a product that was once popular but has fallen out of demand. Examples include the Tickle Me Elmo Doll, portable CD players, and shoes with built-in wheels. Once you have selected a product, research its life cycle. Try to determine when each stage began and ended and what may have caused the product to become obsolete. Create a chart showing each stage of the cycle with corresponding dates.

Teamwork

With a partner, research the price of a gallon of gasoline, a gallon of milk, a movie ticket for an adult, and a loaf of bread over the course of the last 15 years. Create a chart depicting the rise or fall in these prices. Determine what factors may have caused these changes. Predict how the prices may change over the next five years. Present your findings to the class.

Portfolio Development

College and Career Readiness

Schoolwork. Academic information is important to include in a portfolio in order to show your accomplishments in school. Include items related to your schoolwork that support your portfolio objective. These items might be report cards, transcripts, or honor roll reports. Diplomas or certificates that show courses or programs you completed should also be included. Other information can be included as a list, such as relevant classes you have taken.

1. Create a Microsoft Word document that lists notable classes you have taken and activities you have completed. Use the heading "Schoolwork" on the document along with your name.

2. Scan hard copy documents related to your schoolwork, such as report cards, to serve as samples. Place each document in an appropriate folder.

3. Place the hard copy documents in the container for future reference.

4. Update your spreadsheet.

CTSOs

Public Speaking. Public speaking is a competitive event you might enter with your Career and Technical Student Organization (CTSO). This event allows you to showcase your communication skills of speaking, organizing, and making an oral presentation. This is usually a timed event you can prepare for before the competition. You will have time to research, prepare, and practice before going to the competition. Review the specific guidelines and rules for this event for direction as to topics and props you will be allowed to use.

To prepare for a public speaking event, complete the following activities.

1. Read the guidelines provided by your organization. Review the topics from which you may choose to make a speech.

2. Locate a rubric or scoring sheet for the event on your organization's website.

3. Confirm whether visual aids may be used in the presentation and the amount of setup time permitted.

4. Review the rules to confirm if questions will be asked or if you will need to defend a case or situation.

5. Make notes on index cards about important points to remember. Use these notes to study. You may also be able to use these notes during the event.

6. Practice the presentation. You should introduce yourself, review the topic that is being presented, defend the topic, and conclude with a summary.

7. After the practice presentation is complete, ask for feedback from your instructor. You may consider also having a student audience listen and give feedback.

Promotion

Exploring Careers

Promotions Manager

A business must be able to let the public know what products it offers. Companies rely on promotional managers to increase public awareness of their goods and services. Promotions managers plan and coordinate advertising programs, events, and promotional materials. They also organize contests and other events to help make people aware of a company's goods and services.

Typical job titles for this position include *advertising manager*, *promotions and advertising manager*, and *advertising sales manager*. Examples of tasks that advertising and promotions managers perform include:

- plan advertising and promotional campaigns to increase product awareness

- review and approve layouts and advertising copy

- coordinate a campaign team to meet the company's campaign goals

- prepare and monitor advertising and promotion budgets

Promotions manager positions typically require a bachelor degree. Many require experience in advertising or promotions techniques. A basic knowledge of sales and marketing principles, including strategies and tactics for creating interest in a company's goods or services, is also needed.

Reading Prep

Skim the Review Your Knowledge questions at the end of the chapter. Use them to help you focus on the most important concepts as you read the chapter.

College and Career Readiness

Check Your Business IQ

Before you begin the chapter, see what you already know about business by taking the chapter pretest. The pretest is available at www.g-wlearning.com.

Section 12.1

Role of Promotion

?**E**ssential **Q**uestion

What role do promotion strategies play in marketing?

Objectives

After completing this section, you will be able to:

- **Explain** promotion as one of the four Ps of marketing.
- **Explain** the promotional mix.
- **Define** the concept of integrated marketing communications.

Key Terms

promotion
product promotion
institutional
  promotion
persuasion
communication
  process
sender
encoding
channel

receiver
decoding
feedback
promotional mix
advertising
visual
  merchandising
storefront
marquee
public relations (PR)

press release
integrated marketing
  communications
  (IMC)
promotional
  campaign
electronic promotion
participatory
  marketing
AIDA

Promotion Strategies

Promotion is the process of communicating with potential customers in an effort to influence their buying behavior. It is one of the four Ps of marketing, which are product, place, price, and promotion. Promotion includes making people aware about the price of a product and where it is offered.

A **product promotion** is promoting specific products, as shown in Figure 12-1. In contrast, an **institutional promotion** focuses on promoting the company rather than its products. These promotions are designed to create a favorable view of the brand and increase awareness, as shown in Figure 12-2.

Without promotion, customers would not have information about a company or product. It would be difficult for them to make purchases that meet their needs and wants in an efficient manner.

Promotion has definite goals—it is used to inform, persuade, or remind the audience of a message.

A message that *informs* is one that provides information or education. Promotions that inform tell people something they want or need to know. Brochures, ads, e-mails, and catalogs make customers aware of the latest offerings.

A message that *persuades* is one that attempts to change the behavior of the receiver. **Persuasion** uses logic to change a belief or get people to take a certain action. A car advertisement is an example of a message that attempts to persuade the receiver to buy a car. Marketing communication attempts to persuade and change behavior through messages.

Messages that *remind* are those appearing in multiple places over a period of time. The first few times a person sees the message, they may not remember it. Reminder messages repeat

Product Promotion

Goodheart-Willcox Publisher

Figure 12-1 A product promotion makes people aware of a specific product.

Institutional Promotion

Goodheart-Willcox Publisher

Figure 12-2 An institutional promotion promotes the company and the brand.

information that was given earlier. For example, many of the same television commercials are repeated during a single program. Repeating the commercials provides reminder messages.

Marketing uses the communication process to create clear promotional messages for the customer. The **communication process** is a series of actions on the part of the sender and the receiver of a message and the path the message follows. The six elements of the process are the sender, message, channel, receiver, translation, and feedback, as shown in Figure 12-3.

- The person who has a message to communicate is called the **sender**.

- The sender creates the *message*, which is the information to be conveyed. **Encoding** is the process of turning the idea for a message into symbols that can be communicated.

- The **channel** is how the message is transmitted, such as face-to-face conversation, telephone, text, or another method that is appropriate for the situation.

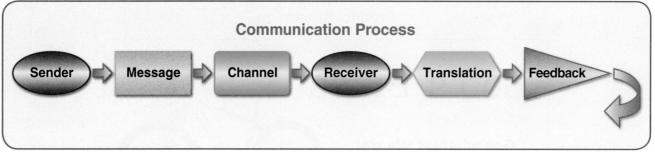

Communication Process

Sender → Message → Channel → Receiver → Translation → Feedback

Figure 12-3 Marketers use the communication process to create messages for the customer.

- The **receiver** is the person who reads, hears, or sees the message.

- Once the message is received, it is decoded. **Decoding** is the translation of a message into terms that the receiver can understand.

- **Feedback** is the receiver's response to the sender and concludes the communication process.

Marketers must consider each step in the communication process when developing a promotion. Understanding the elements of the communication process helps in creating and effectively communicating promotional messages.

Promotional Mix

There are many ways to promote a business or its products. The **promotional mix** is a combination of the elements used in a promotional campaign. Common elements in a promotional mix include advertising, sales promotion, public relations, and personal selling, as shown in Figure 12-4.

Advertising

Advertising is any nonpersonal communication paid for by an identified sponsor. Advertising is a key component of a promotional campaign. Ads provide the features and benefits about a product, including the price, description, and other information that gets reader attention. Effective advertising is aimed at the *target market*, or people

most likely to buy the product. Traditional advertising includes print and broadcast media.

Print media is one of the most effective forms of advertising. It includes all tangible promotional messages. Newspapers, magazines, directories, direct mailings, and outdoor signage are print media. Print also includes *transit promotion*, which is advertising found on public transportation, such as city buses, or in public transportation areas.

Broadcast media includes television and radio. Radio and television ads, known as *commercials*, reach a large number of people daily.

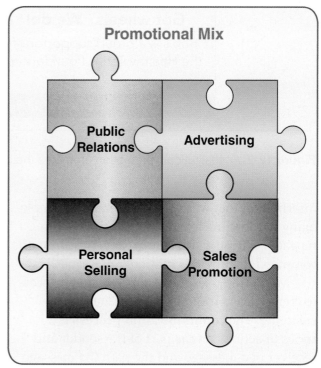

Promotional Mix

Public Relations — Advertising — Personal Selling — Sales Promotion

Figure 12-4 The combination of the elements in a promotional campaign makes up the promotional mix.

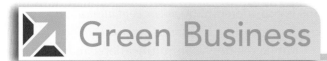

Green Business   Digital Coupons

Many businesses offer convenient digital coupons that are sent directly to customers through e-mail, text messages, or QR codes. Digital coupons eliminate the costs and resources involved in printing and physically distributing coupons. The customer simply presents the coupon or QR code on the screen of their smartphone or tablet device to receive the discount or special offer. Some customer loyalty cards can store digital coupons. When the customer's loyalty card is scanned, any digital coupons loaded onto the card are applied to the total purchase. Digital coupons are a convenient and green solution that benefits both customers and businesses.

These also include infomercials. *Infomercials* are paid product demonstrations that are generally longer in length than typical commercials.

Sales Promotions

Marketers create sales promotions to encourage customers to buy a product as soon as possible. A sales promotion can include coupons, rebates, samples, loyalty programs, contests and sweepstakes, and trade shows. Promotional items, such as water bottles and pens, are sometimes used. Each item has the company information on it so customers think of the company when the items are used. These are also called *marketing premiums* or *specialty media*.

Retailers use visual merchandising as a form of sales promotion. **Visual merchandising** is the process of creating floor plans, displays, and fixtures to attract customer attention and encourage purchases. *Point of purchase (POP) displays* are often used in visual merchandising. Examples of POP displays are the impulse items that are conveniently located at the checkout counter.

The storefront of a business is an important element of visual merchandising. The **storefront** is the store exterior that reflects the image

Leonard Zhukovsky/Shutterstock.com

Advertising on public transportation is an example of transit promotion.

of the business. It is often the first image or impression a customer has of a business. The storefront of a business may be enhanced by a **marquee**, which is an overhanging structure containing a sign at the entrance of the store.

Public Relations (PR)

Public relations (PR) is applying communication skills that promote goodwill between a business and the public. Unlike advertising, public relations is unpaid media coverage.

A press release is an example of public relations communication. A **press release** is a story featuring useful company information written by the company PR contact. Press releases are sent to the public through social media or other forms of mass communication. In some situations, an official representative of the company may hold a press conference and deliver the information in the form of a formal speech. A *formal speech* is a speech that is scripted. The speaker follows the narrative provided by the communications department of the company.

This is considered to be *public communication*, which is speaking to a large group.

Public relations communication can be either proactive or reactive. *Proactive public relations* is when the company presents itself in a positive manner to build an image. Companies issue PR communications to explain their contributions to the community, environment, and other socially responsible activities. *Reactive public relations* is used to counteract a negative public perception about the company. Negative media publicity can be generated for any number of reasons. When negative messages arise, a business must sometimes take action to reestablish the positive image of the company.

Personal Selling

Personal selling is any direct contact between a salesperson and a customer. While the other pieces of the promotional mix are important, most customers prefer personal contact. Personal selling may include formal product demonstration or impromptu speaking about a product. *Impromptu speaking* is talking without advanced notice to plan what will be said.

Nagel Photography/Shutterstock.com

The marquee is an important element of visual merchandising.

Experienced salespeople know their product well and are prepared to provide information and answer customer questions. Chapter 13 covers personal selling in greater detail.

Integrated Marketing Communications

Integrated marketing communications (IMC) is a promotional strategy that combines the elements of the promotional mix to create a unified marketing message. All of the pieces of the promotional mix do not need to be used at one time. However, when multiple components are used, each must complement the other to effectively convey a clear and consistent message. All of the promotional elements used should present a unified image about the product or business.

The coordination of marketing communications to achieve a specific goal is a **promotional campaign**. It is also called a *promotional plan*. Included in the plan is a detailed list of goals, dates, and other activities that are carefully researched and documented. This serves as a guideline to make sure that the business can reach its goals effectively.

A component of the promotional plan is electronic promotion. **Electronic promotion** is any promotion that uses the Internet, e-mail, or other digital technology. It is also called *digital marketing*. Social media is an important part of digital marketing.

Participatory marketing is a promotion strategy that uses multiple elements to communicate and interact with customers. It is also referred to as *engagement marketing*. It requires the strategy of communicating *with* customers rather than communicating *at* customers. This strategy works on the premise that many customers will participate in marketing activities when they think they will benefit. Contests, free samples, and an opportunity to voice an opinion are examples of ways in which customers can participate in marketing activities. Twitter, Facebook, and Instagram are some of the digital vehicles used by marketers to encourage customers to participate virtually.

Promotional plans are designed to encourage customers to buy. Each element of the promotional mix is focused on attracting customer attention, interest, desire, and action. The acronym for these activities is called **AIDA**, which is shown in Figure 12-5.

- *Attention.* Getting customers to look at the product or promotion is the first step in the AIDA process. The design or sound elements used should gain the attention of viewers and listeners. Customers should know exactly what the business offers.

- *Interest.* Customers must be interested in the business or product to make a purchase. The promotion should identify the features and benefits most important to the customers. It should show that the business is interested in the specific needs of customers.

- *Desire.* The promotion should encourage customers to sample, use, or touch the product. This persuades customers to experience and want it.

- *Action.* It should be convenient for customers to buy. The promotion should explain exactly how, where, and when the product can be bought.

AIDA integrates the different elements of the promotional mix. Following the AIDA model helps marketers focus and create effective promotional messages.

wavebreakmedia/Shutterstock.com

IMC requires careful planning to create a unified marketing message.

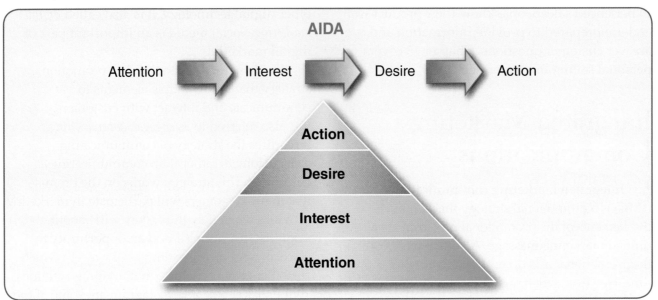

Goodheart-Willcox Publisher

Figure 12-5 AIDA is a four-step process that can help a promotional campaign reach its target audience.

Section 12.1 Review

 Check Your Understanding

1. What are the six elements of the communication process?
2. What are common elements in the promotional mix?
3. Give examples of print media advertising.
4. Explain the importance of a business storefront as an element of visual merchandising.
5. Explain the role of participation as a key element of marketing.

 Build Your Vocabulary

As you progress through this course, develop a personal glossary of key terms. This will help you build your vocabulary and prepare you for a career. Write a definition for each of the following terms and add it to your personal glossary.

promotion
product promotion
institutional promotion
persuasion
communication process
sender
encoding
channel
receiver
decoding
feedback
promotional mix

advertising
visual merchandising
storefront
marquee
public relations (PR)
press release
integrated marketing
    communications (IMC)
promotional campaign
electronic promotion
participatory marketing
AIDA

Advertising

How can a marketer develop an effective advertisement?

Objectives

After completing this section, you will be able to:

- **Explain** how to create an effective advertising campaign.
- **Describe** four elements of an advertisement.
- **Explain** how advertising benefits society.

Key Terms 🔗

advertising campaign
unique selling
   proposition
   (USP)
metrics
creative plan
headline
hook

copy
brand name
logo
tagline
action word
typography
typeface
weight

environmental print
art
layout
white space
signature
Advertising
   Self-Regulatory
   Council (ASRC)

Advertising Campaigns

Advertising is one element of the promotional mix. *Advertising* is any nonpersonal communication paid for by an identified sponsor. A message is relayed to anyone who sees or hears the message. Advertising is everywhere people look—on streets, computers, phones, television, and radio. Advertising can change beliefs and attitudes about products and help people make buying decisions. It may create positive or negative feelings about a product or a company. The main purpose of advertising is to *persuade* receivers to buy a product or accept an idea. It can also *inform* customers about goods and services and *remind* them to take action.

An **advertising campaign** is a coordinated series of linked ads with a single idea or theme.

An advertising campaign is one piece of the overall promotional campaign. Depending on the product and the target market, some types of media may be more appropriate for advertising than others. There is no one medium or mix of media that is the best to use for all advertising situations. Figure 12-6 shows the steps for creating successful advertising campaigns.

Establish Goals

The goals for an advertising campaign should be clearly defined. The goals should be specific and measurable. This enables the business to know if the campaign was effective. For example, campaign goals might include a specific sales goal or to increase brand awareness by 10 percent.

Steps for Creating an Advertising Campaign
1. Set campaign goals.
2. Identify the target audience.
3. Establish the budget.
4. Select the media.
5. Create the message.
6. Establish the metrics.
7. Analyze the results.

Goodheart-Willcox Publisher

Figure 12-6 Carefully following each step in creating an advertising campaign helps ensure success.

Identify the Audience

It is important to identify the target audience for the product or message. The target market will help determine the message and the appropriate media for the advertising campaign.

Establish the Budget

The ad campaign budget must be established before media is chosen. Advertising dollars are just one part of the promotional budget. It is important to be clear on the amount allocated for advertising in particular.

Select the Media

An important step in planning the ad campaign is selecting the appropriate media. The media will depend on the message and the target market. Selection must be carefully made to choose the media that will best communicate the message and reach the audience.

Write the Message

Effective campaigns deliver a marketing message that is valuable to the customer. The unique selling proposition (USP) should be at the heart of the campaign. The **unique selling proposition (USP)** is a statement summarizing the features and benefits of the company or product, how it differs from the competition, and how it is better than the competition. For

example, price, features, benefits, new items, store location, hours, and sale pricing are often included in advertising.

Accuracy is important in communication that goes to the public from an organization. Errors, such as misrepresenting a product or misquoting a price, can cause negative public relations for a business. Grammatical errors, such as misspelling, improper capitalization, and punctuation errors, also negatively affect the public's perception of a business. All communication should be scrutinized for correctness before it is conveyed to an audience. A proofreading process should be in place to verify that the message is accurate and effective.

Establish the Metrics

Metrics are standards of measurement. Metrics are created to track and evaluate promotion activities. Depending on the activity,

lev radin/Shutterstock.com

Mascots are one way marketers advertise a product or brand.

the metrics used to measure success will differ. Sometimes it is easy to tie sales directly to a promotion by using coupons or quick response (QR) codes. Marketers choose the best metrics based on the campaign goals.

Analyze the Results

Once the campaign is complete, the results are evaluated based on the established metrics. If the campaign meets the set metrics, it is considered successful. If it does not meet the established metrics, the results are evaluated and corrections are noted for the next campaign. The evaluation process can be extensive. Marketing promotions are expensive and it is important that dollars are spent wisely to meet the goals of the campaign.

Creating an Advertisement

Creating an advertisement is similar to other business functions. The first step is planning. A **creative plan** outlines the goals, primary message, budget, and target market for different ad campaigns. After the planning process is complete, the advertisement message can be created. The classic structure for an ad has four elements: headline, copy, graphics, and the signature, as shown in Figure 12-7.

Diego Cervo/Shutterstock.com

All advertising pieces should be proofread for effectiveness as well as accuracy.

Headline

A **headline** consists of the words designed to grab attention so viewers will read the rest of the ad. Headlines usually appear in large type or have some other attention-getting graphic element. A general rule recommends that headlines have no more than seven words. Subheadings may also be used.

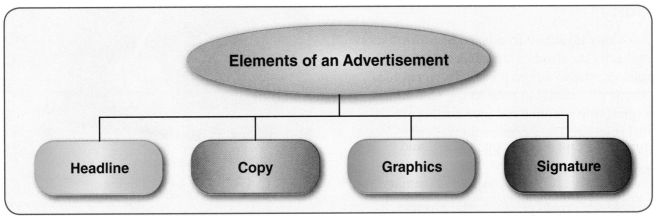

Goodheart-Willcox Publisher

Figure 12-7 While each advertisement is different, most contain a general set of elements.

You Do the Math

Communication and Representation

It is not usually the case that a problem needing to be solved mathematically is presented in the "language" of math. Usually, you will need to look at the problem and identify the mathematical concepts present. Then, determine an appropriate mathematical expression to solve the problem.

Solve the following problems.

1. While driving his route the first day of his six-day workweek, Henry noticed that he filled the gas tank twice, once with 8.3 gallons and once with 7.9 gallons. The total cost of these two fill-ups was $61.24. He also had to pay $7.40 in tolls that day. How much petty cash should Henry request for the rest of the week?

2. A shipping carton contains 28 books. The dimensions of the shipping carton are 11 inches by 17 inches by 16 inches. The weight of the carton is 12.6 pounds, and a palette can hold a maximum of 150 pounds. How many cartons of books can be placed on the palette?

3. A supervisor notices that six workers have created 748 items before lunch on Monday. The order for 12,000 items must be filled by the end of the day on Friday. How many temporary workers must be hired to complete all the items for the order?

The headline uses words to call attention to the ad, much like a lure on a fishing hook. The goal is that by reading the headline, a person is hooked into reading the rest of the ad. In fact, the aspect of an ad that grabs attention is often called the **hook**. Research shows that over 80 percent of readers only read headlines. Because of this, many advertisers think the headline is the most important part of the ad.

The headline and body copy should work together. The headline attracts attention, while the body copy presents the selling message.

Copy

Copy is ad text that provides information and sells the product. In advertising, copy refers to the words in the ad. The term *body copy* is often used to refer to the words that explain the product and give additional information. The person who writes advertising copy, including the headlines, is called a *copywriter*.

Body copy should be brief and clearly give people reasons to purchase the product. It should provide information needed to locate the product and make the buying decision.

Dragon Images/Shutterstock.com

Copywriters are skilled at writing information for advertising purposes.

Gil C/Shutterstock.com

Colorful type is used to create a simple but effective logo that identifies the eBay brand.

Effective advertising copy should do the following:

- create intrigue
- appeal to the senses
- sound newsworthy
- use action words
- meet goals

The brand name should be used in the copy. A **brand name** is the name given to a product consisting of words, numbers, or letters that can be read or spoken. The **logo**, which is a picture, design, or graphic image that represents the brand, may also be used. In addition, taglines are generally part of the copy. A **tagline**, or *slogan*, is a phrase or sentence that summarizes an essential part of the product or business.

When writing copy, the *four Cs of communication* should be applied: clarity, conciseness, courtesy, and correctness. Each line should be proofread and checked for correct grammar, vocabulary, and punctuation. Communication that contains typographical errors or poor language usage negatively reflects on both the copywriter and the business.

Create Intrigue

Copywriters use words to arouse interest, curiosity, and desire. Words like *new, hottest, free, limited offer, sale, bonus,* and *special offer* may be intriguing to readers.

Appeal to the Senses

It is hard to make products seem real on a printed page. Copywriters use descriptive words so the reader can almost see, hear, taste, feel, or smell the product.

Sound Newsworthy

Stating the *who, what, when, where, why,* and *how* of a product can make the copy sound newsworthy. Include information such as statistics, performance results, case histories, comments from satisfied customers, and quotes from experts.

Use Action Words

Action words are verbs that tell the readers what to do. These call-to-action words include *save, join, get, buy, come in, visit, call, e-mail,* and *register,* to name a few. They are joined by adverbs suggesting when or how to act, such as *now, toll-free,* and *today.*

ducu59us/Shutterstock.com

A well-written advertisement includes a call to action that encourages readers to respond to the message.

Meet Goals

Copy should be proofread to evaluate the effectiveness of the message. If the goal has not been accomplished, the material should be rewritten. Advertisements must be 100 percent accurate. The final pages should be proofread to make sure that names are accurate, all words are spelled correctly, and no errors exist. Copy that is incorrect can permanently damage the reputation of a business or organization.

Graphics

Graphics provide visual interest. The graphics are often the first part of the ad a reader notices, especially when colorful or unusual. Graphics include typography, art, and layout.

Typography

Typography is the visual aspect of the words printed on a page. Typography includes decisions about typeface, size, and weight.

- **Typeface** is a particular style for the printed letters of the alphabet, punctuation, and numbers. There are hundreds of typefaces from which to choose.

- Letter size can vary from small to very large. Larger letters have more emphasis. Headlines are usually larger than body copy. Letter size is used to make some words stand out and to emphasize the key ideas.

- In typography, **weight** refers to the thickness and slant of the letters. There are three weights: regular, *italic*, and **bold**. Size and weight are both used to make some words more prominent. Headlines are usually bold and appear in the largest size.

Color may also impact headlines and advertising copy. White or yellow letters on a dark background can make the words stand out. Words in red also pop on a printed page. Blue is often used to attract attention, has a serious look, and suggests reliability.

Designers pay close attention to environmental print. **Environmental print** is print that appears in everyday life. Letters, numbers, and symbols that appear in advertising encourage readers to interact with or respond to the print they see in their surroundings. Environmental print, such as the sign at Target stores, can be the first encounter a young child or person from another country has with English. Selecting the correct typography is an important design consideration.

Rob Hainer/Shutterstock.com

The Toys R Us sign is an example of environmental print in which type, symbols, and color are used in a strategic manner.

Alfie Photography/Shutterstock.com

The advertising message on promotional items should be consistent with the brand.

Art

Art is all of the elements that illustrate the message of an ad. Art includes drawings, photographs, charts, and graphs. Logos, shapes behind print, and abstract images or designs are also considered art. The art used in advertising should be consistent with the brand. In fact, art sometimes helps to define a brand if it is used properly.

A product photograph is the most common type of advertising art. Grocery, fashion, and automobile ads use product photos to make products look attractive. Businesses that sell services also use art to convey the idea of the service. Photos may also show people using the service.

Most people are attracted to photos of other people, particularly children. Celebrities, such as sports figures and actors, are often used in advertising because they are well-known. Shocking, surprising, or amazing art may also be used as a hook. Well-executed drawings are often as effective as photographs.

Layout

Layout is the arrangement of the headline, copy, and art on a page. An ad may have a great headline and fascinating art. However, if they are not placed attractively on the page, the ad might be ineffective.

One of the most useful layout tools is white space. White space is the blank areas on a page where there is no art or copy. White space acts as a frame for the message. It can also separate the parts of an ad so they stand out. Ads with little white space appear cluttered and are hard to read. Graphic designers must create ads that are easy to read so the message will be received.

Signature

The signature identifies the person or company paying for the ad. Signatures usually include the company name and logo. It may also include the company slogan or tagline. An ad signature completes an advertisement much like a signature ends a letter. It may also include location and contact information, such as website, phone number, and street address.

Benefits of Advertising on Society

While advertising clearly benefits business, it also can benefit society. Advertising can:

- help increase employment, which generates sales for businesses
- stimulate competition among businesses so they offer the best products at the lowest prices

Ethics

Advertised Merchandise

It is a deceptive practice for a business to advertise merchandise that it does not have available in its store. Advertising merchandise to draw customers into the store without sufficient stock or a plan to fulfill the consumer's request for merchandise is unethical.

- encourage consumers to seek a higher standard of living

- speed up the acceptance of new products

- inform consumers and businesses about product choices

- provide revenue to pay for broadcast programming and print vehicles

- help people learn about health and social issues

Advertisers have legal and ethical obligations to consumers and business customers. They are responsible for providing honest, accurate information.

Laws and Regulations

Many laws govern the advertising industry. Some of these laws established federal agencies that monitor the actions of advertisers. These agencies also enforce the laws and regulations. The main regulatory agency is the Federal Trade Commission (FTC). Other agencies that regulate advertising include the Food and Drug Administration (FDA) and the Federal Communications Commission (FCC). The US Patent and Trademark Office and the Library of Congress monitor certain advertising and licensing rules. It is the responsibility of marketers to know and follow the laws and regulations for their businesses.

Self-Regulation

Most industries self-regulate advertising in addition to following the law. The advertising industry, however, leads the way in self-regulation. It has many organizations dedicated to monitoring advertising practices. The **Advertising Self-Regulatory Council (ASRC)** establishes the policies and procedures for advertising self-regulation.

The *Better Business Bureau (BBB)* promotes fair advertising and selling practices across all industries. Local BBBs are found in most large cities. They keep records of all advertising and selling complaints. The Council of Better Business Bureaus reviews complaints and recommends solutions.

Associations within the advertising industry also have codes of ethics and standards of practice to monitor member advertising practices. The American Association of Advertising Agencies and the American Advertising Federation work to maintain high advertising standards. The various media outlets also have advertising standards. Each newspaper and magazine sets standards for the kind of advertising it will accept. The network television stations have some of the strictest advertising standards. These standards change over time to reflect changes in public viewpoints.

Ethics

Even with federal laws in place, advertisers have a great deal of freedom. *Ethics* are rules of behavior based on ideas about what is right and wrong. Advertising ethics follow the rules of truth and accuracy at all times.

Sometimes it is hard to tell what is ethical. A company may learn it has behaved unethically only after the public reacts to its advertising. For example, it is legal for a lumber company to advertise home-repair services after a natural disaster. However, the company should be careful *not* to give the impression it is using the disaster for gain.

Gil C/Shutterstock.com

The Better Business Bureau is a reliable source of consumer information and assistance.

Social Responsibility

Social responsibility is behaving with sensitivity to social, environmental, and economic issues. A business also has a duty to help others and to improve society in general. For example, Toms Shoes supports a One for One® program. For each product purchased, Toms makes a donation to help a person in need. One of the company's goals is to improve lives around the world.

Several national professional organizations in the advertising industry work with advertisers to assist them in helping their communities. Some of these organizations include the Ad Council, American Association of Advertising Agencies, and American Advertising Federation. Through these organizations, advertisers donate time and money to civic events and community projects. They often create professional ads and commercials free of charge for these events.

rnl/Shutterstock.com

Slogans, or taglines, can become an important and memorable element of a public service advertising campaign.

Section 12.2 Review

 Check Your Understanding

1. List examples of unique selling propositions often included in advertising.
2. Why is accuracy important in advertising?
3. What are five expectations of effective advertising copy?
4. What is the function of white space in layout?
5. Identify five federal agencies or offices that are involved in advertising laws and regulations.

 Build Your Vocabulary

As you progress through this course, develop a personal glossary of key terms. This will help you build your vocabulary and prepare you for a career. Write a definition for each of the following terms and add it to your personal glossary.

advertising campaign
unique selling
   proposition (USP)
metrics
creative plan
headline
hook
copy
brand name
logo
tagline
action word

typography
typeface
weight
environmental print
art
layout
white space
signature
Advertising
   Self-Regulatory
   Council (ASRC)

Review and Assessment

Chapter Summary

Section 12.1 Role of Promotion

- Promotion is the process of communicating with potential customers in an effort to influence their buying behavior. It is one of the four Ps of marketing and includes making people aware about the price and place of a product and where it is offered. Promotion is used to inform, persuade, or remind the audience of a message through use of the communication process.

- The promotional mix combines all the elements used in a promotional campaign. It includes advertising, sales promotion, public relations, and personal selling. The mix of promotional elements helps a business reach its target market and business goals.

- Integrated marketing communications (IMC) combines the elements of the promotional mix to create one unified marketing message. A promotional plan is a part of the IMC and is the coordination of marketing communications to achieve a specific goal. Understanding the AIDA customer buying process model helps to develop an effective promotional plan.

Section 12.2 Advertising

- An advertising campaign is a coordinated series of linked ads with a single idea or theme. The steps for creating a successful advertising campaign are: establish goals, identify the audience, establish the budget, select the media, write the message, establish the metrics, and analyze the results.

- A creative plan outlines the goals, primary message, budget, and target market for different ad campaigns. The four elements of the classic structure for an advertisement include the headline, copy, graphics, and signature.

- Advertising benefits society, as well as business. It can help increase employment, stimulate competition, and encourage a higher standard of living. Society is protected by laws and regulations that monitor and control the actions of advertisers.

Online Activities

Complete the following activities to help you learn, practice, and expand your knowledge and skills.

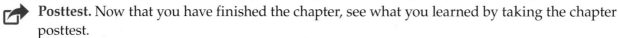

Posttest. Now that you have finished the chapter, see what you learned by taking the chapter posttest.

Vocabulary. Practice vocabulary for this chapter using the e-flash cards, matching activity, and vocabulary game until you are able to recognize their meanings.

Review Your Knowledge

1. Explain promotion as one of the four Ps of marketing.
2. Describe each of the elements of the communication process.
3. Differentiate between proactive public relations and reactive public relations.
4. Describe the concept of integrated marketing communications.
5. How does AIDA apply to the promotional mix?
6. What are the steps for creating an advertising campaign?
7. Why is it important to identify the target audience of an advertising campaign?
8. Describe the four elements of the classic structure of an advertisement.
9. How does the advertising industry self-regulate?
10. Explain how advertising can benefit society.

Apply Your Knowledge

1. List three examples of institutional advertising you have seen in the media. For each example, identify:
   - where you saw the ad
   - the related company or business
   - the message of the ad
   - if the ad was effective
2. Describe an infomercial you have seen on television. What did the infomercial do to grab viewer attention? Explain how infomercials influence or persuade viewers.
3. Advertising is considered negative by some individuals. However, others think advertising is beneficial for the consumer. Make a list of the pros and cons of advertising that you have observed. After you have completed the lists, write a sentence that supports your viewpoint, whether positive or negative, of advertising.
4. Name a store that you frequently visit and know well. Select one department in the store. Recall the visual merchandising strategies used to create a positive shopping experience. Describe the techniques used and indicate if they are effective or ineffective. Are there certain aspects of being in the store that make you want to return?
5. Create a new ad idea for a product with which you are familiar. Create a catchy headline, ad copy, sketch any graphics, and include the signature in the ad. Proofread your ad for correct and appropriate information, as well as grammar and spelling. What is the unique selling proposition (USP) at the heart of the ad? How is your ad different or better than existing ads for the product?

Communication Skills

College and Career Readiness

Speaking. Rhetoric is the study of writing or speaking as a way of communicating information or persuading someone. It is important to be prepared when you are speaking to an individual or to an audience. Style and content influence how the listener understands your message. Make an informal presentation to your class about the importance of integrated marketing communication.

Reading. Analyze the quality of the information presented in this chapter about creating advertisements. Is the information coherent? Is concrete evidence presented? Report your opinion to the class.

Writing. Revision is the key to effective writing. Select a product for which you will write a promotional message. Decide if the message will inform, persuade, or remind the audience. Write the first draft of the message. Refine and organize the message so it flows logically. Ask a classmate to review your work and help you use language in a more effective and precise manner.

Internet Research

Ad Performance. Analyzing the performance of an advertising campaign is an important task for businesses. Marketing dollars must be spent wisely and contribute to the overall sales performance of a company. There are many metrics that are used to analyze the effectiveness of promotions for a business. Using the Internet, research ways to analyze advertising campaigns. List and describe three different effective methods of analyzing ad performance.

Teamwork

Working as a team, research a popular promotion that was widely publicized. Within your group, discuss what made this promotion popular. Delegate one person to record the group's collective ideas. Next, select a promotion that was poorly received. Compare and contrast the two campaigns. Why do you think one was well received and the other was not? Be prepared to share with the class.

Portfolio Development

College and Career Readiness

Skills and Talents. Include samples of your work that show your skills or talents. Look at past school or work assignments you have completed. Include a research paper, letter, electronic slide show, or other items that illustrate your business communication skills. Select a book report, essay, poem, or other work that demonstrates your writing talents. Look for projects that show your skills related to critical thinking and problem solving. Have you completed a long or complicated project? What career area interests you most? Select completed work from classes that will help prepare you for jobs or internships in that area.

1. Create a Microsoft Word document that lists your skills and talents. Use the heading "Skills and Talents" along with your name. Next to each skill or talent listed, write a description of an assignment and explain how your skill or talent was involved in completing it.

2. Scan hard-copy documents related to your skills and talents to serve as samples. Save the documents in an appropriate folder.

3. Place the hard copies in the container for future reference.

4. Update your spreadsheet.

CTSOs

Case Study. A case study presentation may be part of a Career and Technical Student Organization (CTSO) competitive event. The activity may be a decision-making scenario for which your team will provide a solution. The presentation will be interactive with the judges.

To prepare for a case study event, complete the following activities.

1. Conduct an Internet search for *case studies.* Your team should select a case that seems appropriate to use as a practice activity. Look for a case that is no more than a page long. Read the case and discuss it with your team members. What are the important points of the case?

2. Make notes on index cards about important points to remember. Team members should exchange note cards so that each evaluates the other person's notes. Use these notes to study. You may also be able to use these notes during the event.

3. Assign each team member a role for the presentation. Ask your instructor to play the role of competition judge as your team reviews the case.

4. Each team member should introduce himself or herself, review the case, make suggestions for the case, and conclude with a summary.

5. After the presentation is complete, ask for feedback from your instructor. You may also consider having a student audience listen and give feedback.

Selling

Exploring Careers

Sales Manager

For companies that do business nationally or internationally, coordinating sales efforts is important to keep sales functions running smoothly and efficiently. These companies often divide their sales territories into regions and employ a manager to direct the activities in each region. Sales managers hire, train, and direct salespeople to meet company sales goals. They establish quotas for representatives and monitor sales potential. Sales managers also help establish inventory requirements.

Typical job titles for this position also include *director of sales*, *sales supervisor*, and *sales executive*. Examples of tasks sales managers perform include:

*   monitor customer preferences to help focus the efforts of sales representatives

*   prepare sales budgets

*   complete performance evaluations of sales representatives

*   resolve customer complaints

Sales manager jobs typically require a bachelor degree, as well as considerable experience or on-the-job training. Knowledge of selling techniques and sales principles is necessary. The ability to think critically to solve problems is also desirable.

Reading Prep

College and Career Readiness

Write all of the key terms for this chapter on a sheet of paper. Highlight the words that you do not know. Before you begin reading, look up the highlighted words in the glossary and write the definitions.

Check Your Business IQ

Before you begin the chapter, see what you already know about business by taking the chapter pretest. The pretest is available at www.g-wlearning.com.

Role of Sales

What steps do salespeople take to make a sale?

Objectives

After completing this section, you will be able to:

- **Discuss** the value of personal selling.
- **Describe** ways to prepare to sell.
- **Explain** the steps in the sales process.

Key Terms 📲

personal selling
telemarketing
call center
preapproach
feature-benefit selling
lead
cold calling

sales process
approach
service approach
greeting approach
merchandise
   approach
combination approach

substitute selling
objections
excuses
close
buying signals
overselling
suggestion selling

Personal Selling

Personal selling is direct contact with a prospective customer with the objective of selling a product. It is an important element in the promotional mix. Personal selling provides information that a marketing brochure or website cannot provide. A salesperson can persuade a customer to make a decision about how to meet a need or want. Personal contact can be important to a customer when making a buying decision.

Business-to-Business (B2B) Selling

Business-to-business selling (B2B) is a business selling to another business. B2B sales may also be called *field sales*, *industrial sales*, or *organizational sales*. Companies that sell equipment and raw

materials to manufacturers are involved in B2B sales. Manufacturers that sell finished products to retailers are involved in B2B sales.

B2B sales may include governmental and institutional sales. When a business sells to a government, it is often referred to as *governmental sales*. When a business sells to a nonprofit organization, such as a school or hospital, it is often called *institutional sales*.

There are typically two types of sales positions for B2B sales: inside salesperson and outside salesperson. An *inside salesperson* communicates with customers via phone or e-mail. An *outside salesperson* visits with the customer at his or her place of business. Some sales communication is made by phone or e-mail, but the primary contact is face-to-face and relationship selling. *Relationship selling* focuses on building long-term relationships with customers.

mangostock/Shutterstock.com

Pharmaceutical sales are an example of outside salespeople who personally visit the offices of customers.

Business-to-Consumer (B2C) Selling

Business-to-consumer (B2C) selling is selling to consumers. Retail is a typical example of business in the B2C market. Most retail sales are made by a salesperson in the place of business. However, some retail businesses conduct the selling process by telephone. **Telemarketing** is personal selling done over the telephone.

Many larger retailers have call centers for the telemarketing function. A **call center** is an office that is set up for the purpose of receiving and making customer calls for an organization. Some call centers specialize in *inbound* calls, which is when customers call into the center. For example, Lands' End is a company that sells clothing, luggage, and home products. When customers want to place a phone order for items from Lands' End, their calls go to an inbound call center.

Other call centers specialize in *outbound* calls, which is when salespeople make customer calls. For example, a newspaper might have a telemarketing call center that calls local

Blend Images/Shutterstock.com

When customers place phone orders for products from a catalog, the calls are answered by an inbound call center.

businesses to ask them to advertise in the newspaper. Many nonprofit organizations use outbound call centers to raise money for their organizations. The people who make these calls are usually called *fund-raisers*, but their tasks are very similar to a telemarketer.

The Internet can also be used for personal selling. The customer can visit a website where a salesperson interacts with the customer in real time. If the customer visits a website and does not interact with a salesperson in real time, then it is not considered to be personal-selling.

Preparing to Sell

There are specific tasks that must be completed before making contact with the customer. The **preapproach** consists of tasks that are performed before contact is made with a customer. Preapproach tasks include product training and identifying potential customers.

Product Training

Product training is the first step to prepare for personal selling. It is important that the salesperson understands the product and can answer customer questions accurately. Reviewing a competitive analysis helps the sales team understand how products compare with the competition. Product pricing is explained in product training so customer questions can be answered.

The marketing team provides catalogs, brochures, and other materials that present the features and benefits of the products. **Feature-benefit selling** is the method of showing the major selling features of a product and how it benefits the customer. This is also known as *solution selling*. It is vital that the salesperson can convey how the product satisfies the needs of customers and makes their lives better or easier.

Some products, such as financial investments, may require more formal training and certification.

Learning about the product is an important part of sales team training.

To gain this certification, accredited classes may be required at a local university. This training may take weeks or months to complete. Other types of formal training may be provided by the company in a class or workshop format. A product expert may offer classes on a product, such as a piece of equipment, so that the salesperson understands how the product works.

Informal training takes place on an individual level. Salespeople may study on their own to become familiar with the catalog, brochures, and information on the website about how to use the product. Most products are sold with printed information, such as care tags, content labels, and user manuals. Other print sources may include publications from manufacturers, consumer publications, and trade publications. Manufacturers often provide videos, booklets, and samples of their products.

Identify Potential Customers

The next step in the preapproach stage of selling is identifying potential customers. This is also called *prospecting*. Potential customers are often called **leads** or *prospects*. For a salesperson in a retail setting, the customers may walk into the store. However, salespeople who need to call on customers must start with a list of contacts.

Identifying sales leads is used most often in B2B sales. Customer leads are generated in a variety of ways. Customers visiting a trade show may ask for someone to contact them about more information. People who visit a website or call customer support may ask for a salesperson to call them. Large companies may have dedicated sales staff that generates leads. Some companies purchase names of potential sales leads. Cold calling is another way to prospect. **Cold calling** is the process of making contact with people who are not expecting a sales contact. Most often, a combination of methods is used to generate sales leads.

Once a sales lead is identified, it is important to gather additional information. Learning about the customer is called *qualifying the lead*. Both the customer's and salesperson's time is valuable. Calling on people who are not interested in buying a product is not typically a productive

use of time. It is important to know that the lead is qualified and may generate a sale.

Sales Process

The **sales process** is a series of steps that a salesperson goes through to help the customer make a satisfying buying decision. There are generally six steps in the process, as shown in Figure 13-1.

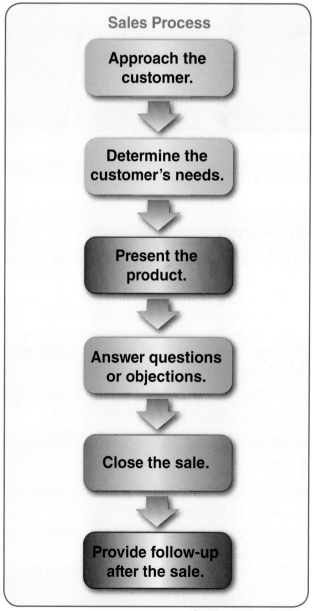

Goodheart-Willcox Publisher

Figure 13-1 Salespeople generally use six steps in helping customers make buying decisions.

Edyta Pawlowska/Shutterstock.com

When approaching a customer, business etiquette requires that the salesperson lead with a handshake.

Approach the Customer

The **approach** is the step in which the salesperson makes the first in-person contact with a potential customer. A salesperson should always lead with a handshake and an introduction. It is customary to give the customer a business card. When approaching a customer, the salesperson should always:

- be appropriately dressed
- have good posture
- smile
- have pleasant tone of voice and clear speech
- make direct eye contact
- focus on the customer

Many sales experts say that customers decide whether they want to continue working with a salesperson within four minutes. In those four minutes, a salesperson must:

- get the customer's attention
- project a positive, professional image of self and products

- show true concern and interest in the needs of the customer
- show trustworthiness and honesty
- make the customer feel comfortable

The customer's first impression of a salesperson can be critical in making the sale.

Business-to-Business (B2B)

In business-to-business sales calls, the salesperson typically makes an appointment so the customer expects the visit. It is important for the salesperson to be on time and prepared to present the product, offer brochures, and answer any questions the customer may have. B2B sales are often based on relationship selling, so it is acceptable to talk about current events or other conversation starters.

Business-to-Consumer (B2C)

B2C calls typically take place in a retail environment. Three types of approaches are often used in this setting: service approach, greeting approach, and merchandise approach.

The **service approach** starts with the phrase "May I help you?" It is the most common sales approach and works well in many situations.

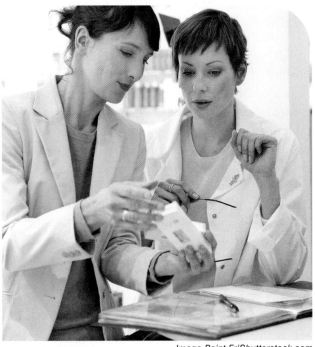

Image Point Fr/Shutterstock.com

Brochures with product descriptions are commonly offered by salespeople to potential B2B customers.

You Do the Math
Problem Solving and Reasoning

In business and at home, you may be tasked with checking the work of others. When the work includes figures, it is often a good idea to check the solution for accuracy and effectiveness. For example, a business calculates the fuel economy of its delivery truck to be 19 miles per gallon. However, the fuel used on a 20-mile delivery run is four gallons. This means that either the calculation is incorrect or the reported usage is incorrect.

Solve the following problems.

1. A business sells 387 units for an average of $27.48 each. Its reported gross sales are $10,634.78. Is the reported sales figure correct?

2. Harris drives 687 miles in 16 hours. He uses 18.5 gallons of gasoline. He states that his car gets 47 miles to the gallon. Is he correct?

3. A business spent a total of $43.87 on office supplies in one month and has decided to wait one month to pay the charge. The credit account charges 19.7 percent on outstanding balances. The business estimates the finance charge will be $2.25. Is this correct?

The **greeting approach** consists of a friendly welcome to the store or department. Words, such as "hi," "hello," or "good afternoon," should be used. A genuine smile and eye contact help make a positive impression.

With the **merchandise approach**, the conversation starts with a comment about the product. This approach works well when the salesperson takes notice of which product the customer is considering. For example, a customer in a sporting goods store is holding a running shoe. The salesperson might walk up to the customer and say, "That shoe is on sale today for half price."

A **combination approach** often works best. This approach combines the greeting and merchandise approaches. The salesperson makes the customer feel welcome and provides information that might help sell the item.

Determine the Customer Needs

The marketing concept of meeting customer needs is very important in the selling process. In a B2B selling situation, needs may be defined during the qualifying process. In a B2C selling situation, needs are usually determined during the approach. There are many reasons why customers buy a product.

- *Rational buying motives* are based on reason.

- *Emotional buying motives* are based more on feelings than reason.

- *Loyalty buying motives* are based on customer loyalty to a company with which they always do business.

There are three ways to determine customer needs and wants: observation, questioning, and listening. All three of these skills intersect, as shown in Figure 13-2.

Determining Customer Needs

Observation

Questioning   Listening

Goodheart-Willcox Publisher

Figure 13-2 Salespeople observe, question, and listen to customers to determine their needs.

Observation is the first step in learning about the customer. Much can be learned through nonverbal communication. *Nonverbal communication* is the expression or delivery of messages through actions, rather than words. This is often called *body language*. Behavior is also a part of nonverbal communication. An example of behavior is avoiding eye contact. Silence on the part of a customer is also a nonverbal cue that is related to behavior.

The goal of *questioning* is to learn about the needs and wants of different customers. A salesperson should use customer answers to determine which products to offer to satisfy those needs and wants.

Listening combines hearing with evaluating. Hearing is a physical process, while listening is an intellectual process. Active listening is fully participating while processing what other people have said.

Questioning is useless if the salesperson does not listen to the response. A salesperson must carefully listen to what the customer does and does *not* say in order to improve sales and customer satisfaction. Listening often leads to learning more information. Anything that prevents clear, effective communication is a listening barrier and must be overcome. Focus must be on the customer and distractions ignored.

michaeljung/Shutterstock.com

Listening is an important part of the selling process.

Present the Product

The product presentation stage is the heart of the sales process. This is where desire is created for the product. It is a chance to tell the customer about the product, show how that product meets needs, and answer any questions or objections. It is the main opportunity for a salesperson to influence the customer to buy the product. Making a sales presentation is similar to an actor on a stage. The performance should be professional and polished.

Select the Product

One of the keys to good selling is to select the appropriate products to show the customer. Knowing which products to show requires careful listening and extensive product knowledge on the part of the salesperson.

Substitute Sell

Sometimes, a customer may be looking for a specific brand that is not carried or is out of stock. **Substitute selling** is the technique of showing products that are different from the originally requested product. The goal is to get the customer to buy a different product that still fits the need. It is important that the customer not be pressured into buying something he or she does not really want. The customer must believe that the substitute product is acceptable and that it will satisfy the original need.

Prepare the Presentation

In B2C sales, product presentations are usually informal. For example, in a retail store, the presentation may be to show an item off a rack and give the price. For an automobile dealer, it might involve offering a test-drive and providing printed materials that describe features and benefits of the car.

In B2B sales, the salesperson often makes a formal presentation to a group of customers. A *formal presentation* is a planned speech. It may include a slide show or short video that focuses on the features and benefits of the product. Presentations using appropriate media can engage and inform the audience.

Canadapanda/Shutterstock.com

During the product presentation, a salesperson has an opportunity to influence the customer's purchase decision.

Product samples or marketing promotional items, such as branded notepads and water bottles, may be distributed. Marketing materials, like catalogs, brochures, or sales sheets, may also be given to the audience.

A presentation may include a demonstration of the product or website. Demonstrations are most effective when the customer can actually try the product. While trying out the product, customers often sell themselves on its benefits.

It is often effective to create a product display similar to, but smaller than, the one used for a trade show. Customers appreciate browsing the products offered by the company. Having the opportunity to touch the product and get a firsthand look is beneficial to the sales process.

Answer Questions or Objections

During and after the presentation, the customer should be asked for comments and questions. Customers need to know why they should buy the product. It is important to

reinforce the features and benefits of the product and how the purchase will make the individual's life easier or better.

lightpoet/Shutterstock.com

Making a formal presentation, or speech, is common when selling to a large group of customers.

Green Business   Lunch

Lunchtime is an opportunity for a business to go green. The most environmentally friendly lunch option is to encourage employees to bring lunch in a reusable container. Businesses can provide the option to recycle paper, plastic, and aluminum for any packaging that needs disposal. Providing inexpensive reusable utensils, cups, and plates that can be washed and reused saves on waste.

When employees need to get out at lunch and take a break, businesses can offer incentives for carpooling rather than each employee driving his or her own car to a restaurant. Group lunch orders can save the amount of packaging that is needed to prepare a takeout order.

A salesperson should be prepared to overcome customer objections and excuses. **Objections** are concerns or other reasons a customer has for not making a purchase. Objections give a salesperson insight into a customer's concerns. They also provide an opportunity to give information specific to that customer's needs. **Excuses** are personal reasons not to buy.

It is important to listen, observe body language, and maintain eye contact. The customer should be allowed enough time to express the objection. After the customer is finished speaking, the salesperson should pause. A pause shows respect for the customer and the objection. It gives the salesperson time to consider the objection and compose a response that meets this particular customer's needs.

Close the Sale

The goal of all sales activities is to close the sale. The **close** is the moment when a customer agrees to buy a product. It can occur at any point

Tyler Olson/Shutterstock.com

The close is when a customer agrees to buy a product.

during the sales process. Some customers make decisions quickly and decide to make a purchase soon after the approach or during a presentation.

The salesperson's job is to determine when the customer is ready to buy and then close the sale. **Buying signals** are verbal or nonverbal signs that a customer is ready to purchase. Buying signals include comments, facial expressions, and actions. Buying signals often indicate mental ownership. *Mental ownership* occurs when the customer acts and speaks as if the product is already his or hers.

There are many ways to close a sale. However, salespeople should always avoid overselling, which is unethical. **Overselling** is promising more than the product or the business can deliver. The result might be a returned product, a customer who will never buy from the company again, or even a lawsuit.

After the sale is closed, the salesperson may use suggestion selling. **Suggestion selling** is the technique of suggesting additional items to go with merchandise requested by a customer. Suggestion selling occurs most often after the customer makes the choice to purchase a specific

item or items. For example, if a man buys a suit, the salesperson might recommend a shirt, tie, and belt that go well with it. Often, the suggested item is something the customer needs, but would have forgotten to buy. Customers are usually very appreciative when the salesperson knows enough to suggest appropriate merchandise.

Follow Up after the Sale

After the transaction is complete, it is important for a salesperson to follow up with the customer. The purpose of following up after a sale is to ensure customer satisfaction. Customers have a large number of product choices and many places to buy them. Research shows that it is much more costly to find new customers than to keep current ones. One of the ways to keep customers is to follow up with them after a sale and make sure they are satisfied. Following up after the sale is part of relationship selling in marketing. From a marketing perspective, the customer relationship starts at the approach, continues indefinitely, and includes many purchases.

Section 13.1 Review

 Check Your Understanding

1. What is the difference between B2B selling and B2C selling?
2. What are two tasks that are a part of preapproach in preparing to sell?
3. List the six steps of the sales process.
4. What are three ways to determine customer needs and wants?
5. Explain the purpose of following up after a sale.

 Build Your Vocabulary

As you progress through this course, develop a personal glossary of key terms. This will help you build your vocabulary and prepare you for a career. Write a definition for each of the following terms and add it to your personal glossary.

personal selling	greeting approach
telemarketing	merchandise approach
call center	combination approach
preapproach	substitute selling
feature-benefit selling	objections
lead	excuses
cold calling	close
sales process	buying signals
approach	overselling
service approach	suggestion selling

After the Sale

Essential Question

What is the benefit of providing customer service after a sale is closed?

Objectives

After completing this section, you will be able to:

- **Explain** the importance of customer service to the success of a business.
- **Describe** the functions of a customer support team.
- **Explain** the role of customer service in handling customer complaints.

Key Terms 📤

customer service
customer-service mindset

transaction
customer support team
online support

frequently asked questions (FAQ) pages

Customer Service

Customer service is the way in which a business provides services before, during, and after a purchase. Successful businesses also provide good customer service. Good customer service should be provided by all employees in a company as a part of the marketing concept. Company image is often projected through employee performance.

Customer service is provided in some form whenever any employee has direct or indirect contact with a customer. It could be as simple as answering a question or saying *hello* when someone enters a store. The sales team is the first line of contact with a customer. The salesperson in a retail store or a restaurant probably has the first encounter with customers.

A successful business expects quality customer service from its sales team. *Quality customer service* meets customer needs, as well as the standards for customer service set by the company. *Exceptional customer service* is service that meets and exceeds

customer needs. The phrase "going above and beyond" is often used to refer to exceptional customer service. Every business can provide exceptional customer service.

Production Perig/Shutterstock.com

An upset customer may post negative comments on social media or the company's website that will affect the purchasing decisions of other customers.

High-Pressure Selling

Employees working in sales have quotas that are expected to be met. Sometimes, because of the pressure to meet these goals, sales associates will put pressure on customers to purchase a product. High-pressure selling techniques are an unethical practice. Pressuring a customer into a purchase that he or she does not want to willingly make is not only unethical, but could cost the company future business.

Businesses that are committed to the marketing concept focus their energies on the customer, including quality customer service. Businesses that succeed in providing exceptional customer service develop a customer-service mindset in all their employees. A **customer-service mindset** is the attitude that customer satisfaction always comes first.

Customer service includes many services provided during and after a sale. Examples of customer services include the following:

- vehicle repair and maintenance services
- clothing alterations
- appliance delivery and installation
- convenient store hours
- gift registries
- personal shopper services

These services are meant to increase customer satisfaction with both the business and the product.

An important part of customer service is efficient order processing. After the sale is complete, the product is transferred to the customer. In a retail situation, the customer typically leaves with the purchase. A **transaction** is the exchange of payment and product. In retail sales, the transaction happens immediately. The merchandise is carefully packed and the customer pays with cash, check, credit card, or debit card. Larger sales, such as an automobile, may require that the customer obtain loans.

A B2B sale generally involves a purchase order. The purchasing agent making the purchase may take the product immediately if he or she is in the store at the time of the transaction. However, these sales are usually large or bulky and delivery is normally expected. Shipping is arranged for the order and any specific directions needed are given.

In telemarketing or business sales, the transaction includes taking and processing an order, as well as arranging for shipment and payment. Courtesy and efficiency are important in this step. Paperwork must be handled quickly and accurately. An error made in an item number or price will create problems for the customer.

Customer Support Team

Even though customer service is provided by all employees, an organized customer support team is usually a part of the sales and marketing department. The **customer support team** consists of employees who assist customers, take orders, and answer questions that come into the company via phone or website.

Receiving information from the customer is just as important as giving information. Customer support training usually includes suggestions on how specific feedback can be gained from customers. For example, the customer may be asked how he or she learned about the product that is being ordered. If it was from a brochure, the support person may ask for the number on the brochure. This information can then be sent to marketing to track metrics and evaluate the success of a marketing campaign.

A customer support person may also ask for feedback about a product that the customer ordered. Customers may be asked about their likes and dislikes or what could be improved about the product. This information may then be sent to a product development team to help create better product.

Many organizations provide 24/7 customer support online. **Online support** is information and resources available to customers through the Internet. Online support can take several different forms and offer many types of information. This support is usually provided through a website, social media, or discussion board. Customers have the option of using the support type with which they are most comfortable. Some company websites offer many forms of online customer support. Other organizations can only offer one or two. Online support is convenient for customers because they can find answers at the best times for them.

Websites

The website of a business is typically accessible 24 hours a day, every day of the year. In addition to providing company and product information, many websites offer online support resources. Common types of online support include FAQ pages, e-mail support, product tracking, and online chat.

FAQ Pages

Frequently asked questions (FAQ) pages are the part of a website that gives detailed answers to questions or issues that show up most often. FAQ pages are effective in answering customer questions quickly without taking the time of a support person. If new questions or issues are raised through e-mail or by phone, they can be added to the FAQ page.

E-Mail Support

Many issues can be solved through e-mail, which is a fast and efficient online support option. However, when using e-mail support, the turnaround time to answer customer inquiries and issues is critical. A business must have sufficient personnel to respond to customer e-mails.

Product Tracking

Customers appreciate the ability to track their orders. When orders are placed, the tracking information and link is sent to the customers by e-mail. The link provides a way to check the shipping progress at any time.

Online Chat

Perhaps the fastest-growing form of online customer support is the ability to chat online with a support rep. Customers interact with staff dedicated to answering their questions and solving problems.

Kzenon/Shutterstock.com

Some businesses strive for exceptional customer service by providing special services, like custom interior design, to meet a customer's unique needs.

An advantage to online chat support is that responses are immediate and problems can usually be solved quickly.

Social Media

Social media is a great way to address customer issues directly. Facebook and Twitter allow customers to post both positive and negative feedback. The person in charge of monitoring the company's social media accounts can immediately address any questions and solve problems.

Discussion Boards

Discussion boards are public. Any customer or product user can answer questions posted by other customers. Discussion boards free the support staff to work with other customers. They can also be used to post timely announcements, much like using social media.

Handling Customer Complaints

Customers bring many different opportunities with them. Customers also create new opportunities when they disagree with store policies or make demands. The following are some common customer service problems:

- product is out of stock
- store does not have the right size or color
- salesperson does not speak the customer's language
- customer becomes angry or upset over a store policy
- not enough staff is available to efficiently help customers

Customer service reps are trained to be polite and carefully handle unhappy customers. Company policies detail how to address specific customer complaints. The following behaviors are expected when customer service reps handle unhappy customers.

- Be polite and friendly when greeting the customer.
- Listen to the customer's issue.
- Clarify the issue to be sure that it is clearly understood.
- Offer solutions to the customer.

If the customer service rep is unable to resolve the issue and satisfy the customer, the issue is often transferred to a supervisor.

Section **13.2** Review

 Check Your Understanding

1. What is the difference between *quality* customer service and *exceptional* customer service?

2. List examples of customer services provided after a sale.

3. What kind of feedback might a customer support person receive from a customer?

4. List examples of online support that are commonly available through websites.

5. What are the behaviors expected from customer service reps when handling unhappy customers?

 Build Your Vocabulary

As you progress through this course, develop a personal glossary of key terms. This will help you build your vocabulary and prepare you for a career. Write a definition for each of the following terms and add it to your personal glossary.

customer service

customer-service mindset

transaction

customer support team

online support

frequently asked questions (FAQ) page

Review and Assessment

Chapter Summary

Section 13.1 Role of Sales

- Personal selling is an important element in the promotional mix. It provides information that a marketing brochure or website cannot. Inside salespeople and outside salespeople provide personal selling in B2B sales.

- To prepare for selling, preapproach tasks must be addressed. Preapproach tasks include product training and identifying potential customers.

- The sales process is a series of steps that a salesperson goes through to help the customer make a satisfying buying decision. There are generally six steps in the process: approach the customer, determine customer needs, present the product, answer questions or objections, close the sale, and follow up after the sale.

Section 13.2 After the Sale

- Customer service is the way in which a business provides services before, during, and after a purchase. Customer service is provided in some form whenever any employee has direct or indirect contact with a customer. Businesses that are committed to the marketing concept focus their energies on the customer, including quality customer service.

- The customer support team assists customers, takes orders, and answers questions that come into the company via phone or website. Customer support may also get feedback from customers that can be used by marketing to track metrics, evaluate the success of a marketing campaign, or improve a product.

- Customer service reps are trained to be polite and carefully handle unhappy customers. They should follow company policies on addressing customer complaints, listen carefully to the customer, and offer solutions.

Online Activities

Complete the following activities to help you learn, practice, and expand your knowledge and skills.

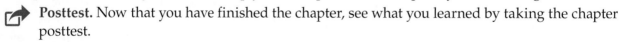

Posttest. Now that you have finished the chapter, see what you learned by taking the chapter posttest.

Vocabulary. Practice vocabulary for this chapter using the e-flash cards, matching activity, and vocabulary game until you are able to recognize their meanings.

Review Your Knowledge

1. Discuss the value of personal selling.
2. How are sales leads generated?
3. List three sales approaches used in B2C sales.
4. List and explain three reasons why B2C customers buy a product.
5. When does *mental ownership* occur in the sales process?
6. Explain the importance of customer service to the success of a business.
7. Why is order processing an important part of customer service?
8. How does order processing for a B2B purchase differ from that of a B2C purchase?
9. What is the advantage of using online chat for customer support?
10. Give examples of common customer service problems.

Apply Your Knowledge

1. Reflect on the last experience you had when shopping and needed the assistance of a salesperson. Did the salesperson provide you with important information? How would you rank the value of personal selling for the store in which you were shopping?
2. In your own words, explain the selling process. In your opinion, what are some of the most important items a salesperson should remember about selling to a customer?
3. Feature-benefit selling is an important approach that businesses use to help a customer understand why he or she should buy a specific product. Select a product with which you are familiar, such as a digital device. Make a list of the features and benefits of that product. Next, try to sell the product to your classmate. Were you an effective salesperson?
4. Write a one-page summary of what you believe to be the difference between quality customer service and exceptional customer service. Provide at least two examples.
5. Customer services are important to everyone who makes a purchase in a store or online. As a customer, which services are most important to you? List three services and describe why you chose each.

Communication Skills

College and Career Readiness

Writing. Rhetoric is the study of writing or speaking as a way of communicating information or persuading someone. Identify rhetoric that could be used to persuade a customer to purchase a tennis racquet. Write a script in a step-by-step format for presenting the item to an adult customer.

Speaking. It is important to be prepared when you are speaking to an individual or to an audience. Style and content influences how the listener understands your message. Using the script you developed in the last activity, convince a classmate to buy a tennis racquet. Make use of visuals or demonstrations to enhance the presentation. Adjust your presentation length to fit the attention of the audience.

Listening. Active listening is fully participating as you process what others are saying. Salespersons must practice active listening in order to fully understand a customer's need. Make a list of listening strategies that could be used to enhance listening comprehension. Examples might include monitoring the message for what is being said or focus on the message.

Internet Research

Customer Service. Customer service is an important asset for a business. Using the Internet, search for *customer service training manual*. Review several examples of customer service training manuals available online. Take notes on the important information you find that can help a business have superior customer service representatives. What do you think are the top five customer support actions that are important to a business?

Teamwork

"The customer is always right." How many times have you heard this phrase? Discuss the meaning of this saying with your team. What, exactly, does this mean? Give examples of when the customer may not always be right.

Portfolio Development

College and Career Readiness

Talents. You have collected documents that show your skills and talents. However, some skills and talents are not effectively represented using only documents. Do you have a special talent in an area such as art, music, or design? Have you taken part in volunteer activities? Create a video to showcase your talents and activities. For example, if you are an artist, create a video that shows your completed works. If you are a musician, create a video with segments from your performances. If you have taken part in a volunteer or service activity, create a video that tells viewers about it. (Be sure you have permission to include other people in your video.)

1. Place the video file in an appropriate subfolder for your digital portfolio.
2. Print selected screen shots from the video.

3. Create a Microsoft Word document with a heading and your name. In the document, describe the video. State that the video will be made available upon request or identify where it can be viewed online. Indicate that sample screenshots are attached. Save the document in an appropriate file format.

4. Place hard copies in the container for future reference.

5. Update your master spreadsheet.

CTSOs

Communication Skills. Competitive events may also judge communications skills. Presenters must be able to exchange information with the judges in a clear, concise manner. This requirement is in keeping with the mission of CTSOs: to prepare students for professional careers in business. Communication skills will be judged for both the written and oral presentation. The evaluation will include all aspects of effective writing, speaking, and listening skills.

To prepare for the business communications portion of an event, complete the following activities.

1. Visit the organization's website and look for specific communication skills that will be judged as a part of a competitive event.

2. Spend time to review the essential principles of business communication, such as grammar, spelling, proofreading, capitalization, and punctuation.

3. If you are making a written presentation, ask an instructor to evaluate your writing. Review and apply the feedback so that your writing sample appears professional and correct.

4. If you are making an oral presentation, ask an instructor to review and listen for errors in grammar or sentence structure. After you have received comments, adjust and make the presentation several times until you are comfortable with your presentation.

5. Review the Communication Skills activities that appear at the end of each chapter of this text as a way to practice your reading, writing, listening, and speaking skills.

6. To practice listening skills, ask your instructor to give you a set of directions. Then, without assistance, repeat those directions to your instructor. Did you listen closely enough to be able to do what was instructed?

UNIT 4

Business Finance

Focus on Finance

Finance is all activities involving money. It is one of the four functions of business that is taken seriously by the management team. The decisions they make directly affect the profitability and security of a business. Finance activities involve financial exchange. *Financial exchange* is the process of transferring money from an individual or organization to another. Money is exchanged for consumer, business, and government transactions. Financial institutions, such as banks, help facilitate financial exchange by offering banking services to its customers and keeping money moving in the economy.

Not all financial exchange happens with cash. Credit is a medium of financial exchange that allows individuals, businesses, and governmental agencies to buy goods or services now and pay for them later. Businesses may extend credit to individual consumers and to business customers. This offers customers a convenient form of payment and builds customer loyalty for the business.

Sound financial decisions involve careful planning of all the resources of a business, including products, people, and finances. A business or organization must apply financial management techniques to make effective financial decisions. *Financial management* is a process used to manage the financial resources of a business. It starts with being prepared for risks that may be encountered. Risk management includes identifying potential business risks and developing plans to avoid, reduce, transfer, or assume them. A business can apply risk management strategies to help protect its profitability and security.

Following sound accounting practices supports the financial management activities of a business. Through the use of accounting systems, records of transactions can be kept and financial statements created for review on regular basis. Businesses must have accurate, up-to-date financial records in order to determine profitability and plan future business activities.

Social Media for Business

With more than one billion users, Facebook is a must for most businesses, both large and small. Businesses and organizations create pages to share their stories and to connect with people. These pages can be customized by posting stories, sharing photos, hosting events and contests, and more. People who follow the page using the **Like** button will have access to updates from the business.

According to Facebook, there are over 550,000 active apps businesses can use on the Facebook platform. Many were created to improve business practices or more efficiently integrate Facebook into a company's operations. For example, there are surveys, contacts, blogging, testimonials, contests, and sweepstakes apps, to name just a few. Many business apps are free. Even fee-based apps offer a basic service at no charge. Many large brands use custom apps because they enhance the user experience.

952.91

662.25

While studying, look for the activity icon ⬀ for:

- Pretests and posttests
- Vocabulary terms with e-flash cards and matching activities
- Self-assessment

G-WLEARNING.com

CHAPTER 14

Risk Management

In This Chapter

Exploring Careers

Finance

Insurance Sales Agent

An insurance sales agent is a client's first contact when buying insurance. Agents sell insurance to individual customers, as well as businesses. They spend most of their time working with clients. Clients may come into the insurance business office, or agents may travel to the client's home or place of business. Insurance sales agents have flexible schedules to fit the needs of their clients and often work nights and weekends.

Typical job titles for this position also include *insurance agent* and *insurance broker*. Examples of tasks that insurance sales agents perform include:

- find potential customers
- determine types of insurance that fit the customer's requirements and needs
- facilitate the application process and submit the information to an underwriter
- prepare reports and maintain records

Insurance sales agent positions likely require a bachelor degree. Most states also require agents to hold a professional license. Insurance sales agents need to have excellent communication skills, expertise with financial products, the ability to work without supervision, and computer skills.

College and Career Readiness

Reading Prep

Before reading this chapter, read the opening pages and section titles for this chapter. These can help prepare you for the topics that will be presented. What does this tell you about what you will be learning?

Check Your Business IQ

Before you begin the chapter, see what you already know about business by taking the chapter pretest. The pretest is available at www.g-wlearning.com.

Understanding Risk

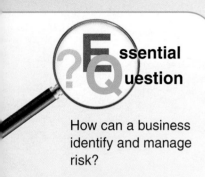

Objectives

After studying this section, you will be able to:

- **Identify** various types of risk.
- **Explain** the concept of risk management.

Key Terms

risk	risk management	insurance
natural risk	controllable risks	uninsurable risk
economic risk	uncontrollable risks	
market risk	pure risk	
human risk	speculative risk	

Identifying Risk

The activities of all businesses and organizations involve risk. A **risk** is the possibility of loss, damage, or injury. *Business risk* is the possibility of loss or injury that affects a business. To be prepared, management should identify potential risks that may be encountered. The four basic types of risk are natural, economic, market, and human, as shown in Figure 14-1.

- **Natural risk** is a situation caused by acts of nature. This is a controllable risk and insurance can help recover the losses from damage.

- **Economic risk** is a situation that occurs when business activities suffer due to changes in the US or world economy. Local, national, and world economic and political conditions can affect the success of a business. Economic risk is hard to predict and is uncontrollable.

- **Market risk** is the potential that the target market for new goods or services is much

less than originally projected. Planning helps reduce this risk, but it is uncontrollable and cannot be insured.

- **Human risk** is a negative situation caused by the actions of people. These risks include shoplifting, embezzlement, and using stolen credit cards. It also includes risks caused by employees such as fraudulent behavior. Being prepared can help reduce losses. Some human risks are insurable.

Risk management is the process of evaluating risk and finding ways to minimize or manage loss. Businesses are liable for their risks. *Liable* means responsible. When discussing the damages and responsibility related to risks, *liability* means legal responsibility for actions and costs.

Controllable and Uncontrollable Risks

Controllable risks are situations that cannot be avoided, but can be minimized by purchasing insurance or creating a risk management plan.

Basic Types of Risk

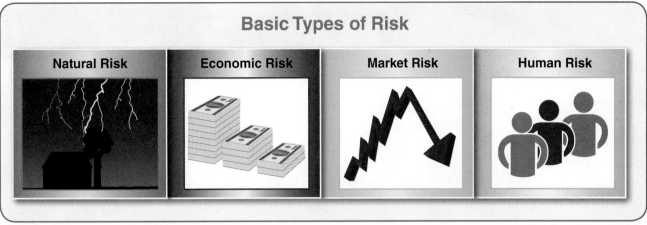

| Natural Risk | Economic Risk | Market Risk | Human Risk |

Goodheart-Willcox Publisher

Figure 14-1 The four basic types of risk can cause loss, damage, or injury.

For example, to reduce the risk of loss from viruses attacking the computer network of a business, firewalls and antivirus software can be installed. Network issues may not be entirely preventable, but a business can take steps to reduce losses.

Uncontrollable risks are situations that cannot be predicted or covered by purchasing insurance. An uncontrollable risk cannot be minimized by taking certain actions. For example, an extreme downturn in the economy can affect the profits of many businesses. This is an uncontrollable and uninsurable risk.

Pure and Speculative Risks

Potential business risks can be categorized as either pure risks or speculative risks. A **pure risk** is a risk with a possibility of loss, but no possibility of gain. Insurance protection is needed to cover pure risk losses. Pure risk includes personal risks, property risks, and liability risks.

- *Personal risks* directly affect an individual, such as illness or disability.

- *Property risks* affect personal or business property. Property risks include events such as theft of a car or fire in an office building.

Kyrien/Shutterstock.com

Acts of nature are not avoidable, but the losses that result can be controlled by purchasing insurance.

Monkey Business Images/Shutterstock.com

Buying and selling stocks is a speculative risk because money can either be made or lost.

- *Liability risks* result from the possibility of losing money, property, or other assets as a result of legal proceedings.

A **speculative risk** is a risk that can result in either financial gain or financial loss. Most speculative risks are not insurable because they are taken willingly in hopes of making a gain. For example, buying gold or stocks may result in a profit or a loss when the property is sold. Businesses take speculative risks when they purchase merchandise that may or may not sell. They also take risk when they spend money on advertising that may or may not generate more customers.

Managing Risk

There are basic ways that risk management can be applied by a business. By identifying the potential risks that a business may encounter, plans can be made to handle them if they arise. As shown in Figure 14-2, many of the risks identified can be avoided, reduced, transferred, or assumed.

Avoid Risk

One of the first steps in risk management is to assess the risks, and determine if they can be avoided. *Avoidance* is taking steps to eliminate risk. For example, the physical location of a business may present risks. To avoid the risk of certain types of

dizain/Shutterstock.com

Figure 14-2 Businesses can take any of these actions to manage identified risks.

You Do the Math   Statistical Reasoning

Qualitative data include things that can be observed, but not measured. Smell, taste, color, appearance, and texture are all examples of types of qualitative data. On the other hand, quantitative data include things that can be measured. Distance, weight, cost, speed, and temperature are all examples of types of quantitative data.

Solve the following problems.

1. The catalog description of a product reads as follows: attractive, blue product has a smooth finish, fits in a space 5 inches wide, and weighs 14 ounces. List the qualitative data and quantitative data in this description.

2. A business describes its customer service staff as follows: a staff of 17 pleasant and helpful representatives includes five certified technicians and two master technicians. List the qualitative data and quantitative data in this description.

3. Look around your classroom. Describe your classmates using only quantitative data.

property damage, the geography and surrounding areas of potential locations can be researched. Locations in flood-prone areas or floodplains can be eliminated to avoid this type of risk.

Reduce Risk

Reducing a risk is a strategy of minimizing risks that cannot be avoided. For example, a business that identifies the potential for human risk can put safeguards in place. Many businesses suffer losses due to theft. If this is considered a potential risk, a business may put strict employee procedures in place or hire security. These safeguards could reduce some of the loss potential.

Transfer Risk

Some risks can be transferred so that the owner shares the risk with others. Insurance is the most common way of transferring risk. **Insurance** is a financial service used to protect against loss. Individuals who purchase insurance become members of a large group of people who transfer risk to an insurance company.

aodaodaodaod/Shutterstock.com

To help reduce the risk of theft, some businesses install security systems.

Green Business   Reusable Bags

Reusable shopping bags can reduce some of the one trillion plastic bags that are used every year around the world. Plastic shopping bags pose an environmental problem because a single plastic bag can take up to 1,000 years to break down in a landfill. Simply throwing these bags in the trash can be harmful to wildlife and contaminate soil and water.

In the United States, only 1 percent of plastic bags are recycled.

Alternatively, reusable bags save thousands of pounds of landfill waste every year. Many stores are now offering incentives to customers who take their purchases home in reusable bags.

Assume Risk

Unfortunately, insurance may not be available to cover all the risks a business identifies. An **uninsurable risk** is one that an insurance company will not cover. In this case, businesses must assume the full risk. They are responsible for losses associated with risks that cannot be avoided or insured, such as economic and market risks.

A business may choose to self-insure by saving money to cover the financial losses of some risks. One way to self-insure is by setting up a bank account specifically for this purpose. Money can be automatically deposited into the account each month to cover a future loss. Setting up a special account is similar to paying a premium to an insurance company. The difference is that the premium is paid to the business, and the business assumes 100 percent of the risk. If an uninsured risk event happens, the self-insurance money is available to cover losses. State regulations may require a business to prove it can finance self-insurance before allowing it to self-insure rather than purchase insurance.

Section 14.1 Review

Check Your Understanding

1. What is business risk?
2. List four basic types of risk.
3. What are some examples of pure risks?
4. Why are speculative risks not insurable?
5. Once risks have been identified, how can they be managed?

Build Your Vocabulary

As you progress through this course, develop a personal glossary of key terms. This will help you build your vocabulary and prepare you for a career. Write a definition for each of the following terms and add it to your personal glossary.

risk	controllable risks
natural risk	uncontrollable risks
economic risk	pure risk
market risk	speculative risk
human risk	insurance
risk management	uninsurable risk

Business Insurance

Objectives

After studying this section, you will be able to:

- **Explain** the role of insurance companies in helping customers managing risk.
- **Identify** the types of insurance.
- **Describe** common insurance coverage for businesses.

Key Terms ↗

insurance policy
premium
claim
deductible
general liability insurance
product liability insurance
professional liability insurance

commercial insurance
liability insurance
business interruption insurance
fidelity bond
directors and officers insurance

data breach insurance
property insurance
workers' compensation insurance
unemployment insurance
disability insurance

Insurance Companies

Insurance companies are licensed for-profit businesses. They are required to follow regulations enforced by the federal government and individual state departments of insurance.

The most well-known service provided by insurance companies is financial protection through insurance policies. The insurance company, the *insurer*, protects the *insured*, the policyholder. For a fee, the insurer provides the insured with protection against economic loss.

Ken Wolter/Shutterstock.com

For a fee, insurance companies offer financial protection through insurance policies.

An **insurance policy** defines the type of losses that are covered, amount of coverage in dollars, and other conditions to which the two parties agree.

By purchasing insurance, a policyholder becomes a member of a large pool of customers. Each customer's risk is transferred to the insurance company. The insurance company charges its customers premiums to assume their risk. The **premium** is the amount the insured pays for insurance coverage. The money collected from policy premiums is invested in the stock market, bonds, and other types of investments. Earnings from the investments are used to pay claims of insured customers. Earnings above the amount needed for policy claims are profit for the company.

When the insured suffers a loss, a claim is made. A **claim** is the process of documenting a loss against an insurance policy. Most policies have a deductible when a claim is made. The **deductible** is the amount the insured is responsible for paying when a claim is made. In general, the higher the amount of the deductible, the lower the premium.

Businesses and individuals typically purchase insurance from an insurance agent. There are two types of insurance agents: independent and contract. An *independent agent* is an insurance agent who works for multiple insurance companies. Independent agents are also called *brokers*. Insurance brokers can compare the products offered by various companies to find the insurance policy that best fits the needs of their customers. A *contract agent* is an insurance agent who works for only one insurance company. This type of agent can offer customers only the insurance products available from a single insurance company.

Selecting an agent is an important part of buying insurance coverage. The agent should understand the needs of each customer. Insurance agents may specialize in business or consumer insurance, which makes them a knowledgeable resource when selecting a policy.

An insurance agent should be able to help customers determine the appropriate amount of insurance to buy. Having the right amount of insurance is important to financial security. Customer service is also a key factor when choosing an insurance company and agent. Policy information should be easy to access. Assistance and information from the company or agent should be readily available to customers. An efficient process for filing claims is important. If a loss occurs, customers should be able to easily navigate the claims process to make use of their policy coverage. Business, as well as individuals, should shop for the best insurance company and policy that fits their needs.

Types of Insurance

Risk is a factor in all types of businesses. The fact that a business operates every day is a risk. A business that wants to stay in operation must be prepared for potential losses that might occur.

Robert Crum/Shutterstock.com

When an insured suffers a loss, a claim is made against the corresponding insurance policy.

Businesses can buy insurance to protect against specific types of financial losses. The Small Business Administration (SBA) defines several types of insurance, including general liability, product liability, professional liability, and commercial.

General liability insurance protects against financial losses that result from legal issues. This includes lawsuits for accidents and injuries that occur on business premises. The number of personal injury law suits in the US is exceptionally high. General liability insurance can protect the owners and their business.

Product liability insurance protects against financial losses due to a product defect that may cause injury to the user of the product. Companies that manufacture, wholesale, distribute, and sell a product may be liable for its safety.

Professional liability insurance protects service-based businesses from financial losses caused by errors and negligence in how a service is provided. It is also called *malpractice insurance.*

kurhan/Shutterstock.com

Many healthcare professionals are covered by professional liability insurance to protect them against malpractice suits.

Many states require business in certain professions, such as healthcare professionals and lawyers, to carry professional liability insurance.

Commercial insurance is insurance that protects commercial property from risks, such as fire, theft, and natural disaster. The following are some examples of commercial insurance.

- *Commercial property insurance* covers buildings and other assets of the business. It generally covers losses due to fire, accidents, and other specified losses.

- *Commercial auto insurance* protects the vehicles owned by a business from accidents and other losses. This coverage applies to vehicles used to transport employees. It also applies to transporting equipment or products for business purposes.

- *Inland marine insurance* offers protections for property being transported for business, such as tools or equipment. This insurance also provides coverage to property belonging to others when that property is in the possession of the insured.

- *Equipment breakdown insurance* covers property damage and productivity losses due to the accidental breakdown of business machinery and equipment.

- *Ordinance or law insurance* covers losses caused when local building ordinances or laws are enforced. For example, a new building ordinance may require the electrical system to be upgraded in buildings 100 years and older.

Business Insurance

The insurance coverage needed by a business depends on the size of the business, type of business operations, and probable risks. The National Association of Insurance Commissioners (NAIC) is a good source for obtaining information about insurance. Their website provides an abundance of information to help make insurance buying decisions. Most businesses have coverage for liability, property, vehicles, and employees of the business.

Liability

Liability insurance covers financial losses caused by the actions or negligence of a person or business. Insurance companies offer many different types of liability insurance. The most common types for business are general liability, product liability, and professional liability, as described earlier in this section. There are many insurance policies that specifically cover business liability losses. The following are examples:

- **Business interruption insurance** covers the lost income and related expenses caused by a property damage loss.

- **Fidelity bonds** cover financial and property losses caused by employee actions, such as theft or embezzlement.

- **Directors and officers insurance** protects a business from financial losses caused by the actions of the company's executive officers.

- **Data breach insurance** covers the legal fees and other financial losses sustained when a company's data files are accessed without permission. Typically, this type of coverage applies to both electronic data and paper files.

Liability insurance covers lawsuits brought against a business. This type of insurance can be expensive, but can be a wise investment.

Property

Property insurance covers losses and damage to the assets of a business caused by a variety of events, such as floods, fire, smoke, and vandalism. The definition of *property* is broad. In addition to covering physical business assets, property insurance also covers income lost from lack of sales due to property losses. For example, a fire causes a retail business to close for two months while repairs are made. Property insurance may cover the income lost by the business during the time it was closed due to damage from the fire.

Vehicles

Vehicle insurance covers all types of commercial vehicles owned by the business. This includes trucks, cars, and trailers. The coverage includes damage to the vehicles, property damaged as a result of the vehicles, and injuries to individuals resulting from accidents.

Employees

Businesses may offer various types of insurance coverage to employees as part of employment benefits. These can include health insurance, life insurance, and dental insurance.

Hurst Photo/Shutterstock.com

Certain actions taken by executive officers can cause financial losses for a company. Director and officers insurance protects a business from this risk.

However, there are certain types of insurance that businesses with employees are required by law to carry. Workers' compensation, unemployment insurance, and disability insurance are a few that may be required.

- **Workers' compensation insurance** covers medical expenses and lost wages for employees who are injured at work. Each state has a workers' compensation commission or board that enforces these laws.

- **Unemployment insurance** provides certain benefits to workers who have lost their jobs through no fault of their own. Businesses pay for this insurance through a payroll tax, and the benefits are managed by the state government.

- **Disability insurance** provides some financial income to employees who become sick or injured due to a nonwork related event or condition. This type of insurance is not required in all states.

The guidelines and requirements for business insurance can vary by state and industry. It is important for business owners to research local requirements.

Phil Date/Shutterstock.com

Workers' compensation insurance covers losses for employees injured while on the job.

Section **14.2** Review

 Check Your Understanding

1. Explain the most well-known service provided by insurance companies.
2. Name two types of insurance agents.
3. How does the Small Business Administration (SBA) categorize some types of insurance needs?
4. List examples of types of common insurance coverage for businesses.
5. List three examples of coverage provided by employers for employees.

 Build Your Vocabulary

As you progress through this course, develop a personal glossary of key terms. This will help you build your vocabulary and prepare you for a career. Write a definition for each of the following terms and add it to your personal glossary.

insurance policy
premium
claim
deductible
general liability insurance
product liability insurance
professional liability insurance
commercial insurance
liability insurance

business interruption insurance
fidelity bond
directors and officers insurance
data breach insurance
property insurance
worker's compensation insurance
unemployment insurance
disability insurance

Review and Assessment

Chapter Summary

Section 14.1 Understanding Risk

- All businesses activities involve risk. A risk is the possibility of loss, damage, or injury. Types of risk include natural risk, economic risk, market risk, and human risk. Potential business risks can be pure or speculative, as well as controllable and uncontrollable.

- Many of the risks identified can be avoided, reduced, transferred, or assumed. Risks can be managed through smart business strategies and by purchasing insurance.

Section 14.2 Business Insurance

- Insurance companies are for-profit businesses. The most well-known service provided by insurance companies is financial protection through insurance policies. The insurance company, the *insurer*, protects the *insured*, the policyholder. For a fee, the insurer provides the insured with protection against economic loss. Businesses and individuals typically purchase insurance from an insurance agent.

- Businesses buy insurance to protect against specific types of financial losses. Types of business insurance include general liability, product liability, professional liability, and commercial insurance.

- Most businesses have coverage for liability, property, vehicles, and employees of the business. Certain types of insurance are required by law when a business has employees.

Online Activities

Complete the following activities to help you learn, practice, and expand your knowledge and skills.

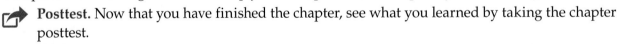 **Posttest.** Now that you have finished the chapter, see what you learned by taking the chapter posttest.

Vocabulary. Practice vocabulary for this chapter using the e-flash cards, matching activity, and vocabulary game until you are able to recognize their meanings.

Review Your Knowledge

1. Describe the four basic types of risk.
2. Explain the concept of risk management.
3. Differentiate between controllable and uncontrollable risks.
4. Differentiate between pure and speculative risks.
5. Explain how businesses can self-insure.
6. Explain the role of insurance companies in managing risk.

7. Identify the common types of commercial insurance that a business might purchase.

8. Identify and describe types of liability insurance that a business might purchase.

9. Describe the coverage provided by commercial vehicle insurance.

10. What types of insurance are required by law for businesses to provide for their employees?

Apply Your Knowledge

1. Make a list of some tasks and activities in which students participate on a daily basis in your school environment. Examples could be as basic as walking down the hall or as involved as playing on the football team. Next to each activity in your list, identify a potential natural risk, economic risk, market risk, and human risk that could occur. What did you learn from this exercise?

2. Many of the risks identified by a business can be avoided, reduced, transferred, or assumed. Select a business with which you are familiar, such as a local retail store or restaurant. Create a chart with three columns. Label the columns as Avoid/Reduce, Transfer, and Assume. Identify specific risks your chosen business might encounter. Sort the risks into the appropriate columns on the chart, indicating if each risk can be avoided, reduced, transferred, or assumed.

3. Security risks are an important consideration for all businesses, especially retail businesses. To avoid or reduce risk, some businesses install security systems. Make a list of the types of business risks that can be avoided or reduced by installing a security system.

4. Select a business in your area with which you are familiar. Identify the activities that the business performs, as well as the location of the business. Make a list of items that would be covered by property insurance for this business.

5. Employees pose various risks to their employers. How can a business plan to reduce risks that pertain to employees?

Communication Skills

College and Career Readiness

Listening. Engage in a conversation with someone you have not spoken with before. Ask the person how he or she manages risk in personal circumstances and more formal circumstances such as at school or a job. Actively listen to what that person is sharing. Next, summarize and retell what the person conveyed in conversation to you. Did you really hear what was being said?

Reading. Figurative language is used to describe something by comparing it with something else. Locate an advertisement for insurance services. Scan the information for figurative language about the product. Compare this with a description using literal language. Did the use of literal or figurative language influence your opinion of the services? Did the advertisement help you understand the service or company?

Writing. Everyone has a stake in protecting the environment. Taking steps as an individual to become more environmentally conscious is a behavior of responsible citizens. From a business standpoint, it may also help a company be more profitable. Make a list of actions a business can take to minimize risk to the environment.

Internet Research

Risk Management. Choose a research topic related to the risk management for business. After you have refined the topic, complete the research using the Internet. Take appropriate notes so that you can write a two-page report on your findings. Devise a time line for completing the research and writing the paper.

Teamwork

Working with your team, identify examples of natural, economic, human and market risks that a business might face. How might a business manage each? Share your opinions with the class.

Portfolio Development

College and Career Readiness

Technical Skills. Your portfolio should showcase your technical skills. Are you exceptionally good working with computers? Do you have a talent for creating videos? Technical skills are important for succeeding in school or at work.

1. Create a Microsoft Word document that describes the technical skills you have acquired. Use the heading "Technical Skills" and your name. Describe the skill, your level of competence, and any other information that will showcase your skill level. Save the document file.

2. Update your master spreadsheet.

CTSOs

Business Law. Business law is a competitive event you might enter with your Career and Technical Student Organization (CTSO). Business law is an individual event in which participants take an objective test that covers multiple legal topics. Participants are usually allowed one hour to complete the event. One of the topics that may be included on the test is *insurance as a means of risk management.*

To prepare for a business law event, complete the following activities.

1. Visit the organization's website well in advance of the date of the event.

2. Download any posted practice tests.

3. Conduct research on the Internet regarding the legal topics that will be covered on the test. Print out the information you find to use as study material.

4. Visit the organization's website often to make sure information regarding the event has not changed.

CHAPTER 15

Money and Banking

Exploring Careers

Financial Analyst

Financial analysts study the economy and the financial information of a business in order to advise its leaders. They analyze the financial affairs of a business and develop a plan to meet its financial goals for the future. Financial analysts advise businesses on investments, insurance, and taxes. They may be a member of a private practice or provide services through an investment firm, bank, or financial service firm.

Other typical job titles for a financial planner are *investment planner* and *financial consultant*.

Some examples of tasks that financial analysts perform include:

- analyze financial statements

- advise businesses on ways to achieve their financial goals

- provide investment and tax advice

- monitor investments, tax strategies, and risk management for the business

Financial analyst jobs often require a bachelor degree in finance, economics, or business or law school. They must also pass the General Securities Representative Qualification Examination Series 7 and any additional exams required by individual states. Two or more years of work experience in financial services or a related field are needed.

Reading Prep

College and Career Readiness

Arrange a study session to read the chapter aloud with a classmate. At the end of each section, discuss any words you do not know. Take notes of words you would like to discuss in class.

Check Your Business IQ

Before you begin the chapter, see what you already know about business by taking the chapter pretest. The pretest is available at www.g-wlearning.com.

Understanding Money

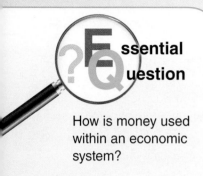

How is money used within an economic system?

Objectives

After studying this section, you will be able to:

- **Explain** the concept of money.
- **Identify** the responsibilities of the Federal Reserve.
- **Discuss** the importance of financial exchange.

Key Terms

money
banknote
security
government bond
treasury note

treasury bill
medium of exchange
unit of value
store of value
monetary system

financial exchange
credit card
debit card
electronic funds transfer (EFT)

Money

Money is anything of value that is accepted in return for goods or services. Money is also known as *currency*. In ancient times, people exchanged goods for other goods instead of using a standard currency. This is called bartering. To *barter* is to exchange one good or service for another good or service. Some businesses still barter today. For example, an accounting business may exchange its services with the services of an automobile repair business. No money is exchanged, but both parties receive an economic benefit.

Currency can be in the form of paper money or coins. In the United States, the dollar is the official currency used for financial exchange. It is *legal tender* that must be accepted "for all debts, public and private." Paper money is produced by the US Treasury, and coins are produced by the United States Mint. Paper money is also referred to as a banknote. A **banknote** is a type of a document guaranteeing the payment of a specific amount of money, either on demand or at a set time, with the payer named on the document.

Jason Stitt/Shutterstock.com

Paper money is also referred to as a banknote.

Banknotes are considered legal tender and are used in exchange for goods and services.

Government bonds, treasury notes, and treasury bills are securities issued by the US government when it borrows money. A **security** is a type of financial investment issued by a corporation, government, or other organization. Bonds, treasury notes, and treasury bills are issued as a promise to pay interest and repay the money that was borrowed when the security matures. Investors in government securities include individuals, businesses, and other governments. A **government bond** is a security that pays interest over terms of ten to thirty years. A **treasury note** is a security that pays interest over terms ranging from two to ten years. A **treasury bill** is a security that matures in a year or less. Some economists consider treasury bills to be part of the money supply. Government debt is highly marketable, which means it can be sold and converted to currency that can be used in the economy.

Functions of Money

Money allows business transactions to take place and goods and services to be exchanged. In this way, money has a function, or serves a purpose. As shown in Figure 15-1,

money serves three functions in our economy: medium of exchange, unit of value, and store of value.

As a **medium of exchange**, money is used in exchange for goods and services needed by individuals, businesses, and governments. Compared to bartering, money is more convenient for trading. Money is the basis of our economy and necessary for economic activities.

Unit of value means that money is a common measure of the worth or price of a good or service. The value represented by currency is different in each country. In the United States, everyone knows what a dollar is and how much it is worth. Using money as a unit of value is an easy way to place a price that is understood on an item or service.

Money also functions as a **store of value**, which means it can be saved and used at a later date. An item that holds its value over a period of time is said to have a good store of value. The value of currency is generally stable. However, it can lose some of its purchasing power over time. Money received today is worth more than the same amount received in the future. This is because money received today can be invested or deposited in the bank to earn interest. This concept is called the *time value of money*.

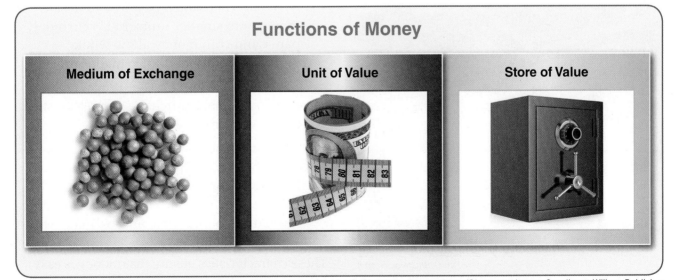

Magone./Shutterstock.com; Lisa S./Shutterstock.com; dencg/Shutterstock.com; Goodheart-Willcox Publisher

Figure 15-1 Money serves three functions in our economy.

You Do the Math

Problem Solving and Reasoning

When solving word problems, you must identify the elements of the math problem and solve it. However, an important key to solving word problems is to make sure enough information has been provided to solve the stated problem. If some information is not provided, the problem cannot be solved.

Solve the following problems.

1. A business sells smartphones across the nation. Each phone comes in packaging that measures 6 inches by 4 inches by 1 inch. The products are shipped to resellers in cartons that measure 18 inches by 12 inches by 12 inches. The cartons can hold a maximum of 15 pounds. The company wants to know how much each full carton weighs. Is there enough information to solve this problem? If not, what information is missing?

2. Darren orders office supplies every Monday. This week he must order 23 reams of paper, 2000 envelopes, and 12 boxes of tape. He wants to know how much this will cost. Is there enough information to solve this problem? If not, what information is missing?

3. Laura travels for work. On Monday, she drove 48 miles. On Tuesday, she drove 37 miles. On Thursday, she drove 76 miles. She is reimbursed for gasoline at a rate of 53 cents per mile. Laura wants to determine how many miles per gallon she averaged while traveling. Is there enough information to solve this problem? If not, what information is missing?

Properties of Money

To be useful and meaningful in an economy, money must have certain characteristics. Money should be stable, easily recognized, divisible, portable, and durable.

Fablok/Shutterstock.com

The US dollar is the most widely recognized currency around the world.

- *Stable.* Money must maintain its value over time in order for it to be widely accepted. People in an economy are confident to use and accept money that has consistent value.

- *Recognized.* To be accepted, authentic money must be immediately recognizable. The US dollar is the most widely recognized currency around the world.

- *Divisible.* There must be a way to divide money into smaller units. In US currency, paper and coin money allow whole dollars to be divided into smaller units of currency.

- *Portable.* To make purchases, people must be able to carry money with them.

- *Durable.* Money is handled many times by many people. It needs to be strong and last a long time. US paper bills are made out of a special blend of cotton and linen rather than paper. US coins are made with a blend of metals.

These characteristics ensure that money is easy to use and can be used with confidence for business transactions in an economy.

Federal Reserve

The Federal Reserve System, often called *the Fed*, was created by the United States Congress in 1913 as our nation's central bank. The Fed supervises and regulates banks in the country. National banks are required to be a part of the Federal Reserve System. State banks are not required to join, but they have the option to join. Banks that are part of the Federal Reserve System are known as *member banks*.

The Federal Reserve System is divided into 12 districts. The map in Figure 15-2 shows the 12 Federal Reserve districts. Each district has a Federal Reserve bank. In addition, there are 25 Federal Reserve branch banks located throughout the country. With 12 Federal Reserve banks and 25 branch banks, the US is the only industrialized country that does not have a single central bank.

The Fed is responsible for the monetary system in the United States. A **monetary system** is the mechanism a nation uses to provide and manage money for itself. The Federal Reserve has the following four core functions:

- establish monetary policy
- supervise and regulate financial institutions
- maintain the stability of the nation's financial system
- provide financial services

Monetary Policy

Monetary policy is action taken to manage the supply of money and interest rates in an economy. The Fed establishes monetary policies, which influence money and credit conditions in the economy. For example, when the economy is slow, it may take action to lower interest rates and encourage consumers and business to spend more. In an economy that is growing too fast, the Federal Reserve can take action to slow the economy and avoid inflation.

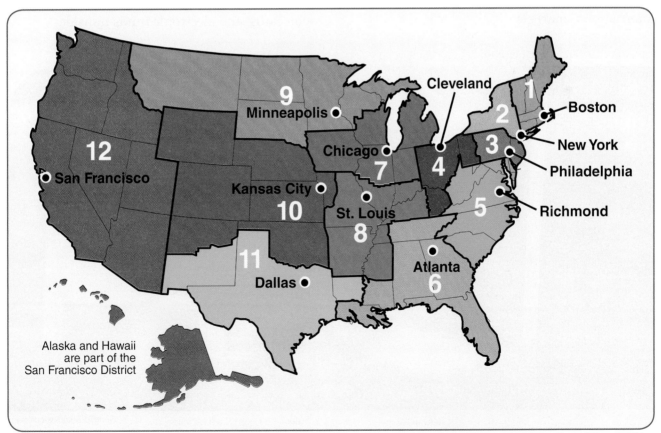

Source: The Federal Reserve Board; Goodheart-Willcox Publisher

Figure 15-2 The twelve Federal Reserve districts are spread across the entire country.

Supervise and Regulate Financial Institutions

The Federal Reserve supervises and regulates financial institutions to ensure the safety and soundness of the country's banking system. It works with the Federal Deposit Insurance Corporation (FDIC), which provides insurance for depositors in insured banks. The Fed also works with the Consumer Advisory Council to protect consumers through various laws related to consumer financial activities.

Maintain Stability of the Nation's Financial System

To maintain the stability of the nation's financial system, the Fed takes actions to control risks in the financial markets. It monitors the economy and makes necessary adjustments to interest rates and in other financial areas. The goal is to avoid foreseeable financial crises and maintain a stable national economy that can positively impact international markets.

Provide Financial Services

The Fed provides financial services to the government and depository institutions, and helps operate and oversee the country's payment systems. It provides a variety of payment services, including collecting checks, electronically transferring funds, and distributing paper money and coins. The Federal Reserve also lends money to member banks in order to meet temporary needs for cash.

Financial Exchange

Financial exchange is the process of transferring money from one individual or organization to another. Money is exchanged for consumer, business, and government transactions.

Types of Financial Exchange

There are many types of financial exchange. Some basic examples include cash, credit cards, debit cards, and electronic funds transfer.

GongTo/Shutterstock.com

In 2014, Janet Louise Yellen became the first woman to hold the office of Chair of the Board of Governors of the Federal Reserve.

Cash

Cash transactions are made with paper money and coins. Using cash is simple and practical for many types of transactions, especially small purchases. Businesses benefit from cash transactions because they can be made quickly and easily. There are no third-party services or fees involved, such as with bank checks and credit cards. One disadvantage of cash is that it must be carefully handled and monitored, which may be time-consuming. Businesses often take steps to verify that currency is genuine and not counterfeit before accepting it. Cash can also be easily lost or stolen.

Credit Cards

A **credit card** is a plastic card that allows the holder to make credit purchases up to an authorized amount. It allows consumers and businesses to make purchases without cash. Using a credit card is like borrowing money from the financial institution that issued the card.

Goodluz/Shutterstock.com

Credit cards enable consumers and businesses to make purchases without cash.

There are fees and interest charges that apply to purchases made using a credit card. Credit cards have a credit limit, which is a maximum amount of money that can be borrowed at one time. Each month, a minimum payment must be made to the credit card company toward the total amount owed.

Debit Cards

A bank-issued **debit card** allows customers to pay for purchases directly from their checking account. The card is swiped like a credit card, and the money is taken out of the owner's checking account when the transaction is complete. Charges may be involved when using debit cards.

Electronic Funds Transfer

An **electronic funds transfer (EFT)** is a transfer of money from one bank account to another. It is often used to make large payments to avoid sending checks through the mail. Businesses often use EFT transactions to pay employee wages and make payments to vendors. EFT transactions are faster than mailing checks. They are also generally more convenient and less costly to process.

Legal Responsibilities of Financial Exchange

Our free enterprise system is based on the voluntary exchange of goods and services. However, laws and regulations are necessary to help facilitate financial exchanges and protect buyers and sellers from fraud and other illegal behavior. The *legal responsibilities of financial exchange* cover many areas, including privacy, disclosure, fraud, consumer rights, and interest rates.

The terms of exchange in a financial transaction are determined by state and federal laws. In a business transaction, the buyer and seller must reach a legal agreement when trading money for goods or services. This is known as a contract and is legally enforced. Ethically and legally, both parties must fulfill their obligations as part of their legal responsibilities associated with the financial exchange.

For example, buyers must pay the agreed upon amount for a purchase of goods or services. It is illegal and unethical for a buyer to write a check that has insufficient funds or pay with counterfeit money. There are laws covering criminal and civil penalties for these actions. Sellers must provide the agreed upon good or service. They cannot sell stolen or illegal items and cannot write sales contracts that contain terms that violate the law.

Financial institutions also have legal responsibilities for financial exchanges. These financial exchanges can include checks, electronic fund transfers, and credit cards. For example, the fees banks charge for writing bad checks are regulated at the federal level. Electronic fund transfers must be made accurately and securely. There are also state and federal laws that limit credit card fees, interest rates, and the disclosure of information.

Stephen Coburn/Shutterstock.com

Legal responsibilities of financial exchange apply to both the buyer and the seller in a transaction.

Section 15.1 Review

 Check Your Understanding

1. What are the three functions of money?
2. List five properties of money.
3. List the four core functions of the Federal Reserve.
4. List some basic examples of financial exchange.
5. Why are laws and regulations necessary regarding financial exchange?

 Build Your Vocabulary

As you progress through this course, develop a personal glossary of key terms. This will help you build your vocabulary and prepare you for a career. Write a definition for each of the following terms and add it to your personal glossary.

money	unit of value
banknote	store of value
security	monetary system
government bond	financial exchange
treasury note	credit card
treasury bill	debit card
medium of exchange	electronic funds transfer (EFT)

Banking

?Essential Question

How do financial institutions serve business customers?

Objectives

After studying this section, you will be able to:

- **Describe** two types of financial institutions.
- **Identify** financial services provided by banks.
- **Explain** the importance of banking regulations.

Key Terms

financial institution
depository institution
deposit
credit union
savings and loan
   institution

nondepository
   institution
securities firm
investment bank
finance company

checking account
check
savings account
line of credit
letter of credit

Financial Institutions

A **financial institution** is any organization that provides services related to money. Financial institutions help facilitate financial exchange. They help keep money moving in the economy for consumers, businesses, and government. The two main types of financial institutions are depository and nondepository.

Depository Institutions

A **depository institution** is a financial institution that accepts money from customers and deposits it into the customer's account. A **deposit** is money placed into an account. A *depositor* is a customer who makes the deposit.

Commercial Banks

Commercial banks are the largest category of deposit institution. They are generally owned by stockholders and operate to make a profit. Commercial banks vary in size from

Ken Wolter/Shutterstock.com

Financial institutions provide many services for their consumer, business, and government customers.

small community banks to large regional and national banks. They service both individual and business customers. The size of a bank often determines the range of services it offers.

Green Business   Commuting

Employees must get to work using some mode of transportation. According to the United States Census Bureau, over 75 percent of American workers drive to work alone on a commute that is an average of 25 minutes. This adds up to billions of gallons of gas burned and billions of hours wasted driving each year.

Much of this time and fuel can be saved when workers consider other options for commuting. By participating in a carpool or using public transportation, fuel is conserved and time spent commuting can be used in other ways. Many metropolitan areas also have car sharing services. In some cities, employers give bonuses or perks to employees who commute to work in an environmentally friendly way.

Smaller banks typically make consumer and small-business loans and offer simple deposit accounts. Larger banks offer many other services like money management, foreign exchange services, transaction processing, and large commercial loans.

Credit Unions

A **credit union** is a nonprofit financial institution that is privately owned and provides banking services for its members. Membership is restricted to people who are affiliated with a specific employer or organization. Some examples of people who are eligible to join credit unions might include employees of a participating business, members of a union, or people who live within a certain community. Credit unions are focused on consumer banking, but most offer a wide range of services.

Savings and Loan Institutions

A **savings and loan institution** is a financial institution that offers savings and loan services. These financial institutions were originally created to help people save money and borrow money. They include *thrift institutions* and *mutual savings banks*. Savings and loan institutions accept savings deposits and make loans, with emphasis on home mortgages. Some savings institutions are operated like commercial banks and are owned by stockholders. Others are owned by the depositors and borrowers of the institution, which is called *mutual* ownership.

Nondepository Institutions

A **nondepository institution** is a financial institution that does not accept deposits. These institutions generate profits by selling services. Four major types of nondepository institutions are insurance companies, securities firms, investment banks, and finance companies.

Insurance Companies

An *insurance company* is a for-profit business that primarily sells insurance products. They offer protection for customers from risks that can result in financial distress, such as accidents and death.

vinnstock/Shutterstock.com

Savings and loan institutions accept savings deposits and make loans.

Customers pay policy premiums to the insurance company. The premium dollars are pooled together and invested. When customers make claims against their policies, the insurance company pays using money from the premium pool. Any remaining money is profit for the company.

Securities Firms

A **securities firm** is a financial institution that is involved in trading securities in financial markets. These businesses charge clients fees to invest their money, buy and sell securities, and provide financial advice.

Investment Banks

An **investment bank** is a financial institution that provides services for businesses. This nondepository institution helps businesses raise money for expansion or maintenance of the business. Investment banks also provide businesses with advice and research on complex financial transactions, such as mergers and acquisitions.

Finance Companies

A **finance company** is a financial institution that makes money by issuing loans. It is also known as a *loan company*. The two types of finance companies are *consumer finance companies* and *business finance companies*. Lending money to consumers and businesses is the only service finance companies provide. Loans can be issued for many different reasons. For example, some customers of a finance company may need money to cover short-term financial emergencies. Others may need a loan to purchase various goods and services.

Financial Services

Financial institutions provide many services for their consumer, business, and government customers. Some services are customized for certain types of customers. For example, certain types of bank accounts and loans are offered to meet the unique needs of business customers.

Milles Studio/Shutterstock.com

Investment bankers help businesses raise money and provide advice on complex transactions.

Ethics

Customer Data

Some financial institution websites gather personal and confidential information from customers, such as credit card numbers or phone numbers. Sharing or tampering with personal information is not only unethical, but may also be illegal. Protecting customer data helps protect the reputation of the business.

Other bank services are tailored to meet the needs of consumers. The variety of services offered to customers by financial institutions are called *banking products.*

General Banking Services

General banking services are those services offered by financial institutions to all types of customers. Various forms of checking and savings accounts, electronic banking options, and bank cards are available for both consumer and business customers.

Checking Accounts

A **checking account** is a bank account that allows the account owner to make deposits, write checks, and withdraw money. A **check** is a written order for the bank to pay a specific amount to the person or organization to which the check is written. Checking accounts are also known as *demand accounts* because money can be withdrawn at any time. Banks charge customers various fees to use and maintain checking accounts.

Savings Accounts

A **savings account** is a bank account used by depositors to accumulate money for future use. The money deposited into savings accounts is used by the financial institution to make loans to customers. In return for using the depositor's money, the bank pays interest on the amount in the savings account.

Electronic Banking

Electronic banking is a popular banking service offered by most financial institutions when a customer opens a checking account. Online banking and direct deposit are two examples of electronic banking.

Online banking allows customers to conduct financial transactions on a secure website owned by the financial institution. Customers can transfer funds, apply for loans, and monitor account information.

Online banking also allows for electronic funds transfers. An *electronic funds transfer (EFT)* is the movement of money electronically from one financial institution to another. *Direct deposit* is a type of EFT transaction in which money is deposited directly into a customer's checking account. Direct deposits are most commonly made by businesses to pay employee wages and make payments to suppliers. Another type of EFT transaction is an *automatic bill payment.* This is a regular payment made from a customer's bank account to a vendor or supplier. With an automatic bill pay arrangement, the customer allows the vendor to take payment directly from the bank account.

Odua Images/Shutterstock.com

Electronic banking is a common banking service provided by financial institutions to all types of customers.

Bank Cards

Banks and credit unions typically issue bank cards to their customers when a checking account is opened. A bank-issued debit card allows customers to pay for purchases directly from their checking account. The bank cards may also be used at an ATM to withdraw cash. Charges may be involved when using bank cards.

Most banks and credit unions also offer credit cards such as Visa and MasterCard. A credit card is not automatically given to the customer in the same way that a debit card is issued. A credit card requires the customer to apply and meet certain conditions.

Business Banking Services

Banks serve a diverse range of business customers, from small local service and retail companies to large corporations with operations across the country. Businesses have banking needs that are much different than individuals. Some businesses use cash management services to handle financial collections and disbursements. Businesses may also use bank services to get letters of credit, manage payroll, and pay taxes. Some common services provided by financial institutions to business customers are business checking accounts, business lines of credit, long-term business loans, and international banking services.

Business Checking Accounts

Business checking accounts are structured and operate much the same as personal checking accounts. However, businesses typically write many more checks and make more deposits each month than individuals. Bank fees may depend on the number of transactions made on the account, as well as other factors specific to the financial institution.

Business Lines of Credit

A **line of credit** is a prearranged amount of credit that is available for a business to use as needed. Business lines of credit can be established either through a business credit card or a bank account that can be used to write checks or make electronic payments. Interest is charged on the amount borrowed against the credit card or bank account. There may be fees charged to maintain the credit line even when no money is borrowed. Some businesses may be required to secure lines of credit with collateral.

Long-Term Business Loans

Businesses generally need loans at some point in their operation. Loans may be needed when starting a business or when expanding an existing business. Long-term business loans are normally used to fund asset purchases, such as equipment and building remodeling. These loans typically have a fixed interest rate. Businesses typically make monthly or quarterly payments on long-term loans.

International Banking Services

Businesses that sell goods or service in the global market require special banking services. International business requires special documents, currency exchange, and other legal processes that require the services of a bank.

Goodluz/Shutterstock.com

Business lines of credit and long-term business loans are common banking services provided to business customers.

An example of a document that may be required for international business is a letter of credit. A **letter of credit** is a document guaranteeing that a buyer will pay the seller the agreed-upon amount and within the time specified. This is a legal document issued by the bank that protects both the buyer and seller. The buyer is guaranteed receipt of merchandise before paying. The seller is guaranteed receipt of payment once the merchandise is accepted.

There are additional documents that a bank can provide a business for international business activities. International banking services are only offered by large banks.

Banking Regulations

Financial institutions must comply with many federal and state regulations. Federal regulators include the Federal Reserve System, Comptroller of the Currency, Federal Deposit Insurance Corporation (FDIC), Office of Thrift Supervision, and National Credit Union Administration (NCUA). Financial institutions are regulated to be sure they are financially sound and comply with consumer protection laws. Figure 15-3 describes some of the consumer protection laws related to banking and credit.

Almost every depository institution is a member of either the FDIC or NCUA. These are independent government agencies that provide deposit insurance in the event of a bank failure. The FDIC and NCUA cover up to $250,000 on qualifying accounts per owner, per single account. The FDIC also examines and supervises financial institution policies and operations. Its goal is to help maintain consumer and business confidence in the banking system. When customer deposits are federally insured, it means the bank, savings and loan, or credit union is regularly checked. The institution must pass ongoing examinations of its financial holdings, operations, and management. FDIC insurance guarantees that depositors are protected if the bank fails or cannot repay deposits on demand.

Many consumer protection laws ensure that banks provide fair and equitable service

Consumer Protection Laws	
Law	How it Protects Consumers
Truth in Lending Act (1968)	Requires disclosure of all terms of a loan in a clear way
Fair Credit Reporting Act (1970)	Provides consumers the right to examine their own credit report and correct inaccuracies
Fair Credit Billing Act 1974)	Protects consumers against unfair charges and provides a way to challenge incorrect bills
Equal Credit Opportunity Act (1975)	Prohibits credit grantors from discriminating against consumers on the basis of sex, marital status, race, national origin, religion, age, or the receipt of public assistance
Electronic Fund Transfer Act (1978, amended 2009)	Sets guidelines for electronic transfers and payments, including ATM transactions and online payments
Overdraft Protection Act (2013)	Requires banks to disclose all terms and charges related to overdraft protection, sets overdraft fee limits, and prohibits deceptive practices intended to create overdrafts on accounts

Goodheart-Willcox Publisher

Figure 15-3 There are many US regulations that establish and protect consumer rights for financial transactions.

to consumers. Banks are required to give consumers clear and accurate information about savings accounts, loan products, and other services. The *Truth in Lending Act* requires clear disclosure of finance charges and annual percentage rates on loans. It also limits customer liability on lost or stolen credit cards.

Another area of bank regulation involves equal opportunity lending. Congress passed the *Equal Credit Opportunity Act* in 1974, which makes it unlawful to discriminate against any credit applicant based on race, color, religion, national origin, sex, marital status, or age. The *Community Reinvestment Act* enacted in 1977 requires that financial institutions help meet the credit and development needs of the community. This includes customers in lower and moderate income areas. The Federal Reserve reviews the efforts of financial institutions in meeting these regulations.

Section 15.2 Review

 Check Your Understanding

1. What are two main types of financial institutions?
2. List three examples of depository institutions.
3. Define general banking services as offered by financial institutions.
4. Identify four examples of general banking services.
5. Name the two types of federal regulators that almost every depository institution is a member.

 Build Your Vocabulary

As you progress through this course, develop a personal glossary of key terms. This will help you build your vocabulary and prepare you for a career. Write a definition for each of the following terms and add it to your personal glossary.

financial institution
depository institution
deposit
credit union
savings and loan
    institution
nondepository institution
securities firm

investment bank
finance company
checking account
check
savings account
line of credit
letter of credit

Review and Assessment

Chapter Summary

Section 15.1 Understanding Money

- Money is anything of value that is accepted in return for goods or services and allows business transactions to take place and goods and services to be exchanged. Money serves as a medium of exchange, unit of value, and store of value. To be meaningful, money must be stable, recognized, divisible, portable, and durable.

- The Federal Reserve System was created by the United States Congress in 1913 as our nation's central bank. It is responsible for the monetary system in the United States. The Federal Reserve supervises and regulates banks in the country.

- Financial exchange is the process of transferring money from one individual or organization to another. Methods of financial exchange include cash, credit cards, debit cards, and electronic funds transfer. Financial exchanges must be conducted within guidelines established by federal law.

Section 15.2 Banking

- Financial institutions help facilitate financial exchange and keep money moving the economy for consumers, businesses, and government. The two main types of financial institutions are depository and nondepository.

- Financial institutions provide many services to their customers. General banking services checking accounts, savings accounts, electronic banking, and bank cards. For business customers, banks typically offer business checking accounts, business lines of credit, long-term business loans, and international banking services.

- Financial institutions must comply with many federal and state regulations. Regulations ensure that banks provide fair and equitable services to consumers for accounts, loan products, and other services. Regulations also provide for equal opportunity lending.

Online Activities

Complete the following activities to help you learn, practice, and expand your knowledge and skills.

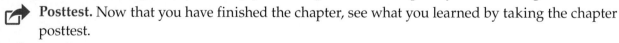

Posttest. Now that you have finished the chapter, see what you learned by taking the chapter posttest.

Vocabulary. Practice vocabulary for this chapter using the e-flash cards, matching activity, and vocabulary game until you are able to recognize their meanings.

Review Your Knowledge

1. Explain the concept of money.
2. Explain each of the properties of money.
3. Describe the responsibilities of the Federal Reserve.
4. Explain legal responsibilities associated with financial exchanges.
5. What is the difference between credit card and debit card financial exchanges for the consumer?
6. Differentiate between the two main types of financial institutions.
7. List and describe four major types of nondepository institutions.
8. What financial services are commonly available to business customers?
9. Explain why a business would need international banking services.
10. Explain the importance of banking regulations.

Apply Your Knowledge

1. Create a chart with three columns. In the first column, list the following forms of exchange: paper money (banknotes), coins, government bonds, treasury notes, credit, debit, electronic funds transfer. In column two, describe each item. In column three, give an example of each.
2. List the primary types of currency and define each. What do they all have in common? Which do you use most often?
3. List three financial institutions in your area. Identify each as depository or nondepository. For each, give examples of the services and financial products the institution provides.
4. Assume you are planning to open a checking account and trying to decide which bank to use. What banking services do you consider most important in making that decision?
5. The FDIC was established in 1933 as a result of legislation put in place during the Great Depression. How does the FDIC help ensure that the citizens of the United States will always have their money available to them?

Communication Skills

College and Career Readiness

Writing. Generate your own ideas relevant to using financial exchange in an appropriate manner. Use multiple authoritative print and digital sources and document each. Write several paragraphs about your findings to demonstrate your understanding about the topic.

Reading. Review the vocabulary list at the beginning of this chapter. Sight words are those words that you recognize automatically. Identify the sight words with which you are familiar. For those words that are unfamiliar, write context clues that will help you decide the meaning of those words.

Speaking. Businesses use technology on a daily basis. Brainstorm ways that a business can use the services of financial institutions to enhance its productivity. Prepare a speech that details two technological services offered by financial institutions to business customers. Explain how these services can improve the productivity of a business.

Internet Research

Financial Exchange. Financial exchange implies a certain amount of financial responsibility from the buyer and seller. Using the Internet, research a financial exchange that was either unethical or illegal. Describe the situation and give your opinion on the legal responsibilities that were involved.

Money Supply. The money supply is the total amount of money available at any given time in an economy. The money supply has three measures. M1 is the most commonly used measure of the money supply. It is the money we use for everyday transactions. Using the Internet, research M1, M2, and M3. Evaluate the validity and reliability of your sources. Next, create a chart to explain what each is and its importance to the money supply for the US economy.

Teamwork

Financial exchange is the process of transferring money from one individual or organization to another. Working with your team, create a new form of financial exchange. Describe how money is exchanged with this new form. How is your new form an improvement over current forms of financial exchange?

Portfolio Development

College and Career Readiness

Clubs and Organizations. Being involved in academic clubs or professional organizations will help you make a good impression. You can also learn a lot that will help you with your studies or your career. While in school, you may belong to clubs, such as National Honor Society and Future Business Leaders of America. When you are employed, you may belong to professional organizations related to your career area, such as the American Nurses Association.

1. Identify clubs or organizations to which you belong. Create a Microsoft Word document to list the name of each organization. Use the heading "Clubs and Organizations" and your name. Briefly describe the organization, your level of involvement, and how long you have been a member. Save the document.

2. Update your master spreadsheet.

CTSOs

Community Service Project. Many competitive events for CTSOs include a community service project. This project is usually carried out by the entire CTSO chapter and will take several months to complete. This project will probably span the school year. There are two parts to this event, written and oral. The chapter will designate several members to represent the team at the competitive event. To prepare for a community service project, complete the following activities.

1. Read the guidelines provided by your organization.

2. Contact the association immediately at the end of the state conference to prepare for next year's event.

3. As a team, select a theme for your chapter's community service project.

4. Decide which roles are needed for the team. There may be one person who is the captain, one person who is the secretary, and any other roles necessary to create the plan. Ask your instructor for guidance in assigning roles to team members.

5. Identify your target audience, which may include business, school, and community groups.

6. Brainstorm with members of your chapter. List the benefits and opportunities of supporting a community service project.

CHAPTER 16

Credit

Exploring Careers

Credit Analyst

When a credit application is submitted, the business or financial institution must assess the risks involved. This assessment is done by a credit analyst. Credit analysts study credit and financial data to decide if and how much credit should be extended. They examine financial records, advise on financial matters, and prepare reports to illustrate the degree of risk involved in extending credit to a particular person or business. Financial analysis software is typically used to assist in this process.

Typical job titles for this position also include *analyst*, *credit administrator*, and *risk analyst*. Examples of tasks that credit analysts perform include:

- analyze credit data to determine the risk involved in extending credit

- evaluate the financial status of customers

- evaluate the profitability of an organization

Most credit analyst positions require a bachelor or master degree. A strong background in mathematics, economics, and accounting is necessary. Credit analysts must also have critical-thinking, decision-making, and communication skills.

In This Chapter

College and Career Readiness

Reading Prep

Before reading this chapter, review the table of contents for this text. Create a graphic organizer that traces the content from simple to complex ideas.

Check Your Business IQ

Before you begin the chapter, see what you already know about business by taking the chapter pretest. The pretest is available at www.g-wlearning.com.

Credit Basics

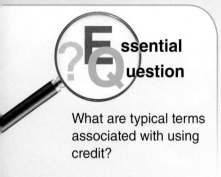

Objectives

After completing this section, you will be able to:

- **Summarize** the purpose and importance of credit.
- **Identify** the types of credit available to individuals and businesses.
- **Describe** the charges associated with using credit.
- **Discuss** the possible outcomes of using credit unwisely.

Key Terms

credit
creditor
debtor
consumer credit
business credit

trade credit
closed-end credit
secured credit
installment loan
principal

finance charge
open-end credit
unsecured credit
annual percentage rate (APR)

What Is Credit?

Credit is an agreement between two parties in which one party lends money or provides goods or services to another party with the understanding that payment will be made at a later date. In every credit transaction, there is a party who extends credit and a party who receives credit. The party extending credit is known as the **creditor**, or the *lender*. The creditor is the party to whom money is owed. The party receiving credit is known as the **debtor**, or the *borrower*. The debtor is the party who owes money to a creditor.

All credit is based on trust. A *debtor-creditor relationship* is a legal relationship that exists between the two parties. This relationship is based on good faith that both parties will uphold their end of the agreement. The debtor must repay the creditor based on the terms of the agreement.

Consumer credit is credit granted to individual consumers by a retail business. **Business credit** is credit granted to a business by a financial institution or another company. **Trade credit** is a business granting a line of credit to another business for a short period of time to purchase its goods and services.

The purpose of credit is to serve as a medium of exchange that allows individuals, businesses, and governmental agencies to buy goods or services now and pay for them later. Without credit, purchases would have to be made with cash. This could prevent businesses or individuals from buying goods and services needed to operate on a daily basis. Credit provides the following benefits:

- ability to use goods and services as they are being paid for
- opportunity to buy costly items
- source of funding for emergency or unexpected expenses

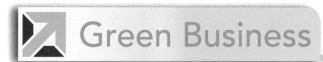

Green Business | Energy Star

Have you noticed the Energy Star label that appears on products such as lightbulbs, computers, and other electronic devices? The US Environmental Protection Agency established the Energy Star program in 1992 to rate the energy efficiency of products. The Energy Star label guarantees the product meets a certain level of energy efficiency. Using energy efficient products helps to reduce energy consumption, which reduces the negative impact on the environment and lowers energy bills.

- convenience of carrying a credit card instead of cash or a checkbook

Credit is also important to the economy. It provides consumers, businesses, and government additional buying power needed to support production and distribution of products. Credit keeps cash flowing through the economy and drives economic growth.

Types of Credit

Various types of credit are available to individuals and businesses. The most common types are closed-end credit and open-end credit.

Closed-End Credit

Closed-end credit is a loan for a specific amount that must be repaid with interest by a specified date or according to a specified schedule. *Interest* is the amount paid by a borrower to a lender for the use of credit.

Loans usually require that collateral is pledged when the loan is granted. *Collateral* is property that a borrower promises to give up in case of default. Credit loans that require collateral are known as **secured credit**. Obtaining a loan for a building is an example of a secured loan because collateral would be required.

Most closed-end credit is offered in the form of installment loans. An **installment loan** is a loan for a specific amount of money that is repaid with interest in regular installments. The **principal** is the amount of money borrowed. A contract is signed stating the principal of the loan, interest rate, length of the loan, and other provisions of the agreement.

Installment loans are repaid with a set amount for each payment, or installment.

Andresr/Shutterstock.com

Buying supplies for use in business is an example of a B2B sale. The credit extended by the store for that business purchase is considered business credit.

An *amortization table* is a schedule that shows the amount of interest and principal for each payment so the loan can be repaid within a specific period of time. The amortization table in Figure 16-1 shows a $1,000 installment loan using an interest rate of 9 percent that will be paid off in 12 months.

Loans are granted by commercial banks, credit unions, finance companies, insurance companies, credit card agencies, and individuals. Finance charges vary with the size of the loan, interest rate, and repayment period. The **finance charge** is the total amount paid by a borrower to a lender for the use of credit. Interest rates vary among different lenders and with the collateral pledged.

Open-End Credit

Open-end credit is an agreement that allows the borrower to use a specific amount of credit over a period of time. A maximum amount of credit is established, along with a repayment schedule. An example of open-end credit is a credit card. The borrower has a specified amount of credit that can be used at any time. Monthly payments are made against the balance owed.

Benjamin Haas/Shutterstock.com

A business seeking a loan might use the company's fleet of vehicles as collateral.

Month	Payment	Principal	9% Interest	Principal Balance
1	$87.45	$79.95	$7.50	$920.05
2	87.45	80.55	6.90	839.50
3	87.45	81.15	6.30	758.35
4	87.45	81.76	5.69	676.59
5	87.45	82.38	5.07	594.21
6	87.45	82.99	4.46	511.22
7	87.45	83.62	3.83	427.60
8	87.45	84.24	3.21	343.36
9	87.45	84.87	2.58	258.49
10	87.45	85.51	1.94	172.98
11	87.45	86.15	1.30	86.83
12	87.48	86.83	0.65	0.00

Goodheart-Willcox Publisher

Figure 16-1 An amortization table shows the amount of interest and principal applied with each payment scheduled during the period of a loan.

Because the account does not automatically close when the balance is paid off, it is referred to as a "revolving account."

Open-end credit is typically unsecured. **Unsecured credit** is credit granted based on a signed credit agreement. No collateral is required, just the promise to pay and signature of the borrower. Open-end credit is also referred to as a *line of credit* or *revolving line of credit*.

Credit Terms

Using credit is not free; it can come with hefty charges. An **annual percentage rate (APR)** is the annual cost of credit charged by a lender. The higher the APR, the larger the finance charges. The finance charge for the use of credit

Stasique/Shutterstock.com

Accountants carefully review the terms of purchase when a business is applying for credit.

has two parts: interest and fees. The *interest rate* represents the cost of the loan and is expressed as a percent of the amount borrowed. *Fees* include items such as application fees and other necessary processing costs.

The APR includes all fees and charges that otherwise may be hidden from the borrower. The APR reveals the true cost of credit and helps to compare different loans and other sources of credit. Money lenders and credit card companies are required by the federal *Truth in Lending Act* to state the APR of loans when they advertise a rate. The total amount paid for the use of credit is based primarily on three factors:

- *Interest rate charged.* The APR is based on items such as the type of loan, current market rate of interest, and borrower's credit score.

- *Amount of credit used.* Interest is money paid for the use of a lender's money. The more money a person borrows, the more he or she will pay in interest.

- *Length of the repayment period.* Interest accrues for as long as the credit account has a balance. The debtor is responsible to make payments as long as the account is open and has a balance greater than zero.

Simple interest is one formula used when calculating the cost of a loan. The formula is based on the principal, interest rate, and length of time of the loan. The formula is as follows.

Principal (P) × Rate (R) × Time (T) = Interest

For example, an APR of 12 percent means that $12 interest will be paid per year on each $100 borrowed. If a business pays for a $700 vehicle repair using a credit card that charges a 12 percent annual interest rate, the repair will actually cost $784.

Principal (P) × Rate (R) × Time (T) = Interest

$700 × .12 × 1 = $84

Principal (P) + Interest = Repayment Amount

$700 + $84 = $784

Syda Productions/Shutterstock.com

Consumers who overuse credit run the risk of late payments, low credit scores, and even bankruptcy.

Consumer credit transactions are regulated on the federal and state levels. Credit laws address finance charges, late fees, cash advances, and other issues to protect consumers.

Businesses that extend credit must comply with both federal laws and laws issued by the state in which the businesses operate. Some of these laws are described in Figure 16-2.

Credit Laws	
Truth in Lending Act (1968)	Requires businesses and financial institutions to disclose precise credit terms and costs
Fair Credit Billing Act (1974)	Protects consumers from billing errors and provides outlets to challenge incorrect statement
Equal Credit Opportunity Act (1974)	Prohibits creditors from discriminating against an applicant on the basis of race, color, religion, national origin, gender, marital status, age, or whether the applicant receives public assistance as income
Fair Credit Reporting Act (1970)	Gives consumers the right to receive a copy of their credit reports and to dispute inaccurate information within it
Fair Debt Collection Practices Act (1977)	Establishes legal protection against abusive debt collection practices
Credit Card Accountability Responsibility and Disclosure Act (2009)	Makes the rates and fees of credit cards more transparent and prohibits unfair practices related to credit card rates and fees

Goodheart-Willcox Publisher

Figure 16-2 Consumer credit transactions are regulated by federal and state credit laws.

When to Use Credit

When used wisely, credit helps the buyer to obtain items when they are needed. If used unwisely, it can create financial disasters.

Consumers who overuse credit run the risk of not being able to make payments on time. Not making timely payments lowers the credit score of the consumer. A lower credit score makes additional credit more difficult to obtain. It also results in higher interest rates for credit that can be obtained. In addition, the improper use of credit can lead to personal bankruptcy.

Businesses that overuse credit run the risk of cash flow problems. If most of the cash of a business is going toward loan payments, money may not be available to pay business expenses. Paying business expenses late or not at all could result in lawsuits and the inability to obtain additional business credit.

Section **16.1** Review

 Check Your Understanding

1. Explain the debtor-creditor relationship.
2. Why is credit important in the economy?
3. What are the most common types of credit available to individuals and businesses?
4. What is the formula used to calculate simple interest?
5. What is the risk of overusing credit for a business?

 Build Your Vocabulary

As you progress through this course, develop a personal glossary of key terms. This will help you build your vocabulary and prepare you for a career. Write a definition for each of the following terms and add it to your personal glossary.

credit
creditor
debtor
consumer credit
business credit
trade credit
closed-end credit
secured credit

installment loan
principal
finance charge
open-end credit
unsecured credit
annual percentage rate (APR)

Business and Credit

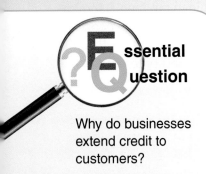

Objectives

After completing this section, you will be able to:

- **Discuss** the costs and benefits of extending credit to customers.
- **Explain** how businesses obtain and use credit.

Key Terms

proprietary credit card
credit policy
three Cs of credit
credit report

credit bureau
credit score
credit risk
accounts receivable

accounts receivable aging report
collection agency
five Cs of banking

Extending Credit to Customers

Some businesses extend credit by accepting credit cards from their customers. Credit cards are a convenient form of payment for customers and may enable customers to spend more than if using cash.

Consumer credit is sometimes issued in the form of a proprietary credit card. A **proprietary credit card** is one that can only be used in the stores of the company that issued it. Most large department stores and gasoline companies issue proprietary credit cards. Examples of companies that issue proprietary credit cards include Macy's, Sears, Target, and ExxonMobil. If a business sells big-ticket items, like appliances or home furnishings, consumer credit may be offered in the form of an installment loan.

It is sometimes preferable for a business to accept bank-issued credit cards, such as MasterCard and Visa. An advantage to accepting these cards is that the financial institution is responsible for collecting the money owed, not

the business. The financial institution pays the business immediately and then collects the money owed for the sale from the customer.

Susan Law Cain/Shutterstock.com

Most major department stores issue proprietary credit cards that may only be used in the stores of that company.

This service is not free for either the business or the customer. Credit card companies charge businesses a fee to process credit transactions. A business may be charged 2 to 3 percent of each purchase by the financial institution. In addition, customers pay monthly interest on unpaid balances to the bank that issued the credit card.

There are many costs involved when businesses extend or accept credit. These costs may directly affect profit. The following are examples of the costs associated with extending credit to customers.

- If accepting credit or debit cards, the business pays transaction fees to the financial institution that issued the cards.

- If extending trade credit to businesses, cash is tied up while waiting for payments. The cash could be used to operate the business.

- Customers who do not pay their credit balances create bad debts, which decrease the net income of a business.

- Extending credit requires additional paperwork, which takes time for management or employees to process.

For these reasons, many businesses add an additional percentage, or markup, to the price of products to cover the cost of credit. *Cost of credit* is a variable expense that influences the pricing decisions for products.

Credit Policy

Before making the decision to extend credit to customers, a business should establish a credit policy. A **credit policy** is a written set of guidelines used by an organization to determine how many and which customers will be approved for credit. A credit policy establishes limits for the amount of credit that will be extended for installment loans and trade credit. Specific terms of repayment are included, as well as interest rates, late fees, penalties, and actions for nonpayment. Limits and guidelines are also established for the company as to how much credit the business can afford to extend.

Tyler Olson/Shutterstock.com

Individual businesses must decide if extending credit to customers is a good decision for their business.

You Do the Math   Functions

Both businesses and individuals invest money and take out loans. Compound interest is exponential. This means that previously earned interest itself earns interest in the future. This can be thought of as interest on interest. The future value of a balance with compound interest is calculated by multiplying the present value by one plus the annual interest rate taken to the power of the number of terms.

$$FV = PV \times (1 + r)^n$$

In this equation, *FV* is the future value, *PV* is the present value, *r* is the annual interest rate, and *n* is the period of time over which interest is compounded.

Solve the following problems.

1. A business has placed $10,000 in a certificate of deposit (CD) that earns 3.78 percent interest per year. The term of the CD is three years. How much money will the business have at the end of the term?

2. Elija has taken out a small business loan of $25,000 for a term of five years. The interest rate is 2.9 percent annually. How much interest will have been paid at the end of the loan?

3. A florist needs to purchase a new delivery van. The amount that will be financed is $36,575. The dealership is offering three financing options: 4.9 percent for 48 months, 1.9 percent for 60 months, and 0.9 percent for 72 months. Which option results in the lowest total interest paid?

Having a policy in place can help guide a business through the process of extending credit. Company policies vary by the type of credit extended to individual customers. Each business must decide if extending credit to customers is a good business decision. Some businesses choose to accept only cash or checks to avoid the transaction fees related to credit payments. When granting credit to customers, it is important to establish a credit process that reduces potential risk.

Three Cs of Credit

Businesses that extend credit to customers should check the financial background of each applicant. A credit application that includes personal and financial information is typically completed by the applicant. Depending on the loan amount or trade credit extended, financial statements showing net worth and financial status may be required. Bank statements may also be requested. Before extending credit to customers, a business should consider the three Cs of credit. The **three Cs of credit** are

criteria used to evaluate the creditworthiness of consumer credit applicants.

- *Character.* Current debt, payment history, and credit scores are considered when evaluating the financial character of an individual.

- *Capacity.* Lenders review finances to determine if the individual receives a regular paycheck and how long he or she has been employed.

- *Capital.* All of an individual's assets and liabilities are evaluated to determine net worth.

A copy of the credit terms should be provided to all customers who are approved for a credit account. Specific terms of repayment, interest rates, late fees, penalties, and actions for nonpayment should be included. In addition, credit amount limits for the account should be noted. The Truth in Lending Act requires that businesses provide this information to customers before the first transaction. If the customer is *not* approved for credit, the business should convey the denial.

Credit Report

Before extending credit to an individual or business, the creditor typically requests a credit report. A **credit report** is a record of credit history and financial behavior for a business or individual. The credit history may provide information on how likely the business or individual is to repay the credit. A credit report shows:

- the number and types of credit accounts and indicates any that are past due
- how promptly credit cards and loans were paid in full
- timely payment of other bills, such as rent, taxes, and utilities
- current total outstanding debts
- amount of available credit on credit cards and home equity loans

Consumer credit reports are issued by credit bureaus. A **credit bureau** is a private firm that maintains consumer credit data and provides credit information to businesses for a fee. There are three national credit-reporting agencies: Equifax, Experian, and TransUnion LLC.

Consumers also are given a credit score. A **credit score** is a numerical measure of a loan applicant's creditworthiness at a particular point in time. Credit scores may vary depending on which credit bureau reports the number. A credit score is also known as the *FICO score*. It is named for the Fair Isaac Corporation that developed the rating system. FICO scores are calculated for consumers on the five categories of information shown in Figure 16-3.

A credit report for a business may be provided by one of the three credit reporting agencies. Dun & Bradstreet also provides credit reports for businesses. This organization provides credit building and solutions for businesses.

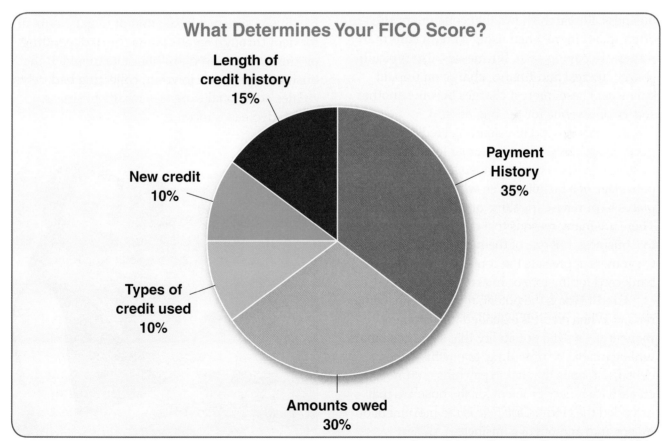

Source: Fair Isaac Corporation; Goodheart-Willcox Publisher

Figure 16-3 Consumer FICO credit scores consider length of credit history, payment history, amounts owed, types of credit used, and new credit.

Ethics

Information

Don't believe everything you read. Just because you read an article or advertisement in a magazine or newspaper, don't assume it is correct, legal, or ethical. Ethical communication is based on an individual's perception, either on the part of the writer or the reader. Analyze the information based on your own personal ethics.

Rewards and Risks of Extending Credit

When credit is extended to customers, there are many rewards. The greatest reward for a business is the generation of sales. Offering credit through credit cards, installment loans, and trade credit can create steady income for a business. Research shows that consumers will often spend more when using a credit card than if they are paying cash. Businesses also typically charge interest and finance charge on unpaid balances. These interest charges become another source of revenue for the business.

Another reward of extending credit to customers is building customer loyalty. *Customer loyalty* is the continued and regular patronage of a business even when there are other places to purchase the same or similar products. There are many reasons that customers are loyal to a business, but one of them is convenience. Customers appreciate the convenience of using a bank card for in-store or Internet purchases.

Credit risk is the potential of credit not being repaid. When credit is extended to customers, there is always the possibility that some customers will be unable, or unwilling, to pay his or her debt. Customers that fail to pay bills on time may create a cash-flow problem for the business that extended the credit. *Cash flow* is the movement of money into and out of a business.

A business that extends credit should carefully monitor cash flow. If the business receives more cash than it spends, the cash flow is positive. If it spends more cash than it receives, the cash flow is negative.

One important financial management task is to keep track of when the accounts receivable are due or overdue. The **accounts receivable** is a list of the individuals or businesses that owe money to a company. This activity is critical to maintaining enough cash flow to keep the business open. Customers who are late making payments should be sent reminders urging them to pay.

An **accounts receivable aging report** shows when accounts receivables are due, as well as the length of time accounts have been outstanding. An aging report typically shows receivables as *current, 30 days, 60 days, 90 days,* and *120 days and over.* The purpose of an aging report is to indicate which receivables are more urgent to collect because they have been past due for a longer amount of time.

The accounts of customers who do not pay after repeated attempts to collect may be turned over to a collection agency. A **collection agency** is a company that collects past-due bills for a fee. Businesses may also attempt to get payment for debt through small claims court, depending on the amount owed and the state in which the business operates. However, collecting bad debts creates additional expenses for the business, which decreases income.

Ikonoklast Fotografie/Shutterstock.com

A reward of extending credit to customers is building customer loyalty.

Obtaining Business Credit

Most businesses need credit at some point in their operation. Small businesses need credit for start-up costs and to grow operations. Large businesses also need credit for growth and expansion.

For short-term credit needs, many small businesses use bank-issued credit cards, such as Visa and MasterCard. According to the US Small Business Administration (SBA), over 65 percent of small businesses regularly use credit cards. Using credit cards is convenient and can help a small business build a credit history and obtain loans. Large companies also use credit cards. Some large companies provide managers with corporate credit cards to pay for travel-related business expenses.

For long-term credit needs, many businesses borrow from banks. To qualify for a bank loan, a business must prove it has the ability to repay. To determine if a business has the ability to repay a loan, lenders consider the five Cs of banking. The **five Cs of banking** are criteria lenders use to evaluate the creditworthiness of businesses.

- *Cash flow.* Cash flow is the movement of money into and out of a business. Lenders want to know that a business can generate enough positive cash flow to repay the loan on time.

- *Capacity.* Capacity is the ability of a business to repay a loan. To assess capacity, banks look at factors such as the credit history of the business, amount of current earnings, and other debt of the business.

- *Capital.* Capital is the owners' investment in the business. The greater the amount of capital, the more likely the business can get a loan. Capital is also referred to as *equity*.

©iStock.com/DragonImages

To qualify for a bank loan, lenders evaluate a business to determine if it has the ability to repay the loan.

- *Collateral.* Collateral is the property a business uses to secure a loan. This may be buildings or equipment owned by the business, or the personal property of the business owner. Collateral may also be a *co-signer*, which is someone who guarantees to pay the loan.

- *Conditions.* Conditions relate to the overall environment in which the business operates. To assess conditions, lenders evaluate the strength of the national economy, local economy, and industry in which the business competes. They review the level of demand for the goods or services provided by the business. Lenders also determine if there are any legal problems associated with the business or the goods or services it provides. A business is more likely to receive a loan when economic and industry conditions are good, and its competitive position is strong.

A business that does not meet the five Cs of banking can be turned down for a loan.

When this situation occurs, it may mean that the business is not a good credit risk and may not be financially able to maintain operations.

Types of Business Credit

Virtually all businesses use some form of credit. Even very large and profitable businesses use credit on a regular basis. Examples of sources of business credit are supplier financing and bank financing.

Supplier Financing

Businesses may use credit provided by suppliers. Credit extended by a business to another business is called *trade credit*. It occurs when a business buys goods or services on credit from another business, called the *supplier*. Trade credit allows businesses to acquire goods to sell without making an immediate payment. In many cases, this allows a business to buy goods and then resell the goods before actually paying the supplier. Trade credit is sometimes called *supplier financing* or *vendor financing*.

©iStock.com/DragonImages

Using trade credit, a business can buy goods and then resell the goods before actually paying the supplier.

For trade credit, terms of the line of credit is most often 30 or 60 days. This means that the purchase is interest free for 30 or 60 days. Full payment is expected at the end of the time period. If the bill is paid in full by the specified date, no interest is charged. However, if the bill is not paid or not paid in full by the specified date, interest charges are applied. Common credit terms are *n/30* and *n/60*, which means the buyer has 30 or 60 days from the date of purchase to pay the net amount of the purchase. The *net amount* is the total amount of the purchase less returns, if any.

Sometimes suppliers offer a discount for early payments. For example, the credit term might be stated as *2/10, net 30*. This means the buyer can deduct a 2 percent discount if the bill is paid within 10 days of sale. Otherwise, the buyer must pay the total net amount within 30 days.

Bank Financing

Banks provide two main types of business financing: business loans and lines of credit.

A *business loan* is money borrowed from a bank for a specific purpose. It is usually used to start a new business or to expand the operations of an existing business. Business loans have an established repayment schedule over a definite period of time. These loans usually carry a fixed interest rate that remains the same over the term of the loan.

A *business line of credit* is an established amount of money a bank makes available for a business to use whenever the money is needed. The business can use all or a portion of the money from a line of credit and pay it back on a regular basis.

The Small Business Administration (SBA) is an agency of the federal government that assists small businesses with financing. The SBA does not actually make loans, but guarantees loans up to 80 percent made by private lenders. The most common SBA loan is the General Small Business Loan, which is for all start-up costs. To qualify for a General Small Business loan, the business must meet the guidelines set by the SBA.

Section 16.2   Review

 Check Your Understanding

1. Why do some businesses prefer to accept bank-issued credit cards, such as MasterCard and Visa?
2. List the three Cs of credit that help evaluate a customer's creditworthiness.
3. Identify the rewards of extending credit to customers.
4. What are the five Cs of banking that lenders use to evaluate a business seeking credit?
5. Explain the meaning of the trade credit term *n/30*.

 Build Your Vocabulary

As you progress through this course, develop a personal glossary of key terms. This will help you build your vocabulary and prepare you for a career. Write a definition for each of the following terms and add it to your personal glossary.

proprietary credit card
credit policy
three Cs of credit
credit report
credit bureau
credit score

credit risk
accounts receivable
accounts receivable aging
   report
collection agency
five Cs of banking

Review and Assessment

Chapter Summary

Section 16.1 Credit Basics

- Credit is an agreement between two parties in which one party extends credit and another party receives credit. The purpose of credit is to serve as a medium of exchange that allows individuals, businesses, and governmental agencies to buy goods or services now and pay for them later. Credit is also important to the economy because it keeps cash flowing and drives economic growth.

- Various types of credit are available to individuals and businesses. The most common types are closed-end credit and open-end credit. Installment loans are a common type of closed-end credit. An example of open-end credit is a credit card.

- Using credit is not free. The finance charge for the use of credit includes interest and fees. The total amount paid for the use of credit is based primarily on the interest rate charged, amount of credit used, and length of the repayment period. Businesses that extend credit must comply with both federal and state credit laws.

- Using credit unwisely can create financial disasters. Consumers who overuse credit run the risk of not being able make payments on time, which results in a lower credit score and higher interest rates. Businesses that overuse credit may not be able to pay business expenses and risk lawsuits.

Section 16.2 Business and Credit

- There are both costs and benefits to extending credit to customers. The costs may directly affect the profit of a business. Many businesses add a markup to the price of products to cover the cost of credit. The greatest benefit to offering customers is the generation of sales. Offering credit can create steady income for a business. Building customer loyalty is another benefit of extending credit to customers. Customers appreciate the convenience of using credit for purchases.

- Most businesses need credit at some point in their operation. For short-term credit needs, many businesses use bank-issued credit cards. Bank loans may be needed for long-term credit needs. To determine if a business has the ability to repay a loan, lenders evaluate businesses based on the five Cs of banking. Types of business credit include supplier financing and bank financing.

Online Activities

Complete the following activities to help you learn, practice, and expand your knowledge and skills.

 Posttest. Now that you have finished the chapter, see what you learned by taking the chapter posttest.

 Vocabulary. Practice vocabulary for this chapter using the e-flash cards, matching activity, and vocabulary game until you are able to recognize their meanings.

Review Your Knowledge

1. Identify some of the benefits of credit.
2. What is an amortization table?
3. Describe the charges associated with using credit.
4. What are the three factors that contribute to the total amount paid for using credit?
5. Discuss the possible outcomes of using credit unwisely.
6. Discuss the costs and benefits of extending credit to customers.
7. What information is provided about business or individual on a credit report?
8. How do accounts receivable affect the cash flow of a business?
9. How do conditions affect the ability of a business to repay a loan?
10. What are the most common terms for using trade credit?

Apply Your Knowledge

1. Credit serves many purposes for consumers and businesses alike. Write several paragraphs that summarize the purpose of credit in our economy.
2. Credit has a different level of importance for individual consumers and businesses. Explain the importance of credit for consumers and businesses. What is the recurring theme for both parties?
3. As a consumer, when is it acceptable to use credit? When is it unacceptable to use credit?
4. When considering a customer for credit, lenders review all the information on the credit application and credit report. What kind of information do you think could hurt a customer's chance of getting credit? Make a list of five items that could reflect negatively on someone's creditworthiness. Briefly describe how to fix or avoid each.
5. List the five Cs of banking used to evaluate the ability of a business to repay a loan. Describe what information a business can provide or may be requested to provide for each item listed.

Communication Skills

College and Career Readiness

Listening. Engage in a conversation with someone you have not spoken with before. Ask the person how he or she manages personal credit. Actively listen to what that person is sharing. Build on his or her ideas by sharing your own. Try this again with other people you have not spoken to before. How clearly were different people able to articulate themselves? How do you think having a conversation with someone you do not normally speak with is different from a conversation you might have with a friend or family member you speak with every day?

Speaking. Etiquette is the art of using good manners in any situation. Etiquette is especially important when making phone calls since the two parties cannot interact face-to-face. Create a script for a telephone conversation to convince a loan officer that you are a good candidate for an automobile loan. Make a list of the important facts that support why you should be granted a loan. Use "please" and "thank you" when appropriate. Ask a classmate to assume the role of the loan officer. Practice your telephone conversation. How would you rate your use of good manners? How does your classmate rate your speech?

Writing. Identity theft is a serious problem for business, as well as consumers. What responsibility do you think financial institutions have in preventing and addressing identity theft? Write a report consisting of several paragraphs that describes your opinion.

Internet Research

Credit Card Interest Rates. Credit is not free, and it can come with a hefty cost. This applies to both businesses and consumers. Using the Internet, search for current credit card rates. What rates did you find?

Credit Card Calculator. Search the Internet for a credit card calculator. Insert $1,000 at 13 percent interest. What is the total amount calculated?

Teamwork

With a small group of classmates, discuss how you will use credit in the future. What types of businesses will be involved in your use of credit? What is the maximum amount of credit debt you are willing to carry? Why did you choose that amount? Be prepared to share your discussion findings with the class.

Portfolio Development

College and Career Readiness

Networking. *Networking* means talking with others and establishing relationships with people who can help you achieve career, educational, or personal goals. You have probably already begun to build one, even if you have not thought of it in these terms. People in your network include your instructors, employers, coworkers, or counselors who know about your skills and interests. Those who participate with you in volunteer efforts, clubs, or other organizations can also be part of your network. These people may help you learn about open positions and may be able to give you information that will help you get a position.

1. Identify people who are part of your network.

2. Create a spreadsheet that includes information about each person. Include each person's name, contact information, and relationship to you. For example, the person might be a coworker, employer, or fellow club member. Save the file. This will be used for your personal use and not included in your portfolio.

CTSOs

Event Preparation. No matter which CTSO competitive events you participate in, you have to be well organized and prepared. Of course, you will have studied the content exhaustively before the event. You must also make sure all the tools you need for the event have been secured and travel arrangements to the event have been made. Confirming details well in advance of an event decreases stress and leaves you free to concentrate on the event itself.

To prepare for a competition, complete the following activities.

1. Pack appropriate clothing, including comfortable shoes and professional attire.

2. Prepare all technological resources, including anything that you might need to prepare or compete. Double check to make sure that any electronic presentation material is saved in a format that is compatible with the machines that will be available to you at the event.

3. If the event calls for visuals, make sure you have them prepared in advance and that they are packed and ready to take with you.

4. Bring registration materials, including a valid form of identification.

5. Bring study materials, including flash cards and other materials you have used to study for the event. If note cards are acceptable when making a presentation, make sure your notes are complete and easy to read. Have a back-up set in case of an emergency.

6. At least two weeks before you go to the competition, create a checklist of what you need for the event. Include every detail down to a pencil or pen. Use this checklist before you go into the presentation so that you do not forget anything.

CHAPTER 17

Financial Management

Exploring Careers

Accountant

Most companies are in business to make money. As a result, knowing the financial standing of a company is important information. Accountants are responsible for understanding and assessing this information. They also analyze financial information so they can advise business owners and managers. Business owners rely on accountants to help them make sound business decisions.

Typical job titles for this position also include *certified public accountant (CPA)*, *staff accountant*, and *cost accountant*. Examples of tasks accountants perform include:

- gather information to prepare financial reports
- create and maintain financial reports
- analyze financial reports to create forecasts and budgets
- communicate financial standing of company to managers or business owners
- compute taxes owed and prepare tax returns

Accounting positions require a bachelor degree in accounting, business administration, or a related field. Many companies require applicants to have a master degree in a related field, as well. The CPA certification is also required for many accounting jobs.

Reading Prep

Arrange a study session to read the chapter with a classmate. After you read each section independently, stop and tell each other what you think the main points are in the section. Continue with each section until you finish the chapter.

College and Career Readiness

Before you begin the chapter, see what you already know about business by taking the chapter pretest. The pretest is available at www.g-wlearning.com.

Section 17.1

Basic Accounting Procedures

?Essential Question

What are the basic accounting procedures businesses should practice?

Objectives

After completing this section, you will be able to:

- **Explain** the finance function of business.
- **Identify** types of daily business transactions.
- **List** the components of payroll.
- **Explain** double-entry accounting procedures.

Key Terms

financial planning
revenue
expense
financial management
accounting
generally accepted
  accounting
  principles (GAAP)
audit
business entity
fiscal period
budget

sales forecast budget
sales forecast
start-up budget
operating budget
cash budget
source document
sale on account
purchase on account
merchandise
payroll
withholding allowance
dependent

employee's earnings
  record
payroll register
gross pay
account
chart of accounts
double-entry
  accounting
journal
journalizing
ledger
posting

Finance

The finance function of business includes all activities that involve money. Finance is one of the four functions of business, as shown in Figure 17-1. An important part of finance is planning. **Financial planning** is the process of setting financial goals and developing plans to reach them. Business goals can be short-term or long-term and should be written as SMART goals.

The primary goal of business is to generate revenue. **Revenue** is the earnings that a business receives for the goods and services it sells. Successful businesses have three core goals. Each relates to generating adequate revenue:

- *Pay debts.* Banks and others who have extended credit to the business must be paid. These debts must be paid on time.

- *Provide return for investors.* Those who have a stake in a business expect to get returns on their investments.

- *Finance future growth.* For a business to continue, money must be available to finance future growth.

Goodheart-Willcox Publisher

Figure 17-1 Finance is the function of business that involves monetary activity.

Another important goal for a business is to control expenses. **Expenses** are the costs involved in operating a business. *Profit* is the difference between the income earned and expenses incurred by a business during a specific period of time.

Proper financial management helps businesses to remain profitable. **Financial management** is a process used to manage the financial resources of a business. It includes accounting, budgeting, and risk management. Risk management is covered in Chapter 14.

Accounting

Following sound accounting practices is the first step to good financial management. **Accounting** is the system of recording business transactions and analyzing, verifying, and reporting the results. The purpose of accounting is to keep records of transactions and to create financial statements and reports on a regular basis. Businesses must have accurate, up-to-date financial records in order to make good decisions that help the businesses grow and thrive.

Accounting is often called the *language of business.* No matter the type of business or its form of ownership, the accounting process produces reports and statements that are used to communicate financial information about a business to those who need the information. Those who use accounting information include managers, lending institutions, and taxing authorities.

Accounting is guided by **generally accepted accounting principles (GAAP)**. These are the rules, standards, and practices businesses follow to record and report financial information. By following GAAP, all businesses prepare statements and reports according to the same standards. The accounting records of businesses are audited to make certain that they have been in accordance to GAAP. An **audit** is a review of the financial statements of a business and the accounting practices that were used to produce them.

According to GAAP, for accounting purposes, each business is considered to be an independent business entity. A **business entity** is an organization that exists independently of the owner's personal finances.

Dragon Images/Shutterstock.com

Accountants keep accurate, up-to-date financial records that businesses use to make decisions and plans.

This applies whether the business is a sole proprietorship, partnership, or corporation. Business financial records must be kept separate from the owner's personal financial records. For example, if a business owns the building and vehicles used for business operations, these items would be listed only on the financial records of the business, not the owner's personal records. Likewise, personal property, like a home and personal car, are not included on business financial reports.

A **fiscal period** is the period of time for which a business summarizes accounting information and prepares financial statements. It may also be called an *accounting period*. The fiscal period for a business may be one month, one quarter, or one year. For tax purposes, most businesses use one year as the fiscal period.

An auditor reviews the financial statements of a business to confirm that standard practices have been followed and verify the financial data.

This is called the *fiscal year*. Businesses often use the *calendar year* of January 1 through December 31 as their fiscal year. However, a fiscal year can be any consecutive 12-month period.

There are two accounting methods used to record business transactions: cash-basis accounting and accrual basis accounting. Under the *cash-basis accounting*, revenue is not recorded until cash is received. Expenses are not recorded until cash is paid. For example, a business sells a $600 computer to a customer. The invoice for the sale may request payment in 30 days. Using the cash-basis accounting, the sale is not recorded until the business receives payment from the customer. Usually, only small service businesses use the cash-basis method.

Under the *accrual-basis accounting*, revenues and expenses are recorded when they occur. For example, the sale of a $600 computer is recorded when the sale happens, regardless of when payment is received. Most businesses use the accrual-basis method. Any business that carries an inventory must use accrual-basis accounting.

Budgets

A **budget** is a financial plan that reflects anticipated revenue and shows how it will be allocated in the operation of the business. Budgets are an important function of accounting. They are often used during financial planning. Business owners and managers must determine which expenses and other costs are necessary to keep the business operating successfully and which ones are not.

Budgets are typically created by each department of a business and then combined to create the overall company budget. This is the basis of making sound financial decisions. Business owners and managers are responsible for making financial decisions that directly influence the success of a business. The budgeting process provides a guide in carrying out the operations of the business.

Cost control is monitoring costs to stay within the planned budget. At the end of the year, managers compare the actual income, expenses, and other costs with the budgeted amounts. The budgets are then compared with the actual performance at the end of a financial time period.

Green Business | Reusable Water Bottles

Drinking water is good for a person's health. However, using disposable water bottles is bad for the environment and can also be bad for a person's health. According to National Geographic, over 80 percent of water bottles end up in landfills. Just like plastic bags, plastic water bottles do not biodegrade. Instead, they leak harmful chemicals into the soil and water.

The plastic used to bottle water may also be harmful to a person's health. The type of plastic used to bottle water is typically safe when used one time. However, when the bottle gets reused, it leaches harmful chemicals and bacteria with each sip. A more healthful choice is to use a reusable water bottle made from a safe, durable plastic that is washed frequently.

A *discrepancy* is the difference between the budgeted amount and the actual amount. This comparison provides management with a tool for planning the next year's budget. If there are financial issues which need attention, managers can make adjustments. For example, if expenses are higher than projected, a plan can be put into place to monitor and control them for the coming year.

kurhan/Shutterstock.com

Individual departments create budgets which are combined to create the overall company budget.

Common budgets used in financial planning include sales forecast, start-up, operating budgets, and cash budgets.

Sales Forecast Budget

Since revenue is the most important component of the budget, a sales forecast budget must be considered. The sales and marketing team usually creates this budget. The **sales forecast budget** is the projected sales units and revenue dollars for the period. The information for this budget starts with a sales forecast. A **sales forecast** is a prediction of future sales based on past sales. It also includes a market analysis for a specific time period. Sales forecasting is generally based on previous sales history, projections of sales from the sales team, and other factors specific to the business. The sales forecast helps guide the success of the business. Forecasts are also used to project the number of units of product needed to fill orders so that the business does not run out of stock.

Start-up Budget

A **start-up budget** is a budget created in the planning stages for a new business. This budget helps a new business project revenues and expenses until the business is profitable. It is typically part of the financial plan section of the business plan. A start-up budget includes information such as equipment needs, buildings, and any services required to get the business underway. Information for the budget is obtained from the pro forma financial statements that were created for the business plan.

Operating Budget

Once the business is in full operation, an operating budget may be used to project operations for the business. An **operating budget** is a projection of the sales revenue that will be earned and the expenses that will be incurred during a future period of time. The operating budget usually covers a period of twelve months. It allows a business to plan its expected revenue and expenses for the period of time covered by the budget. In a large business, each department may create its own operating budget. Each department is responsible for meeting its own sales and revenue projections.

Cash Budget

A **cash budget** is used to estimate the amount of money coming into and going out of the business. Estimates are based on the amount of revenue the business anticipates generating and expenses that will be incurred. These numbers are based on past history, as well as on other budgets.

Pablo Calvog/Shutterstock.com

The IRS requires businesses to maintain documentation for business transactions.

Accounting Transactions

A *business transaction* is any activity that affects the business. However, not all transactions involve cash. For example, a business may purchase equipment on credit or sell goods on credit to customers. A typical business has many types of transactions every day.

The *accounting equation* is the foundation of all accounting records. The accounting equation is stated as:

assets = liabilities + owner's equity

Assets are the property or items of value a business owns. Examples of assets are cash, inventory, buildings, and office and manufacturing equipment. A business also generally has *liabilities*, which are debts owed to others. Examples of liabilities are accounts payable, which are amounts owed to vendors. The difference between the assets of a business and its liabilities is called *owner's equity*. Owner's equity is also known as *net worth*.

Source documents are records that prove a business transaction occurred. This includes purchase orders, invoices, and other documents. All transactions must be documented with a physical source document, such as a printed receipt, purchase order, or invoice. The IRS requires that a business maintain proper documentation.

ra2studio/Shutterstock.com

An operating budget projects sales and expenses during a future period of time.

Source documents are necessary to prove the transaction actually happened. Examples of daily accounting transactions are:

- cash sales, credit sales, sales on account

- cash purchases, purchases on account

- cash paid for expenses

Sales

Cash sales are transactions in which cash is received by the business at the time of the sale. Some customers pay cash or write a check for their purchases. The business gives a copy of the sales receipt to the customer and keeps a copy for its records. Customers may use a bank-issued credit card or debit card to make a purchase. These are treated as cash sales. The business gives the customer a sales receipt and keeps a copy of the same receipt. The daily credit and debit card sales receipts are used to verify how much will be received from the credit card companies. The business also uses these records to calculate the monthly service charges owed to the credit card companies.

A **sale on account** is a transaction for which cash for the sale is received at a later date. These transactions are usually a business-to-business (B2B) customer. A sales invoice is sent to the customer and a copy is kept for the business. The customer account is known as an *account receivable*. Accounts receivable are considered assets.

Purchases

A **purchase on account** is a transaction for which merchandise purchased is paid to the vendor at a later date. **Merchandise** is an item, or items, that are bought with the intention of reselling to a customer.

A purchase order is sent to the vendor and a copy is kept for the business. The vendor account is known as an *account payable*. Accounts payable are liabilities. Sometimes a business will pay cash for merchandise. These transactions are called *cash purchases*.

After merchandise is purchased, it is stored as inventory. Inventory is the assortment or selection of items that a business has on hand at a particular point in time. Merchandise can be one of the largest assets a company owns. Because a large amount of cash, as well as storage, is tied up in merchandise, careful management is necessary.

wavebreakmedia/Shutterstock.com

When businesses purchase merchandise, they may make the purchase on account or pay cash.

Expenses

Expenses are the costs involved in operating a business. Rent, utilities, and gasoline are examples of expenses that a business incurs. Cash, checks, or credit cards are usually used to pay normal expenses of a business.

Payroll

An important responsibility of a business is to pay its employees. The **payroll** is a list of all employees working for the business and their earnings, benefits, taxes withheld, and other deductions. Employees are typically paid weekly, biweekly, or monthly. Payroll is generally the largest expense for a business and generates multiple types of financial transactions. These transactions are recorded when the payroll is completed for the pay period. Two important components of payroll are employee records and employer records.

Employee Records

Managing payroll requires the company to have accurate information for each employee. Payroll records include personal information about an employee, such as Social Security number, addresses, number of dependents, and other details related to compensation.

antoniodiaz/Shutterstock.com

Managing payroll involves recording personal information about each employee.

Recording employee information starts with the federal Form W-4. This form records an employee's address, Social Security number, and the number of withholding allowances claimed. A **withholding allowance** is an amount of income that is not subject to income taxes. An employee is allowed to claim a personal allowance and an allowance for each legal dependent. A **dependent** is an individual who relies on someone else for financial support, such as a child, a spouse, or an elderly parent.

The **employee's earnings record** is an individual record maintained for each employee. It shows the employee's payroll information year-to-date. Information from the earnings records of employees is used to complete reports required by federal and state law.

Employer Records

By law, employers must keep accurate records of earnings and payments to employees. Most employers do this with a payroll register. A **payroll register** is a summary of the earnings, payroll deductions, and net pay for all employees recorded for each payroll period. The payroll register can be prepared manually or using a payroll software program. Once completed, it becomes the basis for recording the payroll and issuing checks to employees. An example of a payroll register is shown in Figure 17-2.

Employees earn a wage or a salary which becomes an expense of the business. A *wage* is the dollar amount per hour that an employee is paid for work. Employees who work over 40 hours and earn a wage, are usually paid an additional wage for any overtime worked. A *salary* is a fixed amount paid for an employee's work and is usually paid monthly or twice a month. Managers are typically paid a salary and often work more than 40 hours a week. They are not usually entitled to overtime pay. In addition to paying for work, employers usually provide certain benefits for their employees. *Benefits* are a form of non-cash compensation received in addition to a wage or salary. Examples of benefits are sick days, vacation days, and insurance.

In general, withholdings are deducted from an employee's gross pay. **Gross pay** is the amount of

PAYROLL REGISTER

PERIOD ENDED: January 17, 20--   DATE OF PAYMENT: January 23, 20--

	EMPL. NO.	EMPLOYEE'S NAME	MARITAL STATUS	NO. OF ALLOW-ANCES	EARNINGS REGULAR	OVERTIME	TOTAL	FEDERAL INCOME TAX	SOC. SEC. TAX	MEDICARE TAX	HEALTH INSURANCE	OTHER	TOTAL	NET PAY	CHECK NO.	
					1	2	3	4	5	6	7	8	9	10		
1	203	Daniels, Bill	M	2	820.00	85.00	905.00	76.93	27.15	13.57	28.00		145.65	759.35	3900	1
2	228	Emery, Ethan	S	2	475.00		475.00	40.38	14.25	7.12	28.00		89.75	385.25	3901	2
3	266	Guerin, Kim	S	1	800.00	150.00	950.00	80.75	28.50	14.25	20.00		143.50	806.50	3902	3
4	267	Ramirez, Lupe	M	4	625.00	50.00	675.00	57.38	20.25	10.12	45.00		132.75	542.25	3903	4
5	235	Rogachevsky, Scott	M	3	520.00		520.00	44.20	15.60	7.80	45.00		112.60	407.40	3904	5
6	222	Sanders, Renee	S	1	750.00		750.00	63.75	22.50	11.25	20.00		117.50	632.50	3905	6
7																7
8																8
9																9
10																10
			TOTALS		3,990.00	285.00	4,275.00	363.39	128.25	64.11	186.00		741.75	3,533.25		

Goodheart-Willcox Publisher

Figure 17-2 A payroll register shows the earnings, deductions, and net pay for all employees for each payroll.

income earned before taxes and other deductions are withheld. Paycheck withholdings include:

- *FICA taxes.* These payroll taxes are paid in part by both employees and employers. FICA taxes finance Social Security and Medicare programs for those who are retired, disabled, or have other specific conditions.

- *Income taxes.* Income taxes are withheld from each employee's gross pay. They include federal income tax and state and local where required by law. Income taxes are used to provide governmental services.

- *Employee benefits.* Employers may cover all or a portion of the cost of the employee benefits offered, such as health and life insurance premiums. If the employee pays a portion, the amount is deducted from the gross pay.

Employers pay unemployment taxes for their employees. Unemployment taxes are used by the government to pay employees who have been laid off from their jobs. These taxes are paid by the employers only.

Employers must follow the provisions of the *Federal Insurance Contribution Act (FICA)* and other payroll tax laws. These laws ensure taxes are properly deducted from the payroll and forwarded to the appropriate agencies. The business sends the employee tax withholdings

to the local, state, and federal governments. Other deductions, such as insurance premiums, are forwarded to the insurance company or other institutions that should receive the amounts. Depending on the amount, payroll taxes withheld from employee earnings are sent to the federal government weekly, monthly, or quarterly. State taxes and other withholdings are usually paid quarterly.

©iStock.com/Art-Of-Photo

Withholdings, such as taxes and insurance, are deducted from an employee's gross pay.

After the payroll is complete, payroll checks are issued for each employee. Most companies make an electronic funds transfer (EFT) for the payroll. A direct deposit is made into each employee's bank account for his or her net pay. Each employee receives a payment record similar to a pay stub. This record shows gross amount, withholdings, and net pay.

Double-Entry Accounting

The first step in recording a transaction is to identify which accounts are affected. An **account** is an individual record that summarizes information for a single category, such as cash or sales. The name of the account is called the *account title*. A list of all accounts in the business is called the **chart of accounts**, as shown in Figure 17-3.

Every transaction affects at least two separate accounts. For example, if a customer buys a computer, the business not only has a sale, but it also receives money. The two accounts involved for this transaction are cash and sales. At least one account will be debited and one account will be credited. *Debit* is the left side of an account and *credit* is the right side of an account, as shown in Figure 17-4.

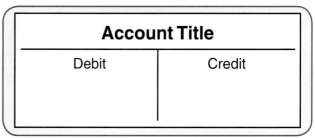

Account Title	
Debit	Credit

Goodheart-Willcox Publisher

Figure 17-4 Each transaction has a debit and a credit.

Cook's Computer Warehouse
Chart of Accounts

ASSETS

101   Cash
102   Accounts Receivable
103   Equipment

LIABILITIES

201   Accounts Payable
202   Notes Payable

OWNER'S EQUITY

301   David Cook, Capital
302   David Cook, Drawing

REVENUE

401   Sales

EXPENSES

501   Advertising Expense
502   Rent Expense
503   Insurance Expense
504   Supplies Expense
505   Utilities Expense

Goodheart-Willcox Publisher

Figure 17-3 A chart of accounts is a list of all business accounts.

Recording the debit and credit parts of a transaction is called **double-entry accounting.** Increases are recorded on the normal balance side of an account.

- Asset and expense account types have *debit balances*. For these accounts, debits *increase* the balance and credits *decrease* the balance.

- Liability, revenue, and owner's equity account types have *credit balances*. For these accounts, credits *increase* the balance and debits *decrease* the balance.

After a transaction is analyzed to determine the debits and credits, it is then recorded in a journal.

Journals

A **journal** is a form used to record business transactions in chronological order. **Journalizing** is the process of recording business transactions in a journal. A business selects the journals that best fit its needs. Some businesses use special journals. A *special journal* is used to record only one type of transaction. For a business with a large number of transactions, special journals are an efficient way to journalize. There are four special journals.

- *Cash receipts journals* are used for all receipts of cash.

- *Cash payments journals* are used for all payments of cash.

- *Sales journals* are used for all sales of merchandise on account transactions.

- *Purchases journals* are used for all purchases on account transactions.

Not all transactions are recorded in special journals. For example, when a customer returns merchandise that was bought on credit, that transaction would not be recorded in a special journal. A return is not a cash receipt, cash payment, sale, or purchase and would not be recorded in one of the special journals. As a result, another journal is needed. The journal used for any transaction that cannot be recorded in a special journal is called a *general journal*. A general journal can also be used to record all business transactions.

Some businesses prefer to use only a general journal rather than multiple special journals. Because the general journal requires the account name of the debit and credit to be written, it can accommodate any type of transaction. An example of a general journal is shown in Figure 17-5.

Ledgers

A group of accounts is called the **ledger.** The general ledger has individual accounts for each asset, liability, and owner's equity accounts.

Businesses also create individual accounts for customers who owe money, as well as accounts for the vendors to whom the business owes money. Individual accounts for customers and vendors are called *subsidiary ledgers*.

		GENERAL JOURNAL				PAGE 3		
						1	2	
			DOC.	POST.		GENERAL		
	DATE	ACCOUNT TITLE	NO.	REF.		DEBIT	CREDIT	
1	Mar 1	Cash				100 00		1
2		Sales					100 00	2
3		Receipt 101						3
4								4
5								5
6								6

Figure 17-5 A general journal can be used to record all business transactions.

After transactions are recorded in the journals, the information is transferred to the general ledger and the subsidiary ledgers, as shown in Figure 17-6. The transferring of information from the journals to the ledger is called **posting**. By posting to the ledgers, the business can obtain specific information about each account in the business. For example, if the business wants to know how much it owes to vendors, the Accounts Payable account will show the current balance. Businesses generally post at the end of each business day so that the accounts are up-to-date.

ACCOUNT	SALES					ACCOUNT NO.	410
			POST.			BALANCE	
DATE	ITEM		REF.	DEBIT	CREDIT	DEBIT	CREDIT
Mar 1			G1		100 00		100 00

Figure 17-6 The process of posting transactions to ledgers allows the business to obtain specific information about each account.

Section 17.1 Review

Check Your Understanding

1. The finance function of business includes what types of activities?
2. State the accounting equation.
3. What is the first step in recording a transaction?
4. What are subsidiary ledgers?
5. After transactions are recorded in the journals, where is the information transferred?

Build Your Vocabulary

As you progress through this course, develop a personal glossary of key terms. This will help you build your vocabulary and prepare you for a career. Write a definition for each of the following terms and add it to your personal glossary.

financial planning
revenue
expense
financial management
accounting
generally accepted accounting principles (GAAP)
audit
business entity
fiscal period
budget
sales forecast budget
sales forecast
start-up budget
operating budget
cash budget

source document
sale on account
purchase on account
merchandise
payroll
withholding allowance
dependent
employee's earnings record
payroll register
gross pay
account
chart of accounts
double-entry accounting
journal
journalizing
ledger
posting

Financial Records

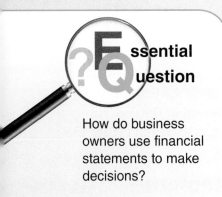

How do business owners use financial statements to make decisions?

Objectives

After completing this section, you will be able to:

- **State** the importance of financial statements for a business.
- **Explain** why financial statement analysis is performed.

Key Terms

accounting cycle
stakeholder
balance sheet
cash flow statement
income statement

financial ratio
working capital
current asset
current liability

current ratio
debt ratio
net profit ratio
operating ratio

Financial Statements

Financial statements are used to report information for the business. They are completed at the end of the accounting cycle. The **accounting cycle** is the sequence of steps businesses follow to record, summarize, and report financial information. By progressing through each step of the accounting cycle, the transactions of the business are recorded and summarized and financial statements can be produced.

Creating financial statements is one part of the financial management process. Businesses use financial statements to determine profitability and to help plan future business activities. Financial statements are also used when completing tax returns. Accurate statements make the tax process go smoothly and efficiently.

For those who have invested in a business, financial statements are important. People with a stake in the business need to see how their investments are doing. Financial statements give **stakeholders**, who are the people with interest in the business, updates about the status of the business. Lenders, such as a bank, want to know loans will be repaid on time.

Financial statements vary depending on if the business is a proprietorship, partnership, or corporation. However, for all businesses, financial statements are created on a regular basis, either monthly or quarterly. Financial statements are also prepared at the end of the fiscal year.

When a business is applying for funding, *pro forma statements* may be created. Pro forma statements are projections of future business transactions. Four pro forma statements typically created are the balance sheet, cash flow, income statement, and owner's equity. After the business is operating, the same types of financial statements will be created to reflect the actual transactions that have occurred in the business.

Balance Sheet

The **balance sheet** reports the assets, liabilities, and owner's equity. Assets are property or items of value owned by a business. Liabilities are the debts of the business. Owner's equity reflects the net worth of the business.

The balance sheet gives a snapshot of the financial condition of the business for a specific date. An example of a balance sheet is shown in Figure 17-7.

Cash Flow Statement

A **cash flow statement** reports how cash moves in to and out of a business. If the business is receiving more cash than it is spending, the cash flow is positive. The reverse is negative cash flow. A cash flow statement indicates how well a business is managing its expenses as they relate to income.

Income Statement

An **income statement** reports the revenue and expenses of a business for a specific time period and shows a net income or net loss. The revenue reflects the total amount of sales for the period. Expenses show amounts incurred to keep the business operating. The net income is the amount of profit at the end of the time period.

The income statement is also known as a *profit and loss (P & L) statement*. Figure 17-8 is an example of an income statement for a service business.

Owner's Equity Statement

The *owner's equity statement* summarizes changes in the owner's equity during a fiscal period. It is important for business owners to know what the equity was at the beginning of the accounting period as well as the end. An owner's equity statement is shown in Figure 17-9.

Financial Statement Analysis

Financial statement analysis is the process of reviewing information provided in financial statements to analyze the performance of the business. **Financial ratios** evaluate the overall financial condition of the business by showing the relationships between selected figures on financial statements.

Cook's Computer Warehouse
Balance Sheet
December 31, 20--

ASSETS

Cash	$36,000	
Accounts Receivable	22,000	
Equipment	15,000	
Total Assets		$73,000

LIABILITIES

Accounts Payable	$24,000	
Notes Payable	18,000	
Total Liabilities		$42,000

OWNERS' EQUITY

David Cook, Capital		31,000
Total Liabilities and Owner's Equity		$73,000

Goodheart-Willcox Publisher

Figure 17-7 A balance sheet shows all assets, liabilities, and owner's equity.

Cook's Computer Warehouse
Income Statement
For Year End December 31, 20--

Revenue

Sales		$68,000

Operating Expenses

Advertising Expense	$ 5,000	
Rent Expense	20,000	
Insurance Expense	6,000	
Supplies Expense	200	
Utilities Expense	1,800	
Total Expenses		33,000
Net Income		$35,000

Goodheart-Willcox Publisher

Figure 17-8 An income statement reports the revenue and expenses of a business.

Cook's Computer Warehouse
Owner's Equity Statement
For Year End December 31, 20--

David Cook, Capital, January 1		$10,000
Plus Net Income	35,000	
Less Withdrawals	14,000	
Net Increase in Capital		21,000
David Cook, Capital, December 31		$31,000

Goodheart-Willcox Publisher

Figure 17-9 All changes in the owner's equity during a fiscal period are reported on an owner's equity statement.

By analyzing financial ratios, owners can identify areas in which the business is strong and where improvements need to be made. Financial ratios provide a benchmark of company performance that can be compared to earlier years of the business. Ratios are also a good way to show comparisons with competitors in the same industry.

Balance Sheet

The balance sheet shows the financial strength of the business. In order to plan for the future, a business must have enough resources to pay debts and still have money to invest in the business. A business can measure its financial strength by analyzing the balance sheet and determine its working capital, current ratio, and debt ratio.

An important analysis for a business is to determine working capital. **Working capital** is the difference between current assets and current liabilities of a business. A **current asset** is cash or any asset that will be exchanged for cash or used within one year. Examples of current assets include inventory, accounts receivable, and supplies.

Pressmaster/Shutterstock.com

Creating financial statements is part of the financial management process. They are used to determine profitability and help plan future business activities.

A **current liability** is a short-term debt that must be paid within one year. Working capital is a measure of how well a business can meet its short-term debts.

current assets − current liabilities = working capital

$$\$58{,}000 - \$24{,}000 = \$34{,}000$$

The working capital is $34,000.

A **current ratio** shows the relationship of current assets to current liabilities. This ratio shows how capable a company is to pay its current liabilities.

current assets ÷ current liabilities = current ratio

$$\$58{,}000 \div \$24{,}000 = 2.42{:}1$$

The current ratio of 2.42:1 shows that assets are 2.42 times larger than liabilities. The business can compare this ratio with those of other similar businesses to see if it meets industry norms. Knowing this information can help the owner determine if the business is doing well or needs improvement.

A **debt ratio** shows the percentage of dollars owed as compared to assets owned.

total liabilities ÷ total assets = debt ratio

$$\$42{,}000 \div \$73{,}000 = .58{:}1$$

This ratio shows that for every dollar of assets, the business owes creditors 58 cents. The business can compare this ratio with industry guidelines to see if the ratio is healthy.

Income Statement

A business must analyze its progress on a regular basis to see if it is performing to industry standards and meeting the company's goals. *Profit margin ratios* are an important indicator of progress. Profit margin ratios include the net profit ratio and the operating ratio.

You Do the Math
Numeric Reasoning

To multiply whole numbers and decimals, place the numbers, called the *factors*, in pairs in a vertical list. When multiplying a percentage, move the decimal two places to the left. To find the number of decimal places needed in the final product, add the number of places in each number. Two decimal places plus three decimal places means the product must have five decimal places.

Solve the following problems.

1. Shelia earns $12 an hour and earns time and a half (1.5×) for hours worked over 40. Last week, Shelia worked a total of 42 hours. What is her gross pay?

2. You live in an area that has a general sales tax rate of 8.5 percent on most purchases. How much sales tax would you pay for the following goods?
   - $150 three-in-one computer printer
   - $30 box of printer paper
   - $4 package of pens

3. A business must pay a 2 percent fee on all credit card transactions. What is the total fee for all of these transactions: $24.76, $52.76, and $29.35?

Net profit ratio illustrates how much profit is generated per dollar of sales.

net income ÷ sales = net profit ratio

$35,000 ÷ $68,000 = .51:1

This ratio shows that for every dollar of sales, the business is producing 51 cents in profit.

Comparing expenses to sales is another important ratio. **Operating ratio** shows the relationship of expenses to sales.

expenses ÷ sales = operating ratio

$33,000 ÷ $68,000 = .49:1

This ratio shows that for every dollar of sales, 49 cents goes toward expenses.

Section 17.2 Review

 Check Your Understanding

1. When are financial statements completed for a business?
2. Which financial statement provides the financial condition of the business on a specific date?
3. For what purpose does the owner's equity statement serve?
4. List three financial ratios that are calculated from the balance sheet.
5. List two financial ratios that are calculated from the income statement.

 Build Your Vocabulary

As you progress through this course, develop a personal glossary of key terms. This will help you build your vocabulary and prepare you for a career. Write a definition for each of the following terms and add it to your personal glossary.

accounting cycle
stakeholder
balance sheet
cash flow statement
income statement
financial ratio
working capital

current asset
current liability
current ratio
debt ratio
net profit ratio
operating ratio

Review and Assessment

Chapter Summary

Section 17.1 Basic Accounting Procedures

- Finance is one of the four functions of business. Financial management is a process used to manage the financial resources of a business. It includes accounting, budgeting, and risk management. Financial planning is the process of setting financial goals and developing plans to reach them.

- A business transaction is any activity that affects the business. All daily business transactions must have a source document to prove it happened. The accounting equation is used to analyze business transactions.

- Businesses use double-entry accounting to record transactions. Every transaction has at least two parts, or two accounts. Transactions are recorded in journals then posted into ledgers.

- An important responsibility of a business is to pay its employees. The regular payroll generates multiple types of financial transactions. These transactions are recorded as the payroll is completed.

Section 17.2 Financial Records

- Financial statements are important to all the stakeholders in a business. These statements provide information about the financial status of the business. Creating financial statements is one part of the financial management process.

- The information provided in financial statements is used to analyze the performance of the business by calculating financial ratios. Financial statement analysis provides benchmarks for making decisions about the business.

Online Activities

Complete the following activities to help you learn, practice, and expand your knowledge and skills.

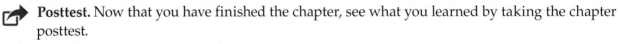 **Posttest.** Now that you have finished the chapter, see what you learned by taking the chapter posttest.

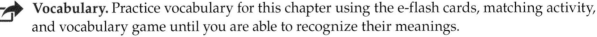 **Vocabulary.** Practice vocabulary for this chapter using the e-flash cards, matching activity, and vocabulary game until you are able to recognize their meanings.

Review Your Knowledge

1. Explain three core goals of a successful business.
2. Describe common budgets used in financial planning.
3. Explain a cash sale.
4. Describe two components of payroll.

5. List and describe four special journals used to record transactions.

6. Explain why financial statements are important to a business owner.

7. Define financial statement analysis.

8. What does the balance sheet show?

9. How is debt ratio calculated?

10. What do profit margin ratios indicate?

Apply Your Knowledge

1. Pay a visit to the accounting teacher in your school. Ask for examples of each of the basic journals typically used by a business. Create a poster of each with captions on the type of journal and its purpose.

2. A net profit ratio illustrates how much profit is generated per dollar of sales. Village Bicycle Shop has a net income of $62,000 and $107,000 in sales. Using the formula presented in the chapter, calculate the net profit ratio for Village Bicycle Shop. Explain what the resulting ratio means.

3. Acceptable accounting principles dictate that personal records be kept separately from the records of a business. Explain why this is important. What kinds of issues could arise from a business that does not follow this standard?

4. Using the balance sheet in Figure 17-7, interpret the nature of the statement. What does it show? Why should an investor analyze the balance sheet of a business? Interpret what the balance sheet reveals about a business.

5. Income statements provide important financial information for a business. What is the nature of income statements? Interpret the information that an income statement reveals about a business.

Communication Skills

College and Career Readiness

Reading. After reading this chapter, what insights did you gain about accounting processes that could be applied in a future career? Write several paragraphs describing what you learned.

Listening. Active listening is fully participating as you process what others are saying. Practice active listening skills while listening to your teacher present this chapter on financial management. Analyze the following aspects of the lecture: point of view, reasoning, stance, word choice, tone, points of emphasis, and organization.

Writing. It is important for an employee to apply both technical and academic skills in the workplace. Understanding basic financial information is a workplace skill that is applied each day in personal and work life. Write a paragraph describing why understanding finance is considered a workplace skill. How do you think that understanding finance will help you in your professional career?

Internet Research

Federal Accounting Standards Advisory Board. Visit the website of the Federal Accounting Standards Advisory Board (FASAB). Write a paragraph of the services that FASAB provides the accounting industry. Why do you think this organization is important for our economy?

Teamwork

Working with your team, create a tutorial for your classmates on the process of analyzing accounting transactions. Use visuals, such as a flow chart, to describe the steps in the process. Show examples of source documents that are used to document each financial transaction. Package the presentation in document format that a person unfamiliar with analyzing transactions could use.

Portfolio Development

College and Career Readiness

References. An important part of any portfolio is a list of references. A *reference* is a person who knows your skills, talents, or personal traits and is willing to recommend you. References will probably be someone from your network. These individuals can be someone for whom you worked or with whom you provided community service. Someone you know from your personal life, such a youth group leader, can also be a reference. However, you should not list relatives as references. Consider which references can best recommend you for the position for which you are applying. Always get permission from the person before using his or her name as a reference.

1. Ask several people from your network if they are willing to serve as a reference for you.

2. Create a Microsoft Word document with the names and contact information for your references. Use the heading "References" and your name. Save the document.

3. Update your master spreadsheet.

CTSOs

 **Business Financial Plan.** Creating a business financial plan is a competitive entrepreneurship event that may be offered by your Career and Technical Student Organization (CTSO). This may be an individual or team event. There may be two parts to this event: the written plan and the oral presentation of the plan.

The event calls for the development of a written business plan that will likely be judged prior to the competition. Written events can be lengthy and take a lot of time to prepare. Therefore, it is important to start early.

The rules for this event are similar to other business plan presentations. However, writing this plan requires research on the means of financing a business and the institutions and individuals that provide such financing.

To prepare for writing a financial plan, complete the following activities.

1. Read the guidelines provided by your organization. There will be specific directions given as to the parts of the business plan and how each should be presented. All final format guidelines will also be given, including how to organize and submit the business plan. Be sure to ask any questions about points that you do not understand.

2. Read the research topic assigned by your CTSO. Do your research early. Research may take days or weeks, and you do not want to rush the process.

3. Study this chapter to learn about financial plans.

4. Visit the website of your CTSO and create a checklist of the guidelines you must follow. Ask yourself: Does this event still interest me? Can I do what is necessary to be successful at the event? If you answered "yes," move forward with the writing process.

6. Set a deadline for yourself so that you write at a comfortable pace.

7. After you write your first draft, ask a teacher to review it and give you feedback.

8. Once you have the final version of your finance plan, review the checklist you prepared. Make sure you have addressed all the requirements. Your score will be penalized if a direction is not followed exactly.

9. Practice presenting the presentation.

Personal Finance

Focus on Personal Finance

Personal financial management is a process used by individuals to manage their limited income and meet unlimited personal needs and wants. Financially capable individuals know how to manage their resources to reach personal goals. Being *financially capable* means having the ability to understand basic topics related to finance. Understanding topics related to personal finance, such as earning money, spending money, and saving money, will help you reach your goals.

Financial fitness begins with identifying the values and goals most important to you. Values and goals will direct your financial decisions and help you to wisely manage your income throughout your life. You must first decide what you want most and then create a plan to use your resources to accomplish it.

Earning money from a career that is personally satisfying is the first step in gaining independence. Your financial success depends more on how you manage the money you earn, than how much money you earn. Through savings, investments, and managing risk you can learn to make wise choices that will help you reach your financial goals.

Social Media for Business

Twitter is a useful tool for communicating with customers. Businesses can connect in real time with customers who are using their product or visiting their booth at an exhibit. Customers can find information instantly about the company, a product launch, or another business announcement. The company can hear what customers are saying about the product, the company, the industry, or a particular topic. This line of communication also helps gather intelligence about the competition. Twitter is a good way to network and expand the customer base of a business.

A twitter post is called a *tweet* and is limited to 140 characters. Businesses that use Twitter can optimize their tweets by posting pictures and using the hashtag symbol (#). Twitter converts any word or URL with a hashtag in front of it into a searchable term. For example, if a business wanted to promote a new product called OrcaWater, it would include #OrcaWater in every tweet to create a searchable stream of relevant tweets about the product. Event organizers often use a hashtagged term to keep all tweets about an event in a single, searchable stream. Anyone searching Twitter for a topic can find all tweets containing the hashtagged word in a single location. People who search hashtags on Twitter often become Twitter followers of related businesses. Increasing the number of Twitter followers also increases the number of potential customers for a business!

While studying, look for the activity icon for:

- Pretests and posttests
- Vocabulary terms with e-flash cards and matching activities
- Self-assessment

G-WLEARNING.com

357

Exploring Careers

Tax Preparer

Preparing a tax return can be confusing for many people. A tax preparer completes tax returns for clients. This includes completing all supporting schedules, inserting all appropriate information, and calculating amount of money to be paid to or received from the IRS. Preparers may specialize in one area, such as individual returns, business returns, estates and trusts, tax planning, and tax appeals. Typical job titles for this position also include *tax advisor*, *tax consultant*, and *tax specialist*. Examples of tasks that tax preparers perform include:

- consult and advise clients on their taxes

- research tax laws and regulations

- input data into computer programs

- help clients develop plans to reduce taxes

- prepare all tax documentation for clients, such as return forms

Tax preparer jobs typically require a bachelor degree in accounting. To receive an Enrolled Agent (EA) designation from the IRS, tax preparers must complete 10 years of working for the IRS or pass a three-part comprehensive exam. A tax preparer spends a lot of time working directly with clients, so they must have excellent communication skills. They should have strong computer skills, knowledge of tax laws and regulations, and the ability to work without supervision in a fast-paced environment.

In This Chapter

College and Career Readiness

Reading Prep

The summary at the end of the chapter highlights the most important concepts. Read the chapter and write a summary of it in your own words. Then, compare your summary to the summary in the text.

Check Your Business IQ

Before you begin the chapter, see what you already know about business by taking the chapter pretest. The pretest is available at www.g-wlearning.com.

Income

?**E**ssential **Q**uestion

Why is it important to understand how to make wise personal financial decisions?

Objectives

After completing this section, you will be able to:

- **Explain** the importance of financial management.
- **Describe** different forms of earned income.
- **Identify** payroll deductions.
- **Explain** the steps involved in creating a budget.

Key Terms

personal financial
   management
financially capable
earned income
minimum wage

overtime wage
tip
payroll deduction
allowance
net pay

FICA taxes
fixed expense
variable expense
variance

Personal Financial Management

Financial management is a process used by businesses to manage financial resources to accomplish business goals. **Personal financial management** is a process used by individuals to manage limited income to meet personal unlimited needs and wants. **Financially capable** means having the ability to understand basic topics related to finance. These topics include earning money, as well as spending, saving, and investing money.

Personal financial management begins when an individual receives money. The money may be received as a gift or as earnings from a job. Money could be from winning a contest or some other source. Having money creates the need for making decisions. Personal values, priorities, and goals influence the decisions an individual makes. Should the money be spent, saved, or invested?

Cheryl Savan/Shutterstock.com

Personal financial management begins when a person receives money. Money received as a gift, in a paycheck, or any other source creates financial decisions.

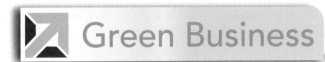

Green Business Unplug Electronics

If electronics and appliances are turned off at night, will the electric bill be less? The answer is a potential "no." Electronics that are plugged into an outlet use standby power, which is the minimum power usage when the item is plugged in. That means that even if it is turned off, it is still drawing power and costing money to run, just because it is plugged into an outlet. To make sure that computers, monitors, printers, photocopiers, and other electronics will not waste power, unplug them entirely.

It is a common practice in Europe to unplug equipment that is not in use, including lights and computers. Up to 25 percent can be saved on energy costs by just turning off and unplugging equipment at the end of the day. Less energy usage also reduces negative effects on the environment.

Every financial decision has a cost. Choosing one option means giving up other options that may have been available. A *trade-off* is an item given up in order to gain something else. A trade-off then creates an opportunity cost. *Opportunity cost* is the value of the next best option that was not selected. The decision-making process can help an individual make wise financial decisions. By using the steps in Figure 18-1, a systematic approach can be applied to analyze trade-offs and opportunity costs.

Learning how to manage your money also includes understanding your rights as a consumer. There are many resources available that provide information for making wise decisions about spending money. Consumer advocacy groups promote consumer rights and interests. The government provides regulatory and law enforcement agencies to deal with dishonest and fraudulent business practices. The Better Business Bureau (BBB) is a non-profit group that promotes ethical business practices and can offer support for consumers who need assistance. There are many resources available on the Internet to assist buyers before making spending decisions. Contracts and consumer protection laws are discussed in Chapter 3.

Earned Income

Earned income is the income received from employment or from self-employment. For most people, employment is the primary way to earn income. Earned income can be a wage, salary, or commission. It also includes tips, bonuses, and income from self-employment.

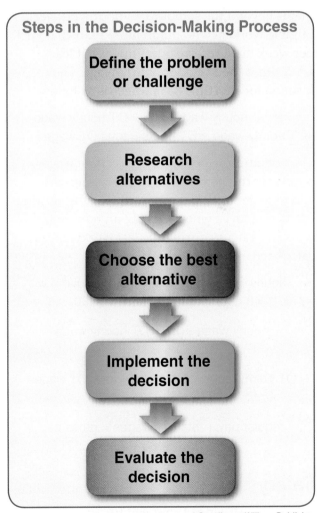

Steps in the Decision-Making Process

Define the problem or challenge

Research alternatives

Choose the best alternative

Implement the decision

Evaluate the decision

Goodheart-Willcox Publisher

Figure 18-1 A systematic decision-making process can be a helpful tool when making economic decisions.

Wage

A *wage* is payment for work and is usually calculated on an hourly, daily, or weekly basis. A wage is paid on a schedule which is often every week or every two weeks. Many unskilled and beginning workers are paid the minimum wage. The **minimum wage** is the lowest hourly wage employers can pay most workers by law. The US government sets and enforces the minimum wage through the Fair Labor Standards Act (FLSA). The total amount of earnings before deductions is known as *gross pay*. The formula for gross pay is as follows.

hourly wage × hours worked = gross pay

Most wage earners are covered by the overtime provisions of the FLSA. **Overtime wage** is the amount paid for working time in a week that is beyond the standard 40-hour workweek. Eligible workers who put in more than 40 hours per week must receive overtime pay at least 1 1/2 times their regular hourly wage. The formula for overtime (OT) wages is as follows.

hourly wage × 1.5 = OT hourly wage
OT hourly wage × OT hours = total OT wages

For employees who earn overtime wages, regular earnings plus overtime earnings are added to get gross pay. For example, the earnings for an employee who earns $12 an hour and worked 44 hours during the last workweek is calculated as follows.

hourly wage × hours worked = regular pay
40 hours × $12 per hour = $480

hourly wage × 1.5 = OT hourly wage
$12 × 1.5 = $18

OT hourly wage × OT hours = total OT wages
$18 × 4 = $ 72

regular pay + total OT wages = gross pay
$480 + 72 = $552

Salary

A *salary* is a fixed payment for work and is usually expressed as an annual figure. It is paid in periodic equal payments. The payment period is usually weekly, biweekly (every other week), semimonthly (twice a month), or monthly. Salaried workers are expected to put in as much time as it takes to do the job. Therefore, most professionals who are on salary are not paid overtime.

Commission

A *commission* is income paid as a percentage of sales made by a salesperson. Some people may work on a commission-only basis. Others may receive a combination of their regular salary plus commission. Salespeople usually work on commission.

Tips

A **tip** is money paid for service beyond the payment that is required. A customer leaves a tip as a reward for good service. A tip is also known as a *gratuity*. Tips also provide an incentive for workers to provide good service. This money belongs to the worker, not the employer.

Aigars Reinholds/Shutterstock.com

Wages are typically earned per hour of work.

Bonus

A *bonus* is money added to an employee's base pay. It is usually a reward for performance or a share of business profits. Bonuses are incentives to encourage workers to perform better. Bonus income is usually based on worker performance, length of time with the company, or company performance.

Self-Employment Income

A growing proportion of the US workforce is self-employed. Unlike employees who perform services for their employer, self-employed individuals work for themselves. The form of income earned is called *profit* or *self-employment income.*

Payroll Deductions

A **payroll deduction** is a subtraction from gross pay. Some deductions are mandatory, such as Social Security taxes, Medicare taxes, and income taxes. Other payroll deductions are optional, such as health insurance and retirement savings plans.

The federal income tax system is built on a pay-as-you-earn concept. This means a working person pays taxes from each paycheck instead of in one lump sum each year. State and local income taxes usually work this way, as well.

Employees complete a Form W-4 when they begin a job. Form W-4 is the Employee's Withholding Allowance Certificate that helps the employer determine how much income tax to withhold from an employee's paychecks as payroll deductions. Figure 18-2 shows a completed Form W-4.

The amount of income tax withheld from a paycheck depends on how much is earned, marital status, and the number of allowances that are claimed. An **allowance** is an amount of earnings not subject to income taxes. Taxpayers may take an allowance for themselves and for each of their dependents. The more allowances claimed, the smaller the amount of tax that will be withheld from a paycheck by the employer.

Net pay is gross pay minus payroll deductions. It is also known as *take-home pay.* For an example of common payroll deductions, see the paycheck stub in Figure 18-3.

gross pay − payroll deductions = net pay

Source: US Department of the Treasury/Internal Revenue Service; Goodheart-Willcox Publisher

Figure 18-2 Employees complete the Form W-4. It provides information employers use to determine how much federal tax to withhold from paychecks.

Town Department Store 111 Broadway Avenue Franklin, IL 65432		Pay Period: 03/08/-- through 03/21/--		Employee: Kristy A. James 1027 Cedar Street Franklin, IL 65432	
Gross Pay	Federal Income Tax Withheld	State Income Tax Withheld	Social Security Tax Withheld	Medicare Tax Withheld	Net Pay
$ 345.00	$ 18.06	$ 13.80	$ 21.39	$ 5.00	$ 286.75
Gross Pay Year-to-Date	Federal Year-to-Date	State Year-to-Date	Social Security Year-to-Date	Medicare Year-to-Date	Net Pay Year-to-Date
$ 8,484.50	$ 444.16	$ 339.38	$ 526.04	$ 123.03	$ 7,051.89

Goodheart-Willcox Publisher

Figure 18-3 This paycheck stub shows some of the common payroll deductions from income.

FICA Tax

Most workers in the United States are covered by the Federal Insurance Contributions Act (FICA). **FICA taxes** are taxes paid by the employee and employer that are used to finance the federal Social Security and Medicare programs. Total FICA taxes are 7.65 percent, which includes 6.2 percent for Social Security taxes and 1.45 percent for Medicare. Employers withhold FICA taxes from each employee's paycheck. There is an annual cap on the amount of income that is subject to the Social Security portion of FICA taxes. However, there is no cap on income that is taxed for Medicare.

The FICA tax is a matching tax. This means that employers must match the amount of FICA taxes that their employees pay. Employers add their share of the FICA tax and pay the total to the government under the employee's name and Social Security number.

For individuals who are self-employed, they must pay both the employer and employee percentages on the income that they make. That means they pay double the tax that an individual working for an employer pays.

Federal, State, and Local Withholding Taxes

The amount deducted for taxes is based on earnings, marital status, and withholding allowances that an employee claims. Federal income taxes are taxes withheld from the employee's gross pay and forwarded to the federal government. The taxes collected are used for many purposes, such as national security and other governmental functions.

State income taxes are taxes withheld from the employee's gross pay and are forwarded to the state government. Most states have an income tax. These taxes are used for roads, education, and other state-specific purposes.

Some local governments, such as cities and counties, also have income taxes. Local withholding taxes are withheld from the employee's gross pay and forwarded to the local government. These taxes are used for police departments, roads, and other local services.

Other Deductions

Voluntary deductions may be withheld for health care, dental care, vision care, and other insurance that employees purchase through their employers. These deductions might also include charitable contributions, which are donations made to a charitable organization.

Budgeting Your Earnings

Once you begin working, it is important to learn how to manage earnings. An important step of financial management is to create a budget.

You Do the Math   Connections

Many calculations related to income and taxes involve percentages. A percentage (%) means a part of 100, and is the same as a fraction or decimal. For example, 15 percent is the same as 15 ÷ 100 or .15. To calculate the percentage of a number, change the percentage to a decimal and multiply by the number.

For example, 15 percent of 200 = 15/100 × 200 or .15 × 200 = 30

Solve the following problems.

1. Riley has been working as an office assistant for 3 years making a salary of $19,500. During his recent performance review, he was given an 11 percent raise. What is Riley's new salary?

2. Social security tax is one of the standard withholdings from employee paychecks. Marin earns $650 per week before withholdings. Social Security tax is 6.2 percent. How much will be withheld from Marin's paycheck for Social Security?

3. Local currency exchange businesses offer check cashing services for a fee. To cash checks written for amounts between $500.00 and $2,000.00, the currency exchange charges 2 percent of the check amount. If you cash a check written for $575.00 at a currency exchange, how much money will you be given?

A *budget* is a financial plan used by business to project anticipated revenue and show how it will be allocated in the operation of the business. A *personal budget* is a financial plan used by individuals to project anticipated earnings and shows how they will be allocated. It is a financial plan for controlling spending and building wealth for your future. A well-developed budget serves as a guide that helps an individual stay on track to achieve personal and financial goals.

A budget can be prepared using paper and pencil, electronic spreadsheet programs, or with personal finance software programs. Personal finance software programs are inexpensive and include Quicken®, BankTree, and AceMoney.

A budget should be created based on SMART goals. If the goals are not measurable, they will be hard to accomplish. The budget process involves the following basic steps:

1. Set a budget period.

2. List estimated income.

3. List estimated expenses.

4. Track spending.

5. Compare budgeted amount with actual amounts.

Step 1: Set a Budget Period

Any period of time can be selected as a budget period. However, personal budgets are usually prepared on a monthly basis. This is because most major household expenses are paid monthly.

Andrey_Popov/Shutterstock.com

Creating a personal budget helps control spending and build wealth.

Step 2: List Estimated Income

The process of developing a budget starts with listing income. Only income that is available for current living expenses should be included. Income reserved for future use, such as retirement savings, should not be included.

Step 3: List Estimated Expenses

Expenses are cash expenditures made during the budget period. Savings amounts are also listed in this category as it is money that should be put aside each budget period. Savings can include any bank account or other investments such as an Individual Retirement Account (IRA).

The key to controlling spending is being aware of exactly where your money is going. For planning and control, it is helpful to classify expenses as fixed and variable. A **fixed expense** is one that is equal in amount each budget period. Fixed expenses do not change with fluctuations in income. Examples of common fixed expenses are car payments and rent. A **variable expense** is an expense that can go up and down during the budget period. Examples of variable expenses are costs for clothing and entertainment.

Step 4: Track Spending

Budgeting is an ongoing process and progress must be continuously monitored. Each time money is spent or received, the amount should be recorded in the *Actual Amount* column. It is also a good idea to keep receipts as a record of spending.

Step 5: Compare

At the end of the budget period, compare actual amounts with budgeted amounts. The difference between the actual amounts and the budgeted amounts is referred to as a **variance**. Variances can be favorable or unfavorable. For example, if less money is spent than budgeted, it is a *favorable variance*. On the other hand, if more money is spent than the budgeted amount, it is an *unfavorable variance*.

A personal budget for a married couple with two incomes is shown in Figure 18-4.

• The *Budgeted Amount* column shows the estimated income and expenses for the month. The amounts in this column are estimated and entered at the start of the month.

mangostock/Shutterstock.com

A car payment is a fixed expense that is the same amount in each budget period.

CATEGORY	Budgeted Amount	Actual Amount	Variance
INCOME:			
John's take home pay	$3,255	$3,255	$--
Susan's take home pay	2,878	2,878	--
Monthly interest from investments	200	290	90
Income subtotal	$6,333	$6,423	*$90*
EXPENSES:			
House payment	$1,317	$1,317	$--
Car payment	425	425	--
Life insurance premium	50	50	--
Auto insurance premium	85	123	-38
Health insurance	300	300	--
College Funds	200	200	--
IRA contributions	400	400	--
Heating and electricity	200	242	42
Telephone	90	110	-20
Water and sewer	50	58	-8
Lawn care	40	40	--
Gasoline/oil	250	305	-55
Auto repairs	0	40	-40
Clothing	100	80	20
Entertainment	200	170	30
Internet and cable	82	82	--
Groceries	400	456	-56
Eating out	200	212	-12
Gifts/Donations	300	240	60
Expenses subtotal	$4,689	$4,850	-$161
Remainder (income – expenses)	$1,644	$1,573	$71

Figure 18-4 A budget shows estimated income and expenses. Make adjustments to variable expenses when an unfavorable variance occurs.

- Amounts in the *Actual Amount* column show the actual figures for income and expenses during the month. These amounts are entered as each occurs. However, some people prefer to record all amounts at the end of the month.

- The third column, the *Variance* column, shows the difference between the budgeted amounts and the actual amounts. Note that actual income

exceeded budgeted income. The result is a favorable income variance of $90. On the other hand, actual expenses exceeded budgeted expenses. The result is an unfavorable expense variance of $161. Unfavorable variances should be studied closely to determine why they happened.

Overall, the budget was favorable. Even though expenses were higher than projected, the income was still higher than expenses.

Section 18.1 Review

 Check Your Understanding

1. What does earned income include?
2. What is the formula for calculating gross pay? For net pay?
3. Which payroll deductions are mandatory?
4. List examples of items that are considered payroll deductions.
5. List the five steps of the budget process.

 Build Your Vocabulary

As you progress through this course, develop a personal glossary of key terms. This will help you build your vocabulary and prepare you for a career. Write a definition for each of the following terms and add it to your personal glossary.

personal financial management	payroll deduction
financially capable	allowance
earned income	net pay
minimum wage	FICA taxes
overtime wage	fixed expense
tip	variable expense
	variance

Section 18.2

Taxes

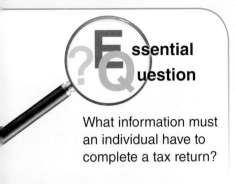

?**E**ssential **Q**uestion

What information must an individual have to complete a tax return?

Objectives

After completing this section, you will be able to:

- **Differentiate** the forms used in filing an income tax return.
- **Explain** how to calculate taxable income.
- **Explain** how to prepare a Form 1040EZ.
- **Identify** where tax information and assistance can be found.

Key Terms 📤

tax return
Form W-2 Wage and
   Tax Statement
unearned income

taxable income
tax deduction
itemized deduction

standard deduction
exemption
tax credit

Filing an Income Tax Return

The individual income tax is the federal government's largest source of revenue. The Internal Revenue Service (IRS) is the government agency responsible for collecting federal income taxes. Approximately 200 million individuals file a tax return each year. A **tax return** is a report containing information used to calculate taxes owed by the taxpayer. Tax returns must also be filed with most tate governments. In some areas, a city tax return may also need to be filed. Not filing a tax return is a crime.

Individuals must file a tax return when his or her income reaches a level established by law. If income is not great enough to file a tax return but income taxes were withheld, a return should be filed so a refund can be obtained. Refunds are never automatic. A tax return must be filed in order to receive a refund.

Tax returns must be filed no later than April 15 of the year after the income was earned.

If April 15 falls on a Saturday, a Sunday, or a national holiday, the filing date is extended to the next business day. Those who owe taxes and file late are charged a penalty.

Africa Studio/Shutterstock.com

Individuals must file tax returns with the federal government.

In addition to filing on time, it is important to provide accurate information on a tax return form. Being *accurate* means to give factual, error-free information. Providing *inaccurate* information could extend the processing of the tax return, delay the tax refund, and may prompt the IRS to investigate the tax return in a process called an audit. An *audit* is the review of financial records and statements to make sure the information is accurate as reported.

It is easy to make an error when recording numbers. To ensure accuracy, double-check the entries and the calculations. Being accurate also means recording truthful information. Intentionally providing false information on a tax return form is a crime. An individual caught providing false information faces financial penalties, fines, and even criminal prosecution.

A Form W-2 is needed to complete a tax return. A **Form W-2 Wage and Tax Statement** shows earnings and tax deductions withheld during the year. A Form W-2 is shown in Figure 18-5. This statement is automatically sent each January by employers to their employees. Other documentation, such as interest statements from the bank for savings accounts, is also needed to complete a return.

The three basic forms used to file income taxes are 1040, 1040A, and 1040EZ. Forms and instructions are available for download on the IRS website at www.irs.gov. Printed forms can be picked up at community locations, such as public libraries and post offices.

- *Form 1040* is commonly referred to as the *long form*. It must be used by taxpayers with a taxable income more than $100,000. It must also be used by taxpayers who have business or rental income, income or losses from selling assets, or itemized tax deductions.

- *Form 1040A* is commonly referred to as the *short form*. It can be used by taxpayers with a taxable income less than $100,000 who have

22222	a Employee's social security number 987-65-4321	OMB No. 1545-0008		
b Employer identification number (EIN) XX-XXXXXXX		1 Wages, tips, other compensation 28956.98	2 Federal income tax withheld 3020.42	
c Employer's name, address, and ZIP code Town Department Store 111 Broadway Avenue Franklin, IL 65432		3 Social security wages 28956.98	4 Social security tax withheld 1795.33	
		5 Medicare wages and tips	6 Medicare tax withheld 419.88	
		7 Social security tips	8 Allocated tips	
d Control number 123456789		9 Advance EIC payment	10 Dependent care benefits	
e Employee's first name and initial Last name Suff. Kristy A. James 1027 Cedar Street Franklin, IL 65432		11 Nonqualified plans	12a	
		13 Statutory employee ☐ Retirement plan ☐ Third-party sick pay ☐	12b	
		14 Other	12c	
			12d	
f Employee's address and ZIP code				
15 State Employer's state ID number IL XX-XXXXXXX	16 State wages, tips, etc. 28956.98	17 State income tax 1362.40	18 Local wages, tips, etc.	19 Local income tax	20 Locality name

Form **W-2** Wage and Tax Statement   **20--**   Department of the Treasury—Internal Revenue Service

Copy 1—For State, City, or Local Tax Department

Figure 18-5 A Form W-2 shows how much an employee was paid during a year and the payroll deductions that were withheld.

no business income and who choose not to itemize deductions. Most taxpayers who have dependents, but are not homeowners, use Form 1040A.

- *Form 1040EZ* is the simplest form to use. This form is for individuals with a taxable income less than $100,000. They must also file as single or married filing jointly and claim no dependents. Income can only be from employee compensation, unemployment compensation, and interest.

Electronic filing (e-filing) allows filing of an income tax return online. A variety of computer software programs are available that enable a return to be filed using a personal computer. These programs can be purchased on CD or downloaded from the web page of the company that produces the program. E-filing programs provide information, advice, and step-by-step directions for the filing process. The IRS also offers a free e-filling service.

Income

Gross income includes earned and unearned income. *Earned income* is earnings from employment. This includes earned income of wages, salary, commission, tips, and bonuses.

Andrey_Popov/Shutterstock.com

Tax returns can be conveniently filed online through e-filing.

Unearned income is earnings from sources other than work. Unearned income includes interest on savings accounts, earnings from investments, and rental income. It also includes Social Security and retirement income, alimony, and unemployment compensation. Lottery winnings or other contest winnings are also considered as unearned income.

Taxable income is the amount on which taxes are calculated. Taxes are not calculated based on gross income, but can be reduced by adjustments. Adjustments are government-approved reductions in gross income. This helps to reduce the amount of tax that must be paid. For example, students or their parents can deduct the interest paid on student loans. *Adjusted gross income* is calculated by subtracting adjustments from total income.

A **tax deduction** is an amount that is subtracted from adjusted gross income, which further reduces taxable income. When filing a tax return, deductions may be itemized or a standard deduction can be used. An **itemized deduction** is an allowed expense that can be deducted from adjusted gross income. Typical itemized deductions are interest paid on home loans, taxes paid on the value of a home, state income taxes paid, and contributions to recognized charities and churches.

Taxpayers who do not have enough itemized deductions to benefit from them can choose the standard deduction. The **standard deduction** is a fixed amount that may be deducted from adjusted gross income. The standard deduction amount is set by law. It will vary according to the taxpayer's filing status (single, married, or head of household).

Taxpayers also are allowed tax exemptions. An **exemption** is an amount that a taxpayer can claim for each person who is dependent on that person's income. There are two types of exemptions: personal and dependent. *Personal exemptions* are those claimed for the taxpayer or the taxpayer and spouse, if married and filing together. *Dependent exemptions* are those claimed for children or other individuals supported by the taxpayer.

Hurst Photo/Shutterstock.com

Receipts for itemized deductions should be kept in an organized manner throughout the year.

A **tax credit** is an amount that is subtracted from the taxes an individual owes, if eligible. Tax credits provide a greater advantage than tax deductions. Deductions reduce taxable income, but a credit reduces taxes. For example, taxpayers with income under a designated amount can take a $1,000 tax credit for each dependent child under the age of 17. Tax advisors or the IRS can advise taxpayers which tax credits might be available to them.

Preparing a Form 1040EZ

The first step to complete a tax return is to fill in the personal information. An example of Form 1040EZ is shown in Figure 18-6. Accuracy is important in recording information. If any information contains errors, the taxpayer's refund check could be delayed. A taxpayer can also face fines, penalties, and interest if inaccurate information results in an excessive refund.

Personal Information

The taxpayer's name, current address, and Social Security number should be clearly written in the space provided.

Income

Income from wages, salaries, and tips should be recorded. Taxable interest and unemployment compensation should be entered. Next, calculate the adjusted gross income. The taxpayer can claim him- or herself as an exemption and a spouse, if married. The taxable income can then be figured.

Payments, Credits, and Tax

Federal income tax that has been withheld and recorded on the Form W-2 is recorded.

Department of the Treasury—Internal Revenue Service

Form 1040EZ

Income Tax Return for Single and Joint Filers With No Dependents (99)   **20--**

OMB No. 1545-0074

Your first name and initial
Kristy A.

Last name
James

Your social security number
987 65 4321

If a joint return, spouse's first name and initial

Last name

Spouse's social security number

Home address (number and street). If you have a P.O. box, see instructions.
1027 Cedar Street

Apt. no.

▲ Make sure the SSN(s) above are correct.

City, town or post office, state, and ZIP code. If you have a foreign address, also complete spaces below (see instructions).
Franklin, IL 65432

Presidential Election Campaign
Check here if you, or your spouse if filing jointly, want $3 to go to this fund. Checking a box below will not change your tax or refund. ☑ You ☐ Spouse

Foreign country name

Foreign province/state/county

Foreign postal code

Income Attach Form(s) W-2 here. Enclose, but do not attach, any payment.	1	Wages, salaries, and tips. This should be shown in box 1 of your Form(s) W-2. Attach your Form(s) W-2.	1	28,956	98
	2	Taxable interest. If the total is over $1,500, you cannot use Form 1040EZ.	2	850	00
	3	Unemployment compensation and Alaska Permanent Fund dividends (see instructions).	3		
	4	Add lines 1, 2, and 3. This is your **adjusted gross income.**	4	29,806	98
	5	If someone can claim you (or your spouse if a joint return) as a dependent, check the applicable box(es) below and enter the amount from the worksheet on back. ☐ You ☐ Spouse If no one can claim you (or your spouse if a joint return), enter $10,150 if **single;** $20,300 if **married filing jointly.** See back for explanation.	5	10,150	00
	6	Subtract line 5 from line 4. If line 5 is larger than line 4, enter -0-. This is your **taxable income.** ▶	6	19,656	98
Payments, Credits, and Tax	7	Federal income tax withheld from Form(s) W-2 and 1099.	7	3,020	42
	8a	**Earned income credit (EIC)** (see instructions)	8a		
	b	Nontaxable combat pay election. 8b			
	9	Add lines 7 and 8a. These are your **total payments and credits.** ▶	9	3,020	42
	10	**Tax.** Use the amount on **line 6 above** to find your tax in the tax table in the instructions. Then, enter the tax from the table on this line.	10	2,498	00
	11	Health care: individual responsibility (see instructions) Full-year coverage ☑	11		
	12	Add lines 10 and 11. This is your **total tax.**	12	2,498	00
Refund Have it directly deposited! See instructions and fill in 13b, 13c, and 13d, or Form 8888.	13a	If line 9 is larger than line 12, subtract line 12 from line 9. This is your **refund.** If Form 8888 is attached, check here ▶ ☐	13a	522	42
	▶ b	Routing number	▶ c Type: ☐ Checking ☐ Savings		
	▶ d	Account number			
Amount You Owe	14	If line 12 is larger than line 9, subtract line 9 from line 12. This is the **amount you owe.** For details on how to pay, see instructions. ▶	14	0	00

Third Party Designee
Do you want to allow another person to discuss this return with the IRS (see instructions)? ☐ **Yes.** Complete below. ☑ **No**

Designee's name ▶

Phone no. ▶

Personal identification number (PIN) ▶

Sign Here
Joint return? See instructions. Keep a copy for your records.

Under penalties of perjury, I declare that I have examined this return and, to the best of my knowledge and belief, it is true, correct, and accurately lists all amounts and sources of income I received during the tax year. Declaration of preparer (other than the taxpayer) is based on all information of which the preparer has any knowledge.

Your signature
Kristy A. James

Date
3/1/--

Your occupation
Sales Clerk

Daytime phone number
(123) 456-7890

Spouse's signature. If a joint return, **both** must sign.

Date

Spouse's occupation

If the IRS sent you an Identity Protection PIN, enter it here (see inst.)

Paid Preparer Use Only

Print/Type preparer's name

Preparer's signature

Date

Check ☐ if self-employed

PTIN

Firm's name ▶

Firm's EIN ▶

Firm's address ▶

Phone no.

For Disclosure, Privacy Act, and Paperwork Reduction Act Notice, see instructions.

Cat. No. 11329W

Form **1040EZ** (20--)

Figure 18-6 The 1040EZ is the simplest income tax return form.

The amount of tax owed is then identified on the tax tables. A partial 1040EZ tax table is shown in Figure 18-7. In this example, Kristy's taxable income ($19,656.98) falls in the income bracket *At least 19,650, But less than 19,700*. The tax in that bracket for a single person is $2,498. Kristy entered that amount on Line 10 of 1040EZ.

The Patient Protection and Affordable Care Act, passed in 2013, requires that each person have health care coverage. On the 2014 income tax returns, a new line called Health Care: Individual Responsibility was added. This item must be addressed by all taxpayers. Before completing an income tax return, taxpayers should read filing instructions provided by the IRS to make sure this item, as all items on a return, are addressed properly. Tax laws change from year to year, so it is important to read all directions that accompany the form.

Tax Refund or Amount Owed

If the amount of taxes already paid is more than owed, the taxpayer will receive a refund. If the amount is less, the taxpayer must pay the difference.

If Form 1040EZ, line 6, is–		And you are–	
At least	But less than	Single	Married filling jointly
		Your tax is–	
19,500	19,550	2,475	2,021
19,550	19,600	2,483	2,029
19,600	19,650	2,490	2,036
19,650	19,700	2,498	2,044
19,700	19,750	2,505	2,051
19,750	19,800	2,513	2,059
19,800	19,850	2,520	2,066
19,850	19,900	2,528	2,074
19,900	19,950	2,535	2,081
19,950	20,000	2,543	2,089

Source: US Department of the Treasury/Internal Revenue Service; Goodheart-Willcox Publisher

Figure 18-7 A 1040EZ tax table categorizes levels of taxable income with the corresponding tax amounts.

Ethics

Tax Returns

It is unethical to file a fraudulent tax return. In a fraudulent tax return, a person deliberately reports information that is not correct. A person who intentionally files a tax return that is not accurate may be subject to penalties, interest, and possible prison time.

Signature

A return must always be signed before it can be processed. An unsigned returned will be returned for a signature. If a refund is due, this could delay the return by several weeks. If taxes are owed, it could result in penalties and interest.

Sources of Tax Information and Assistance

Many sources are available for tax planning information and assistance in filing a return. As income increases, finances become more complicated. There are professionals who can advise on tax matters.

Internal Revenue Service (IRS)

The IRS publishes free instruction booklets annually. The office also operates a system of recorded phone messages with tax information on a variety of questions. The agency offers a website and a toll-free hotline for specific questions. Walk-in service is available at some IRS offices across the country.

Volunteer Income Tax Assistance (VITA) Program

The VITA Program is an IRS service that offers free tax help to lower income people who need assistance in preparing their tax returns. IRS-certified volunteers provide free basic income tax return preparation to qualified individuals in local communities.

VITA sites are generally located at community and neighborhood centers, libraries, schools, shopping malls, and other convenient locations. Most locations also offer free electronic filing.

Tax Counseling for the Elderly (TCE) Program

The IRS TCE Program provides free tax assistance to individuals who are age 60 and older. Certified by the IRS, TCE volunteers provide free tax assistance to elderly individuals who qualify for the service. Tax assistance is provided at community locations across the nation. Many of these community locations also offer free electronic filing services.

Tax Preparation Services

Many tax attorneys and certified public accountants specialize in tax matters. They prepare tax returns based on records and receipts provided by the taxpayer. Services of this type range from one-person offices to nationwide firms specializing in tax preparation.

Tax Preparation Guides

Each year, tax guides are published by various sources and are available for purchase.

These guides are also available at many public libraries. Most news and financial periodicals run articles on tax filing, as well. These articles appear in the weeks and months before April 15 each year.

racorn/Shutterstock.com

There are many online tax resources for individuals filing tax returns.

Section 18.2 Review

Check Your Understanding

1. By what date must a tax return be filed?
2. List three basic forms used to file income taxes.
3. Which taxpayers benefit from a standard deduction?
4. What information is included on a Form 1040EZ?
5. List some examples of resources for tax planning and assistance.

Build Your Vocabulary

As you progress through this course, develop a personal glossary of key terms. This will help you build your vocabulary and prepare you for a career. Write a definition for each of the following terms and add it to your personal glossary.

tax return
Form W-2 Wage and Tax Statement
unearned income
taxable income
tax deduction
itemized deduction
standard deduction
exemption
tax credit

Review and Assessment

Chapter Summary

Section 18.1 Income

- It is important for each individual to learn to become financially capable. A financially capable adult knows how to manage personal financial resources. Financial management is a process used to manage those personal financial resources and make decisions.. These decisions involve trade-offs and opportunity costs.

- Earned income is income received from employment or self-employment and can take various forms. It can be wages, salary, commission, tips, bonuses, and income from self-employment.

- Payroll deductions are subtractions from a person's gross pay. Some of these deductions go toward the federal government to finance federal programs, such as Social Security and Medicare. Other deductions are optional, such as health insurance and retirement savings plans.

- When a person is employed, it is important for him or her to know how to budget earnings. Budgeting helps a person anticipate revenue and see how it will be allocated. It also helps for controlling spending and building wealth. A well-developed budget serves as a guide that helps keep an individual stay on track to achieve personal and financial goals.

Section 18.2 Taxes

- A Form W-2 is needed to complete a tax return. This form shows earnings and tax deductions withheld during the year. Depending on income and dependents, Form 1040, Form 1040A, or Form 1040EZ is used to complete a tax return.

- Taxable income is the amount on which taxes are calculated. This figure is adjusted through tax deductions, credits, and exemptions to reach a person's adjusted gross income.

- When preparing a Form 1040EZ, accuracy is important. If there are any errors, the taxpayer's refund check could be delayed, or the taxpayer could be fined. The form should contain a person's personal information, income, and any payments or credits. The taxpayer's refund or amount owed is calculated on the form. All forms must be submitted by April 15 of the year after the income was earned.

- There are professionals and services available for tax planning and filing assistance. The IRS, Volunteer Income Tax Assistance Program, Tax Counseling for the Elderly Program, tax preparation services, and tax preparation guides are all available for taxpayers to use when filing income tax.

Online Activities

Complete the following activities to help you learn, practice, and expand your knowledge and skills.

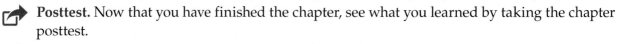

- **Posttest.** Now that you have finished the chapter, see what you learned by taking the chapter posttest.

- **Vocabulary.** Practice vocabulary for this chapter using the e-flash cards, matching activity, and vocabulary game until you are able to recognize their meanings.

Review Your Knowledge

1. When should financial management begin?

2. Differentiate different forms of earned income.

3. On what concept is our federal income tax system built?

4. What is the equation for calculating net pay?

5. How do variances apply to budgeting?

6. Explain the importance of providing accurate information on an income tax return.

7. Differentiate three forms used for filing income tax returns.

8. How is adjusted gross income calculated?

9. Explain the steps in preparing a Form 1040EZ.

10. What was added to the 2014 income tax forms due to the Patient Protection and Affordable Care Act?

Apply Your Knowledge

1. It is important to learn to become a financially capable adult. Summarize the qualities you believe a financially capable individual possesses. Describe how the qualities you identified contribute to a person's financial capabilities.

2. Suzanne DelGrosso worked 40 hours during a week plus 4 overtime hours. Her regular hourly rate is $15.75. What was her gross pay before overtime pay? What was her total earnings for the week? Suzanne had to pay state taxes of $47.03, federal taxes of $137.57, and local taxes of $19.60. She did not have any other deductions. What was her net pay for the week? Show your calculations for gross pay and net pay.

3. FICA taxes are withheld from each employee's paycheck at a rate of 6.2 percent of gross pay. In addition, employers must match the amount of FICA taxes that their employees pay. How much is deducted for FICA taxes from an employee who earns $750 each week in gross pay? What is the employer's annual matching amount for this employee?

4. What government services would you be willing to pay higher taxes to support? Explain your reasoning.

5. Describe one of your financial goals. Explain how a well-planned budget can help you reach that goal.

6. Which income tax return form will you use to file your taxes this year? Explain your decision.

7. In order to complete an income tax return, there are many sources of personal information that is necessary. A Form W-2 is needed along with various other statements of earnings and expenditures. Make a list of the documentation that you will need to complete your income tax return.

8. Providing accurate information is important when completing government forms, providing information to your employer, and many other business situations. Why do you think that accurate information is important? What could be some of the consequences of not providing adequate information or truthful information when requested?

Communication Skills

College and Career Readiness

Writing. Generate ideas that relate to the importance of accurate information. Make a list of reasons you would provide when explaining to a co-worker why accurate information is important when filing an income tax return.

Listening. Hearing is a physical process. Listening combines hearing with evaluation. Effective leaders learn how to listen to their team members. Listen to your instructor as the financial management material of this chapter is presented. Listen carefully and take notes about the main points. Then, organize the key information that you heard. What points would you reiterate if you were presenting the chapter?

Speaking. Participate in a one-on-one communication with a classmate about the benefits of using electronic filing for personal income tax. Keep in mind that your style of presentation can influence the opinion of the listener.

Internet Research

Tax Forms. The website of the Internal Revenue Service provides tax forms and information for individuals and businesses. Go to www.irs.gov. Locate Forms 1040, 1040A, and 1040EZ. Create a poster displaying each form. Write captions that describe the different purpose of each form.

Preparing an Individual Tax Return. The website of the Internal Revenue Service provides tax forms and information for individuals and businesses. Navigate to www.irs.gov and download Form 1040EZ. You may print the form or complete the process online. Next, you will complete an imaginary income tax return. Follow the instructions in the chapter for completing Form 1040EZ. However, omit your social security number. Assume your wages were reported on a W-2 statement from your employer. Your total wages were $30,150. Federal tax withheld was $3,100. State income tax was $1,400. Claim that you are single and no one can claim you on another income tax return. Follow the steps in this chapter for completing a return. What is your refund?

Teamwork

To become financially capable, an individual must be responsible for his or her financial decisions. Learning to create and live within a budget can be a challenge. Working with your team, make a list of potential expenses that a college student would encounter. Next to each expense, classify each as fixed or variable. After the list is complete, ask the following question about each expense: Is this something I need or want? What did you and your team members learn from this exercise?

Portfolio Development

College and Career Readiness

Soft Skills. Employers and colleges review various qualities of candidates. For example, the ability to communicate effectively, get along with customers and coworkers, and solve problems are important skills for many jobs. These types of skills are often called *soft skills*. Make an effort to learn about and develop the soft skills needed for your chosen career field.

1. Conduct research about soft skills and their value in helping people succeed.

2. Create a Microsoft Word document and list the soft skills important for a job or career that you currently possess. Use the heading "Soft Skills" and your name. For each soft skill, write a paragraph that describes your abilities. Give examples to illustrate your skills. Save the document.

3. Update your master spreadsheet.

CTSOs

Business Calculations. The business calculations event is an objective test that covers multiple problems related to various business applications. Participants are usually allowed one hour to complete the event.

To prepare for a business calculations test, complete the following activities.

1. Well in advance of the date of the event, visit the organization's website.

2. Download any posted practice tests.

3. Time yourself taking the tests with the aid of a non-graphing calculator. Check the answers and correct any mistakes you may have made.

4. Review the Math Skills Handbook in this text.

5. Visit the organization's website often to make sure information regarding the event has not changed.

Personal Banking and Investments

Exploring Careers

Bank Teller

When an individual walks into a bank, the first person he or she encounters is likely a bank teller. Bank tellers assist in the services offered at the bank and help customers with their existing accounts. Tellers handle cash transactions, communicate with the customers, and balance the cash drawer at the end of the day.

Typical job titles for this position also include *teller*, *account representative*, and *personal banking representative*. Examples of tasks bank tellers perform include:

- cash checks and pay out the corresponding money
- receive checks and cash for deposit
- enter customer transactions into computers
- examine checks for endorsements and verify information
- count currency, coins, and checks received
- receive and count daily inventories of cash, drafts, and travelers' checks
- prepare and verify cashier's checks

Bank teller jobs often require a high school diploma, though a college degree is preferred. Tellers receive training in bank policies and procedures, including emergency operations. Tellers must have excellent math skills, as well as good communication skills, people skills, honesty, and integrity.

In This Chapter

Reading Prep

Scan this chapter and look for information presented as fact. As you read this chapter, try to determine which topics are fact and which are the author's opinion. After reading the chapter, research the topics and verify which are facts and which are opinions.

College and Career Readiness

Check Your Business IQ

Before you begin the chapter, see what you already know about business by taking the chapter pretest. The pretest is available at www.g-wlearning.com.

Personal Banking

?Essential Question

How do the banking products offered by financial institutions help individuals manage their money?

Objectives

After studying this section, you will be able to:

- **Identify** personal banking products and services commonly offered by financial institutions.
- **Describe** electronic banking options offered by financial institutions.
- **Explain** how to open and use a personal checking account.

Key Terms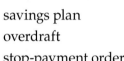

savings plan	certified check	payee
overdraft	money order	postdated check
stop-payment order	traveler's check	bank statement
cashier's check	endorsement	reconcile

Banking Products and Services

When earning a regular income, consumers typically look to a financial institution to help manage their money. A financial institution is an organization that provides services related to money. The variety of products and services offered to customers by financial institutions are called *banking products and services*.

Types of financial institutions include commercial banks, savings and loan associations, and credit unions. When choosing a financial institution, an important factor is knowing that the money is safe. The Federal Deposit Insurance Corporation (FDIC) is an independent agency created by the federal government to protect bank customers by insuring their deposits. The FDIC insures accounts at national banks and other banks that choose to enroll in the program.

Banking Products

Banking products may be defined differently by each financial institution. Examples of banking products include checking and savings accounts and credit and debit cards.

Monkey Business Images/Shutterstock.com

A banker can help customers open their own bank account.

Checking Accounts

A *checking account* is a bank account that allows the owner to make deposits, write checks, and withdraw money. A *check* is a written order for the bank to pay a specific amount to the party to whom the check is written. Checking accounts are also called *demand deposit accounts* because cash can be withdrawn or checks written on demand.

Writing checks from a checking account is a convenient way to buy goods and services and pay bills. It also provides a record of deposits and receipts of payments. However, there are some restrictions and penalties when using a checking account. Some accounts have minimum balance requirements, withdrawal limitations, and penalties for overdrafts. These items can increase the cost of services and make managing your money more complicated. Fees may include a maintenance fee, charges for ATM use, low-balance penalties, check-writing fees, and check-printing charges. These can vary among financial institutions and different types of accounts. Higher minimum balance accounts usually reduce or eliminate many of these fees.

Responsible use of checking accounts aids in money management. It also helps a consumer build a sound credit rating.

Bank Cards

Banks and credit unions issue various types of cards to account holders. Debit cards are generally issued automatically to checking account customers. To obtain a credit card, an application must be completed to determine creditworthiness. Not everyone will be approved for the same bank cards or rates.

Debit Cards. A *debit card* is a card that allows the user to electronically access funds in his or her account at an ATM or to pay for goods and services from a business. Using a debit card has the same result as writing a check because the amount of the purchase comes directly from the checking account. These transactions are automatic and deducted almost immediately from the account. A debit card can also be used at most ATMs to make withdrawals, deposits, and transfer money from one account to another.

Dual-purpose debit cards can also be used for credit purchases. A purchase can be made by swiping the card through a *point-of-sale (POS)* terminal at the merchant's checkout counter. The cardholder will be asked if the purchase is to be recorded as a debit or as a credit. If debit is chosen, a PIN is entered to authorize the transaction. The money comes directly from the checking account. If credit is chosen, a sales slip is signed rather than entering a PIN. The transaction is treated as a credit purchase. The money still comes from the checking account, but it may be several days before the merchant receives the money.

An advantage of using debit cards is the convenience that they provide. Carrying a debit card is safer than carrying cash and more convenient than writing a check. A disadvantage of a debit card is that when used as cash, the money is immediately withdrawn from the checking account. There is no grace period, so the user has to be careful not to overdraw.

Syda Productions/Shutterstock.com

Debit and credit cards are convenient banking products offered to customers.

Credit Cards. Most banks and credit unions also offer credit cards, such as Visa and MasterCard. A credit card is not given automatically to customers in the same way that a debit card is issued. Issuing a credit card requires the customer to apply and meet certain conditions. Unlike debit cards, money does not come directly out of a checking account when a purchase is made. Instead, monthly payments are made based on the balance of the account. Some credit cards carry an annual fee. Interest is charged on the average unpaid daily balance for all credit cards.

Credit cards, like debit cards, offer convenience of not having to carry cash. Many consumers find it much easier to use credit cards than cash. Credit cards give the user time to pay for purchases rather than spend available cash. They also provide consumer protection. If there is problem with an item purchased using a credit card, the credit card company will help resolve the issue.

A disadvantage of credit cards is the high interest rates most cards charge. If the balance is not paid at the end of the month, large interest fees accumulate. For example, suppose a consumer had a $1,000 credit card balance that carries a 21 percent interest rate. If the consumer made only the minimum monthly payment and made no additional purchases, it would take about 5.75 years to pay off the balance. Care must be taken to avoid abusing credit and ending up with credit card balances that an individual cannot afford to pay.

Savings Plans

A **savings plan** is a strategy for using money to reach important goals and to advance financial security. A *savings account* is a bank account used by depositors to accumulate money for future use. They are a good way to get in the habit of saving money. Financial institutions offer several different types of savings accounts. These accounts are liquid, which means that money can be withdrawn at any time. However, a disadvantage of savings accounts is that they typically pay low interest.

Banking Services

In order to take advantage of banking services, an individual must own an account at the bank, such as a checking or savings account. Examples of banking services are safe deposit boxes, loans, account services, and various special payment services.

Safe-Deposit Boxes

Some financial institutions rent boxes within their vaults to customers for the storage of valuables. Jewelry, birth records, insurance policies, and other important items are often kept in safe-deposit boxes. Rental charges for these boxes vary. The contents of a safe-deposit box are *not* insured by the FDIC. However, some banks provide insurance if the contents of a box are lost or destroyed.

Loans

Making loans has always been one of the primary services provided by banks and other financial institutions. Individuals can borrow money to finance the purchase of cars, homes, and other items. Owners of businesses can borrow money to expand operations, purchase inventory, develop new products, buy new equipment, and for many other purposes.

Alexander A. Kataytsev/Shutterstock.com

Many bank customers use safe-deposit boxes to store valuable items and documents.

Tyler Olson/Shutterstock.com

Banks and other financial institutions offer loans, including student loans, as part of their banking services.

Account Services

Many financial institutions offer special payment services to their customers. Although overdrafts are not encouraged, some banks offer overdraft protection. An **overdraft** is a check written for an amount greater than the balance of the account. This is often called a *bounced check.* Banks charge an insufficient funds fee to cover an overdraft transaction. This fee can be costly. With overdraft protection service, a financial institution will honor a check even if it exceeds the account balance. Money from the customer's savings account is automatically moved to the checking account to cover the amount of the check. However, this service is not free. A charge is applied to the account for each instance.

Consumers must sign up for overdraft protection service with their bank. The *Consumer Overdraft Protection Fair Practices Act of 2009* requires consumers to sign an agreement with their depository institutions to cover and charge for overdrafts.

A **stop-payment order** is a request for a financial institution to refuse to honor a check

written, if the check has not already cleared the account and been paid. This service is useful if a check is lost or stolen, to prevent others from cashing it. A stop-payment order is also useful when there is a grievance about goods or services paid for by check. The best way to place a stop-payment order is to go directly to the bank and make the request in person. A stop-payment order may also be made by phone. Forms and processes provided by the bank must be followed.

Special Payment Services

Banks offer services that provide customers with alternative ways of making payments. Some examples of payment services offered by financial institutions include cashier's checks, certified checks, money orders, and traveler's checks.

- A **cashier's check** is a special type of check that the bank guarantees to pay. A cashier's check is purchased from a bank and used to make a payment to a person or a business. A cashier's check cannot be forged and will not bounce.

- A **certified check** is a personal check that the bank certifies is genuine and that there is enough money in the account to cover the check. A written check is taken to the bank where a bank official signs and stamps the word *certified* on it. The money is immediately deducted from the account and becomes unavailable for any other purpose.

- A **money order** is a payment order for a specific amount of money payable to a specific payee. People who do not have checking accounts may use money orders to safely send payments by mail. Money orders do not contain personal information, and the purchaser is not responsible if one is lost or stolen.

- A **traveler's check** is a special form of check that functions as cash. Traveler's checks can be cashed at many places around the world. If the checks are lost or stolen, they can be replaced at the nearest bank or by the agency selling them.

Electronic Banking Options

There are many ways to carry out banking activities that are alternatives to traditional methods. Electronic banking is a popular banking service offered by most financial institutions when a customer opens a checking account.

Online Banking

Online banking services allow bank customers to conduct financial transactions on a secure website owned by the financial institution. With online banking, account holders can:

- pay bills
- transfer money between accounts
- view account balance and statements
- access their accounts 24 hours a day
- view checks and deposits
- review account history

Goodluz/Shutterstock.com

Traveler's checks can be cashed at places around the world and replaced if lost or stolen.

Many banks offer a student checking account with minimal fees. This may be a good option for students opening their first checking account.

An *interest-bearing checking account* is a combination savings and checking account. Money earns interest and checks can be written on the account. In credit unions, these accounts are called *share drafts*. In banks and savings and loan associations, they are called *negotiable orders of withdrawal* or *NOW accounts*. Financial institutions offer this type of account with varying interest rates, minimum-balance requirements, and service charges.

Lifeline checking accounts are intended for low-income customers. In some states, banks are required by law to make these accounts available. They feature low minimum deposit and minimum balance requirements, low monthly fees, and limits on the number of checks that may be written per month. Electronic services may also be limited, unless the account holder pays additional fees.

Opening a Checking Account

Opening a checking account requires only a few simple steps. Some banks require a parent or guardian to be listed on an account for an individual under 18 years old.

- Complete the application and provide the bank with personal information, such as a Social Security number, birth date, address and other contact information, and employment information.

- Supply a personal ID for identity confirmation.

- Sign a signature card, as shown in Figure 19-2. This is the only signature the financial institution will honor on checks and withdrawal slips. If another party has check-cashing privileges on the account, he or she also needs to sign a signature card. If an account is shared with a parent or a spouse, it becomes a joint account. Completing this form requires a clear understanding of who will write checks and how records of transactions will be kept.

- Answer security questions. If information is accessed about the account on a mobile device or a computer, security questions help verify customer identity.

- Accept or decline a credit, debit, or ATM card.

Bank Checking Draft Signature Card		
Submit one card to establish an optional check redemption privilege, which allows you to write checks against your account.		
Name of Account		
Account Number	Date	
The registered owner(s) of this account must sign below. By signing this card, the signatory(ies) agree(s) to all the terms and conditions set forth on the reverse side of this card.		
Signature	Signature	
Signature	Signature	
Institutional Accounts: ❑ Check here if any two signatures are required on checks ❑ Check here if only one signature is required on checks	Joint Tenancy Accounts: ❑ Check here if both signatures are required on checks ❑ Check here if only one signature is required on checks	

Figure 19-2 A signature card is completed when a checking account is opened. This is the signature that should be used for all transactions on the bank account.

Once all the necessary information is gathered and recorded, the bank assigns a checking account number. The customer is usually given a starter pack of checks, deposit slips, and a checking account ledger to record all transactions.

Making a Deposit

After the account is open, a deposit must be made so there is money in the account in order to write checks. To deposit money in a checking account, a deposit slip is completed as a record of the transaction. A deposit slip states what is being deposited (currency, coins, or checks) and the amount of each item, as shown in Figure 19-3.

If a payroll check or other type of check is cashed or deposited, it must first be endorsed. An **endorsement** is a signature on the back of a check. Its purpose is to transfer ownership of the check from the receiver to the bank. An endorsement should be signed exactly as the name appears on the front of the check. There are three ways to endorse a check, as shown in Figure 19-4.

- *Blank endorsement.* This endorsement requires only the signature of the payee.

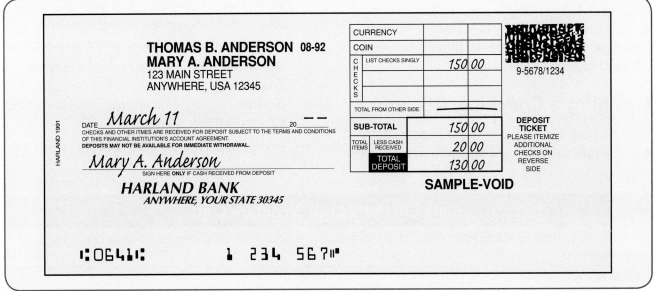

Goodheart-Willcox Publisher

Figure 19-3 A deposit slip is a record of money put into an account.

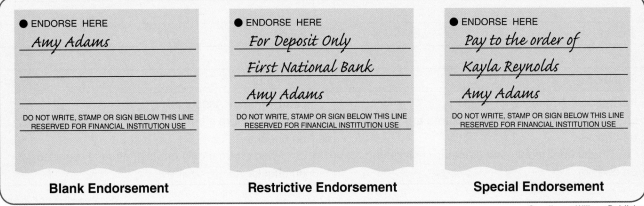

Goodheart-Willcox Publisher

Figure 19-4 Three types of endorsements are commonly used on checks.

The **payee** is the person, business, or organization to whom the check is written. A check endorsed this way may be cashed by anyone. This type of endorsement should be made only at the time and place the check will be cashed or deposited.

- *Restrictive endorsement.* A check with a restrictive endorsement may be used only for the specific purpose stated in the endorsement. For example, when "For Deposit Only" is written on the back of a check it means that the check cannot be cashed. The check can only be deposited into the account. Restrictive endorsements are often used when banking by mail or depositing at an ATM.

- *Special endorsement.* A special endorsement is used to transfer a check to another party. Only the person named in the endorsement can cash the check. To use a special endorsement, the words "Pay to the order of" are written. This indicates the name of the party to receive the check.

Writing Checks

A blank check has important information on it. This information helps financial institutions process checks correctly. For checks to be processed, they must also be written correctly. When writing a check, the following items should be recorded in the correct spaces, as shown in Figure 19-5.

- date

- name of the payee

- amount of the check in numbers

- amount of the check in words

- reason for writing the check on the *Memo* line

- signature of the drawer (person writing the check)

Checks should be written in black ink. The check number, date, payee, and amount should be recorded in the check register. To avoid errors in a checking account balance, all transactions and fees should also be recorded in the check register. Keeping receipts is also helpful.

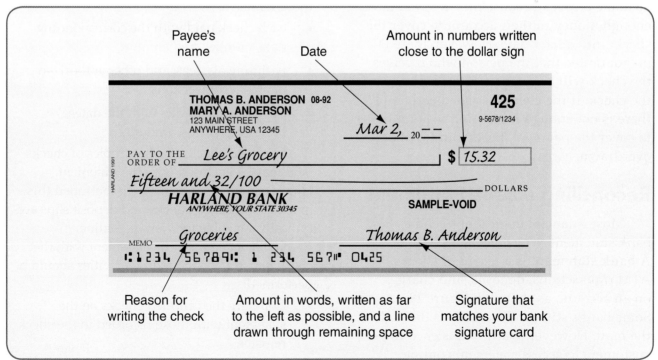

Goodheart-Willcox Publisher

Figure 19-5 Checks should be written neatly and carefully to avoid mistakes in processing the payment.

You Do the Math

Communication and Representation

When solving an equation, it is important to make sure the units match. For example, when calculating fuel economy in miles per gallon (MPG), the final unit must be miles over gallons. So, the equation must be the number of miles divided by the number of gallons. If the equation is incorrectly expressed as the number of miles *times* the number of gallons, the final unit would be mile-gallons, not miles/gallon.

Solve the following problems.

1. A business must calculate the number of sales dollars generated per sales representative ($/rep).

Is this the correct equation for this calculation: dollars × reps? If not, what is the correct equation?

2. What is the final unit for this equation: 12.8 feet × 3.6 feet ÷ 7.6 seconds?

3. A shipping box is rated to hold 65 pounds. A company ships products that weigh 1.3 pounds each. The company uses the following formula to determine how many products can be placed in one box: pounds per product × pound per box. Is this the correct equation? If not, what is the correct equation?

Corrections should never be made on a check. Instead, the check should be voided and a new one written. A destroyed check should be recorded in the check register by writing its number and the word *void*.

A **postdated check** is a check written with a future date. Some people choose to postdate a check because they will not have enough money in their account to cover the check until a later date. However, there is no guarantee that the person who receives the check will hold it until the date on the check. If the check is cashed early and there is not enough money in the account to cover the payment, the account will be overdrawn.

Reconciling a Bank Statement

Most financial institutions send a bank statement to customers each month. A **bank statement** is a record of checks, ATM transactions, deposits, and charges on an account, as shown in Figure 19-6. Some banks still send statements through the mail. However, many banks encourage customers to access statements online. When the bank statement is received, it should be reconciled. **Reconcile** means to

compare the check register to balance the checking account.

A bank statement usually begins with a summary of the account. It shows the beginning balance, total amount of checks cleared and other payments made, total of deposits and credits, and ending balance. The summary is followed by a detailed listing of these items:

- each check paid with the corresponding date, number, and amount

- withdrawals, fees, and other authorized payment transactions

- deposits and credits with the dates, descriptions, and amounts

Canceled checks or photocopies of checks paid may be enclosed with the statement. However, many banks have discontinued this practice. Cancelled checks and deposit slips are typically available for viewing online.

To reconcile the bank statement with the check register, the following activities should be performed:

- Compare the canceled checks on the statement with those recorded in the check register.

- Compare the deposits on the statement with those recorded in the check register.

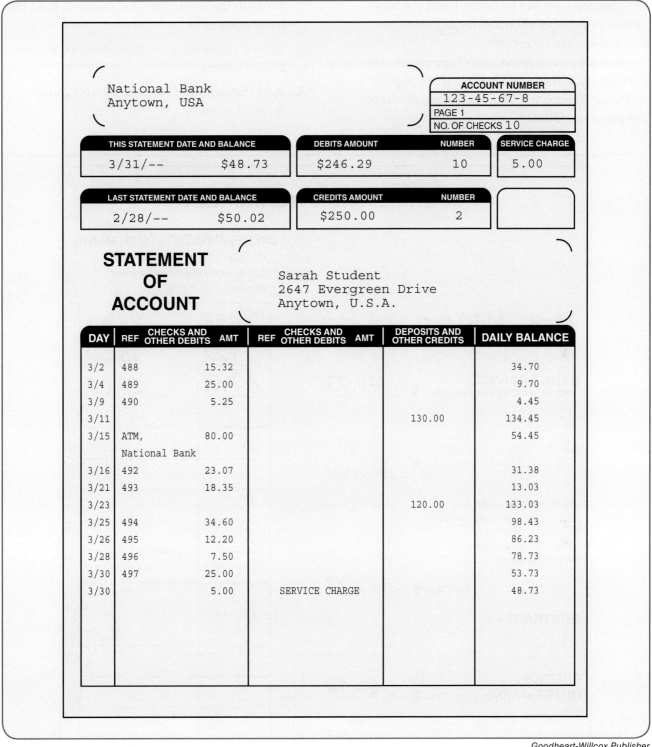

National Bank
Anytown, USA

ACCOUNT NUMBER
123-45-67-8
PAGE 1
NO. OF CHECKS 10

THIS STATEMENT DATE AND BALANCE	DEBITS AMOUNT	NUMBER	SERVICE CHARGE
3/31/-- $48.73	$246.29	10	5.00

LAST STATEMENT DATE AND BALANCE	CREDITS AMOUNT	NUMBER	
2/28/-- $50.02	$250.00	2	

STATEMENT
OF
ACCOUNT

Sarah Student
2647 Evergreen Drive
Anytown, U.S.A.

DAY	REF	CHECKS AND OTHER DEBITS	AMT	REF	CHECKS AND OTHER DEBITS	AMT	DEPOSITS AND OTHER CREDITS	DAILY BALANCE
3/2	488		15.32					34.70
3/4	489		25.00					9.70
3/9	490		5.25					4.45
3/11							130.00	134.45
3/15	ATM, National Bank		80.00					54.45
3/16	492		23.07					31.38
3/21	493		18.35					13.03
3/23							120.00	133.03
3/25	494		34.60					98.43
3/26	495		12.20					86.23
3/28	496		7.50					78.73
3/30	497		25.00					53.73
3/30			5.00		SERVICE CHARGE			48.73

Figure 19-6 A bank statement is a record of all the transactions on an account during the statement period.

- Verify that ATM transactions and fees recorded in the register match those on the statement.
- Check ATM transactions and deposits that have not yet appeared on the statement.
- Confirm debit card purchases.
- Subtract service charges listed on the statement from the balance shown in the register.

The bank should be contacted if the bank statement lists questionable fees or items of which there are no records.

Many bank statements include reconciliation worksheets that can be used for this purpose, as shown in Figure 19-7. The worksheet can be completed as follows:

1. Write in the closing balance as shown on the bank statement.

2. Record deposits made that are not listed on the statement.

3. Add the amount from steps 1 and 2 and record the total.

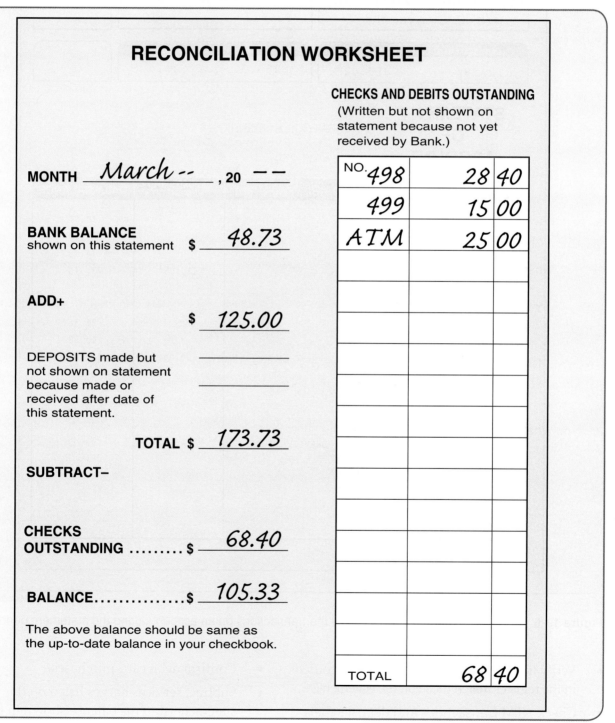

RECONCILIATION WORKSHEET

CHECKS AND DEBITS OUTSTANDING
(Written but not shown on statement because not yet received by Bank.)

MONTH _March --_ , 20 _ --_

BANK BALANCE
shown on this statement $ _48.73_

ADD+
                          $ _125.00_

DEPOSITS made but not shown on statement because made or received after date of this statement.

TOTAL $ _173.73_

SUBTRACT−

CHECKS OUTSTANDING ....$ _68.40_

BALANCE................$ _105.33_

The above balance should be same as the up-to-date balance in your checkbook.

NO.		
498	28	40
499	15	00
ATM	25	00
TOTAL	68	40

Figure 19-7 This type of worksheet and directions for reconciling an account appear on the back of most bank statements.

4. Record the number and amount of any checks and ATM withdrawals not included on the statement. These amounts should be added together and entered as a total outstanding amount.

5. Subtract the amount in step 4 from the amount in step 3. Enter the balance.

The balance on the worksheet should match the current balance in the check register. If they do not agree, review the steps and check the math. If the figures still do not agree or come close, contact the bank for assistance.

baranq/Shutterstock.com

Monthly bank statements should be reconciled with the check register and the balances should match.

Section **19.1** Review

Check Your Understanding

1. What are the variety of products and services offered to customers by financial institutions called?

2. What are three common types of checking accounts?

3. Describe three ways to endorse a check.

4. List the six items that must be filled in on a check.

5. What information is typically included on a bank statement?

Build Your Vocabulary

As you progress through this course, develop a personal glossary of key terms. This will help you build your vocabulary and prepare you for a career. Write a definition for each of the following terms and add it to your personal glossary.

savings plan	traveler's check
overdraft	endorsement
stop-payment order	payee
cashier's check	postdated check
certified check	bank statement
money order	reconcile

Savings and Investments

Essential Question

What are the options available for personal saving and investing?

Objectives

After studying this section, you will be able to:

- **Differentiate** the various types of savings plans.
- **Explain** the concept of investments.
- **Describe** the function of estate planning.

Key Terms

interest-bearing savings account

high-yield savings account

money market account (MMA)

certificate of deposit (CD)

investing

personal investment plan

investment portfolio

diversification

mutual fund

individual retirement account (IRA)

traditional IRA

Roth IRA

annuity

estate

executor

will

Savings Plans

Financial institutions offer several products to help customers save their money and develop a savings strategy. Savings accounts are a popular savings option and are available in many different forms.

An **interest-bearing savings account** is a type of demand deposit account that pays interest and allows for regular deposits and withdrawals. Interest-bearing savings accounts have no set maturity date. Withdrawals can be made at any time.

Regular savings accounts, also called *basic savings accounts*, pay interest and allow deposits and withdrawals. These savings accounts generally offer the lowest interest earnings of all savings options. They also have the most liquidity of savings options.

OLJ Studio/Shutterstock.com

Savings accounts are popular banking products that help customers save their money and develop a savings strategy.

Green Business Digital ID Cards

The process of producing and distributing membership cards, credit cards, and other identification cards uses a great deal of energy and resources. Many companies are replacing plastic and laminated cards with digital ID cards. A digital format may be available for customer loyalty cards, fitness club membership cards, proof of auto insurance ID cards, and even credit cards.

A digital ID card can be stored on a smart phone and often includes a barcode or QR code. Smartphone apps, such as Google Wallet and Apple Passbook, are available to help organize and access digital cards of all kinds. Offering digital ID cards is a resource-saving step for businesses and a great convenience for customers.

A **high-yield savings account** is an account that pays a higher interest rate than basic savings accounts. To get the higher rate, however, the bank requires a larger initial deposit and a higher minimum balance. The number of times withdrawals can be made in a year may also be limited.

A **money market account (MMA)** is a type of savings account that requires a higher minimum balance than a regular savings account, but offers a higher interest rate. The minimum balance in a money market account is usually $500, but can be as high as $10,000. Some MMAs pay a flat rate of interest regardless of the balance. Others use a tier structure that pays a higher interest rate on accounts with higher balances. Most MMAs offer check-writing privileges. However, there is a limit on the number of checks that can be written per month. There is also a minimum amount for each check, which can be as much as $500.

A **certificate of deposit (CD)** is a savings account that requires a fixed deposit amount for a fixed period of time, or *term*. When the term is up, the money can be kept in the CD, deposited into another CD, or taken out. A CD is sometimes called a *time deposit* or *time account*. Since CDs require a commitment of money for a period of time, they pay a higher rate of interest than money market and savings accounts. CDs are not liquid. *Liquidity* refers to how easy it is to convert an asset into cash without losing value. In order to get the highest interest earnings, money must be left in a CD until the term is up. This term may be as little as one month or as much as seven years. If CDs are cashed before the time period is over, a significant amount of interest is lost. Also, there is a penalty for early withdrawal.

Investments

Investing is purchasing a financial product or valuable item with the goal of increasing wealth over time in spite of possible loss. Investments generally offer greater returns or profit on money than savings accounts. However, they also present an element of risk. Investments are not insured and are considered financial risks.

To increase wealth is a goal that many people aspire to achieve. A **personal investment plan** is a plan to develop investment growth. It is an important step in meeting long-term goals and achieving financial security. There are many formats and methods used to create an investment plan.

Figure 19-8 shows an example of steps to take in creating an investment plan. An investment plan is an evolving document that should be reviewed on a regular basis.

An **investment portfolio** is a collection of securities and other assets a person owns. Successful investors diversify their portfolios. **Diversification** is the process of spreading risk by putting money in a variety of investments. Building a diversified portfolio involves gathering information, considering strategies, and selecting investment methods.

Some types of investments disperse earnings on a regular basis by sending checks to investors. Other types of investments offer continuous interest payments to investors. Owners of rental property, for example, can earn income from monthly rent payments collected from tenants. The earnings from some investments are tax exempt, such as interest received from bonds issued by state and local governments. When earnings from an investment are not taxed, the investor has more money available for personal use or to make additional investments.

Stephen Coburn/Shutterstock.com

Many people use investments to help achieve their goal of increasing wealth.

Creating an Investment Plan	
1. Write SMART goals.	Define short-term and long-term investment goals. Is your goal to invest for the short term, such as purchasing a car? Or for the long term, such as purchasing a house or planning for retirement?
2. Determine the date you will need funds from your investments.	The date you need the money will determine what types of investments to make. Low-risk investments, such as bank CDs, are usually purchased for short-term goals. For long-term goals, stocks, and other higher growth investments are usually purchased.
3. Research investment opportunities.	Make a list of appropriate investments that will allow you to meet your goals.
4. Decide how much risk you are willing to take.	Weigh the pros and cons of risk taking. High-risk investments normally grow faster than low-risk investments. However, high-risk investments typically lose more in a bad economy.
5. Determine how much money is needed for investing.	Set up an investment plan and start investing to reach your target goal. Most investment plans can be funded on a monthly basis.
6. Review the plan regularly.	Review investment plans at least once a year to determine if you are on track to achieve your goals.
7. Use your funds.	Withdraw money from the plan to meet your goal.

Goodheart-Willcox Publisher

Figure 19-8 Creating a personal investment plan is important in meeting financial goals.

Securities

A *security* is a type of investment issued by a corporation, government, or other organization. The most popular investments, stocks, bonds, and mutual funds are considered securities.

A *stock* is a share in the ownership of a corporation. The person buying the stock becomes a stockholder, or shareholder, of the corporation. A *dividend* is a portion of a company's earnings that is paid to stockholders. Dividends are paid only when declared by the company's board of directors. The *board of directors* is a group of individuals who represent stockholders and oversee the major policy decisions of the company. Dividends are not guaranteed. They are only paid when the board of directors believes it is in the best interest of the company. Instead of paying dividends, some companies put profits back into the company in the hope of increasing its growth and stock value.

A *bond* is a type of security issued by a corporation, government, or other organization that pays interest over time. The owner of a bond lends money to the issuer of the bond. Until the bond matures, the bondholder is a creditor. The issuer owes the face value of the bond plus interest.

US government bonds are issued by the US Treasury and are the safest bonds that can be bought. When a government bond is purchased, the money is loaned to the federal government. Treasury bills, notes, and bonds sell in increments of $100.

A **mutual fund** is an investment created by pooling the money of many people and investing it in a collection of securities. Think of a mutual fund as a "basket" of securities. Professional managers at investment firms purchase securities and place them in the basket. Shares of ownership in the basket are then sold to investors. Each investor in the fund owns a tiny part of every security in the basket. Mutual funds may invest in stocks, bonds, commodities, gold, and other securities.

Valuable goods and real estate can also be investments. They can be attractive investments because their value is not eroded by inflation as money can be. Valuable goods include rare and usually expensive items, and include the following:

- *Collectibles.* Collectibles are objects purchased for the pleasure of ownership and because they are expected to increase in value. Common collectibles include rare coins, books, stamps, art, antiques, sports memorabilia, and vintage automobiles.

- *Precious metals.* Precious metals include gold, silver, platinum, and other metals. These are purchased from banks and dealers in the form of pieces of jewelry, coins, or bars. Gold is a store of value, and it lasts forever. It does not tarnish, corrode, or degrade. Gold is in demand worldwide and is a way to diversify an investment portfolio.

- *Gemstones.* Precious gemstones include diamonds, emeralds, sapphires, and others. They are collected as loose stones or as pieces of jewelry.

Buying real estate, either land or buildings, is another way to invest for future profit. This type of investment usually requires enough money for a down payment plus payments on a long-term loan.

bikeriderlondon/Shutterstock.com

Gemstones are valuable goods that can be purchased and included in an investment portfolio.

Retirement Plans

Retirement planning is a key element of financial security. Retirement programs can be employer sponsored in which employees can participate. There are also personal retirement programs that individuals set up for themselves.

A *401(k)* plan is an employer-sponsored retirement plan. The plan is funded with before-tax salary contributions. In addition, employers often match employee salary contributions. The *403(b)* plan is a type of retirement plan available to employees of nonprofit organizations, such as public schools, colleges, hospitals, and public libraries. It has many of the same characteristics as the 401(k) plan.

An **individual retirement account (IRA)** is a personal retirement investment account created by a person. An IRA is *not* an investment, but a vehicle that holds the investments that are chosen. Investments in an IRA can include stocks, bonds, mutual funds, bank CDs (certificates of deposit), and even real estate. There are two primary types of IRAs: traditional IRA and Roth IRA.

A **traditional IRA** is an individual retirement account that allows individuals to contribute pre-tax income to investments that will grow tax deferred. Contributions to a traditional IRA are tax deductible. A **Roth IRA** is an individual retirement account in which individuals contribute after-tax income and qualified withdrawals are not taxed. Contributions to a Roth IRA are made with after-tax earnings.

Self-employed individuals can open a *simplified employee pension (SEP)* plan or a *Keogh plan*. Each is a personal retirement plan that has its own set of qualifications and guidelines.

An annuity is another form of investment that can be used in personal retirement planning. An **annuity** is a contract with an insurance company that provides regular income for a set period of time, usually for life. Some annuities also provide death benefits. Investors make payments into an annuity over many years or in one large payment. Both the money invested and the interest it earns accumulates in the annuity. The principal and earnings on an annuity are not taxed until money is either withdrawn or paid out at a future time.

Planning for retirement is a key element of financial security.

Estate Planning

Estate planning is part of an overall financial plan. An **estate** consists of the assets and liabilities a person leaves when he or she dies. It includes property, savings, investments, and insurance benefits. *Estate planning* is the active management of these assets with directives for managing and distributing them when the owner dies. An **executor** is a person appointed to carry out the terms outlined in a will. A **will** is a legal document stating a person's wishes for his or her estate after death. If a person dies without naming an executor, the court will appoint one. Through the process of estate planning, an individual can:

- decide how assets should be managed after his or her death
- provide for dependents
- minimize tax liabilities
- name an executor
- assign a power of attorney
- prepare a will
- prepare a trust

Many estate planning tasks involve preparing various forms and documents. Assistance from a legal or financial professional can be beneficial. Like the overall financial plan, all the pieces of estate planning should be reviewed regularly and revised as needed.

Section 19.2 Review

 Check Your Understanding

1. List examples of types of savings accounts.
2. Identify examples of securities.
3. What are some valuable goods considered as investments?
4. What are two types of retirement plans?
5. What is estate planning?

 Build Your Vocabulary

As you progress through this course, develop a personal glossary of key terms. This will help you build your vocabulary and prepare you for a career. Write a definition for each of the following terms and add it to your personal glossary.

interest-bearing savings account

high-yield savings account

money market account (MMA)

certificate of deposit (CD)

investing

personal investment plan

investment portfolio

diversification

mutual fund

individual retirement account (IRA)

traditional IRA

Roth IRA

annuity

estate

executor

will

Review and Assessment

Chapter Summary

Section 19.1 Personal Banking

- Financial institutions offer a variety of services to customers known as *banking products and services*. Banking products include checking accounts, bank cards, and savings plans. Banking services are available only to bank customers and may include safe-deposit boxes, loans, and special payment services.

- Electronic banking is a popular banking product offered by most financial institutions. Products include online banking and mobile banking options which offer account access via the Internet. Electronic funds transfer (EFT), peer-to-peer payments (P2P) and automated teller machines (ATMs) are other examples.

- Financial institutions offer a variety of checking accounts with different features, restriction, and fees. After opening a checking account, it is important to manage the money in the account responsibly and reconcile bank statements regularly.

Section 19.2 Savings and Investments

- Savings accounts are bank accounts used by depositors to accumulate money for future use. Financial institutions offer several types of savings accounts, including interest-bearing savings accounts, high-yield savings accounts, money market accounts, and certificate of deposit (CD) accounts.

- Investing is purchasing a financial product or valuable item with the goal of increasing wealth over time in spite of possible losses. An investment portfolio is a collection of securities and other assets a person owns. Investments include stocks, bonds, mutual funds, real estate, and valuable goods. There are certain investments that are specifically for retirement planning. These include 401(k) plans, 403(b) plans, IRAs, simplified employee pension plans, Keogh plans, and annuities.

- Estate planning is part of an overall financial plan. Through the process of estate planning, a person can decide how assets should be managed after his or death, provide for any dependents, minimize tax liabilities, name an executor, assign a power of attorney, prepare a will, and prepare a trust.

Online Activities

Complete the following activities to help you learn, practice, and expand your knowledge and skills.

Posttest. Now that you have finished the chapter, see what you learned by taking the chapter posttest.

Vocabulary. Practice vocabulary for this chapter using the e-flash cards, matching activity, and vocabulary game until you are able to recognize their meanings.

Review Your Knowledge

1. Identify banking products and services commonly offered by financial institutions.
2. Give an example of an advantage and disadvantage of using a debit card.
3. Describe electronic banking options offered by financial institutions.
4. Describe the steps in opening and maintaining a checking account.
5. Explain how to reconcile a bank statement.
6. Differentiate the various types of savings plans.
7. Explain the concept of investments.
8. Describe popular investments that are also considered securities.
9. Explain four common retirement plans.
10. What is the purpose of estate planning?

Apply Your Knowledge

1. Create a chart with three columns. In column one, list the following banking services: credit cards, debit cards, online banking, mobile banking, EFT, and ATM. In column two, write the advantages of each banking service listed. In column three, write the disadvantages of each banking service listed. Analyze each service considering its advantages and disadvantages.
2. If a person prefers to pay for everything in cash, is having a checking account necessary? Explain your reasoning.
3. Alex's bank statement shows a beginning balance of $573.28 and the following transactions:
   - three deposits: $25, $150, and $30
   - posted checks: number 110 for $45.00, number 111 for $500, and number 113 for $10.75
   - ATM withdrawal of $10.00
   - service fee of $2.00

   Her checkbook also lists a deposit for $300 and check number 112 written for $54.87. Using the bank reconciliation worksheet in Figure 19-7 as an example, reconcile her bank statement and find her ending balance.
4. Review the process of opening a checking account in Section 19.1. The process of opening a savings account is similar. Make a list of all the information you need to provide to open a checking account. Can you provide all the required information?
5. Using the steps to create an investment plan in Figure 19-8, create your own investment plan. Be specific in your financial goals, the amount of money involved, and the steps you will take to reach your goal or goals.

Communication Skills

College and Career Readiness

Speaking. Select three of your classmates to participate in a discussion panel. Acting as the team leader, name each person to a specific task such as time-keeper, recorder, etc. Discuss the topic of investing for your future. Keep the panel on task and promote democratic discussion. The recorder should make notes of important information that was discussed. The notes should be edited and a final document created for distribution to the class.

Reading. Select several chapters of this textbook. Identify two generic features that are used in each chapter. Compare and contrast how each feature is used. Why do you think the author chose those particular features to apply in multiple chapters?

Writing. Attending to your personal and financial well-being is an important step in becoming a contributing member of society. Why do you think it is important to create an investment plan while you are still in high school? What advantages can starting a plan now provide you as an adult?

Internet Research

Opening a student checking account. Search the Internet to find a bank that offers student checking accounts. Record the URL of the website for the bank. Examine the requirements for opening a basic checking account with no limit on the number of checks written. As a practice exercise, write the information on a separate sheet of paper that is requested for opening a checking account. To protect against identify theft, do not write your social security number on this sheet of paper. If the website permits, practice completing the application online.

Maintaining a student checking account. In the last exercise, you chose a bank at which you could potentially open a student checking account. List the requirements for maintaining a basic checking account with the bank. Identify the benefits and restrictions that must be followed.

US Savings Bonds. Some savings choices offer less liquidity and require a commitment of funds for a longer period of time. A popular choice among these is US savings bonds. There are two types of US savings bonds: EE Bonds and I Bonds. EE Bonds earn a fixed interest rate and are purchased at full face value in amounts of $25 or more. I Bonds are sold at face value in denominations ranging from $25 to $10,000. I Bonds pay a fixed interest rate plus a semiannual inflation add-on rate. Research the unique characteristics of EE Bonds and I Bonds. Create a visual to explain the two types of savings bonds. Cite your sources and do not violate any copyright laws using material that you find.

Teamwork

Form a team of classmates and develop a plan for investing $5,000 over the length of this course. Use the Internet, current financial publications, and books on financial planning for information on developing your plan. Factors to identify and consider include your objectives, types of investments, expected returns, risk tolerance, liquidity, and diversification. Describe your plan in terms of these factors. In the final week of class, compare the results of your team's plans with those of other teams in the class.

Portfolio Development

College and Career Readiness

Hard Skills. Employers review candidates for various positions and colleges are always looking for qualified applicants. When listing your qualifications, you may discuss software programs you know or machines you can operate. These abilities are often called *hard skills*. Make an effort to learn about and develop the hard skills you will need for your chosen career.

1. Conduct research about hard skills and their value in helping people succeed.

2. Create a Microsoft Word document and list the hard skills that are important for a job or career that currently you possess. Use the heading "Hard Skills" and your name. For each hard skill, write a paragraph that describes your abilities. Give examples to illustrate your skills. Save the document.

3. Update your master spreadsheet.

CTSOs

Personal Finance. Personal finance is a competitive event you might enter with your Career and Technical Student Organization (CTSO). The personal finance competitive event may include an objective test that includes banking topics. If you decide to participate in this event, you will need to review basic banking concepts to prepare for the test.

To prepare for a personal finance event, complete the following activities.

1. Read the guidelines provided by your organization. Make certain that you ask any questions about points you do not understand. It is important to follow each specific item that is outlined in the competition rules.

2. Review the vocabulary terms at the beginning of each chapter.

3. Review the Checkpoint questions at the end of each section of the text.

4. Review the end-of-chapter activities for additional practice.

5. Ask your instructor to give you practice tests for each chapter of this text. It is important that you are familiar with answering multiple choice and true/false questions. Have someone time you as you take a practice test.

CHAPTER

20

Insurance

Exploring Careers

Claims Adjuster

When a person files a claim with his or her insurance company, the first person he or she speaks with is a claims adjuster. Claims adjusters determine whether an insurance claim is covered by an insured's policy. They inspect property damage, estimate repair costs, and assess the financial responsibility of the insurance company.

Typical job titles for this position also include *insurance adjuster*, *claims analyst*, and *claims specialist*. Examples of tasks claims adjusters perform include:

- plan and schedule the work required to process a claim
- interview witnesses and claimants
- review police and hospital records
- inspect property damage
- develop reports that are used to evaluate claims
- negotiate with the claimant to settle the claim
- work with attorneys and witnesses to defend the insurer's position

Claims adjuster jobs require a high school diploma, though a college degree is preferred. Adjusters must have excellent communication and interview skills, as well as good people skills, honesty, and integrity.

College and Career Readiness

Reading Prep

Before reading this chapter, write down everything you know about the topic. As you read, make a list of things you have learned that you did not know before. When you finish the chapter, compare the two lists and share with the class.

Check Your Business IQ

Before you begin the chapter, see what you already know about business by taking the chapter pretest. The pretest is available at www.g-wlearning.com.

Section 20.1

Health and Life Insurance

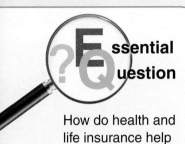

?EQ Essential Question

How do health and life insurance help manage personal risk?

Objectives

After completing this section, you will be able to:

- **Describe** personal risks and how they can be managed.
- **Identify** health insurance coverage options.
- **Differentiate** life insurance coverage options.

Key Terms

coinsurance
exclusion
preexisting condition
preauthorization
utilization review
regular medical
  insurance

inpatient
major medical
  insurance
comprehensive
  medical insurance
dental insurance
vision care insurance

managed care plan
copayment
beneficiary
term life insurance
whole life insurance
endowment insurance

Personal Risk

Life involves risk. *Risk* is the possibility of loss, damage, or injury. Some risks are predictable, such as growing older. Other risks are unpredictable. These include serious illnesses or injuries, car accidents, house fires, and theft. Some events can limit an individual's ability to earn a living or may wipe out personal assets.

There are various types of risks an individual will likely face in a lifetime. Some risks have little consequences, such as planning a trip to the beach on a day when there is only a 10 percent chance of rain. Other risks can have much more serious consequences, such as driving a car without insurance. Examples of risks include the following.

- *Personal risks* are those that affect a person directly, such as illness or disability or the illness or disability of an immediate family member.

- *Property risks* are those that affect personal or real property. A car theft and a house fire are examples of property risk.

- *Liability risks* result from the possibility of losing money or other property as a result of legal proceedings. Liability risks are also called *legal risks*. For example, if a friend falls and is injured on someone's property, the property owner may be legally liable for any injuries sustained by the injured party.

Risk Management

Financial security depends in part on risk management. *Risk management* is the process of measuring risk and finding ways to minimize or manage loss. Four common methods of risk management include avoid, reduce, transfer, and assume, as shown in Figure 20-1.

- *Avoid* risk by taking steps to eliminate the risk. For example, suppose a trail marker warns "Do not go beyond this point!" Hikers may avoid injury by obeying the warning.

Tiramisu Studio/Shutterstock.com

Some risks can be avoided simply by being aware of your surroundings.

- To *reduce* risk involves a strategy of minimizing risks that cannot always be avoided. For example, wearing a seat belt while driving reduces the chance of injury or death in the event of an accident.

Goodheart-Willcox Publisher

Figure 20-1 Risk management involves identifying potential risks and choosing a method to handle them.

- *Transfer* risk by shifting the risk to someone else. The most common way to do this is to buy insurance. By purchasing insurance, the insured becomes a member of a large pool of people and risk is transferred to the insurance company. Insurance is a common method of risk management.

- *Assume* risk by assessing the risk and making financial preparations for possible future loss. It is also called *self-insuring*. For example, a person may set aside money in a savings account to use in case he or she becomes unemployed. By setting aside extra money before a loss occurs, that money will be available when needed.

Insurance

Insurance is a financial service used to protect against loss. The *insurer*, the insurance company, receives money from the *insured*, or the policyholder. A *premium* is an amount of money regularly paid to an insurance company for a policy.

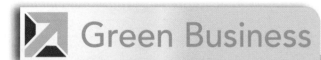

Green Business   Recycle and Save

Many socially responsible businesses work with the community to encourage participation in recycling efforts. Several have in-store recycling bins for customers to deposit used batteries, CFL light bulbs, used ink cartridges, and plastic shopping bags.

Some retailers offer incentives for recycling items in the store. For example, Apple offers customers Apple Store gift cards for the value of old, reusable electronics. Best Buy offers a trade-in

credit for unwanted video games and electronics. Both Apple and Best Buy responsibly recycle electronics that do not have any trade-in value at no charge to the customer.

A great number of businesses have realized the importance of being environmentally conscious. Offering convenient recycling options benefits the existing customers and may help attract new customers.

A portion of the money collected from premiums is placed in a state-required reserve account to pay claims of insured persons. Insurance companies also invest some of the premium money received. The insured receives an insurance policy that defines the type of losses that are included and the coverage provided for those losses.

The main purpose of insurance is to provide protection against specific types of financial losses. Events that could put an individual's finances at risk include illness or injury, accidents, death, and property losses. Insurance pays for losses that would be difficult or impossible for an individual to pay. Taking a careful look at risks and making a plan to manage them with insurance and other resources are basic steps in any financial plan. The National Association of Insurance Commissioners (NAIC) is a good source for obtaining information about insurance. Their website provides an abundance of information to help make insurance buying decisions.

The type and amount of insurance needed varies from person to person. It depends on the risks being covered, amount available to pay for losses, and financial obligations of the insured persons. For example, an unmarried person without children generally needs less coverage than a head of a family with several children. Protection needs increase with each additional dependent a person acquires. Protection needs also increase as additional assets are acquired or if the value of assets already owned has increased. Types of insurance that protect against financial risks include health, disability, life, home, and automobile insurance.

Health Insurance

Health insurance offers protection by covering specific medical expenses created by illness, injury, and disability. Many of these plans are available through a *group health insurance* policy. Group insurance may be available through an employer, union, or another organization. Companies often pay a portion or all of the premiums for their employees. Group coverage is often provided as a benefit by an employer. In most cases, this type of coverage costs less than an individual policy for the same amount of coverage.

People who are not eligible for group insurance may purchase health insurance on their own. Many health insurance companies sell individual plans. The application process includes completing a medical history questionnaire and may involve medical tests or a complete physical exam.

The policyholder is responsible for a deductible and coinsurance. A *deductible* is the amount paid toward medical expenses before the insurance company begins to pay. For example, if a plan has an annual $500 deductible, the first $500 of medical expenses must be paid by the policyholder. Once the deductible is met, the insurance company begins to pay on qualified expenses above the deductible. **Coinsurance** is a percentage of the service costs that patients pay. For example, if a medical service costs $100 and the coinsurance is 20 percent, the patient's cost would be $20.

Kzenon/Shutterstock.com

Coinsurance is the amount patients must pay for medical services.

Some insurance plans may contain exclusions. An **exclusion** is a medical service that is not covered in an insurance plan. Examples include dental care or treatment of preexisting conditions. A **preexisting condition** is an illness or an injury a person has before signing up for health insurance. Generally, these conditions are not covered by a new plan for a stated period of time, if at all.

Plans also may require preauthorization and utilization reviews for certain services. A **preauthorization** is an approval from the plan before receiving certain procedures and treatments. A **utilization review** is an insurance company's examination of requests for medical treatments and procedures to make sure they are covered and the patient truly needs them.

Examples of health insurance plans include regular medical, major medical, comprehensive medical, dental, and vision care insurance.

- **Regular medical insurance** coverage includes prescriptions, hospital stays, and inpatient tests. An **inpatient** is a person whose care requires a stay in a hospital. It does not cover surgeries.

- **Major medical insurance** typically covers the costs of serious illnesses and injuries, as well as high-cost procedures.

- **Comprehensive medical insurance** combines basic and major medical protection in one policy.

- **Dental insurance** covers specified dental services, such as exams and teeth cleaning.

- **Vision care insurance** covers specified eye care services, such as eye exams, glasses, and contact lenses.

Managed Care Plans

A **managed care plan** is a type of health-care plan in which the insurance company contracts with specific doctors, hospitals, and other health-care providers to deliver medical services and preventive care to members at reduced cost.

The choice of service providers is limited to those who participate in the plan, except for referrals to necessary specialists outside the plan.

Three forms of managed care are health maintenance organizations (HMOs), preferred provider organizations (PPOs), and point-of-service (POS) plans.

- *Health maintenance organizations (HMOs)* provide a list of participating physicians from which the insured selects a primary care doctor. This doctor coordinates the patient's health care and carries out routine exams and treatments. The primary care doctor makes referrals to a specialist for specialized treatments, consultations, or procedures. The plan normally covers only the treatments provided by doctors who participate in the plan.

- *Preferred provider organizations (PPOs)* arrange with specific doctors, hospitals, and other caregivers to provide services at reduced costs to plan members. The insured may choose providers outside the plan for an extra cost.

- *Point-of-service (POS) plans* connect the insured with a primary care doctor who participates in the plan and is the "point of service" provider. That doctor supervises patient care and makes referrals, as necessary, to participating or nonparticipating specialists.

Tyler Olson/Shutterstock.com

In addition to medical care, health insurance plans can also cover dental and vision care.

The insured and/or the employer pay a set amount in monthly premiums. The insured also pays any required deductibles, coinsurance payments, or copayments. A **copayment** is a flat fee the patient must pay for medical services. Copayments are due at the time of service. For example, a doctor's appointment or a prescription may require copayment at the time of service. Copayment amounts are determined by the health-care plan.

Coverage for Young Adults

Many health insurance plans cover the policyholder's children until they reach a certain age. The Patient Protection and Affordable Care Act includes provisions for young adults to remain on family policies until age 26. Young adults may remain on their parents' insurance plan until they turn 26 years old, even if they are married or do not live with their parents.

Many colleges offer student medical insurance for major medical expenses. For routine health problems, students can visit free or low-cost campus health and mental health clinics. Young people who do not go to college often get health coverage through an employer. However, health coverage is usually not available to part-time, temporary, and contract employees.

Government-Sponsored Health Insurance

The government offers health insurance to certain eligible people, including older adults, people with disabilities, low-income families, and children. The amount each person pays depends on various factors.

- *Medicare* covers specific health-care expenses for eligible citizens age 65 and older. It also covers those under age 65 with certain diseases or disabilities. The governmental funding for Medicare comes from payroll taxes.

- *Medicaid* is a health insurance program for eligible low-income persons and those with certain disabilities. It is a state-administered program financed by federal and state tax revenues.

Monkey Business Images/Shutterstock.com

College students may have health insurance coverage through their parents or student medical insurance offered by many colleges.

- Many American families earn too much to qualify for Medicaid, but not enough to afford private health insurance premiums. The *Children's Health Insurance Program (CHIP)* gives federal funds to states to provide health insurance coverage for children ages 18 and younger. The program rules vary slightly among states.

Disability Insurance

Disability insurance pays a portion of income lost to a worker who is unable to work for a prolonged period because of a nonwork related illness or injury. Many employers provide limited disability insurance to their workers as a benefit. The employer pays the premium for these group plans. If an employee wants a higher level of insurance through the group plan, he or she may be able to pay for it. Consumers may buy this type of coverage independently if they are not part of employer health-care plans or other insurance programs.

Lisa S./Shutterstock.com

Workers lose income when they are injured and cannot work. Disability insurance and workers' compensation insurance cover some of the lost income and expenses.

Workers' compensation insurance is another type of disability insurance. Employers in every state are required to provide this type of insurance. Workers' compensation provides a safety net for workers with work-related illnesses or injuries. It covers medical care and pays for a portion of lost wages. Workers' compensation also pays for medical treatment and rehabilitation that injured workers may require. The entire cost of the insurance is usually paid by the employer. When workers are permanently disabled, they may receive benefits for life. If injuries and illnesses are fatal, workers' compensation provides death benefits to survivors.

Life Insurance

The right life insurance choices can help provide financial security for you and your family. Life insurance protects dependents from loss of income and helps pay expenses after the death of the insured person. When an insured person dies, the face value of his or her policy is paid to the beneficiary. The *face value* is the amount for which the policy is written. A **beneficiary** is a person or organization named by a policyholder to receive the death benefit of an insurance policy after the policyholder's death.

There are three traditional types of life insurance policies: term life, whole life, and endowment. Each type is available in slightly different forms and with different features.

Term Life

Term life insurance is a type of insurance that provides protection only for a specific period of time. This time period may be 1, 5, 10, or 20 years, or until a specified age. When the term ends, so does the protection. Term policies often include a renewable option that allows you to renew the coverage at the end of the term, usually at higher rates.

The advantage of term insurance is that it offers the most protection for the insurance dollar. Policies that offer only a death benefit cost less than policies with cash value features. Cash value is the amount of money a policyholder would receive if the policy were surrendered before

death or maturity. For those people who really need insurance and cannot afford high premiums, term coverage may be the best choice.

Whole Life

Whole life insurance is a type of insurance that provides basic lifetime protection, as long as premiums are paid. Whole life insurance is also called *straight life insurance*. The death benefit amount is paid to beneficiaries upon the death of the insured. In addition to the death benefit, the policy builds cash value over the years. Whole life policies include limited payment policies, variable life, adjustable life, and universal life.

Limited Payment Policies

Limited payment policies offer lifetime protection. They require premium payments over a stated period of time, such as 20 years, or until you reach a certain age. During the payment period, premiums are higher and cash value builds faster than for standard whole life coverage.

Golden Pixels LLC/Shutterstock.com

Life insurance helps protect family members from financial losses and expenses after the death of the insured person.

Variable Life

Variable life insurance premiums are fixed. The insurance protection is combined with an investment feature. The face value varies with the performance of the fund in which the premiums are invested. However, the face amount may not fall below the original amount of the insurance. These policies guarantee a minimum death benefit. The benefit may be higher than the guarantee, depending on the earnings of the premium dollars invested.

Adjustable Life

An adjustable life insurance policy lets the policyholder revise the policy as personal needs change. Within limits, the policyholder may raise or lower the premiums, face value, and premium payment period. Coverage may start with term insurance for a given amount, premium, and term. All these factors may change as needed. Flexibility is the key advantage of adjustable life coverage.

However, the need to constantly monitor coverage may be considered a disadvantage.

Universal Life

Universal life insurance allows premiums, face value, and level of protection to be adjusted. In addition, it offers a cash value feature. The cash value of the policy builds based on the current interest rate. An annual statement shows the current level of protection, cash value, and interest earned. The statement also includes a breakdown of how premiums are allocated to protection and expenses.

Endowment Insurance

Endowment insurance is a type of insurance that pays the face value of the policy to beneficiaries if the insured dies before the endowment period ends. It pays the face value amount to the insured if he or she lives beyond the endowment period.

Section 20.1 Review

 Check Your Understanding

1. Identify three types of risk.
2. List four methods of risk management.
3. List examples of health insurance plans.
4. Name three forms of managed care plans.
5. What are the three traditional types of life insurance policies?

 Build Your Vocabulary

As you progress through this course, develop a personal glossary of key terms. This will help you build your vocabulary and prepare you for a career. Write a definition for each of the following terms and add it to your personal glossary.

coinsurance

exclusion

preexisting condition

preauthorization

utilization review

regular medical insurance

inpatient

major medical insurance

comprehensive medical insurance

dental insurance

vision care insurance

managed care plan

copayment

beneficiary

term life insurance

whole life insurance

endowment insurance

Personal Property Insurance

What should an individual consider when buying insurance for personal property?

Objectives

After completing this section, you will be able to:

- **Explain** the importance of property insurance.
- **Describe** types of auto insurance coverage.
- **Identify** the options to consider when buying insurance.

Key Terms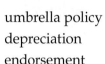

umbrella policy
depreciation
endorsement

bodily injury liability
property damage
  liability

no-fault auto
  insurance

Property Insurance

Personal property has monetary value and personal importance to its owner. Whether living in a house that is owned or an apartment that is rented, personal property should be insured against loss. Homeowners and renters insurance are available to protect the resident.

Homeowners Insurance

Homeowners insurance provides coverage for liability and damage to property under certain conditions. It provides two basic types of coverage: property protection and liability protection.

Property coverage insures the policyholder against financial loss due to damage to or loss of a dwelling, personal property, and possessions, such as clothes and furnishings. It may also pay for additional living expenses if the insured needs to move out of the dwelling because of damage to the property. The specific losses covered depend on the type of policy purchased. Floods and earthquakes are not covered by property and casualty insurance. Coverage for these events is purchased separately.

Denise Lett/Shutterstock.com

Homeowners insurance covers damage to property and offers liability protection.

Ethics

Computer Ethics

While you are at work or school, it is important to be respectful in your use of computer equipment. The computer is available for your use as a tool for research or to accomplish a task. It is unethical to use the computer to download copyrighted material or harass others. Unapproved use of computers may open up the computer network to viruses and other issues that may jeopardize the integrity of the network as well as have legal implications.

Homeowners liability coverage protects a homeowner if others are injured on the policyholder's property. For example, if someone falls and is hurt in someone's home, liability coverage pays for losses incurred if the insured is liable. This also covers accidental damage to the property of others caused by the policyholder's family, pet(s), or property. Homeowners liability coverage pays for the legal costs of defense if the insured is sued because of injuries or damages.

Additional liability coverage can be purchased through an umbrella policy, also known as an *extended liability policy*. An **umbrella policy** is an insurance policy that covers loss amounts that are higher than those covered by primary policies.

The first step in buying the right homeowners coverage is to find out how much it would cost to rebuild the home. This may be more or less than the price paid for the home or its current market value. The cost of rebuilding a home depends on local building costs and the type of home that is owned.

To keep insurance coverage up to date, the insurance agent should be informed of any major home improvements. Also, adding an inflation-guard clause on the policy automatically adjusts policy renewal coverage to reflect current rebuilding costs.

Personal property can also be insured for replacement cost or actual cash value. **Depreciation** is a decrease in the value of property as a result of age or wear and tear.

Replacement value covers the cost of replacing what is lost without deducting depreciation. *Actual cash value* is the replacement cost minus depreciation.

Renters Insurance

Many renters mistakenly believe they do not need insurance because the policy of the property owner will cover any loss they may suffer. However, the property owner's policy does not cover the personal items of a renter. The property owner only carries coverage on the dwelling itself. To cover their personal items, it is a good idea for renters to purchase a renters insurance policy.

Renters insurance covers losses due to damage or loss of personal property and possessions. Examples of personal items include electronics, furniture, and bedding. It is also advisable to purchase a policy that includes liability insurance. If guests are harmed in a rented home or apartment, liability insurance covers any expenses for which the resident is responsible.

Ermolaev Alexander/Shutterstock.com

Renters insurance covers the personal belonging of renters, such as furniture, electronics, and clothes.

College students living in a dorm or renting an apartment may need renters insurance to protect their possessions. However, an endorsement to their parents' homeowners insurance may cover a child's personal possessions while living in a dorm. An **endorsement** is an attachment to an existing insurance policy to provide coverage for items not included on the original policy.

Auto Insurance

Auto insurance gives policyholders coverage for liability and property damage under specified conditions. All 50 states have financial responsibility laws that require drivers to show proof of their ability to pay certain minimum amounts in damages after an accident. Most states also have auto insurance laws that require car owners to buy a minimum amount of bodily injury and property damage liability insurance in order to legally drive their cars. An auto insurance policy may include several types of coverage for the insured vehicle or driver.

Bodily injury liability is insurance coverage that protects a person who is responsible for an auto accident that results in the injury or death of other parties. **Property damage liability** is insurance coverage that protects a person who is responsible for an auto accident that results in damage to property of others.

These coverages on an auto insurance policy cover the policyholder and any person driving the car with the owner's permission. They pay damages to other parties involved in an accident that the insured caused. Both types of liability coverage pay the legal fees for settling claims. They also pay for damages assessed against the insured, up to the limits stated in the policy. These damages include injuries to other parties or damage to the property of others. The following are types of auto insurance coverage that pay the insured.

- *Medical payments* coverage pays the medical expenses resulting from an accident in the insured car, regardless of who is at fault. It is also known as *personal injury protection (PIP)*. It covers the insured and any person injured in or by the insured car.

Dmitry Kalinovsky/Shutterstock.com

All states have auto insurance coverage requirements which provide financial protection in case of an accident.

You Do the Math

Problem Solving and Reasoning

Insurance is a financial service used to protect against loss. The insurance company charges its customers to assume their risk. The charge is called a *premium*. When a claim is made, the policyholder is responsible to pay a certain amount toward the loss before the insurance company begins to pay. This amount is called a *deductible*. Once the deductible is met, the insurance company begins to pay for covered losses above the deductible amount.

Solve the following problems.

1. Scott's auto insurance has a deductible of $500. Scott is in an accident that affects only his car and requires $3,000 worth of repairs. How much will both he and the insurance company pay toward the repairs?

2. Angela's auto insurance premium is $1,500 annually. She wants to increase her property damage coverage limit from $100,000 to $150,000. Her insurance agent says this will raise her premium by 6 percent. How much more will Angela pay each month with her new premium?

3. Ahmed's car insurance premium is $1,889.50. He is eligible for a 15% discount. After the discount is applied, how much will Ahmed's premium be?

- *Collision* coverage pays the insured for damage to his or her car due to an auto accident or collision with another car or object.

- *Comprehensive physical damage* coverage pays the insured for loss or damage to his or her car resulting from fire, theft, falling objects, explosions, earthquakes, floods, riots, civil commotions, and collisions with a bird or animal.

- *Uninsured motorist* coverage pays the insured for injuries caused by an uninsured or hit-and-run driver. *Underinsured motorist* coverage protects the insured for losses caused by a driver whose insurance will not cover all the damaged incurred. They cover insured persons while they are driving, riding, or walking. This means that the insured is covered if he or she is injured as a pedestrian. It also covers passengers in the insured person's car.

- *Roadside assistance* and *rental reimbursement* coverage are additional types of coverage that may be purchased. These pay the insured for certain expenses.

No-fault auto insurance is a type of insurance plan that eliminates the fault-finding process in settling claims. When an accident occurs, each policyholder makes a claim to his or her own insurance company. Each company pays its own policyholder regardless of who is at fault. No-fault insurance is designed to simplify and speed up payments to accident victims.

State legislators decide whether their state adopts a no-fault insurance plan and what form it takes. Most states with a no-fault plan have a combination no-fault and liability insurance. The no-fault pays for claims up to a set amount, called a *threshold*. However, in most states individuals can sue for additional damages when an accident involves severe injuries, death, or major medical bills. Liability insurance pays for damages over and above the threshold amount.

Auto accidents can be avoided by keeping the car in good running condition, driving within the speed limit, and minimizing distractions while driving, such as eating, drinking, texting, and talking on a cell phone.

An insurance agent should clearly explain different types of coverage and help policyholders evaluate their coverage needs.

Buying Insurance

When buying insurance for a home or vehicle, always select a company that is respected within the insurance industry, by its policyholders, and by people in the financial field. The company should be licensed to operate and have a good reputation for settling claims fairly and promptly.

The insured should look closely at policies that offer the benefits and options important to his or her situation. Premiums charged by different companies for the same types and amounts of coverage should be compared.

The insurance agent is also important. Very often, the agent is the key to the quality of service received. All states require a special license to sell insurance. The initials following an agent's name indicate completion of specific studies in the insurance field:

- *CLU* indicates a Chartered Life Underwriter

- *ChFC* indicates a Chartered Financial Consultant

- *LUTCF* indicates a Life Underwriters' Training Council Fellow

Members of the National Association of Life Underwriters subscribe to the ethical standards of that group.

An agent should be chosen who can clearly explain the different types of coverage and benefits available. A good agent advises clients honestly about the type and amount of coverage needed. He or she helps policyholders evaluate coverage needs and financial charges. A responsible agent also handles policy revisions and claims promptly.

After a policy is purchased and delivered, it should be reviewed carefully. If a life insurance policy does not meet expectations, most companies allow the client to return it within ten days without obligation.

Buying Auto Insurance

Auto insurance is a costly service. As shown in Figure 20-2, coverage for young drivers is particularly high because they tend to have more accidents. Premium rates and service for the same coverage may vary greatly from company to company. It pays to carefully shop several insurance companies.

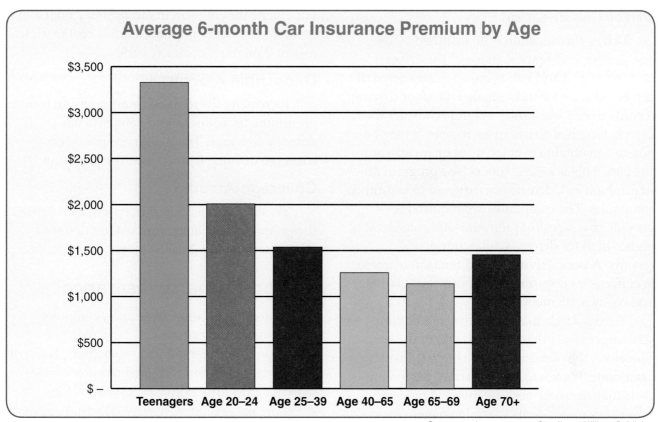

Source: carinsurance.org; Goodheart-Willcox Publisher

Figure 20-2 Auto insurance premiums for young drivers tend to be higher than those for older, experienced drivers.

To compare insurance costs, check the cost of coverage with several reliable insurance companies. In most states, proof of insurance coverage must be in the vehicle. The guidelines in Figure 20-3 can help you select the automobile insurance you need. The cost of auto insurance depends on driver classification, rating territory, discount eligibility, type of vehicle, deductible amount, and coverage amount.

Suggestions for Buying Automobile Insurance

- Decide the types and amounts of coverage you need. If you now have a policy, review your coverage and its cost before renewal time.

- Check with several reputable insurers. Keep in mind that the least expensive coverage is not necessarily the best for you. Consider such things as the company's reliability and its reputation for service, including claims handling. If you are in doubt about a company, check with the Department of Insurance for your state.

- Consider the amount you would save by paying a higher deductible. You may find it pays in the end to take care of small losses yourself.

- Check with your agent regarding your eligibility for premium discounts.

- Consider special coverages or higher policy limits if you frequently drive other commuters to work or groups of children to school or other events.

- Consider reducing or dropping collision coverage as cars get older.

Goodheart-Willcox Publisher

Figure 20-3 The guidelines in this chart can help you select auto insurance.

Driver Classification

Driver classification is determined by the age, gender, and marital status of the driver. Driving record and habits are also considered. It can be difficult for individuals with poor driving records to buy insurance. Insurers consider these drivers too great a risk. In such cases, it may be possible to obtain coverage through an *assigned risk plan*. This is a state-supervised program in which high-risk drivers are assigned to insurance companies. The companies are required to provide coverage, but premiums are considerably higher than for drivers with better driving records. A poor driving record tends to increase premiums, as does a record of previous claims and costly settlements.

Young, single males are involved in more serious accidents than other classes of drivers. Therefore, they tend to pay the highest insurance premiums. If a young man marries, his insurance costs may decrease because married men have fewer serious accidents than single men. Rates for women, single and married, are lower than rates for males.

Rating Territory

The number and amount of claims an insurance company processes in an area determines rates for auto insurance. Premiums are higher in frequent claim areas, such as big cities and high traffic districts.

Discount Eligibility

Some companies offer discounts to drivers with the following characteristics:

- have a safe driving record
- get good grades (if still in school)
- have installed antitheft devices
- are over a certain age
- have two or more cars on a policy
- have a good credit score

Type of Vehicle

Cars that are costly to repair or that are favorite targets of thieves cost more to insure. Premiums are higher for luxury, sports, and new cars than for standard models and older cars.

For older cars, collision insurance may not be cost effective. Very popular models cost more to insure than more ordinary cars.

Deductible Amount

Increasing the deductible amount can reduce premiums for collision and comprehensive damage coverage. The higher the policy or coverage deductible, the lower the premium.

Coverage Amount

The more protection purchased, the higher the premium. However, the cost per dollar of coverage is usually less for more coverage.

Buying Property Insurance

Like other types of insurance, company reputations for honoring and promptly processing claims should be researched. The cost of protecting a home and personal possessions depends primarily on the following factors:

- *Type and amount of coverage.* The higher the amount of protection purchased and the more perils covered, the higher the premium will be. A policy with replacement value coverage is more expensive than one with cash or market value protection.

VGstockstudio/Shutterstock.com

Getting good grades in school can help reduce the cost of auto insurance.

- *Size of the deductible.* The higher the deductible is, the lower the insurance premium will be.

- *Risk factors of neighborhood.* The type of home and its location influence premium rates. For example, fire protection for a frame house is higher than on a brick house. Protection against theft and vandalism in high-crime areas are more costly than in low-crime areas.

- *The insurance company.* The cost of insurance premiums varies from company to company.

- *Opportunity for discounts.* Insurance companies offer premium reductions for having more than one policy with the company, such as home and auto policies. Also, discounts may be available for protective devices, such as a smoke detector or burglar alarm, for nonsmoker policyholders, or for long-term policyholders.

Section 20.2 Review

 Check Your Understanding

1. List two basic types of coverage provided by a homeowners insurance policy.
2. Why is renters insurance a good idea?
3. Name five types of auto insurance coverage that pay the insured.
4. What factors are used when determining the cost of auto insurance?
5. What factors are used when determining the cost of protecting a home and personal possessions?

 Build Your Vocabulary

As you progress through this course, develop a personal glossary of key terms. This will help you build your vocabulary and prepare you for a career. Write a definition for each of the following terms and add it to your personal glossary.

umbrella policy	bodily injury liability
depreciation	property damage liability
endorsement	no-fault auto insurance

Review and Assessment

Chapter Summary

Section 20.1 Health and Life Insurance

- Risk is unavoidable. Some risks are predictable and others are unpredictable. Examples of risk include personal, property, and liability risks. Risk management is a key aspect of minimizing or managing loss. It includes avoiding, reducing, assuming, and transferring risk. Buying insurance is a common way of transferring risk.

- Health insurance offers protection by covering specific medical expenses created by illness, injury, and disability. Health insurance plans can include regular medical, major medical, comprehensive, dental, and vision care insurance. Plans can be purchased privately, through government-sponsored programs, or may be available through an employer.

- Life insurance protects dependents from loss of income and helps pay expenses after the death of the insured person. There are three traditional types of life insurance policies: term life, whole life, and endowment. Each type has different features regarding premiums, value, and investment options.

Section 20.2 Personal Property Insurance

- Property insurance covers the personal property of an insured. Policies are available for both homeowners and renters. Homeowners insurance provides coverage for liability and damage to property under certain conditions. Renters insurance covers a renter against losses due to damage or loss of personal property and possessions. The owner of the rental property only carries coverage on the dwelling itself, not on property of the residents.

- Auto insurance covers the policyholder for liability and property damage in the event of an accident. Coverage can include bodily injury liability, property damage liability, medical payments, collision insurance, comprehensive physical damage, uninsured and underinsured motorists, roadside assistance, and rental reimbursement.

- When purchasing insurance for a home or vehicle, it is important to research the insurance company, the insurance agents who work for that company, and the types of policies offered. The cost of auto insurance depends on driver classification, rating territory, discount eligibility, type of vehicle, deductible amount, and coverage amount. Similarly, the cost of property insurance depends on the type and amount of coverage, size of the policy deductible, risk factors of the neighborhood, the insurance company, and discounts.

Online Activities

Complete the following activities to help you learn, practice, and expand your knowledge and skills.

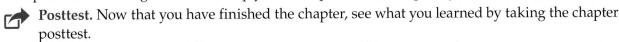 **Posttest.** Now that you have finished the chapter, see what you learned by taking the chapter posttest.

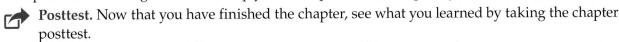 **Vocabulary.** Practice vocabulary for this chapter using the e-flash cards, matching activity, and vocabulary game until you are able to recognize their meanings.

Review Your Knowledge

1. Explain different types of risk that an individual might encounter.
2. What factors of a person's life must be considered when selecting the type and amount of insurance needed?
3. What is the difference among HMOs, PPOs, and POS plans?
4. List and describe three examples of government-sponsored health insurance.
5. Explain the different types of whole life insurance policies that are available.
6. Explain the purpose of homeowners insurance.
7. How does the insured benefit from uninsured and underinsured motorist coverage?
8. Explain how claims are handled with a no-fault auto insurance plan.
9. What qualities should an individual look for in an insurance agent?
10. How does driver classification affect the cost of auto insurance?

Apply Your Knowledge

1. Think about specific risks in your life right now. Make a list of the risks for which you would be willing to assume financial responsibility. Explain your plan for assuming these risks.
2. For the risks you are not willing to assume, explain how you can avoid, reduce, or transfer them. Use this information to develop a personal risk management plan.
3. Write a summary of the factors that would be important to you when choosing a health insurance plan.
4. Identify possible hazards that pose the greatest threat of property loss or damage in the area in which you live. Explain the types of insurance policies that cover these hazards and the specific types of property covered.
5. Workers' compensation insurance provides benefits for workers with work-related illnesses or injuries. Think of a large business in your area. List some of the potential work-related illnesses or injuries associated with the business.

Communication Skills

College and Career Readiness

Listening. Active listening is fully participating as you process what others are saying. Practice active listening skills while participating in a one-on-one discussion with a classmate. Consider the person's point of view, reasoning, stance, word choice, tone, points of emphasis, and organization. What did you learn from this activity?

Writing. Now that you have completed reading multiple chapters in this text, analyze the themes and structures that the author used. Create a concept map that illustrates how the themes of this text are related.

Reading. Read the Ethics features presented throughout this book. What role do you think that ethics and integrity have in risk management? Think of a time when you used your ideals and principles to make a decision that involved some type of risk. What process did you use to make the decision? In retrospect, do you think you made the correct decision? Did your decision have any consequences?

Internet Research

Automobile Insurance. The law requires that drivers carry certain types and amounts of auto insurance coverage. These requirements vary among states. Using the Internet, find the legal requirements of your state. Gather information from relevant sources, such as an insurance company or government site. Do you believe the requirements are sufficient? Why or why not?

Teamwork

In this chapter, you learned about various types of risk and how insurance helps an individual manage personal risk. Working with a teammate, discuss the types of insurance you each think are important to a high school student. Write several paragraphs to support your opinions.

Portfolio Development

College and Career Readiness

Introduction. As you assemble your final portfolio, compose an introduction that gives an overall snapshot of who you are. This will be the first page of the portfolio that sets the stage for your presentation, so you want to make a good impression. Tell the reader who you are, your goals, and any biographical information that is relevant. You may want to highlight information by making references to sections or page numbers. There may be a website or URL to direct the reader to examples or documents of importance.

In addition to the items you have already collected, there are some additional ones that you might include.

- *Résumé.* An updated résumé may be appropriate for the situation. If you have already submitted a résumé separately, it is not necessary to include.

- *Letters of recommendation.* If you have letters from instructors, employers, or others who have praised your performance, include these in this introductory section.

- *Photo.* Photos are not required. However, a photo will help the interviewer remember who you are after the interview when evaluating potential candidates.

- *Table of contents.* A table of contents will give a professional appearance to your documents. Consider title pages for each section to add clarity.

CTSOs

Proper Attire. Some Career and Technical Student Organization (CTSOs) require appropriate business attire from all entrants and those attending the competition. This requirement is in keeping with the mission of CTSOs: to prepare students for professional careers in business.

To be sure that the attire you have chosen to wear at the competition is in accordance with event requirements complete the following activities.

1. Visit the organization's website and look for the most current dress code.

2. The dress code requirements are very detailed and gender specific. Some CTSOs may require a chapter blazer to be worn during the competition.

3. Do a dress rehearsal when practicing for your event. Are you comfortable in the clothes you have chosen? Do you present a professional appearance?

4. In addition to the kinds of clothes you can wear, be sure the clothes are clean and pressed. You do not want to undermine your appearance or event performance with wrinkled clothes that may distract judges.

5. Make sure your hair is neat and worn in a conservative style. If you are a male, you should be clean-shaven. Again, you do not want anything about your appearance detracting from your performance.

6. As far in advance of the event as is possible, share your clothing choice with your organization's advisor to make sure you are dressed appropriately.

6

Managing Your Career

Focus on Your Career

As a young adult, one of the keys to your personal success will be your ability to transition from school to a career. Now is the time to begin creating a career plan to guide you as you prepare to pursue future career opportunities. The career you choose will determine the people you meet, the places you travel, and the amount of money that you earn. It is one of the most important decisions you will make in your lifetime.

Pursuing employment is a major step for most individuals. Finding a first job is challenging and can be a lengthy process. Job seekers can increase their chances of being hired by becoming aware of standard job application practices. These practices include writing a résumé, cover letter, and completing a job application form.

Once you are employed, it is important to understand what is expected on the job. Your employer will have standards that all employees are expected to honor. In addition, learning how to be a productive digital citizen is one way to help you gain success in the workplace.

Social Media for Business

A *blog* is an informational or discussion-based website that consists of a series of dated posts in reverse chronological order. The word blog is short for *web log*. Many businesses use blogs to write narrative updates about their products and services. Blogs also provide information about a company. There are many blog platforms available, such as WordPress and Blogger. Companies often have blogs built into their own websites.

Customers can follow a blog, which means they will receive an e-mail when a new blog post is published. Bloggers should aim to highlight the strengths of the business by using narratives and pictures. Featuring success stories on a blog is one way to connect with customers.

- Posts should be short to maintain the reader's attention. Even though blogs do not have a character limit, it is common to keep blog posts between 300 and 1,000 words. An ideal length is 500 words.

- A professional tone should be used, abbreviations avoided, and the basics of professional communication applied.

- Using creative titles will catch a potential reader's attention. Getting a reader to click on the blog is the first step, and a good title will help.

- Placing multimedia elements, such as video clips, photos, illustrations, and links, in the post will help break up the text.

While studying, look for the activity icon ↗ for:

- Pretests and posttests
- Vocabulary terms with e-flash cards and matching activities
- Self-assessment

G-WLEARNING.com

21

Career Planning

Exploring Careers

Public Relations

Business Management & Administration

Presenting a positive image to customers and others is important to the success of an organization. People who work in public relations (PR) help businesses and other organizations make a favorable public impression. Public relations professionals may work for businesses, governmental agencies, or other organizations.

Typical job titles for these positions include *public relations director*, *communications specialist*, and *community affairs manager*. Examples of tasks that PR professionals perform include:

- work with others to promote an organization's image, activities, or brands

- prepare press releases, write newsletters, maintain blogs, give presentations, and answer questions from the media or the public

- arrange for company executives to give speeches or presentations, which they may also help to write

- work with community groups or charities sponsored by the organization

Public relations positions require a bachelor degree in communications, public relations, marketing, or related studies. On-the-job experience may be required for management positions. PR professionals need strong communications and human-relations skills. Computer skills in word processing, desktop publishing, and webpage creation are also important.

Reading Prep

College and Career Readiness

The summary at the end of the chapter highlights the most important concepts. Read the chapter and write a summary in your own words. Then, compare your summary to the summary provided in the text.

Check Your Business IQ

Before you begin the chapter, see what you already know about business by taking the chapter pretest. The pretest is available at www.g-wlearning.com.

Choosing a Career

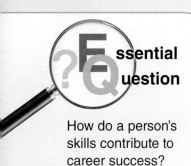

How do a person's skills contribute to career success?

Objectives

After completing this section, you will be able to:

- **Determine** the skills needed for the workplace.
- **Describe** how to create a career plan.
- **Explore** sources of career information.
- **Summarize** how CTSOs can prepare a student for a career.

Key Terms

job
career
skill
employability
skills
career cluster

career pathway
career plan
aptitude
ability
values
interest

networking
informational
interviewing
career and technical
student organization
(CTSO)

Skills for the Workplace

A **job** is the work a person does regularly in order to earn money. A **career** is a series of related jobs in the same profession. A job may be a part-time position you go to after school. A career is a position for which you prepare by attending school or completing specialized training. Over time, a job can turn into a career.

All employment opportunities require skills. A **skill** is something an individual does well. Skills are the foundational elements of all career fields. *Job-specific skills* are critical skills necessary to perform the required work-related tasks of a position. Job-specific skills are acquired through work experience and education or training. Without them, an individual will be unlikely to perform the job successfully.

Employability skills are applicable skills used to help an individual find a job, perform in the workplace, and gain success in a job or career. Employability skills are known as *foundation skills*. They are also known as *transferrable skills*. You have already acquired many of these skills. However, some of them are gained through life experience. Others may be gained from working at a job. Some of these may be gained in social situations. These skills are not specific to one career but are transferrable to many different jobs and professional positions. Examples of employability skills are shown in Figure 21-1.

Career Clusters

Studying the career clusters is a good way to begin analyzing the principles of career fields.

Employability Skills			
Basic skills	Reading Writing	Speaking Listening	Technology Mathematics
Thinking skills	Decision making Creative thinking	Problem solving Visualization	Reasoning
People skills	Social perceptiveness Leadership	Teamwork Cultural competence	
Personal qualities	Self-management Integrity	Honesty Sociability responsibility	

Goodheart-Willcox Publisher

Figure 21-1 Employability skills can help lead to success in the workplace.

The **career clusters**, shown in Figure 21-2, are 16 groups of occupational and career specialties. Career clusters are centered around related career fields.

Within each of the 16 career clusters are multiple career pathways. **Career pathways** are subgroups within the career clusters that reflect occupations requiring similar knowledge and skills. These pathways include careers ranging from entry-level to those that require advanced college degrees and many years of experience. All of the careers within the pathways share a foundation of common knowledge and skills.

Levels of Careers

In each career area, there are many opportunities for employment. Positions are generally grouped by skill level or education. There are five levels of careers that make up a career ladder as shown in Figure 21-3.

- An *entry-level* position is usually a person's first or beginning job. It requires very little training.

- A *career-level* position requires an employee to have the skills and knowledge for continued employment and advancement in the field.

- A *specialist-level* position requires specialized knowledge and skills in a specific field of study. However, someone in this position does not supervise other employees.

- A *supervisory-level* position requires specialized knowledge and skills. It also has management responsibility over other employees.

- An *executive-level* position is the highest level. This position is responsible for the planning, organization, and management of a company.

Career Planning

Planning for your career can be exciting. Your career choice will direct many other decisions in your life. It will affect decisions about your education and even where you will live. To determine the careers that will be enjoyable for you, you must first learn about yourself.

A **career plan** is a list of steps on a time line to reach each of your career goals. It is also known as a *postsecondary plan*. A career plan should include education options. Education options include four-year colleges, two-year colleges, or technical schools. It should also address current job opportunities in your career of interest.

There is no set format for writing a career plan. Many free career plan templates can be found on the Internet. Figure 21-4 illustrates action items for a career plan. To create a plan, you should first conduct a self-assessment and then set SMART goals. You will continue revising the career plan as you achieve your goals and set new ones.

The 16 Career Clusters

Careers involving the production, processing, marketing, distribution, financing, and development of agricultural commodities and resources. 	Careers involving management, marketing, and operations of foodservice, lodging, and recreational businesses. 
Careers involving the design, planning managing, building, and maintaining of buildings and structures. 	Careers involving family and human needs. 
Careers involving the design, production, exhibition, performance, writing, and publishing of visual and performing arts. 	Careers involving the design, development, support, and management of software, hardware, and other technology-related materials. 
Careers involving the planning, organizing, directing, and evaluation of functions essential to business operations. 	Careers involving the planning, management, and providing of legal services, public safety, protective services, and homeland security. 
Careers involving the planning, management, and providing of training services. 	Careers involving the planning, management, and processing of materials to create completed products. 
Careers involving the planning and providing of banking, insurance, and other financial-business services. 	Careers involving the planning, management, and performance of marketing and sales activities. 
Careers involving governance, national security, foreign service, revenue and taxation, regulation, and management and administration. 	Careers involving the planning, management, and providing of scientific research and technical services. 
Careers involving planning, managing, and providing health services, health information, and research and development. 	Careers involving the planning, management, and movement of people, materials, and goods. 

Goodheart-Willcox Publisher; Source: States' Career Clusters Initiative 2008

Figure 21-2 Each of the 16 career clusters contains multiple career pathways.

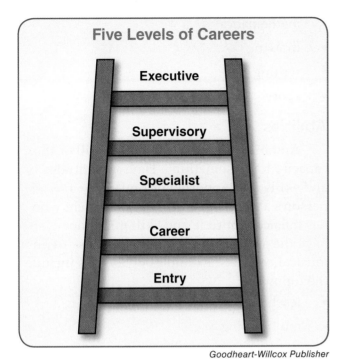

Five Levels of Careers

Executive

Supervisory

Specialist

Career

Entry

Goodheart-Willcox Publisher

Figure 21-3 Most careers have different levels of positions based on years of experience, education, and technical skills.

Conducting a Self-Assessment

A *self-assessment* is the first step in evaluating your aptitudes, abilities, values, and interests. By conducting a self-assessment, you can focus your energy on what is necessary for you to become successful in a career. Some self-assessment techniques are thinking or writing exercises. Others are in the form of tests, such as a personality test. Your career counselor can help you conduct a self-assessment.

Consider what you like to do and what you do well. This can give you clues to aid your self-assessment. If you always do well in math class, you may find success in a career that requires you to work with numbers. On the other hand, if you do not do well in English class, a career that requires writing may not be your best match. Identifying a career that you will enjoy and excel in begins with finding out what you like to do.

Action Items for a Career Plan: Public Relations Specialist			
	Extracurricular and Volunteer Activities	**Work Experience**	**Education and Training**
During Junior High School	• Help nonprofit groups and local youth groups with public relations efforts • Prepare press kits for nonprofit groups and local youth groups	• Choose a part-time job or volunteer position that allows application of business communication skills	• Participate in a CTSO • For optional or extra credit work, select topics and projects related to business communication and writing techniques
During High School	• Be a contributor for the school newspaper or yearbook • Write and edit press releases for school	• Work as an intern in a public relations capacity at a local business	• Enroll in business classes in addition to required course work for graduation
During College	• Help student, nonprofit, or local groups identify the best strategies to maximize their public relations efforts	• Work as a part-time public relations employee for a local business	• Follow the bachelor degree path for Business Management & Administration
After College	• Become a member of a public relations team in a local business • Attend local business professionals and chamber of commerce events	• Work as a public relations specialist	• Participate in appropriate professional development opportunities • Consider obtaining a master degree in Business

Goodheart-Willcox Publisher

Figure 21-4 This table illustrates action items to use for a potential career plan in the Business Management & Administration career cluster.

What is your *work style*? Some individuals prefer to work independently. Others need constant direction to accomplish a task. Mornings are more productive for some workers, where as others perform better in the afternoons. Casual dress influences some people to perform well. Business dress makes others more effective on the job.

When taking a self-assessment, you strive to identify your aptitudes, abilities, values, and interests. Learning this information can reveal careers for which you are well-suited.

Aptitudes

An **aptitude** is a characteristic that an individual has developed naturally. Aptitudes are also called *talents*. When a person naturally excels at a task without practicing or studying, he or she has an aptitude for it. For example, a person with an aptitude for music may be very good at accurately humming a tune or keeping a beat, even if he or she has never studied music.

Knowing your aptitudes can lead to job success. Some examples of aptitudes are:

- mathematics
- drawing
- writing
- sports

Abilities

An **ability** is the mastery of a skill or the capacity to do something. Having aptitudes and skills are supported or limited by a person's abilities. For instance, a student who has musical aptitude and skill might not have the ability to perform under pressure in musical concerts. Examples of abilities include the following:

- teaching others
- multitasking
- thinking logically
- speaking multiple languages

While an aptitude is something a person is born with, an ability can be acquired. Often, it is easier to develop abilities that match your natural aptitudes. For example, someone with

Goodluz/Shutterstock.com

By conducting a self-assessment, an individual can focus on what is necessary to become successful in a desired career.

an aptitude for acquiring languages may have the ability to speak French. A person without an aptitude for acquiring language can also learn to speak French, but it may be more difficult. Aptitudes and abilities do not always match. Someone with an aptitude for repairing machines may not enjoy doing this type of work and never develop the ability.

Values

The principles and beliefs that an individual considers important are **values**. They are beliefs about the things that matter most to an individual. Values are developed as people mature and learn. Your values will affect your life in many ways. They influence how you relate to other people and make decisions about your education and career.

Your work values can provide great insight into what kind of career will appeal to you. For some individuals, work values include job security. For others, the number of vacation days is important. Everyone has a set of work values that are taken into consideration when choosing a career path. For example, a person who values the environment may want to pursue a career in green energy or conservation. Examples of values include:

- perfection
- equality
- harmony
- status

Closely related to values are family responsibilities and personal priorities. These can have a direct impact on career choice. For example, if you expect to have a large family, you may decide that time is a family responsibility. You may want to spend as much time as possible with your children as they grow. This may mean choosing a career that does not typically require travel or working long hours. On the other hand, it may be important to you to live in an expensive house and drive an expensive car. This personal priority will require a career with an income level that supports these choices.

Ethics

Confidential Information

It is unethical for an employer to share personal information about a job applicant. Information that appears on a résumé or discussed during an interview is confidential. It is unethical to share confidential information about employees and doing so may end in a lawsuit. Depending on the confidentiality of the topic, sharing the information may be considered slanderous.

Interests

An **interest** is a feeling of wanting to learn more about a topic or to be involved in an activity. Your interests might include a subject, such as history. You may be interested in local politics or cars. Your interests can also include hobbies, such as biking or cooking. There is a good chance there is a career that would allow you to do what you enjoy as a profession.

Your interests may change over time. You may find new hobbies or topics that interest you. Try to determine if there is a uniting theme to your interests. When considering your interests, look at the "big picture." For example, you may enjoy being on the cross country team right now. In a few years, a career as an arborist might suit you because you enjoy physical activity and being outdoors. Examples of interests include:

- art and creativity
- technology
- sports and adventure
- collecting

Setting SMART Goals

Another step in the career-planning process is to set goals. A *goal* is something a person wants to achieve in a specified time period. There are two types of goals: short term and long term. A *short-term goal* is one that can be achieved in less than one year. An example of a short-term goal may be getting an after-school job for the fall semester. A *long-term goal* is one that will take a longer period of time to achieve, usually more than one year. An example of a long-term goal is to attend college to earn a four-year degree.

Goal setting is the process of deciding what a person wants to achieve. Your goals must be based on what you want for your life. Well-defined career goals follow the SMART goal model. Recall that *SMART goals* are specific, measurable, attainable, realistic, and timely, as illustrated in Figure 21-5.

Specific

A career goal should be specific and straightforward. For example, "I want to have a career" is not a specific goal. Instead, you might say, "I want to have a career in writing." When the goal is specific, it is easier to track progress.

Measurable

It is important to be able to measure progress so you know when you have reached your goal. For example, "I want to earn a bachelor degree in journalism." This goal can be measured. When you earn the degree, you will know the goal has been reached.

Attainable

Goals need to be attainable. For example, "I want to be editor-in-chief at a newspaper when I graduate from college." This is not reasonable for that point in a person's career. Gaining work experience is necessary before obtaining an executive position. This goal becomes more attainable when coupled with a plan to gain the necessary aptitudes, skills, and experience.

Realistic

Goals must be realistic. Obtaining a position as editor-in-chief at a newspaper may be practical with proper planning. It is not realistic for a new college graduate. Finding an entry-level position as a reporter and working your way up to editor-in-chief over a period of years makes this a realistic goal.

Timely

A goal should have a starting point and an ending point. Setting a time frame to achieve a goal is the step most often overlooked. An end date can help you stay on track. For example, you may want to be editor-in-chief by the time you are 35 years old. Aiming to get the experience

Goodheart-Willcox Publisher

Figure 21-5 Well-defined career goals follow the SMART goal model.

and education to achieve this position by a specific age will help you remain motivated to reach the goal on time.

Finding Career Information

There are many resources for career research. They will help you evaluate which careers make the best use of your talents, skills, and interests.

Internet Research

The Internet is a good place to start when you begin researching your future career. Researching various professions, employment trends, industries, and prospective employers provides insight to careers that may interest you. Many postsecondary schools have websites that provide career information.

The Occupational Information Network (O*NET) is a valuable resource for career information. The most comprehensive database of occupational information, O*NET Online, was created by the US Department of Labor and is updated regularly. This website contains data on salary, growth, openings, education requirements, skills and abilities, work tasks, and related occupations for more than 1,000 careers. The database can be searched by career cluster.

The Internet is also a great tool to use when you begin applying for jobs. You can search for available jobs in almost any career field. When you find a job that interests you, you can submit a résumé, job application, and cover letter via the Internet.

Career Handbooks

The US Bureau of Labor Statistics publishes the *Occupational Outlook Handbook* and the *Career Guide to Industries*. An *industry* is a group of businesses that produce the same type of goods or services. These handbooks describe the training and education needed for various jobs. They provide up-to-date information about careers, industries, employment trends, and even salary outlooks. The average person spends 30 percent of his or her time working every day. Understanding the industry of a chosen career is an important step to take. Career handbooks offer a great place to begin researching specific careers, their industries, and the areas of the country or world in which these industries thrive.

Networking

Networking means talking with people you know and making new contacts. Networking with family and friends can lead to job opportunities. The more contacts you make, the greater your opportunities for finding career ideas. Talking with people you know can help you evaluate career opportunities. It may also lead to potential jobs.

Informational Interviews

Informational interviews can give you unique insight into a career. **Informational interviewing** is a strategy used to interview a professional to ask for advice and direction, rather than for a job opportunity. This type of interview will help you get a sense of what it is like to work in that profession.

wavebreakmedia/Shutterstock.com

There are many resources for information on careers.

It can also be a valuable networking opportunity. By talking with someone in the field, you can learn more about what is expected. You can also learn what types of jobs are available and other information about an industry.

At informational interviews, be as professional and polite as you would in any other interview situation. Follow up with your contact after an interview. Send a thank-you message to show appreciation for his or her time.

Career and Technical Student Organizations

Career and technical student organizations (CTSOs) are national student organizations with local school chapters that are related to career and technical education (CTE) courses. CTSO programs are tied to various course areas. Internships and other cooperative work experiences may be a part of the CTSO experience. CTSOs can help prepare high school graduates for their next step, whether it is college or a job.

CTSO Goals

The goal of CTSOs is to help students acquire knowledge and skills in different career and technical areas. They also help students develop leadership skills and gain work experience important for professional development. These organizations guide student members to become competent, successful members of the workforce.

michaeljung/Shutterstock.com

Participating in CTSO program activities can promote a lifelong interest in community service.

Support for local CTSO chapters is often coordinated through each state's education department. Local chapters elect officers and establish a program of work. The CTSO advisors help students run the organization and identify the best programs that meet the goals of the educational area.

CTSO Opportunities

Competitive events are a main feature of most CTSOs. Competing in various events enables students to show mastery of specific content. These events also measure the use of decision-making, problem-solving, and leadership skills. Students may receive recognition awards for participating in events. In some cases, scholarships may be awarded if students win at state and national-level competitions.

Participating in a CTSO program and its activities can promote a lifelong interest in community service and professional development. Student achievement in specific areas, such as leadership or patriotism, is recognized with certificates or through award ceremonies. Other professional development opportunities may include:

- completing a school or community project related to the field of study
- training in the field
- supporting a local or national philanthropic organization
- attending CTSO state meetings
- participating in leadership conferences

Your participation in a CTSO can help you learn more about a profession. These organizations give students firsthand experience with the demands of a career.

Section 21.1   Review

 Check Your Understanding

1. Explain the difference between a job and a career.
2. Describe the relationship between career clusters and career pathways.
3. Explain the importance of setting SMART goals.
4. Name and describe three types of organizations of business.
5. Summarize how CTSOs can prepare you for a career.

 Build Your Vocabulary

As you progress through this course, develop a personal glossary of key terms. This will help you build your vocabulary and prepare you for a career. Write a definition for each of the following terms, and add it to your personal glossary.

job	ability
career	values
skill	interest
employability skills	networking
career cluster	informational interviewing
career pathway	career and technical
career plan	student organization
aptitude	(CTSO)

Planning for Your Education

Essential Question

Why is planning for education, training, or certification worthwhile?

Objectives

After completing this section, you will be able to:

- **Describe** the role of education, training, and certification on career choices.
- **Explain** the term college access.
- **Identify** sources of funding for pursuing an education.

Key Terms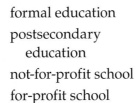

formal education
postsecondary
   education
not-for-profit school
for-profit school

occupational training
internship
apprenticeship
certification
college access

529 plan
scholarship
work-study program
need-based award

Education, Training, and Certification

There are many steps you will take as you plan your career. Your educational needs will depend on your career interests and goals. Some careers require a high school diploma followed by technical training or a bachelor degree. Others require a master degree, as well. Still others require professional certification. Early career planning can help you make decisions about your education.

Education

Formal education is the education received in a school, college, or university. Most careers require a college degree. However, for an entry-level position, a high school diploma may get you in the door. Jobs higher on the career ladder often require additional formal education.

Blend Images/Shutterstock.com

A person's education, training, and certification needs depend on his or her career goals.

Green Business   Green Job Search

Technology has made finding and applying for jobs more eco-friendly than ever before. Before the widespread availability of the Internet, job seekers read through the want ads in piles of newspapers. They needed to either mail their résumés or travel to multiple business locations to complete job applications. This required a lot of resources, such as paper and fuel.

Using the Internet, job seekers can now locate and apply for open job positions online by electronically uploading and e-mailing their résumés in response to a job posting. Many websites allow job seekers to complete and submit their applications online. Some companies even conduct online interviews, using Skype or similar technology. This saves on travel costs. Searching and applying for jobs electronically saves employers and job seekers time and money.

High School

During high school, a variety of subjects are covered. This gives students a well-rounded education to serve as a foundation for life-long learning. English, history, and science are some of the subjects all students study in high school. At the end of four years, students graduate and receive a *high school diploma*.

Postsecondary Education

Postsecondary education is any education achieved after high school. This includes all two- and four-year colleges and universities. Common postsecondary degrees are an associate degree and a bachelor degree. An associate degree is a two-year degree. A bachelor degree is a four-year degree.

Area of Study. Students in postsecondary schools choose an area of study that suits an interest or meets a career goal. This is referred to as a *major*. For example, a student who wants to become an elementary school teacher may major in education.

When considering a major, research the income potential of the career. Some careers start at a low salary and steadily increase over the course of the career. Other careers may start high and continue to increase. In addition to income potential, look into the number of jobs that are available in the area, both for new graduates and for those with experience.

In addition to major areas of study, postsecondary students are typically required to take a wide variety of classes in other subjects. These courses are referred to as *general education courses*. They cover many of the same subject areas as high school courses. The courses also cover subjects not often offered at the high-school level, such as political science and psychology.

Not-for-Profit and For-Profit Schools. A postsecondary school may be either a not-for-profit school or a for-profit school. A **not-for-profit school** is one that returns the money it earns back into the school. These schools receive funding from student tuition and fees, donations, and governmental programs. A not-for-profit school is what most people think of in terms of "college." It may be public, such as a state university. Others may be private, such as a private college or a community college. Not-for-profit schools tend to encourage academic exploration and personal growth beyond the specific requirements of a student's major.

A **for-profit school** is one that is set up to earn money for investors. It provides a product, which is education. In return for providing education, for-profit schools receive money from their customers, which are students. For-profit schools are also known as *proprietary schools*. They tend to focus on specific skills and do not require general education courses. A trade school is an example of a for-profit school. They typically offer a two-year degree specialized in a field of trade, such as automotive repair or cosmetology. Some for-profit schools offer bachelor degree programs.

Requirements and Costs. When considering a college or university, be aware of what is needed to apply. Requirements may include:

- official transcripts
- college exam test scores
- essays
- interviews

For all requirements, be sure to know the deadlines for completing and submitting the information. Missing a deadline can mean not being accepted to the school.

The costs of a postsecondary education must be considered. In addition to tuition, there are fees for many classes. Some majors include many laboratory classes. These classes can have more fees than other courses. Living expenses must also be considered as part of the cost of a postsecondary education.

Graduate and Postgraduate Education

Education received after an individual has earned a bachelor degree is *graduate education.*

Master degrees are graduate degrees. Education beyond a master degree is called *postgraduate education.* Doctorate degrees are postgraduate degrees.

Graduate study often builds on the same subject area or a closely related subject in which the bachelor degree was earned. For example, a student who earned a Bachelor of Science in computer programming may pursue a Master of Science degree in information technology.

Continuing Education

Some careers that have professional licenses require *continuing education* classes. These classes are completed to maintain the license. Completing these classes earns the student *continuing education units (CEUs).* If you are a teacher, for example, your school system may require that you earn a specified number of CEUs every year.

Another form of continuing education is more commonly called *adult education* or *adult ed.* These classes are for people age 18 or older

Many careers require additional education beyond a bachelor degree.

You Do the Math   Geometric Reasoning

Slope is the angle of a line measured in relation to a horizontal axis. It is the ratio of rise over run (rise/run). The rise is the distance of a line above or below the horizontal axis. The run is the length of a line measured along the horizontal axis. The greater the slope, the steeper the line. Two lines are parallel if their slopes are identical. If the slopes are not identical, the lines will intersect.

Solve the following problems.

1. Line A has a run of 2 inches and a rise of 1 inch. Line B has a run of 12 inches and a rise of 6 inches. Are these parallel or intersecting lines?

2. The roof on house A has a slope of 4/12. What is the rise of this roof? What is the run?

3. Hill A has a slope of 8/4. Hill B has a slope of 8/6. Which hill is steeper?

and traditionally focus on basic skills. Classes are offered in a wide variety of topics. They can range from learning computer skills to the English language.

Training

A college degree is not necessary for all career paths. Before taking on the expense of college classes, decide if college is right for you and your goals. There are many options for career training, including occupational training, internships, apprenticeships, and military service.

Occupational Training

Training for a specific career can be an option for many technical, trade, and technology fields. **Occupational training** is education that prepares you for a specific type of work. This type of training typically costs less than a traditional college education. It can also be completed in less time.

Internships

An **internship** is a short-term position with a sponsoring organization that gives the intern an opportunity to gain on-the-job experience in a certain field of study or occupation. Internships can be paid or unpaid. Often, high schools, colleges, and universities offer school credit for completing internships. Internships are an opportunity to gain work experience while working on an education.

Apprenticeships

An **apprenticeship** is a combination of on-the-job training, work experience, and classroom instruction. Apprenticeships are typically available to those who want to learn a trade or a technical skill. The apprentice works on mastering the skills required to work in the trade or field under the supervision of a skilled tradesperson.

Military Service

Service in the military can provide opportunities to receive skilled training, often in highly specialized technical areas. In addition to receiving this training, often it can be translated into college credit or professional credentials. After completing military service, there are many benefits available to veterans. For example, the *GI Bill* is a law that provides financial assistance for veterans pursuing education or training. Other forms of tuition assistance are also available.

Some people choose to enter the armed forces through the *Reserve Officers Training Corp (ROTC)*. Each branch of the military has an ROTC program at selected colleges and universities. Some high schools have Junior ROTC programs. The purpose of the ROTC program is to train commissioned officers for the armed forces. It can provide tuition assistance in exchange for a commitment to military service. Students enrolled in this program take classes just like other college students. The program is considered an elective. However, students also receive basic military and officer training.

Information is available on the *Military Career Guide Online* at www.todaysmilitary.com. Also, opportunities available in the armed forces are outlined in the *Occupational Outlook Handbook*.

Professional Certification

Some professional organizations offer certifications. **Certification** is a professional status earned by an individual after passing an exam focused on a specific body of knowledge. The individual usually prepares for the exam by taking classes and studying content that will be tested.

Some jobs require a professional certification. There are many types of certifications in most industries and trades, as shown in Figure 21-6. For example, a financial planning agency might require a financial planner to be certified as a qualification for the job. Other employers may prefer, but not require, certification.

There are certifications that must be renewed on a regular basis. For example, many certifications sponsored by Microsoft are only valid for the specific version of software. When the next version is released, another exam must be taken to be certified for the update. Other certifications require regular continuing

Certifications by Industry	
Administrative	Certified Professional Secretary (CPS) Certified Administrative Professional (CAP)
Automotive	ASE Certified Medium/Heavy Truck Technicians ASE Master Certified Automobile Technician
Financial Planning	Certified Financial Planner (CFP)
Health Support	Certified EKG/ECG Technician (CET) Certified Nurse Technician (CNT)
Hospitality	Certified Hospitality Accountant Executive (CHAE) Certified Hospitality Supervisor (CHS)
Human Resources	Professional in Human Resources (PHR) Senior Professional in Human Resources (SPHR)
Information Technology	Cisco Certified Network Professional Microsoft Certified Systems Administrator Sun Certified Java Programmer
Internal Auditing	Certified Internal Auditor (CIA) Certification in Control Self-Assessment (CCSA)
Manufacturing	Certified Manufacturing Technologist (CMfgT) Certified Engineering Manager (CEM)
Project Management	Project Management Professional (PMP) Certified Associate in Project Management (CAPM)
Real Estate	Certified Commercial Real Estate Appraiser (CCRA) Certified Residential Specialist (CRS)
Workplace Safety	Certified Environmental Health and Safety Management Specialist (EHS) Certified Safety Auditor (SAC)
Workplace Skills	National Career Readiness Certificate (NCRC)

Goodheart-Willcox Publisher

Figure 21-6 Certifications are available in many different industries.

education classes to ensure individuals are current with up-to-date information in the profession.

Some certifications are not subject-specific. Instead, they verify that an individual has employability skills. These certifications confirm that the person possesses the skills to be a contributing employee. The focus of these certifications is on workplace skills. Individuals who earn this type of certification have demonstrated they possess the qualities necessary to become effective employees.

College Access

College access refers to building awareness about college opportunities, providing guidance regarding college admissions, and identifying ways to pay for college. College access includes access to many types of postsecondary institutions. This includes colleges, universities, and trade schools. Attending a postsecondary school to further your education can be a critical step in your career plan. However, preparing to go to college can present challenges to students and families, both academically and financially. The sooner you begin planning, the better. It is never too early.

Academic preparation includes taking the right classes and doing your best. If you have always been a good student, keep up the good work. If you have not been performing to your potential, demonstrate your abilities and commitment by showing improvement. Along with strong academics, involvement in organizations at your high school or in your community will also provide greater access to college. Most schools are looking for well-rounded individuals. As you plan for your education, learn as much as possible about what it takes to be admitted to the college of your choice.

Many websites provide information to help you gain access to college. You can begin by searching the Internet for resources offered in your state. Search using the term *college access* plus the name of your state. If you have already

been thinking about a specific school, check its official website to learn about admission requirements and to find out what financial help might be available to you. The US Department of Education, the College Board, and the National College Access Program Directory have websites that include a wealth of information about college access. Topics include applying to college and paying for college. If you have not already done so, talk to your family, friends, and guidance counselor today for information to begin planning for college.

Funding Your Education

As you are making decisions on your education, you will need to create a financial plan for paying for your education. Whether you attend a trade school, community college, or university, someone has to pay the cost of the education. Funds to pay for education can come from a variety of sources. Each student's financial situation is different. You will need to figure out which sources are available to you and which ones fit your needs.

Many online college cost calculators can help you estimate how much money you will need to fund your education. Once you have an idea of how much it will cost to go to college, you need to figure out how you will pay for it.

Some families can afford to pay for college with current income or savings. If your parents or other family members are able and willing to pay for a college education for you, take advantage of their generosity. Thank them by studying hard and earning your degree.

Someone in your family may have established a 529 plan to fund your college education. A **529 plan** is a savings plan for education operated by a state or educational institution. These plans are tax-advantaged savings plans and encourage families to set aside college funds for their children. These funds may be used for qualified colleges across the nation. Each state now has at least one 529 plan available. Plans vary from state to state because every state sets up its own plan.

There are restrictions on how this money can be used, so make sure you understand how the plan works. There are penalties if money invested in a 529 plan is used for anything other than college expenses.

Even if your family has a 529 plan, the amount saved might not be enough to pay for all your college expenses. Many families pay for college using savings, current income, and loans. Parents, other family members, and students often work together to cover the cost of college. You might contribute money you have saved, money you earn if you work while attending school, and money for loans you will have to repay. More than half of students attending college get some form of financial aid. Figure 21-7 shows potential sources of funding for your education.

Financial aid is available from the federal government, as well as from nonfederal agencies. There is more than $100 billion in grants, scholarships, work-study, need-based awards, and loans available each year. Some states also offer college money to attend a state school, if you have good grades in high school.

Potential Sources of Funding a College Education		
Source	**Brief Description**	**Repayment**
529 Plan	Tax-advantage savings plan designed to encourage saving for future college costs. Plans are sponsored by states, state agencies, and educational institutions.	No repayment.
Grants	Money to pay for college provided by government agencies, corporations, states, and other organizations. Most grants are based on need and some have other requirements.	No repayment.
Scholarships	Money to pay for college based on specific qualifications including academics, sports, music, leadership, and service. Criteria for scholarships vary widely.	No repayment.
Work-study	Paid part-time jobs for students with financial need. Work-study programs are typically backed by government agencies.	No repayment.
Need-based awards	Aid for students who demonstrate financial need.	No repayment.
Government education loans	Loans made to students to help pay for college. Interest rates are lower than bank loans.	Repayment is required. Repayment may be postponed until you begin your career.
Private education loans	Loans made to students to help pay for college. Interest rates are higher than government education loans.	Repayment is required.
Internships	Career-based work experience. Some internships are paid and some are not. In addition to experience, you will likely earn college credit.	No repayment.
Military benefits	The US Military offers several ways to help pay for education. It provides education and training opportunities while serving and also provides access to funding for veterans. The US Reserve Officers' Training Corps (ROTC) programs and the military service academies are other options to consider.	No repayment, however a service commitment is required.

Figure 21-7 There are multiple alternatives for funding a college education.

A *grant* is a financial award that does not have to be repaid and is typically provided by a nonprofit organization. Grants are generally need-based and usually tax exempt. A Federal Pell Grant is an example of a government grant.

A **scholarship** is financial aid that may be based on financial need or some type of merit or accomplishment. There are scholarships based on standardized test scores, grades, extra-curricular activities, athletics, and music. There are also scholarships available for leadership, service, and other interests, abilities, and talents.

It is surprising how many scholarships and grants go unused because no one has applied for them. Do not fail to apply for help just because you do not want to write the essay or fill out the application. Talk to your school counselor. Be persistent if you think you might qualify for a scholarship.

Work-study programs are part-time jobs on a college campus. They are subsidized by the government. Wages earned at a work-study job go toward paying for tuition and other college expenses.

Need-based awards are financial-aid awards available for students and families who meet certain economic requirements. Income and other demographics are used to determine if a student qualifies for this assistance.

Section 21.2 Review

 ### Check Your Understanding

1. What are three ways an individual can meet his or her educational needs for a career?
2. Describe the role formal education can play in career preparation.
3. How is an apprenticeship different from an internship?
4. Explain the importance of college access.
5. Give several examples of financial aid that might be available for high school students.

 ### Build Your Vocabulary

As you progress through this course, develop a personal glossary of key terms. This will help you build your vocabulary and prepare you for a career. Write a definition for each of the following terms, and add it to your personal glossary.

formal education	certification
postsecondary education	college access
not-for-profit school	529 plan
for-profit school	scholarship
occupational training	work-study program
internship	need-based award
apprenticeship	

Review and Assessment

Chapter Summary

Section 21.1 Choosing a Career

- Employers require both job-specific skills and employability skills. Job-specific skills are those that are specific to the tasks related to a position. Employability skills are not specific to one career, but rather transferrable to any career. Studying the career clusters is a good way to learn about the different types and levels of careers.

- Creating a career plan will help you reach your goals. Conducting a self-assessment is the first step to discover who you are and what your interests are. Next, setting SMART goals will help you as you write your career plan.

- There are many resources for career research to help evaluate which careers would make the most of your talents, skills, and interests. The Internet is a good place to start. Career handbooks and informational interviews are also a way to gain insight into a career.

- Career and technical student organizations (CTSOs) are national student organizations that are related to career and technical education (CTE) courses. The goal of CTSOs is to help students acquire knowledge and skills in different career and technical areas, as well as related leadership skills and work experience.

Section 21.2 Planning for Your Education

- Your educational needs will depend on your career interests and goals. Most careers require a college education. However, there are many options for career training, including occupational training, internships, and apprenticeships. The military is also a career option.

- College access refers to building awareness about college opportunities, providing guidance regarding college admissions, and identifying ways to pay for college. It includes access to many types of postsecondary institutions, including colleges, universities, and trade schools.

- As you are making decisions on your education, it is important to create a financial plan for paying for your education. A 529 plan is a savings plan and is one way to pay for an education. There are also grants, scholarships, work-study, need-based awards, and loans available to help students and their families.

Online Activities

Complete the following activities to help you learn, practice, and expand your knowledge and skills.

Posttest. Now that you have finished the chapter, see what you learned by taking the chapter posttest.

Vocabulary. Practice vocabulary for this chapter using the e-flash cards, matching activity, and vocabulary game until you are able to recognize their meanings.

Review Your Knowledge

1. What is the difference between job-specific skills and employability skills?
2. Describe what should be included in a career plan.
3. Why is self-assessment important when considering career choices?
4. Explain the relationship between aptitudes and abilities.
5. What is O*NET?
6. What is the goal of informational interviewing?
7. Individuals preparing for careers may seek formal education, training, and potential certification opportunities. Describe each option.
8. Describe how military service provides career training.
9. College access is important to any student considering educational opportunities. What are some sources of information for building college awareness?
10. Explain the difference between grants and scholarships.

Apply Your Knowledge

1. Skills are the foundational elements of all career fields. Two important types of skills that are foundational to your career are job-specific skills and employability skills. Create a chart with two columns. In column one, list the job-specific skills you currently possess. In column two, list the employability skills that you possess. Use this chart as a source of information when you create a career plan.
2. Analyzing the principles of various clusters will help you select a career in which you are interested. Refer to the Career Clusters in Figure 21-2. Review the Business Management and Administration career cluster, Marketing career cluster, and Finance career cluster. Select a career cluster to analyze. How are the different careers within the cluster related to one another?
3. Conduct an informal self-assessment by defining your work style, aptitudes, values, and interests. Next, evaluate your individual talents, abilities, and skills. This will help prepare you to write a career plan.
4. Your interest can be a first step in determining career opportunities that would be a good fit for you. Take time to analyze your interests and how you can turn these into SMART career goals. Write three of your career goals as SMART goals. Specify how each of these goals is specific, measurable, attainable, realistic, and timely.
5. A career plan is a list of steps to reach a career goal. Write a list of action items for a career plan for the next five years that you might consider following. Use Figure 21-4 as an example. Include your career objectives and the strategies you will use to accomplish your goals.

6. Research the costs in tuition and fees of a college you would like to attend. Next, research scholarships and grants for which you may be eligible. Build a plan to fund your first year of attendance and present your plan to the class.

Communication Skills

College and Career Readiness

Speaking. The way you communicate with others will have a lot to do with the success of the relationships you build. Create a speech that will introduce you to a counselor at a local college. The counselor should be a person you have never met. Deliver the speech to your class. How did the style, words, phrases, and tone you used influence the way the audience responded to the speech?

Writing. Many postsecondary applications, such as applications to colleges, require an essay as part of the application process. Write a 500-word essay that explains why your chosen career is the perfect one for you. Identify the audience and determine an effective approach and technique that will clearly state your purpose.

Reading. Most people use technology on a daily basis. Using technology in the workplace can help employees be more productive. In other instances, technology can be a distraction. Read about types of technology and how people can use each to be more productive in the workplace. What did you learn?

Internet Research

Employment Opportunities. Using the Internet, explore a career that is of interest to you. Research the education, training, and certification requirements of the career. Next, compare this career with a career in the same career cluster. What opportunities are currently available for each career? Evaluate salaries, career paths, and demand for the careers. Does the future look promising for either pathway?

Career Match. Self-assessment tools can help decide which career opportunities might be a good fit for you. Visit the O*NET Resource Center online and select the assessment called Career Exploration Tools. After locating the tool, use it to identify a career that is matched to the skills you currently possess. Use the results from the survey to research the career using O*NET. Write several paragraphs about the career to which you were matched. Design an effective report that will share your findings with the class.

Career Exploration. As a student, you will be planning for your future career. Research the Business Management and Administration career cluster, the Finance career cluster, and the Marketing career cluster. Which career cluster appeals to you? Write several paragraphs to explain how and why you chose a specific cluster.

Career Plan. It is important that you take ownership of a career plan that matches your interests and skills. Using the Internet, research how to create a career plan. Select a template that meets your needs. Create a career plan that aligns a career pathway to your educational goals. Using your list of SMART goals, create a career plan for the next five years.

Teamwork

By joining a CTSO, you can participate in student leadership and learn how to prepare for school and career opportunities. Working with your team, make a list of the CTSOs that are available at your school. What leadership activities are provided for students in each organization? What professional development activities are available? How can your school CTSOs help you prepare for life after graduation? Share your findings with the class.

Portfolio Development

College and Career Readiness

Organizing Your Portfolio. You have collected various items for your portfolio and tracked them in your master spreadsheet. Now is the time to organize the contents. Review the items and select the ones you want to include in your final portfolio. There may be documents that you decide not to use.

Next, create a flow chart to lay out the organization for your portfolio. Your instructor may have specific guidelines for you to follow.

1. Review the documents you have collected. Select the items you want to include in your portfolio.

2. Check the quality of each item in your folders. Make sure that the documents you scanned are clear. Do a final check of the documents you created to make sure they are high quality in form and format.

3. Create the flow chart. Revise until you have an order that is appropriate for the purpose of the portfolio.

CTSOs

Careers. Many competitive events for CTSOs competitions offer events that include various careers. This competitive event may include an objective test that covers multiple topics. Participants are usually allowed one hour to complete the event.

To prepare for the careers component of an event, complete the following activities.

1. Read the careers features in each chapter of the text. As you read about each career, note an important fact or two that you would like to remember.

2. Conduct an Internet search for *careers*. Review careers that may be a choice for the event. Make notes on important facts about each.

Exploring Careers

Collector

When individuals or businesses do not pay their bills, other businesses suffer. Collectors find and contact people who are behind on their bills. They arrange to have the person or business pay the money owed. Collectors use mail, telephone, or in-person visits to solicit payment. If payment is not provided, the person in this job starts the process to stop the service or reclaim the product or property.

Typical job titles for this position also include *debt collector*, *credit clerk*, and *accounts receivable specialist*. Examples of tasks collectors perform include:

- find customers who have delinquent accounts
- use mail, telephone, e-mail, or personal visits to solicit payment
- work with customers to create a plan for repayment
- use a computer to identify and monitor overdue accounts
- monitor the efforts to collect on accounts

Most collector positions require a minimum of a high school diploma. Some positions provide training on the specific computer software used to record the status of collection accounts. Interpersonal skills are needed, as well as general computer skills.

Reading Prep

Before reading the chapter, skim the photos and their captions. As you read, determine how these concepts contribute to the ideas presented in the text.

College and Career Readiness

Check Your Business IQ

Before you begin the chapter, see what you already know about business by taking the chapter pretest. The pretest is available at www.g-wlearning.com.

Résumés, Cover Letters, and Applications

Essential Question

What can a person's résumé reveal about his or her potential career success?

Objectives

After completing this section, you will be able to:

- **Describe** a résumé.
- **Explain** how to submit a résumé.
- **Describe** how to write a persuasive cover message to accompany a résumé.
- **Explain** how to apply for a job in person and online.

Key Terms

résumé
career objective
chronological résumé

reference
keyword
cover message

portfolio
job application

Writing a Résumé

When looking for your first job, you must sell your talents and skills to a potential employer. You must persuade the hiring manager that your skills and experience match the qualifications of the job you are seeking. A **résumé** is a document that profiles a person's career goals, education, and work history. Think of a résumé as a snapshot that shows who you are and why you would be an asset as an employee.

A résumé is the first impression that potential employers will have of you. It must be well-written and error free. The *four Cs of communication* of clarity, conciseness, courtesy, and correctness should be applied when writing for employment. When finished, each line should be proofread and checked for correct grammar, vocabulary, and punctuation. Communication that contains typographical errors or poor language usage negatively reflects on both the applicant.

A general rule of thumb is that a résumé should be one page. Résumés have standard parts that employers expect to see. A résumé is illustrated in Figure 22-1.

Name and Personal Information

The top of the résumé page should present your name, address, telephone number, and e-mail address. Use an e-mail address that is your real name, or at least a portion of it. E-mails with nicknames or screen names do not make a professional impression. Before you begin applying for jobs through e-mail, set up an e-mail address that you will use only for professional communication.

Career Objective

A **career objective** is a summary of the type of job for which the applicant is looking. An example of an objective is, "To gain industry experience as a sales associate while earning my business degree."

Work Experience

The work experience section of a résumé includes details about an individual's work history. The information in this section is typically the main focus of the employer's attention.

Jake Barton
123 Eastwood Terrace
Saratoga Springs, NY 60123
518-555-9715
jbarton@e-mail.edu

CAREER OBJECTIVE
A mature and responsible high school senior seeks an entry-level job as an accountant's assistant.

WORK EXPERIENCE
Saratoga Springs City Online Newspaper, Saratoga Springs, NY
September 2016 to present
Accounting Intern

- Track subscriptions revenue for newspaper.
- Assist with the setup of billing processes.
- File invoices as needed.
- Prepare accounts receivable and payable schedules.

Hunter High School, Saratoga Springs, NY
September 2015 to September 2016
Student Office Volunteer

- Answered telephone calls.
- Sorted and filed vendor invoices as they were received.
- Updated spreadsheets to track student fees.
- Recorded fees for parking permits.

EDUCATION
Hunter High School, Saratoga Springs, NY
Expected graduation date: May 2017
Relevant coursework: Accounting I and II, Financial Math

HONORS

- Hunter High School Honor Roll, 8 quarters
- FBLA Most Valuable Student of the Year, 2014

ACTIVITIES

- Saratoga High School FBLA, two years

Goodheart-Willcox Publisher

Figure 22-1 A chronological résumé has standard sections that employers expect to see.

As you begin composing this section, list your current or most recent employer first. This format is known as a chronological résumé. A **chronological résumé** lists information in reverse chronological order, with the most recent employer listed first.

For each work experience entry, include the company name, your job title, and the duration of time you worked there. List the responsibilities and details about the position you held. Do not list the addresses or telephone numbers of previous employers. This contact information will be provided on a job application form.

Volunteer work may also be listed as work experience. Employers are especially interested in community-oriented applicants who do volunteer work. Be certain to list any volunteer activities and the length of time you have participated in the activities.

Education

List the name of your high school and where it is located. Indicate the year in which you will graduate. Briefly describe any courses you have taken that are relevant to the job for which you are applying. List any certifications you have earned, special courses or training programs completed, and any other educational achievements related to the job you are seeking.

Honors, Activities, and Publications

Employers look for well-rounded individuals. Include information on your résumé that shows your involvement in activities outside of work or school. These can be separate sections, or they can be combined into one section. List applicable honors, activities, or publications with the corresponding year in which each occurred. If you have been a leader in an organization, note that experience. If you are a member of career and technical student organization (CTSO), include the name of the organization and number of years you have been a member.

References

A **reference** is a person who can comment on the qualifications, work ethic, personal qualities, and work-related aspects of another

Monkey Business Images/Shutterstock.com

A teacher or mentor is a good choice to ask to be a reference when applying for a position.

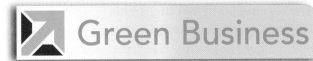

Green Business   Cleaning Products

Products used to clean buildings and workstations can have an impact on the environment. Toxic chemicals in many traditional cleaning products can pollute water sources and other business assets. They are also hazardous for employees to use, as the chemicals are poisonous. Instead, many businesses use green cleaning products in their facilities. Employees who clean the building can do just as good of a job with nontoxic green cleaners as they can with hazardous chemical cleaners.

Chemical cleaners should also be avoided when cleaning computer screens and work areas. These chemicals are hard on the equipment. If used improperly, chemical cleaners can damage computer equipment. On the other hand, green cleaning products are safe to use on almost any surface and are also safer for the employee using them.

person's character. Your references should be three or four people for whom you have worked and one person who knows you socially. Your list of references should present each person's name, title, and contact information. Get permission from the people you intend to use as references. Do not list relatives.

It is customary for references to be provided only on request. For that reason, your list of references should be separate from your résumé. To be prepared, bring copies of your list of references to the job interview. Employers who require references in advance usually indicate this in the job advertisement. Otherwise, you will be told during the interview process when references are needed.

Submitting a Résumé

The traditional way to submit a résumé is by mail or in person. However, most people submit résumés online. To do this, you may need to send your résumé as an e-mail attachment or upload it to a website. In some cases, you will need to copy and paste your résumé into an online application form. Be aware that this process usually strips out formatting, such as tabs, indentations, and bold type. You may need to make adjustments to the layout of your résumé after uploading it into an online application form.

Employers may use a software program to screen the résumés submitted electronically. These programs look for keywords to screen applicants. A **keyword** is a word or term that specifically relates to the functions of the position for which the employer is hiring. Keywords are typically nouns rather than verbs. For example, keywords for an accounting position may include spreadsheets, financial statements, and net profit. Be sure to include keywords in your résumé to increase your chance of being offered the position.

Singkham/Shutterstock.com

A résumé can be submitted by mail, in person, or online.

Writing Cover Messages

A **cover message** is a letter or e-mail sent with a résumé to introduce the applicant and summarize his or her reasons for applying for a job. It is a sales message written to persuade the reader to grant an interview. A cover message provides an opportunity to focus a potential employer's attention on your background, skills, and work experience that match the job you are seeking.

Writing a cover message is an important part of applying for a job. It sets the tone for the résumé that follows. A cover message should focus on your qualifications without being boastful. It does not repeat the details in the résumé. Rather, it highlights your key qualifications that are specific to the job for which you are applying. The message also explains how you heard about the position.

If you are submitting an application by mail, follow the rules for formatting a letter. However, most applications for jobs are submitted online. Figure 22-2 shows an example of a cover message that is sent by e-mail.

Introduction

A cover message should begin with an introduction that tells the employer who you are and why you are applying for the position. If responding to an advertisement, mention

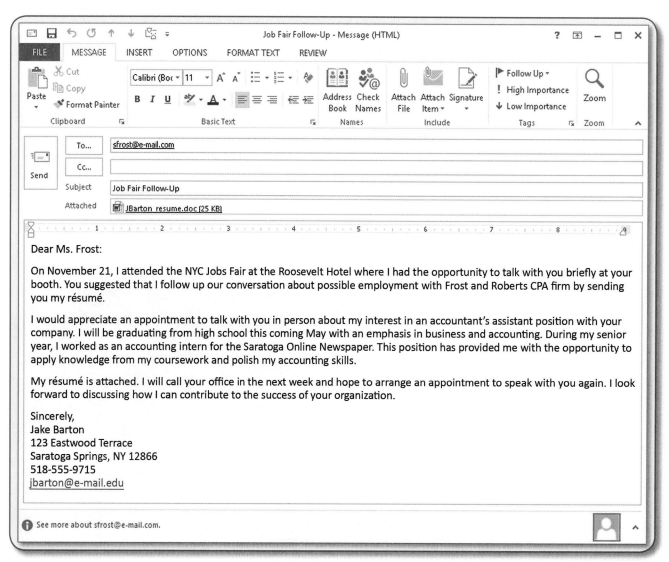

Goodheart-Willcox Publisher

Figure 22-2 A cover message sent in an e-mail should also have the résumé included as an attachment.

You Do the Math   Probabilistic Reasoning

Probability is the likelihood of an event occurring. In general, probability is stated as the number of ways an event can happen over the total number of outcomes. Flipping a coin, for example, can result in either heads or tails. The probability of the result being heads is one in two (1/2). There is only one side of the coin with heads, and there are two total possible outcomes. Probability can be expressed as a percentage. In the case of a flipped coin: $1/2 = .5 \times 100 = 50\%$ chance of being heads.

Solve the following problems.

1. A local office supply store offers a random discount to its regular customers. The discount may be 2 percent, 4 percent, 6 percent, or 25 percent. The discount is randomly selected by the cash register computer. What is the probability that a customer will receive the 25 percent discount?

2. The manager in a shoe store has observed that of 100 pair sold, 42 were blue. What is the probability percentage that the next customer will buy shoes in a color other than blue?

3. At a combination supermarket and retail store, 47 customers purchased only groceries, 13 customers purchased groceries and items from the retail area, and 62 customers purchased items only from the retail area. What is the probability that a customer will purchase groceries?

the position title and where you found the ad. For example, you might be responding to an online job posting. If sending a general letter of application, explain in specific terms how you identified the company and why you are interested in working there. If someone gave you the name of the employer to contact, mention the person and his or her connection to the company in your message.

Body

In the body of the cover message, demonstrate your positive work behaviors and qualities that make you employable, such as your ambition, determination, and abilities. Focus on the positive traits and skills that the employer seeks, as highlighted in the job description. Explain why you are qualified and how your skills and experience make you the best candidate for the job. Do not expect the reader to infer why you are the right person to hire—point it out. Remember that your résumé accompanies the cover message, so it is not necessary to repeat the facts in it. Give enough information to encourage the reader to read the résumé. Show genuine interest in the business.

Conclusion

The conclusion has two purposes: to request an interview and to make it easy for the reader to grant that interview. Leave no doubt in the reader's mind about your desire to be contacted for an interview. State how and when you can be reached or indicate how and when you will follow up. Supply the employer with the information necessary to arrange an interview.

Applying for Employment

Most job applicants apply in person or online. Employers have application guidelines that are usually stated in the job advertisement. When you connect with a potential employer, confirm the process with him or her.

Before applying, it is important to do one final review of your résumé and cover message. Make sure both are accurate and error free. Some job advertisements might request candidates to submit a portfolio as part of the application process. A **portfolio** is a selection of related materials that an individual collects and organizes to show qualifications, skills, and talents to support a career or personal goal. You have been creating a portfolio throughout this course. Each chapter in this text has a Portfolio Development activity as part of the end-of-chapter exercises. Your finished portfolio can be a part of the application materials that you might need to apply for a job.

Applying in Person

The traditional way to apply for employment is to print your résumé, cover

Blue or black ink should be use when completing a job application by hand.

message, and portfolio and hand deliver them to a potential employer. All documents should be on the same high-quality white or off-white paper using a laser printer. Do not fold or staple the documents. Instead, use a large envelope or paper clip the pages together. If using an envelope, print your name on the outside and list the components.

When you arrive at the employer, be prepared to complete an application. A **job application** is a form with spaces for contact information, education, and work experience. Have your personal data, information about your citizenship status, and locations and names of past employers handy. Use blue or black ink, and use your best printing. Like a résumé or cover message, an employment application needs to be free of spelling, grammar, and usage errors. Carefully review the form before submitting it.

Applying Online

Most employers encourage job applications online. The first step may be to complete an online application. Next, you may be required to upload a résumé or copy and paste information into a résumé form on the site. When pasting text, avoid any formatting and use plain text. Formatting can make the information difficult to read when the employer accesses the application.

Section 22.1 Review

 Check Your Understanding

1. What is the purpose of a résumé?
2. List the standard sections of a résumé.
3. Explain the purpose of a cover message.
4. Name two ways to apply for a job.
5. What information is needed to complete a job application?

 Build Your Vocabulary

As you progress through this course, develop a personal glossary of key terms. This will help you build your vocabulary and prepare you for a career. Write a definition for each of the following terms and add it to your personal glossary.

résumé	keyword
career objective	cover message
chronological résumé	portfolio
reference	job application

Job Interviews and the Employment Process

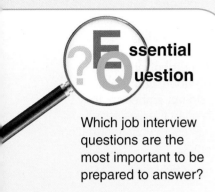

Which job interview questions are the most important to be prepared to answer?

Objectives

After completing this section, you will be able to:

- **Discuss** how to prepare for a job interview.
- **Describe** the employment process.

Key Terms

job interview
verbal communication
mock interview

hypothetical question
behavioral question

employment verification
background check

Job Interview

A **job interview** is the employer's opportunity to review a candidate's résumé and ask questions to see if he or she is qualified for the position. This is your opportunity to sell yourself in person and demonstrate professionalism. Your answers to interview questions are important in the employer's decision-making process.

The first step in preparing for a job interview is to learn as much as you can about the job and the company. There are several ways to do this. If the company has a website, thoroughly study the site. Pay special attention to the *About Us* section for an overview of the company. Look for press releases, annual reports, and information on its products or services.

While a company website can be a valuable source of information, do not limit your research to just the company site. Use your network of friends and relatives to find people who are familiar with the employer. Get as much information as you can from them.

Call the company's human resources department. The human resources department often has materials specifically for potential employees.

wavebreakmedia/Shutterstock.com

The job interview is an opportunity to convince the employer that you are a match for the position.

Use your best *telephone etiquette* while speaking with the person who answers the phone. Introduce yourself, state your purpose for calling, and be prepared with a list of questions to ask. Say "please" and "thank you" when speaking with each person so that you project a positive impression.

Interview Questions

Interview questions are intended to assess your skills and abilities and explore your personality. Your answers to interview questions help determine whether you will fit in with the company team and the manager's leadership style. Interviewers also want to assess your critical-thinking skills. They may ask you to cite specific examples of projects you have completed or problems you have solved.

Verbal communication is speaking words to communicate. It is also known as *oral communication*. In the course of a workday, most people spend at least some portion of time talking with coworkers, supervisors, managers, or customers. This communication involves a variety of situations, such as conversations about work tasks, asking and answering questions, making requests, giving information, and participating in meetings. Communicating effectively in an interview requires specific skills to be mastered.

Questions Likely to Be Asked

Before the interview, try to anticipate questions the interviewer is likely to ask you. The following are some common interview questions.

- What are your strengths?

- What are your weaknesses?

- What about this position interests you?

- What do you plan to be doing five years from now?

- Why do you want to work for this organization?

Write down your answers to these questions and practice them in front of a mirror. To prepare for an interview, conduct a mock interview with a friend or an instructor. A **mock interview** is a practice interview conducted with another

Ethics

Applications and Résumés

When applying for a job, to a college, or for a volunteer position, it is important to be truthful in your application and résumé. Fabricating experience or education is unethical and could cost you the opportunity to be a part of that organization. This means always telling the truth about your skills, experience, and education. Do not embellish. Play up your strengths without creating the illusion of being someone you are not. Present your information in a positive light, but be honest.

person. Practice until you can give your planned responses naturally and without reading them off the page. The more prepared you are, the more relaxed, organized, competent, and professional you will appear to the interviewer.

Hypothetical Questions

Interviewers may also ask hypothetical questions. **Hypothetical questions** are questions that require a candidate to imagine a situation and describe how he or she would act. Frequent topics of hypothetical questions relate to working with and getting along with coworkers. For example, "How would you handle a disagreement with a coworker?" You cannot prepare specific answers to these questions, so you need to rely on your ability to think on your feet.

For these types of questions, the interviewer is aware that you are being put on the spot. In addition to what you say, he or she considers other aspects of your answer as well. Body language is first and foremost. Avoid fidgeting and looking at the ceiling while thinking of your answer. Instead, look at the interviewer and calmly take a moment to compose your thoughts. Keep your answer brief. If your answer runs on too long, you risk losing your train of thought. Try to relate the question to something that is familiar to you and answer honestly. Do not try to figure out what the interviewer wants you to say. Showing that you can remain poised and project confidence carries a lot of weight, even if your answer is not ideal.

Behavioral Questions

Interviewers may ask behavioral questions. **Behavioral questions** are questions that draw on an individual's previous experiences and decisions. Your answers to these types of questions indicate past behavior, which may be used to predict future behavior and success in a position. The following are some examples of behavioral questions.

- Tell me about a time when you needed to assume a leadership position in a group. What were the challenges, and how did you help the group meet its goals?

- Describe a situation where you needed to be creative in order to help a client with a problem.

- Describe a situation when you made a mistake. Tell me how you corrected the mistake and what measures you put in place to ensure it did not happen a second time.

Again, you cannot prepare specific answers to these questions. Remain poised, answer honestly, and keep your answers focused on the question. Making direct eye contact with the interviewer can project a positive impression.

Questions an Employer Should Not Ask

State and federal laws prohibit employers from asking questions on certain topics. It is important to know these topics so you can be prepared if such a question comes up during an interview. It is illegal for employers to ask questions about a job candidate's religion, national origin, gender, or disability. Questions about age can only be asked if a minimum age is required by law for a job. The following are some examples of questions an employer is not permitted to ask a candidate.

- What is your religion?
- Are you married?
- What is your nationality?
- Are you disabled?
- Do you have children?
- How much do you weigh?

If you are presented with similar questions during the interview, stay professional. You are not obligated to provide an answer. You could respond, "Please explain how that relates to the job." Or you could completely avoid the question by saying, "I would rather not answer personal questions."

Questions to Ask the Employer

Write down any questions you have about the job, salary, benefits, and company policies. Keep in mind that the questions you ask reveal details about your personality. Asking questions can make a good impression. Questions show that you are interested and aware. Good questions cover the duties and responsibilities of the position. Be aware of how you word questions. Some questions are not appropriate until after you have been offered the job. In the early stages of the interview process, your questions should demonstrate that you would be a valuable employee and are interested in learning about the company.

Bronwyn Photo/Shutterstock.com

Prepare for the questions asked in an interview by rehearsing your answers. The more prepared you are, the more relaxed and professional you will appear to be.

The following are some questions you may want to ask.

- What are the specific duties of this position?
- What is company policy or criteria for employee promotions?
- Do you have a policy for providing on-the-job training?
- When do you expect to make your hiring decision?
- What is the anticipated start date?

Usually, the interviewer will tell you the hourly rate or salary for the position. Sometimes, however, an interviewer asks what salary you want or expect. Prepare for questions about salary by researching the industry. If you are unsure, you can simply tell the interviewer that the salary is negotiable.

Dressing for the Interview

An interview is a meeting in which you and the employer discuss the job and your skills. Interviews are usually in person, but initial interviews are sometimes conducted by phone. A face-to-face interview is typically the first time you are seen by a company representative. First impressions are important, so dress appropriately. You should be well-groomed and professionally dressed. Your appearance communicates certain qualities about you to the interviewer. When dressing for an interview, consider what you wish to communicate about yourself.

The easiest rule to follow is to dress in a way that shows you understand the work environment and know the appropriate attire. It is better to dress more conservatively than to dress in trendy clothing. Employers understand that interviewees want to put their best foot forward. Dressing more conservatively than needed is not likely to be viewed as a disadvantage. However, dressing too casual, too trendy, or wearing inappropriate clothing is likely to cost you the job.

Evaluating the Interview

Evaluate your performance as soon as you can after the interview. Every job interview is an opportunity to practice. If you discover that you are not interested in the job, do not feel your time was wasted. Make a list of the things you feel you did right and things you would do differently next time. Asking yourself the following questions can help in evaluating your performance.

- Was I adequately prepared with knowledge about the company and the position?
- Did I remember to bring copies of my résumé, a list of references, my portfolio, and any other requested documents to the interview?
- Was I on time for the interview?
- Did I talk too much or too little?
- Did I honestly and completely answer the interviewer's questions?
- Did I dress appropriately?
- Did I display nervous behavior, such as fidgeting, or forgetting things I wanted to say?

Phase4Studios/Shutterstock.com

Professional dress is a must for a job interview.

- Did I come across as composed and confident?
- Which questions could I have handled better?

Writing Follow-Up Messages

Immediately after the interview, write a *thank-you message* to the person who interviewed you. Thank the interviewer for taking the time to talk with you about the job and your career interests. Restate any important points that were made, and if you are still interested, reinforce your enthusiasm for the job. A thank-you may be in the form of a printed letter sent through the mail or an e-mail. Business thank-you letters should be keyed and formatted in business style. Keep the letter brief and to the point. Remind the interviewer of your name and reiterate your enthusiasm, but do not be pushy. An example of a thank-you message is shown in Figure 22-3.

Employment decisions can take a long time. Some companies notify all applicants when a decision has been made, but some do not. If you have not heard anything after a week or two, it is appropriate to send a brief follow-up message. Be sure your tone is positive. Avoid sounding impatient or demanding. Simply restate your interest in the job and politely inquire whether a decision has been made.

Accepting a job is one of the most fulfilling messages you will ever write. Think of this as your first official act as a new employee. It remains important to present an image of intelligence, organization, courtesy, and cooperation. In writing an acceptance message, let your natural enthusiasm show. Be positive and thank the person who has been the bearer of good news. Say that you look forward to the job.

Employment Process

The employment process can take a substantial amount of time. There are tasks that the employer completes to make sure a candidate is a fit for the position. In addition, there are forms that the employee must complete before starting a position.

Employment Verification

The employer will complete an employment verification using the information on your application or résumé. **Employment verification** is a process through which the information provided on an applicant's résumé is checked to verify that it is correct. Employers typically verify only the dates of employment, position title, and other objective data. Most employers will not provide opinions about employees, such as whether or not he or she was considered a good worker.

Dear Ms. Frost:

Thank you for the opportunity to discuss the position of accountant assistant.

I am very excited about the possibility of working for Frost and Roberts CPA firm. The job is exactly the sort of challenging opportunity I had hoped to find. I believe my educational background and internship experience will enable me to make a contribution, while also learning and growing on the job.

Please contact me if you need any additional information. I look forward to hearing from you.

Sincerely,

Goodheart-Willcox Publisher

Figure 22-3 A thank-you message is an appropriate way to follow up the interview. Thank the interviewer for taking the time to meet with you, and restate your interest in the job.

Another important part of the employment process is a background check. A **background check** is an investigation into personal data about a job applicant. This information is available from government records and other sources. This includes public information on the Internet. Sometimes employers also run a check of your credit. You must give employers permission to conduct background and credit checks on you.

Many employers use Internet search engines, such as Google, to search for your name. Employers may also check social networking websites, such as Facebook and Twitter. Be aware of this before posting any personal information or photos. These checks might work to your advantage or against you, depending on what the employer finds. It is up to you to ensure that the image you project on social networking sites is not embarrassing or, worse, preventing you from achieving your career goals.

Employment Forms

You will spend a considerable amount of time in the human resources department completing necessary forms for your employment. Come prepared with the personal information required for a multitude of forms. You will need your Social Security Number, contact information for emergencies, and other personal information.

Form I-9

A *Form I-9 Employment Eligibility Verification* is used to verify an employee's identity and that he or she is authorized to work in the United States. This form is from the US Citizen and Immigration Services, a government agency within the US Department of Homeland Security. Both citizens and noncitizens are required to complete this form. An example of a Form I-9 is shown in Figure 22-4.

The Form I-9 must be signed in the presence of an authorized representative of the human resources department. Documentation of identity must be presented at the time the form is signed. Acceptable documentation commonly used includes a valid driver's license, a state-issued photo ID, or a passport.

Form W-4

A *Form W-4 Employee's Withholding Allowance Certificate* is used by the employer for the information necessary to withhold the appropriate amount of taxes from an employee's paycheck. Deductions are based on marital status and the number of dependents claimed, including the employee. The amounts withheld are forwarded to the appropriate government agency.

At the end of the year, the employer sends the employee a *Form W-2 Wage and Tax Statement* to use when filing income tax returns. This form summarizes all wages and deductions for the year for an individual employee.

Benefits Forms

The human resources department will provide a variety of forms that are specific to the compensation package offered by the employer. Be prepared to complete multiple forms on your first day.

wavebreakmedia/Shutterstock.com

Employment verification can include a background check, credit check, and completing a variety of forms.

Employment Eligibility Verification

Department of Homeland Security
U.S. Citizenship and Immigration Services

USCIS
Form I-9
OMB No. 1615-0047
Expires 03/31/20XX

▶ **START HERE.**   Read instructions carefully before completing this form. The instructions must be available during completion of this form.
ANTI-DISCRIMINATION NOTICE.   It is illegal to discriminate against work-authorized individuals. Employers **CANNOT** specify which document(s) they will accept from an employee. The refusal to hire an individual because the documentation presented has a future expiration date may also constitute illegal discrimination.

Section 1. Employee Information and Attestation *(Employees must complete and sign Section 1 of Form I-9 no later than the **first day of employment**, but not before accepting a job offer)*

| Last Name *(Family Name)* | First Name *(Given Name)* | Middle Initial | Other Names Used *(if any)* |

| Address *(Street Number and Name)* | Apt. Number | City or Town | State | Zip Code |

| Date of Birth *(mm/dd/yyyy)* | U.S. Social Security Number | E-mail Address | Telephone Number |

I am aware that federal law provides for imprisonment and/or fines for false statements or use of false documents in connection with the completion of this form.

I attest, under penalty of perjury, that I am (check one of the following):

☐ A citizen of the United States

☐ A noncitizen national of the United States *(See instructions)*

☐ A lawful permanent resident (Alien Registration Number/USCIS Number): _____

☐ An alien authorized to work until (expiration date, if applicable, mm/dd/yy) _____. Some aliens may write "NA" in this field. *(See instructions)*

For aliens authorized to work, provide your Alien Registration Number/USCIS Number **OR** *Form I-94 Admission Number:*

Goodheart-Willcox Publisher; Source: US Department of Homeland Security

Figure 22-4 The Employment Eligibility Verification Form I-9 confirms an employee's identity. All new employees are required to complete this form.

Section 22.2 Review

Check Your Understanding

1. Explain the purpose of a job interview for both the employer and the applicant.

2. How can a job seeker prepare for questions that an interviewer might ask?

3. What is the easiest rule to follow when dressing for an interview? Explain.

4. What should be included in a follow-up message after an interview?

5. List the forms that must be completed by a newly hired employee.

Build Your Vocabulary

As you progress through this course, develop a personal glossary of key terms. This will help you build your vocabulary and prepare you for a career. Write a definition for each of the following terms and add it to your personal glossary.

job interview
verbal communication
mock interview
hypothetical question

behavioral question
employment verification
background check

Review and Assessment

Chapter Summary

Section 22.1 Résumés, Cover Messages, and Applications

- A résumé is a document that provides potential employers with a profile of a person's career goals, work history, and job qualifications. The most important part of a résumé is the listing of work experience and achievements. Other parts of the résumé, however, are essential to presenting a complete profile for the employer.

- After writing a résumé, the next step is to submit it. A résumé may be mailed or submitted online.

- A cover message is a selling or persuasive message. A cover message provides an introduction to who you are and why you are the right person for the position you are seeking. Writing a cover message provides an opportunity to focus a potential employer's attention on the fact that you are the best candidate for the job.

- Most job applicants apply for a job either in person or online. The traditional way to apply for employment is in person by hand delivering a printed version of a résumé, cover message, and portfolio. Applying online can vary by employer, but it typically includes uploading documents and completing forms on a company website.

Section 22.2 Job Interviews and the Employment Process

- The job interview is your opportunity to sell yourself. To prepare for the interview, rehearse answers to questions likely to be asked during the interview. The *About Us* section of the company website is also a good source of information to use in preparing for the interview. At the interview, it is important to dress appropriately and professionally. Immediately after your interview, follow up with a thank-you letter or e-mail to the person who interviewed you.

- The employment process can take a substantial amount of time. Employers must conduct employment verification and a background check to make sure the candidate is qualified for the position. In addition, employment forms must be complete by an employee when beginning a new job.

Online Activities

Complete the following activities to help you learn, practice, and expand your knowledge and skills.

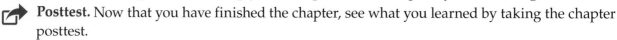 **Posttest.** Now that you have finished the chapter, see what you learned by taking the chapter posttest.

Vocabulary. Practice vocabulary for this chapter using the e-flash cards, matching activity, and vocabulary game until you are able to recognize their meanings.

Review Your Knowledge

1. What should be included in the name and personal information section of a résumé?
2. How is a résumé submitted?
3. Explain keywords and the role they play in writing the experience section of a résumé.
4. Why is the cover message important?
5. Describe the purposes of a conclusion to a cover message.
6. Describe ways a person can learn about a company when preparing for a job interview.
7. Why is it beneficial to ask questions during an interview?
8. What should an applicant do to evaluate his or her performance after a job interview?
9. What steps should be taken by an applicant after a job interview?
10. Describe what happens during employment verification.

Apply Your Knowledge

1. Prepare to write a personal résumé for a business position of your choice. Make a list of all your past work experiences. Write a brief description of your job responsibilities to demonstrate your positive work behaviors and qualities that make you employable. Use appropriate keywords. If you have any special licenses or certifications, note these also. Next, list your educational background and any other information you think should be included on your résumé.

2. Create a draft of your résumé. After your draft is complete, format the document. Using Figure 22-1 as an example, create your final résumé. Demonstrate use of appropriate content, concepts, and vocabulary. Check the final document for grammar.

3. A résumé may be required during the application process for college or a community service position for which you are applying. How would you modify your résumé for a college application? For a volunteer position?

4. Write a cover message that you would attach with your résumé if applying for a business position. Use the example as shown in Figure 22-2. Explain how your positive work behaviors and other qualities make you employable. Demonstrate use of appropriate content, concepts, and vocabulary. Check the final document for grammar and formatting.

5. Write an answer for each of the following potential interview questions.
   - What makes you a good employee?
   - What are your strengths?
   - What are your weaknesses?

6. Create a list of five questions you might ask during the interview. Be aware of how you word questions to make the best impression.

7. Ask a friend, teacher, or family member to conduct a mock interview with you. Dress as you would for an actual job interview. Before the interview begins, give your résumé to the interviewer. As you answer questions for the interviewer, demonstrate your professionalism by applying appropriate oral skills and conducting yourself in a manner that is acceptable in the workplace.

8. You have recently been interviewed for the position of assistant manager at a local business. Write a thank-you message to the interviewer.

Communication Skills

College and Career Readiness

Reading. Read a magazine, newspaper, or online article about the importance of professional communication. Take notes to identify the purpose of the article and the intended audience. Determine the central ideas of the article and review the conclusions made by the author. Demonstrate your understanding of the information by summarizing what you read, making sure to analyze the audience, purpose, and message of the article.

Speaking. Business careers require that individuals be able to participate and contribute to one-on-one discussions. Developing intrapersonal communication skills is one way to achieve career opportunities. As your instructor lectures on this chapter, contribute thoughtful comments when participation is invited.

Writing. As a student, you will be planning for your future career. It is important that you take ownership of a career plan that matches your interests and skills. Review and update your plan to align your personal educational goals to a career path. Consult with counselors or other professionals who can help guide you in the process.

Internet Research

Online Job Advertisement. Using the Internet, locate job advertisements for a company that is hiring for positions that interest you. Select one that would fit your criteria if you were to apply for it. Summarize how you found this particular job using the Internet, such as what search terms you used.

Lawful Interview Questions. Research the term *lawful interview questions*. Give examples of federal laws regarding employment interviews. Write several paragraphs explaining what you learned from this research.

Multiple Intelligence. Multiple intelligence research indicates that intelligence is not just I.Q. Individuals exhibit how smart they are by exhibiting behaviors in various ways. Using the Internet, research the topic of multiple intelligence. Write several paragraphs about your findings, and evaluate the validity and reliability of sources.

Teamwork

Work in pairs or teams as assigned by your teacher to conduct mock interviews. Take turns acting as the interviewer and the interviewee. Refer to the typical interview questions given in this chapter, but come up with your own questions as well. When all interviews are completed, write a brief summary evaluating how you performed in the interview. Describe what you could do better in the future.

Portfolio Development

College and Career Readiness

Presenting Your Portfolio. You have organized the components of the portfolio. Now, you will create the final product. Start with a flow chart to create the order of your documents. Next, prepare a table of contents for the items. This will help the person reviewing the portfolio.

Your instructor may have examples of digital portfolios you can review for ideas. Search the Internet for articles about how to organize a digital portfolio.

1. Review the documents you have collected. Select the items you want to include in your portfolio.
2. Create the slide show, web pages, or other medium for presenting your e-portfolio.
3. View the completed e-portfolio to check the appearance.
4. Present the portfolio to your instructor, counselor, or other person who can give constructive feedback.
5. Review the feedback you received. Make necessary adjustments and revisions.

CTSOs

Job Interview. Job interviewing is an event you might enter with your CTSO. By participating in the job interview, you will be able to showcase your presentation skills, communication talents, and ability to actively listen to the questions asked by the interviewers. For this event, you will be expected to write a letter of application, create a résumé, and complete a job application. You will also be interviewed by an individual or panel.

To prepare for a job interview event, complete the following activities.

1. Use the Internet or textbooks to research the job application process and interviewing techniques.
2. Write your letter of application and résumé, and complete the application form (if provided for this event). You may be required to submit this before the event or present the information at the event.
3. Make certain that each piece of communication is complete and free of errors.
4. Solicit feedback from your peers, instructor, and parents.

CHAPTER 23

Digital Citizenship

Exploring Careers

Webmaster

Most companies have a website through which they do at least some of their marketing and selling. Logically, a website that looks interesting and is easy to use will be more successful than a poorly designed one. A webmaster manages website development, design, and maintenance after it becomes active.

Other typical job titles for webmasters include *web developer*, *web designer*, and *corporate webmaster*. Examples of tasks that webmasters perform include:

- work with web-development teams to provide an easy-to-use interface and solve usability issues

- troubleshoot web page and server problems and keep downtime to a minimum

- implement and monitor firewalls and other security measures

- update content and links as requested or needed by the company

Most jobs in this field require a bachelor degree in web design or a related field. Training at a vocational school or an associate degree may be a suitable substitute in some cases. Exceptional skill with computers and computer programs is a must. Webmasters must be proficient in application-server software, graphics software, payment-processing software, and web page-creation software. They need a good understanding of graphic design, website design, programming, and problem solving. They must also have good customer service, communication, and math skills.

Reading Prep

Arrange a study session to read the chapter aloud with a classmate. Take turns reading each section. Stop at the end of each section to discuss what you think its main points are. Take notes of your study session to share with the class.

College and Career Readiness

Check Your Business IQ

Before you begin the chapter, see what you already know about business by taking the chapter pretest. The pretest is available at www.g-wlearning.com.

©iStock.com/Aldo Murillo

475

Communicating in a Digital Society

Essential Question

What implications does digital citizenship have for society as a whole?

Objectives

After completing this section, you will be able to:

- **Describe** the elements of digital communication.
- **Explain** intellectual property and what it includes.
- **Discuss** the importance of the Electronic User's Bill of Rights.

Key Terms

digital communication
digital citizen
digital literacy
digital citizenship
cyberbullying
etiquette

netiquette
slander
libel
digital footprint
intellectual
  property

plagiarism
piracy
infringement
public domain
open source

Digital Communication

Digital communication is the exchange of information through electronic means. Using technology to communicate in the workplace, as well as in one's personal life, requires users to be responsible. A **digital citizen** is someone who regularly and skillfully engages in the use of technology, such as the Internet, computers, and other digital devices. This requires the knowledge and skills to successfully navigate the Internet to interact with individuals and organizations. Digital communication is composed of digital literacy and digital citizenship.

Digital Literacy

Digital communication requires digital literacy skills. **Digital literacy** is the ability to use technology to locate, evaluate, communicate, and create information. According to the US federal government, digital literacy skills include the following:

- using a computer or mobile device, including the mouse, keyboard, icons, and folders
- using software and applications to complete tasks, such as word processing and creating spreadsheets, tables, and databases
- using the Internet to conduct searches, access e-mail, and register on a website
- communicating online, including sharing photos and videos, using social media networks, and learning to be an informed digital citizen
- helping children learn to be responsible and make informed decisions online

To learn more about digital literacy skills, visit the Digital Literacy website for information, resources, and tools. This website is supported by various departments of the US government.

StockLite/Shutterstock.com

Digital literacy skills are necessary when working in a business environment.

Digital Citizenship

Digital citizenship is the standard of appropriate behavior when using technology to communicate. Good digital citizenship focuses on using technology in a positive manner rather than using it for negative or illegal purposes. People who participate in the digital society have a legal responsibility for their online actions, whether those actions are ethical or unethical. *Ethics* are the principles of what is right and wrong that help people make decisions. Ethical actions are those that apply ethics and moral behavior. Unethical actions are those that involve immoral behavior, crime, or theft while online. These actions can be punishable by law.

It is important to understand the difference between ethical and unethical electronic activities. For example, it is sometimes difficult for a reader to know where joking stops and bullying starts. **Cyberbullying** is using the Internet to harass or threaten an individual. It includes using social media, text messages, or e-mails to harass or scare a person with hurtful words or pictures. A victim of cyberbullying cannot be physically seen or touched by the bully.

However, this does not mean the person cannot be harmed by his or her actions. Cyberbullying is unethical and can be prosecuted.

wavebreakmedia/Shutterstock.com

Digital citizens respect their employer and only use office equipment for business purposes.

You Do the Math   Connections

The margin of error is an allowance permitted to account for changes in circumstances or miscalculations. Margin of error is commonly seen in surveys, but may also be applied to calculations to allow for rounding errors. For example, a political survey may compare the percentage of voters favoring one candidate over another. These surveys, called polls, almost always state a margin of error, such as ±3 percent. In this case, the margin of error means the stated percentages may be 3 percent too high or too low.

Solve the following problems.

1. A business calculates its weekly expenses as $12,054 with a margin of error of ±2.5 percent. What is the maximum the weekly expenses should be?

2. A survey states that 45.6 percent of American households will purchase a new smartphone in the next year. The survey has a margin of error of ±8 percent. When estimating how many smartphones will be sold, what is the lowest percentage of households that can be assumed to make this purchase within the next year?

3. A survey of families planning to take a vacation over the upcoming holiday weekend states that 73.6 percent will drive at least 500 miles. The margin of error is ±4.6 percent. Allowing for the margin of error, what is the range of percentages of families that will drive at least 500 miles?

Another unacceptable behavior is flaming. *Flaming* is purposefully insulting someone and inciting an argument on social media. Spamming is equally unethical. *Spamming* is sending unwanted mass e-mails or intentionally flooding an individual's social media site or e-mail inbox with unwanted messages.

Etiquette is the art of using good manners in any situation. **Netiquette** is etiquette used when communicating electronically. It is also known as *digital etiquette*. Netiquette includes accepted social and professional guidelines for Internet communication. These guidelines apply to e-mails, social networking, and other contact with customers and peers via the Internet during work hours. For example, using all capital letters in a message, which has the effect of yelling, is not acceptable. Always use correct capitalization, spelling, and grammar.

Having poor netiquette can also have legal ramifications. **Slander** is speaking a false statement about someone that causes others to have a bad opinion of him or her. **Libel** is publishing a false statement about someone that causes others to have a bad or untrue opinion of him or her. Slander and libel can be considered

crimes of defamation. It is important to choose words carefully when making comments about others, whether online or in person.

What you post on the Internet never really goes away. A **digital footprint** is a data record of all an individual's online activities. Even if you delete something you have posted on the Internet, it is still stored in your digital footprint. Always think before posting to social media sites or sending an e-mail. What you post online today could risk your future college and job opportunities.

Intellectual Property

The Internet provides countless sources for obtaining text, images, video, audio, and software. Even though this material is easily obtainable, this does not mean it is available for you to use any way you choose. Laws exist to govern the use of media and creative works. The creators or owners of this material have certain legal rights. **Intellectual property** is something that comes from a person's mind, such as an idea, invention, or process.

Intellectual property laws protect a person's or a company's inventions, artistic works, and other intellectual property.

Plagiarism is claiming another person's material as your own, which is both unethical and illegal. If you must refer to someone else's work, follow intellectual property laws to ethically acquire the information. Use standard methods of citing sources. Citation guidelines in *The Chicago Manual of Style* and the Modern Language Association's *MLA Handbook* can be helpful.

Piracy is the unethical and illegal copying or downloading of software, files, and other protected material. Examples of protected material include images, movies, and music. Piracy carries a heavy penalty, including fines and incarceration.

Copyright

A *copyright* acknowledges ownership of a work and specifies that only the owner has the right to sell the work, use it, or give permission for someone else to sell or use it.

lightpoet/Shutterstock.com

Reusing material without permission, such as photocopying pages out of a textbook, is unethical.

Any use of copyrighted material without permission is called **infringement**. The laws cover all original work, whether it is in print, on the Internet, or in any other form of media. Scanning a document does not make the content yours.

Copyrighted material is indicated by the © symbol or the statement "copyright by." Lack of the symbol or statement does not mean the material is not copyrighted. All original material is automatically copyrighted as soon as it is in a tangible form. An idea cannot be copyrighted. A copyright can be registered with the US Copyright Office, which is part of the Library of Congress. However, original material is still legally protected whether or not the copyright is registered.

Most information on the Internet is copyrighted, whether it is text, graphics, illustrations, or digital media. This means it cannot be reused without obtaining permission from the owner. Sometimes, the owner of the material places the material on the Internet for others to reuse. However, if this is not explicitly stated, assume the material is copyrighted and cannot be freely used.

Many websites list rules, called the *terms of use*, which must be followed for downloaded files. The agreement may come up automatically, for example, if you are downloading a file or software application. If, however, you are copying an image or a portion of text from a website, you will need to look for the terms of use information. Unless the terms of use specifically state that you are free to copy and use the material provided on a website, assume the material is copyrighted. You cannot reuse the material without permission.

Fair use doctrine allows individuals to use copyrighted works without permission in limited situations under very strict guidelines. Fair use doctrine allows copyrighted material to be used for the purpose of describing or reviewing the work. For example, a student writing about the material in an original report is an example of fair use. Another example is a product-review website providing editorial comment. Fair use doctrine does not change the copyright or ownership of the material used under the doctrine.

In some cases, individuals or organizations may wish to allow others to use their intellectual property without needing permission. This type of use assignment may be called *copyleft*, which is a play on the word *copyright*. One popular method of allowing use of intellectual property is a Creative Commons license.

A *Creative Commons (CC) license* is a specialized copyright license that allows free distribution of copyrighted work. If the creator of the work wants to give the public the ability to use, share, or advance his or her original work, a Creative Commons license provides that flexibility. The creator maintains the copyright and can specify how the copyrighted work can be used. For example, one type of Creative Commons license prohibits commercial use.

Public domain refers to material that is not owned by anybody and can be used without permission. Material can enter the public domain when a copyright expires and is not renewed. Much of the material created by federal, state, or local governments is often in the public domain. This is because taxpayer money was used to

create it. Additionally, the owner of the material may choose to give up ownership and place the material in the public domain.

Patent

A *patent* gives a person or company the right to be the sole producer of a product for a defined period of time. Patents protect an invention that is functional or mechanical. The invention must be considered useful and inoffensive, and it must be operational. This means that an idea may not be patented. A process can be patented under certain conditions. The process must be related to a particular machine or transform a substance or item into a different state or thing.

Trademark

A *trademark* protects taglines, slogans, names, symbols, and any unique method to identify a product or company. A *service mark* is similar to a trademark, but it identifies a service rather than a product. Trademarks and service marks do not protect a work or product. They only protect the way in which the product is described. The term "trademark" is often used to refer to both trademarks and service marks. Trademarks never expire.

The symbols used to indicate a trademark or service mark are called *graphic marks*. Some graphic marks can be used without being formally registered, as shown in Figure 23-1.

License Agreement

A *licensing agreement* is a contract that gives one party permission to market, produce, or use the product or service owned by another party.

Twin Design/Shutterstock.com

Most brand logos, such as those seen on social media websites, are trademarks.

Correct Usage of Trademark Symbols	
™	Trademark, not registered
SM	Service mark, not registered
®	Registered trademark

Goodheart-Willcox Publisher

Figure 23-1 Graphic marks are symbols that indicate legal protection of intellectual property.

Ethics

Intellectual Property

Did you know you must cite any information you use that was written by someone else? Intellectual property is anything that belongs to someone else—copyrighted material, trademarks, music, just to name a few examples. If you quote material for a blog, website, or even a PowerPoint® presentation, you must give the owner credit for that material. It is unethical to present information as your own when it is not and can be illegal. It is also unethical to misrepresent data. Search the Internet for the proper use of intellectual material.

The agreement grants a license in return for a fee or royalty payment. When buying software, the purchaser agrees to follow the terms of a license. A *license* is the legal permission to use a software program. All software has terms of use that explain how and when the software may be used. Figure 23-2 explains the characteristics of different software licensing.

Alternative usage rights for software programs are typically covered by the *GNU General Public License (GNU GPL)*. The GNU GPL guarantees all users the freedom to use, study, share, and modify the software. The term **open source** applies to software that has had its source code made available to the public at no charge. Open-source software can be downloaded and used for free and can be modified and distributed by anyone. However, part or all of the code of open-source software may be owned by an individual or organization.

Electronic User's Bill of Rights

The *Electronic User's Bill of Rights* details the rights and responsibilities of both individuals and institutions regarding the treatment of digital information. It was originally proposed in 1993 by Frank W. Connolly of American University. It is modeled after the original United States Bill of Rights, although it contains only four articles. The articles are not legally binding, but contain guidelines for the appropriate use of digital information. The articles in the Electronic User's Bill of Rights include the following.

- *Article I: Individual Rights* focuses on the rights and freedoms of the users of computers and the Internet. It states "citizens of the electronic community of learners" have the right to access computers and informational resources. They should be informed when their personal information is being collected. They have the right to review and correct the information that has been collected. Users should have freedom of speech and rights of ownership for their intellectual property.

- *Article II: Individual Responsibilities* focuses on the responsibilities that come with those rights outlined in Article I. A citizen of the electronic community is responsible for seeking information and using it effectively. It is also the individual's responsibility to honor the intellectual property of others. This includes verifying the accuracy of information obtained electronically.

Characteristics	Software Type		
	For-Purchase	**Freeware**	**Shareware**
Cost	• Must be purchased to use • Demo may be available	Never have to pay for it	• Free to try • Pay to upgrade to full functionality
Features	Full functionality	Full functionality	Limited functionality without upgrade

Goodheart-Willcox Publisher

Figure 23-2 Each type of software has specific licensing permissions.

A citizen of the digital community is expected to respect the privacy of others and use electronic resources wisely.

- *Article III: Rights of Educational Institutions* states the right of educational institutions to access computers and informational resources. Like individuals, an educational institution retains ownership of its intellectual property. Each institution has the right to use its resources as it sees fit.

- *Article IV: Institutional Responsibilities* focuses on the responsibilities that come with the rights granted in Article III. Educational institutions are held accountable for the information they use and provide. Institutions are responsible for creating and maintaining "an environment wherein trust and intellectual freedom are the foundation for individual and institutional growth and success."

Section 23.1 Review

 Check Your Understanding

1. List the components of digital communication.
2. What actions are considered cyberbullying?
3. Name two unethical uses of another person's intellectual property.
4. What does a licensing agreement allow?
5. What does the Electronic User's Bill of Rights provide?

 Build Your Vocabulary

As you progress through this course, develop a personal glossary of key terms. This will help you build your vocabulary and prepare you for a career. Write a definition for each of the following terms and add it to your personal glossary.

digital communication	libel
digital citizen	digital footprint
digital literacy	intellectual property
digital citizenship	plagiarism
cyberbullying	piracy
etiquette	infringement
netiquette	public domain
slander	open source

Internet Use in the Workplace

Essential Question

How can unacceptable Internet use by an employee affect a company as a whole?

Objectives

After completing this section, you will be able to:

- **Explain** how employers ensure appropriate use of the Internet in a professional setting.
- **Describe** the importance of digital security.

Key Terms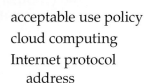

acceptable use policy
cloud computing
Internet protocol
    address

hacking
cookies
phishing
malware

spyware
software virus
firewall
identity theft

Using the Internet

An important aspect of digital citizenship is respecting your employer's property and time. Internet access provided by the company should be used only for business purposes. For example, checking personal e-mail or playing a game online is not acceptable. Most companies have an established acceptable use policy. An **acceptable use policy** is a set of rules that explains what is and is not acceptable use of company-owned and company-operated equipment and networks. Employees are typically made aware of acceptable use policies during training, before they are allowed access to the company's computers and network.

Many organizations allow cloud computing to support collaboration and working remotely. **Cloud computing** is using remote servers to store and access data over the Internet rather than on a personal computer or local server. This allows users to access personal content, such as saved files, from anywhere with a Wi-Fi connection. Cloud computing makes private digital information accessible from

any device. However, before using Internet access for cloud computing at work, make certain that your employer has given you permission to do so. Some companies and schools to use *filters* that prevent unauthorized Internet surfing or visiting selected websites during working hours. If you have not been given explicit permission before accessing the cloud at work, it may be considered unauthorized use in the workplace.

Censorship is the practice of examining material, such as online content, and blocking or deleting anything considered inappropriate. Employers are legally allowed to censor information that employees read on the Internet during work hours.

Whether at work or home, each time you access a search engine or visit a web page, the computer's identity is revealed. The **Internet protocol address**, known as an *IP address*, is a number used to identify an electronic device connected to the Internet. While your personal information cannot be easily discovered, an IP address can reveal your approximate geographic location. Any e-mails you send from your computer or mobile devices have an IP address attached to them. Use caution when doing so.

One way to protect yourself online is to ensure that you are transmitting data over secure web pages. When transmitting private information to a website, check that the site is secure. A secure URL begins with https. The s stands for secure. This is not 100 percent foolproof, but generally is a sign of protection. Secure websites may also display an icon somewhere in the browser to indicate that the communication is secure. Be wary of uploading personal information to sites that do not display the protection icon.

Public Wi-Fi hotspots should be avoided. While convenient, these networks are generally not secure and put your devices at risk of inadvertently exposing data. One definition of **hacking** is illegally accessing or altering digital devices, software, or networks.

Hackers can also create illicit hotspots in locations where free or paid public Wi-Fi exists. Users unknowingly connect to the incorrect network, which allows the hacker access to any data being transmitted over that connection. The signal with the best strength may not always be the legitimate hotspot. An easy way to avoid illicit hotspots is to check with an employee of the business providing it. Ask the employee for the name of the network and the access key. If a Wi-Fi authentication screen asks for credit card information, confirm that the Wi-Fi connection is legitimate.

Cookies

Cookies are bits of data stored on your computer that record information about the websites you have visited. Cookies may also contain the personal information you enter on a website. Most cookies are from legitimate websites and will not harm your computer. Some advertisers place them onto your computer without your knowledge or consent. Marketers use the information for research and selling purposes. If a hacker gains access to your cookies, you are at risk. The cookies can be used to steal personal information you have entered on a website. Cookies also can be used to target you for a scam based on your Internet history.

As a precaution, there are ways to protect your computer from cookies. One way is to prevent them from being accepted by the browser. Most Internet browsers allow you to set a preference to never accept cookies. Check your browser for specific instructions. Another way to protect your computer is to delete cookies on a regular basis. Cookies can also be removed by running a disk cleanup utility.

Phishing

Phishing is the use of fraudulent e-mails and copies of valid websites to trick people into providing private and confidential data. A common form of phishing is sending a fraudulent e-mail that appears to be from a legitimate source, such as a bank. The e-mail asks for certain information, such as a Social Security number or bank account number.

Lighthunter/Shutterstock.com

Use caution and protect your privacy when using technology to communicate.

Green Business — Computer Technology

Advances in computer technology have improved hardware capabilities and performance. Often, terminals can be set up at several workstations and connected to a single server where the applications actually run. Sharing the computing power of a single server reduces the need for multiple computers, which reduces the amount of power used by a business.

Newer computers and printers are also more efficient, using less energy to power them. Some businesses are replacing desktop computers with laptop or notebook computers to save energy. Laptops are 30% more energy efficient than desktop computers. By upgrading to new equipment, businesses not only save the environment but save money on operating expenses.

Sometimes it provides a link to a web page. The linked web page looks real, but its sole purpose is to collect private information that will be used to commit fraud.

Most legitimate organizations do not use e-mail to request this type of information. Never provide confidential information in response to an unsolicited e-mail. Avoid clicking a link to a website in an e-mail. It is better to manually enter the website URL into a web browser. Never open an e-mail attachment that you are not expecting.

Malware

Malware, short for *malicious software*, is a term given to software programs that are intended to damage, destroy, or steal data. Beware of an invitation to click on a website link for more information about an advertisement, as the link may trigger malware. One click can activate a code, and your computer could be hacked or infected. Malware comes in many forms including spyware, Trojan horses, worms, and viruses.

- *Spyware.* **Spyware** is software that spies on a computer. Spyware can capture private information, such as e-mail messages, usernames, passwords, bank account information, and credit card information. Often, affected users are not aware that spyware is on their computer.

- *Trojan horses* are malware usually disguised to appear as a useful or common application in order to convince people to download and use the program. However, the Trojan horse performs malicious actions on the user's computer, such as destroying data or stealing information. Trojan horses do not self-replicate, nor do they infect other files.

- *Worms* are similar to Trojan horses, except they do self-replicate. Worms self-replicate so they can infect other computers and devices. Like Trojan horses, worms do not infect other files.

- *Software virus.* A **software virus** is a computer program designed to negatively impact a computer system by infecting other files. A virus may destroy data on the computer, cause programs to malfunction, bring harm to a network, or steal information. Viruses can be introduced to a computer in many ways, such as by downloading infected files from an e-mail or website.

Virus-protection software helps safeguard a computer and should be used on any computer or electronic device that is connected to the Internet or any type of network. Virus-protection software is also referred to as *antivirus* or *antimalware* software.

Virus-protection software should also have a firewall. A **firewall** is a program that monitors information coming into a computer. It helps ensure that only safe information gets through.

Digital Security

Do not be lulled into a false sense of security when communicating with others online. Be especially careful with those whom you do not know personally. Avoid opening e-mails that look suspicious. Use common sense when deciding what personal details you share, especially your address and Social Security number. Resist the urge to share too much information that could be stolen.

Avoid Identity Theft

Identity theft is an illegal act that involves stealing someone's personal information and using that information to commit theft or fraud. There are many ways that your personal information can be stolen without your knowing. A lost credit card or driver's license can provide thieves with the information they need to steal a person's identity. Criminals also steal physical mail to commit identity theft. This method is often called *dumpster diving*. However, computer technology has made identity theft through digital means the most prevalent.

Be wary of how much information you share on social networking websites. If you suspect your identity has been stolen, visit the Identity Theft website provided by the Federal Trade Commission for resources and guidance. Time is of the essence, so if this unfortunate situation happens to you, act immediately.

Create a Security Plan

A security plan should be in place for your computer in general, any databases you maintain, and any mobile devices you have. Your employer will assist in creating a plan for your workplace equipment. If you have any suspicions about communicating with someone or giving your information via a website, do not proceed. Investigate the person or the company with whom you are dealing. You may be able to avoid a scam before it is too late.

Consider downloading and running antivirus software for your mobile device. Many people rely on mobile devices. It is important to guard them against viruses that would disrupt a primary means of communication and expose personal data.

You must also plan to protect your mobile devices from theft. If you become careless and leave your smartphone or other device in an unexpected location, your identity can be stolen. You may also be stuck with a large telephone bill. If it is an employer-issued device, you may be responsible for replacing it using your personal funds. To protect your mobile device from use by a thief, create a password to lock it. Have the number of your mobile device in a safe place so that if the unexpected happens, you can contact your service provider.

Secure Passwords

Unfortunately, many people have weak passwords for even their most important accounts, such as banking or credit card accounts.

Kues/Shutterstock.com

A security plan includes storing backup of important digital files in a fireproof container.

Your employer will have guidelines for creating passwords for work accounts. When creating new passwords, use the tips shown in Figure 23-3.

Security Settings

Become familiar with the security settings and features of your browser when accessing the Internet from your computer. Change your settings to protect your computer and your information. Enabling a *pop-up blocker* prevents your browser from allowing you to see pop-up ads, which can contain malware.

Back Up Your Computer

An important part of a security plan is backing up the data on your computer. If a virus invades your computer or the hard disk crashes, it may be too late to retrieve your files and computer programs.

Your employer will request regular backups of files on your work computer. For your

personal computer, put a plan in place to perform regular backups. Decide on a storage device and method for backing up your files. Place the backup in a fireproof container and store it at a location other than your home.

Secure Passwords

- Do not be careless or in a hurry.
- Do not use passwords that contain easily guessed information.
- Do not use the same passwords for multiple accounts or profiles.
- Do change your passwords often.
- Do record your passwords on a dedicated and secure hard-copy doccument.

Goodheart-Willcox Publisher

Figure 23-3 Use these tips to create safe, secure passwords.

Section 23.2 Review

 Check Your Understanding

1. Explain why following an acceptable use policy is an example of ethical behavior.
2. Why should a digital citizen be aware of his or her IP address?
3. Discuss the importance of digital security.
4. Explain how to protect a mobile device from theft.
5. Why should a computer be backed up on a regular basis?

 Build Your Vocabulary

As you progress through this course, develop a personal glossary of key terms. This will help you build your vocabulary and prepare you for a career. Write a definition for each of the following terms and add it to your personal glossary.

acceptable use policy	malware
cloud computing	spyware
Internet protocol address	software virus
hacking	firewall
cookies	identity theft
phishing	

Review and Assessment

Chapter Summary

Section 23.1 Communicating in a Digital Society

- Digital communication is the exchange of information through electronic means. It requires digital literacy skills and appropriate digital citizenship behavior.

- Intellectual property is something that comes from a person's mind, such as an idea, invention, or process. Copyrights, patents, and trademarks can protect intellectual property rights. Material that is in the public domain refers to material that is not owned by anyone and can be used without permission. Products or services can be protected by issuing a licensing agreement which is a contract that gives one party permission to use a product or service owned by someone else.

- The Electronic User's Bill of Rights details the rights and responsibilities of both individuals and institutions regarding the treatment of digital information.

Section 23.2 Internet Use in the Workplace

- Internet access provided by a company should be used only for business purposes. Most companies have an acceptable use policy that explains what is and is not acceptable use of company-owned and company-operated equipment.

- Identity theft is an illegal act that involves stealing someone's personal information and using that information to commit theft or fraud. It is important to protect equipment, data, and your digital footprint against theft by putting a security plan in place.

Online Activities

Complete the following activities to help you learn, practice, and expand your knowledge and skills.

 Posttest. Now that you have finished the chapter, see what you learned by taking the chapter posttest.

 Vocabulary. Practice vocabulary for this chapter using the e-flash cards, matching activity, and vocabulary game until you are able to recognize their meanings.

Review Your Knowledge

1. Give two examples of digital literacy skills.
2. Explain the importance of digital citizenship.
3. Explain what intellectual property is and what it includes.
4. What is fair use doctrine?

5. How does open-source software differ from other forms of software?

6. Describe measures companies put in place to ensure their employees use the Internet appropriately while at work.

7. How can a digital citizen protect his or her computer from cookies?

8. Describe the most common form of phishing.

9. How does virus protection software help safeguard a computer?

10. Why is it important to back up a computer?

Apply Your Knowledge

1. Create a list of acceptable behaviors that are considered to be good examples of netiquette. Next to each, explain why these behaviors are necessary in a digital society.

2. Select a topic related to digital citizenship, such as social media use or identity theft. Prepare a presentation to illustrate the implications of your topic on individuals, society, and businesses. Give your presentation to the class.

3. Analyze the legal and ethical responsibilities required as a professional in the business workplace.

4. Photocopying copyrighted material is illegal and unethical. What is your opinion of a friend photocopying a text book chapter instead of buying the textbook? Do you think that duplicating copyrighted materials is illegal, unethical, or both? Do you think the fair use doctrine would apply in this situation?

5. Professional marketing communication regularly involves persuasive messages. Advertisements that claim weight loss overnight or white teeth in four hours attempt to persuade the audience to purchase a product. How do these communication messages impact society? Does the advertiser's point of view sway the audience? What social responsibilities does marketing have to society? Write several paragraphs discussing your opinion.

6. When shopping online, you may notice that with each new site you browse, you see advertisements for previous sites and products that you have searched. This is due to the presence of cookies on your computer. Marketers use this information for selling purposes. That is why you are likely to see those products appear repeatedly when shopping online. Is this an ethical practice? Why or why not?

Communication Skills

College and Career Readiness

Reading. Imagery is descriptive language that indicates how something looks, feels, smells, sounds, or tastes. After you have read this chapter, find an example of how the author used imagery to appeal to the five senses. Analyze the presentation of the material. Why did you think this appealed to the senses? How did this explanation create imagery? Did it influence the reader's mood?

Writing. Generate your own ideas relevant to using digital technology in the appropriate manner. Use multiple authoritative print and digital sources and document each. Write several paragraphs about your findings to demonstrate your understanding of digital citizenship.

Speaking. Most people in the United States act as responsible and contributing citizens. How can a person demonstrate social and ethical responsibility in a digital society? Can you think of ways that are not discussed in this chapter? Share your opinions with the class.

Internet Research

Copyright. Copyright laws protect intellectual property. Conduct an Internet search for *copyright law violation example*. Select an example and discuss the law and how it was violated. What copyright issues were at stake? Write your findings and cite your sources using *The Chicago Manual of Style* or your choice of reference guide.

Teamwork

Working with your team, identify and analyze examples of ethical responsibilities that a professional person in business has to society. Make a list of applicable rules your team thinks is appropriate for professional conduct. How can a professional exhibit ethical conduct?

Portfolio Development

College and Career Readiness

Printed Portfolio. There may be an occasion where a print portfolio is required rather than a digital one. The organization process is similar to the digital version. Your instructor may have examples of printed portfolios that you can review for ideas. You can also search the Internet for articles about how to organize a printed portfolio.

1. Review the documents you have collected. Select the items you want to include in your portfolio. Make copies of certificates, diplomas, and other important documents. Keep the originals in a safe place.

2. Place the items in a binder, folder, or other container.

3. Give the portfolio to your instructor, counselor, or other person who can give constructive feedback.

4. Review the feedback you received. Make necessary adjustments and revisions.

CTSOs

Day of the Event. You have practiced all year for this CTSO competition, and now you are ready. Whether it is for an objective test, written test, report, or presentation, you have done your homework and are ready to shine.

To prepare for the day of the event, complete the following activities.

1. Get plenty of sleep the night before the event so that you are rested and ready to go.

2. Use your event checklist before you go into the presentation so that you do not forget any of your materials that are needed for the event.

3. Find the room where the competition will take place and arrive early. If you are late and the door is closed, you will be disqualified.

4. If you are making a presentation before a panel of judges, practice what you are going to say when you are called on. State your name, your school, and any other information that will be requested. Be confident, smile, and make eye contact with the judges.

5. When the event is finished, thank the judges for their time.

Math Skills Handbook

Table of Contents

Getting Started

Math skills are needed in everyday life. You will need to be able to estimate the cost of purchases, calculate sales tax, and large quantities of materials. This section is designed to help develop your math proficiency for better understanding of the concepts presented in the textbook. Using the information presented in the Math Skills Handbook will help you understand basic math concepts and their application to the real world.

Using a Calculator

There are many different types of calculators. Some are simple and only perform basic math operations. Become familiar with the keys and operating instructions of your calculator so calculations can be made quickly and correctly.

Shown below is a scientific calculator that comes standard with the Windows 8 operating system. To display this version, select the **View** pull-down menu and click **Scientific** in the menu.

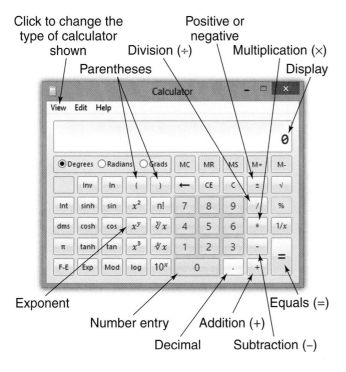

Click to change the type of calculator shown

Parentheses

Division (÷)

Positive or negative

Multiplication (×)

Display

Exponent

Number entry

Decimal

Addition (+)

Equals (=)

Subtraction (−)

Solving Word Problems

Word problems are exercises in which the problem is set up in text, rather than presented in mathematical notation. Many word problems tell a story. You must identify the elements of the math problem and solve it.

There are many strategies for solving word problems. Some common strategies include making a list or table; working backward; guessing, checking, and revising; and substituting simpler numbers to solve the problem.

Strategy	How to Apply
List or table	Identify information in the problem and organize it into a table to identify patterns.
Work backward	When an end result is provided, work backward from that to find the requested information.
Guess, check, revise	Start with a reasonable guess at the answer, check to see if it is correct, and revise the guess as needed until the solution is found.
Substitute simpler information	Use different numbers to simplify the problem and solve it, then solve the problem using the provided numbers.

Number Sense

Number sense is an ability to use and understand numbers to make judgments and solve problems. Someone with good number sense also understands when his or her computations are reasonable in the context of a problem.

Example
Suppose you want to add three basketball scores: 35, 21, and 18.
- First, add 30 + 20 + 10 = 60.
- Then, add 5 + 1 + 8 = 14.
- Finally, combine these two sums to find the answer: 60 + 14 = 74.

Example
Suppose your brother is 72 inches tall and you want to convert this measurement from inches to feet. You use a calculator to divide 72 by 12 (number of inches in a foot) and the answer is displayed as 864. You recognize immediately that your brother cannot be 864 feet tall and realize you must have miscalculated. In this case, a multiplication operation was entered instead of a division operation. The correct answer is 6.

Numbers and Quantity

Numbers are more than just items in a series. Each number has a distinct value relative to all other numbers. They are used to perform mathematical operations from the simplest addition to finding square roots. There are whole numbers, fractions, decimals, exponents, and square roots.

Whole Numbers

A whole number, or integer, is any positive number or zero that has no fractional part. It can be a single digit from 0 to 9, or may contain multiple digits, such as 38.

Place Value

A digit's position in a number determines its *place value.* The digit, or numeral, in the place farthest to the right before the decimal point is in the *ones position.* The next digit to the left is in the *tens position,* followed by the next digit in the *hundreds position.* As you continue to move left, the place values increase to thousands, ten thousands, and so forth.

Example

Suppose you win the lottery and receive a check for $23,152,679. Your total prize would be *twenty-three million, one hundred fifty-two thousand, six hundred seventy-nine dollars.*

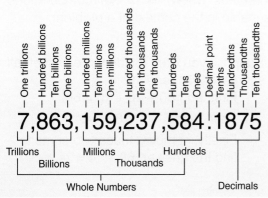

Addition

Addition is the process of combining two or more numbers. The result is called the *sum.*

Example

A plumber installs six faucets on his first job and three faucets on his second job. How many faucets does he install in total?

$$6 + 3 = 9$$

Subtraction

Subtraction is the process of finding the *difference* between two numbers.

Example

A plumber installs six faucets on her first job and three faucets on her second job. How many more faucets did she install on the first job than the second? Subtract 3 from 6 to find the answer.

$$6 - 3 = 3$$

Multiplication

Multiplication is a method of adding a number to itself a given number of times. The multiplied numbers are called *factors,* and the result is called the *product.*

Example

Suppose you are installing computers and need to purchase four adapters. If the adapters are $6 each, what is the total cost of the adapters? The answer can be found by adding $6 four times:

$$\$6 + \$6 + \$6 + \$6 = \$24$$

However, the same answer is found more quickly by multiplying $6 times 4.

$$\$6 \times 4 = \$24$$

Division

Division is the process of determining how many times one number, called the *divisor,* goes into another number, called the *dividend.* The result is called the *quotient.*

Example

Suppose you are installing computers and buy a box of adapters for $24. There are four adapters in the box. What is the cost of each adapter? The answer is found by dividing $24 by 4:

$$\$24 \div 4 = \$6$$

Decimals

A decimal is a kind of fraction with a denominator that is either ten, one hundred, one thousand, or some power of ten. Every decimal has three parts: a whole number (sometimes zero), followed by a decimal point, and one or more whole numbers.

Place Value

The numbers to the right of the decimal point indicate the amount of the fraction. The first place to the right of a decimal point is the tenths place. The second place to the right of the decimal point is the hundredths place. As you continue to the right, the place values move to the thousandths place, the ten thousandths place, and so on.

Example

A machinist is required to produce an airplane part to a very precise measurement of 36.876 inches. This measurement is *thirty-six and eight hundred seventy-six thousandths* inches.

36.876

Addition

To add decimals, place each number in a vertical list and align the decimal points. Then add the numbers in each column starting with the column on the right and working to the left. The decimal point in the answer drops down into the same location.

Example

A landscaper spreads 4.3 pounds of fertilizer in the front yard of a house and 1.2 pounds in the backyard. How many pounds of fertilizer did the landscaper spread in total?

$$\begin{array}{r} 4.3 \\ + \ 1.2 \\ \hline 5.5 \end{array}$$

Subtraction

To subtract decimals, place each number in a vertical list and align the decimal points. Then subtract the numbers in each column, starting with the column on the right and working to the left. The decimal point in the answer drops down into the same location.

Example

A landscaper spreads 4.3 pounds of fertilizer in the front yard of a house and 1.2 pounds in the backyard. How many more pounds were spread in the front yard than in the backyard?

$$\begin{array}{r} 4.3 \\ - \ 1.2 \\ \hline 3.1 \end{array}$$

Multiplication

To multiply decimals, place the numbers in a vertical list. Then multiply each digit of the top number by the right-hand bottom number. Multiply each digit of the top number by the bottom number in the tens position. Place the result on a second line and add a zero to the end of the number. Add the total number of decimal places in both numbers you are multiplying. This will be the number of decimal places in your answer.

Example

An artist orders 13 brushes priced at $3.20 each. What is the total cost of the order? The answer can be found by multiplying $3.20 by 13.

$$\begin{array}{r} \$3.20 \\ \times \quad 13 \\ \hline 960 \\ + \ 3200 \\ \hline \$41.60 \end{array}$$

Division

To divide decimals, the dividend is placed under the division symbol, the divisor is placed to the left of the division symbol, and the quotient is placed above the division symbol. Start from the *left* of the dividend and determine how many times the divisor goes into the first number. Continue this until the quotient is found. Add the dollar sign to the final answer.

$$\begin{array}{r} 3.20 \\ 3\overline{)9.60} \\ \underline{9} \quad \text{Product of } 3 \times 3 \\ 06 \quad \text{Bring down the 6} \\ \underline{6} \quad \text{Product of } 2 \times 3 \\ 0 \quad \text{No remainder} \end{array}$$

Example

An artist buys a package of three brushes for $9.60. What is the cost of each brush? The quotient is found by dividing $9.60 by 3.

$$\begin{array}{r} 3.20 \\ 3\overline{)9.60} \\ \underline{-9} \\ 06 \\ \underline{} \\ 00 \end{array}$$

Rounding

When a number is rounded, some of the digits are changed, removed, or changed to zero so the number is easier to work with. Rounding is often used when precise calculations or measurements are not needed. For example, if you are calculating millions of dollars, it might not be important to know the amount down to the dollar or cent. Instead, you might *round* the amount to the nearest ten thousand or even hundred thousand dollars. Also, when working with decimals, the final answer might have several more decimal places than needed.

To round a number, follow these steps. First, underline the digit in the place to which you are rounding. Second, if the digit to the *right* of this place is 5 or greater, add 1 to the underlined digit. If the digit to the right is less than 5, do not change the underlined digit. Third, change all the digits to right of the underlined digit to zero. In the case of decimals, the digits to the right of the underlined digit are removed.

Example

A company's expense for utilities last year was $32,678.53. The owner of the company is preparing a budget for next year and wants to round this amount to the nearest 1,000.

Step 1: Underline the digit in the 10,000 place.

$$\$3\underline{2},678$$

Step 2: The digit to the right of 2 is greater than 5, so add 1.

$$2 + 1 = 3$$

Step 3: Change the digits to the right of the underlined digit to zero.

$$\$33,000$$

Fractions

A fraction is a part of a whole. It is a numerator that is divided by a denominator.

$$\frac{\text{numerator}}{\text{denominator}}$$

The *numerator* specifies the number of equal parts that are in the fraction. The *denominator* shows how many equal parts make up the whole.

Proper

In a *proper fraction,* the numerator is less than the denominator.

Example

A lumber yard worker cuts a sheet of plywood into four equal pieces and sells three of them to a carpenter. The carpenter now has 3/4 of the original sheet. The lumber yard has 1/4 of the sheet remaining.

Improper

An *improper fraction* is a fraction where the numerator is equal to or greater than the denominator.

Example

A chef uses a chili recipe that calls for 1/2 cup of chili sauce. However, the chef makes an extra-large batch that will serve three times as many people and uses three of the 1/2 cup measures. The improper fraction in this example is 3/2 cups of chili sauce.

Mixed

A mixed number contains a whole number and a fraction. It is another way of writing an improper fraction.

Example

A chef uses a chili recipe that calls for 1/2 cup of chili sauce. However, the chef makes an extra-large batch that will serve three times as many people and uses three of the 1/2 cup measures. The improper fraction in this example is 3/2 cups of chili sauce. This can be converted to a mixed number by dividing the numerator by the denominator: The remainder is 1, which is 1 over 2. So, the mixed number is 1 1/2 cups.

Reducing

Fractions are reduced to make them easier to work with. Reducing a fraction means writing it with smaller numbers, in *lowest terms.* Reducing a fraction does not change its value.

To find the lowest terms, determine the largest number that *evenly* divides both the numerator and denominator so there is no remainder. Then use this number to divide both the numerator and denominator.

Example

The owner of a hair salon asks ten customers if they were satisfied with the service they recently received. Eight customers said they were satisfied. So, the fraction of satisfied customers is 8/10. The largest number that evenly divides both the numerator and denominator is 2. The fraction is reduced to its lowest terms as follows.

$$\frac{8}{10} = \frac{8 \div 2}{10 \div 2} = \frac{4}{5}$$

Addition

To add fractions, the numerators are combined and the denominator stays the same. However, fractions can only be added when they have a *common denominator.* The *least common denominator* is the smallest number to which each denominator can be converted.

Example

A snack food company makes a bag of trail mix by combining 3/8 pound of nuts with 1/8 pound of dried fruit. What is the total weight of each bag? The fractions have common denominators, so the total weight is determined by adding the fractions.

$$\frac{3}{8} + \frac{1}{8} = \frac{4}{8}$$

This answer can be reduced from 4/8 to 1/2.

Example

Suppose the company combines 1/4 pound of nuts with 1/8 pound of dried fruit. To add these fractions, the denominators must be made equal. In this case, the least common denominator is 8 because $4 \times 2 = 8$. Convert 1/4 to its equivalent of 2/8 by multiplying both numerator and denominator by 2. Then the fractions can be added as follows.

$$\frac{2}{8} + \frac{1}{8} = \frac{3}{8}$$

This answer cannot be reduced because 3 and 8 have no common factors.

Subtraction

To subtract fractions, the second numerator is subtracted from the first numerator. The denominators stay the same. However, fractions can only be subtracted when they have a *common denominator.*

Example

A snack food company makes a bag of trail mix by combining 3/8 pound of nuts with 1/8 pound of dried fruit. How much more do the nuts weigh than the dried fruit? The fractions have common denominators, so the difference can be determined by subtracting the fractions.

$$\frac{3}{8} - \frac{1}{8} = \frac{2}{8}$$

This answer can be reduced from 2/8 to 1/4.

Example

Suppose the company combines 1/4 pound of nuts with 1/8 pound of dried fruit. How much more do the nuts weigh than the dried fruit? To subtract these fractions, the denominators must be made equal. The least common denominator is 8, so convert 1/4 to its equivalent of 2/8. Then the fractions can be subtracted as follows.

$$\frac{2}{8} - \frac{1}{8} = \frac{1}{8}$$

This answer cannot be reduced.

Multiplication

Common denominators are not necessary to multiply fractions. Multiply all of the numerators and multiply all of the denominators. Reduce the resulting fraction as needed.

Example

A lab technician makes a saline solution by mixing 3/4 cup of salt with one gallon of water. How much salt should the technician mix if only 1/2 gallon of water is used? Multiply 3/4 by 1/2:

$$\frac{3}{4} \times \frac{1}{2} = \frac{3}{8}$$

Division

To divide one fraction by a second fraction, multiply the first fraction by the reciprocal of the second fraction. The *reciprocal* of a fraction is created by switching the numerator and denominator.

Example

A cabinetmaker has 3/4 gallon of wood stain. Each cabinet requires 1/8 gallon of stain to finish. How many cabinets can be finished? To find the answer, divide 3/4 by 1/8, which means multiplying 3/4 by the reciprocal of 1/8.

$$\frac{3}{4} \div \frac{1}{8} = \frac{3}{4} \times \frac{8}{1} = \frac{24}{4} = 6$$

Negative Numbers

Negative numbers are those less than zero. They are written with a minus sign in front of the number.

Example

The number −34,687,295 is read as *negative thirty-four million, six hundred eighty-seven thousand, two hundred ninety-five.*

Addition

Adding a negative number is the same as subtracting a positive number.

Example

A football player gains nine yards on his first running play (+9) and loses four yards (−4) on his second play. The two plays combined result in a five yard gain.

$$9 + (-4) = 9 - 4 = 5$$

Suppose this player loses five yards on his first running play (−5) and loses four yards (−4) on his second play. The two plays combined result in a nine yard loss.

$$-5 + (-4) = -5 - 4 = -9$$

Subtraction

Subtracting a negative number is the same as adding a positive number.

Example

Suppose you receive a $100 traffic ticket. This will result in a −$100 change to your cash balance. However, you explain the circumstance to a traffic court judge and she reduces the fine by $60. The effect is to subtract −$60 from −$100 change to your cash balance. The final result is a −$40 change.

$$-\$100 - (-\$60) = -\$100 + \$60 = -\$40$$

Multiplication

Multiplying an odd number of negative numbers results in a *negative* product. Multiplying an even number of negative numbers results in a *positive* product.

Example

If you lose two pounds per week, this will result in a −2 pound weekly change in your weight. After five weeks, there will be a −10 pound change to your weight.

$$5 \times (-2) = -10$$

Suppose you have been losing two pounds per week. Five weeks ago (−5) your weight was 10 pounds higher.

$$(-5) \times (-2) = 10$$

Division

Dividing an odd number of negative numbers results in a *negative* quotient. Dividing an even number of negative numbers results in a *positive* quotient.

Example

Suppose you lost 10 pounds, which is a −10 pound change in your weight. How many pounds on average did you lose each week if it took five weeks to lose the weight? Divide −10 by 5 to find the answer.

$$-10 \div 5 = -2$$

Suppose you lost 10 pounds. How many weeks did this take if you lost two pounds each week? Divide −10 by −2 to find the answer.

$$-10 \div -2 = 5$$

Percentages

A percentage (%) means a part of 100. It is the same as a fraction or decimal.

Representing Percentages as Decimals

To change a percentage to a decimal, move the decimal point two places to the left. For example, 1% is the same as 1/100 or 0.01; 10% is the same as 10/100 or 0.10; and 100% is the same as 100/100 or 1.0.

Example

A high school cafeteria estimates that 30% of the students prefer sesame seeds on hamburger buns. To convert this percentage to a decimal, move the decimal point two places to the left.

$$30\% = 0.30$$

Representing Fractions as Percentages

To change a fraction to a percentage, first convert the fraction to a decimal by dividing the numerator by the denominator. Then convert the decimal to a percentage by moving the decimal point two places to the right.

Example

A high school cafeteria conducts a survey and finds that three of every ten students prefer sesame seeds on hamburger buns. To change this fraction to a percentage, divide 3 by 10, and move the decimal two places to the right.

$$3 \div 10 = 0.30 = 30\%$$

Calculating a Percentage

To calculate the percentage of a number, change the percentage to a decimal and multiply by the number.

Example

A car dealer sold ten cars last week, of which 70% were sold to women. How many cars did women buy? Change 70% to a decimal by dividing 70 by 100, which equals 0.70. Then multiply by the total number (10).

$$0.70 \times 10 = 7$$

To determine what percentage one number is of another, divide the first number by the second. Then convert the quotient into a percentage by moving the decimal point two places to the right.

Example

A car dealer sold 10 cars last week, of which seven were sold to women. What percentage of the cars were purchased by women? Divide 7 by 10 and then convert to a percentage.

$$7 \div 10 = 0.70$$

$$0.70 = 70\%$$

Ratio

A ratio compares two numbers through division. Ratios are often expressed as a fraction, but can also be written with a colon (:) or the word *to*.

Example

A drugstore's cost for a bottle of vitamins is $2.00. It sells the bottle for $3.00. The ratio of the selling price to the cost can be expressed as follows.

$$\frac{\$3.00}{\$2.00} = \frac{3}{2}$$

$$\$3.00{:}\$2.00 = 3{:}2$$

$$\$3.00 \text{ to } \$2.00 = 3 \text{ to } 2$$

Measurement

The official system of measurement in the United States for length, volume, and weight is the US Customary system of measurement. The metric system of measurement is used by most other countries.

US Customary Measurement

The following are the most commonly used units of length in the US Customary system of measurement.

- 1 inch
- 1 foot = 12 inches
- 1 yard = 3 feet
- 1 mile = 5,280 feet

Example

An interior designer measurers the length and width of a room when ordering new floor tiles. The length is measured at 12 feet 4 inches (12′ 4″). The width is measured at 8 feet 7 inches (8′ 7″).

Example

Taxi cab fares are usually determined by measuring distance in miles. A recent cab rate in Chicago was $3.25 for the first 1/9 mile or less, and $0.20 for each additional 1/9 mile.

Metric Conversion

The metric system of measurement is convenient to use because units can be converted by multiplying or dividing by multiples of 10. The following are the commonly used units of length in the metric system of measurement.

- 1 millimeter
- 1 centimeter = 10 millimeters
- 1 meter = 100 centimeters
- 1 kilometer = 1,000 meters

The following are conversions from the US Customary system to the metric system.

- 1 inch = 25.4 millimeters = 2.54 centimeters
- 1 foot = 30.48 centimeters = 0.3048 meters
- 1 yard = 0.9144 meters
- 1 mile = 1.6093 kilometers

Example

A salesperson from the United States is traveling abroad and needs to drive 100 kilometers to meet a customer. How many miles is this trip? Divide 100 kilometers by 1.6093 and round to the hundredth place.

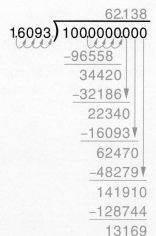

Estimating

Estimating is finding an *approximate* answer and often involves using rounded numbers. It is often quicker to add rounded numbers, for example, than it is to add the precise numbers.

Example

Estimate the total miles a delivery truck will travel along the following three segments of a route.

- Detroit to Chicago: 278 miles
- Chicago to St. Louis: 297 miles
- St. Louis to Wichita: 436 miles

The mileage can be estimated by rounding each segment to the nearest 100 miles.

- Detroit to Chicago: 300 miles
- Chicago to St. Louis: 300 miles
- St. Louis to Wichita: 400 miles

Add the rounded segments to estimate the total miles.

$$300 + 300 + 400 = 1,000 \text{ miles}$$

Accuracy and Precision

Accuracy and precision mean slightly different things. *Accuracy* is the closeness of a measured value to its actual or true value. *Precision* is how close measured values are to each other.

Example

A machine is designed to fill jars with 16 ounces of peanut butter. The machine is considered accurate if the actual amount of peanut butter in a jar is within 0.05 ounces of the target, which is a range of 15.95 to 16.05 ounces. A machine operator tests a jar and measures the weight to be 16.01 ounces. The machine is accurate.

Suppose a machine operator tests 10 jars of peanut butter and finds the weight of each jar to be 15.4 ounces. The machine is considered precise because it fills every jar with exactly the same amount. However, it is not accurate because the amount differs too much from the target.

Algebra

An *equation* is a mathematical statement that has an equal sign (=). An *algebraic* equation is an equation that includes at least one variable. A *variable* is an unknown quantity.

Solving Equations with Variables

Solving an algebraic equation means finding the value of the variable that will make the equation a true statement. To solve a simple equation, perform inverse operations on both sides and isolate the variable.

Example
A computer consultant has sales of $1,000. After deducting $600 in expenses, her profit equals $400. This is expressed with the following equation.

$$sales - expenses = profit$$
$$\$1,000 - \$600 = \$400$$

Example
A computer consultant has expenses of $600 and $400 in profit. What are her sales? An equation can be written in which sales are the unknown quantity, or variable.

$$sales - expenses = profit$$
$$sales - \$600 = \$400$$

Example
To find the value for sales, perform inverse operations on both sides and isolate the variable.

$$
\begin{array}{rcl}
sales - \$600 &=& \$400 \\
+ \ \$600 &+& \$600 \\
\hline
sales &=& \$1,000
\end{array}
$$

Order of Operations

The order of operations is a set of rules stating which operations in an equation are performed first. The order of operations is often stated using the acronym *PEMDAS.* PEMDAS stands for parentheses, exponents, multiplication and division, and addition and subtraction. This means anything inside parentheses is computed first. Exponents are computed next. Then, any multiplication and division operations are computed. Finally, any addition and subtraction operations are computed

to find the final answer to the problem. The equation is solved from left to right by applying PEMDAS.

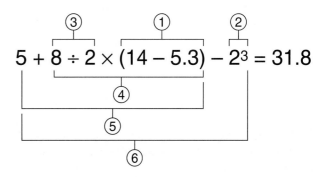

$$5 + 8 \div 2 \times (14 - 5.3) - 2^3 = 31.8$$

Recursive Formulas

A *recursive formula* is used to determine the next term of a sequence, using one or more of the preceding terms. The terms of a sequence are often expressed with a variable and subscript. For example, a sequence might be written as a_1, a_2, a_3, a_4, a_5, and so on. The subscript is essentially the place in line for each term. A recursive formula has two parts. The first is a starting point or seed value (a_1). The second is an equation for another number in the sequence (a_n). The second part of the formula is a function of the prior term (a_{n-1}).

Example
Suppose you buy a car for $10,000. Assume the car declines in value 10% each year. In the second year, the car will be worth 90% of $10,000, which is $9,000. The following year it will be worth 90% of $9,000, which is $8,100. What will the car be worth in the fifth year? Use the following recursive equation to find the answer.

$$a_n = a_{n-1} \times 0.90$$

$$\text{where } a_1 = \$10,000$$

$$a_n = \text{value of car in the } n^{th} \text{ year}$$

Year	Value of Car
n = 1	$a_1 = \$10,000$
n = 2	$a_2 = a_{2-1} \times 0.90 = a_1 \times 0.90 = \$10,000 \times 0.90$ $= \$9,000$
n = 3	$a_3 = a_{3-1} \times 0.90 = a_2 \times 0.90 = \$9,000 \times 0.90$ $= \$8,100$
n = 4	$a_4 = a_{4-1} \times 0.90 = a_3 \times 0.90 = \$8,100 \times 0.90$ $= \$7,290$
n = 5	$a_5 = a_{5-1} \times 0.90 = a_4 \times 0.90 = \$7,290 \times 0.90$ $= \$6,561$

Geometry

Geometry is a field of mathematics that deals with shapes, such as circles and polygons. A *polygon* is any shape whose sides are straight. Every polygon has three or more sides.

Parallelograms

A *parallelogram* is a four-sided figure with two pairs of parallel sides. A *rectangle* is a type of parallelogram with four right angles. A *square* is a special type of parallelogram with four right angles (90 degrees) and four equal sides.

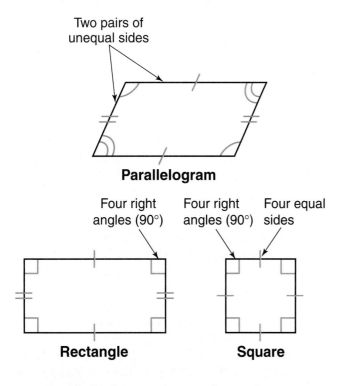

Parallelogram

Rectangle   **Square**

Example
Real-life examples of squares include ceramic floor and wall tiles. Real-life examples of a rectangle include a football field, pool table, and most doors.

Triangles

A three-sided polygon is called a *triangle.* The following are four types of triangles, which are classified according to their sides and angles.

- *Equilateral:* Three equal sides and three equal angles.
- *Isosceles:* Two equal sides and two equal angles.
- *Scalene:* Three unequal sides and three unequal angles.
- *Right:* One right angle; may be isosceles or scalene.

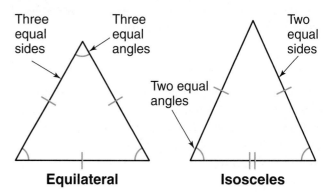

Equilateral   **Isosceles**

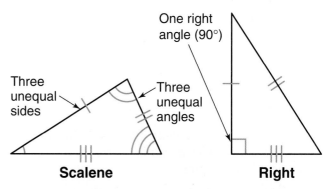

Scalene   **Right**

Example
Real-life examples of equilateral triangles are the sides of a classical Egyptian pyramid.

Circles and Half Circles

A *circle* is a figure in which every point is the same distance from the center. The distance from the center to a point on the circle is called the *radius.* The distance across the circle through the center is the *diameter.* A half circle is formed by dividing a whole circle along the diameter.

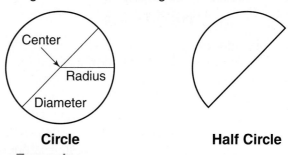

Circle   **Half Circle**

Example
Real life examples of circles include wheels of all sizes.

Perimeter

Perimeter is a measure of length around a figure. Add the length of each side to measure the perimeter of any figure with sides that are all line segments, such as a parallelogram or triangle. The perimeter of a circle is called the *circumference*. To measure the perimeter, multiply the diameter by pi (π). Pi is approximately equal to 3.14. The following formulas can be used to calculate the perimeter of various figures.

Figure	Perimeter
parallelogram	2 × width + 2 × length
square	4 × side
rectangle	2 × width + 2 × length
triangle	side + side + side
circle	π × diameter

Example

A professional basketball court is a rectangle 94 feet long and 50 feet wide. The perimeter of the court is calculated as follows.

2 × 94 feet + 2 × 50 feet = 288 feet

Example

A tractor tire has a 43 inch diameter. The circumference of the tire is calculated as follows.

43 inches × 3.14 = 135 inches

Area

Area is a measure of the amount of surface within the perimeter of a flat figure. Area is measured in square units, such as square inches, square feet, or square miles. The following formulas can be used to calculate the area of the corresponding figures.

Figure	Area
parallelogram	base × height
square	side × side
rectangle	length × width
triangle	1/2 × base × height
circle	π × radius^2 = π × radius × radius

Example

An interior designer needs to order decorative tiles to fill the following spaces. Measure the area of each space in square feet.

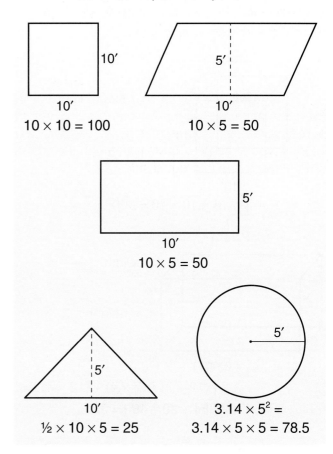

10 × 10 = 100   10 × 5 = 50

10 × 5 = 50

½ × 10 × 5 = 25   3.14 × 5^2 =
                        3.14 × 5 × 5 = 78.5

Surface Area

Surface area is the total area of the surface of a figure that occupies three-dimensional space, such as a cube or prism. A *cube* is a solid figure that has six identical square faces. A *prism* has bases or ends that have the same size and shape and are parallel to each other, and each of whose sides is a parallelogram. The following are formulas to find the surface area of a cube and a prism.

Object	Surface Area
cube	6 × side × side
prism	2 × [(length × width) + (width × height) + (length × height)]

Example

A manufacturer of cardboard boxes wants to determine how much cardboard is needed to make the following size boxes. Calculate the surface area of each in square inches.

Cube

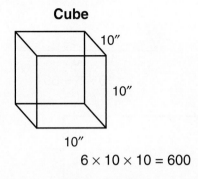

10″

10″

10″

$$6 \times 10 \times 10 = 600$$

Prism

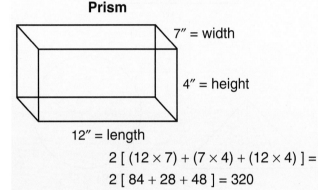

7″ = width

4″ = height

12″ = length

$$2\,[\,(12 \times 7) + (7 \times 4) + (12 \times 4)\,] =$$
$$2\,[\,84 + 28 + 48\,] = 320$$

Volume

Volume is the three-dimensional space occupied by a figure and is measured in cubic units, such as cubic inches or cubic feet. The following formulas can be used to calculate the volume of the corresponding figures.

Solid Figure	Volume
cube	$side^3 = side \times side \times side$
prism	$length \times width \times height$
cylinder	$\pi \times radius^2 \times height = \pi \times radius \times radius \times height$
sphere	$4/3 \times \pi \times radius^3 = 4/3 \times \pi \times radius \times radius \times radius$

Example

Find the volume of packing material needed to fill the following boxes. Measure the volume of each in cubic inches.

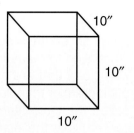

10″

10″

10″

$$10 \times 10 \times 10 = 1000$$

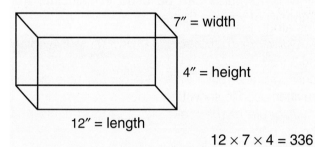

7″ = width

4″ = height

12″ = length

$$12 \times 7 \times 4 = 336$$

Example

Find the volume of grain that will fill the following cylindrical silo. Measure the volume in cubic feet.

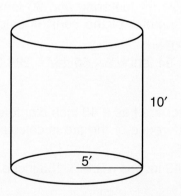

10′

5′

$$3.14 \times 5 \times 5 \times 10 = 785$$

Example

A manufacturer of pool toys wants to stuff soft material into a ball with a 3 inch radius. Find the cubic inches of material that will fit into the ball.

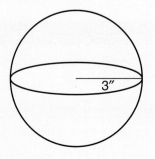

3″

$$\frac{4}{3} \times 3.14 \times 3 \times 3 \times 3 = 113$$

Data Analysis and Statistics

Graphs are used to illustrate data in a picture-like format. It is often easier to understand data when shown in a graphical form instead of a numerical form in a table. Common types of graphs are bar graphs, line graphs, and circle graphs.

A *bar graph* organizes information along a vertical axis and horizontal axis. The vertical axis runs up and down one side and the horizontal axis runs along the bottom.

A *line graph* also organizes information on vertical and horizontal axes. However, data are graphed as a continuous line rather than a set of bars. Line graphs are often used to show trends over a period of time.

A *circle graph* looks like a divided circle and shows how a whole object is cut up into parts. Circle graphs are also called *pie charts* and are often used to illustrate percentages.

Example

A business shows the following balances in its cash account for the months of March through July. These data are illustrated below in the line graph.

Month	Account Balance	Month	Account Balance
March	$450	June	$800
April	$625	July	$900
May	$550		

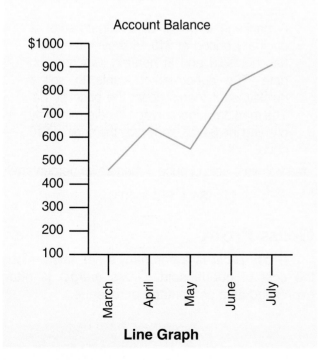

Line Graph

Example

A business lists the percentage of its expenses in the following categories. These data are displayed in the following circle graph.

Expenses	Percentage
Cost of goods	25
Salaries	25
Rent	21
Utilities	17
Advertising	12

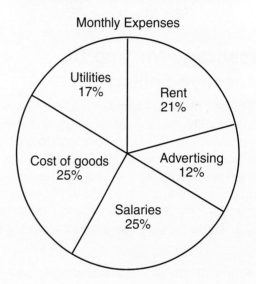

Monthly Expenses

Circle Graph

Math Models for Business

Math skills used in business are the same math skills required in everyday life. The ability to add, subtract, multiply, and divide different types of numbers is very important. However, this type of math is often focused on prices, taxes, profits, and losses.

Markup

Markup is a term for the amount by which price exceeds the cost. One way to express markup is in dollars. Another way to express markup is percentage. The *markup percentage* is the amount of the markup as a percentage of the cost.

Example

A retailer pays $4 for a pair of athletic socks and prices them for sale at $7. The dollar markup is $3.

selling price − cost = dollar markup

$$\$7 - \$4 = \$3$$

Example

A pair of athletic socks costs $4 and is priced at $7. The dollar markup is $3. To find the markup percentage, divide $3 by $4. The markup percentage is 75%.

markup dollars ÷ cost = markup percentage

$$\$3 \div \$4 = 0.75 = 75\%$$

Percentage Markup to Determine Selling Price

The selling price of an item can be determined if you know the markup percentage and the cost. First, convert the markup percentage to a decimal. Next, multiply the cost by the decimal. Then, add the markup dollars to the cost to determine the selling price. Another way to find the selling price is to convert the markup percentage to a decimal and add 1.0. Then, multiply this amount by the cost.

Example

A pair of athletic socks costs $4, which the retailer marks up by 75%. Find the selling price.

1. Convert the markup percentage to a decimal.

$$75\% = 0.75$$

2. Multiply the cost by the markup.

cost × markup = dollar markup

$$\$4 \times 0.75 = \$3$$

3. Add the $3 markup to the $4 cost to find the selling price. The selling price is $7.

$$\$4 + \$3 = \$7$$

Example

A pair of athletic socks costs $4, which the retailer marks up by 75%. Find the selling price.

1. Convert the 75% markup percentage to 0.75 and add 1.0.

$$0.75 + 1.0 = 1.75$$

2. Multiply 1.75 by the $4 cost to find the selling price.

$$\$4 \times 1.75 = \$7$$

Markdown

A *markdown* is the amount by which the selling price of an item is reduced. Sometimes a markdown is also called a *discount.* To find the amount of a markdown, subtract the new or discounted price from the original price. A markdown can also be expressed as a percentage of the original price. Sometimes this is called a *percentage discount.*

Example

A package of meat at a supermarket is originally priced at $10. However, the meat has not sold and is nearing its expiration date. The supermarket wants to sell it quickly, so it reduces the price to $6. This is a markdown of $4.

selling price − discounted price = dollar markdown

$$\$10 - \$6 = \$4$$

Example

A package of meat at a supermarket is originally priced at $10. However, the meat has not sold and is nearing its expiration date. The supermarket wants to sell it quickly, so it marks down the price by $4. The markdown percentage is determined by dividing the $4 markdown by the original $10 price.

markdown ÷ selling price = markdown percentage

$$\$4 \div \$10 = 40\%$$

Gross Profit

Gross profit is a company's net sales minus the cost of goods sold. *Gross margin* is often expressed as a percentage of revenue.

Example

A wristband manufacturer generated net sales of $100,000 last year. The cost of goods sold for the wristbands was $30,000. The net sales of $100,000 minus the $30,000 cost of goods sold leaves a gross profit of $70,000.

net sales − cost of goods sold = gross profit

$$\$100,000 - \$30,000 = \$70,000$$

Example

The gross profit of $70,000 divided by the net sales of $100,000 is 0.70, or 70%.

gross profit ÷ net sales = gross margin percentage

$$\$70,000 \div \$100,000 = 0.70 = 70\%$$

Net Income or Loss

Net income or loss is a company's revenue after total expenses are deducted from gross profit. Total expenses include marketing, administration, interest, and taxes. A company earns a *net income* when gross profit exceeds expenses. A *net loss* is incurred when expenses exceed gross profit.

Example

A wristband manufacturer had a gross profit of $70,000. In addition, expenses for marketing, administration, interest, and taxes were $50,000. Net profit is calculated by subtracting the total expenses of $50,000 from the gross profit of $70,000. The net profit was $20,000.

gross profit on sales − total expenses = net income or loss

$$\$70,000 - \$50,000 = \$20,000$$

Break-Even Point

A *break-even point* is the number of units a company must sell to cover its costs and expenses and earn a zero profit. Use the following formula to find a company's break-even point.

total costs ÷ selling price = break-even point

Sales Tax

Sales tax is a tax collected on the selling price of a good or service. The sales tax rate is usually expressed as a percentage of the selling price. Sales tax is calculated by multiplying the sale price by the tax rate.

Example

Suppose you buy a T-shirt for $10.00. How much is the sales tax if the tax rate is 5%? Convert 5% to a decimal (.05) and multiply it by the sale price.

sale price × sales tax rate percentage = sales tax

$$\$10 \times 0.05 = \$0.50$$

Return on Investment

Return on investment (ROI) is a calculation of a company's net profit as a percentage of the owner's investment. One way to determine ROI is to divide net profit by the owner's investment.

Example

Suppose you start a dry-cleaning business with a $100,000 investment, and you earn a $20,000 net profit during the first year. Divide $20,000 by $100,000, which equals a 20% return on your investment.

net income ÷ owner's investment = return on investment (ROI)

$$\$20,000 \div \$100,000 = 0.20 = 20\%$$

Glossary

529 plan. Savings plan for education operated by a state or educational institution. (21)

A

ability. Mastery of a skill or the capacity to do something. (21)

absolute advantage. When a country can produce goods more efficiently and at a lower cost than another country. (5)

acceptable use policy. Set of rules that explains what is and is not acceptable use of company-owned and company-operated equipment and networks. (23)

acceptance. Element of a contract stating that all parties involved must agree to the terms of contract. (3)

account. Individual record that summarizes information for a single category, such as cash or sales. (17)

accounting. System of recording business transactions and analyzing, verifying, and reporting the results. (17)

accounting cycle. Sequence of steps businesses follow to record, summarize, and report financial information. (17)

accounts receivable. List of the individuals or businesses that owe money to a company. (16)

accounts receivable aging report. Report that shows when accounts receivables are due, as well as the length of time accounts have been outstanding. (16)

action word. Verb that tell the readers what to do. (12)

advertising. Nonpersonal communication paid for by an identified sponsor. (12)

advertising campaign. Coordinated series of linked ads with a single idea or theme. (12)

Advertising Self-Regulatory Council (ASRC). Establishes the policies and procedures for advertising self regulation. (12)

AIDA. Focus of elements of the promotional mix to attract customer attention, interest, desire, and action. (12)

allowance. Amount of earnings not subject to income taxes. (18)

angel investors. Private investors who fund start-up businesses. (6)

annual percentage rate (APR). Annual cost of credit charged by a lender. (16)

annuity. Contract with an insurance company that provides regular income for a set period of time, usually for life. (19)

antitrust laws. US laws that promote fair trade and competition among businesses. (2)

apprenticeship. Combination of on-the-job training, work experience, and classroom instruction. (21)

approach. Step in the sales process in which the salesperson makes the first in-person contact with a potential customer. (13)

aptitude. Characteristic that an individual has developed naturally; also called *talents*. (21)

arbitration. Occurs when a third party reviews the case made by both sides of a negotiation. (9)

art. All of the elements that illustrate the message of an ad. (12)

assets. Property or items of value a business owns. (6)

audit. Review of the financial statements of a business and the accounting practices that were used to produce them. (17)

B

background check. Investigation into personal data about a job applicant. (22)

bait and switch. Practice of advertising one product with the intent of persuading customers to buy a more expensive item when they arrive in the store. (11)

balance of payments. Total amount of money that comes into a country, minus the total amount of money that goes out for a specific period of time. (5)

balance of trade. Difference between a nation's exports and its imports. (5)

balance sheet. Reports the assets, liabilities, and owner's equity. (17)

bank statement. Record of checks, ATM transactions, deposits, and charges on an account. (19)

banknote. Document that guarantees the payment of a specific amount of money, either on demand or at a set time, with the payer named on the document. (15)

base price. General price at which a company expects to sell a product. (11)

behavioral question. Questions that draw on a person's previous experiences and decisions. (22)

behavioral segmentation. Dividing a market by the relationships between customers and the good or service. (10)

beneficiary. Person or organization named by a policyholder to receive the death benefit of an insurance policy after the policyholder's death. (20)

benefit. Form of noncash compensation received in addition to a wage or salary. (9)

blue-collar worker. Worker whose job involves physical labor. (9)

board of directors. Group of individuals who make high-level management decisions for a business and establish company policies. (4)

bodily injury liability. Insurance coverage that protects a person who is responsible for an auto accident that results in the injury or death of other parties. (20)

bond. A certificate of debt issued by an organization or government. (2)

bonus. Money added to an employee's base pay. (9)

brand. Name, term, or design that sets a product or business apart from its competition. (8)

brand name. Name given to a product consisting of words, numbers, or letters that can be read or spoken. (12)

breach of contract. When one or more parties do not follow the agreed terms of a contract without having a legitimate reason. (3)

break-even point. Point at which revenue from sales equals the costs. (11)

budget. Financial plan that reflects anticipated revenue and shows how it will be allocated in the operation of the business. (17)

bulk-breaking. Process of separating a large quantity of goods into smaller quantities for resale. (11)

business. Term for all the activities involved in developing and exchanging products. (1)

business credit. Credit granted to a business by a financial institution or another company. (16)

business cycle. Alternating periods of expansion and contraction in the economy. (2)

business entity. Organization that exists independently of the owner's personal finances. (17)

business interruption insurance. Covers the lost income and related expenses caused by a property damage loss. (14)

business market. Consists of customers who buy products for use in a business. (4)

business plan. Written statement of goals and objectives for a business with a strategy to achieve them. (6)

business-to-business (B2B). Business that sells primarily to other businesses. (4)

business-to-consumer (B2C). Business that sells primarily to individual consumers. (4)

buying signals. Verbal or nonverbal signs that a customer is ready to purchase. (13)

C

call center. An office that is set up for the purpose of receiving and making customer calls for an organization. (13)

capacity. A person is legally able to enter into a binding agreement. (3)

capital. All the tools, equipment, and machinery used to produce goods or provide services. (1)

capital goods. Products businesses use to produce other goods. (1)

capital structure. Refers to the way a business is financed. (6)

capitalism. An economic system where the economic resources are privately owned by individuals rather than the government. (1)

career. Series of related jobs in the same profession. (21)

career and technical student organization (CTSO). National student organizations with local school chapters that are related to career and technical education (CTE) courses. (21)

career clusters. Groups of occupational and career specialties. (21)

career objective. Summary of the type of job for which the applicant is looking. (22)

career pathways. Subgroups within career clusters that reflect occupations requiring similar knowledge and skills. (21)

career plan. List of steps on a time line to reach a career goal; also called *postsecondary plan*. (21)

cash budget. Used to estimate the amount of money coming into and going out of the business. (17)

cash flow. Movement of money into and out of a business. (6)

cash flow statement. Reports how cash moves into and out of a business. (17)

cashier's check. Special type of check that the bank guarantees to pay. (19)

certificate of deposit (CD). Savings account that requires a deposit of a fixed amount of money for a fixed period of time or term; also called a *time deposit* or *time account*. (19)

certification. Professional status earned by an individual after passing an exam focused on a specific body of knowledge. (21)

certified check. Personal check that the bank certifies is genuine and that there is enough money in the account to cover the check. (19)

chain of command. Authority structure in a company from the highest to the lowest levels; also called the *line of authority*. (7)

channel. How a message is transmitted. (12)

channel of distribution. Path that goods take through the supply chain. (11)

chart of accounts. List of all accounts in the business. (17)

check. Written order for the bank to pay a specific amount to the person or organization to which the check is written. (15)

checking account. Bank account that allows the account owner to make deposits, write checks, and withdraw money. (15)

chronological résumé. Résumé that lists information in reverse chronological order, with the most recent employer listed first. (22)

claim. Process of documenting a loss against an insurance policy. (14)

close. Moment when a customer agrees to buy a product. (13)

closed-end credit. Loan for a specific amount that must be repaid with interest by a specified date or according to a specified schedule. (16)

cloud computing. Using remote servers to store and access data over the Internet rather than on a personal computer or local server. (23)

code of conduct. Handbook that outlines expectations of employee behavior. (3)

code of ethics. Document that dictates how business should be conducted. (3)

coinsurance. Percentage of the service costs that patients pay. (20)

cold calling. Process of making contact with people who are not expecting a sales contact. (13)

collaboration skills. Skills that enable individuals to work with others to achieve a common goal. (7)

collateral. Asset pledged that will be claimed by the lender if the loan is not repaid. (6)

collection agency. Company that collects past-due bills for a fee. (16)

collective bargaining. Formal negotiation process between management and unions to resolve issues. (9)

college access. Building awareness about college opportunities, providing guidance regarding college admissions, and identifying ways to pay for college. (21)

collusion. When two or more businesses work together to remove their competition, set prices, and control distribution. (2)

combination approach. B2C approach that combines the greeting and merchandise approaches. (13)

command economy. An economy in which the government makes all the economic decisions for its citizens. (1)

commerce. The activities involved in buying and selling goods on a large scale. (2)

commercial insurance. Protects commercial property from risks, such as fire, theft, and natural disaster. (14)

commercialization. Introduction stage of a new product. (8)

commission. Income paid as a percentage of sales made by a salesperson. (9)

communication process. Series of actions on the part of the sender and the receiver of a message and the path the message follows. (12)

comparative advantage. When a country specializes in producing a product at which it is relatively more efficient. (5)

compensation. Payment to an employee for work performed including wages or salaries, incentives, and benefits. (9)

competition. Actions taken by two or more businesses attempting to attract the same customers. (1)

comprehensive medical insurance. Combines basic and major medical protection in one policy. (20)

compromise. Giving up an individual idea, or part of an idea, so that the group can come to a solution. (7)

confidentiality. Specific information about a company or its employees is never shared, except with those who have clearance to receive it. (3)

conflict management. Process of recognizing and resolving team disputes in a balanced and effective way. (7)

conflict-resolution skills. Skills required to resolve a situation that could lead to hostile behavior. (7)

consideration. Element of a contract stating that something of value must be promised in return. (3)

consumer. Customers who purchase goods and services for their own use. (1)

Consumer Bill of Rights. Basic expectations of fair treatment of consumers. (3)

consumer credit. Credit granted to individual consumers by a retail business. (16)

consumer market. Consists of customers who buy products for their own use. (4)

consumer price index (CPI). Measure of the average change in the prices paid by consumers for typical consumer goods and services over time. (2)

contingency plans. Backup plans that outline alternative actions that can be taken if the organization's other plans are unsuccessful. (7)

contract. Legally binding agreement between two or more people or businesses. (3)

contract law. Regulates how contracts are written, executed, and enforced. (3)

controllable risks. Situations that cannot be avoided, but can be minimized by purchasing insurance or creating a risk management plan. (14)

controlling. Continuous process of evaluating the progress in reaching goals and making corrections to plans, when necessary. (7)

conversion. Process of changing and improving resources to create goods or services. (8)

cookies. Bits of data stored on a computer that record information about the websites visited. (23)

cooperative. Business that is owned and operated by those using its services; also called a *co-op*. (4)

copayment. Flat fee the patient must pay for medical services. (20)

copy. Ad text that provides information and sells the product. (12)

corporate culture. How the owners and employees of a company think, feel, and act as a business. (3)

corporate social responsibility. All the actions taken by a business to promote social good. (3)

corporation. Business that is legally separate from its owners and has most of the legal rights of an actual person. (4)

cover message. Letter or e-mail sent with a résumé to introduce an applicant and summarize his or her reasons for applying for a job. (22)

creative plan. Outlines the goals, primary message, budget, and target market for different ad campaigns. (12)

credit. Agreement between two parties in which one party lends money or provides goods or services to another party with the understanding that payment will be made at a later date. (16)

credit bureau. Private firm that maintains consumer credit data and provides credit information to businesses for a fee. (16)

credit card. Plastic card that allows the holder to make credit purchases up to an authorized amount. (15)

credit policy. Written set of guidelines used by an organization to determine how many and which customers will be approved for credit. (16)

credit report. Record of credit history and financial behavior for a business or individual. (16)

credit risk. Potential of credit not being repaid. (16)

credit score. Numerical measure of a loan applicant's creditworthiness at a particular point in time; also known as the *FICO score*. (16)

credit union. Nonprofit financial institution that is privately owned and provides banking services for its members. (15)

creditor. Party extending credit; also called the *lender*. (16)

critical-thinking skills. Ability to analyze a situation, interpret information, and make reasonable decisions. (7)

culture. Shared beliefs, customs, practices, and social behavior of a particular group or nation. (5)

current asset. Cash or any asset that will be exchanged for cash or used within one year. (17)

current liability. A short-term debt that must be paid within one year. (17)

current ratio. Shows the relationship of current assets to current liabilities. (17)

custom manufacturing. Converting resources to a product that fits the specifications of a particular customer. (8)

customer. Individual or group who buys products. (1)

customer profile. Detailed description of the typical consumer in a market segment. (10)

customer relationship management (CRM). System to track contact and other information for current and potential customers. (10)

customer service. Way in which a business provides services before, during, and after a purchase. (13)

customer-service mindset. Attitude of a business and employees that customer satisfaction always comes first. (13)

customer support team. Employees who assist customers, take orders, and answer questions that come into the company via phone or website. (13)

cyberbullying. Using the Internet to harass or threaten an individual. (23)

D

data breach insurance. Covers the legal fees and other financial losses sustained when a company's data files are accessed without permission. (14)

database marketing. System of gathering, storing, and using customer data for marketing directly to customers based on their histories. (10)

debit card. Allows customers to pay for purchases directly from their checking account. (15)

debt financing. Borrowing money that must be repaid for use in the business. (6)

debt ratio. Shows the percentage of dollars owed as compared to assets owned. (17)

debtor. Party receiving credit; also called the *borrower.* (16)

deceptive pricing. Pricing products in a way that intentionally misleads customers. (11)

decoding. Translation of a message into terms that the receiver can understand. (12)

deductible. Amount the insured is responsible for paying when a claim is made. (14)

deflation. General decline in prices throughout an economy. (2)

demographic segmentation. Dividing the market of potential customers by their personal statistics. (10)

dental insurance. Covers specified services such as exams and teeth cleaning. (20)

dependent. Individual who relies on someone else for financial support. (17)

deposit. Money placed into an account. (15)

depository institution. Financial institution that accepts money from customers and deposits it into the customer's account. (15)

depreciation. Decrease in the value of property as a result of age or wear and tear. (20)

depression. Period of economic contraction that is severe and lasts a long time. (2)

digital citizen. Someone who regularly and skillfully engages in the use of technology, such as the Internet, computers, and other digital devices. (23)

digital citizenship. Standards of behavior when using technology to communicate. (23)

digital communication. Exchange of information through electronic means. (23)

digital footprint. Data record of all an individual's online activities. (23)

digital literacy. Ability to use technology to locate, evaluate, communicate, and create information. (23)

direct channel. Path of selling goods or services directly from a manufacturer to end users without using intermediaries. (11)

direct materials inventory. Raw materials needed to produce a finished product. (8)

directors and officers insurance. Protects a business from financial losses caused by the actions of the company's executive officers. (14)

disability insurance. Provides some financial income to employees who become sick or injured due to a nonwork related event or condition. (14)

discrimination. Occurs when an individual is treated unfairly because of his or her race, gender, religion, national origin, disability, or age. (9)

diversification. The process of spreading risk by putting money in a variety of investments. (19)

diversity. Having people from different backgrounds, cultures, or demographics coming together in a group. (5)

dividend. Portion of a corporation's earnings distributed to stockholders. (4)

division of labor. Specialization of individuals who perform specific tasks. (8)

domestic business. All the business activity involved in making, buying, and selling product within a nation's borders. (5)

double-entry accounting. Recording the debit and credit parts of a transaction. (17)

E

earned income. Income received from employment or from self-employment. (18)

economic risk. Situation that occurs when business activities suffer due to changes in the US or world economy. (14)

economic system. Organized way in which a nation chooses to use its resources to create goods and services. (1)

economics. Science that examines how goods and services are produced, sold, and used. (1)

electronic data interchange (EDI). Standard transfer of electronic data for business transactions between organizations. (8)

electronic funds transfer (EFT). Movement of money electronically from one financial institution or account to another. (15)

electronic promotion. Any promotion that uses the Internet, e-mail, or other digital technology; also called *digital marketing*. (12)

embargo. Government order that prohibits trade with a foreign country. (5)

employability skills. Applicable skills used to help an individual find a job, perform in the workplace, and gain success in a job or career. (21)

employee's earnings record. Individual payroll record maintained for each employee. (17)

employer identification number (EIN). Number assigned by the IRS for businesses to use for income tax purposes. (3)

employment contract. Describes the terms of employment between a business and an employee. (3)

employment verification. Process through which the information provided on an applicant's résumé is checked to verify that it is correct. (22)

encoding. Process of turning the idea for a message into symbols that can be communicated. (12)

endorsement. Signature on the back of a check. (19) Attachment to existing insurance policy to provide coverage for items not included on the original policy. (20)

endowment insurance. Insurance that pays the face value of the policy to beneficiaries if the insured dies before the endowment period ends. (20)

English as a second language (ESL). Use of English by people with a different native language. (5)

entrepreneur. Person who starts a new business or purchases an existing business. (1)

entrepreneurship. Willingness and ability to start a new business. (1)

environmental print. Print that appears in everyday life. (12)

equity financing. Capital brought into a business in exchange for a percent of ownership in the business. (6)

ergonomics. Science concerned with designing and arranging things people use so that they can interact efficiently and safely. (9)

estate. Consists of the assets and liabilities a person leaves when he or she dies. (19)

e-tailer. Retailer that sells products through websites. (11)

ethics. Rules of behavior based on a group's ideas about what is right and wrong. (3)

etiquette. Art of using good manners in any situation. (23)

exclusion. Medical service that is not covered in an insurance plan. (20)

excuses. Personal reasons not to buy. (13)

executor. Person appointed to carry out the terms outlined in a will. (19)

exemption. Amount that a taxpayer can claim for each person who is dependent on that person's income. (18)

expansion. Period when economy is growing and the GDP is rising. (2)

expense. Cost involved in operating a business. (17)

exports. Goods and services that are produced within a country's borders and sold in another country. (5)

extensive buying decision. Purchase that involves a great deal of research and planning. (10)

external influence. Motivator or change factor from outside the business. (10)

extractor. Business or person that takes natural resources from the land. (4)

F

factors of production. Economic resources a nation uses to make goods and supply services for its population. (1)

false advertising. Overstating the features and benefits of products or making false claims about them. (3)

family leave. Time off work for certain life events. (9)

feature. Fact about a good or service. (11)

feature-benefit selling. Sales method of showing the major selling features of a product and how it benefits the customer. (13)

Federal Reserve System. The central bank of the United States that is responsible for the country's monetary system. (2)

feedback. Receiver's response to the sender; concludes the communication process. (12)

FICA taxes. Taxes paid by the employee and the employer that are used to finance the federal Social Security and Medicare programs. (18)

fidelity bond. Covers financial and property losses caused by employee actions. (14)

finance charge. Total amount paid by a borrower to a lender for the use of credit. (16)

finance company. Financial institution that makes money by issuing loans. (15)

financial exchange. Process of transferring money from one individual or organization to another. (15)

financial institution. Any organization that provides services related to money. (15)

financial management. Process used to manage the financial resources of a business. (17)

financial planning. Process of setting financial goals and developing plans to reach them. (17)

financial ratio. Evaluates the overall financial condition of a business by showing the relationships between selected figures on financial statements. (17)

financially capable. Having the ability to understand basic topics related to finance. (18)

finished goods inventory. Assortment or selection of finished items for sale that a business has in stock. (8)

firewall. Program that monitors information coming into a computer. (23)

first-line management. Level of management that coordinates and supervises the activities and duties of employees. (7)

fiscal period. Period of time for which a business summarizes accounting information and prepares financial statements; also called *accounting period*. (17)

fiscal policy. Tax and spending decisions made by the president and Congress. (2)

five Cs of banking. Criteria lenders use to evaluate the creditworthiness of businesses, including cash flow, capacity, capital, collateral, and conditions. (16)

fixed expense. Expense that is equal in amount each budget period. (18)

flextime. Policy allowing employees to adjust work schedules to better match personal schedules. (9)

floating currency. Currency with an exchange rate set by the market forces of supply and demand in the foreign exchange market. (5)

for-profit business. Organization that generates revenue. (4)

for-profit school. A school that is set up to earn money for investors. (21)

foreign exchange rate. Cost to convert one currency into another. (5)

Form W-2 Wage and Tax Statement. Statement that shows earnings as well as tax deductions withheld during the year. (18)

formal education. Education received in a school, college, or university. (21)

four Ps of marketing. Marketing elements of product, price, place, and promotion. (10)

franchise. Right to sell a company's goods or services in a specific area. (5)

franchisee. Person or company that buys the rights to use a brand. (5)

franchisor. Parent company that owns a chain and the brand. (5)

freight forwarder. Company that organizes shipments. (11)

frequently asked questions (FAQ) page. Part of a website that gives detailed answers to questions or issues that show up most often. (13)

G

general liability insurance. Protects against financial losses that result from legal issues. (14)

generally accepted accounting principles (GAAP). Rules, standards, and practices businesses follow to record and report financial information. (17)

geographic segmentation. Segmenting a market based on where customers live. (10)

globalization. Connections made among nations when economies freely move goods, labor, and money across borders. (5)

goal. Something to be achieved in a specified period of time. (7)

good. Physical item that can be touched. (1)

government bond. Security that pays interest over terms of ten to thirty years. (15)

government market. Customers include national, state, and local government offices and agencies. (4)

greeting approach. B2C approach that consists of a friendly welcome to the store or department. (13)

gross domestic product (GDP). Market value of all final products produced in a country during a specific time period. (2)

gross pay. Amount of income earned before taxes and other deductions are withheld. (17)

guarantee. Promise that a product has a certain quality or will perform in a specific way. (11)

H

hacking. Illegally accessing or altering digital devices, software, or networks. (23)

harassment. Uninvited conduct toward a person based on his or her race, color, religion, sex, national origin, age, or disability. (9)

headline. Consists of the words designed to grab attention so viewers will read the rest of the ad. (12)

high-yield savings account. Account that pays a higher interest rate than basic savings accounts. (19)

hook. Aspect of an ad that grabs attention. (12)

human resources management (HRM). Process of hiring, training, and developing employees. (9)

human resources. Employees who work for a business. (9)

human risk. Negative situation caused by the actions of people. (14)

hypothetical question. Questions that require a candidate to imagine a situation and describe how he or she would act. (22)

I

identity theft. Illegal act that involves stealing someone's personal information and using that information to commit theft or fraud. (23)

image. Idea that people have about someone or something. (8)

imports. Goods, services, and capital that are brought into a country from outside its borders. (5)

impulse buying decision. Purchase made with no planning or research. (10)

incentive. Type of compensation based on performance; also known as *pay for performance*. (9)

income statement. Reports the revenue and expenses of a business for a specific time period and shows a net income or net loss. (17)

indirect channel. Uses intermediaries to get the product from the manufacturer to the end users. (11)

individual retirement account (IRA). Personal retirement investment account created by a person. (19)

inflation. General rise in prices throughout an economy. (2)

inflation rate. Rate of change in prices calculated on a monthly or yearly basis. (2)

informational interviewing. Strategy used to interview a professional to ask for advice and direction, rather than asking for a job opportunity. (21)

infringement. Any use of copyrighted material without permission. (23)

inpatient. Person whose care requires a stay in a hospital. (20)

inseparable. Service cannot be separated from the person who performs it. (11)

installment loan. Loan for a specific amount of money that is repaid with interest in regular installments. (16)

institution. Nonprofit organization that may be either public or private. (4)

institutional promotion. Focuses on promoting the company rather than its products. (12)

insurance. Financial service used to protect against loss. (14)

insurance policy. Defines the type of losses that are covered, amount of coverage in dollars, and other conditions to which the two parties agree. (14)

intangible. Something that cannot be touched. (11)

integrated marketing communications (IMC). Promotional strategy that combines the elements of the promotional mix to create a unified marketing message. (12)

integrity. Honesty of a person's actions. (3)

intellectual property. Something that comes from a person's mind, such as an idea, invention, or process. (23)

intercultural communication. Process of sending and receiving messages between people of various cultures. (5)

interest. Amount a borrower pays to a lender for a loan. (2) A feeling of wanting to learn more about a topic or to be involved in an activity. (21)

interest-bearing savings account. Type of demand deposit account that pays interest and allows for regular deposits and withdrawals. (19)

interest rate. The cost of a loan, expressed as a percent of the amount borrowed. (2)

intermediary. Person or business that sells the goods and services from producers to customers. (4)

internal influence. Motivator or change factor that comes from within a business itself. (10)

international trade. Buying and selling of goods and services across national borders; also known as *world trade* and *international business*. (5)

Internet protocol address. Number used to identify an electronic device connected to the Internet; also known as an *IP address*. (23)

internship. Short-term position with a sponsoring organization that gives the intern an opportunity to gain on-the-job experience in a certain field of study or occupation. (21)

interpersonal skills. Skills that help people communicate and work well with each other. (7)

inventory. Assortment or selection of items that a business has on hand at a particular point in time. (8)

inventory management. Area of management involved in ordering goods, receiving them into stock on arrival, and paying the vendor. (8)

inventory shrinkage. Difference between the perpetual inventory and the physical inventory. (8)

investing. Purchasing a financial product or valuable item with the goal of increasing wealth over time in spite of possible loss. (19)

investment bank. Financial institution that provides services for businesses. (15)

investment portfolio. Collection of securities and other assets a person owns. (19)

itemized deduction. Allowed expense that can be deducted from adjusted gross income. (18)

J

job. Work a person does regularly in order to earn money. (21)

job analysis. Process that identifies the job requirements for a position, employee qualifications, and how success will be evaluated. (9)

job application. Form with spaces for contact information, education, and work experience. (22)

job description. Defines the position and expectations of the job. (9)

job interview. Employer's opportunity to review a candidate's résumé and ask questions to see if he or she is qualified for the position. (22)

job sharing. Arrangement where two part-time employees handle the responsibilities of a single full-time position. (9)

job-specific skills. Critical skills necessary to perform the required work-related tasks of a position. (6)

joint venture. Partnership of two or more companies that work together for a specific business purpose. (5)

journal. Form used to record business transactions in chronological order. (17)

journalizing. Process of recording business transactions in a journal. (17)

just-in-time (JIT) inventory-control system. Method of managing inventory that keeps a minimal amount of raw materials on hand to meet production needs. (8)

K

keyword. Word or term that specifically relates to the functions of the position for which an employer is hiring. (22)

L

labor. Work performed by people in organizations, also called *human resource.* (1)

labor force. All of the people in a nation who are capable of working and want to work. (2)

labor union. Group of workers united as a single body to protect and advance the rights and interests of its members; also called *organized labor.* (9)

law of supply and demand. An economic principle that states the price of a product is determined by the relationship of the supply of the product and the demand for the product. (1)

layout. Arrangement of the headline, copy, and art on a page. (12)

lead. Potential customer; also called *prospect.* (13)

leadership. Ability to influence others to reach a goal. (6)

leading. Process of influencing others to work toward common goals. (7)

lease. Contract to rent something. (3)

ledger. Group of accounts. (17)

letter of credit. Document guaranteeing that a buyer will pay the seller the agreed-upon amount and within the time specified. (15)

liability. Legal responsibility. (4)

liability insurance. Covers financial losses caused by the actions or negligence of a person or business. (14)

libel. Publishing a false statement about someone that causes others to have a bad or untrue opinion of him or her. (23)

licensing. When a business sells the right to manufacture its products or use its trademark. (5)

limited buying decision. Purchase that requires some amount of research and planning. (10)

limited liability company (LLC). Form of business ownership that combines the benefits of a corporation with those of proprietorships and partnerships. (4)

line of credit. Prearranged amount of credit that is available for a business to use as needed. (15)

list price. Established price printed in a catalog, on a price tag, or in a price list. (11)

listening skills. Ability to hear what a person says and understand what is being said. (7)

logistics. Planning and managing the flow of goods, services, and people to a destination. (5)

logo. Picture, design, or graphic image that represents the brand. (12)

loss leader. Pricing an item much lower than the current market price or the cost of acquiring the product. (11)

M

major medical insurance. Typically covers the costs of serious illnesses and injuries, as well as high-cost procedures. (20)

malware. Term given to software programs that are intended to damage, destroy, or steal data; short for *malicious software*. (23)

managed care plan. Health-care plan in which the insurance company contracts with specific doctors, hospitals, and other health-care providers to deliver medical services and preventive care to members at reduced cost. (20)

management. Process of controlling and making decisions about a business. (7)

manufacturer. Business that uses supplies from other producers to make products. (4)

manufacturer's suggested retail price (MSRP). Price recommended by the manufacturer. (11)

market. Anywhere buyers and sellers meet to buy and sell goods and services. (1) All the people and organizations that might purchase a product. (6)

market economy. An economy in which individuals are free to make their own economic decisions, also known as *free enterprise* or *private enterprise*. (1)

market research. Gathering and analyzing information about a business. (6)

market risk. Potential that the target market for new goods or services is much less than originally projected. (14)

market segmentation. Process of dividing the market into smaller groups. (10)

market structure. How a market is organized based on the number of businesses competing for sales in an industry. (2)

marketing. Consists of dynamic activities that identify, anticipate, and satisfy customer demand while making a profit. (10)

marketing concept. Approach to business that focuses on satisfying customers as the means of achieving profit goals. (10)

marketing mix. Strategy for using the elements of product, price, place, and promotion. (10)

marketing plan. Document describing business and marketing objectives and the strategies and tactics to achieve them. (10)

marketing strategy. Plan that helps a business meet its overall goals and objectives. (10)

markup. Amount added to the cost of a product to determine the selling price. (11)

marquee. Overhanging structure containing a sign at the entrance of the store. (12)

mass marketing. Marketing to a larger group of people who might buy a product. (10)

mass production. Manufacturing goods in large quantities using standard techniques. (8)

materials processing. Changing the form of raw materials for another use. (8)

mediation. Process in which a neutral person meets with each side of a negotiation in an attempt to find a solution that both sides will accept. (7)

medium of exchange. Money is used in exchange for goods and services needed by individuals, businesses, and governments. (15)

mentor. Someone with experience who can provide advice, suggestions, and ideas. (6)

merchandise. Item or items that are bought with the intentions of reselling to a customer. (17)

merchandise approach. B2C approach in which the conversation starts with a comment about the product. (13)

metrics. Standards of measurement. (12)

middle management. Consists of a company's division managers and department heads. (7)

minimum wage. Lowest hourly wage employers can pay most workers by law. (18)

mission statement. Sentence in a business plan that describes the purpose of the business. (6)

mixed economy. An economy in which both the government and individuals make decisions about economic resources. (1)

mock interview. Practice interview conducted with another person. (22)

monetary policy. Policy that regulates the supply of money and interest rates by a central bank in an economy. (2)

monetary system. Mechanism a nation uses to provide and manage money for itself. (15)

money. Anything of value that is accepted in return for good or services. (15)

money market account (MMA). Type of savings account that requires a higher minimum balance than regular savings accounts, but offers a higher interest rate. (19)

money order. Payment order for a specific amount of money payable to a specific payee. (19)

money supply. Total money circulating at any one time in a country. (2)

monopolistic competition. Large number of businesses selling similar, but not the same, products and at different prices; also known as *imperfect competition.* (2)

monopoly. Market structure with one business that has complete control of a market's entire supply of goods or services. (2)

morals. Individual's ideas of what is right and wrong. (3)

multi-channel retailer. Retailer that sells products through both brick-and-mortar stores and online sites. (11)

multinational corporation. Business that operates in more than one country. (5)

mutual fund. Investment created by pooling the money of many people and investing it in a collection of securities. (19)

N

natural risk. Situation caused by acts of nature. (14)

need. Something a person must have to survive. (1)

need-based award. Financial-aid awards available for students and families who meet certain economic requirements. (21)

negotiation. When individuals involved in a conflict come together to discuss a compromise. (7)

net pay. Gross pay minus payroll deductions. (18)

net profit ratio. Illustrates how much profit is generated per dollar of sales. (17)

netiquette. Etiquette used when communicating electronically; also known as *digital etiquette.* (23)

networking. Talking with people a person knows and making new contacts. (21)

new product. Product that is different in some way from existing products. (8)

no-fault auto insurance. Insurance plan that eliminates the faultfinding process in settling claims. (20)

nondepository institution. Financial institution that does not accept deposits. (15)

nonprice competition. Competitive advantage based on factors other than price. (2)

nonstore retailer. Business that sells directly to consumers in ways that do not involve a physical store location. (11)

nonverbal skills. Ability to communicate effectively using body language, eye contact, personal space, behavior, and attitude. (7)

North American Industry Classification System (NAICS). Numeric system used to classify businesses and collect economic statistics; pronounced *nākes.* (4)

not-for-profit organization. Organization that exists to serve some public purpose. (4)

not-for-profit school. A school that returns the money it earns back into the school. (21)

O

objections. Concerns or other reasons a customer has for not making a purchase. (13)

occupational training. Education that prepares a person for a specific type of work. (21)

offer. Element of a contract that is a proposal to provide a good or service. (3)

oligopoly. Market structure with a small number of businesses selling the same or similar products. (2)

online support. Information and resources available to customers through the Internet. (13)

open source. Applies to software that has source code freely available to the public. (23)

open-end credit. Agreement that allows the borrower to use a specific amount of credit over a period of time. (16)

operating budget. Projection of the sales revenue that will be earned and the expenses that will be incurred during a future period of time. (17)

operating ratio. Shows the relationship of expenses to sales. (17)

operational plans. Designed to reach the day-to-day goals of a business. (7)

operations management. Area of management responsible for the activities necessary to produce goods and services. (8)

opportunity cost. The value of the next best option that was not selected. (1)

organizing. Coordination of activities and resources needed to reach its goals. (7)

organization chart. Diagram that shows the structure of an organization. (7)

organizational chart. Diagram showing how each employee position within a company interacts with others in the chain of command. (7)

overdraft. Check written for an amount greater than the balance of the account, also known as a *bounced check*. (19)

overselling. Promising more than the product or the business can deliver. (13)

overtime wage. Amount paid for working time in a week that is beyond the standard 40-hour workweek. (18)

P

packaging. Protects products until customers are ready to use them. (11)

participatory marketing. Promotion strategy that uses multiple elements to communicate and interact with customers. (12)

partnership. Association of two or more persons who co-own a business with the objective of earning a profit. (4)

partnership agreement. Written contract that establishes a partnership; also called the *articles of partnership*. (4)

payee. Person, business, or organization to whom a check is written. (19)

payroll. List of all employees working for a business and their earnings, benefits, taxes withheld, and other deductions. (17)

payroll deduction. Subtraction from gross pay. (18)

payroll register. Summary of the earnings, payroll deductions, and net pay for all employees recorded for each payroll period. (17)

peak. Highest point in the business cycle and marks the end of the expansion. (2)

perfect competition. Characterized by a large number of businesses selling the same product at the same prices. (2)

periodic inventory-control system. Method of measuring inventory that involves taking a physical count of merchandise at regular periods. (8)

perishable. Services cannot be stored for later use. (11)

perpetual inventory-control system. Method of counting inventory that shows the quantity on hand at all times. (8)

personal financial management. Process used by individuals to manage limited income to meet personal unlimited needs and wants. (18)

personal influence. Influence that makes each individual unique. (10)

personal information management (PIM). System used to acquire, organize, maintain, retrieve, and use information. (7)

personal investment plan. Plan to develop investment growth. (19)

personal leave. Days each year employees can use for personal reasons. (9)

personal selling. Direct contact with a prospective customer with the objective of selling a product. (13)

persuasion. Use of logic to change a belief or get people to take a certain action. (12)

philanthropy. Promoting the welfare of others. (3)

phishing. Use of fraudulent e-mails and copies of valid websites to trick people into providing private and confidential data. (23)

piecework. Wage based on a rate per unit of work completed. (9)

pipeline. Line of connected pipes that are used for carrying liquids and gases over a long distance. (11)

piracy. Illegal copying or downloading of software, files, or other protected material, including images, movies, and music. (23)

place. Includes the activities involved in getting goods and services to customers. (10)

plagiarism. Claiming another person's material your own, which is both unethical and illegal. (23)

plan. Outline of the actions needed to accomplish a goal. (7)

planning. Process of setting goals and deciding how to accomplish them. (6)

policy. Outlines how company decisions are made. (7)

portfolio. Selection of related materials that an individual collects and organizes to show qualifications, skills, and talents to support a career or personal goal. (22)

postdated check. Check written with a future date. (19)

posting. Transferring information from the journal to the ledger. (17)

postsecondary education. Any education achieved after high school. (21)

preapproach. Tasks that are performed before contact is made with a customer. (13)

preauthorization. Approval from the plan before receiving certain procedures and treatments. (20)

predatory pricing. Setting very low prices to remove competition. (11)

preexisting condition. Illness or injury a person has before signing up for health insurance. (20)

premium. Amount the insured pays for the insurance coverage. (14)

press release. Story featuring useful company information written by the company PR contact. (12)

price. Amount of money requested or exchanged for a product. (10)

price ceiling. Maximum price set by the government for certain goods and services it believes are priced too high. (11)

price competition. When a lower price is the main reason for customers to buy from one business over another. (2)

price discrimination. Occurs when a company sells the same product to different customers at different prices based on personal characteristics. (11)

price fixing. Occurs when two or more businesses in an industry agree to sell the same good or service at a set price, which eliminates price competition. (2)

price floor. Minimum price set by the government for certain goods and services it believes are priced too low. (11)

price gouging. Raising prices on certain kinds of goods to an excessively high level during an emergency. (11)

pricing objectives. Goals defined in the business and marketing plans for the overall pricing policies of the company. (11)

principal. Amount of money borrowed. (16)

pro forma balance sheet. Financial statement that reports the assets, liabilities, and net worth of the business. (6)

pro forma cash flow statement. Financial statement that reports anticipated sources and uses of cash from operations, investing, and financing activities. (6)

pro forma financial statements. Financial statements based on estimates of future business performance, sales, and expenses. (6)

pro forma income statement. Financial statement that projects revenues and expenses to show whether or not a business is profitable. (6)

procedure. Describes how tasks should be completed. (7)

producer. Business that creates goods and services. (4)

product. Anything that can be bought or sold. (1)

product depth. Number of product items within a product line. (11)

product item. Specific model, color, or size of products in a line. (11)

product liability insurance. Protects against financial losses due to a product defect that may cause injury to the user of the product. (14)

product life cycle. Series of stages a product goes through from its beginning to end. (8)

product line. Group of closely related products within the product mix. (11)

product mix. All of the goods and services that a business sells. (11)

product planning. Process of deciding which products will be most strategic for an organization to produce. (8) Process of deciding which products will appeal to the target market. (11)

product promotion. Promoting specific products. (12)

product width. Number of product lines a company offers. (11)

production process. All the activities required to create a product. (8)

productivity. Measure of a worker's production in a specific amount of time. (2)

professional development. Education for people who have already completed their formal schooling and training. (9)

professional liability insurance. Protects service-based businesses from financial losses caused by errors and negligence in how a service is provided; also called *malpractice insurance.* (14)

profit. The difference between the income earned and expenses incurred by a business during a specific period of time. (1)

promotion. Process of communicating with potential customers in an effort to influence their buying behavior. (10)

promotional campaign. Coordination of marketing communications to achieve a specific goal. (12)

promotional mix. Combination of the elements used in a promotional campaign. (12)

property damage liability. Insurance coverage that protects a person who is responsible for an auto accident that results in damage to the property of others. (20)

property insurance. Covers losses and damage to the assets of a business caused by a variety of events, such as floods, fire, smoke, and vandalism. (14)

proprietary credit card. A credit card that can only be used in the stores of the company that issued it. (16)

proprietary information. Any work created by company employees on the job that is owned by that company. (3)

proprietorship. Business that is owned and often operated by a single individual. (4)

prototype. Working model of a new product for testing purposes. (8)

psychographic segmentation. Dividing the market by certain preferences of lifestyle choices. (10)

psychological influence. Influence that comes from within a person or why a person has specific needs and wants. (10)

psychological pricing. Pricing techniques that create an image of a product and entice customers to buy. (11)

public domain. Refers to material that is not owned by anybody and can be used without permission. (23)

public relations (PR). Applying communication skills that promote goodwill between a business and the public. (12)

purchase on account. Transaction for which merchandise purchased is paid to the vendor at a later date. (17)

pure risk. Risk with a possibility of loss, but no possibility of gain. (14)

Q

quality. Indicator of a product's excellence. (11)

quality control. Activity of checking products as they are produced or received to ensure the quality meets expectations. (8)

quota. Limit on the amount of a product imported into a country during a specific period of time. (5)

R

recall. Order to remove or repair unsafe products in the market. (3)

receiver. Person who reads, hears, or sees a message. (12)

recession. Period of significant decline in total output, income, employment, and trade in an economy. (2)

reconcile. Compare the check register to balance the checking account. (19)

reference. Person who can comment on the qualifications, work ethic, personal qualities, and work-related aspects of another person's character. (22)

regular medical insurance. Coverage includes prescriptions, hospital stays, and inpatient tests. (20)

relationship selling. Focuses on building long-term relationships with customers. (10)

repackaging. Using new packaging on an existing product. (8)

repositioning. Marketing an existing product in a new way to create a new opinion or view of the product in the minds of customers to increase sales. (8)

résumé. Document that profiles a person's career goals, education, and work history. (22)

retailer. Business that buys products from wholesalers or directly from producers, and sells them to consumers to make a profit. (4)

revenue. Earnings that a business receives for the goods and services it sells.

risk. Possibility of loss, damage, or injury. (14)

risk management. Process of evaluating risk and finding ways to minimize or manage loss. (14)

Roth IRA. Individual retirement account in which individuals contribute after-tax income and qualified withdrawals are not taxed. (19)

routine buying decision. Purchase made quickly and with little thought. (10)

S

salary. Fixed payment for work; expressed as an annual figure. (9)

sale on account. Transaction for which cash for the sale is received at a later date. (17)

sales and service contract. Lists the goods or services provided by a business and the price the customer paid in exchange. (3)

sales forecast. Predication of future sales based on past sales. (17)

sales forecast budget. Projected sales units and revenue dollars for the period. (17)

sales process. Series of steps that a salesperson goes through to help the customer make a satisfying buying decision. (13)

savings account. Bank account used by depositors to accumulate money for future use. (15)

savings and loan institution. Financial institution that offers savings and loan services. (15)

savings plan. Strategy for using money to reach important goals and to advance financial security. (19)

scarcity. When demand is higher than the available resources. (1)

scholarship. Financial aid that may be based on financial need or some type of merit or accomplishment. (21)

secured credit. Credit loans that require collateral. (16)

securities firm. Financial institution that is involved in trading securities in financial markets. (15)

security. Type of financial investment issued by a corporation, government, or other organization. (15)

selling price. Actual price customers pay for a product after any discounts or coupons are deducted. (11)

sender. Person who has a message to communicate. (12)

service. Action or task that is performed, usually for a fee. (1)

service approach. B2C approach that starts with the phrase "May I help you?" (13)

service business. Business that earns profits by providing consumers with services that meet their needs and wants. (4)

signature. Identifies the person or company paying for the ad. (12)

situational influence. B2C influence that comes from the environment. B2B influence that comes from the environment in which the business exists. (10)

skill. Something an individual does well. (21)

slander. Speaking a false statement about someone that causes others to have a bad opinion of him or her. (23)

SMART goal. Goal that is specific, measurable, attainable, realistic, and timely. (7)

social influence. Influence that comes from the society in which a person lives. (10)

social responsibility. Behaving with sensitivity to social, environmental, and economic issues. (3)

software virus. Computer program designed to negatively impact a computer system by infecting other files. (23)

source document. Record that proves a business transaction occurred. (17)

sourcing. Finding suppliers of materials needed for the production of a product. (8)

specialization. Focusing on the production of specific goods so that more products can be produced with the same amount of labor. (2)

speculative risk. Risk that can result in either financial gain or financial loss. (14)

spyware. Software that spies on a computer. (23)

staffing. Process of recruiting, hiring, training, evaluating, and compensating employees. (7)

stakeholder. Person with interest in a business. (17)

standard deduction. Fixed amount that may be deducted from adjusted gross income. (18)

standard of living. Level of material comfort measured by the goods, services, and luxuries available. (1)

start-up budget. Budget created in the planning stages for a new business to help project revenues and expenses until the business is profitable. (17)

start-up capital. Money necessary to start and open a business; also called *seed capital*. (6)

stock. Share of ownership in a corporation. (4)

stock market. System and marketplace for buying and selling stocks. (2)

stop-payment order. Request for a financial institution to refuse to honor a check written, as long as the check has not cleared the account and already been paid. (19)

store of value. When money is saved and used at a later date. (15)

storefront. Store exterior which reflects the image of the business. (12)

strategic plans. Created for the long-term goals of an organization. (7)

strike. Occurs when union workers temporarily refuse to work. (9)

substitute selling. Sales technique of showing products that are different from the originally requested product. (13)

suggestion selling. Sales technique of suggesting additional items to go with merchandise requested by a customer. (13)

supplier. Business that sells materials, supplies, or services to an organization that creates product; also called a *vendor*. (8)

supply chain. Businesses, people, and activities involved in turning raw materials into products and delivering them to end users. (11)

systematic decision-making. Process of choosing an option after evaluating the available information and weighing the costs and benefits of your alternatives. (1)

T

tactical plans. Developed for the short-term goals of a company. (7)

tagline. Phrase or sentence that summarizes an essential part of the product or business; also called a *slogan*. (12)

target market. Specific group of customers whose needs a company will focus on satisfying. (10)

tariff. Governmental tax on imported goods. (5)

tax credit. Amount that is subtracted from the taxes an individual owes, if eligible. (18)

tax deduction. Amount that is subtracted from adjusted gross income, which further reduces taxable income. (18)

tax return. Report containing information used to calculate taxes owed by the taxpayer. (18)

taxable income. Amount on which taxes are calculated. (18)

team. Group of two or more people working together to achieve a common goal. (7)

teamwork. Cooperative efforts by individual team members to achieve a goal. (7)

telecommuting. Arrangement where employees work away from the business site. (9)

telemarketing. Personal selling done over the telephone. (13)

term life insurance. Insurance that provides protection for a specific period of time. (20)

test marketing. Introducing a new product to a small portion of the target market to learn how it will sell. (8)

three Cs of credit. Criteria used to evaluate the creditworthiness of consumer credit applicants, including character, capacity, and capital. (16)

time management. Practice of organizing time and work tasks to increase personal efficiency. (7)

tip. Money paid for service beyond the payment that is required. (18)

top management. Consists of a company's board of directors, president, and other high-ranking managers. (7)

trade agreement. Document listing the conditions and terms for importing and exporting products between countries. (5)

trade barrier. Any government action taken to control or limit the amount of imports. (5)

trade credit. Line of credit granted from one business to another for a short period of time to purchase goods and services. (16)

trade industry. Provides labor based on specialized knowledge and skills. (11)

trade-off. When something is given up in order to gain something else. (1)

trade policy. Body of laws related to the exchange of goods and services for international trade. (5)

trade sanction. Embargo that affects only certain goods. (5)

trade secret. Confidential information a company needs to keep private and protect from theft. (3)

trade show. Large gathering of businesses for the purpose of displaying goods and services for sale. (8)

trading bloc. Group of countries that join together to trade as if they are a single country. (5)

traditional economy. An economy in which economic decisions are based on a society's values, culture, and customs. (1)

traditional IRA. Individual retirement account that allows individuals to contribute pre-tax income to investments that grow tax deferred. (19)

trait. Distinguishing characteristic or quality that makes each person unique. (6)

transaction. Exchange of payment and product. (13)

transferable skills. Skills gained through life experience or working on a job that help an individual perform in the workplace or gain success in a career; also known as *foundation skills*. (6)

transportation. Physical movement of products through the channel of distribution. (11)

traveler's check. Special form of check that functions as cash. (19)

treasury bill. Security that matures in a year or less. (15)

treasury note. Security that pays interest over terms ranging from two to ten years. (15)

trial run. Testing a service on a few select customers to make sure that everything runs smoothly. (8)

trough. Lowest state of a business cycle and marks the end of a recession. (2)

typeface. Particular style for the printed letters of the alphabet, punctuation, and numbers. (12)

typography. Visual aspect of the words printed on a page. (12)

U

umbrella policy. Insurance policy that covers loss amounts that are higher than those covered by primary policies; also known as an *extended liability policy*. (20)

uncontrollable risks. Situations that cannot be predicted or covered by purchasing insurance. (14)

unearned income. Earnings from sources other than work. (18)

unemployment insurance. Provides certain benefits to workers who have lost their jobs through no fault of their own. (14)

unemployment rate. Percentage of the civilian labor force that is unemployed. (2)

uninsurable risk. Risk that an insurance company will not cover. (14)

unique selling proposition (USP). Statement summarizing the features and benefits of the company or product, how it differs from the competition, and how it is better than the competition. (12)

unit of value. Money is a common measure of what something is worth or what something costs. (15)

unsecured credit. Credit granted based on a signed credit agreement alone; also referred to as a *line of credit* or *revolving line of credit*. (16)

utility. Characteristics of a product that satisfy wants and needs. (1)

utilization review. Insurance company's examination of requests for medical treatments and procedures to make sure they are covered and the patient truly needs them. (20)

V

value proposition. Explains the value of a product over others that are similar. (11)

values. Principles and beliefs that a person considers important. (21)

variable. Each service is almost always unique. (11)

variable expense. Expense that can go up and down during the budget period. (18)

variance. Difference between a budgeted dollar amount and the actual dollar amount. (18)

venture capital. Money invested in a business by investors who form partnerships or groups to pool investments. (6)

verbal communication. Speaking words to communicate; also known as *oral communication*. (22)

verbal skills. Ability to communicate effectively using spoken or written words. (7)

vision care insurance. Covers specified services, such as eye exams, glasses, and contact lenses. (20)

visual merchandising. Process of creating floor plans, displays, and fixtures to attract customer attention and encourage purchases. (12)

W

wages. Money earned in exchange for work. (1)

want. Something that a person desires, but can live without. (1)

warranty. Written document that states the quality of a product with a promise to correct certain problems that might occur. (11)

weight. Refers to the thickness and slant of letters. (12)

white-collar worker. Worker who primarily uses mental abilities and knowledge acquired in higher education. (9)

white space. Blank areas on a page where there is no art or copy. (12)

whole life insurance. Insurance that provides basic lifetime protection, as long as premiums are paid; also called *straight life insurance*. (20)

wholesaler. Business that purchases large quantities of products directly from producers and sells the products in smaller quantities to retailers; also known as a *distributor*. (4)

will. Legal document stating a person's wishes for his or her estate after death. (19)

withholding allowance. Amount of income that is not subject to income taxes. (17)

work environment. Location, physical conditions, and emotional atmosphere in which employees work. (9)

work in process inventory. Consists of products that are partially completed, also called *unfinished product*. (8)

worker's compensation insurance. Covers medical expenses and lost wages for employees who are injured at work. (14)

working capital. Difference between current assets and current liabilities of a business. (17)

work-study program. Part-time job on a college campus that is subsidized by the government. (21)

Index

E

e-commerce, 47
e-mail support, 270
e-tailer, 226
earned income, 361–363, 371
    bonus, 363
    commission, 362
    salary, 362
    self-employment income, 363
    tips, 362
    wage, 362
economic activity, 22–37
economic freedom, 14
economic growth rate, 25
economic measurement, 24–32
economic output, 24. *See also*
    gross domestic product
economic problem, 11–12
economic recovery, 32
economic resources, 10–11
economic risk, 280
economic system, 12–15
    command, 13
    market, 14
    mixed, 14
    traditional, 13
economics, 10
    introduction to, 4, 10
EDI. *See* electronic data
    interchange
education funding, 447–449
    529 plan, 447
    grant, 449
    need-based awards, 449
    scholarship, 449
    work-study programs, 449
EEOC. *See* US Equal Employment
    Opportunity Commission
effective business organization,
    124–126
EFT. *See* electronic funds transfer
EIN. *See* employer identification
    number
electronic banking, 306, 386–388
    automated teller machines
       (ATMs), 388
    electronic funds transfer (EFT), 387
    mobile banking, 387
    online banking, 386
    peer-to-peer (P2P) payments, 387
electronic data interchange (EDI),
    148
electronic funds transfer (EFT),
    301, 306, 387
electronic promotion, 241
Electronic User's Bill of Rights,
    481–482
    Article I: Individual Rights, 481

Article II: Individual
    Responsibilities, 481
Article III: Rights of Educational
    Institutions, 482
Article IV: Institutional
    Responsibilities, 482
elements of a contract, 44–45
    acceptance, 44
    consideration, 44
    legal consequences, 45
    offer, 44
embargo, 88
emergency procedures, 176
emotional buying motives, 263
employability skills, 432
employee benefits, 343
employee health and safety, 50
employee motivation, 173–174
    Maslow's Hierarchy of Needs, 173
    motivation/hygiene theory, 173
    two-factor theory, 173
employee payroll records, 342
employee's earnings record, 342
employer/employee relationships,
    174
employer identification number
    (EIN), 48
employer payroll records, 342–344
employment contract, 46
employment forms, 468–469
    Form I-9 Employment Eligibility
       Verification, 468
    Form W-2 Wage and Tax
       Statement, 468
    Form W-4 Employee's
       Withholding Allowance
       Certificate, 468
employment process, 467–469
    employment forms, 468–469
    employment verification, 467–468
employment verification, 467
    background check, 468
encoding, 237
end user, 65. *See also* consumer
endorsement, 390, 418
    blank, 390
    restrictive, 391
    special, 391
endowment insurance, 415
engagement marketing, 241. *See
    also* participatory marketing
environmental protection, 48–49
English as a second language
    (ESL), 93
entering global market, 94–95
entrepreneur, 11, 104
    traits and skills, 106–108
entrepreneurship, 11, 104–111
    five Ps, 104–106

entry-level position, 433
environmental print, 248
Environmental Protection Agency
    (EPA), 49
EPA. *See* Environmental
    Protection Agency
Equal Credit Opportunity Act, 309
Equal Employment Opportunity
    laws, 50
equilibrium, 15
equipment breakdown insurance,
    287
equity, 327
equity financing, 117
ergonomics, 176–177
ESL. *See* English as a second
    language
estate, 400
estate planning, 401
ethics, 53, 250, 477
Ethics
    Accountability, 116
    Advertised Merchandise, 249
    Applications and Résumés, 464
    Bias-Free Language, 163
    Bribes, 126
    Business Ethics, 7
    Checks, 387
    Code of Ethics, 152
    Collusion, 35
    Computer Ethics, 417
    Confidential Information, 437
    Consumer Data, 306
    Ethical Messages, 45
    Expense Accounts, 341
    Going Out of Business Sale,
       215
    High-Pressure Selling, 269
    Information, 326
    Insurance Claims, 286
    Integrity, 64
    Intellectual Property, 481
    Sourcing, 94
    Tax Returns, 374
    Using Social Networking Media,
       199
ethics and social responsibility,
    53–57
etiquette, 478
euro, 90
European Union (EU), 89
evaluation, 155
even pricing, 217
exceptional customer service, 268
exclusion, 411
excuses, 266
executive summary, 114
executive-level position, 433
executor, 401

high-yield savings account, 397
high school diploma, 443
HMO. *See* health maintenance organization
homeowners insurance, 416–417
　liability coverage, 417
　property coverage, 416
homeowners liability coverage, 417
honesty, 55
hook, 246
HR. *See* human resources department
HRM. *See* human resources management
human resources, 10, 130, 162
　role of, 162–169
human resources (HR) department, 130, 162
human resources management (HRM), 162
　compensation, 165–167
　legal compliance, 168–169
　performance evaluation, 167–168
　recruiting and hiring, 162–164
　training, 164–165
human resources planning, 162
human risk, 280
hygiene factors, 173
hyperinflation, 27
hypothetical question, 464

I

idea generation, 152–153
idea screening, 153
identity theft, 486
ILAB. *See* US Bureau of International Labor Affairs
image, 154
IMC. *See* integrated marketing communications
impasse, 170
imperfect competition, 33. *See also* monopolistic competition
import duty, 88. *See also* tariff
imports, 84–85
impromptu speaking, 240
improving productivity, 149–150
inaccurate, 370
incentive, 166
income, 360–368, 371–372
　earned, 361, 371
　　gross, 371
　　taxable, 371
　　unearned, 371
income statement, 348, 350–351
income taxes, 343
independent agent, 286

indicator, 24
indirect channel, 222
individual retirement account (IRA), 400
　Roth IRA, 400
　traditional IRA, 400
industrial sales, 258. *See also* business-to-business selling
industry, 66, 439
inflation, 26–27
　double-digit, 27
inflation rate, 26–27
influence, 194
infomercials, 239
information utility, 7
informational interviewing, 439
infringement, 479
inland marine insurance, 287
inpatient, 411
inseparable, 206
inside salesperson, 258
installation, 208
installment loan, 317
institution, 68
institutional promotion, 236
institutional sales, 258
instructions, 208
insurance, 283, 409–410
　brokers, 286
　business, 285–289
　buying, 420–423
　companies, 283
　contract agent, 286
　for employees, 288–289
　independent agent, 286
　policy, 286
　types of, 286–287
insurance broker, 286
insurance companies, 285–286, 304
insurance policy, 286
insured, 285, 409
insurer, 285, 409
intangible, 206
integrated marketing communications (IMC), 241–242
integrity, 53
intellectual property, 478–481
　copyright, 479–480
　license agreement, 480–481
　patent, 480
　trademark, 480
intercultural communication, 93
interest, 27–28, 317, 437
interest-bearing checking account, 389
interest-bearing savings account, 396

interest rate, 27–28, 319
intermediaries, 65, 224–226
　agents, 226
　retailers, 225–226
　wholesalers, 224–225
internal influences, 197
Internal Revenue Service (IRS), 48, 369, 374
international banking services, 307–308
international business, 84
international trade, 84
Internet in the workplace, 483–487
Internet protocol (IP) address, 483
internship, 445
interpersonal skills, 134
　collaboration skills, 134
　critical-thinking skills, 134
　listening skills, 134
　nonverbal skills, 134
　verbal skills, 134
interpreter, 93
introduction stage, 216
inventory, 147
inventory management, 147
　just-in-time inventory-control system (JIT), 149
　periodic inventory-control system, 148
　perpetual inventory-control system, 148
inventory shrinkage, 148
investing, 397
investment bank, 305
investment portfolio, 398
investments, 397–400
　retirement plans, 400
　securities, 399
IP address. *See* Internet in the workplace
IRA. *See* individual retirement account
IRS. *See* Internal Revenue Service
itemized deduction, 371

J

JIT. *See* just-in-time inventory-control system
job, 432
job-specific skills, 106–107, 432
job analysis, 163
job application, 462
job description, 163
job interview, 463–467
　evaluate, 466–467
　follow-up message, 467
　interview questions, 464–466

R

rack jobbers, 224. *See also* wholesaler
rail transportation, 229
rating territory, 422
rational buying motives, 263
raw materials, 65, 222. *See also* natural resources
raw-materials manufacturers, 65, 224
raw-materials producers, 65, 224
reactive public relations, 240
recall, 52
receiver, 238
recession, 32
reconcile, 392
reconciling bank statements, 392–395
recruiting, 163
reduce risk, 283
reference, 458–459
regular medical insurance, 411
relationship selling, 193, 258
rental reimbursement coverage, 419
renters insurance, 417–418
repackaging, 151–152
replacement value, 417
repositioning, 151
Reserve Officers Training Corp (ROTC), 445
restrictive endorsement, 391
résumé, 456
  chronological, 458
  submitting, 459
  writing, 456–459
retailer, 65, 225
retirement plans, 400
  401(k), 400
  403(b), 400
  individual retirement account (IRA), 400
  Keogh plan, 400
  simplified employee pension (SEP), 400
revenue, 336
revolving line of credit, 319. *See also* open-end credit
risk, 280, 408
  business, 280
  controllable, 280–281
  economic, 280
  human, 280
  identifying, 280–282
  liability, 408
  managing, 282–284
  market, 280
  natural, 280

personal, 408
property, 408
pure, 281
speculative, 282
uncontrollable, 281
understanding, 280–284
risk management, 280, 408–409
  assume, 409
  avoid, 408
  reduce, 409
  transfer, 409
road transportation, 228
roadside assistance coverage, 419
Robinson-Patman Act, 47
role of legal system, 47–49
  business finances, 48
  e-commerce, 47
  environmental protection, 48–49
  fair competition, 47
role of government in economy, 34–37
  correct for externalities, 37
  manage economy, 35–36
  promote competition, 37
  provide legal framework, 36
  provide public goods, 36
  provide public services, 36
  provider, 35
  regulator, 35
ROTC. *See* Reserve Officers Training Corp
Roth IRA, 400

S

S corporation, 75–76
safe-deposit boxes, 384
safety inspections, 208
salary, 166, 342, 362
sale on account, 341
sales
  process, 261–267
  promotions, 239–240
  role of, 258–267
sales and service contract, 45
sales-below-cost (SBC) laws, 219
sales forecast, 339
sales forecast budget, 339
sales journals, 345
sales process, 261–267
  answer questions or objections, 265–266
  approach the customer, 262–263
  close the sale, 266–267
  determine customer needs, 263–264
  follow up after the sale, 267
  present the product, 264–265
sales promotions, 239–240

satisfiers, 173. *See also* motivation factors
savings account, 306, 384
savings and loan institution, 304
savings plan, 384, 396–397
SBA. *See* US Small Business Administration
scarcity, 11. *See also* economic problem
scheduling, 146
scholarship, 449
SCORE. *See* Service Corps of Retired Executives
screening interview, 164
seasonal discount, 218
SEC. *See* US Securities and Exchange Commission
secure passwords, 486–487
secured credit, 317
securities, 399
securities firm, 305
securities laws, 48
security, 297, 399
security settings, 487
seed capital, 116. *See also* start-up capital
self-assessment, 435
self-employment income, 363
self-insuring, 409
self-regulation, 250
selling, 188
selling price, 213, 216
sender, 237
service, 6
service approach, 262
service businesses, 66, 226
Service Corps of Retired Executives (SCORE), 110
service mark, 480
share drafts, 389. *See also* interest-bearing checking account
Sherman Antitrust Act, 37, 47
short form, 370. *See also* Form 1040A
short-term goal, 125, 437–438
shortage, 16
signature, 249
simple interest, 319
simplified employee pension (SEP), 400
situational influences, 194, 197
Six Sigma, 150
skill, 134, 432
  employability, 432
  goal setting, 134
  interpersonal, 134
  job-specific, 432
  time management, 134

government market, 67–68
institutions, 68
types of insurance, 286–287
commercial, 287
general liability, 287
product liability, 287
professional liability, 287
typography, 248

U

umbrella policy, 417
uncontrollable risks, 281
underinsured motorist coverage, 419
understanding money, 296–302
unearned income, 371
unemployment insurance, 289
unemployment rate, 28
employed, 28
full employment, 28
unemployed, 28
unfair pricing, 219–220
bait and switch, 219
deceptive pricing, 219
loss leader, 219
predatory pricing, 219
price discrimination, 219
price fixing, 219
price gouging, 219
unfavorable variance, 366
unfinished product, 147. *See also* work in process inventory
uninsurable risk, 284
uninsured motorist coverage, 419
unique selling proposition (USP), 244
unit of value, 297
United States Mint, 296
universal life insurance, 415
unlimited liability, 71
unsecured credit, 319
US Bureau of International Labor Affairs (ILAB), 91
US Bureau of Labor Statistics, 26, 439
US Citizen and Immigration Services, 468
US Consumer Product Safety Commission (CPSC), 51–52
US Copyright Office, 479
US Department of Education, 447
US Department of Homeland Security, 468
US Department of Labor (DOL), 49, 171, 439
US Department of Treasury, 48, 296

US Endangered Species Act, 89
US Equal Employment Opportunity Commission (EEOC), 49–50, 175
US Food and Drug Administration (FDA), 250
US Patent and Trademark Office, 250
US Securities and Exchange Commission (SEC), 48
US Small Business Administration (SBA), 109–110, 287, 327, 329
usage, 208
installation, 208
instructions, 208
technical support, 208
USP. *See* unique selling proposition
utility, 7, 145
form, 7
information, 7
place, 7
possession, 7
time, 7
utilization review, 411

V

value, 11, 213
values, 437
value proposition, 213
value quality, 207
variable, 206
variable expense, 366
variable life insurance, 415
variance, 366, 368
favorable, 366
unfavorable, 366
vendor, 146. *See also* supplier
vendor financing, 328
venture capital, 117
verbal communication, 464
verbal skills, 134
vision, 112
vision care insurance, 411
visual merchandising, 239
voluntary exchange, 14
Volunteer Income Tax Assistance (VITA) Program, 374–375

W

wage, 165, 342, 362
wages, 8
want, 7
warranty, 209
water transportation, 229
coastal ships, 229

inland ships, 229
ocean-going ships, 229
websites, 270
weight, 248
white-collar worker, 169
white space, 249
whole life insurance, 414–415
adjustable life, 415
limited payment policies, 414
universal life, 415
variable life, 415
wholesaler, 65, 224
will, 401
withholding allowance, 342
work-life balance, 172–173
work-study program, 449
work environment, 174–177
emergency procedures, 176
ergonomics, 176–177
workplace conduct, 175
workplace safety, 175–176
work in process inventory, 147
work style, 436
workers' compensation insurance, 289
working capital, 349
workplace conduct, 175
workplace diversity, 174
workplace environment, 172–176
workplace laws, 49–50
compensation, 49
employee health and safety, 50
equal employment opportunity, 49–50
labor relations, 49
workplace safety, 175–176
workplace skills, 432–433
world trade, 84
worms, 485

Y

You Do the Math
Algebraic Reasoning, 27, 55
Communication and Representation, 246, 392
Connections, 149, 365, 478
Functions, 210, 324
Geometric Reasoning, 107, 445
Measurement Reasoning, 88, 135
Numeric Reasoning, 16, 351
Probabilistic Reasoning, 166, 461
Problem Solving and Reasoning, 71, 263, 298, 419
Statistical Reasoning, 197, 283